# AMERICAN FOREIGN POLICY

## PAST, PRESENT, AND FUTURE

### THIRTEENTH EDITION

## GLENN P. HASTEDT

**JAMES MADISON UNIVERSITY**

ROWMAN & LITTLEFIELD
Lanham • Boulder • New York • London

Executive Acquisitions Editor: Michael Kerns
Assistant Editor: Elizabeth Von Buhr
Sales and Marketing Inquiries: textbooks@rowman.com

Credits and acknowledgments for material borrowed from other sources, and reproduced with
permission, appear on the appropriate pages within the text.

Published by Rowman & Littlefield
An imprint of The Rowman & Littlefield Publishing Group, Inc.
4501 Forbes Boulevard, Suite 200, Lanham, Maryland 20706
www.rowman.com

86-90 Paul Street, London EC2A 4NE

British Library Cataloguing in Publication Information Available

**Library of Congress Cataloging-in-Publication Data**
Names: Hastedt, Glenn P., 1950- author.
Title: American foreign policy : past, present, and future / Glenn P. Hastedt, James Madison
   University.
Description: Thirteenth edition. | Lanham : Rowman & Littlefield, [2023] | Includes bibliographical
   references and index.
Identifiers: LCCN 2022054836 (print) | LCCN 2022054837 (ebook) | ISBN 9781538173756
   (paperback) | ISBN 9781538173763 (epub)
Subjects: LCSH: United States—Foreign relations—Textbooks. | United States—Foreign
   relations—1945-1989—Textbooks. | United States—Foreign relations—1989—Textbooks. |
   United States—Foreign relations administration—Textbooks.
Classification: LCC E183.7 .H27 2023 (print) | LCC E183.7 (ebook) | DDC 327.73—dc23/
   eng/20221207
LC record available at https://lccn.loc.gov/2022054836
LC ebook record available at https://lccn.loc.gov/2022054837

*To Thomas and Matthew*

# Brief Contents

Preface   xv

1   Defining American Foreign Policy Problems   1

2   The Global Context   20

3   The American National Style   40

4   Learning from the Past   60

5   Society   85

6   Congress   111

7   Presidency   137

8   Bureaucracy   160

9   Policy-Making Models   185

10   Diplomacy   206

11   Economic Instruments   230

12   Military Instruments: Big Wars   254

13   Military Instruments: Small Wars   277

14   Alternative Futures   299

Glossary   A-1
Notes   B-1
Photo Credits   C-1
Index   D-1
About the Author   E-1

# Contents

Preface    xv

## 1 Defining American Foreign Policy Problems    1

Learning Objectives    2

On the Agenda: Leaving Afghanistan    2

Thinking about Foreign Policy Problems    3

Choices    4
  What Do Americans Want in Foreign Policy?    4
  The National Interest    5

Costs    6

Building Consensus    8

Selecting a Policy Instrument    9
  Hard Power and Soft Power    9
  Unilateral or Multilateral Action    9

■ HISTORICAL LESSON: Into Afghanistan    10

Presidential Foreign Policy Doctrines    11
  The Truman Doctrine    12
  The Nixon Doctrine    12
  The Carter Doctrine    13
  The Reagan Doctrine    13
  The Bush Doctrine    14
  In Search of the Trump Doctrine    15
  Is There a Trump Foreign Policy Legacy?    16

Assessing Foreign Policy Results    16
  Intellectual Coherence    17
  The Dominance of Domestic Politics    17
  Consistency of Application    18

Over the Horizon: The Future of Grand Strategy    18

Critical Thinking Questions | Key Terms    19

## 2 The Global Context    20

Learning Objectives    21

On the Agenda: The Ukraine War    21

**Thinking about the World**  23
  Realism  24
  Neoliberalism  24
  Constructivism  24

**International System: Structural Constants**  25
  Decentralization  25
  Self-Help System  25
  A Stratified System  26

**International System: Evolutionary Trends**  27
  Diffusion of Power  27
  Issue Proliferation  27
  Actor Proliferation  28

■ **HISTORICAL LESSON: NATO**  29
  Regional Diversity  30

**Dominant Features Today**  31
  Terrorism  31

■ **BOX 2.1: Snapshot of Global Terrorism, 2021**  32
  Globalization  34
  American Hegemony  35
  America and the World: Attitudes and Perceptions  37

**Over the Horizon: 2040**  38

**Critical Thinking Questions | Key Terms**  39


**3  The American National Style**  40

**Learning Objectives**  41

**On the Agenda: The Mexican Border**  41

**The Importance of Ideas**  43

**Isolationism versus Internationalism**  45

**Historical Sources of the American National Style**  46

**Patterns**  48
  Unilateralism  48
  Moral Pragmatism  49
  Legalism  51

**Consequences of the American National Style**  52

■ **HISTORICAL LESSON: The Bracero Program**  52

**Voices from the Past**  55

**Over the Horizon: A Millennial Foreign Policy?**  57

**Critical Thinking Questions | Key Terms**  58

4   **Learning from the Past   60**

Learning Objectives   61

On the Agenda: COVID-19   61

How Do Policy Makers Learn from the Past?   64

Events from Which Policy Makers Learn   65

Types of Calculations Made   66

Lessons Learned   67

▓ HISTORICAL LESSON: Ebola   68

Case Studies   69
  The Vietnam War   69
  The Iraq War   76

Over the Horizon: Searching for Lessons from Afghanistan   83

Critical Thinking Questions | Key Terms   84

5   **Society   85**

Learning Objectives   86

On the Agenda: Quincy Institute for Responsible Statecraft   86

Public Awareness of Foreign Policy Issues   87

Public Opinion   88
  Trends and Content   88
  Public Opinion and the Use of Force   90
  Impact of Public Opinion   92

Elections   93
  Voting and Foreign Policy   93
  Impact of Elections   94

Interest Groups   96
  Types of Interest Groups   96

▓ HISTORICAL LESSON: The America First Committee, 1940   96
  Impact of Interest Groups   103

Political Protest   103

The Media and American Foreign Policy   104
  Newspapers and Television   104
  The New Media and American Foreign Policy   105
  Shaping the Public's View   106

States and Cities: The New Foreign Policy Battleground   107

Policy Makers' Responses  108

Over the Horizon: An Intelligence-Industrial Complex?  109

Critical Thinking Questions | Key Terms  109


6  **Congress  111**

Learning Objectives  112

On the Agenda: Aid for Ukraine  112

Constitutional Powers  114
 Treaty-Making Power  114
 Appointment Powers  117
 War Powers  117

▓ Historical Lesson: War Powers Act  118
 Commerce Powers  121

▓ BOX 6.1: Excerpt: House Resolution Authorizing the Use of Military Force against Iraq, October 2, 2002  122

Congressional Structure and Foreign Policy  123
 Blunt Foreign Policy Tools  123

▓ BOX 6.2: Investigating Russia's Involvement in the 2016 Presidential Election  127
 The Absence of a Single Voice  128
 Policy Entrepreneurship  129
 Staff Aides  129

Influence of Party and Region  130

Outsourcing Foreign Policy  131

Congress and the President: The Changing Relationship  132

Over the Horizon: A New War Powers Act?  134

Critical Thinking Questions | Key Terms  136


7  **Presidency  137**

Learning Objectives  138

On the Agenda: Biden's First One Hundred Days  138

▓ Historical Lesson: John F. Kennedy's First One Hundred Days  139

Weak President or Strong President  140

Presidential Power and Supreme Court Decisions  141

**The President and the Foreign Affairs Constitution   141**
Executive Agreements   142
Signing Statements   143
Executive Orders, Spending, and Administrative Powers   143
Informal Ambassadors   144
Undeclared Wars   145

**When Does the President Matter?   146**
Presidential Personality   147
Presidential Managerial Style   149

**The National Security Council   151**

**Other White House Voices   154**
The Vice President   154
The U.S. Trade Representative   155
The White House Chief of Staff   156
The First Lady   157

**Over the Horizon: Improving Presidential Transitions   157**

**Critical Thinking Questions | Key Terms   159**


**8   Bureaucracy   160**

**Learning Objectives   161**

**On the Agenda: Fixing the State Department   161**

**Presidents and the Bureaucracy   163**

**The State Department   163**
Structure and Growth of the State Department   163
The State Department's Value System   164
Impact of the State Department on Foreign Policy   166

**The Department of Defense   167**
Structure and Growth of the Department of Defense   167

**Historical Lesson: Integrating the Military   169**
The Value System of the Department of Defense   172
Impact of the Defense Department on Foreign Policy   173

**The CIA and the Intelligence Community   174**
Structure and Growth of the CIA and the Intelligence Community   174
The Intelligence Community's Value System   177
Impact of the CIA and the Intelligence Community on Foreign Policy   179

**The Domestic Bureaucracies   179**
Treasury, Commerce, and Agriculture   180
Homeland Security   181

Policy Makers' Response to Bureaucracy   182

Over the Horizon: U.S. Space Command   182

Critical Thinking Questions | Key Terms   184


9   **Policy-Making Models   185**

Learning Objectives   186

On the Agenda: Ukraine War Decision Making   186

Foreign Policy Decisions and Models   188

The Rational Actor Model   189

The Bureaucratic Politics Model   190

The Small-Group Decision-Making Model   191

Elite Theory and Pluralism   194

■ HISTORICAL LESSON: The War to End All Wars   196

Integrating Models   197

The Cuban Missile Crisis   198
   The Crisis: An Overview   198
   Applying the Rational Actor Model to the Crisis   201
   Applying the Bureaucratic Politics Model to the Crisis   202
   Applying the Small-Group Decision-Making Model to the Crisis   203

Models: A Policy Maker Critique   204

Over the Horizon: Individual-Centered Models   204

Critical Thinking Questions | Key Terms   205


10   **Diplomacy   206**

Learning Objectives   207

On the Agenda: The Paris Agreement   207

Diplomacy: Choices and Dilemmas   208
   The Diplomatic Tool Kit   208
   Bilateralism versus Multilateralism   210
   Process versus Product   210
   Incentives versus Sanctions   211

Bilateral Diplomacy: Allies, Friends, and Adversaries   211

Shuttle Diplomacy   212

Summit Diplomacy  213
Economic Summits  214
East-West Superpower Summits  215

Conference Diplomacy  216
The General Agreement on Tariffs and Trade and the World Trade Organization  216

◼ HISTORICAL LESSON: The Kyoto Protocol and Copenhagen Accord  217
Environmental Conferences  219
Human Rights Conferences  219
Global Health Conferences  220

UN Diplomacy  221

Public Diplomacy and Digital Diplomacy  222

The Political Use of Force  223
Coercive Diplomacy  223
Nuclear Diplomacy  225

Arms Transfers  225

Over the Horizon: Coalitions of the Willing  228

Critical Thinking Questions | Key Terms  228

## 11  Economic Instruments  230

Learning Objectives  231

On the Agenda: United States–Mexico–Canada Agreement (USMCA)  231

Economic Statecraft  232

Inventory of Options  233

Strategic Outlooks  234
Free Trade  234
Strategic Trade  235
Monetary Strategies  235

Varieties of Trade Agreements  236
Bilateral Trade Agreements  236
Regional Trade Agreements  237
Global Trade Agreements  238

The China Trade War  239

Economic Sanctions  240
Using Sanctions  240
Sanctions in Action: Iran, Cuba, Russia  242

Foreign Aid  245

Types of Foreign Aid   246
Cold War Foreign Aid   248
Post–Cold War Foreign Aid   249

■ **Historical Lesson: NAFTA**   249
Post-9/11 Foreign Aid   250
Contemporary Foreign Aid   251

**Over the Horizon: How Trade Wars End**   252

**Critical Thinking Questions | Key Terms**   253


**12  Military Instruments: Big Wars   254**

**Learning Objectives**   255

**On the Agenda: North Korean Denuclearization**   255

**Cold War Nuclear Thinking**   257
The U.S. Cold War Strategic Arsenal   257
U.S. Cold War Nuclear Strategy   258

■ **HISTORICAL LESSON: The Baruch Plan**   260

**Post–Cold War Nuclear Thinking**   261
The U.S. Post–Cold War Strategic Nuclear Arsenal   261
U.S. Post–Cold War Nuclear Strategy   262

**Bridging the Nuclear-Conventional Divide**   263
Deterrence   264
Preemption   265

**Using Large-Scale Conventional Military Force**   266

**Reducing the Danger of War: Arms Control and Disarmament**   268
The Cold War Record   269
The Post–Cold War Record   270

**Defense**   273
The Strategic Defense Initiative   273
National Missile Defense Systems   274

**Over the Horizon: A New Age of Nuclear Proliferation**   275

**Critical Thinking Questions | Key Terms**   276


**13  Military Instruments: Small Wars   277**

**Learning Objectives**   278

**On the Agenda: Cyber Warfare**   278

**Separating Big Wars from Small Wars**   279

Exiting Small Wars  280

Types of Small Wars  281
Hybrid Warfare  281
Counterinsurgency  282
Counterterrorism  283

The Return of Small Wars?  284

Small Wars by Other Means  286
Cold War Covert Action  286
Post–Cold War Covert Action  288
The Covert War against Osama bin Laden  289
Cyber Warfare  289

Small Wars for Peace  290
Humanitarian/Peacekeeping Operations  290
▓ HISTORICAL LESSON: The Path to Mogadishu  291
Stability Operations  292

Conventional, Cyberspace, and WMD Arms Control  293
Chemical and Biological Weapons  293
Recovering Loose WMD Material  294
Cyberspace  295
Conventional Weapons  295

Counterproliferation  296

Over the Horizon: Drone Wars  297

Critical Thinking Questions | Key Terms  298

14 **Alternative Futures  299**

Learning Objectives  300

On the Agenda: The South China Sea  300

Foreign Policy Visions  302
The United States as an Ordinary State  302
Reformed America  303
Pragmatic America  305
American Crusader  306
America the Balancer  307
Disengaged America  308

▓ HISTORICAL LESSON: The First Asian Pivot: Commodore Perry's Opening of Japan  308

Over the Horizon: A New Cold War?  310

Critical Thinking Questions | Key Terms  311

Glossary   A-1

Notes   B-1

Photo Credits   C-1

Index   D-1

About the Author   E-1

# Preface

This thirteenth edition of *American Foreign Policy* comes at a time when U.S. foreign policy finds itself being pulled in multiple directions at the same time. One debate is whether it should turn back from Donald Trump's America First agenda or continue to embrace it. A second debate is over whether it is entering a new cold war. Underlying both debates is an increasingly polarized domestic landscape that presents potential obstacles to the success of any foreign policy.

Like its predecessors, this thirteenth edition does not try to present students with an answer on how best to move American foreign policy forward. Rather, it is designed to help students cultivate the critical thinking skills they need to develop their own answers and participate in current and future debates about the conduct and content of U.S. foreign policy. We do this by raising four key sets of questions over the course of the book: (1) What do we mean by foreign policy and what is the national interest? (2) How did we get here and how do we learn from the past? (3) How is foreign policy made? (4) What next?

The thirteenth edition contains all of the essential critical thinking materials found in previous editions. The introductory "On the Agenda" section introduces students to the material being covered by providing them with a short contemporary case study. The "Historical Lessons" section provides a historical context for students to understand current U.S. foreign policy issues and is linked to the "On the Agenda" section. The "Over the Horizon" section concludes each chapter with a speculative view to the future to spur student thinking about how American foreign policy might evolve in the coming years. Each of these critical thinking sections has been updated, and in some cases a new topic has been added to better capture the current U.S. foreign policy agenda. When this is the case, sometimes the material has been moved to another chapter.

This edition updates information presented in the twelfth and introduces students to key facets of Joe Biden's foreign policy. New topics in the "On the Agenda," "Historical Learning," and "Over the Horizon" sections include:

- COVID-19
- the Ukraine War (various aspects are addressed in several of these sections)
- exiting Afghanistan
- Biden's first one hundred days
- nuclear proliferation
- NATO
- the Quincy Institute for Responsible Statecraft

Important topics from the twelfth edition that are also found in these sections include:

- the South China Sea
- the Paris Climate Agreement
- the Mexican border

- the United States–Mexico–Canada Agreement
- the future of grand strategy
- North Korean denuclearization

Special thanks to the reviewers for the thirteenth edition: Lynda K. Barrow, Coe College; Scott Duryea, La Roche University; Ronald Lee, Rockford University; David Mitchell, Bucknell University; Kanishkan Sathasivam, Salem State University; and others who wish to remain anonymous.

And to those at Rowman & Littlefield who worked on this edition: Michael Kerns, executive editor; Elizabeth Von Buhr, assistant editor; Ami Reitmeier, senior marketing manager; Alden Perkins, production editor; and Matt Evans copy editor.

# Defining American Foreign Policy Problems 1

## Learning Objectives

Students will be able to:

1. Describe the presidential grand strategies introduced in the chapter.
2. Identify the key considerations that must be made in selecting a foreign policy option.
3. Evaluate the merits of the criteria used to evaluate foreign policy.
4. Assess to what extent the exit from Afghanistan is an argument for or against the value of grand strategies.

## On the Agenda: Leaving Afghanistan

Stating that "it's time to end America's longest war," on April 14, 2021, President Joe Biden announced plans for the full withdrawal of all U.S. troops in Afghanistan by September 11, 2021, the twentieth anniversary of the September 11, 2001, al-Qaeda terrorist attacks on the United States. That target date was not reached. Nor was the promise that there would be no repeat of the chaotic withdrawal that occurred when South Vietnam unexpectedly fell to North Vietnam. Instead, on August 15, 2021, the Taliban returned to power. They had ruled Afghanistan in 2001 and provided a safe haven for al-Qaeda to conduct its terrorist campaign before being forced out of power by U.S. military operations. Chaos gripped Kabul, Afghanistan's capital, as Americans, foreigners, and Afghanis desperately sought to flee from the Taliban.

That the Taliban ultimately would regain control over the Afghan government following the U.S. withdrawal was not unexpected. Military and intelligence estimates at the time Biden announced his decision generally anticipated that it would take twelve to eighteen months after U.S. troops left Afghanistan for the Taliban to achieve a military victory allowing it to return to power. As the summer progressed, intelligence assessments began to raise doubts about this time line. Desertions were increasing in the Afghan army, and those remaining showed little ability or interest in fighting the Taliban. For its part, the Taliban arranged for the surrender of government forces, took over military bases, and obtained a large supply of weapons using a strategy of coercion and persuasion. In April, the Taliban controlled seventy-seven of some four hundred districts in Afghanistan. In early August, it controlled 223 districts. Foreign volunteers from Pakistan had swelled the Taliban's military strength from sixty or seventy thousand to over one hundred thousand fighters. These successes gave rise to a growing sense of inevitability of a Taliban victory and the withdrawal of public support for the government and defections to the Taliban. An early revision of this intelligence assessment concluded that Kabul could fall in as little as six months after U.S. troops left. That time line was next reduced to ninety days and then in early August down to a matter of days or weeks.

The end came with lightning speed. The Taliban entered Kabul on August 15 facing little resistance after President Ashraf Ghani fled to the United Arab Emirates. Less than two weeks earlier, it did not control a single provincial capital. In one week it took control of the second- and third-largest cities in Afghanistan, leaving Kabul as the only major city under government control.

A variety of explanations have been put forward as to how the sudden and unexpected ending to the U.S. presence in Afghanistan caught the Biden administration by surprise. One set of explanations asserts that it was due to carelessness on the part of the administration. It did not pay enough attention to the situation in Afghanistan and operated on the basis of false assumptions. Officials countered this in two ways. First, most of the key assumptions guided both its policy to Afghanistan as well as the policies of previous presidents. Second, the National Security Council met thirty-six times to discuss the Afghan situation following Biden's April announcement that U.S. forces would leave Afghanistan on September 11, 2022; the military openly discussed its concerns with Biden; the White House held more than fifty meetings on embassy security and evacuations; and in early August the Pentagon looked at "significantly negative case scenarios."

A second explanation is that it was not so much the fault of the Biden administration but the reality that policy makers do not always have the ability to control and shape events. This is particularly the case for rapidly evolving events where their powers to act are limited by such factors as time, distance, and the need to rely on others to act in specific ways. Biden, it is noted, was extremely unhappy with Afghan president Ghani for not having managed to effectively construct and manage a plan to consolidate his military forces to protect key cities.

A third explanation is that Biden's foreign policy options toward Afghanistan were seriously restricted by the decisions of previous presidents, in particular those of Donald Trump. This is an argument Biden made: "I inherited a deal cut by my predecessor . . . which left the Taliban in the strongest position militarily since 2001 and imposed a May 1, 2021, deadline on U.S. forces." Biden continued that he had a choice to accept that deal or "ramp up our presence and send more American troops to fight once again in another country's civil conflict."

This chapter examines six key tasks in constructing a foreign policy: (1) problems must be defined, (2) choices must be made, (3) costs must be assessed, (4) public support must be built, (5) a course of action must be designed, and (6) results must be assessed. It will also examine presidential grand strategies as a source of guidance in making foreign policy. The "Historical Lesson" section of this chapter will review the process by which the United States entered Afghanistan.

## Thinking about Foreign Policy Problems

In thinking about foreign policy problems, presidents discover three political truths very quickly. First, most foreign policy problems contain a bundle of distinct policy problems or issues that intersect in complicated ways. This makes deciding how to approach a problem difficult because of uncertainty over the nature of the problem or how attacking one aspect will affect its other dimensions. In 2004, National Security Advisor Condoleezza Rice told the 9/11 Commission, "You didn't have an approach against al-Qaeda because you didn't have an approach against Afghanistan. And you didn't have an approach against Afghanistan because you didn't have an approach against Pakistan. And until we could get that right, we didn't have a policy."[1]

Second, foreign policy problems are seldom ever "solved." George Shultz, President Ronald Reagan's secretary of state, noted that policy making does not involve confronting "one damn thing after another . . . it involves confronting the same damn thing over and over."[2] This is due in part to the difficulty of fashioning policies that accurately capture the problem's complexity. The necessity of dealing with the same problem over and over again may also occur because it has no solution. Problems without solutions are often characterized as *wicked problems.* Terrorism is seen by many as a wicked problem because no permanent solution exists. Terrorism can be deterred, targets can be protected, and the terrorist threat can be managed, but the potential for terrorism always exists.

Third, it is important to realize that the history and origin of foreign policy problems differ in their political history. Some foreign policy problems are inherited from previous administrations, but others are the result of a president's own policy. The key dilemma faced by U.S. presidents is whether to endorse the policy line of their predecessor or move in a new direction. Deciding which direction to go involves strategic and political considerations. The key strategic consideration centers on the success of the inherited policy: should it be continued or changed? The central political consideration involves who gets credit or is blamed for the policy. Only inherited policy problems can be blamed on one's predecessor. President Trump frequently cited the "mess" he inherited from President Obama in justifying his foreign policy decisions. As noted in the "On the Agenda" section, President Biden placed responsibility for the chaotic exit from Afghanistan at the doorsteps of the peace agreement Trump agreed to with the Taliban.

# Choices

Foreign policy is about choices: what goals to pursue, what threats to protect against, what costs to bear, and who should bear those costs. Choices always exist. When asked if the president ever had a last card to play in foreign policy before having to walk away and accept defeat, President George W. Bush replied, "There is always another card." However, those choices might not always be great ones. In reflecting on the four military options presented to him on Afghanistan, Obama noted that two were basically alike and two were unclear.[3] Trump has expressed similar frustration with the military options given to him in dealing with North Korea and Iran.

Just as there are always options once a conflict is underway, so too there are always choices about which problems to place on the foreign policy agenda. Two different lines of thinking have been used to make foreign policy choices: asking what Americans want, and asking what the United States should do. Answers to the first are generally found in public opinion polls. Answers to the second are typically sought by referring to the concept of the national interest.

## What Do Americans Want in Foreign Policy?

Determining what the American public wants is not always easy. The answer can depend on how the question is framed. A 2022 Gallup poll asked the public to identify the top threats facing the United States. Cyberterrorism was identified as the top threat by 82 percent. This was followed in order by the development of nuclear weapons by North Korea (78 percent), the development of nuclear weapons by Iran (76 percent), and international terrorism (71 percent).[4] A 2021 Pew Foundation poll asked the public to rank their foreign policy priorities. At the top of the list was protecting the jobs of American workers, which was cited by 75 percent. It was followed in order by protecting the United States from terrorist attacks (71 percent), reducing the spread of infectious diseases (71 percent), and preventing the spread of weapons of mass destruction (64 percent).[5]

This listing of priorities has remained relatively stable, but it also shows signs of change. In a November 2018 public opinion poll, 71 percent said protecting the jobs of American workers was very important;[6] 81 percent identified this goal as important in 2013, and 78 percent in 1978. In 2018 this priority came in second to protecting the United States from terrorist attacks (72 percent). It was also the second-ranked goal in 2014. Change is also evident at the other end of the public opinion spectrum. In 2018, only 17 percent identified promoting human rights as a priority. Compare this to 2013, when 33 percent prioritized it. Table 1.1 presents an overview of how Americans evaluated the significance of national security threats facing the United States just prior to the Russian invasion of Ukraine.

## The National Interest

For those who pose the question of selecting goals in terms of the demands of foreign policy rather than the wishes of the American people, the answer is found in defending and pursuing the **national interest**, the fundamental goals and objectives of a country's foreign policy. This term is unmatched in its emotional impact and ability to shape a foreign policy debate. It conveys a sense of urgency, imminent threat, and higher purpose. All other foreign policy objectives pale in comparison to those promoting the national interest. It is advanced with great certainty and talked about as if there could be no doubt about its meaning.

Students of world politics have struggled—with little success—to give concrete meaning to the term "national interest."[7] Various formulations are used to separate threats and problems into different categories. Some employ a pyramid with a few core national interest problems at its apex. Beneath it are larger numbers of long-range societal goals and goals that advance the interests of specific groups. Others use the same logic to divide foreign policy problems into three categories: *A-list threats* pose a direct and immediate challenge to U.S. survival. *B-list threats* involve challenges to immediate U.S. interests but not to U.S. survival. *C-list threats* indirectly affect the U.S. national interest but are not immediate or direct.

The implication of both frameworks is the same. Policy makers need to concentrate resources on addressing the most important foreign policy issues so they do not jeopardize

| Table 1.1 | Public Perception of Top U.S. International Security Threats | | |
| --- | --- | --- | --- |
| *Threat* | *Critical (%)* | *Important (%)* | *Not Important (%)* |
| Cyber terrorism | 82 | 16 | 2 |
| Development of nuclear weapons by North Korea | 78 | 19 | 2 |
| Development of nuclear weapons by Iran | 76 | 19 | 4 |
| International terrorism | 71 | 25 | 3 |
| Military power of China | 67 | 29 | 4 |
| Spread of infectious diseases | 64 | 31 | 5 |
| Military power of Russia | 59 | 35 | 6 |
| Economic power of China | 57 | 34 | 8 |
| Climate change/global warming | 55 | 25 | 20 |
| Conflict between Russia and Ukraine | 52 | 37 | 11 |

*Source:* Jeffrey Jones, "Terrorism, Nuclear Weapons, China Viewed as Top US Threats," Gallup Poll, March 7, 2022. Polls conducted February 1–17, 2022.

the U.S. national interest. The ever-present danger is that not enough resources will be available to successfully deal with a core national interest problem or A-list threat should it appear.

Regardless of approach, the fundamental problem remains: deciding in which category to place a foreign policy problem. This is a judgment call that has led to two major lines of dissent in discussing the national interest. One argues that, since it is not possible to rank the importance of foreign policy goals in some abstract fashion, the national interest should be defined by a country's actions. If a country is willing to allocate significant resources to a problem, then solving that problem is in the national interest. A second voice, which calls for reexamination of the issues included in these ranking schemes, wants greater attention paid to **public goods**. These are goods—such as a clean environment—that are not owned by any one country. Because they belong to everyone in the international community, public goods tend to be devalued in discussions of the national interest.

## Costs

Two different broad types of foreign policy have been identified. Each comes with a price tag. **Declaratory policy** consists of proclamations that state the intent of the United States to pursue a line of action. It establishes and raises expectations about what the United States will do. **Action policy** is what the United States actually does. The perennial danger exists that declaratory and action policies will be out of sync, creating what some refer to as the "say-do" problem.[8]

The most notable example during the Obama administration came with his bold statement about a "red line" warning to Syria over the use of chemical weapons. Five times he warned the Syrian government about the consequences, yet no action was taken. A "say-do gap" was commonplace in the Trump presidency as he frequently exhibited a significant gap between his declaratory and action policies. It is also a problem that the Biden administration had to deal with. In its declaratory policy, frequent reference was made to moving away from Trump's foreign policy, yet on many occasions its actions were very consistent with those of Trump. One major occurrence of the say-do problem occurred in the exit from Afghanistan. U.S. allies felt slighted and endangered when, contrary to Biden's frequent comments about working with allies rather than ignoring them as Trump had frequently done, he did not warn them of the impending collapse of the Afghan government. As a result, they were unable to move many of their citizens to safety.

The greater the gap between declaratory and action foreign policies and the more frequently this gap exists, the more difficult and costly it becomes to get other states to join in on foreign policy initiatives. Trump discovered this in trying to get Europe and other states to support his withdrawal from the Iranian nuclear agreement. The lack of fit between declaratory and action foreign policy in the areas of human rights and democracy promotion has repeatedly dogged presidents. These issues often have received a great deal of declaratory policy support but little action policy support. Beyond creating the say-do gap, many argue that this discrepancy also undermines American global leadership by denying presidents "the global bully pulpit" from which to build a global consensus for action.[9] This too is a criticism leveled at Trump's foreign policy.

At the most basic level, the price tag of action policy can be calculated readily in human and monetary terms. An estimated 2,324 American soldiers died in combat operations in the

**Table 1.2** Estimated Direct War Deaths in Afghanistan and Pakistan, October 2011–August 2021

|  | *Afghanistan* | *Pakistan* | *Total* |
|---|---|---|---|
| U.S. military | 2,324 | — | 2,324 |
| U.S. DOD civilian | 6 | — | 6 |
| U.S. contractors | 3,917 | 90 | 4,007 |
| National military and police | 69,095 | 9,431 | 78,526 |
| Other allied troops | 1,144 | — | 1,144 |
| Civilians | 46,319 | 24,099 | 70,418 |
| Opposition fighters | 52,893 | 32,838 | 85,731 |
| Journalists and media workers | 74 | 87 | 161 |
| Humanitarian aid workers | 446 | 105 | 551 |
| Total | 176,206 | 66,650 | 242,856 |
| Total rounded | 176,000 | 67,000 | 243,000 |

*Source:* Watson Institute of International and Public Affairs, Brown University, "Costs of War," September 2022, https://watson.brown.edu/costsofwar/figures/2021/human-and-budgetary-costs-date-us-war-afghanistan-2001-2022.

Afghan War. Additionally 4,007 U.S. contractors and 551 humanitarian aid workers died. As seen in table 1.2, the deaths of Afghanis was much greater, resulting in an overall death total of 243,000. The overall monetary cost of the Afghan War has been placed at $2.313 trillion.

Two additional dimensions of the cost problem also must be taken into account when examining action policy: opportunity cost and blowback. **Opportunity cost** means that resources devoted to one foreign policy problem cannot be used to address other foreign policy or domestic problems. Resources are limited, but the foreign and domestic policy goals that policy makers may decide to pursue have no natural limits. The difference between the resources (power) available and the list of goals being pursued is often referred to as the **Lippmann gap** in honor of columnist Walter Lippmann, who in 1947 observed that a recurring problem in American foreign policy was an imbalance between American power and the goals it sought.[10] When this imbalance occurred, he found American foreign policy to be mired in domestic conflict and to be ineffective abroad. Most notably, there was inadequate preparation for conflicts, and peace agreements were too hastily constructed.

The second additional dimension of the cost problem is that policies have unintended consequences. **Blowback**, the term commonly used to capture the essence of this phenomenon,[11] was first used by the CIA to characterize problems that came about as a result of covert action programs. An example can be found in the War on Terrorism. After defeating Iraq, the United States instituted a policy of de-Ba'athification, removal of the Ba'ath Party's influence. Iraq's military was dissolved. All soldiers were dismissed but were allowed to keep their weapons. With no possibility of employment, many joined ISIS and came to hold important military leadership positions. Diplomacy can also produce blowback. Biden experienced major blowback following the announcement of a 2021 nuclear submarine agreement between the United States, Great Britain, and Australia. Under its terms, the two countries would help Australia build nuclear submarines, which it would then deploy in the Pacific Ocean. The agreement was meant to strengthen the U.S. presence in Asia, counter the military growth of China in the region, and rebuild ties with U.S. allies. Unexpectedly for the Biden administration, it also created a major crisis in U.S.-France relations. The agreement meant that Australia would cancel a $66 million agreement recently signed with France to buy French-built submarines, dealing a deep blow to the French economy and its standing in Asia. France characterized the deal as a "unilateral, brutal, unpredictable decision," one that Trump would have made.

## Building Consensus

In order to succeed, a foreign policy must be supported by the American public. American policy makers have long recognized this reality. Dean Acheson, who served as secretary of state from 1949 to 1953, once commented that 80 percent of the job of conducting foreign policy was managing the domestic ability to make policy.[12] The term long used to convey this sense of support was **bipartisanship**. It referred to the ability of both Democrats and Republicans to unite behind a course of action. Unity at home is seen as sending a message to adversaries that they cannot "wait out" a president in hopes of getting a better deal with their successor, or try to appeal to Congress to undercut their foreign policy. In the absence of unity at home, presidents face three sets of challenges in developing a foreign policy because each can become a point of political controversy: (1) what goals to pursue, (2) what instruments to select, and (3) how to judge the policy's outcome as a success or failure.

Recent presidents have found bipartisanship in increasingly short supply, raising the following question: is bipartisanship normal, or does it only appear under a limited set of conditions? This question received renewed attention in both Trump's and Biden's presidencies as they both struggled in varying ways with exiting from Afghanistan and developing a policy toward Ukraine.

Because it is such a powerful symbol, the national interest is a key instrument that presidents and others have used to build public support for their foreign policies. While it may not dictate a specific course of action, invoking the national interest places opponents on the defensive and serves as a point of consensus for the public to unite behind the president.[13]

At the same time, invoking the national interest in making foreign policy is not without its own costs. Two points are frequently raised against the overuse or misuse of invoking the national interest in conducting foreign policy. First, having justified a course of action as being in the national interest, it is politically difficult to do an about-face and declare that this is no longer the case. Typically in these cases, policy makers insist that their policy is correct but alter the definition of the national interest used as justification. Doing so raises questions about the true intent and commitment of the United States to particular goals. The Iraq War is a case in point. In 2003, President George W. Bush stated that the purpose of the Iraq War was "to disarm Iraq, free its people and defense [*sic*] the world from grave danger [of weapons of mass destruction]." In 2005, he characterized the Iraq War as an effort to quarantine terrorist groups that might otherwise attack the United States. In 2007, he compared America's enemies to communists.[14] Most recently, Trump freely and rapidly changed the direction of the U.S. national interest in his alternating characterizations of North Korea and China as friends and foes. Second, using the concept of the national interest as a means of building public support may also blind presidents to other foreign policy problems. By the end of Bush's presidency, the excessive focus on Iraq began to trouble Secretary of State Condoleezza Rice and others who feared that, by making Iraq the "end-all, be-all test" of American strength, U.S. standing and interests in other parts of the world were being harmed.[15]

# Selecting a Policy Instrument

Policy makers must decide not only which goals to pursue but also how to pursue them. A prime consideration in selecting a policy instrument is the context in which it will operate. Power cannot be used with equal effectiveness everywhere. Economic strategies that worked well when the United States was a hegemonic economic power may prove less useful in a period of economic decline or parity. Similarly, covert action policies successful in one country may fail in another. Beyond these issues, which will be addressed in later chapters, two other fundamental choices must be made: between hard power and soft power, and between unilateral and multilateral action.

## Hard Power and Soft Power

At the most general level, policy makers have two forms of power around which to build their foreign policies. The first, **hard power**, is coercive power that is the traditional means by which states protect and advance their national interests. While most often employed against an enemy, hard power can also be used against a reluctant ally. It is designed to force or compel another state to act in a prescribed fashion. Hard power tries to limit the range of choices open to another state so that the state will act in accordance with U.S. wishes. Hard power is most often associated with the military, but as Trump's foreign policy demonstrated with his frequent invocation of tariffs against allies and adversaries, economic power can also be used to compel.

**Soft power**, the power to influence and persuade, is rooted in the power of attraction. It seeks to convince states to willingly identify with the United States and support the U.S. position. Domination is replaced by cooperation. Examples include using the military for disaster and humanitarian relief efforts and strengthening democratic institutions and civil society in states making the transition to democracy. In each of these cases, the United States can draw on the reservoir of goodwill that is created in carrying out its foreign policy. The United States is not alone in using soft power. China also actively employs it, but for China soft power resides in its economic model, technological advances, and governing competence.[16]

Observers of U.S. foreign policy are divided as to whether the use of hard power or soft power is preferable. Hard power supporters note that soft power is difficult to use. Many of the associated resources, such as the appeal of American values and American democracy, are beyond the control of policy makers and are not easily mobilized. Soft power supporters note that while hard military power can defeat an enemy, it cannot produce peace. Robert Gates, who served in both the George W. Bush and Obama administrations, cautioned that "we cannot kill our way to victory."[17]

## Unilateral or Multilateral Action

A second important choice in selecting a policy instrument is whether to act alone (unilaterally) or as part of a group of states (multilaterally). *Unilateral action* offers the advantage of maximum control over the use of the policy instrument and the maximum benefit of its use. Offsetting this advantage, states acting unilaterally will also bear the greatest burden of failure. In addition, they may not possess the necessary hard and soft power resources to act alone.

*Multilateral action*—through formal alliances, international organizations, or informal coalitions—also presents states with potential problems. One is the *free-rider problem*, in which other states do not contribute their fair share to the joint undertaking, placing a greater burden on the more powerful states. A second potential problem is the *patron's dilemma*. Here, the more powerful state becomes entrapped in the foreign policy initiatives of less powerful states because they need their cooperation. If it supports the initiative, the more powerful state may be dragged into expensive and unwinnable conflicts; if it abandons the ally, its reputation and trustworthiness may come into question, making it harder to act multilaterally in the future.

Debates over the relative merits of pursuing goals largely through multilateral versus unilateral actions came into the forefront of the foreign policy debate in the Trump presidency. From the very beginning of his bid for the presidency, the core theme of Donald Trump's foreign policy was "America First." As we will see in the "Historical Lesson" section of chapter 5, this is not the first time this expression has been employed by those opposed to what they perceive as a dangerous and overly internationalist U.S. foreign policy in need of correction, but it did mark a significant departure and rejection of the foreign policy approach followed by post–World War II presidents. Reversing this break with the past was a major foreign policy objective of Biden, who repeatedly announced his intent to bring the United States "back to the table."

## Historical Lesson

### Into Afghanistan

U.S. involvement in Afghanistan began following the 1979 Soviet invasion. Carried out by some fifty thousand Soviet troops, the Reagan administration saw the invasion as an attempt to increase Soviet influence in the region. Evidence suggests that the Soviet leadership was motivated more by fears of large-scale domestic unrest on its borders. The Soviets had planned to leave the bulk of the fighting to the Afghan army, but soon they were forced to increase their military presence to over 110,000 troops as the Mujahedin, a loose coalition of Islamic forces, proved too strong to defeat. Peace talks began in 1982 leading to the Soviet withdrawal in 1989 along with pledges by the United States and Soviet Union not to intervene in Afghanistan's internal affairs. A major reason for the success of the Mujahedin was $2.1 billion in covert U.S. military support provided by the CIA.

The Mujahedin refused to accept the peace agreement and continued fighting for control of the Afghan government. The communist Afghan government fell in 1992, but that did not bring peace; the fighting continued. In the midst of this fighting, the Taliban, an Islamic fundamentalist movement, came into existence in 1994 with the support of neighboring Pakistan, which saw the Taliban as an Afghan force that would protect its security interests in the ongoing civil war. By 1998, the Taliban had succeeded in taking control over most of Afghanistan. Initially the United States was not opposed to the Taliban because it saw them as capable of returning order to Afghanistan. This soon changed. After the Taliban took control of the government, it began trying to enforce a reform agenda designed to create an Islamic state as well as provide support for al-Qaeda, which fought against Soviet forces following their invasion into Afghanistan. It was given refuge in Afghanistan by the Taliban after it was forced out of Somalia in 1996.

After 9/11, Bush demanded that the Taliban expel bin Laden and al-Qaeda. The Taliban refused Bush's request. On September 14, Bush obtained an Authorization for Use of Military Force (AUMF) from Congress against al-Qaeda and its supporters. Air strikes were begun on October 7, and on October 19, the first special operations forces entered Afghanistan to work with the Northern Alliance, a coalition of anti-Taliban warlords guided by CIA operatives. At first the Taliban were able to turn back the Northern Alliance, but by November, battlefield successes were mounting rapidly in its favor. On November 13, Kabul fell to the Northern Alliance. At a December 10, 2001, news conference, Deputy Secretary of Defense Paul Wolfowitz stated, "We have accomplished one major objective, which is the defeat of the Taliban government." The U.S. military commitment at this point was small. Only 2,500 American troops were in Afghanistan. While U.S. military commanders and Bush administration officials were caught off guard by the rapid collapse of the Taliban, movement was already underway to expand the U.S. goals that lay behind the military victory. In announcing the air strikes, Bush identified two limited objectives: disrupt al-Qaeda's use of Afghanistan as a base of operations and weaken the military capability of the Taliban government. Shortly before the special operations forces entered Afghanistan, a National Security Council strategy paper was approved which stated that the United States should "take steps to contribute to a stable post-Taliban Afghanistan." It also stated that "the U.S. should not commit to any post-Taliban military involvement, since the U.S. will be heavily engaged in the anti-terrorism effort worldwide."

A few days before the announcement by Wolfowitz, a conference of Afghan opposition leaders was held in Bonn, Germany, to establish a new government, the Afghan Interim Authority. Hamid Karzai was selected to head it. The UN announced the creation of an International Security Assistance Force that would be commanded by NATO to aid the new government in providing security. The Taliban were not invited to participate. In March 2002, Secretary of Defense Donald Rumsfeld commented that there had been no point in negotiating with what was left of the Taliban: "The only thing you can do is to bomb them and try to kill them. And that's what we did, and it worked."[18]

From the outset, the new Afghan government struggled to assert and build its legitimacy and expand its power. Taliban forces had fled to Pakistan and into rural areas of Afghanistan to evade capture. By the summer of 2003, they had begun to reassert their presence in Afghanistan. By July 2008, the situation in Afghanistan had deteriorated to the point that the chairman of the Joint Chiefs of Staff characterized it as "precarious and urgent"; thirty-six thousand U.S. troops were present at the time. Three options were presented to President Barack Obama: (1) eighty thousand additional troops for a counterinsurgency to maximize success, (2) forty thousand troops with a medium likelihood of success, and (3) twenty thousand troops to pursue a counterterrorism strategy.

### Applying the Lesson

1. How similar were the U.S. and Soviet experiences in going into Afghanistan? How did they differ?
2. How much changed in U.S. military strategy between the initial entry into Afghanistan and the reentry?
3. What other options might the United States (and Soviets) have pursued to stabilize the situation in Afghanistan?

# Presidential Foreign Policy Doctrines

**Grand strategy** is the linchpin uniting goals and tactics in a government-wide approach that brings together all elements of power. The earliest U.S. grand strategy was put forward in President George Washington's Farewell Address. His call for avoiding entanglement in foreign alliances provided the conceptual foundation for a policy of isolationism that, in various forms, was embraced by many of his successors. Other examples of notable early American foreign policy grand strategies include the *Monroe Doctrine*, which called for a policy of activism and the creation of a U.S. sphere of influence in Latin America in return for involvement in European affairs; *Manifest Destiny*, which was a policy of continental expansion; and the

*Open Door*, a strategy for establishing an American presence in Asia. In this section, five post–World War II foreign policy doctrines that have been particularly important for signaling shifts in the agenda of U.S. foreign policy will be introduced. After discussing them, our attention will turn to questions about whether a Trump grand strategy existed, what the legacy of Trump's foreign policy might be for the future of U.S. foreign policy, and how Joe Biden's foreign policy fits in with that of Donald Trump.

## The Truman Doctrine

The origins of the Truman Doctrine are found in a speech that President Harry S. Truman made to a special joint session of Congress on March 17, 1949, in which he asked for $400 million for economic assistance to Greece and Turkey to help them resist Soviet-inspired aggression. In making his request, he asserted that "it must be the policy of the United States to support free peoples who are resisting attempted subjugation by armed minorities or outside pressures."

Greece was involved in a civil war that pitted a pro-British government against leftist rebels led by the communist-controlled National Liberation Front. Turkey was involved in an ongoing dispute with the Soviet Union over control of the Dardanelles and Bosporus, straits linking Soviet ports along the Black Sea with the Mediterranean Sea. From the Soviet point of view, access to the Mediterranean was crucial to its ability to act as a great power, but it was also a security threat. During World War II, Turkey had permitted German naval forces to enter the Black Sea via the straits. Stalin now insisted on international control over the straits, a demand that Turkey interpreted as a threat to its national sovereignty.

Truman's speech is widely seen as the equivalent of a U.S. declaration of Cold War against the Soviet Union. It firmly rejected the pre–World War II U.S. foreign policy of isolationism and provided a rationale for U.S. activism in world affairs. Truman divided the world into two opposite and competing ways of life, "one based on freedom, another on coercion," and called on Americans to help free people remain free. The Truman Doctrine, as the content of this speech came to be known, also identified a universal enemy with its references to aggression by "totalitarian regimes," a phrase applied almost exclusively to the Soviet Union and its allies.

Although the Truman Doctrine did not specify a set of actions to be taken, its implementation quickly centered on two concepts: containment and deterrence. Central to both was a status quo orientation to events in the world. U.S. foreign policy would not actively seek to roll back the Iron Curtain but focus on stopping the further expansion of the Soviet Union and its sphere of influence.

## The Nixon Doctrine

The Nixon Doctrine, presented in an address to the nation in November 1969, was part of an attempt to formulate a policy that would allow the United States to remain the dominant power in the international system after Vietnam but not require it to send troops abroad to contain the spread of communism. Nixon asserted that "a nation cannot remain great if it betrays is allies and lets down its allies. . . . The United States will keep its treaty commitments . . . we shall look to the nation directly threatened to assume primary responsibility for providing the manpower for its defense." In short, the United States would help free countries defend themselves by providing both military and economic assistance, but those countries must provide for their own military defense. There would be no more Vietnams.

Two major initiatives grew out of this strategy. The most narrowly constructed was *Vietnamization*, which sought to turn over responsibility for defending South Vietnam to the South Vietnamese. In an effort to buy sufficient time for Vietnamization to work, Nixon ordered the invasion of Cambodia and Laos to eliminate communist sanctuaries. That strategy failed. In spring 1972, North Vietnamese forces attacked across the seventeenth parallel into the South, forcing Nixon to "re-Americanize" the war. The second, more broadly conceived policy initiative was **détente**, which sought to engage the Soviet Union and China in a dialogue that would transform their relationship with the United States from competition and open distrust to limited cooperation and muted conflict. The most significant accomplishments of détente were the opening to China and the signing of Strategic Arms Limitation Talks (SALT) arms control agreements with the Soviet Union.

A major consequence of the Nixon Doctrine was a massive increase in the level of arms transfers to regional powers allied with the United States. Indonesia, the Philippines, Saudi Arabia, Iran, Pakistan, and South Korea became prime recipients of this aid.

## The Carter Doctrine

The Carter Doctrine is the name given to the policy announced by President Jimmy Carter in his 1980 State of the Union address following the Soviet Union's December 1979 invasion of Afghanistan. In his speech, Carter stated that the United States would treat an "attempt by any outside force to gain control of the Persian Gulf region as an assault on the vital interests of the United States and such force will be repelled by any means necessary, including military force."

The Carter Doctrine represented an about-face for Carter's original foreign policy toward the Soviet Union. Carter had campaigned on a platform that rejected power politics and promised to replace it with an emphasis on human rights and morality. Shortly after being elected, in 1977 he quickly moved to negotiate a new Panama Canal Treaty that would transfer sovereignty over the canal to Panama. The following year, in September 1978, Carter arranged for a summit conference at the presidential retreat at Camp David between Israeli prime minister Menachem Begin and Egyptian president Anwar Sadat, at which both leaders agreed to a "just, comprehensive and durable settlement for the Middle East conflict." This agenda deemphasized the importance of the Soviet Union to U.S. foreign policy.

The Soviet action caught the Carter administration off guard and called into question the wisdom of Carter's foreign policy agenda of building peace. As part of his response, Carter requested an increase in annual defense spending and expanded the American naval and air presence in the Persian Gulf. Debate over the wisdom of this response was soon overshadowed by the Carter administration's inability to resolve the Iranian hostage crisis and secure the release of the Americans taken hostage in the American embassy.

## The Reagan Doctrine

Unlike Nixon and Carter, for most of his presidency Reagan saw the Soviet Union as a state to be challenged, not an opportunity for cooperation. Early in his administration, he referred to the Soviet Union as an "evil empire," charging that "the only morality they recognize is what will further their cause; meaning they reserve unto themselves the right to commit any crime, to lie, to cheat." A prerequisite for dealing effectively with such a state was a major buildup of American military strength and a toughened stance on arms control. Reagan called for a $16 billion increase in defense spending over five years, the deployment of the MX missile system, the renewed production of poison gas, the development of the neutron bomb, and the beginning of a long-term research plan—the Strategic Defense Initiative ("Star Wars")—to build a missile defense system. On arms control, his administration went public with a series of accusations of Soviet arms control cheating.

In his 1985 State of the Union speech, Reagan asserted, "We must not break faith with those who are risking their lives—on every continent from Afghanistan to Nicaragua—to defy Soviet aggression and secure rights which have been ours from birth. Support of freedom fighters is self-defense." By speaking in this manner, Reagan signaled an important shift in his foreign policy from that of his predecessors. The United States would now do more than contain the spread of communism; it would work actively to remove communists and their allies from power. In fact, the Reagan administration was already doing so.

One case involved organizing and supporting the Contras, opponents of the revolutionary Nicaraguan Sandinista government. The administration's unwavering support for the Contras became one of the most controversial features of its foreign policy. Reagan characterized the Contras as the "moral equivalent of the founding fathers," but human rights groups complained at length about their brutality. In 1984, Congress cut off funding for the Contras. In an effort to circumvent this ban, the Reagan administration undertook a failed secret initiative that became known as the Iran-Contra Affair. The initiative proposed that American weapons intended for Israel would be sold to Iran, and Israel would receive new weapons. In return, Iran would help secure the release of American hostages in Lebanon. Money from the weapons sales would be used to fund the Contras.

The Reagan administration was also deeply involved in Afghanistan. The primary Afghan group opposing the Soviet Union's invasion, the Mujahedin, proved to be a formidable fighting force that tied down Soviet forces. By 1987, the administration had provided the Mujahedin with $630 million. This aid was not without its long-term costs. A large amount of U.S. arms flowed into the hands of Afghan groups that combined forces with the Taliban-led government after the Soviet Union left, and were later used against U.S.-supported interests.

Near the end of his administration, Ronald Reagan did an about-face in his foreign policy. He and Soviet leader Mikhail Gorbachev became regular partners at summit conferences, meeting five times during Reagan's last term. It was their second summit at Reykjavik, Iceland, that provoked the most controversy. The Reagan administration was caught off guard by Gorbachev's proposal that both sides eliminate all offensive strategic nuclear weapons. Reagan initially accepted the proposal but backed off later because of his personal attachment to the Star Wars program.

## The Bush Doctrine

Although the Bush Doctrine first appeared as a unified statement in the September 2002 *National Security Strategy of the United States of America*, its key themes were already visible by that time.[19] Speaking to a joint session of Congress following the 9/11 terrorist attacks, President George W. Bush stated that the United States "would make no distinction between the terrorists who committed these acts and those who harbor them" and that "we will pursue nations that provide aid or safe haven to terrorism. Every nation, in every region, now has a decision to make. Either you are with us or you are with the terrorists." To these observations, the National Security Strategy added that "we cannot let our enemies strike first," that the United States will use its power to encourage free and open societies, and that it will never allow its military supremacy to be challenged.

The Bush Doctrine provided the intellectual framework for launching the Global War on Terrorism, the invasion of Afghanistan to remove the Taliban from power, and the invasion of Iraq. Achieving those objectives provided problematic. Central to the administration's argument for the Iraqi invasion was its possession of weapons of mass destruction, a claim that later proved to be false. The Taliban and Iraq's Saddam Hussein were removed from power with relative ease, but capturing Osama bin Laden and establishing democracy in Iraq proved to be a far greater challenge. It was only near the end of the Bush administration, as it moved its goals away from spreading democracy, that a sense of stability returned to the region.

## In Search of the Trump Doctrine

Not every president has a foreign policy doctrine with their name attached. For some, foreign policy either is not a high priority or largely follows in the footsteps of previous presidents. Others find grand strategies hard to change.[20] Political scientist Richard Betts identifies still another factor complicating the search for presidential grand strategies.[21] He argues that grand strategy rarely guides foreign policy. Often the phrase "grand strategy" is imposed on presidential foreign policy by outside commentators as they seek to describe what they see.

Virtually from the outset of his administration, a debate began over whether a Trump Doctrine existed that would qualify as a grand strategy: did it serve as a coherent plan made in advance of a foreign policy undertaking that would guide its formulation and implementation?[22]

One frequently cited foundation for a Trump Doctrine is the concept of "America First." It was also a key component of his campaign for the White House and had a prominent place in his inaugural address:

> For many decades, we've enriched foreign industry at the expense of American industry; subsidized the armies of other countries while allowing for the very sad depletion of our military; we've defended other nation's borders while refusing to defend our own; and spent trillions of dollars overseas while America's infrastructure has fallen into disrepair and decay. . . . From this day forward, a new vision will govern our land . . . it's going to be America First.

While America First was a highly effective campaign slogan, its value as a guide to foreign policy proved problematic due to disagreements over its definition and frequent invocation to justify different polices and changes in policy. Consequently, many observers have focused more closely on Trump's personal worldview and his approach to conducting foreign policy in order to uncover the ideas underlying a Trump Doctrine. Six factors stand out as particularly influential in his conduct of foreign policy:

1. Trump's clearest focus was on unraveling or reversing polices inherited from previous administrations. He was far less clear or consistent regarding the nature of the concrete policies it hoped to put in their place.

2. Trump saw the world as an arena of zero-sum competition, or winners and losers. A global community did not exist. "America is in the game and American is going to win."
3. In navigating this competitive world, Trump embraced a bilateral transactionalist approach to foreign policy. The objective was to a make a deal that increased U.S. power, not to transform the world.
4. Trump's focus on short-term outcomes was insensitive to the second- and third-order consequences of a decision.
5. For Trump, the key bottom-line measure of winning and losing was found in increasing U.S. economic power and standing.
6. Trump treated foreign policy in instinctive and personalized terms, focusing on personal relationships rather than bureaucratic interactions.

## Is There a Trump Foreign Policy Legacy?

Today, a different question is debated: what is the legacy of Trump's foreign policy? Is it a "one and done" foreign policy that will have no or little influence on Biden's foreign policy and those of his successors, or will its influence continue to be felt at home and abroad in the making and conduct of U.S. foreign policy?

Those who downplay the significance of Trump's foreign policy legacy build their case around such factors as the inconsistency of his foreign policy, his heavy focus on undoing the policies of his predecessors, his impulsive decision-making style, and the short-term focus on his transactionalist approach to foreign policy.

Those who see its influence as potentially long lasting note that his foreign policy did not represent a complete break with the past.[23] Additionally, they point to two other factors. The first lies in domestic politics. Trump and his foreign policy agenda rested on a growing domestic base of populism and American disenchantment with the costs and benefits of global involvement. The second factor lies in global politics. Trump's foreign policy was not viewed in a positive light by many heads of government and left them fearful it would return. Their national interest required taking steps to protect their countries from the costs that America First imposed on them. From the perspective of foreign governments, Trump's foreign policy is "gone but not forgotten" and one from which a return to pre-Trump foreign policy is impossible.[24]

Also factoring into the debate over Trump's foreign policy legacy is the extent to which Biden's foreign policy mirrors it. As we will see throughout our discussion of U.S. foreign policy, a central theme in Biden's conduct of foreign policy has been to reverse Trump's policies. Richard Haass suggests that while there are real differences between the two, at the end of Biden's first year in office four significant points of continuity existed: (1) the central place of great-power rivalries in their foreign policy, (2) the embrace of American nationalism, (3) the policy of withdrawal from the Middle East, and (4) the continuing low place that values, most notably human rights and democracy promotion, held in their foreign policies. On this last point, Haass notes that while Biden pledged to prioritize these values, they have not risen to a prominent level in U.S. foreign policy.[25]

## Assessing Foreign Policy Results

Judging the consequences of a foreign policy is a complicated task. Success and failure are often treated as absolute categories, yet this is seldom the case. Far more typical are situations in which success and failure are both present in varying degrees. A state rarely has a single goal when it undertakes a course of action, and the reality of multiple goals further complicates the calculations of costs and benefits. Estimates of success and failure also depend on time frame. Economic sanctions work slowly, but this does not mean they are any less effective than fast actions. Such slow solutions might even be preferable, because they minimize the risk of miscalculation that occurs during crisis situations.

Political considerations also cloud any evaluation of the effectiveness of a policy instrument. In 2003, Libya announced that it was giving up its pursuit of nuclear weapons. The George W. Bush administration quickly hailed the announcement as evidence of the success of its tough post-9/11 military stance, including the doctrine of preemption. Others countered that the success really should be attributed to years of behind-the-scenes diplomacy and economic sanctions.[26]

Most fundamentally, U.S. foreign policies can be judged in terms of three standards: (1) intellectual coherence, (2) the extent to which they are motivated by domestic politics rather than foreign events, and (3) consistency of application to foreign policy problems. Each of these reference points has been found to be a problem to some extent in the five foreign policy doctrines examined earlier. The following sections include selective examples from these doctrines to illustrate the challenge of evaluating foreign policy.

## Intellectual Coherence

Does the foreign policy build on a sound and consistent set of ideas? Does it contain contradictory assumptions and lines of action? The Truman Doctrine and the policy of containment were grounded in two very different views of the Soviet Union, both of which could not be correct. One view, championed by George Kennan, saw Soviet expansion largely as defensive and reactionary, with Soviet leaders more concerned with staying in power than with spreading communism. The authors of National Security Council document 68 (NSC-68) rejected this perspective. They saw Soviet hostility to the United States as unrelenting and based on Marxist-Leninist ideological principles. Nixon's policy of détente was firmly rooted in National Security Advisor Henry Kissinger's belief that the most stable international system was one in which all major powers viewed the international system as legitimate, which the Soviet Union and China could not do as long as they were the target of American containment efforts.[27] At the other end of the continuum, Carter's foreign policy was characterized by sympathetic observers as "the hell of good intentions" for its immature and mistaken belief that it could push U.S.-Soviet relations to the sidelines while addressing human rights problems.[28]

## The Dominance of Domestic Politics

As a popular slogan goes, "Domestic politics stops at the water's edge." Foreign policy is about interacting with the world and should not be influenced by domestic politics. This is easier said than done. Truman resisted adopting the changes suggested in NSC-68 because of their budgetary implications, especially the need to fight communism everywhere in the world. Only after the outbreak of the Korean War and the changed domestic climate at home did he embrace a more expansive—and expensive—definition of containment. Reagan represents an interesting case. He pursued aggressive foreign policies and advocated large-scale military spending, yet did not call on the American public to make sacrifices. As one observer put it, the great appeal of Reagan's foreign policy was that it demanded so little from the public while promising to deliver so much.[29] When costs were encountered, such as the attacks on the marine barracks in Lebanon in 1983 that killed 241 marines, Reagan quickly terminated the policy.

## Consistency of Application

Critics have charged that no administration has fully succeeded in using its doctrine as an organizing device to guide all foreign policy decisions. In some cases this is understandable or necessary, because circumstances change. However, in other cases it can undermine the ability of presidents to achieve their foreign policy goals. Carter succumbed to offering arms sales to states with poor human rights records. Reagan did little to aid Eastern European states seeking to break away from the Soviet Union, entered into negotiations with supporters of terrorism as part of the Iran-Contra Affair, and entered into arms control talks with the Soviet Union near the end of his presidency. Bush engaged in a preemptive war with one member of the "axis of evil" (Iraq), but found it necessary to enter into negotiations with another member (North Korea) that had obtained nuclear weapons, and struggled to obtain support from the international community to block the efforts of the third (Iran) to procure nuclear weapons.

# Over the Horizon: The Future of Grand Strategy

As the Trump administration and its predecessors discovered, constructing an effective grand strategy is not an easy task.[30] In 2005, Secretary of State Condoleezza Rice stated that the U.S. strategy in Iraq was to "clear, hold, and build." General George Casey, then the commanding general in Iraq, commented that this was little more than a bumper sticker.[31] It was not a strategy. President Obama once summarized his outlook on foreign policy as "Don't do stupid sh**."

On the table today is the question about the future of U.S. grand strategy. Advocates of having a grand strategy assert that major powers cannot and should not make foreign policy decisions "on the fly," and that achieving foreign policy goals and effectively managing state power requires a plan. In the words of Dean Acheson, Truman's secretary of state, policy makers need to escape a focus on the "thundering present" and instead think about the big picture and ask big questions. No matter how great they are, changes in the structure of the international system and the dynamics of world politics do not eliminate the need for grand strategy. In fact, they only increase that need by providing policy makers with a long-term focus and prioritizing goals.

In place of a grand strategy, Eliot Cohen calls for embracing the concept of *statecraft*.[32] Instead of building foreign policy around strategic ideas that rely on grand principles and simplifications of complex problems, the United States should build its foreign policy around the ability to detect and respond to challenges and opportunities in an effective manner as they arise. What matters in making foreign policy is "sensing, adjusting, exploiting and doing rather than planning and theorizing." According to Cohen, the United States has embraced statecraft before. He identifies Theodore Roosevelt as a president whose foreign policy was built around statecraft.

Political scientist Daniel Drezner raises an even deeper concern about the future of grand strategy. Given the fractured nature of American domestic politics, he wonders whether any viable grand strategy can be created that will last more than one election cycle.[33]

## Critical Thinking Questions

1. Identify ten foreign policy problems facing the United States today. Divide them into A-, B-, and C-list problems. On what basis did you make your decisions?

2. What type of foreign policy problems can best be addressed by hard power? By soft power?

3. Select a foreign policy problem. What standards should be used to evaluate U.S. efforts to address it?

## Key Terms

action policy, 6
bipartisanship, 8
blowback, 7
declaratory policy, 6
détente, 13
grand strategy, 11

hard power, 9
Lippmann gap, 7
national interest, 5
opportunity cost, 7
public goods, 6
soft power, 9

News
War in Ukraine

# We will never surrender our cities, says Zelenskiy, rejecting Russian terms

Jon Henley
Isobel Koshiw Kyiv

Ukraine has said it will never bow to ultimatums to surrender its cities, including the devastated Mariupol, ... thorities in Odesa accused ... residential

**Russia's war in Ukraine: latest developments**

● Under Russian control    Russian-controlled territory    → Russian invasion routes

Russia

Belarus

Chernobyl    Chernihiv    Konotop    Sumy

Poland    Lutsk    Kyiv    Kharkiv

Lviv    Ukraine    Dnipro
River    Dnipro

Ivano-Frankivsk    Zaporizhzhia    Don

...mesens'k    Melitopol

## Learning Objectives

Students will be able to:

1. Identify the constant underlying features of the international system.
2. Contrast the assumptions of the perspectives of realism, liberalism, and constructivism.
3. Assess the relative importance of the three evolutionary trends in the structure of the international system.
4. Explain and rank order the importance of the three dominant features of the international system for our understanding of the Russia-Ukraine War.

# On the Agenda: The Ukraine War

On February 18, 2022, President Joe Biden announced that in the coming days Russia would invade Ukraine. Five days later, Russian forces entered Ukraine on what Russian president Vladimir Putin described as a special operations mission to demilitarize and denazify Ukraine. Within minutes air attacks began, followed by an invasion by ground forces.

In the period leading up to the invasion and after the invasion began, the United States relied on economic sanctions and military aid, including sending additional U.S. troops to Europe to reassure allies but not for combat, to aid Ukraine. By October, it had provided Ukraine with $16.8 billion in aid. Table 2.1 presents a listing of military aid given to Ukraine in the first six months of fighting. Four goals underlay U.S. efforts: (1) maintain Ukraine's independence, (2) make sure the invasion was a strategic failure and had a negative impact on Russian military power, (3) strengthen NATO, and (4) keep the war from escalating.

Here we will review the events leading up to the invasion and the path fighting took leading up to the onset of winter. In the "On the Agenda" section of chapter 9, we will look at the Biden administration's decision making leading up to the invasion. We will also look at congressional funding for Ukraine in chapter 6, and in chapter 13 we will present some of the lessons learned from the Russian war effort with respect to its cyber operations.

Signs of a possible invasion of Ukraine began to surface in March and April 2021 when Russia began a large-scale buildup of military forces along Ukraine's border. This was followed by a second major buildup in October when it placed an estimated one hundred thousand troops there. In many respects this was not the beginning of the conflict. One starting point is 1991 when, with the collapse of the Soviet Union, Ukraine became independent and declared itself to be neutral. During the Cold War, Russia had built a security shield separating itself from Western Europe with the establishment of communist satellite states in Eastern Europe and the Warsaw Pact as a counter to NATO. For background on NATO, see the "Historical Lesson" section. This shield was now gone, and with Ukraine declaring itself neutral the possibility existed of having threatening troops and nuclear weapons stationed right on its borders.

A more recent starting point is 2014 when months of large-scale street protests forced the pro-Russian president Viktor Yanukovych to resign and flee to Russia after he rejected a trade agreement with the European Union in favor of closer ties with Russia. Days later, pro-Russian Ukrainian militia and Russian forces took control of Crimea. In short order a pro-Russian government was established. A referendum followed that led to a declaration of independence and then its incorporation into Russia. Crimea had been part of the Russian Republic of the Soviet Union until 1954 when for political reasons it was made part of the

| Table 2.1 | United States Security Assistance Committed to Ukraine |
|---|---|

- Over 1,400 Stinger antiaircraft systems
- Over 6,500 Javelin antiarmor systems
- Over 20,000 other antiarmor systems
- Over 700 Switchblade tactical unmanned aerial systems
- 126 155mm Howitzers and 260,000 155mm artillery rounds
- 36,000 105mm artillery rounds
- 126 tactical vehicles to tow 155mm Howitzers
- 19 tactical vehicles to recover equipment
- 8 high-mobility artillery rocket systems and ammunition
- 20 Mi-17 helicopters
- Hundreds of armored high-mobility multipurpose wheeled vehicles
- 200 M113 armored personnel carriers
- Over 10,000 grenade launchers and small arms
- Over 59,000,000 rounds of small arms ammunition
- 75,000 sets of body armor and helmets
- 121 Phoenix Ghost tactical unmanned aerial systems
- Laser-guided rocket systems
- Puma unmanned aerial systems
- Unmanned coastal defense vessels
- 22 counter-artillery radars
- 4 counter-mortar radars
- 4 air surveillance radars
- 2 harpoon coastal defense systems
- 18 coastal and riverine patrol boats
- M18A1 Claymore antipersonnel munitions
- C-4 explosives and demolition equipment for obstacle clearing
- Tactical secure communications systems
- Thousands of night vision devices, thermal imagery systems, optics, and laser rangefinders
- Commercial satellite imagery services
- Explosive ordnance disposal protective gear
- Chemical, biological, radiological, nuclear protective equipment
- Medical supplies including first-aid kits
- Electronic jamming equipment
- Field equipment and spare parts
- Funding for training, maintenance, and sustainment

*Source:* U.S. Security Cooperation with Ukraine Fact Sheet, State Department, July 8, 2022.

Ukrainian Republic. Fighting also erupted in the ethnically Russian Donbas region of eastern Ukraine between Ukraine government forces and pro-independence Russian-backed militia. In 2015 the Minsk Peace Agreement brought a formal end to fighting. By terms of the agreement, Russia would pull back its troops and end its interference in Ukraine. In turn, Ukraine would provide a measure of autonomy for Russian-backed militia in eastern Ukraine. The peace was a fragile one as fighting continued in Donbas, with each side accusing the other of failing to abide by its terms.

In the immediate run-up to the invasion of Ukraine, the size of the Russian forces on Ukraine's border reached some two hundred thousand troops. Putin also actively engaged in public diplomacy, citing historic ties between Russians and Ukrainians and referring to them as "one people." He asserted that the United States had installed an anti-Russian regime in Ukraine and provided it with weapons, creating a "critical threat to Russian security" and "an existential threat to world peace." Two days before the invasion, Putin recognized the Donetsk and Luhansk oblasts (provinces) in the Donbas region as independent countries, a move that was followed by their request for Russian military support against Ukraine.

Russia's invasion of Ukraine was a broadly constructed blitzkrieg operation designed to place Russian troops in control of most of Ukraine and lead to the rapid collapse of the government. Neither happened. Russian forces were not up to the military task, resistance from the Ukrainian people was far greater than Russia anticipated, and foreign military and economic aid began arriving, something a quick victory would have prevented. Just over one month into the invasion, Russia announced it was redirecting its military efforts to focus on liberating the Donbas region. Military successes were achieved by Russia with this change, but they were described as "uneven and incremental" and came at a high cost of personnel and equipment. High casualty rates, low morale, an insufficient number of troops, poor leadership, and limited stocks of weapons all took their toll. Increasingly Russia had to rely on mercenaries (such as the Wagner Group) and antiquated weapons, such as 1960s tanks and inaccurate missiles. In the coming months it would rely on Iranian drones and North Korean artillery. Ukraine also successfully took back some territory it had lost, but also at a high human and economic cost. The United States estimates that by mid-April, 5,500–10,000 Ukrainian soldiers and 16,000 Russian soldiers had died. International reports placed the number of Ukrainian civilian losses at some 5,000 killed and 6,520 injured.

It was then expected that a third phase of the war would begin, one in which each side tried to wear down the other in a lengthy war of attrition.[1] Instead, in late summer, after a brief lull, the Ukraine war entered an *action-reaction* phase of escalating violence. The Ukraine launched a successful counteroffensive, severely damaged a key Russian bridge in Crimea, and retook key cities such as Kherson. Putin called up some 300,000 reservists, staged referendums in occupied parts of the Ukraine that supported his call for annexing them into Russia, was linked to sabotaging Nord Stream gas pipelines, and engaged in stepped-up missile strikes of civilian targets and the power infrastructure of Kyiv and other cities. Most significantly, Putin raised the prospect of using nuclear weapons, stating at one point: "With a threat to the territorial integrity of our country, to protect Russia and our people, we of course will use all the means at our disposal. This is not a bluff."

This chapter lays the foundation for developing a deeper understanding of foreign policy problems facing the United States today by presenting three broad international political perspectives used to study world politics and then identifying key structural features in world politics. Attention then turns to the contemporary international system, examining three important issues (terrorism, globalization, and American hegemony) and comparing American and non-American views of the world today.

## Thinking about the World

Disagreements about the causes and consequences of foreign policy decisions are an enduring feature of the commentary on American foreign policy. A basic reason for these disagreements is the existence of different and conflicting theoretical perspectives about the fundamental nature of world politics. Three perspectives are particularly important for understanding the larger debate over what American foreign policy should and can be: realism, neoliberalism, and constructivism.

## Realism

The first theoretical perspective is **realism**.[2] For realists, world politics involves a constant struggle for power carried out under conditions that border on anarchy. There is little room for embracing universal principles or taking on moral crusades. The acknowledged founding voice of American realism was Hans Morgenthau, who captured the essence of realism in stating that leaders "think and act in terms of interests defined as power." For realists, peace—defined as the absence of war—is possible only when states follow their own narrowly defined national interests. Early realists stressed human nature as the central driving force in world politics. Later realists focused attention on the central role played by the structure of the international system. Once in place, the international system becomes a force that states cannot control; instead, it controls the states.

## Neoliberalism

A second theoretical perspective is **neoliberalism**.[3] While conceding that the international system is anarchic in many respects, neoliberalism rejects the pessimistic realist conclusion that world politics is essentially a conflictual process from which there is no escape. Instead, neoliberalism sees world politics as an arena in which all participants (states and nonstate actors) can advance their own interests peacefully without threatening others. This becomes possible by creating conditions that allow the inherent rationality of individuals to come to the forefront. Among the primary factors that promote peaceful intercourse are democracy, respect for international laws, participation in international organizations, restraints on weapons, and free trade. Although many of his views are closer to traditional liberalism, President Woodrow Wilson, who championed the League of Nations after World War I, is the American statesperson most associated today with neoliberalism. Long dismissed by realists as idealistic, Wilsonianism began to reassert itself as a powerful voice in American foreign policy after the Vietnam War.

## Constructivism

The third theoretical perspective relevant to American foreign policy is **constructivism**.[4] While realism and neoliberalism differ in their interpretations of the essential features of world politics, they both share the conviction that the nature of world politics is fixed and that objective rules for conducting foreign policy can be derived from it. Constructivists take issue with this idea, asserting that international politics is not shaped by fixed underlying forces but by our perceptions. Ideas and cultural and historical experience give meaning to what we see. Free trade is not inherently a force for peace or a cause of war. How it is evaluated depends on personal and societal experiences with it.

Perceptions of the world change over time and as we interact with others. An entire generation of Americans has grown up after the end of the Cold War and sees American global dominance as natural. As a result, many in the United States have trouble understanding how revolutionary and unnatural such dominance can appear to others.[5] One year after it was announced, a commentator noted that, from China's perspective, Obama's Asian pivot "was pulled right out of the old Cold War playbook. . . . Washington is trying to inflame new tensions by isolating it and emboldening the countries China has territorial disputes with."[6] The administration soon quietly dropped the phrase "Asian pivot" and begin speaking about the U.S. "rebalancing" to Asia.

# International System: Structural Constants

This section and the following two present an overview of the forces in the international system most often seen as driving state behavior: structural constants, evolutionary trends, and the dominant features of today's international system. While realists, neoliberals, and constructivists would disagree on how to rank their relative importance, all would agree that an effective U.S. foreign policy requires thinking critically about each of them. Structural constants include decentralization, the self-help nature of the international system, and stratification.

## Decentralization

The first enduring feature of the international system is *decentralization*. From the realist perspective, no central political institutions exist to make laws or see to their enforcement in the international arena. There is no common political culture to anchor an agreed-on set of norms governing the behavior of states. The result is a highly competitive international system with a constant expectation of violence and very little expectation that international law or appeals to moral principles will greatly influence the resolution of an issue.

Decentralization does not mean anarchy. For realists, *ordered anarchy* would be a more apt characterization. Enforceable laws and common values may be absent, but there are rules limiting permissible behavior and directions to follow in settling disputes, lending a measure of predictability and certainty to international transactions. Rules are less permanent than laws, are more general in nature, and tend to be normative statements rather than commands. They grow out of the basic principles of self-help and decentralization and are rooted in the distribution of power in the international system. As power distribution changes, so will the rules.

Neoliberals hold a different interpretation. In their view, rules are negotiated, voluntarily entered into, and obeyed by states trying to advance their national interests. Once established, rules often demonstrate a remarkably long life span that outlasts the specific problem they were designed to address or the identity and power of those who negotiated them into existence.

Constructivism takes exception to both realism and liberalism, arguing that "anarchy is what states make of it." To constructivists, anarchy lacks a fixed definition. States may see anarchy as requiring more power or requiring cooperation, depending on the values they hold and their past experiences.

## Self-Help System

The second structural constant in the international system grows out of the first. According to realists, the international system is a self-help system. A state must rely on itself to accomplish its foreign policy goals. To do otherwise runs the risk of manipulation or betrayal at the hands of another state. It is important to stress that great powers as well as smaller powers both need to avoid excessive dependence on others.

The self-help principle challenges policy makers to bring goals and power resources into balance. Pursuing more goals than the available resources allow or squandering resources on secondary objectives saps the vitality of the state and makes it unable to respond effectively to future challenges. Many argue that Vietnam is a classic example of the crippling consequences of an inability to balance goals and resources. American policy produced steady increases in the level of U.S. commitment to the war, but it did not bring the United States any closer to victory. Instead, the reverse occurred: the longer the United States remained in Vietnam and the greater its commitment, the more elusive victory became.

Neoliberals reject the emphasis on self-help. From their perspective, the ability of states and individuals to recognize the costs and benefits of different strategies allows them to pursue cooperative, mutually beneficial solutions to problems and avoid the use of force in settling disputes. Constructivism offers a cautionary perspective, suggesting that self-help can be interpreted as taking risks or acting cautiously to keep goals and resources in balance; it can mean acting alone or in cooperation with others. The perspective adopted reflects societal norms, values, and ideas; as those change, so will policy.

## A Stratified System

The third structural constant in the international system is its stratified nature. The equality of states embedded in the concept of **sovereignty** is a legal myth. The principle of sovereignty dates back to the Treaty of Westphalia and the beginnings of the modern state system in 1648. It holds that no legal authority exists above the state, except that which the state voluntarily accepts. The reality of international politics is quite different; sovereignty is a matter of degree rather than an absolute. States are "born unequal."[7] The resources from which states draw their power are distributed unequally across the globe. As such, the ability of states to accomplish their foreign policy objectives (and their very choice of objectives) varies from state to state.

The principle of stratification leaves open the question of how unevenly power is distributed. The three most commonly discussed forms of stratification are **unipolar, bipolar**, and **multipolar**. In a unipolar system, one state possesses more power than any other. No other state or alliance of states can match it. In a bipolar system, two relatively equal states have more power than all others. Typically, permanent alliance systems form around the two states. A multipolar system is characterized by the presence of a core group of states that are relatively equal in power; floating coalitions—rather than permanent alliances—form as states join and leave to accomplish goals and protect their interests.

Neoliberals would argue that this picture is overdrawn. Rather than being organized around the global or regional distribution of power, the international system should be seen as organized around issue areas, or *regimes*, each of which is organized around its own set of rules and norms. Here again, enlightened self-interest is expected to produce regimes based on accommodation rather than domination. As a perspective for studying foreign policy and international politics, constructivism urges caution in creating fixed power hierarchies and classifying states and is reluctant to provide firm guidance on which policy to adopt or how to define the global context in which states act. This is seen by its advocates as a major contribution to American foreign policy and by its detractors as a major limitation.

# International System: Evolutionary Trends

Although the basic structure of the international system has endured over time, the system itself is not unchanging. Four post–World War II trends are especially notable for their ability to influence the conduct of U.S. foreign policy: diffusion of power, issue proliferation, actor proliferation, and regional diversity.

## Diffusion of Power

Power, the ability to achieve objectives, is typically viewed as something we possess—a commodity to be acquired, stored, and manipulated. However, it must also be viewed as a relational concept. Ultimately, it is not how much power a state has, but how much power it has on a specific issue compared to those with whom it is dealing.

The postwar era has seen a steady diffusion of power. The causes for this are many. After examining the decline of empires throughout history, Robert Gilpin asserts that a cycle of hegemonic decline can be identified.[8] As the cycle progresses, the burdens of imperial leadership, the increased emphasis on the consumption of goods and services, and the international diffusion of technology conspire to sap the strength of the imperial state and bring about its decline.

Foreign policy success and failures can contribute to the diffusion of power. The effect of foreign policy failures is relatively easy to anticipate. In the wake of defeat, the search for scapegoats, disillusionment with the task undertaken, and a desire to avoid similar situations can be followed. The Vietnam War is held by many to have been responsible for destroying the postwar domestic consensus on the purpose of American power. Economic sanctions directed against Fidel Castro in Cuba in the 1960s failed to bring down his regime and only made him more dependent on Soviet support.

American foreign policy successes have also hastened the decline of U.S. dominance. The reconstructions of the Japanese and Western European economies rank as two truly remarkable achievements. In a sense, U.S. foreign policy was *too* successful. These economies became major economic rivals of the U.S. economy and often outperform it. However, the Japanese case also illustrates that there is nothing inevitable about the process of power diffusion. In the 1960s, observers spoke of the Japanese economic miracle and the threat it presented to U.S. economic power. In the 1990s, reference was instead being made to Japan's lost decade and the many economic problems it faced.

## Issue Proliferation

The second area of evolutionary change in the international arena is issue proliferation. Not long ago, there was a relatively clear-cut foreign affairs issue hierarchy. At the top were a relatively small number of high-politics problems involving questions of national security, territorial integrity, and political independence. At the bottom were the numerically more prevalent low-politics issues of commerce, energy, environment, and so on. Although largely intuitive, the line between high and low politics was well established, and the positions occupied by issues in this hierarchy were relatively fixed, allowing policy makers to become familiar with the issues before them and the options open to them. Today, this is no longer the case.

The high-politics category has become crowded. Natural resource scarcity moved from a low-politics to a high-politics foreign policy problem after the 1973 OPEC oil embargo. In

2014, the Defense Department's **Quadrennial Defense Review** and other studies pointed to the growing national security threat posed by global climate change. Issues may also change position in the hierarchy for political reasons. Human rights, which were a major concern for the United States when Jimmy Carter was president, returned to a low-politics position when Reagan took office. Its importance has continued to fluctuate over time, more recently returning to a low-politics position under Trump.

Accompanying the high-low politics division is a long-standing distinction between foreign and domestic policy, which has become increasingly difficult to maintain. How, for example, do we classify attempts to fight international drug cartels? On one level, this is a foreign policy problem. The United States is actively engaged with helping the Mexican government combat the drug cartels operating out of that country. These organizations realize more than $20 billion in profits from U.S. sales alone. Yet this is also a matter of domestic policy, as some states have legalized the recreational use of marijuana.

A term increasingly being used to characterize these and other issues with significant domestic and international dimensions is **intermestic** (*inter* from "international" and *mestic* from "domestic").[9] Among the high-profile examples of intermestic policy areas are protecting the climate, pandemics, and food safety. Climate and pandemics, notably COVID, will be discussed in some detail in later chapters (10 and 4, respectively). Food safety has long been treated as a domestic policy matter. This is no longer realistic, as food production has become globalized. Between 2000 and 2006, the value of U.S. food imports doubled, to $2.2 trillion; yet the Food and Drug Administration (FDA) inspects less than 1 percent of the imported food products under its jurisdiction.

## Actor Proliferation

The third evolutionary feature of the international system is actor proliferation. On the one hand, actor proliferation has taken the form of an expansion in the number of states. Today, there are 190 countries, compared to fifty-eight states in 1930. The United States has diplomatic relations with all but three (four if Taiwan is counted). This expansion in the number of states has brought with it a corresponding expansion in the number of views that can be found on any given problem. Eighty-four states attended the first United Nations Conference on the Law of the Sea in 1958. In contrast, 185 countries attended the 2015 Paris Climate Summit conference; adding the European Union and others brought the total number of participants to 196. The vast number of states and the diversity of views expressed in these global meetings now present great obstacles to achieving an agreement.

Although the growth in the number of new states has slowed, continued growth is taking place in a second area: nonstate actors. While states have never been the only actors in world politics, it is only comparatively recently that nonstate actors have appeared in sufficient numbers and possessed control over enough resources to be significant actors in world politics. Statistically, the growth in the number of nonstate actors has been explosive. On the eve of World War I, there were only 49 intergovernmental organizations (IGOs) and 170 nongovernmental organizations (NGOs). By 1951 the numbers had grown to 123 IGOs and 832 NGOs. The 2015/2016 edition of the *Yearbook of International Organizations* identified 273 conventional IGOs and 3,189 conventional NGOs.[10]

Three categories of nonstate actors may be identified: intergovernmental organizations, such as the United Nations, NATO, and the Organization of American States;

nongovernmental organizations, such as General Motors, the International Red Cross, the Catholic Church, and the Palestine Liberation Organization; and subnational actors, such as the U.S. Defense Department, New York City, and Texas. The "Historical Lesson" section provides an overview of the founding and growth of NATO.

## Historical Lesson

### NATO

On April 9, 1949, the United States and ten allies met in Washington, DC, to establish the North Atlantic Treaty Organization (NATO). The key provision in the NATO Treaty was Article 5, which stated that an attack on one or more members of NATO would be considered an attack against all. Article 5 did not mandate a specific response. It stated that all members would take "such action as it deems necessary, including the use of force." This wording was necessary so as not to infringe on Congress's constitutional power to declare war.

A number of objections to the treaty were raised in the Senate debate over its approval. Some complained that it was too much of an "old-fashioned treaty." Amendments were introduced prohibiting the stationing of U.S. troops in or the transfer of weapons to Europe. In his testimony before the Senate, Henry Wallace, who served one term as vice president under Franklin Roosevelt, argued that NATO would anger Russia and turn it into "a wild and cornered beast." On July 21, the Senate gave its approval by a vote of 82–13. The NATO Treaty went into effect on August 2, 1949.

A number of recurring issues have dominated relations among NATO members, often creating internal conflicts and tension. One issue is membership in NATO. Not every expansion of NATO has produced conflict, but some have. The first involved admitting West Germany to NATO. Its membership was seen by many as desirable after the onset of the Korean War and growing fears about the size of Russian conventional forces in Europe. France, however, objected to German rearmament and the possible stationing of German soldiers in France. It was not until 1955 that West Germany became a member of NATO. Membership again became a high-profile issue

with the fall of the Soviet Union and the collapse of the Warsaw Pact, the military alliance Russia had created to oppose NATO. The question became, should the former members be allowed to join NATO, and if so, how soon? Russia strongly opposed NATO expansion to its borders. In 1994, a halfway house toward expansion was created with the Partnership for Peace. States joining it could consult with NATO but would not be protected by its defense agreement. This debate was revisited as countries once part of the Soviet Union sought membership.

A second issue is burden sharing. In the early years of its existence, it was inevitable that the United States would assume the major share of NATO's costs. This changed with European economic recovery from World War II. By the 1960s, calls for burden sharing became pronounced, and NATO allies were often described as free riders. These concerns surfaced again in the 1970s as legislation was passed requiring NATO members to help offset the cost of stationing U.S. troops in Europe.

A third reoccurring issue is the scope of NATO operations. Initially the debate focused on military matters: Is NATO confined to the defense of Europe, or are out-of-area operations permissible? The United States initially opposed the idea of out-of-area operations. Matters came to a head when the United States refused to support French and British efforts to take control of the Suez Canal away from Egypt. During the Vietnam War, there were occasional calls for NATO to help the United States or at least pick up a greater portion of the cost to defend Europe.

After the end of the Cold War, the question of the scope of NATO's operations took on a different shape. The issue was NATO's involvement in peacekeeping operations in the Balkans. While still within Europe, peacekeeping was not a core mission of NATO at its founding. NATO's involvement in Bosnia and the Yugoslav War began in 1992 when it began supporting UN peacekeeping efforts including monitoring the establishment of no-fly zones. As fighting continued and intensified, NATO's mission changed from monitoring to enforcement. In 1994, NATO fighters shot down Serbian jets, marking the first combat operation in NATO's history. By 1995, NATO was engaged in large-scale bombing campaigns. With the signing of the Dayton Accords peace agreement in 1995, NATO's mission returned to peacekeeping. It agreed to commit sixty thousand troops to a NATO-led international peacekeeping effort. This tension between peacekeeping and combat operations reappeared when NATO became involved in Afghanistan beginning in 2001, its first involvement in military action outside of Europe.

### Applying the Lesson

1. Can any of the three ongoing challenges NATO has faced be solved? If so, how?
2. Is a new NATO needed? What would it look like? What would be its mission?
3. Was Henry Wallace correct in the argument he made to the Senate in 1949?

Actor proliferation has altered in three ways the context in which American foreign policy decisions are made. First, it has changed the language used in thinking about foreign policy problems. The state-centric language of the Cold War now competes for the attention of policy makers with the imagery of interdependence and globalization. Second, nonstate actors often serve as potential instruments of foreign policy. By not being identified as part of a state, their actions may be better received by other actors. Third, nonstate actors often limit the options open to policy makers. Their ability to resist and frustrate state initiatives can necessitate consideration of courses of action that states otherwise would likely reject, including inaction.

## Regional Diversity

As a superpower, the United States is concerned not only with the structure and operation of the international system as a whole, but also with the operation of its subsystems, three of which are especially important. Each presents different management problems and thus requires different solutions.[11] While the language used to describe them comes out of the Cold War era, the differences they highlight remain relevant to the way international politics is conducted and the foreign problems that are considered important.

The first subsystem, the Western system, is made up of the advanced industrial states of the United States, Canada, Western Europe, and Japan. The principal problem in the Western system is managing interdependence. At issue is the distribution of costs and benefits. U.S. leadership and initiative in the realm of national security policy, once so eagerly sought by its allies, is now often resisted. Even before Trump became president, many in the United States had begun to question the costs of leadership and sought to have its allies pick up a larger share of the defense burden. A similar situation holds for underwriting a free trade system or accepting economic discrimination in the name of alliance unity.

The second subsystem is the North-South system. Instead of expectations of sharing and mutual gain, the South views matters from a perspective rooted in the inequalities and exploitation of colonialism. When NATO and U.S. forces intervened in Libya and removed Muammar Gaddafi from power in the name of responsibility to protect, many in the South saw this humanitarian doctrine as nothing but a cover for another instance of Western imperialism. In contrast to solutions to the problems of interdependence, which lie in the fine-tuning of existing international organizations and practices, solutions to the problems of dependence and domination require constructing a new system that the South is willing to accept as legitimate and in which it is treated as an equal.

The third subsystem of concern to the United States is the remnants of the Cold War East-West system. Its fundamental management problem is reintegration. The Cold War divided the East and West into two largely self-contained, competing military and economic parts. In the 1970s, détente brought about a limited reintegration of the East and West through arms control and trade agreements. The opportunity for full-scale integration of these states into the international system came with the demise of communism and the collapse of the Soviet Union, which has to some extent been realized. Russia became a member of the Group of Eight (G8), and both China and Russia joined the World Trade Organization (WTO). Still, the task of reintegration is incomplete, as evidenced by Russia's military intervention into Ukraine and its covert use of social media to influence the outcome of U.S. elections, China's growing assertiveness in the South China Sea and its aggressive overseas economic policies, and ongoing concerns about the status of human rights in both countries.

## Dominant Features Today

In many ways, the contemporary international system lacks a defining identity. For some, it is the post-9/11 era. Others argue that not much has changed in world politics since 9/11.[12] Still others see the current international system as having entered into a new period marked by the resurgence of great-power politics. Regardless of how it is defined, it is clear that the structure of the international system has become more complex. It has become a three-dimensional chessboard, with different problems and dynamics on each board. Disagreement exists over how to rank them in importance. There is a traditional hard-power-driven security chessboard, a soft-power-driven economic chessboard, and a third chessboard dominated by the activities of nonstate actors, where power is diffuse and hard to define. Not only does each chessboard present its own set of challenges and opportunities to the United States, but they also interact to establish a set of underlying international system dynamics to the United States, which can greatly complicate (and frustrate) efforts to accomplish foreign policy objectives. In the following sections, one challenge on each chessboard is identified: terrorism, economic globalization, and American hegemony.[13] As will become clear in these discussions, none of these challenges has a fixed content or set of characteristics. Today, the continued significance of each has become questioned as events have altered the shape of each of these chessboards.

### Terrorism

Terrorism continues to dominate the third chessboard, although its global reach has been significantly reduced with the weakening of two major terrorist groups—al-Qaeda and ISIS (the Islamic State of Iraq and Syria)—and their embrace of localization strategies over global strategies in challenging the influence of perceived enemies of Islam. Box 2.1 presents a snapshot of the scope of the terrorism problem as it existed in 2021.

## Box 2.1

### Snapshot of Global Terrorism, 2021

The total number of deaths from terrorism declined in 2021, falling by 1.2 percent to 7,142. This is the fourth consecutive year where deaths from terrorism remained fairly constant.

The number of attacks rose from 4,458 in 2020 to 5,226 in 2021, a 17 percent increase and the highest number of attacks recorded since 2007, largely due to violence in the Sahel region and instability in countries such as Afghanistan.

Conflict has been the primary driver of terrorism since 2007. In 2021, all of the ten countries most impacted by terrorism were involved in an armed conflict in 2021.

Over the past few years, the number of deaths from terrorism in war-afflicted countries has dropped, with the majority of terrorist activity now taking place in countries involved in political instability and minor armed conflict.

JNIM is the fastest growing group globally, recording the largest increase in the number of attacks and deaths in 2021.

Terrorist activity has been concentrated in South Asia and sub-Saharan Africa, with both regions recording more terrorism deaths than the Middle East/North Africa.

Once groups exist for more than twelve years, they are very hard to stop. In contrast to this, over half of all terrorist groups do not survive beyond three years.

The COVID-19 pandemic had very little impact on terrorism in 2020 and 2021.

Ten countries accounted for 61 percent of deaths from terrorism:

1. Afghanistan
2. Burkina Faso
3. Somalia
4. Mali
5. Niger

The four deadliest terrorist groups:

1. Al-Shabaab
2. Islamic State
3. Taliban
4. JNIM

Countries having the most deaths by terrorism

1. Afghanistan
2. Burkina Faso
3. Somalia
4. Mali
5. Niger

Countries that had the greatest decreases in death due to terrorism:

1. Mozambique
2. Nigeria
3. Syria
4. Chad
5. Colombia

Countries that had the greatest increase in deaths due to terrorism:

1. Niger
2. Mali
3. Afghanistan
4. Democratic Republic of the Congo (DRC)
5. Burkina Faso

*Source:* Institute for Economics and Peace, *Global Terrorism Index, 2021*.

Using the term in its most value free and politically neutral sense, **terrorism** is violence for the purpose of political intimidation.[14] Terrorism is not a new phenomenon, nor is it the exclusive tool of any political ideology or political agenda. It does not specify an organizational form. Governments as well as nonstate actors may engage in terrorism.

Today's brand of terrorism, which dates from 1979, is the fourth wave of terrorism that has arisen since the 1880s.[15] The preceding three waves each lasted a generation. If this pattern holds, the current wave of terrorism will not lose its energy until around 2025. The first, anarchist wave of terrorism began in Russia and was set in motion by the political and economic reform efforts of the tsars. The second, anticolonial wave of terrorism began in the 1920s and ended in the 1960s. The third, New Left wave of terrorism was set in motion by the Vietnam War. It was made up of Marxist groups such as the Weather Underground and separatist groups that sought self-determination for minority groups that felt trapped inside larger states, such as the Palestine Liberation Organization.

The defining features of the current wave of terrorism are twofold. The first is its religious base. Islamic extremism is at its core. Its initial energy was drawn from three events in 1979: the start of a new Muslim century, the ouster of the shah in Iran, and the Soviet invasion of Afghanistan. The United States is the special target of this religious wave of terrorism. Iranian leaders have long referred to the United States as the "Great Satan," and the common goal shared by Islamic terrorist groups has been to drive the United States out of the Middle East. Before 9/11, this wave had produced a steady flow of terrorist attacks on U.S. facilities. Marine barracks were attacked in Lebanon in 1983, the World Trade Center was first bombed in 1993, American embassies were attacked in Kenya and Tanzania in 1998, and the USS *Cole* was attacked in 2000. The second defining attribute is the specter of mass casualties. Earlier waves of terror focused on assassinating key individuals or the symbolic killing of relatively small numbers of individuals, but today we also see terrorist attacks resulting in large numbers of deaths.

The military defeats suffered by al-Qaeda and ISIS in the Middle East as well as the ability of the United States to eliminate key leaders does not translate into the end of terrorism as a key feature of the contemporary international system. In judging the significance of terrorism, what matters is not just the quantity of terrorist attacks but the political impact of those attacks: the target of the attack, its timing, and the amount of fear and destruction it creates.

The ability of terrorist organizations to adapt their structure and goals to altered operating conditions is an important contributing factor to their ability to survive and carry out their mission. Al-Qaeda embraced an organizational structure based on concentric circles. At its core was a central leadership group, surrounded by a ring of al-Qaeda affiliates in different countries. The outer ring contained al-Qaeda locals or lone wolves. ISIS operated as a pseudo-state, controlling oil-producing operations in Iraq and Syria, engaging in extortion, collecting taxes, and selling goods such as abandoned U.S. weapons and antiques on the black market.[16] Even before its defeat, ISIS began to decentralize its decision-making structure. It delegated power to mid-level military commanders in Iraq and Syria, sought out foreign affiliates, and actively recruited and trained disenchanted individuals and criminals to return to their home countries and engage in terrorist attacks.

Of special concern to the United States is the growth of terrorism in Central Africa. The most important terrorist group in this region is al-Shabaab, an al-Qaeda affiliate. The United States began military action in Somalia as part of the Global War on Terrorism following the 9/11 attacks. Beginning in 2007, drone strikes and military raids against al-Shabaab became important elements of U.S. antiterrorism policy. President Trump withdrew some 750 U.S. military forces from Somalia in early December 2020 just after the presidential election as part of his policy to end U.S. participation in forever wars. Drone strikes against al-Shabaab were to continue from Kenya. In May 2022, Biden announced that at the request of the Pentagon, about five hundred U.S. Special Forces troops would return to Somalia to help curb al-Shabaab's growing strength in the region. No U.S. forces were to engage in combat.

In Somalia, Syria, Afghanistan, and elsewhere, assessing the ability of the United States to counter terrorism and limit its influence requires that attention be given to the question of how terrorism ends.[17] Numerous possible endings include the capture or killing of leaders, the loss of popular support, the achievement of goals, the transition to legitimate political organizations, and transformation into criminal organizations.

## Globalization

**Globalization** dominates the second chessboard. Most commentators define globalization as an economic process centered on the speed of interactions among economies and the intense and all-encompassing nature of those interactions. From this perspective, economies do not simply trade with one another; they are transformed by their interactions. Globalization's supporters claim that this transformation will lead to economic benefits and prosperity.

Globalization is much more than just an economic process. It is a dynamic mix of economic, political, social, and cultural forces that has the potential to bring about both positive and negative changes within and among states. Globalization may unleash the forces of democracy, but it may just as easily unleash a fundamentalist and defensive cultural backlash by those who feel threatened. Similarly, globalization accelerates the diffusion of technology and knowledge among people, which may help solve global health and environmental problems, but it also allows terrorist groups to communicate with one another, travel more efficiently, and gain access to weapons of mass destruction.

Economic globalization did not arrive on the scene suddenly. It emerged bit by bit over time. Although some commentators trace its foundations back to the eighteenth century, most identify its beginnings with the post–World War II era and the establishment of the Bretton Woods monetary system and its core institutions: the World Bank, the International Monetary Fund, and the General Agreement on Tariffs and Trade (GATT). Together, these institutions laid the foundation for an international economic system that facilitated and encouraged an ever-expanding and accelerating cross-border flow of money, commodities, ideas, and people. This foundation set in motion a chain reaction, producing what Thomas Friedman refers to as the "flattening of the world."[18] The dominant perspective held that globalization was an irreversible process. It was a reality, not a choice.[19] The problem facing the United States was not whether but how to participate in a globalized economy.

Events over the past decade have called this view into question.[20] References to the emergence of identity politics and the triumph of nationalism over globalization point to a weakening of globalization, if not a retreat from it.[21] Nowhere is this trend more noteworthy than in China where President Xi Jinping has placed increasing emphasis on self-reliance, decoupling China from the global economic system over economic openness to the global system. Political economist Dani Rodrik asserts that this weakening of globalization was not inevitable. It was the result of policy decisions that turned globalization in the wrong direction. The result was greater levels of international economic integration and growth at the cost of domestic economic disintegration.[22] As globalization grew stronger, it created a divide between groups at upper and lower socioeconomic levels. Where the rich saw globalization as beneficial, others saw the accompanying job losses as threatening and came to feel that the political elites were not responding to their fears and needs. As these views gained strength within societies, economic nationalism and political populism grew and support for global trade and financial agreements weakened.

Writing in 2005, Niall Ferguson raised the possibility that at some point globalization may collapse and we may enter into a postglobalist era.[23] He saw economic and political parallels between the current period of globalization and the one that existed prior to the outbreak of World War I and the Great Depression of the 1930s. It is also possible that globalization will not end but enter a new phase. Ian Bremmer raises the possibility that globalization will come to be dominated by state capitalism,[24] in which governments rather than private businesses are the driving force behind investment decisions. China is the model for this. The goal here is to increase state power, not maximize profit. Prominent forms of state capitalism include government-owned or controlled natural resource companies, national champions or firms that receive special tax incentives and other benefits from the state, and state-controlled sovereign wealth funds that invest in key firms and industries. Bremmer warns that state capitalist firms are inherently inefficient due to the role that politics plays in their operation and that their investment decisions could harm global economic growth. Still others see globalization as already being replaced by regionalism as the dominant force on the economic chessboard.[25]

## American Hegemony

American **hegemony** is the principal issue on the first chessboard, the traditional hard-power, security-dominated chessboard. The term **hegemony**, which implies control, dominance, or preeminence, was used to describe the United States' position after the end of the Cold War, when for all practical purposes it was the last superpower left standing on the chessboard. Part of the difficulty in making judgments about the present condition of this first chessboard lies in the terms commonly used to describe hegemonic power.

Some observers refer to the United States as an empire. Not surprisingly, this characterization is controversial.[26] In its most neutral sense, an *empire* is a state with a "wide and supreme domain." The political, economic, and military reach of the United States fits that criterion. However, the term also carries very negative connotations of a state that imposes its will on others and rules through force and domination. Military occupation and the arbitrary use of military power typify an empire's foreign policies, charges that have frequently been leveled at American foreign policy. Critics of the empire label assert that the reach of American foreign policy, which is imperial in the sense that it is global, is being confused with the political ambition to control vast expanses of territory beyond U.S. borders, which does not exist.

A quite different view holds that America's unchallenged dominance allows it to act as the functional equivalent of a world government. It provides services needed for the effective functioning of the international system, such as military security, stewardship of the global economy, and emergency humanitarian aid. If the United States did not carry out these and other crucial tasks, the international system might cease to function effectively, because no other state possesses the resources to do so, and a true world government would not likely come into existence. So American hegemony can be seen as beneficial rather than exploitive. As one supporter of this position noted, it is in the interests of both America and the world that American primacy last as long as possible.[27]

Between these contrasting views of American hegemony lies a third perspective that stresses the limits placed on U.S. hegemony by global politics. One variant of this perspective sees the United States as having sat atop a Unipolar Concert for most of the post–Cold War era.[28] The United States did not dominate global politics single-handedly; it did so with the acquiescence of the next two major powers in the international system (China and Russia). Both chose *not* to try to balance the United States because they benefited greatly from the international system as it operated under U.S. leadership.

Each of these three perspectives finds itself challenged by two questions: (1) How accurate a description is it today? (2) How much longer will it hold true?

For those who adopt the American empire perspective, the historical reality is that empires come with expiration dates; they do not last forever. In addition, today's empires tend to have much shorter life spans than ancient and early modern ones. The Roman Empire lasted 829 years. The British Empire lasted 336 years. Twentieth-century empires on average lasted only fifty-seven years.[29] Even prior to Trump's "America First" foreign policy agenda, the United States' status as an empire was easily questioned due to the rise in Chinese economic and military power. Robert Kaplan asserts that we may have already entered the postimperial moment in which world disorder and competition for power and space will grow.[30]

For those who adopt the United-States-as-global-government perspective, the principal challenges facing the United States involve its ability to structure the "rules of the game" by which international politics is played.[31] These challenges take two forms, both tied to the rising number and influence of authoritarian governments and their rejection of the liberal democratic values at the heart of the global system created by the United States. The first challenge is altering the policies of existing international organizations such as the United Nations to bring them more in line with U.S. values. The second is to create parallel international organizations to advance U.S. interests, like China did by establishing the Asian Development Bank and modeling its structure and functions on those of the World Bank.

For those who stress the continuing importance of power politics to U.S. dominance, the key longevity issue is the extent to which credible challengers to U.S. power exist or will surface. Some see the United States as being a remarkably secure country. There are many foreign policy problems, but individually and collectively they do not constitute security threats.[32] Stephen Brooks and William Wohlforth argue that such challenges will not materialize soon.[33] While China's rise in power today is very real, they note that the distance that China must travel from great power to superpower is far bigger than successful challengers have faced in the past.

Others take a more pessimistic view, arguing that power balancing by Russia and China is already underway to the point that the Unipolar Concert has unraveled, bringing with it a series of regional challenges to U.S. influence.[34] The 2022 National Security Strategy spoke to this potential collapse, noting that China seeks to "reshape the international order."[35] The question raised by those taking this view is one of whether or not a new cold war era has begun with the United States and China as the two anchors. The question of a possible new cold war will be taken up in chapter 14.

Finally, it is important to note that another important perspective exists when it comes to making judgments about power and by extension hegemony. It holds that the rise and fall of great powers is driven by domestic factors, most importantly social characteristics that produce dynamism and comparative advantage. Political scientist Michael Mazarr concludes that today the United States is deficient in many of the qualities that led to its rise as a great power over the second half of the twentieth century.[36]

## America and the World: Attitudes and Perceptions

As constructivists remind us, the global setting of American foreign policy involves more than just a series of contemporary problems and underlying structural features. It also consists of attitudes and perceptions about the world. As evidenced by responses to global public opinion polls conducted in the United States and other countries, it is increasingly obvious that Americans and non-Americans do not always see the world the same way.[37] In 2014, 70 percent of Americans polled said that the United States takes into account the interests of other countries in making foreign policy decisions. Little agreement on this point existed abroad. At one extreme, only 13 percent of Pakistanis indicated that the United States considers their country's interests a great deal or a fair amount. At the other extreme, 85 percent of Filipinos felt that the United States considers their country's interests.

Global public opinion polls also show differences in how Americans and citizens of other countries view policy problems. A 2021 survey asked respondents in advanced countries what type of impact they expected climate change to have in their lives. In the United States, 60 percent responded that it would have somewhat of an impact or a major impact. In Greece, it was 87 percent, and in Sweden only 44 percent answered this way.[38]

Widely different views also exist on how the United States is viewed. A 2021 global opinion poll found considerable variation in the extent to which individuals around the world viewed the United States as a reliable partner. In Canada, 32 percent viewed it as not all reliable or not too reliable, 57 percent as somewhat reliable, and 11 percent as very reliable. In Japan, 23 percent viewed the United States as not reliable at all or not too reliable, 68 percent viewed it as somewhat reliable, and only 7 percent viewed it as very reliable.[39] Table 2.2 presents a snapshot view of how citizens around the world viewed the United States as an ally.

Another politically significant indicator of differences in global outlook is reflected by the periodic anti-American protests that erupt around the world. In seeking to understand the motivations and logic of such anti-American demonstrations, observers have made distinctions among four different types of anti-Americanism:[40]

**Table 2.2**  **How Well the United States Is Viewed as an Ally**

| Country | Not At All | Not Too | Somewhat | Very |
|---|---|---|---|---|
| Canada | 3 | 13 | 63 | 21 |
| Poland | 2 | 7 | 59 | 27 |
| Germany | 8 | 8 | 53 | 30 |
| United Kingdom | 3 | 14 | 57 | 25 |
| Greece | 20 | 26 | 43 | 10 |
| Israel | 1 | 14 | 51 | 31 |
| South Korea | 1 | 15 | 62 | 21 |
| Japan | 3 | 20 | 68 | 8 |
| Malaysia | 13 | 43 | 34 | 9 |

*Source:* Richard Wike et al., "International Attitudes toward the US, NATO, and Russia in a Time of Crisis," PEW Research Center, June 22, 2022.
*Note:* This is not the entire table found at the above site.

1. Liberal anti-Americanism. At its core this is the charge that the United States repeatedly fails to live up to its own ideals in conducting its foreign policy.
2. Social anti-Americanism. Here, the complaint concerns the United States' attempt to impose its version of democracy and its definition of rights on others while being insensitive to local societal values and norms.
3. Sovereign anti-Americanism. This version focuses on the threats the United States presents to the sovereignty and cultural and political identity of another country. A nationalistic backlash can occur regardless of whether the country is powerful or weak.
4. Radical anti-Americanism. This version defines American values as evil and subscribes to the notion that only by destroying them can the world be made safe.

The world is not solidly anti-American. Pro-American views tend to be most pronounced among those aged sixty and older, a factor many attribute to American foreign policy initiatives during the Cold War. Another group with solidly pro-American sentiments is made up of young people identified as *aspirational* (upwardly mobile or would like to be).[41]

## Over the Horizon: 2040

What, then, might the future hold? According to the National Intelligence Council (NIC) *Global Trends 2040* report, which was produced in 2021, the coming years will test U.S. resilience and require it, as well as all other states, to adapt to the changing landscape of international politics.[42] Among the most prominent elements of this changing landscape that it cites are the following. The most certain challenging trend in the next twenty years will be major demographic shifts. Global population growth will slow, and the world population will age rapidly. Environmental crises will continue and will fall disproportionately on poorer regions. Economic trends such as rising debt and more complex and fragmented trading relations will likely shape conditions inside and relations between states. Human development in such areas as health, education, and poverty reduction will continue to command state attention, but progress may be more difficult to achieve. Technological advances will help mitigate some problems but will also create new tensions within and between states, as there will be a growing mismatch between what publics need and expect and what governments can and will deliver.

The NIC report concludes by identifying five possible scenarios on how these forces may come to interact and shape global relations. The scenarios are not predictions or forecasts but an attempt to help policy makers focus on aspects of the international system that have the potential to shape U.S. foreign policy.

*Renaissance of democracies.* In this scenario there is a resurgence of open democracies led by the United States and its allies. Economic growth and technological achievements lead to a successful response to global challenges that renews public trust in democracy.

*A world adrift.* Here, the world is directionless, chaotic, and volatile as international rules and organizations are largely ignored by major powers like China, major regional powers, and nonstate actors.

*Competitive coexistence.* This is a world where the risk of war is low and global problems are manageable. Economic interdependence exists alongside competition for political power and strategic advantage.

*Separate silos.* In this scenario the world is fragmented into self-contained economic and security blocs that are focused on self-sufficiency, resiliency, and defense.

*Tragedy and mobilization.* Here, a global coalition led by the United States and China works with nongovernmental groups and international organizations to implement far-reaching changes in environmental and human development policy areas caused by climate change and related crises.

## Critical Thinking Questions

1. Which of the three theoretical perspectives (realism, neoliberalism, and constructivism) is best suited for guiding thinking about U.S. foreign policy today, and why?
2. Which of the possible global futures is most likely? How should the United States prepare for it?

3. Which features of the international system are most influential in determining the success or failure of U.S. foreign policies, and why?

## Key Terms

bipolar, 26
constructivism, 24
globalization, 34
hegemony, 35
intermestic, 28
multipolar, 26

neoliberalism, 24
Quadrennial Defense Review, 28
realism, 24
sovereignty, 26
terrorism, 32
unipolar, 26

# The American National Style 3

## Learning Objectives

Students will be able to:

1. Distinguish between the four patterns of the U.S. national style.
2. Evaluate the consequences of the U.S. national style for U.S. foreign policy.
3. Assess the extent to which U.S.-Mexican border policy reflects U.S. national style.
4. Identify the major voices of the past that are used to study U.S. national style.

# On the Agenda: The Mexican Border

In responding to foreign policy challenges, the United States is influenced as much by ideas as events. In the case of border security, the idea that technological, engineering, or legal solutions to political problems exist has been especially influential. The U.S.-Mexico border is 1,969 miles long. It is the world's most frequently crossed international border. During his presidential campaign, Donald Trump embraced a solution for a wall to be built along the border as a means to reduce illegal immigration and drug smuggling from Mexico. Once in office, his proposal brought forward a firestorm of controversy, leading to the longest U.S. government shutdown in history, thirty-five days (December 22, 2018–January 25, 2019). The first construction of a brand-new wall in Texas began in October 2019. By the end of his administration, some 460 miles of new barriers were built along the U.S.-Mexico border. On his first day in office, Joe Biden issued a series of executive orders on Mexican border policy, one of which was to cancel the construction of an additional 250 miles of border wall that Trump had planned. In September 2022, with little fanfare, Biden resumed work on the wall, filling gaps and repairing damage.

A closer look reveals that, for over a decade, the United States was seeking technological solutions to the border problem. In 1994, President Bill Clinton authorized Operation Gatekeeper "to restore integrity and safety to the nation's busiest border" by stopping illegal immigration. Prior to this point, only about some 80 miles of barriers and fencing existed along the U.S.-Mexican border in Texas and California. In 2006, President George W. Bush signed the Secure Fence Act, stating that "this bill will help protect the American people. This bill will make our borders more secure." By 2012, the total length of fencing for pedestrian barriers had increased to 649 miles.

A number of highly controversial issues arose in constructing both Trump's border wall and those of his predecessors. Trump originally proposed that Mexico would pay for the wall. In 2019, it was announced that the Pentagon was transferring $3.6 billion from military construction projects in twenty-three states, nineteen countries, and three U.S. territories to pay for the wall. Eventually this transfer would reach about $11 billion. The projected cost of maintaining the fence system Bush proposed was $65 billion over twenty years.

Second, there is the question of its effectiveness. In a three-year period (2019–2021), smuggler groups sawed through the wall almost 3,300 times, often with power tools that could be bought at retail stores. One breach in the wall found in 2021 was so large that two SUVs could pass through it at the same time. Tunnels below the barriers were also a problem. Once, within a two-week period during the Bush presidency, three smuggling tunnels were found, along with over forty tons of marijuana. The tunnels were equipped with lighting, ventilation, and—in one case—a railcar system.

Data on illegal border crossings fuel the arguments of both defenders and opponents of the border fence system. According to statistics from U.S. Customs and Border Patrol (CBP), over 396,000 undocumented people were caught entering the United States illegally in 2018, compared to 1.6 million people in 2000. Defenders of the border fence system cite the drop as evidence of success. Opponents argue that the underlying pattern of illegal immigration is found in period surges rather than straight lines or cycles. These surges are driven by such factors as natural disasters, poverty, corruption, and violence in migrant home countries as well as economic conditions in the United States. The current surge, the fourth in the past three presidencies, saw border crossing in all nine southwestern border sectors more than double in 2021. Table 3.1 presents these increases. Illegal border crossing also reached a one-month record with 221,300 in March 2022, and it also saw some 79,000 Cubans enter the United States across the southern border, more than twice the number of the past two years combined as economic conditions in Cuba worsened. By September, more than two million illegal immigrants were arrested crossing the border. Significant numbers now came from Venezuela, Cuba, and Nicaragua.

A third point of controversy has been the manner in which the fence was constructed. More than thirty legal waivers were used by presidents to bypass existing laws and regulations. The project received exemptions from acts including the Endangered Species Act, the Clean Water Act, and the National Historic Preservation Act. Michael Chertoff, secretary of the Homeland Security Department under Bush, justified the legal waivers, stating, "Criminal activity does not stop for endless debate or protracted litigation."

The transition from Trump to Biden directed attention to a legal dimension to border policy. In the last two years of his administration, Trump initiated two controversial policies. The first was the "Remain in Mexico" program, which Trump implemented in 2019. Under it, asylum seekers stopped at the border were sent back to Mexico where they often lived under dangerous conditions rather than being allowed to stay in the United States while their case was decided, a process that could take years. Biden suspended the program in January 2021. By then over seventy thousand asylum seekers had been sent back to Mexico. A few months later, the administration announced its intent to terminate the program. A series of court cases followed, and in April 2021, the Supreme Court ruled that the Biden administration had to reinstate the policy rather than terminate it. The administration agreed to abide

| Table 3.1 | Migrant Encounters at Southwest Border Sectors, 2021 |
| --- | --- |
| *Southwest Border Sector* | *Increase in Migrant Encounters (%)* |
| Rio Grande | 509 |
| Del Rio | 54.3 |
| El Paso | 256 |
| Tucson | 189 |
| San Diego | 167 |
| Yuma | 1,200 |
| Laredo | 118 |
| El Centro | 115 |
| Big Bend | 332 |

*Source:* John Gramlich and Alissa Scheller, "What's Happening at the U.S.-Mexico Border in 7 Charts," PEW Research Center, November 9, 2021. Data is from U.S. Customs and Border Protection.

by the decision and began talks with Mexico over how to restart it. The Remain in Mexico program resumed with some modifications in December 2021. In June 2022, the Supreme Court ruled that Biden could terminate the program.

The second policy is known as Title 42. Part of the 1944 Public Health Service Act, it allows the government to prohibit the entry of persons from other countries in order to prevent the spread of communicable diseases into the United States. In March 2020, Trump, through the head of the Centers for Disease Control and Prevention (CDC), invoked Title 42 on the Mexican border, effectively closing it. This was the first time it was invoked. Critics argued that the policy was not intended so much to prevent the spread of COVID as to stop migration across the Mexican border, an argument that gained credence after it became known that the Trump administration considered issuing Title 42 in 2019 after a mumps outbreak in an immigration detention center and the spread of flu in Border Patrol stations. On taking office, Biden left Title 42 in place. In early April 2022, the CDC announced that it was terminating Title 42 because it was no longer necessary. That brought another lawsuit and a lower court decision that the administration could not terminate Title 42.

The Mexican border is not the only border the United States has sought to close off using technology. In 1980, Cuban premier Fidel Castro unexpectedly announced that anyone wishing to leave Cuba for the United States would be permitted to do so. Almost instantly, Cuban Americans in Miami organized an operation that came to be known as the Mariel boatlift. President Reagan ordered the coast guard to stop refugees from reaching the United States by boat after an estimated 125,000 Cubans arrived in Florida on boats of varying sizes and seaworthiness. In 1991–1992, some forty thousand Haitians tried to reach the United States by boat. Poverty and political oppression were the primary forces that produced this mass exodus. President George H. W. Bush ordered that their boats be intercepted before reaching the United States and returned to Haiti. In his 1992 presidential campaign, Bill Clinton promised to change this policy. As Inauguration Day approached, fears grew of another mass exodus from Haiti. Shortly after taking office, Clinton retreated from his pledge and kept in place Reagan's order.

Embracing engineering solutions as a means to deal with political problems is only one of the ways in which ideas shape the content and conduct of U.S. foreign policy. To get a fuller picture, this chapter examines the concept of an American **national style** as it relates to foreign policy, with special attention to the style's sources and consequences. Later, the chapter looks at how past approaches influence the contemporary U.S. debate over foreign policy.

# The Importance of Ideas

Policy makers come and go, but ideas and ways of thinking endure. George W. Bush's major foreign policy innovation, moving from **containment** and **deterrence** to **preemption**, strikes many as a radical departure from the past, but others see in it the long reach of American history.[1] The Bush Doctrine's core ideas of moralism, idealism, exceptionalism, militarism, and global ambition have deep intellectual roots in the American foreign policy tradition.[2] Barack Obama's foreign policy received a great deal of criticism for embracing the idea of "leading from behind." It was rejected by many as ill conceived, un-American, and bound to fail. Regardless of the merits of these critiques, few pointed out the similarities between leading from behind and the post-Vietnam Nixon Doctrine (see chapter 1), which called for providing weapons to regional allies so that American troops would not have to be used to contain the spread of communism.[3] Today, many see similarities in Biden's and Trump's foreign policies, which share a reluctance to commit military force to situations that have the potential for getting out of control and in which exiting is difficult (Afghanistan).

The importance of ideas as a force in foreign policy decision making stems from both their immediate and long-term effects.[4] In the short run, shared ideas help policy makers and citizens cope with the inherent uncertainty involved in selecting among competing policy lines. In the long run, ideas can become institutionalized as organizations and laws are designed around them. As they become anchors for future reform debates, ideas continue to exert an influence on policy long after they may have lost their vitality and after those who espoused them have passed from the scene.

The result of this interplay of policies and ideas is a layered pattern in which policies reflecting different sets of ideas and pulling in different directions are combined, with little overall coherence. This pattern is very much evident in American trade policy. Conventional explanations of American trade policies focus on the political leverage of societal interest groups or the demands of the international system.[5] Others argue that only by looking at ideas can America's movement from a protectionist cycle (which began in the early nineteenth century and culminated in the highly protective tariffs of the 1930s), to a free trade cycle with elements of both free trade and fair trade, to Trump's embrace of fair trade be explained.

The national security policy arena provides an even clearer picture of the influence on American foreign policy of shared ideas and ways of acting. The logic of containment became embodied in a wide range of U.S. foreign policy initiatives, including military alliances, foreign aid programs, and covert action. Even the Nixon administration's much heralded shift to a policy of *détente* at the end of the Vietnam War (see chapter 1) could be comfortably fitted into the larger strategy of containment. Détente was designed to protect U.S. influence as much as possible in an era of lessened power abroad and increasingly isolationist feeling at home. Confrontation and crisis management were now too expensive to be the primary means for stopping Soviet expansion. Détente sought to accomplish this end by creating a framework of limited cooperation within the context of an international order that recognized the legitimacy of both U.S. and Soviet core security goals.[6]

More fundamentally, the importance of ideas lies in how they shape policy makers' and citizens' views of the role of the United States in the world. One theme that dominates this worldview is a sense of *exceptionalism*, the belief that the American political system, values, and historical experiences are unique and are models for others to follow. By one count, the phrase "American exceptionalism" appeared 4,172 times in national U.S. publications from 2010 to 2012.[7] Accompanying exceptionalism is the perceived need for (right to) a leadership role in world affairs, either by example or through transforming the international system.[8]

Not everyone embraces the ideas of exceptionalism and leadership equally. In 1998, Secretary of State Madeleine Albright stated that "if we use force, it is because we are America. We are the indispensable nation. We stand tall. We see farther into the future." Compare this with President Donald Trump's America First foreign policy, which emphasizes the centrality of sovereignty and nationalism. Others disagree quite strongly with this reading of America's role in the world.[9] For some, the United States has been antirevolutionary, seeking to prevent social change and stop Third World revolutionary movements that might threaten its dominant position in world affairs. This view is often expressed in the writings of revisionist historians who find U.S. foreign policy to be imperial in nature and rooted in the expansionist needs of capitalism. Others see U.S. foreign policy as racist, as evidenced by its immigration policy, which historically discriminated against the Chinese and other non–Western Europeans; hesitated to support international human rights conventions; and wavered in its attitude about the suitability of Hawaii, Puerto Rico, and the Philippines for either statehood or independence.

## Isolationism versus Internationalism

U.S. foreign policy is frequently discussed in terms of a tension between two opposing general foreign policy orientations: **isolationism** and **internationalism**. From the isolationist perspective, American national interests are best served by "quitting the world" or, at a minimum, maintaining a healthy sense of detachment from events elsewhere. Isolationism draws its inspiration from Washington's Farewell Address in which he urged Americans to "steer clear of permanent alliances with any portion of the foreign world" and asserted that "Europe has a set of primary interests which to us have none or very remote relations."[10] Among the major foreign policy decisions rooted in the principles of isolationism are the Monroe Doctrine, the refusal to join the League of Nations, the neutrality legislation of the 1930s, and, more loosely, the fear of future Vietnams.

According to the internationalist perspective, protecting and promoting American national interests requires an activist foreign policy. Internationalists hold that the United States cannot escape the world, that events abroad inevitably affect U.S. interests, and that any policy based on the denial of their relevance is self-defeating. Such widely divergent undertakings as membership in the United Nations and NATO, the Marshall Plan, the Helsinki Human Rights Agreement, and involvement in Korea and Vietnam can be traced to the internationalist perspective on world affairs.

The oscillation between isolationism and internationalism has not been haphazard. An underlying logic appears to guide movement from one to the other. Five earlier periods of U.S. foreign policy of twenty to thirty years' duration have been identified, each of which has an introvert (isolationist) and extrovert (internationalist) phase (see table 3.2).[11] According to this line of analysis, the United States is no longer internationalist in outlook. The current isolationist phase began in 2014. It can be expected to end in 2034. Evidence of this shift is readily found in public opinion polls, which indicate that, while the American public remains internationalist, it has become less supportive of the use of military force abroad; in addition, majorities now see both the Afghanistan and Iraq Wars as mistakes.

**Table 3.2** **Periods of American Foreign Policy**

| Period | Introvert (years) | Extrovert (years) |
|---|---|---|
| 1 | 1776–1798 | 1798–1824 |
| 2 | 1824–1844 | 1844–1871 |
| 3 | 1871–1891 | 1891–1918 |
| 4 | 1918–1940 | 1940–1967 |
| 5 | 1967–1987 | 1987–2014 |
| 6 | 2014–2034? | |

In each of these periods, U.S. policy makers had to confront a major foreign policy problem. In period one, it was independence; in period two, issues involving manifest destiny were dominant; and in period three, it was the process of becoming an industrial power. The crisis of world democracy dominated period four, and in the fifth period, the need to create a stable world order was the main challenge facing U.S. foreign policy. In each period, the dominant cycle (introversion or extroversion) imposes limits on the types of solutions that can be considered by policy makers and predisposes the public to accept certain courses of action. The cyclical movement between isolationism and internationalism is seen as spiral in nature; each movement toward internationalism has been deeper than the one before it, and each reversal to isolationism has been less complete than the preceding one.

Disagreement exists over the mechanism that triggers a shift from one phase to the next. One possibility is that shifts in foreign policy orientations may be tied to the business cycle.[12] Some have found that U.S. foreign policy takes on a belligerent tone during periods of economic recovery. The more stable the economy, the more moderate is U.S. foreign policy. In a similar vein, it has been argued that the periodic outward thrust of U.S. foreign policy is a product of domestic frustrations and disappointments.[13] Foreign policy successes are sought as a sign that the American dream is still valid and capable of producing victories.

Whatever the specific trigger, the movement from isolationism to internationalism and back again is made possible because both general foreign policy orientations are very much part of the American national style. It is not that one represents the American approach to world affairs and the other its denial. They are two different ways in which the fundamental building blocks that create the patterns of American foreign policy come together.[14] Both are united in the conviction that the institutions and ideals brought forward by the American experience need protection. The approaches differ on how best to provide for their continued growth and development.

Before proceeding to examine the shared roots of internationalism and isolationism, it should be noted that some argue that internationalism is better defined as *interventionism*: a tendency to intervene in the affairs of other states to a degree far beyond any reasonable definition of U.S. national interest. According to this view, there is no competing theme of isolationism, just opposition to specific cases of intervention on pragmatic or tactical grounds.

## Historical Sources of the American National Style

The term *national style* is used to capture the way in which ideas and experiences from the past shape current policy making. The sources of the American national style are found in many places.[15] Two different approaches are used most often. One focuses on the legacy of the overall historical experience of the United States. The second examines the foreign policy ideas of key figures.

Few nations can look back on as favorable a set of conditions in which to grow and develop as the United States. Its vast size provided an abundance of natural resources on which to build a prosperous economy. Just as important for the development of the American national style is the fact that this economic growth took place without any master plan. Individual self-reliance, flexibility, and improvisation were the cardinal virtues in developing America. Guided by these principles, the United States has become a "how-to-do-it" society, with energies that are largely directed to the problem at hand and with long-range concerns that receive scant attention.[16]

U.S. economic growth also occurred in an era of unparalleled global harmony. With the exception of the Crimean War, from the Congress of Vienna in 1815 until the outbreak of World War I in 1914, the great powers of Europe were largely at peace with one another. The defense of America's continental borders never required the creation of a large standing army or navy. Peace and security seemed to come naturally and were widely accepted as the normal condition of world affairs. The links between American security and developments abroad went unnoticed. Democracy, rather than the strength of the British navy or the European balance of power, was seen as the source of American security.

This faith in the power of democracy reflects the extent to which American political thought is rooted in the eighteenth-century view of human nature. Most important to the development of the ideas that have guided U.S. policy makers is the work of John Locke, who argued that people are rational beings capable of determining their own best interests. The best government was considered to be the one that governed least. To Locke, the historical record indicated that the exercise of power led inevitably to its abuse and corrupted the natural harmony existing among individuals. Conflicts between individuals could be settled without the application of concentrated state power. The wastefulness and destructiveness of war disqualified it as a means of conflict resolution. Negotiation, reason, and discussion should be sufficient to overcome misperceptions and reconcile conflicting interests.

In contrast to war, trade is seen as promoting the peaceful settlement of disputes. The dynamics of the marketplace bind individuals together in mutually profitable exchanges. This is not the case when governments dominate society and control activity for their own advantage. Because commerce creates a vested interest in peace, logic points to limiting government powers. The American historical experience seemed to offer vivid proof of the correctness of the liberal outlook on human affairs.

Much attention of late has also been given to the influence of religion on American foreign policy.[17] Four components of this religious framework are especially important. First is the idea of America as God's "chosen nation." Second is the idea that America has a special mission or calling to transform the world. Third, in carrying out this mission, the United States is engaging in a struggle against evil. Finally, it is an apocalyptic outlook on world affairs. Change will come about not through gradual or subtle adjustments but through a cataclysmic transformation in which evil is encountered and then decisively and permanently defeated.

Not all religions necessarily view world politics or America's role in the world in the same way.[18] Within Protestantism, three different schools of thought speak to the conduct of American foreign policy: fundamentalism, evangelicalism, and liberal Christianity.[19] Liberal Christianity, which provided the worldview for such key members of the founding generation of "Cold Warriors" as Secretaries of State Dean Acheson and John Foster Dulles, is now in decline. It has been replaced by fundamentalism and evangelicalism as the politically dominant Protestant forces. Fundamentalists are deeply pessimistic about the possibility of bringing about a new world order and see a deep divide separating believers and nonbelievers. Defensive and self-confident, they hold an apocalyptic view of the future and are not particularly interested in cooperating with those with whom they disagree. Evangelicals also divide the world into believers and nonbelievers, but they are far more optimistic than fundamentalists in their view about the potential for progress and cooperation among different people.

# Patterns

Three patterns of thought and action growing from these past experiences provide the building blocks from which the American national style emerges: unilateralism, moral pragmatism, and legalism.

## Unilateralism

The first pattern is **unilateralism**, a predisposition to act alone in addressing foreign policy problems.[20] Unilateralism does not dictate a specific course of action. Isolationism, neutrality, activism, and interventionism are all consistent with its basic orientation to world affairs. The unilateralist thrust of U.S. foreign policy represents a rejection of the balance-of-power approach associated with the European diplomatic tradition. It reflects the American sense of exceptionalism and is often perceived by others to be an insensitive and egoistic nationalism.

The best-known statement of the unilateralist position is the Monroe Doctrine. With the end of the Napoleonic Wars, concern arose that Spain might attempt to reestablish its control over the newly independent Latin American republics. Great Britain approached the United States about the possibility of a joint declaration to prevent this from happening. The United States rejected the British proposal, only to turn around and make a unilateral declaration to the same end: the United States would not tolerate European intervention in the Western Hemisphere, and in return, it pledged not to interfere in European affairs. In 1904, the Roosevelt Corollary to the Monroe Doctrine was put forward. Spurred into action by the inability of the Dominican Republic to pay its foreign lenders, President Theodore Roosevelt sent in U.S. forces. The Roosevelt Corollary established the United States as the self-proclaimed policeman of the Western Hemisphere. It would play that role many times. The years 1904–1934 saw the United States send eight expeditionary forces to Latin America, conduct five military occupations ranging in duration from a few months to nineteen years, and take over customs collections duties twice. The legacy of the Monroe Doctrine continued into the post–World War II era. The Central Intelligence Agency (CIA)–sponsored overthrows of the Arbenz government in Guatemala and the Allende government in Chile, U.S. behavior in the Bay of Pigs and the Cuban missile crisis, the 1965 invasion of the Dominican Republic, the 1983 invasion of Grenada, and the 1989 invasion of Panama testify to the continued influence of unilateralism on U.S. behavior in the Western Hemisphere.

The nature of American participation in World War I and the subsequent U.S. refusal to join the League of Nations also reflect the unilateralist impulse. Official World War I documents identify the victors as the Allied and Associated Powers. The only Associated Power of note was the United States. For U.S. policy makers, this was more than a mere symbolic separation from its European allies. Woodrow Wilson engaged in personal negotiations with Germany over ending the war without consulting the Allies about the terms of a possible truce. The United States was also the only major victorious power not to join the League of Nations. This abstention is often attributed to isolationism, but it can also be seen as a triumph of unilateralism.[21] Membership would have committed the United States to a collective security system that could have obliged it to undertake multilateral military action in the name of stopping international aggression.

The impact of unilateralist thinking also comes through clearly in the neutrality legislation of the 1930s. These acts placed an embargo on the sale of arms to warring states. The post–World War II shift from isolationism to internationalism did not bring about an abandonment of unilateralism; it only covered it with a multilateral facade. Control over NATO's nuclear forces remains firmly in the hands of the United States. The presence of the UN flag in Korea and references to SEATO treaty commitments in Vietnam could scarcely conceal the totally U.S. nature of these two wars. In the United Nations, the United States' veto power protects its vital interests from the intrusion of other powers, and the system of weighted voting used in international financial organizations guarantees the United States a preponderant voice in their deliberations.

The American penchant for unilateralism was never far beneath the surface in its dealings with allies during the later years of the Cold War. Nowhere was this more evident than at the Reykjavik summit meeting with Soviet leader Mikhail Gorbachev. James Schlesinger observed at the time that in proposing to eliminate all ballistic missiles within ten years, "the administration suddenly jettisoned 25 years of deterrence doctrine . . . without warning, consultation with Congress or its allies."[22]

The Global War on Terrorism did not change this unilateralist impulse; if anything, it reinforced it. In his January 2002 State of the Union address, President George W. Bush gave notice to the world that he was prepared to act unilaterally against terrorism. "Some governments will be timid in the face of terror. . . . If they do not act, America will." Unilateralism is central to Trump's America First approach to foreign policy and his disdain for working through alliances and international organizations. In his campaign for the presidency, Biden promised to "bring America back to the table" and reestablish relations with allies. In practice, however, unilateralism was never far removed from this decision making. Allies felt ignored and endangered with the handling of the exit from Afghanistan due to a lack of consultation, and France felt deeply slighted by being excluded from a submarine agreement with Australia.

## Moral Pragmatism

The second pattern in American foreign policy is **moral pragmatism**.[23] The American sense of morality involves two elements. The first is that state behavior can be judged by moral standards. The second is that American morality provides the universal standard for making those judgments. By definition, American actions are taken to be morally correct and justifiable. Flawed policy initiatives are routinely attributed to leadership deficiencies or breakdowns in organizational behavior, not to the American values that guided the action. In the aftermath of World War I, the Nye Committee investigated charges that the United States had been led into war by banking interests, and the McCarthy investigations explored alleged communist penetration of the State Department following the "loss of China" in the 1950s. This dimension of moral pragmatism reappears in Trump's foreign policy, in his characterizations of the foreign policies of past administrations as "the worst deal ever."

In judging state behavior by moral standards, the United States typically places responsibility for foreign policy problems on the evil nature of the opponent rather than on the underlying dynamics of world politics or its own actions. George Kennan, the author of the containment doctrine, put it this way: "There seems to be a curious American tendency to search, at all times, for a single external evil, to which all can be attributed."

In line with Kennan's observation, Paul Pillar, a CIA officer who once served as national intelligence officer for the Middle East, has gone so far as to argue that the United States needs a villain in making foreign policy and that it found one in Iran.[24] The end result is that the United States became preoccupied with Iran to a far greater extent than was warranted by the threat. Pillar argues that, by casting an adversary as a villain, several harmful by-products for U.S. foreign policy follow, all of which have surfaced in negotiations to limit Iran's quest for nuclear weapons: (1) denial that any reasonable basis for the adversary's action exists, (2) underestimation of how much support the government may have among its people, and (3) underestimation of the adversary's willingness to compromise.

American pragmatism takes the form of an *engineering approach* to foreign policy problem solving.[25] The preferred method for uncovering the solution is to break the problem into smaller ones—the same way an engineer may take a blueprint and break a large task down into smaller ones. An organizational or mechanical solution is then devised for each of the subproblems. In using the engineering approach, it is not unusual to lose sight of the political context of the larger problem being addressed. When this happens, the result can be the substitution of means for ends, improvisation, or reliance on canned formulas to solve the problem.

U.S. involvement is typically put in terms of "setting things right." It is assumed that a right answer does exist and that it is the American answer. In addition, the answer is seen as permanent. Foreign policy crises can arise when states see problems in different terms. To some, this has been especially evident in U.S.-Soviet arms control talks. The American approach to strategic thinking treated nuclear war as a "mathematical exercise."[26] Operating on the basis of a very different historical experience, the Soviets viewed war in quite different terms, marked by a great deal of uncertainty without a concrete solution.

The neutrality principle and related legislation of the 1930s provides an example of moral pragmatism at work. As first put forward, the legislation was easy to implement but paid little attention to the political realities of the day. Weapons were not to be sold to either side. Yet refusing to sell weapons to either participant guaranteed victory to the stronger side and invited its aggression. Neutrality legislation was repeatedly amended in an effort to close the gap between technique and political reality. In 1937, the president was given the authority to distinguish between civil strife and war. In 1939, legislation permitted the cash-and-carry purchase of weapons by belligerents, allowing the United States to sell weapons to Great Britain but making a mockery of the neutrality principle.

The potential dangers of rooting U.S. foreign policy on a foundation of moral pragmatism came through quite clearly in the Iran-Contra fiasco. Convinced of the moral correctness of the goal of freeing American hostages in Lebanon, the Reagan administration proceeded to sell arms to Iran, then diverted monies gained through these sales to the U.S.-backed Contras fighting the Sandinista government in Nicaragua. More recently, this tendency to solve foreign policy problems by designing blueprints and implementing them is evident in the American propensity to equate building democracy with holding elections and writing a constitution.

A frequent complaint leveled at U.S. Cold War foreign policy was that the anticommunist impulse was used to sanction almost any course of action, no matter how immoral, if it brought about the greater goal of stopping communism.[27] In the view of many, this attitude has carried over to the Global War on Terrorism and was found in Trump's willingness to invoke seldom-used declarations of emergency as the basis for his actions.

## Legalism

The third pattern in U.S. foreign policy, **legalism,** grows out of the rejection of the balance of power as a means for preserving national security and the liberal view that people are rational beings who abhor war and favor the peaceful settlement of disputes.[28] A central task of U.S. foreign policy, therefore, is to create a global system of institutions and rules that allow states to settle their disputes without recourse to war. The primary institutional embodiments of the legalist perspective are the League of Nations and the United Nations. Also relevant are the host of post–World War II international economic organizations that the United States joined (i.e., the World Bank and International Monetary Fund). Just as commerce between individuals binds them together, international trade is assumed to bind states together and reduce the likelihood of war.

The rule-making thrust to legalism is found in the repeated use of the **pledge system** as an instrument of foreign policy.[29] In creating a pledge system, the United States puts forward a statement of principle and then asks other states to adhere to it, either by signing a treaty or by pledging their support for the principle. Noticeably absent is any meaningful enforcement mechanism. The Open Door Notes exemplify this strategy for world affairs problem solving. In the Notes, issued between 1899 and 1900, the United States unilaterally proclaimed its opposition to spheres of influence in China and asked other powers to do likewise, but it did not specify any sanctions against a state that reneged on its pledge. The Washington Naval Disarmament Conference of 1922 and the 1928 Kellogg-Briand Pact are also examples of use of the pledge system. The Washington Naval Disarmament Conference sought to prevent war by establishing a fixed power ratio for certain categories of warships, but it failed to include inspection or enforcement provisions. Its restraining qualities were soon overtaken by a naval arms race in areas left uncovered by the agreement and by a general heightening of international tensions. The Kellogg-Briand Pact sought to outlaw war as an instrument of foreign policy. Yet, true to its unilateralist impulse, the United States stated that signing the pact would not prevent it from enforcing the Monroe Doctrine or obligate it to participate in sanctions against other states. Agreements reached during the Strategic Arms Limitation Talks (SALT I and SALT II) followed the tradition of the pledge system. They specified in broad terms the permissible nuclear inventories of the Soviet Union and the United States without creating any enforcement provisions.

Variations of the pledge system have become a prominent feature of U.S. contemporary bilateral and multilateral trade policy. Confronted with an intransigent Japan in 1993, U.S. negotiators settled for a "framework" agreement that specified how future agreements would seek to resolve issues of trade imbalances and barriers to trade without detailing any particulars. The New Strategic Arms Reduction Treaty (New START), signed in 2010 between the United States and Russia, contained no enforcement procedures. Neither did the 2015 Paris Climate Agreement. Countries were expected to set their own reduction standards, and international shaming was to serve as the enforcement mechanism.

Legalism has also placed a heavy burden on U.S. foreign policy. In rejecting power politics as an approach for providing for U.S. national security, policy makers have denied themselves the use of the "reasons-of-state" argument as a justification for their actions. Instead, they have sought to clothe their actions in terms of legal principles. Post–World War II examples include fighting the Korean War under the UN flag and seeking the approval of the Organization of American States for a blockade during the Cuban missile crisis. This pattern has continued in the post–Cold War era. Obama obtained UN support for his air attacks on Libya, George H. W. Bush moved forward with his military campaign against Iraq after getting UN support, and Clinton did the same for his use of force in Haiti. On the surface it might appear that Trump's foreign policy has abandoned legalism; instead, he has drawn upon it to support his unilateralist impulse repeatedly, arguing that the United States is justified in leaving NATO, trade agreements, and other cooperative ventures because other states have not met their responsibilities and have exploited the United States.

## Consequences of the American National Style

As suggested earlier, these three patterns (unilateralism, moral pragmatism, and legalism) come together to support both isolationism and internationalism. They also produce four consequences for the overall conduct of U.S. foreign policy. The first is a tendency to "win the war and lose the peace." As Robert Osgood wrote in 1957,

> The United States has demonstrated an impressive ability to defeat the enemy. Yet . . . it has been unable to deter war; it has been unprepared to fight war; it has failed to gain the objectives it fought for; and its settlements have not brought satisfactory peace.[30]

For many, his observation still rings true today.

The inability to "win the peace" stems from the American tendency to see war and peace as polar opposites. War is a social aberration, and peace is the normal state of affairs. Strategies and tactics appropriate for one arena have no place in the other. The two categories must be kept separate to prevent the calculations of war from corrupting the principles of peace. In times of peace, the accomplishment of foreign policy objectives relies on reason, discussion, and trade. In times of war, power is the appropriate tool. The absence of a conceptual link between war and peace means that war cannot serve as an instrument of statecraft and that war plans will be drawn up in a political vacuum. The objective of war is to defeat the enemy as swiftly as possible. Only when that is accomplished can we return to the concerns of peace.

One example of the consequences of the American national style is the Bracero Program (see the "Historical Lesson").

### Historical Lesson

### The Bracero Program

World War II led to a significant demand for additional workers in the United States, most notably in agriculture and the railroad industry. Between 1942 and 1964, this demand was filled by Mexican workers, "braceros," who crossed into the United States as part of a guest-worker program negotiated between the two countries officially known as the Mexican Contract Labor Program. The wartime years produced the smallest migrant flow of any of these years, with 49,000–82,000 Mexican workers crossing the border. From 1947 to 1954, the average annual migration was 116,000–141,000 per year. In the last ten years of the Bracero Program, there was an average of 333,000 migrant worker contracts.

This was not the first attempt to regulate the entry of Mexican labor across the border. In 1909, President William Howard Taft signed an executive agreement with Mexico permitting thousands of Mexican contract workers to harvest sugar beets in Colorado and Nebraska. When the United States entered World War I, restrictions were eased, and the number of Mexican workers increased to seventy-three thousand. The Mexican government viewed this situation with some alarm. The Mexican constitution of 1917 contained a provision that sought to safeguard the rights of emigrant workers, and it attempted to discourage workers from going to the United States unless they already had contracts that provided such protections. These efforts were largely ineffective. In 1929, with the Great Depression underway in the United States and large numbers of Mexicans returning home due to lack of jobs, the Mexican government sought but failed to obtain a bilateral agreement with the United States that would allow it to jointly manage the flow of workers across the border.

At the outset of the Bracero Program, Mexico possessed significant bargaining strength that allowed it to insert provisions protecting migrant rights. These included insisting that the braceros be paid the prevailing wage and prohibiting Mexicans from being rejected at "white" restaurants and other facilities in the American South. Mexico blacklisted Texas because of its discrimination policies and would not allow braceros to go there.

Gradually, however, Mexico's leverage began to weaken. One important reason was the growing phenomenon of illegal, or "wetback," immigration into areas such as Texas, where demand for migrant labor was great. In 1943, Congress passed Public Law 45, which gave legal status to the agreement reached with Mexico in 1942. One of its key provisions was that the United States could unilaterally declare an "open border" if need be. This power was used in May 1943 to grant one-year entrance permits. Texas farmers rushed into Mexico and began recruiting migrants, and the process undermined the orderly bilateral recruitment of workers. Lax border control enforcement in the early 1950s further contributed to the flow of illegal migrant workers.

In the late 1940s and early 1950s, the United States sought to deal with the problem of illegal migrant labor by transforming it into legal labor through mass deportations and mass legalizations. The scope of the problem was immense.

In New Mexico, braceros made up 70 percent of the seasonal labor force. From 1947 to 1949, the President's Commission on Migratory Labor estimated that 142,000 deportable Mexicans in the United States were legalized as braceros. In 1950, slightly more than 19,800 new bracero contracts were awarded, but an estimated 96,200 illegal Mexicans were working in the United States. From 1955 to 1959, just 18 percent of all seasonal farm laborers were braceros.

The legacy of the Bracero Program is found in many areas. Getting seasonal and regionally concentrated agricultural jobs, rather than establishing permanent residence, became the norm for Mexicans coming to the United States. Part of the Mexican government's response to the end of the Bracero Program was the creation of jobs along the U.S. border for returning migrants, which became the Border Industrialization or Maquiladora Program. This program has not worked as expected, since firms have preferred to hire young Mexican women rather than returning braceros.

Within the United States, the end of the Bracero Program has not ended the debate over how to address the problem of illegal Mexican workers in the United States or how to provide sanctioned labor to employers. The Reagan administration proposed a pilot program that gave fifty thousand Mexicans temporary work permits each year. The George W. Bush administration floated the idea of a massive amnesty program for illegal Mexican migrants in the months prior to the 9/11 attacks. When the administration dropped these plans, Mexico called for the establishment of a new guest-worker program.

## Applying the Lesson

1. What elements of the American national style can be found in the idea of a fence to control immigration and the Bracero Program?
2. Rate the importance of foreign policy and domestic policy considerations in these two policies.
3. Should we think about immigration primarily as an economic problem or as a national security problem?

The closing stages of World War II illustrate the problem inherent in the war-peace dichotomy. Should U.S. forces have pushed as far as possible eastward for the political purpose of denying the Red Army control over as much territory as possible, or should they have stopped as soon as the purely military objectives of the offensive were realized and not risked the lives of U.S. soldiers on nonmilitary goals? The Cold War East-West boundary in Europe reflected the choice of the latter course of action.

The George W. Bush administration was not immune from this artificial separation of war and peace. A sharp distinction between the two was evident in planning for the Iraq War. According to the original war plan, U.S. troops would be withdrawn within six months of the invasion; planning for the postwar transition to democracy was virtually absent. The presence of a sharp war-peace distinction and another consequence, impatience (to be discussed shortly), are evident in Obama's accelerated efforts to leave Afghanistan as the victor after bin Laden's death and the quick exit of American forces from Libya after Muammar Gaddafi was removed from power.

A second consequence of the American national style is the existence of a double standard in judging the behavior of states. Convinced of its righteousness and the universality of its values, and predisposed to act unilaterally, the United States has often engaged in actions that it condemns when they are taken by other states. The United States can be trusted to test and develop nuclear weapons, but others cannot. Soviet interventions in Afghanistan and Czechoslovakia are condemned as imperialism, while U.S. interventions in the Dominican Republic, Grenada, and Panama are held to be morally defensible. The reverse condition also holds. Activities considered by most states to be acceptable have been viewed as highly controversial by the United States. The clandestine collection of information and covert attempts to influence developments in other states, both long-standing instruments of foreign policy, are cases in point. The notion that different rules might apply to the United States than to other states surfaced after revelations of widespread abuse by American interrogators at Abu Ghraib prison. President Bush dismissed as "absurd" an Amnesty International report charging the administration with having created a gulag at the Guantanamo Bay detention facility.

The third consequence of the American national style is ambivalence toward diplomacy. In the abstract, diplomacy is valued as part of the process by which states peacefully resolve their disputes. It occupies a central place in liberal thinking about the proper forums for conducting foreign relations. The product of diplomacy is viewed with great skepticism, however. If the U.S. position is morally correct, how can it compromise (something vital to the success of diplomacy) without rejecting its own sense of mission and its principles? As political scientist John Spanier notes, under these conditions compromise is indistinguishable from appeasement.[31] Such feelings of mistrust and doubt are evident today across the political spectrum. They can be seen in Trump's rejection of Obama's nuclear agreement with Iran and fears about what Trump and Russian president Vladimir Putin may have discussed in their private meetings.

The fourth consequence of the American national style is impatience. Optimistic at the start of an undertaking and convinced of the correctness of its position in both a moral and a technical sense, Americans tend to want quick results and become impatient when positive results are not soon forthcoming. A common reaction is to turn away in frustration. The next time a similar situation presents itself and U.S. action is needed, none may be taken. Calls for "no more Vietnams" reflect this sense of frustration, as did the demand to get U.S. Marines out of Lebanon following the terrorist attacks on the U.S. compound during the Reagan administration. Impatience was evident in the expectation that the United States could oversee the election of an interim Iraqi government, the writing and ratification of a constitution, and the election of a permanent government in just twelve months. As one columnist noted, the problem is that Iraq does not operate on Washington's clock.[32]

The desire for quick and visible results is seen by many as creating a bias toward the use of the military as an instrument of foreign policy. Neither diplomacy nor economic power offers quick results. Using the military as an instrument of foreign policy can create a vicious circle, however. The demand for quick results leads to a reliance on military power, but the rigid distinction between war and peace makes it difficult to use that power effectively to meet political objectives. If the latter occurs, then diplomacy may be utilized. Yet, here again, the results are likely to be slow in coming and may be viewed with skepticism. Frustration will set in and dominate U.S. foreign policy until a consensus supports new foreign policy initiatives.

## Voices from the Past

Many find that important insights into the development of the American national style can also be found in the foreign policy ideas developed by earlier generations of policy makers.

One of these is President John Adams. According to Adams, American foreign policy should be based on the principle that the United States is "the well-wisher to the freedom and independence of all" but "the champion and vindicator only of her own."[33] Adams was putting forward an argument for nonintervention into the affairs of others and advocating a foreign policy that was to be based on the "power of example." To go further, he warned, would involve the United States in "wars of interest and intrigue, of individual avarice, envy, and ambition."

Conservative internationalists point to the writings of Theodore Roosevelt.[34] He would replace liberal internationalism's conception of humanitarian intervention as a philanthropic exercise with one rooted in a sense of nationalistic patriotism. Before the Spanish-American War, Roosevelt wrote, "The useful member of a community is the man who first and foremost attends to his own rights and duties . . . the useful member of the brotherhood of nations is that nation which is most thoroughly saturated with the national ideal."

Walter Mead identifies four other figures from the past as particularly influential in setting the goals and policies that continue to shape American foreign policy: Woodrow Wilson, Alexander Hamilton, Thomas Jefferson, and Andrew Jackson. For virtually the entire post–World War II era, U.S. foreign policy was organized around a combination of Wilsonian and Hamiltonian principles with occasional periods—such as after Vietnam—when Jeffersonian ideas gained prominence. Most recently we have witnessed a rise in the influence of Jacksonianism on U.S. foreign policy, as evidenced by the manner in which Trump's foreign policy is carried out and the goals that it pursues.

Wilson's core foreign policy ideas are found in his Fourteen Points, which he presented in a speech to Congress in 1918. They constituted an outline for constructing a new world order, one that would be marked by an "open" era of international politics, "a general association of nations," and "political independence and territorial integrity to great and small states alike." Looking beyond the Fourteen Points, **Wilsonianism** rested on four elements. The first was promotion of democracy, the second was encouragement of free trade, and the third was weapons control. Together, these three elements would place restraints on the exercise of government power and provide space for the development of individual liberty. The fourth element, the League of Nations, would provide an alternative to balance-of-power politics in ensuring national security.[35]

Early evaluations of Wilson's foreign policy held it to be naively idealistic and fundamentally flawed. This is no longer the case. His foreign policy principles are now embraced by many as those of a vindicated visionary, one who possessed a "higher realism" in his handling of foreign affairs.[36] After the 9/11 terrorist attack, George W. Bush, who had promised a moderate foreign policy, began to sound very much like Wilson. In his 2002 State of the Union address, Bush stated, "America will lead by defending liberty and justice because they are right and true and unchanging for people everywhere. . . . We have no intention of imposing our culture. But America will always stand firm for the nonnegotiable demands of human dignity."

The renewed interest in Wilsonianism has not met with universal approval. Some opponents assert that the term lacks clear meaning, to the point that virtually all recent presidents could be termed Wilsonians.[37] For example, the Reagan Doctrine (see chapter 1) could be seen as the ultimate embodiment of the Wilsonian legacy given its commitment to expand democracy. David Fromkin poses another problem with Wilsonianism as a model for contemporary American foreign policy.[38] He concludes that one of its core assumptions is the importance of a strong presidency. Wilson saw the president's control of foreign policy as "very absolute." He believed that the Senate had no choice but to ratify any treaty submitted to it by the president, regardless of any doubts about its wisdom or the secrecy with which it may have been negotiated. Wilson also advocated the Espionage Act of 1917. Edward Snowden (NSA leaks), Daniel Ellsberg (Pentagon Papers), and Julius and Ethel Rosenberg (stealing atomic secrets for the Soviet Union) are among those charged with violating this act.

Alexander Hamilton advanced a concept of foreign policy that centered on economic considerations. The first task of U.S. foreign policy was promoting the health of the American economy at home and abroad. To that end, Hamilton emphasized the importance of a strong alliance between big business and government. This positioned the United States to engage in the global economy on favorable terms. He advocated a policy of freedom of the seas and an open-door policy ensuring the free flow of money across borders. In the Hamiltonian perspective on foreign policy, excessive amounts of military power and wars were threats to economic stability and growth. Military power must be used for the appropriate purposes and with care. After World War II, this required an American foreign policy that worked with other states to promote and protect an open international economic order. More recently, Hamiltonians were not opposed to the post-9/11 American military offensive against terrorism because those attacks and their aftershocks threatened the health of American and global economic stability and growth.

Thomas Jefferson's approach to foreign policy is seen by many as the foundation for isolationism. At its core is the belief that the primary mission of U.S. foreign policy is to protect and perfect democracy at home. From the Jeffersonian perspective, excess foreign involvements, whether for building democracy or economic development, represent a danger to American democracy because they foster the creation of a strong government. A strong government weakens the system of checks and balances, promotes secrecy, and threatens individual liberties, especially when it involves the use of military force. From the Jeffersonian perspective, what is needed is a constitutional foreign policy. To that end, Jeffersonians support the War Powers Act, which attempts to limit the president's use of force; oppose fast-track legislation that limits congressional power to amend international agreements; and oppose National Security Agency (NSA) domestic spying programs implemented after the 9/11 attacks. Senator Ron Paul has advanced a libertarian foreign policy agenda that is Jeffersonian in outlook, expressing concern about the corrupting effects of global involvement on American democracy.[39] This has been particularly notable in his opposition to the NSA domestic surveillance program.

The lead figure in the fourth foreign policy worldview impacting the American national style is Andrew Jackson.[40] His writings and actions provide a foundation for those who stress the populist principles of courage, honor, and self-reliance in the conduct of American foreign policy. Rooted in the American frontier experience, Jacksonians draw a clear and firm distinction between members of their community and outsiders. The purpose of government is to protect and promote the interests of community members against outsiders who, by definition, threaten it. These outsiders, who hold different economic and cultural values, are found both beyond America's borders and within the government.[41] Jacksonians value simple and direct solutions to problems, fearing that complex solutions inevitably come to serve the interests of these outsiders rather than the people. Pessimists at heart, Jacksonians see the community as being threatened constantly by outsiders. For that reason, they champion a foreign policy of constant vigilance backed by overwhelming might that may be employed with few, if any, constraints. For Jacksonians, the objective of war is victory, not a negotiated solution or the achievement of limited objectives. Jacksonians are slow to focus on foreign policy issues, which works against the achievement of victory in war and other foreign policy initiatives. Domestic issues take precedence. Additionally, once a foreign policy commitment has been made, Jacksonians find it difficult to change their position.

Jacksonianism never disappeared completely from the political scene. The Tea Party movement is often seen as evidence of its most recent revival, although its foreign policy agenda also contains strains of other voices from the past.[42] Donald Trump's election in 2016 is seen as the culmination of this revival.

## Over the Horizon: A Millennial Foreign Policy?

The American national style should not be viewed as being frozen in place. Change is possible but not inevitable, and its direction is unpredictable. In the eyes of some observers, change might come as a result of the increased presence of women, blacks, and Hispanics in the policy-making process.[43] Their histories read quite differently from those presented in the standardized accounts of the American past, and they may bring to the policy process a very different style of acting and thinking about solutions to foreign policy problems.

A key question looking over the horizon for the U.S. national style is, can it change in a way to adapt to future foreign policy challenges, or will traditional ways of defining problems and solutions continue? For example, will engineering solutions such as building a wall continue to dominate thinking about protecting U.S. borders, or will other approaches be used? Will border policies be rooted in a nationalist or globalist perspective?

At a minimum, two different scenarios present themselves. The first is a continuation of the important role that Jacksonian thinking currently plays regarding border policy. This is consistent with the view that Trump's election is best seen as a reflection of an underlying sense of frustration with the American political scene and not simply as a matter of personality and political style. As such, Trump's Jacksonian political agenda can be expected to outlive his presidency and influence future foreign policy making.

The second scenario involves change. A potential source of change in the American national style is the emergence into political power of a new generation: millennials.[44] Born between 1980 and 1997, they make up almost one-quarter of the adult U.S. population. They reached adulthood after the Cold War ended, so they have few memories of a pre-9/11 world with its terrorist attacks and Middle East wars. In addition, they are far more likely than older generations to see the United States as having provoked 9/11 through its foreign policy actions.

Research shows that millennials differ from older Americans in their foreign policy outlooks in three critical ways: (1) they see the world as significantly less threatening and are less worried about national security; (2) they are more supportive of international cooperation; and (3) while compared to older generations they are more hesitant to support use of military force in specific cases, they do not reject using force out of hand. They are more supportive of multilateral military efforts than unilateral action.

These contrasting generational positions are very evident in millennial views on border crossing. A February 2017 Pew poll showed that 78 percent of those aged eighteen to twenty-nine opposed building a wall, as did 65 percent of those aged thirty to forty-nine. Support for the wall in older age groups dipped below 50 percent. A January 2019 Pew poll found that 73 percent of those aged eighteen to twenty-nine and 63 percent of those aged thirty to thirty-nine opposed expanding the wall, compared with 51 percent of those in the fifty to sixty-four age group and 48 percent of those over sixty-five. Looking to more far-ranging foreign policy issues, a February 2021 Pew poll found that while 49 percent of those over age sixty-five ranked reducing illegal immigration into the United States as a top-priority long-range foreign policy goal, only 24 percent of those aged eighteen to thirty-nine did so.

## Critical Thinking Questions

1. Could the United States become isolationist again? Why or why not?
2. What is the most important element in the American national style for understanding U.S. foreign policy, and why?
3. How difficult would it be for the American national style in U.S. foreign policy to change? Explain your answer.

## Key Terms

containment, 43
deterrence, 43
internationalism, 45
isolationism, 45
legalism, 51
moral pragmatism, 49

national style, 43
pledge system, 51
preemption, 43
unilateralism, 48
Wilsonianism, 56

# Learning from the Past 4

## Learning Objectives

Students will be able to:

1. Identify the types of lessons learned from the past by policy makers and the types of calculations they make.
2. Describe and rank order in importance the lessons from the past used by policy makers in making Vietnam policy.
3. Differentiate between the lessons learned from Vietnam and the lessons learned from the Iraq War.
4. Assess the extent to which policy makers might learn from the COVID-19 crisis in preparing for the next global pandemic.

# On the Agenda: COVID-19

On December 31, 2019, China reported an outbreak of pneumonia cases in Wuhan to the World Health Organization (WHO). On January 3, it informed the United States of the outbreak. On January 7, 2020, it confirmed that the cases involved a novel coronavirus. The first confirmed case in the United States came on January 20. On January 27, the New York Stock Market dropped over 450 points as concerns about the economic impact of the disease grew. The Chinese provinces most affected by the outbreak were home to almost fifty thousand branches and subsidiaries of foreign corporations, including some 9,500 American firms. On January 30, the WHO declared a public health emergency, its highest level of alert. In February 2020, the disease was officially labeled COVID-19 by the WHO, and the following month it declared the COVID-19 outbreak to be a pandemic, a disease that affects the entire global population. Here we look at how global and domestic factors shaped the Trump administration's response to the outbreak of COVID-19.

Upon taking office, President Trump launched a trade war against China, which added considerably to the strained relations between the two countries. On January 15, 2020, shortly after the outbreak of COVID-19 in China was first reported and prior to the first death in the United States, Trump signed what he asserted was a historic and transformative trade deal (the Phase 1 Agreement) with China. According to Trump, China agreed to purchase an additional $200 billion of U.S. exports before December 21, 2021. In a speech on January 21 at the Davos World Economic Forum, Trump stated that relations between the two countries "probably" have never been better. Speaking of China's president Xi Jinping, Trump stated, "He's for China, I'm for the U.S., but other than that, we love each other." Trump continued to praise China and Xi on January 24, 2020, when the second death due to COVID-19 in the United States was confirmed. In a Twitter post, Trump wrote, "China has been working very hard to contain the Coronavirus. . . . The United States greatly appreciates their efforts and transparency. It will all work out well. In particular, on behalf of the American People, I want to thank President Xi!" Trump continued to speak positively about how China and President Xi were dealing with COVID throughout February, at one point stating on Twitter: "Just had a long and very good conversation by phone with President Xi of China. He is strong, sharp and powerfully focused on leading the counterattack on the Coronavirus. . . . Great discipline is taking place in China, as President Xi strongly leads what will be a very successful operation."

Trump's positive evaluation of Xi and China's efforts to stop the spread of COVID ended as the promises of the trade agreement did not materialize, the COVID crisis within the United States deepened, and concern for its possible impact on the November elections grew. Trump came to characterize responding to the U.S. COVID crisis in military terms. It was a "war" with an invisible enemy, and he in a sense was a "wartime president." One of his first wartime actions was to close the U.S.-Mexican border. He invoked Title 42 of the 1944 Public Health Service Act, which allowed him to prohibit the entry of persons from other countries in order to prevent the spread of communicable diseases into the United States.

Trump now laid blame directly on China for "the China virus" and the WHO for "getting it wrong" in underestimating the scope of the problem and becoming "China centric." Punishment now drove the agenda. Between March 2020 and the end of the year, Trump put in place more retaliatory measures against China than had existed in the previous three years, including restrictions of Chinese technology firms, sanctions against Chinese officials, looser regulations on diplomatic contacts with Taiwan, and labeling Chinese repression in Xinjiang as genocide. Trump also raised the possibility of seeking hundreds of millions of dollars in damages from China. In May, he announced that the United States would freeze its funding of the WHO for sixty days and withdraw from it, saying that the United States had not been treated properly. The United States had contributed $893 million in assessments and voluntary contributions in 2018 and 2019. His COVID war agenda reached beyond China and the WHO. In May he also invoked the Defense Production Act, which allowed the government to dictate the production and delivery schedules of private companies, thus preventing the export of protective medical clothing and equipment, a move that Germany and others called "modern piracy." Ventilators were provided to El Salvador and Honduras, two Central American countries that supported his immigration policies, but not to Guatemala, which frequently opposed him.

For its part, China conducted a combative COVID foreign policy from the outset. It withheld information and resisted cooperation with the WHO and with other countries, fearing that should it be held accountable in some fashion for the COVID pandemic, its reputation and influence would suffer greatly. Between January 24 and February 29, behind this shield of silence, China imported over 2.5 billion pieces of pandemic medical equipment, including over two million masks. When the United States announced it was stopping its funding of the WHO, China stepped forward and announced a new $30 million contribution. As part of its vaccine diplomacy, China also offered other support for countries in their efforts to combat COVID.

Looking inward, Trump's COVID foreign policy can be seen as resting upon two different foundations. The first was bureaucratic and informational. The second was Trump's decision-making style. In 2018, Trump's national security advisor John Bolton disbanded the National Security Council team set up by President Barak Obama to oversee U.S. epidemic preparedness. Several key health officials left at that time, leaving a void in the administration's insight into the dynamics of major health crises. In January 2020, Trump announced a coronavirus task force led by secretary of health and human services Alex Azar. In early February he was replaced by Vice President Pence, who would now head the White House response. In late February, he too was replaced. When asked about the absence of a solid base to formulate a COVID policy, Trump responded, "We can get money and we can get staff. We know all the people. We can build up very quickly."

Trump further cut the bureaucratic support base with a budgetary policy that advanced a series of cuts in health agency budgets, among them a nearly 16 percent cut in the budget of the Centers for Disease Control and Prevention (CDC). In 2018 a coalition of global health care organizations operating in thirty-nine countries protested plans to cut back CDC operations. One cutback occurred in the Beijing office of the CDC where it had existed for thirty years. In the two years prior to the outbreak of COVID in China, its staff was reduced from just under fifty staffers to about fifteen.

Information about COVID was not absent. Beginning in January, classified intelligence reports began to warn about the dangers to the United States posed by COVID-19. These warnings were included in daily briefing papers. The challenge was to get Trump's attention and convince him of the seriousness of the situation. Azar was unable to speak with Trump about COVID until January 18, and then by phone. During that conversation, Trump interrupted Azar to ask about vaping and when flavored vaping products would return to the market. In early briefings by Chief of Staff Mick Mulvaney, Trump was characterized as largely dismissive of the issue because he did not see it as being a widespread problem. In February he said that "the coronavirus is very much under control in the United States."

**Table 4.1**   **Global Health Security Index 2021: Top 10 and Bottom 10 Countries**

| *Top 10 Countries (100 points is top score)* | |
| --- | --- |
| United States | 75.9 |
| Australia | 71.1 |
| Finland | 70.9 |
| Canada | 69.8 |
| Thailand | 68.2 |
| Slovenia | 67.8 |
| United Kingdom | 67.2 |
| Germany | 65.5 |
| South Korea | 65.4 |
| Sweden | 64.9 |
| | |
| *Median score* | *38.9* |
| *Bottom 10 Countries (0 points is bottom score)* | |
| Venezuela | 20.9 |
| Niue | 20.1 |
| Tuvalu | 20.0 |
| Central African Republic | 18.6 |
| Nauru | 18.0 |
| Equatorial Guinea | 17.4 |
| Syria | 16.7 |
| Yemen | 16.1 |
| North Korea | 16.1 |
| Somalia | 16.0 |

*Source*: Jenny Lei Ravelo, "World Is Dangerously Unprepared for Future Pandemics GHS Index Finds," DEVEX.com, December 9, 2021.

COVID-19 is not the first global pandemic, and health experts warn that it is not the last. Many are especially concerned that countries are unprepared for it. A first step in laying the ground work to meet a future pandemic is to learn from the past. A 2021 Global Health Security Report concluded that countries were "dangerously unprepared for future epidemic and pandemic threats."[1] The top and bottom ten countries in their preparedness list are presented in table 4.1.

This chapter examines the manner in which policy makers learn from the past, the types of calculations they make, and the lessons learned. It then takes a close look at the lessons learned in the U.S. involvement in Vietnam and Iraq. It concludes with a discussion of lessons from Afghanistan.

## How Do Policy Makers Learn from the Past?

Policy makers learn by matching the known with the unknown.[2] This is not a passive act. They do not sit back and simply accept data as a given, but actively interact with it.[3] In deciding how to respond to the humanitarian crisis in Kosovo, Bill Clinton and his advisors drew upon **analogies** with at least four different events from the past, each of which suggested a different definition of the problem and the response: Vietnam, the Holocaust, Munich, and the outbreak of World War I.[4]

In addition to selecting reference points for evaluating information, policy makers must make judgments about whether a piece of information is important (a **signal**) or unimportant (**noise**). Discriminating between the two is no easy task. Identifying a piece of data as a signal does not tell the policy maker what to do; it only sets in motion the process of learning. Information received in the Philippines before the attack on Pearl Harbor did not tell policy makers that they were the next target or identify the steps to take to defend themselves. In the period immediately before Pearl Harbor, fifty-six separate signals, ranging in duration from one day to one month, pointed toward the Japanese attack, but there was also a good deal of evidence to support all of the wrong interpretations. Surprise occurred not because of a lack of signals, but because there was too much noise.[5]

Policy makers discriminate between signals and noise by making a series of assumptions about what motivates the behavior of others or what constitutes the underlying dynamics of a problem. Consider the intercepted Japanese directive to its U.S. embassy and consulates to burn their codes. In retrospect, this is a clear indication that hostilities were imminent. However, during the first week of December 1941, the United States ordered all of its consulates in the Far East to burn their codes, and no one took this to be the equivalent of a U.S. declaration of war against Japan.

The assumptions that policy makers bring to bear on foreign policy problems are influenced by both long-term experiences and immediate concerns. Long-term experience provides policy makers with a database against which to evaluate an ongoing pattern of behavior. For Franklin Roosevelt and other U.S. policy makers, personal experiences and their reading of history led to a conclusion that the presence of the U.S. fleet at Pearl Harbor was a deterrent to a Japanese attack. They failed to appreciate that it also made a fine target. For their part, Japanese leaders drew on their 1904 war-opening attack in the Russo-Japanese War as the model for how to deal with a more powerful enemy.

Once they are in place, perceptual systems are not readily changed. They easily become obsolete and inaccurate. The principle involved here is **cognitive consistency**.[6] Individuals try to keep their beliefs and values consistent by ignoring some information, actively seeking out other data, and reinterpreting still other information to support their perception of reality. As a result, instead of being a continuous and rationally structured process, learning is sporadic and constrained. Policy makers do not move steadily from a simplistic understanding of an event to a more complex one as their experience and familiarity with it builds. New information and new problems are fitted into already well-established perceptual systems. So learning rarely produces dramatic changes in priorities or commitments, and changes in behavior tend to be incremental.

A well-documented case of this process at work is John Foster Dulles's perception of the Soviet Union.[7] Dulles was Eisenhower's secretary of state and had a **closed belief system**. He saw the Soviet Union as a hostile state and interpreted any data that might indicate a lessening of hostility in such a way that it reinforced his original perceptions. In his view, cooperative Soviet gestures were not a sign of goodwill but the product of Soviet failures, representing only a lull before the Soviet Union would engage in another round of hostilities.

## Events from Which Policy Makers Learn

The sporadic and constrained nature of the learning process means that not all aspects of the past are equally likely to serve as the source of lessons. Two categories of events are especially important lesson sources. The first is the dramatic and highly visible event. Policy makers turn to these events with the conviction that, because they are so dramatic and visible, they must contain more important information than commonplace happenings. The scars they leave in defeat and the praises sung in victory can become deeply entrenched in the collective memory of society. Events of this magnitude are often referred to as **generational events** because an entire generation draws on them for lessons. War is the ultimate generational event. A policy maker need not have been involved in the 1938 negotiations at Munich to invoke the analogy and point to the dangers of appeasement.

The corollary to paying a great deal of attention to highly dramatic events is to all but ignore the nonevent. Nothing is learned from the crisis that *almost* happened. Warnings about the weakness of the shah of Iran were heard as early as 1961, when members of the Senate Foreign Relations Committee warned the incoming Kennedy administration that no number of weapons could save him. Mass unrest and corruption, they argued, doomed him to defeat. Senator Hubert Humphrey declared, "This crowd, they are dead. They just don't know it. . . . It is just a matter of time."[8] The more often a warning is given and no attack occurs, the easier it is for policy makers to dismiss the next one. The November 27, 1941, warning to Pearl Harbor that a Japanese attack was possible was not the first one the United States received. An alarming dispatch had been received in October, but no attack had followed.

The second type of highly influential event is one that the policy maker experienced first-hand, especially those that took place early in the policy maker's career. The lessons drawn from events experienced firsthand tend to be overgeneralized to the neglect of lessons that might otherwise be drawn from the careful analysis of the experiences of others.[9] U.S. thinking about the post–World War II role of the atomic bomb provides an example of the pull of personally experienced events on policy making.[10] The initial decisions were made by the men who had defeated Germany and Japan. In formulating ideas about the applications of the bomb, they drew heavily on those experiences. From 1945 to 1950, the Soviet targets identified for destruction by the atomic bomb duplicated the U.S. World War II policy of targeting commercial and industrial centers. They did not view the atomic bomb as a new weapon requiring development of a new strategy. It would be left to politicians to put forward the first strategy tailored to the political and technological realities of the postwar era.

Firsthand experiences that occur early in a policy maker's career are especially important because perceptual systems are resistant to change. Individuals are most open to competing images of reality when they confront a situation for the first time. Once a label or category is selected, it establishes the basis for future comparisons. These early firsthand experiences are not necessarily related to foreign policy problems. They may be ways of thinking about problems that proved successful in the past, positions taken on issues that produced desired outcomes, or strategies used in winning political office.[11] Early firsthand experiences are also of special significance because of the conditions under which policy makers must try to learn from the past. Henry Kissinger spoke to these problems in his memoirs when he stated that "policy makers live off the intellectual capital they have brought with them into office; they have no time to build more capital."[12]

The importance of early career experiences comes through quite clearly in how Donald Trump and Joe Biden have conducted foreign affairs. Trump came into office with no experience in government or politics. He was a businessperson who ran a private corporation, and his actions were not subject to review by stockholders or others. His foreign policy agenda emphasized short-term wins and losses. Biden had a long career in government and was familiar with the give-and-take of political decision making. Accounts of his foreign policy toward issues such as nuclear weapons and the war in Afghanistan made repeated reference to his views on these subjects earlier in his career in the Senate and his experiences as Obama's vice president.

## Types of Calculations Made

When an event is recognized as a possible source of lessons, policy makers frequently engage in two types of calculations. First, they pay attention to *what* happened, but seldom to *why*. The Iron Curtain descended across Europe, Vietnam fell, and hostages were taken following an attack on the American embassy in Iran. Focusing on what happened rather than on why it took place creates a type of tunnel vision that obscures the differences between the present situation and earlier ones. What can be concluded from the fact that the 1968 invasion of Czechoslovakia, the 1979 invasion of Afghanistan, and the 1981 noninvasion of Poland each required three months of preparation time by the Soviet Union? Perhaps not very much.[13] Policy makers could not assume that the Soviets would need three months to prepare for the next invasion. None of these was an extremely urgent case demanding rapid mobilization or precluded an invasion starting at a higher stage of readiness.

Second, in examining what happened, policy makers tend to dichotomize the outcomes into successes and failures. They tend to forget that most policy initiatives are designed to achieve multiple objectives, that success and failure are rarely ever complete, and that neither is permanent. Problems are not so much solved as redefined and transformed into new challenges and opportunities.

When a policy is defined as a success, policy makers are especially prone to ignore three considerations in applying it as a lesson: (1) its costs, (2) the possibility that another option would have worked better or produced the same result at lesser cost, and (3) the role of accident, luck, and chance in affecting the outcome of events. When an event is defined as a failure, a different set of biases tends to grip policy makers' thinking. There is (1) the presumption that an alternative course of action would have worked better and that policy makers should have known this, and (2) an unwillingness to admit that success may have been unattainable or that surprise is inevitable.[14] The congressional investigation into Pearl Harbor takes up thirty-nine volumes, and the success of the Japanese attack continues to bring forward a never-ending series of books asserting that U.S. policy makers knew of the attack and permitted it to happen.

## Lessons Learned

Three lessons are most often learned by policy makers from their studies of history. First, *expect to see more of the same.* The shah of Iran was expected to continue in power in 1979 simply because he had ruled for so long. Iran without the shah seemed inconceivable. The grain shortage of 1973 caught U.S. policy makers by surprise because for them "the grain problem" was always too much grain. It did not occur to policy makers that the combination of large-scale Soviet purchases of grain plus global drought would send the price of grain skyrocketing.

Second, *expect continuity in the behavior of others.* In part this occurs because policy makers are insensitive to the costs of inaction perceived by another state. The United States made this mistake at Pearl Harbor. U.S. estimates of Japanese behavior were based on the cost of attacking the United States. Insufficient attention was given to the costs that the Japanese would experience if they did nothing and allowed the status quo to continue. For similar reasons, the hostile acts or words of allies surprise policy makers more than the hostility of an enemy.

Third, *avoid policies that fail and repeat policies that bring success.* Two conditions work against the continued success of a policy. First, successful policies get overused and are applied to problems and situations for which they were not intended. Second, a successful policy often changes the situation in ways that will frustrate its future use. In the 1960s, military aid to the shah may indeed have been responsible for averting the coup predicted by members of the Senate Foreign Relations Committee; however, because it also changed the situation, by the late 1970s continued military aid became part of the shah's problem instead of the solution.

These three frequently learned lessons cast a long shadow over U.S. foreign policy making in the lead-up to the Iraq War. First, policy makers expected to see more of the same. According to the dominant view, nuclear proliferation was a "strategic chain reaction," with Iraq under Saddam Hussein being the most recent addition to this chain.[15] Second, it was assumed that Saddam Hussein was evil and could not be trusted to change his policies or—at a minimum—be contained as a security threat. Moreover, Saddam Hussein was engaged in an ongoing game of deception and obstruction with UN weapons inspectors. Why would he do this unless he was trying to hide something? When no weapons of mass destruction were found, an unexamined possibility emerged as the best explanation.[16] Saddam Hussein may have been acting out of a fear that if his bluff was exposed, his enemies within Iraq would be emboldened and his hold on power seriously weakened, or his bluff may have been directed at intimidating neighboring states such as Iran and Saudi Arabia. The George W. Bush administration was determined to avoid what it saw as the central mistake made by George H. W. Bush in the Persian Gulf War; the administration would remove Saddam Hussein from power.

## Historical Lesson

### Ebola

In December 2013, a two-year-old boy died of Ebola in the rain forest of Guinea. By the time the epidemic was declared over in December 2015, some 28,600 people were infected with Ebola, and more than 11,300 died in Guinea, Sierra Leone, and Liberia. The WHO did not identify Ebola as the cause of these deaths and issue health warnings until March 2014. The following month it declared the outbreak was coming to an end. This judgment was challenged by Doctors without Borders (Médecins sans Frontières or MSF). It held that the number of deaths only appeared to be declining because local citizens were not reporting them due to distrust of the government. By mid-June, MSF was reporting that the situation was out of control. Foreign health workers were being attacked by local residents who blamed them for bringing Ebola into their country. Local health workers went on strike. Government health warnings stated that Ebola had no cure.

In May, a meeting of the World Health Assembly which oversees the WHO was held. Ebola was not discussed. The WHO continued to resist labeling it a public health emergency for fear of angering the countries most affected by Ebola on whom it was dependent for cooperation and who might see such a declaration as a hostile act. In August, Liberia declared a state of emergency. Two days later the WHO did likewise. Also in August, President Obama hosted a U.S.-Africa Leaders Summit which focused primarily on economic issues and not health. A global response began to take shape in September when the UN Security Council took up the Ebola crisis. This was only the second meeting ever held by the Security Council to address a disease crisis; the other was on HIV/AIDS. The meeting led to the creation of the first UN emergency health mission.

In August, the Centers for Disease Control and Prevention (CDC) judged the situation in these three countries as well as in Nigeria to be of such a magnitude as to send staffers to assist the WHO and local health officials responding to the outbreak. On September 8, Obama declared the Ebola outbreak to be a potential threat to global security. He announced that the United States would send four thousand military personnel to the region to help set up isolation units, provide safety for health workers, and help transport medical equipment. He also stated that the United States would send four hundred thousand home protective kits to the region. The United States would also provide $750 million to the global relief effort. That same day the Defense Department announced it would provide funding to set up a field hospital in Liberia for health care workers infected by Ebola. The following day the U.S. Agency for International Development (USAID) announced that it would provide support for the African Union, a regional organization made up of African states, to deploy some one hundred health workers to manage and run Ebola treatment centers.

One week later, Obama announced that the Defense Department would be the lead agency in overseeing the U.S. response to the Ebola epidemic and would coordinate with global relief efforts. A military command center would be established in Liberia, and three thousand military personnel would be sent to West Africa at a potential cost of $750 million over the next six months. Operation United Assistance was the first U.S. military operation to support a disease-driven foreign humanitarian assistance mission.

While the outbreak of Ebola was largely confined to Africa, fear and panic did set in within the United States. In total, eleven patients were treated for Ebola in the United States, four of them diagnosed in the United States and the other seven diagnosed in Africa. Two patients died. Health officials repeatedly stated that an Ebola outbreak would not occur given the U.S. health care system and its disease surveillance capabilities. They also argued that a travel ban would make it more difficult for medical supplies to reach affected areas. Nonetheless, an October 2014 public opinion polls reported that some 67 percent of Americans supported a travel panel.

On October 14, Obama rejected an outright travel ban on passengers on flights originating in the affected countries from entering the United States. Days later, as political pressure grew even more intense, Obama altered that policy by stating that all recent travelers to Liberia, Sierra Leone, and Guinea would have to enter via specific U.S. airports where screening procedures would be in place.

This was not the first Ebola outbreak. Earlier epidemics occurred in 1976. A more recent one occurred in 2022. As with the COVID-19 pandemic, international cooperation proved challenging, as did working with domestic governments. The 2014 Ebola outbreak also gave rise to numerous lessons learned studies. Among the recommendations made were (1) the need for a global clinical response corps, (2) strong leadership, and (3) a U.S. government framework for multiagency responses to international incidents.

### Applying the Lesson

1. In what ways was the Ebola outbreak similar to and different from the COVID-19 pandemic?
2. How similar does a previous case need to be in order to learn lessons from the past?
3. Were any of the Ebola lessons learned?

## Case Studies

This chapter now shifts to an examination of two case studies about how to learn from the past: Vietnam and the Iraq War. Through the phrases *Vietnam syndrome* (see chapter 5) and **Iraq syndrome,** these conflicts have become primary reference points for thinking about the war in Afghanistan and the merits of intervention in Libya, Syria, and elsewhere. Vietnam provides a look at the range of lessons used by policy makers in making decisions about how to fight the war and illustrates those that American elites have drawn from U.S. involvement. Lessons can also be drawn from how the Iraq War ended. Joshua Rovner's study led him to conclude that, contrary to popular perception, the United States did not win the war and lose the peace.[17] Instead, it won both the war and the peace that followed, but a combination of domestic politics, diplomatic and strategic considerations, and psychological factors combined to prevent U.S. leaders from recognizing that they had won.

Selecting what cases hold insight to a contemporary problem is no easy task. There is a tendency to look to the most similar cases for insight, but looking at cases that are very dissimilar may also provide insight. Vladimir Putin appears to have looked to his prior use of force in Ukraine and Crimea as cases with lessons for his 2022 invasion of Ukraine. In neither case was significant resistance encountered, nor was outside military help provided. The Russian invasion of Afghanistan would provide a case study where significant resistance was encountered and outside military help was forthcoming.

Before turning to these cases, we introduce another: the Ebola outbreak of 2014. While not a global pandemic as was COVID-19, the outbreak of Ebola in Africa serves as another case where the United States and the global community encountered a major health crisis for which it was unprepared and offers potential lessons for the outbreak of the next pandemic.

### The Vietnam War

America's involvement in Vietnam spanned six presidents. The cost of the war and its level of destruction were enormous: 55,000 Americans dead, a maximum American troop presence of 541,000 men, a total cost of $150 billion, untold numbers of Vietnamese dead and wounded, seven million tons of bombs dropped, and twenty million craters left behind. Despite these grim statistics, much confusion still exists. A public opinion poll taken between March 21 and March 25, 1985, revealed that only three of five Americans knew that the United States supported South Vietnam. In a press conference on February 18, 1982, in response to a question about covert operations in Latin America, President Reagan stated:

> If I recall correctly . . . North and South Vietnam had been, previous to colonization, two separate countries [and] provisions were made that these two countries could, by the vote of their people together, decide whether they wanted to be one country or not. . . . Ho Chi Minh refused to participate in such an election. . . . John F. Kennedy authorized the sending of a division of Marines. And that was the first move toward combat troops in Vietnam.[18]

North and South Vietnam did not exist as separate countries prior to French colonization in the 1880s, it was South Vietnam that rejected the elections, and Kennedy sent Green Berets to Vietnam in 1961.

Table 4.2 presents a chronology of major events in the history of the U.S. presence in Vietnam.

**Table 4.2** **Chronology of U.S. Involvement in Vietnam**

| | |
|---|---|
| September 1940 | France gives Japan right of transit, control over local military facilities, and control over economic resources in return for right to keep nominal sovereignty. |
| March 1945 | Gaullist French forces take over administration of Vietnam from pro-Vichy French troops. |
| September 1945 | Ho Chi Minh declares Vietnam to be independent. |
| February 1950 | United States recognizes French-backed Bao Dai government. |
| March 1954 | French forces defeated at Dien Bien Phu. |
| April 1954 | Geneva Peace Talks begin; end in July. |
| September 1954 | SEATO created. |
| July 1956 | No elections held in Vietnam. |
| October 1961 | Taylor-Rostow mission sent to Vietnam; 15,000 advisors sent in as a result. |
| November 1963 | Diem and Kennedy assassinated. |
| August 1964 | Gulf of Tonkin incident. |
| February 1965 | Pleiku barracks attacked; eight U.S. soldiers dead and sixty injured; Operation Rolling Thunder launched in retaliation. |
| May 1965 | General Westmoreland requests 80,000 troops. |
| July 1965 | President Johnson announces an additional 125,000 troops to be sent to Vietnam. |
| January 1968 | Tet Offensive. |
| March 1968 | Bombing halted; Johnson steps out of presidential race. |
| April 1970 | Cambodia invaded. |
| March 1972 | Major North Vietnamese offensive launched. |
| April 1972 | B-52 bombings of Hanoi and Haiphong. |
| May 1972 | North Vietnamese harbors mined. |
| December 1972 | Peace talks collapse and then resume after heavy bombing. |
| January 1973 | Peace agreement signed. |
| March 1975 | North Vietnamese offensive begins. |
| April 1975 | South Vietnam surrenders. |

*Vietnam Chronology*

The first president to have to deal with Vietnam was Truman. Initially, his views on Indochina resembled those held during World War II by Roosevelt, who was sympathetic to Ho Chi Minh's efforts to establish independence for the region and unsympathetic to French attempts to reestablish their prewar position of colonial domination. In 1947, Truman resisted French requests for U.S. aid; he also urged France to end the war against Ho Chi Minh, who, while being one of the founders of the French Communist Party, had proven himself a valuable ally and nationalist in defeating Japan.

Truman's views were soon to undergo a stark and rapid transformation. By 1952 the United States was providing France with $30 million in aid to defeat Ho Chi Minh, and in 1953, when Truman's presidency ended, the United States was paying one-third of the French war cost. Ho Chi Minh was also redefined from a nationalist threat to a communist threat to U.S. security interests. Nothing had changed in Indochina to warrant this new evaluation of the situation. Dramatic events, however, were taking place elsewhere as Cold War competition took root. France was reluctant to participate in a European Defense System, something the United States saw as vital if Europe was to contain communist expansionist pressures. In a virtual quid pro quo, the United States agreed to underwrite the French war effort in Indochina, and France announced its intent to participate in plans for the defense of Europe.

The Eisenhower administration began by reaffirming Truman's financial commitment to France and then enlarged it. By the end of 1953, U.S. aid rose to $500 million and covered approximately one-half of the cost of the French war effort. For Eisenhower and Secretary of State John Foster Dulles, expenditures of this magnitude were necessary to prevent a Chinese intervention that they both felt was otherwise likely to occur. Unfortunately for the French, U.S. aid was not enough to secure victory, and Eisenhower was unwilling to go beyond financing a **proxy war**.

The end came for the French at Dien Bien Phu. With its forces under siege there, France informed the United States that unless it intervened, Indochina would fall to the communists. With no aid forthcoming, the process of withdrawal began. France's involvement in Indochina officially came to an end with the signing of the 1954 Geneva Peace Accords. According to this agreement, a *provisional demarcation line* would be established at the seventeenth parallel. Vietminh troops (troops loyal to Ho Chi Minh) would regroup north of it, and pro-French Vietnamese forces would regroup south of it. Elections to determine who would rule over the single country of Vietnam were scheduled for 1956. The Geneva Peace Accords provided the French with a necessary face-saving way out of Indochina. Ho Chi Minh's troops controlled three-quarters of Vietnam and were poised to extend their area of control. All parties to the agreement expected Ho Chi Minh to win the 1956 election easily.

The United States did not sign the Geneva Accords but pledged to "refrain from the threat or use of force to disturb" the settlement. However, only six weeks after its signing, the United States helped set up the Southeast Asia Treaty Organization (SEATO) as part of an effort to halt the spread of communism in the wake of the French defeat. A protocol extended coverage to Laos, Cambodia, and "the free people under the jurisdiction of Vietnam." The Vietminh saw the protocol as a violation of the Geneva Accords because it treated the seventeenth parallel as a political boundary, not a civil war truce line. Political developments below the seventeenth parallel supported the Vietminh interpretation. In 1955 the United States backed Ngo Dinh Diem, who had declared himself president of the Republic of Vietnam. With U.S. support, he argued that, because South Vietnam had not signed the Geneva Accords, it did not have to abide by them and hold elections. The year 1956 came and went with no elections. By the time Eisenhower left office, U.S. military aid had reached one thousand U.S. military advisors stationed in South Vietnam.

The landmark decision on Vietnam during the Kennedy administration came in October 1961 with the Taylor-Rostow Report. Receiving contradictory information and advice on how to proceed, Kennedy sent General Maxwell Taylor and Deputy National Security Advisor Walt Rostow to Vietnam on a fact-finding mission. They reported that South Vietnam could only be saved by the introduction of eight thousand U.S. combat troops. Kennedy rejected this conclusion, but he did send an additional fifteen thousand military advisors. Kennedy's handling of the Taylor-Rostow Report is significant for two reasons. First, the decision was typical of those he made on Vietnam. He never gave the advocates of escalation all they wanted, but neither did he ever say no. Some increase in the level of the American military commitment was always forthcoming. Second, in acting on the Taylor-Rostow Report, Kennedy helped shift the definition of the Vietnam conflict from a political problem to a military one. Until this point, Vietnam was seen by the Kennedy administration as a **guerrilla war** in which control of the population was key. Going forward, control of the battlefield would become the priority.

Under President Lyndon Johnson, U.S. involvement in the war escalated steadily. Pressures began building in January 1964 when the Joint Chiefs of Staff (JCS) urged Johnson to put aside the United States' self-imposed restraints so that the war might be won more quickly. The JCS especially pushed for aerial bombing of North Vietnam. In August 1964, bombing began in retaliation for an incident in the Gulf of Tonkin, where two North Vietnamese patrol torpedo (PT) boats purportedly fired on the USS *C. Turner Joy* and the USS *Maddox* in neutral waters. President Johnson went to Congress for a resolution supporting his use of force against North Vietnam. The Gulf of Tonkin Resolution, which passed by a unanimous vote in the House and an 88–2 vote in the Senate, gave the president the authority to "take all necessary measures to repel any armed attack against the forces of the United States and to prevent further aggression." The incident itself is clouded in controversy. Later studies suggest that the incident was staged or that it never occurred. According to the authors of these studies, Johnson was merely looking for an excuse to begin bombing.[19] The Gulf of Tonkin Resolution became the functional equivalent of a declaration of war.

From that point forward, the war became increasingly Americanized. *Operation Rolling Thunder*, a sustained and massive bombing campaign, was launched against North Vietnam in retaliation for the February 1965 Vietcong attack on Pleiku. In June the military sought two hundred thousand ground forces and projected a need for six hundred thousand troops. By 1967, U.S. goals were also changing. A Pentagon Papers memorandum put forward the following priorities: 70 percent to avoid a humiliating defeat; 20 percent to keep South Vietnam from China; and 10 percent to permit the people of South Vietnam to enjoy a better, freer way of life.[20]

In January 1968, a final challenge was brought to the Johnson administration. The Tet Offensive was a countrywide assault by communist forces on South Vietnam that penetrated

Saigon, all of the provincial capitals, and even the U.S. embassy compound. The U.S. response was massive, including expanded bombings of North Vietnam. In the end, the communist forces were defeated. As a final thrust to take control of South Vietnam, the Tet Offensive had been premature, but it did demonstrate the bankruptcy of U.S. policy. Massive bombings and hundreds of thousands of U.S. combat troops had not brought the United States closer to victory. In March 1968, Johnson announced both a halt in the bombings against North Vietnam and that he was not a candidate for reelection.

Establishing détente was Richard Nixon's primary concern (see chapter 1); this policy could be threatened by any weakness or vacillation in U.S. policy on Vietnam. American commitments to Vietnam had to be met if the Soviet Union and China were to respect the United States in the post-Vietnam era. The strategy selected for accomplishing this was called *Vietnamization*. Gradually, the United States would reduce its combat presence such that, by 1972, the South Vietnamese army would be able to hold its own when supported by U.S. economic aid and air and naval power.

The inherent weakness of Vietnamization was that it could succeed only if the North Vietnamese did not attack before the South Vietnamese army was ready. Nixon and Kissinger designed a two-pronged approach to lessen this possibility: (1) Cambodia was invaded with the hope of cleaning out North Vietnamese sanctuaries, and (2) the bombing of North Vietnam was increased. Nevertheless, the potential danger became a reality when, in the spring of 1972, North Vietnam attacked across the demilitarized zone (DMZ). At this point, Nixon was forced to re-Americanize the war in order to prevent the defeat of South Vietnam. The bombing of North Vietnam reached unprecedented levels, and North Vietnamese ports were mined.

The Paris Peace Talks were being carried out against the backdrop of this fighting. They had begun in earnest in 1969 but had made little progress. With the escalation of the war, Nixon also offered a new peace plan, which included a promise to withdraw all U.S. forces after an Indochina-wide cease-fire and exchange of prisoners of war. Progress was now forthcoming. Hanoi was finding itself increasingly isolated from the Soviet Union and China, both of which had become more interested in establishing a working relationship with the United States than in defeating it in Vietnam. South Vietnam now began to object to the peace terms and stalled the negotiating process. In early December 1972, the "final talks" broke off without an agreement. On December 18, the United States ordered the all-out bombing of Hanoi and Haiphong to demonstrate U.S. resolve to both North and South Vietnamese leaders. On December 30, talks resumed, and the bombing ended. A peace treaty was signed on January 23, 1973.

Two years later, President Gerald Ford was in office when South Vietnam fell. What had begun as a normal military engagement ended in a rout. On March 12, 1975, the North Vietnamese attacked across the DMZ. On March 25, Hue fell. Five days later, Da Nang fell. The United States evacuated on April 29, and on April 30, South Vietnam surrendered unconditionally.

*Lessons Used by Policy Makers*

In examining the lessons used by policy makers in their decision making on Vietnam, the focus is on the Kennedy and Johnson administrations because it was during this period that the major escalations in the U.S. commitment took place. Two broad types of lessons of the past held by U.S. policy makers can be identified: political lessons and strategic and tactical ones.

For elected and appointed policy makers, the political lessons of the past had the same bottom line: personal survival in the upper circles of decision making in Washington required creating an image of toughness. The source of this lesson for elected officials was the "loss" of China to Mao Tse Tung and communism when the U.S. ally Chiang Kai Shek fled to Taiwan in 1949. The Republicans had successfully leveled this charge against the Democrats. Kennedy applied the same strategy against Nixon in 1960, accusing the Eisenhower administration of losing Cuba. Politically, Kennedy saw Vietnam as his China. Johnson stated many times that he did not intend to be the first U.S. president to lose a war.

The national security managers also drew on the fall of China for lessons and added decision making in the Korean War. In each case, the implications were the same: a reputation for toughness was the most highly prized virtue to possess.[21] The bureaucratic casualties in the decision-making process on China were those who—even though they were correct—had become identified with the "soft" side of a policy debate. Though wrong, those who had been hawkish emerged relatively unscathed from McCarthyism. To a lesser extent, Korea produced a similar pattern. Dean Rusk, who had failed to predict the Chinese entry into Korea but was staunchly anticommunist, did not pay a price for being wrong. Instead, in 1961 he became Kennedy's secretary of state.

Standing out among the host of strategic and tactical lessons drawn on by Vietnam policy makers was the analogy to Munich and the danger of appeasement. Munich had become a symbol for a generation of policy makers.[22] Its impact was so great that even those with no personal contact with the European peace efforts of the late 1930s could draw on it for insight. For example, Lyndon Johnson viewed the central lesson of the twentieth century as being that the appetite for aggression is never satisfied. It was Dean Rusk who drew most openly and repeatedly on the Munich analogy. Although he recognized that differences existed between the aggressions of Ho Chi Minh and Hitler, the basic point remained the same: "Aggression by any other name was still aggression and . . . must be checked."[23]

Very different lessons could be drawn from the French experience in Indochina, which was on the mind of every participant in the debate on the Taylor-Rostow Report.[24] Yet it had a negligible effect on American thinking, falling far short of being a generational experience on the order of Munich. Only George Ball, who worked for France at the Geneva negotiations, drew actively on its lessons. To him, the war was unwinnable. Ball warned Kennedy that if he sent the recommended fifteen thousand combat troops to Vietnam, the commitment would escalate to three hundred thousand men.

Ball became concerned with U.S. policy in Vietnam because he feared that it was diverting attention from Europe. His Europeanist orientation to world politics was not unique within the Kennedy-Johnson administrations. McGeorge Bundy was "totally a man of the Atlantic." He was also very much a product of the 1950s and the Cold War, so when he entered the debate on Vietnam, he was an advocate of the U.S. presence. Kennedy's first ambassador to Vietnam was also a Europeanist who was ignorant of Asia and Asian communism. The predominance of Europeanists illustrates the interaction of political lessons and strategic and tactical lessons of the past. A president concerned with making sure Vietnam did not become his China had limited options in making appointments because a cloud of doubt continued to hang over the credentials of most Asian experts. Even lacking knowledge about Asian affairs, a president could feel politically safe with Europeanists in key decision-making positions.

The lack of knowledge about Asia comes through in the strategic and tactical lessons that key policy makers drew from Asian events. Kennedy's favored set of lessons of the past was Magsaysay's struggle against the Huk guerrillas in the Philippines and the British experience in Malaysia. Both contests were very different from what was being contemplated in Vietnam. For example, according to the U.S. military, the Malaysian analogy was flawed in at least five respects:

1. Malaysian borders were far more controllable.
2. The racial characteristics of the Chinese insurgents in Malaysia made identification and segregation much simpler than the situation in Vietnam.
3. The relative plenty of food in South Vietnam compared to Malaysia made the denial of food to the guerrillas a far less usable weapon.
4. The British were in actual command of military operations in Malaysia.
5. It took the British twelve years to defeat an insurgency far less strong than the one in South Vietnam.[25]

The professional military also proved unable to draw on Asia for insights into how to fight in Vietnam. General Westmoreland was described as "a conventional man in an unconventional war." Vietcong challenges brought only a request for more and more men and more and more bombing. The approach of JCS chairman General Maxwell Taylor was not very different. While he spoke of the challenge of brushfire wars, he was not really talking in terms of fighting a guerrilla war. His solution was additional troops; political reforms were not mentioned. Taylor's analogy was not with Malaysia but with Korea. He drew favorable comparisons of battlefield conditions and terrain but overlooked the different nature of the two wars. Korea had been a conventional war, begun with a border crossing by uniformed troops that fought in large concentrations.[26] This was not Vietnam in 1964.

Lessons drawn by two other policy makers deserve mention. The first is Walt Rostow, who brought to Vietnam decision making a firm set of beliefs about the necessity of winning the war and how to do it. In his eyes, communist intervention had taken place in South Vietnam, breaking the first rule of peaceful coexistence. The boundaries of the two camps were immutable, and any effort to alter them had to be resisted. His solution was air power. Rostow had selected bombing targets during World War II and was convinced that massive bombing would bring North Vietnam to its knees.

The second policy maker is Lyndon Johnson, who drew heavily on his experience in Texas politics in formulating his Vietnam strategy. He had opposed the idea of a coup against Diem. That simply was not the way things were done in Texas: "Otto Passman and I, we have our differences . . . but I don't plan his overthrow."[27] Beyond that, the United States had given its word to Diem, and in Texas, you don't go back on your word. Johnson also felt that displays of toughness were prerequisites for dealing with the Vietnamese. Here, he drew on analogies to his dealings with Mexicans: "If you don't watch they'll walk right into your yard and take it over . . . but if you say to 'em right at the start, 'Hold on just a minute,' they'll know they are dealing with someone who'll stand up. And after that you can get along just fine."[28]

*Lessons Learned*

Vietnam had a tremendous impact on public opinion and elite attitudes. It destroyed the postwar consensus on the ends and means of U.S. foreign policy and left in its place three competing belief systems: Cold War internationalism, post–Cold War internationalism, and neo-isolationism. The existence of these three competing outlooks would greatly complicate future U.S. foreign policy making.

The specific lessons of Vietnam can be identified by examining the results of a survey conducted by Ole Holsti and James Rosenau.[29] They identify seven groups holding different opinions about the sources, consequences, and lessons of Vietnam, covering the entire range from consistent critics to consistent supporters. Fully 30 percent of the sample falls at the two extremes, confirming the depth of the impact of Vietnam on American attitudes. Looking first at the sources of failure, Holsti and Rosenau were able to identify twenty-one reasons why the United States lost. The depth of disagreement is great. Not only are the sources of failure ranked differently by the various groups, but no one explanation appears among all seven groups. Only three explanations are shared by six of the groups: the United States' lack of clear-cut goals, the presence of Soviet and Chinese aid, and North Vietnamese dedication.

A more coherent picture emerges when we review the consequences of Vietnam. Supporters cited international system-related concerns as the most important consequences, while critics cited Vietnam's domestic impact. Only one consequence was cited by all seven groups (but not with the same relative importance): the United States will limit its conception of its national interest. Yet the picture becomes cloudy again when turning to the lessons of Vietnam. Of the thirty-four lessons cited, not one appears among all seven groups. Only two appear among six of the groups: (1) executive-legislative cooperation is vital, and (2) Russia is expansionist.

## The Iraq War

Before turning to the details of the Iraq War, it is important to understand the six linked phases of military activity described by military planners (see figure 4.1). In the Shape Phase (Phase 0), normal and routine military operations take place. In the Deter Phase (Phase I), military action seeks to deter the enemy by demonstrating resolve and capabilities for action.

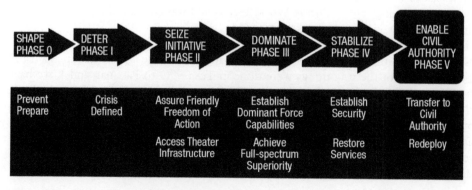

**Figure 4.1   Phase Model of Military Activity**

In the Seize Initiative Phase (Phase II), military force is used to execute offensive operations. In the Dominate Phase (Phase III), military forces focus on breaking the enemy's will for organized resistance by engaging in a full deployment of force. The Stabilize Phase (Phase IV) is required when there is no functioning legitimate government or only a minimally functioning one. In Phase IV, military forces are required to perform limited local governance activities. Finally, in the Enable Civil Authority Phase (Phase V), the objective of the military is to support the civil authorities. Whereas great praise surrounded the initial military operation in Iraq, the lack of connections between the first three phases and Phase IV, as well as the conduct of Phase IV, became the subject of much criticism.[30]

*Iraq War Chronology*

The prelude to the Iraq War found the United States engaged in diplomatic efforts at the UN Security Council to gain its approval for military action against Iraq. President George W. Bush addressed the UN General Assembly in September 2002, calling on it to move quickly to enforce the resolution demanding Iraq's disarmament while making it clear that the United States was prepared to act on its own. With the prospects for an affirmative vote by the UN Security Council virtually nonexistent, on March 16 President Bush met with British prime minister Tony Blair and leaders from Spain and Portugal in the Azores to announce that the "moment of truth" had arrived for Saddam Hussein. The following day Bush issued an ultimatum requiring Saddam to leave Iraq within forty-eight hours, and on March 19 Bush ordered the invasion of Iraq. A **shock-and-awe** military campaign began, designed to overwhelm and demoralize the Iraqi forces and allow coalition forces to move swiftly to Baghdad. On April 9, Baghdad came under the control of U.S. forces, and on May 1 President Bush declared an end to major combat operations. At that point, the administration began Phase IV. A chronology of major events in the Iraq War is presented in table 4.3.

By all accounts, the Bush administration entered Phase IV without a great deal of forethought, expecting it to be completed in about six months. Calls for additional forces were rejected as unnecessary, and postwar planning carried out in the State Department and the CIA received little attention in the Pentagon. On May 12, Paul Bremer arrived in Iraq as head of the new Coalition Provisional Authority (CPA). Bremer's first two orders proved to be highly controversial. CPA Order 1 attempted to "de-Ba'athify" Iraqi society. All full Ba'ath Party members were dismissed immediately from their government positions and banned from future government employment. CPA Order 2 dissolved the Iraqi army, along with Saddam Hussein's bodyguard and special paramilitary. The result of these two decisions was to drive many highly trained individuals into the opposition who had not necessarily been supporters of Saddam Hussein and on whom the United States would have been able to rely to help stabilize the military and political situation.

Establishing political stability proved an elusive goal, as did creating a democratic government. Political milestones were realized, but a functioning government supported by all sectors of the Iraqi population was not created. On May 28, 2004, Iyad Allawi was selected as prime minister of the interim Iraqi government. One month later, sovereignty was transferred, and Paul Bremer left Iraq. On October 13, 2005, a national referendum was held on Iraq's constitution, and in May 2006, Nouri al-Maliki formed Iraq's first permanent, democratically elected government. President Bush praised al-Maliki's government as having "strong leaders that represent all of the Iraqi people" and signaling a "decisive break with the past," but by

| Table 4.3 | Chronology of Major Events in the Iraq War |
|---|---|
| January 2002 | In his State of the Union address, President Bush identifies Iraq, Iran, and North Korea as an "axis of evil." |
| September 2002 | Bush addresses the UN General Assembly and challenges it to confront "the grave and gathering danger" of Iraq or become irrelevant. |
| December 2002 | Bush approves deployment of U.S. forces to the Persian Gulf. |
| February 2003 | The United States, Spain, and Great Britain introduce a resolution in the Security Council authorizing the use of military force against Iraq. Russia, Germany, and France oppose it. |
| March 17, 2003 | Bush gives Saddam Hussein a forty-eight-hour ultimatum to leave Iraq. |
| March 19, 2003 | Operation Iraqi Freedom begins with a "decapitation" air strike against leadership targets in Baghdad. |
| March 21, 2003 | Major fighting begins. |
| May 1, 2003 | Bush declares an end to major combat operations. |
| December 2003 | Saddam Hussein is captured. |
| April 2004 | Photos are aired showing torture and mistreatment of prisoners by U.S. personnel at Abu Ghraib prison. |
| June 2004 | United States transfers power to a new interim Iraqi government. |
| September 2004 | U.S. casualties reach the 1,000 mark. |
| December 2004 | United States announces its plans to expand its military presence in Iraq to 150,000 troops. |
| January 2005 | Iraq holds its first multiparty election in fifty years. |
| May 2006 | Nouri al-Maliki forms Iraq's first permanent democratically elected government. |
| December 2006 | The Iraq Study Group Report (Baker-Hamilton Report) is released. |
| January 2007 | President Bush announces a surge of U.S. forces into Iraq to stem the violence and create conditions for peace. |
| March 19, 2008 | Fifth anniversary of the start of the Iraq War. |
| September 2008 | The United States transfers responsibility for security in Anbar Province, the heart of the Sunni insurgency, to the Iraqi military and police. |
| November 2008 | The Iraq cabinet approves a status of forces agreement that will govern the U.S. presence in Iraq through 2011. |
| January 2009 | Iraq holds local elections that are free from violence. |
| August 2010 | Last U.S. combat brigade leaves Iraq. |
| December 2011 | President Obama declares the Iraq War to be over. |

the end of 2006, U.S. national security advisor Stephen Hadley was questioning its will and capacity to take the necessary military and political steps to bring sectarian violence under control. Al-Maliki's ability to do so was central to the success of Bush's surge plan, announced in January 2007, which sent additional U.S. forces to Iraq.

Bush's decision was controversial because it contradicted the central thrust of the Iraq Study Group's report.[31] The report recommended a phased exit of U.S. forces from Iraq, as well as talks with Syria and Iran. In June it was announced that the surge was complete, with 28,500 more U.S. forces in the country. This brought the total number of U.S. forces in Iraq to 165,000, the largest to date.

U.S. strategy in Iraq began to move in a new direction in 2007 when General David Petraeus took command of its military operation. Prior to assuming this post, he oversaw the writing of the army's new counterinsurgency manual.[32] The first new manual on counterinsurgency (COIN) operations produced by the army in twenty years, it now became the basis of U.S. operations in Iraq. According to the manual, the central issue in insurgencies and counterinsurgencies is political power. The long-term success of COIN requires people to take charge of their own affairs and consent to the government's rule.

The combination of the surge, the change of strategy to COIN, and the "Anbar Awakening" produced by a Sunni tribal uprising altered the military landscape in Iraq. From 2004 until mid-2007, Iraq averaged more than fifteen hundred civilian deaths per month, and the U.S. military experienced almost one hundred dead and seven hundred wounded. By the end of 2007, U.S. fatalities fell to an average of twenty-three per month; from June 2008 to June 2011 this number decreased by just over one half.[33]

By 2013, two years after Obama declared the Iraq War over, a much different scenario was in place. A series of political protests accompanied the insurgency-led violence in Iraq after the withdrawal of U.S. forces. A common focal point was failures of the Iraqi government to end corruption and provide public services. Significant protests in the name of democracy took place in Iraqi Kurdistan. Sunni Arabs protested what they saw to be their marginalization in Iraq's new economic and political order. The net result of this deteriorating situation was that most of the military gains prior to 2011 were gone. Led by al-Qaeda–linked insurgents, suicide attacks were once again common, and in 2013 some 7,800 civilians and 1,000 Iraq security troops died in attacks.

By 2014, references to an Iraq insurgency were increasingly replaced by those identifying the conflict as a civil war. Both politically and militarily, the tipping point came in 2014 with the announcement by the Islamic State of Iraq and the Levant (ISIL/ISIS) of the creation of a worldwide caliphate claiming religious, political, and military authority over all Muslims. In June 2014, ISIS took control of Fallujah and some 70 percent of Anbar Province. In response, Obama sent additional forces to Iraq. Later that year he announced a renewal of significant U.S. military operations in Iraq. It would be 2016 before Fallujah was retaken by Iraqi forces.

### Analogies with Past Conflicts

This section examines three lessons from the past (the Cold War and the Vietnam and Korean Wars) that American policy makers drew upon in making strategic decisions about the Iraq War.

*The Cold War.* The George W. Bush administration cast the Global War on Terrorism as a long war with Iraq as its central front, inviting comparisons with the Cold War. One factor that stands out in many analyses of how the Cold War played out, especially in the Third World, is the challenge that nationalism presented to U.S. foreign policy as it sought to counter the influence of the Soviet Union and communism.[34] Both the Soviet Union and the United States were most effective when they cast their arguments in terms of local conditions and nationalist sentiment, and least effective when trying to couch a local conflict in global terms. The United States also encountered difficulties because it tended to ignore the differences among local enemy forces, grouping them all together under the heading of communists or communist sympathizers and allying with leadership forces often seen by local political forces as part of the problem. This same set of problems was a central challenge that the United States faced in Iraq.

A rather ominous reading of the past is presented by Andrew Bacevich.[35] He sees the Cold War and the Iraq War as firmly linked. In his view, they are World War III and part of World War IV, respectively. Periodically during the Cold War, the Middle East and the Persian Gulf, in particular, had been major concerns of U.S. policy makers, but they were almost always overshadowed by other conflicts. This changed just as the Cold War was ending, with the Soviet invasion of Afghanistan and the Iranian hostage crisis. Bacevich sees President Jimmy Carter as virtually declaring the start of World War IV and Ronald Reagan as fully committing the United States to the region. The first phase of World War IV concluded in 1990. Iran and the Soviet presence in Afghanistan were the main U.S. enemies at this time. A second phase began with Iraq's invasion of Kuwait and ran through the 1990s. World War IV entered its third phase with the terrorist attacks of 9/11.

*The Vietnam War.* There are no shortage of comparisons between the Vietnam War and the Iraq War,[36] nor is there any shortage of controversy over such comparisons. President George W. Bush invoked the Vietnam comparison in 2007, stating that "one unmistakable legacy of Vietnam is that the price of America's withdrawal was paid by millions of innocent citizens." Senator Edward Kennedy (D-MA) countered, saying, "The president is drawing the wrong lessons from history."[37] Among the most often noted differences are those involving the nature of the military conflict. In Vietnam, the United States entered into an ongoing national war of liberation in which the enemy operated as a unified political-military force, engaging in both conventional military battles and insurgency operations. Violence rarely spread into major South Vietnamese cities. The United States also carried the war on the ground and in the air to North Vietnam and neighboring states that it accused of aiding the enemy. More recently, it has been suggested that the need to learn the political lessons of the Vietnam War still exists. Four lessons have been suggested by John Kerry, John McCain, and Bob Kerry: (1) do not confuse a war with the warriors; (2) be honest with Congress and the American people; (3) exercise humility in assuming knowledge about foreign cultures; and (4) with sufficient effort and will, seemingly unbridgeable differences can be reconciled.[38]

The Iraq War began with an American invasion. Conventional battles soon ended, and the conflict became almost entirely a combination of terrorist and insurgency attacks. Opposition forces operated not as a unified political-military front, but as militias, terrorist bands, and death squads under the leadership of a host of leaders. In the process, cities became the battleground and civilians the frequent targets as the various sides fought for dominance and to settle feuds both old and new. The United States did not expand the Iraq War beyond that country's borders, even though it asserted that Iran and Syria were harboring and supporting Iraqi insurgents.

Commentators see far more parallels of the political side of the Iraq War with the Vietnam War, although not all agree on what they are. Melvin Laird, who served as secretary of defense under Nixon during Vietnam, observed one point of similarity: Both wars were launched on the basis of faulty intelligence and "possibly outright deception."[39] By "possible deception," he was referring to the weapons-of-mass-destruction charge leveled against Saddam Hussein and the Gulf of Tonkin incident.

Similarities are also found in the decisions made by presidents early in the war and then as it became clear that victory no longer seemed attainable. For Kennedy and Bush, Vietnam and Iraq became testing grounds for new strategic doctrines.[40] For Kennedy, it was an opportunity to move away from Eisenhower's doctrine of massive retaliation to one of graduated escalation. Massive retaliation, with its emphasis on the all-out use of nuclear weapons, left presidents with few options in dealing with regional threats like Vietnam. For Bush, Iraq provided a test case for preemption as the new American strategic doctrine as a replacement for deterrence, which was judged as too passive and unable to dissuade leaders of rogue states.

Nixon and Bush also used similar language in explaining an American exit strategy to the public. Nixon said, "As South Vietnamese forces become stronger, the rate of American withdrawal can become greater." Bush asserted, "As the Iraqi security forces stand up, coalition forces can stand down."[41] However, political differences are present. The depth of support for the Vietnam War was far wider and deeper than that for the Iraq War. In the early 1960s, few questioned the domino theory and the need for an American presence in Vietnam. No equivalent rationale for action existed at the outset of the Iraq War. Unlike the war in Afghanistan that preceded it, the link to the global spread of terrorism did not seem as evident to most.

*The Korean War.* In June 2007, the Bush administration publicly raised the possibility of a long-term deployment of U.S. troops in Iraq after the end of the present mission. The historical analogy put forward is South Korea, where U.S. forces continued to be based for decades after the Korean conflict formally ended. The Korean model was presented by both Bush and Secretary of Defense Robert Gates as superior to the Vietnam model, in which U.S. forces left "lock, stock, and barrel." The analogy is attractive because of the economic prosperity and political stability that South Korea has experienced since the armistice was signed. However, critics quickly pointed out that, given the animosity toward American forces in Iraq, the continued presence of U.S. troops would likely be a lightning rod in domestic Iraqi politics and a target of military and terrorist attacks. Beirut in the 1980s, where U.S. Marines established a presence after fighting between Lebanon and Israel, was cited as a better analogy. At first the U.S. military forces were welcomed by all factions, but a suicide bomber driving a truck struck the marine barracks in 1983, killing 241 soldiers.

### Operations Decisions

The United States faced two sets of operations decisions about how to fight the Iraq War: counterinsurgency and rebuilding Iraq.

*Fighting COIN operations.* The recognized differences between the political and military battlefields of Vietnam and Iraq noted earlier have led to a major debate over the military lessons of Vietnam for Iraq when it comes to fighting COIN operations. On one side are those who argue that the most relevant strategy in Vietnam was the abandoned "strategic hamlet" program, in which the United States sought to pacify specific areas and then gradually expand control outward. In Iraq this has been referred to as the "oil spot" strategy.[42] At the other end of the spectrum are those who argue that the different political situations in Iraq and Vietnam negate the relevance of any Vietnam COIN strategy for Iraq. They argue that the issue in Iraq is not the people against a government so much as it is a security problem driven by the mutual fear of all people about what will happen if the opposing group(s) seizes control. Winning the hearts and minds of the people does not address this problem, nor does promoting democracy. In fact, democratization may only further polarize the situation by increasing anxieties over what the new government will do.[43]

The search for lessons from the past that the United States can use in fighting insurgents in Iraq also yields a cautionary note. David Kilcullen argues that today's insurgents differ greatly from their predecessors in terms of policy, strategy, operational art, and tactics.[44] For example, given the global and instantaneous nature of communications today, the success of the insurgents may not ride on the legitimacy of the local government but on the ability to mobilize public support around the world for their cause. Kilcullen continues by saying that, whereas it was once believed that COIN operations were 25 percent military and 75 percent political, they may be 100 percent political today. He concludes by echoing the observation of Bernard Fall, a noted Vietnam-era COIN specialist: "If it works, it is obsolete."

### Rebuilding Iraq

The post–World War II American occupations of Germany and Japan were put forward by the George W. Bush administration as the starting points for thinking about rebuilding Iraq. Bush observed, "America has made and kept this kind of commitment before. . . . After defeating enemies, we did not leave behind occupying armies, we left constitutions and parliaments."[45] A closer reading of the American experience in Germany and Japan would have provided reason for utilizing caution with regard to both process and outcome. Douglas Porch maintains that, for nearly a full decade, many of those involved in these reconstruction programs considered their efforts to be nearly a complete failure.[46] Rather than encountering a welcoming population, they found resentment and resistance. Actions taken to bring about reform were often counterproductive. General Lucius Clay, who was in charge of the American occupation zone in Europe, called de-Nazification his biggest mistake. It was in his mind a "hopelessly ambiguous procedure" that linked together small and big Nazis and engendered the hostility of the population at large because implementation often appeared arbitrary and hypocritical. Yet the United States moved quickly to "de-Ba'athify" Iraq by dismissing party members from government positions and decommissioning the army.

It can be argued that the reasons for the ultimate success of the occupations of Germany and Japan had little to do with American foreign policy or the presumed natural inclination of people liberated from tyranny for democracy. Rather, it had to do with factors such as enlightened domestic leadership, economic miracles fueled by the Marshall Plan in Europe, and the Korean War in Asia, along with the prior experience of democracy and entrepreneurship in these two states. The key American contribution was creating domestic and regional security, laying the ground rules for democratic reform, and then getting out of the way.

Germany and Japan were not the only efforts at reconstruction (or, more broadly, nation building) that might have been looked to for lessons. Fourteen other cases exist, including Cuba (1898–1902, 1906–1909, and 1917–1922), the Dominican Republic (1916–1924, 1965–1966), South Vietnam, Cambodia, and Afghanistan.[47] In only two cases, Panama (1989) and Grenada, was democracy in place after ten years. In seven cases, the United States established governments that almost totally depended on the United States for survival. In none of these cases did democracy emerge. One lesson drawn from these experiences is that the ideal form of transition involves a quick transfer of power to legitimately elected local leaders, but this presupposes a functioning electoral system and moderate local leaders who have genuine support among the populace.

Standard discussions of the lessons of the Iraq War, such as those presented here, stress the legacy of the manner in which the United States entered the conflict and then became trapped as a result of poorly conceived strategies and a failure to understand the political and historical context in which it was operating. An alternative view argues that Iraq was winnable and that the problems (and lessons to be learned) were ones of execution. In particular, it is argued that Obama's decision to withdraw U.S. troops sealed defeat.[48]

# Over the Horizon: Searching for Lessons from Afghanistan

Learning from the past is not easy.[49] Past successes and failures are often obscured by the pressing foreign policy issues of the day. Not long after 9/11, Deputy Secretary of State Richard Armitage gave voice to this political reality when he asserted, "History starts today."[50] Yet the pull of the past is never completely gone. As much as Obama wished to escape the Vietnam syndrome, he could not. When members of his administration brought up Vietnam, all Obama could say was "ghosts."[51]

As we look over the horizon, the need to learn from the past can be seen in many aspects of U.S. foreign policy. This chapter began by introducing one such area: anticipating and responding to global pandemics such as COVID. We conclude by looking at a second area: lessons from the U.S. involvement in Afghanistan. The entrance to and exit from Afghanistan were discussed in chapter 1. The search for lessons is already underway and will continue. Here, we highlight some of the most frequently cited aspects of the Afghan War that are leading the search for lessons.[52]

- Level of commitment. Two different lines of lessons are found here. One argues that the military and political commitment was not firm enough. The second argues that the commitment was too great given Afghanistan's lack of strategic importance and the enemy it was directed against.
- The amount of money spent. Rather than create a positive base on which to build a government and economy, the money directed to Afghanistan only intensified the level of corruption and further separated the government from the people.
- The lack of understanding of Afghan culture and society. The United States was always an outside bystander. The U.S. military sought to create an Afghan military in its own image and using its sophisticated weapons rather than building an Afghan military. It demonized the enemy and failed to understand its motivations or roots in society.
- The lack of clarity in pursing the war effort. A number of factors are cited here. Some point to bureaucratic conflict within the U.S. government over how to proceed and the lack of a coherent strategy. Others assert that in viewing the Afghan War as a good war and morally justified, the United States lost sight of its evolving nature. Still others argue that there was a fundamental lack of honesty in how progress of the war effort (or lack thereof) was portrayed to the American public.

## Critical Thinking Questions

1. What is the most important lesson that can be learned from the U.S. experiences in Vietnam and Iraq for avoiding future Afghanistans?

2. What lessons from the past should policy makers try to learn?

3. What are the dangers of looking to the past for lessons on how to deal with current foreign policy problems?

## Key Terms

analogies, 64
closed belief system, 65
cognitive consistency, 64
generational events, 65
guerrilla war, 72

Iraq syndrome, 69
noise, 64
proxy war, 71
shock and awe, 77
signal, 64

# Society 5

## Learning Objectives

Students will be able to:

1. Compare the ability of political parties and interest groups to influence U.S. foreign policy.
2. Describe the content and impact of public opinion on U.S. foreign policy.
3. Explain how policy makers respond to the public's input into foreign policy.
4. Assess the relative influence of newspapers, television, and social media on public thinking about U.S. foreign policy.

# On the Agenda: Quincy Institute for Responsible Statecraft

In 2019 a new **think tank** was established in Washington, DC: the Quincy Institute for Responsible Statecraft. Its stated mission is to "promote ideas that move U.S. foreign policy away from endless war and toward vigorous diplomacy in pursuit of international peace." It seeks to help bring into existence "a world where peace is the norm and war the exception" by serving as a resource for members of Congress, grassroots organizations, and emerging leaders in Washington, across the country, and across both political parties.

The Quincy Institute is named for John Quincy Adams, the sixth president, secretary of state under James Monroe, a diplomat, and member of Congress. In a speech delivered on July 4, 1821, Adams asserted that the United States "goes not abroad, in search of monsters to destroy." He warned that if it did so, the United States "would involve herself beyond the power of extrication." "She might become the dictatress of the world" and would be "no longer the ruler of her own spirit."[1]

Andrew Bacevich, a former career military officer who serves as president of the Quincy Institute, holds that John Quincy Adams's fears are valid today. He sees that U.S. foreign policy has become consumed with searching for "monsters to destroy" and in the process is undermining American leadership in the world. Moreover, the search for monsters to destroy has led to an overmilitarized foreign policy and has produced endless war in Afghanistan and Iraq as well as military interventions in Syria, Libya, and Yemen.

The founders of the Quincy Institute believe that bringing about this change in the nature and direction of U.S. foreign policy requires broadening the debate taking place in Washington by injecting new ideas into those discussions. Existing think tanks are seen as producing foreign policy ideas within the narrow context of existing paradigms rather than reassessing "the first principles of American foreign policy."

Among the foreign policy ideas put forward by the Quincy Institute in its early foreign policy briefs are the following:

- The United States needs to end its overreliance on military superiority and intervention and instead put creative and persistent diplomacy in the lead by promoting locally owned solutions.
- What is needed is far-reaching changes in the way diplomats are recruited, trained, and promoted.

- Some competition between the United States and China is probably inevitable. But this competition does not present an existential threat to the United States and therefore must not be allowed to prevent necessary cooperation in addressing the major threats of the twenty-first century: population movements, pandemics, and climate change.
- U.S. nuclear posture is on a dangerous path that imperils national security. . . . A safer nuclear policy entails, among other steps, reducing the number of deployed strategic warheads by one-third.

Two aspects of the Quincy Institute that have drawn considerable attention are the sources of its funding and the conceptual base on which that agenda rests. In terms of funding sources, the Quincy Institute announced that it would not accept funds from foreign governments, something that has become a problem for several think tanks. It receives funds from a number of frequent supporters of its foreign policy agenda: the Rockefeller Brothers Fund (which supports global peace and justice), the Area Foundation (a supporter of human rights), and the Ploughshares Fund (which advocates the elimination of nuclear weapons). Its most talked about funding sources are the Charles Koch Foundation, which is a strong supporter of the Republican Party and libertarian groups, and George Soros's Open Society Foundation, which provides financial support for liberal and progressive causes. Normally found on opposite sides of the political aisle, what unites Soros and Koch under the umbrella of the Quincy Institute is a strong desire to end America's "endless wars."

Regarding the second aspect, as seen in Soros and Koch working together, supporters of the Quincy Institute's agenda have come to be described as the "Quincy Coalition" because rather than sharing a common view of what U.S. foreign policy should look like, they tend to hold different and often conflicting perspectives.[2] Three stand out: (1) realists who emphasize the importance of power for promoting national security, (2) libertarians who seek to establish an international order that places few regulations or restraints on state actions, and 3) anti-imperialist and anti-intervention progressive democrats.

The founding of the Quincy Institute has produced numerous commentaries. One view expressed is that it embraces a Trump "America First" agenda. This has been challenged by those who note that while seeking to avoid endless wars, it does advocate American involvement in addressing global problems and is not transactionalist in spirit. A second view holds that its agenda is antiliberalism in outlook and that its restraint policy is misplaced and inadequate to the challenges of the contemporary international system.[3] Still another perspective holds that the Quincy Institute's agenda is not without supporters in other think tanks. Cato, the Center for the National Interest, and New America are seen as sharing parts of its foreign policy outlook.[4]

This chapter examines the major avenues available to the public in exercising its voice on foreign policy matters: elections, public opinion, interest group activity, and political movements. It also takes a look at the role of the media in formulating public perceptions, the increasing involvement of states in foreign policy, and how policy makers view the public voice in making foreign policy. The chapter begins by evaluating awareness of the public on matters related to American foreign policy.

## Public Awareness of Foreign Policy Issues

Not everyone is equally interested in or aware of foreign policy issues. A commonly used framework divides the American public into four groups based on level of awareness and action. First, one large group is unaware of all but the most significant international events and at best have vague and weak opinions. Second, another large group is aware of many major international events but is not deeply informed about them. The remainder of the American public, comprising about 25 percent, are generally knowledgeable about foreign policy issues and hold relatively firm convictions. Within this group, referred to as *opinion holders,* a smaller set of activists (1–2 percent) serve as *opinion mobilizers* for the other segments of the public.

It matters where the public gets its information. Opinion polling in the months following the invasion of Iraq found that many Americans were wrong about key facts, such as the existence of evidence linking Iraq and al-Qaeda (45–52 percent of Americans said it existed) and the discovery of weapons of mass destruction (about 25 percent believed this finding). Fox was the news source of choice for those with the most misperceptions, while NPR listeners held the fewest. Another study found that those who are not very attentive to foreign affairs tended to hold isolationist attitudes and got most of their news about international events from talk shows that emphasized soft news stories.[5]

Still, even though the public may not know the facts about a foreign policy issue, it tends to feel confident about what ought to be done. This holds true for both the substance and making of policy. A classic example with regard to the substance of American foreign policy comes from a 1988 poll in which less than 50 percent of Americans could locate South Africa on a map. Nonetheless, 87 percent disapproved of its policy of apartheid.

## Public Opinion

Public opinion provides a first avenue for the public to express its views on foreign policy. Every president since Richard Nixon has employed pollsters to learn just that.[6] Yet the public is not convinced that anyone is listening. A 2014 poll found that, from the American public's point of view, the gap between the views of the American public and the decisions taken by policy makers was considerable: 42 percent said it was very large and 45 percent said it was somewhat large.[7]

Interpreting public opinion polls is not always easy. The public's response can easily be swayed by the wording of a question. For example, before the Persian Gulf War, when asked if the United States should take all action necessary—including military force—to make sure Iraq withdrew from Kuwait, 65 percent said yes. However, only 28 percent said yes when asked if the United States should initiate a war to force Iraq out of Kuwait. Questions on trade policy show a similar sensitivity to wording; responses vary depending on whether the question is about exports or imports or about the impact of trade on wages or economic growth.[8]

### Trends and Content

Because of this sensitivity to wording, analyzing the responses to questions over time is better than looking at onetime polls as a way of uncovering what Americans think about foreign policy issues. Such analysis has captured several turning points in American public opinion about foreign affairs issues.

The pivotal event for the first shift was World War II. Public opinion polls before World War II suggested a strongly isolationist outlook. In 1939, 70 percent of opinion holders said that American entry into World War I was a mistake, and 94 percent felt that the United States should "do everything possible to stay out of foreign wars" rather than try to prevent one. The outbreak of fighting in Europe had little impact on U.S. attitudes.[9] This changed dramatically following the attack on Pearl Harbor when internationalist sentiment came to dominate public perceptions about the proper U.S. role in the world. Between 1949 and 1969, 60–80 percent of the American public consistently favored active U.S. participation in world affairs.[10]

Before the Vietnam War, virtually all internationalists were in fundamental agreement on several key points: The United States had both the responsibility and the capability to create a just and stable world order, peace and security are indivisible, the Soviet Union was the primary threat to world order, and containment was the most effective way of meeting the Soviet challenge.[11] Foreign policy based on these beliefs could expect to receive the support of the American people. When disagreements arose, they tended to be about the process of making foreign policy rather than its substance.

Vietnam changed public attitudes.[12] It produced a steady and steep erosion of internationalist sentiment. In 1964, 65 percent of the public was defined as internationalist. This fell to 41 percent in 1974. That year also saw a dramatic increase in the number of isolationist responses, from 9 percent in 1972 to 21 percent.

Internationalism only reemerged as the majority perspective in 1980. No single pivotal event is associated with its rebirth. Instead, the American public gradually came to see the international system as threatening and out of control and developed a renewed willingness to use U.S. power and influence to protect national interests. Among the events that contributed to this shift were the 1979 Iranian coup and the 1979 Soviet invasion of Afghanistan.

The renewed embrace of internationalism was short-lived. The Pew Research Center characterized the public mood in the months preceding the 2016 election as one of isolationism with a "very, very big stick."[13] Polls then showed that a majority of the American public (57 percent) favored letting other countries deal with their own problems and concentrating on problems in the United States; only 46 percent had held this view in 2010. In 2016, only 17 percent of Americans felt the next president should concentrate on foreign policy over domestic policy, in contrast to 60 percent in 2008. Yet 55 percent of the American public still favored policies that would allow the United States to maintain its status as the only world superpower. Only about one-third saw it as acceptable for another country to rival the United States as a superpower. This outlook was reflected in a twelve-point increase in the number of Americans favoring increased defense spending between 2013 and 2016. The pendulum swung again in 2022. At the outset of the Ukraine War, 49 percent of Republicans and 38 percent of Democrats called for the United States to do more. By September these numbers fell to 16 percent and 20 percent, respectively.

Recent public opinion polls show that the American public is closely divided on questions of global involvement and leadership. A 2019 poll by the Center for American Progress concluded that the public was not isolationist but not fully internationalist in outlook. It characterized the public as favoring *restrained engagement*. It favored diplomatic, economic, and political action over military action. Fifty-one percent said the United States was stronger when it took a leading role in world affairs and worked to protect the national interest by advancing goals it shared with allies. Forty-four percent supported the view that the United States was stronger when it focused on its own problems instead of inserting itself into other countries' problems.[14] A Pew 2021 poll produced similar findings. It showed that 54 percent of the public felt that many U.S. problems could be solved by working with other states. Fifty-four percent said few problems could be solved by doing so.[15]

It also appears that significant divisions exist. In the 2019 Pew poll, 49 percent of white Americans said it was important for the United States to be active in world affairs, compared to 39 percent of Hispanics and 29 percent of blacks. A 2022 poll found that 17 percent of blacks considered China to be an enemy compared to 22 percent of Hispanics and 32 percent of white Americans.[16] In 2018, a Pew poll found that only 29 percent of younger Americans felt that limiting Russian power and influence should be a top foreign policy priority, compared to 54 percent of those aged sixty-five and older.[17]

## Public Opinion and the Use of Force

A particularly important question for policy makers is the willingness of the public to support the use of military force. Here, too, attention must be paid to wording and context. A 2012 poll regarding U.S. policy toward Syria showed that almost 75 percent of Americans opposed military action, but 62 percent supported the creation of no-fly zones.[18] A similar response pattern emerged in the early stages of Russia's invasion of Ukraine. A Chicago Council on Global Affairs poll in March 2022 found that 79 percent of Americans supported sending arms and military aid to Ukraine. Only 41 percent favored enforcing a no-fly zone, and even fewer, 36 percent, supported sending U.S. troops to fight in Ukraine.[19]

The conventional wisdom inherited from the Vietnam War era (see chapter 4) is that the public is unwilling to support the use of force if it results in casualties. Known as the **Vietnam syndrome**, the policy implication of this reading of the public led policy makers to either avoid the use of force altogether or use it only quickly and in an overwhelming fashion in highly controlled settings to ensure a short conflict with few American casualties.

The accumulated evidence on the use of force from the 1960s through the 1990s now points in a different direction, raising questions about the policy implications of the Vietnam syndrome. The public is not totally gun-shy. It will support the use of military force, even when casualties occur, depending on (1) the policy purpose behind its use, (2) the success or failure of the undertaking, and (3) the degree of leadership consensus.

Of particular relevance to policy purpose is a study undertaken by Bruce Jentleson,[20] who found that the American public is most likely to approve military force when its purpose is to restrain the foreign policy actions of a hostile state; it is least likely to do so when the purpose is to bring about internal political change. A 2019 Chicago Council poll provides support for this view. When asked if the United States should use troops to overthrow a dictator, only 35 percent said yes, compared to 70 percent that supported their use to stop another country from obtaining nuclear weapons.

Public support for U.S. military involvement in the Middle East fits this pattern. During the Persian Gulf War, support was highest for Operation Desert Shield and Operation Desert Storm, which were designed primarily to curb Iraqi foreign policy adventurism by defending Saudi Arabia and liberating Kuwait. Public support dropped sharply when the question posed was the overthrow of Saddam Hussein. Similarly, when asked about the Libyan military operation, 65 percent said they supported military action to protect civilians from Gaddafi, but only 48 percent supported the use of military force to remove him from power.

Studies also suggest that the public is sensitive to the domestic costs of foreign policy activism. The more serious the domestic problems relative to the external challenge, the more powerful will be the public's isolationist impulse. So the weaker the economy, the less support a president is likely to find for an activist foreign policy. This logic helps explain support for the Iraq War, which was fought without a tax hike and cost less than 1 percent of the gross domestic product (GDP). In comparison, the Vietnam War cost 9 percent of the GDP, and at one point the Korean War cost 14 percent of the GDP.[21]

A number of other factors also influence public opinion on the use of force. Foremost among them are race, gender, and party identification. When the Iraq War started, only 29 percent of blacks supported it. Hispanics were also far less likely than whites to support it; over 60 percent of all Hispanics disapproved of the Iraq War.[22] A similar pattern held in 2014, when a poll questioned Americans on their support for air strikes against Sunni insurgents in Iraq. Fifty-eight percent of whites voiced their support for air strikes, while only 50 percent of blacks and 43 percent of Hispanics did so.[23]

Gender differences were also evident.[24] The 2014 poll cited earlier showed that 64 percent of men but only 44 percent of women supported air strikes against the Sunni insurgents. On average, regardless of the purpose, women are less supportive of the use of military force. They are also more sensitive to humanitarian concerns and the loss of life. Having said this, women by and large are not pacifists. The differences between men and women on the use of force tend to occur at the margins and are a response to specific circumstances. Table 5.1 presents an overview of gender differences on the use of force over time.

The use of force in Afghanistan and Syria highlights divisions along party lines. In 2013, 67 percent of Democrats believed that the war was not worth fighting, while only 54 percent of Republicans took this position. Only three years earlier, when Bush was president, a mere 27 percent of Republicans thought that the Afghan War was not worthwhile. On Syria, 80 percent of Democrats supported Obama's decision to delay air strikes against Syria, while only 56 percent of Republicans did. Table 5.2 presents on overview of the current partisan divide on defining long-term foreign policy goals.

**Table 5.1  Gender Differences on the Use of Military Force**

| Use-of-Force Situation | Males Supporting (%) | Women Supporting (%) | Difference (%) |
|---|---|---|---|
| World War II | 62 | 53 | −9 |
| Korean War | 54 | 43 | −11 |
| Vietnam War | 42 | 33 | −9 |
| Haiti occupation | 42 | 31 | −11 |
| Sudan/Afghanistan missile strikes | 78 | 68 | −10 |
| Iraq War | 48 | 39 | −9 |
| Syria | 38 | 32 | −6 |
| Libya NATO intervention | 49 | 43 | −6 |
| Israel/Palestine peacekeeping | 37 | 40 | +3 |
| Lebanon marines | 44 | 33 | −12 |
| Somalia | 61 | 53 | −9 |
| Nicaragua | 41 | 24 | −17 |

*Source:* Richard Eichenberg, *Gender, War and World Order* (Ithaca, NY: Cornell University Press, 2019), 58.

| Table 5.2 | Partisan Divides on Top Priorities as Long-Term Foreign Policy Goals | |
|---|---|---|
| **Foreign Policy Goal** | **Republican (%)** | **Democrats (%)** |
| Dealing with climate change | 14 | 70 |
| Strengthening United Nations | 19 | 39 |
| Reducing U.S. commitment overseas | 29 | 29 |
| Reducing U.S. trade deficit | 33 | 48 |
| Aid refugees fleeing violence | 14 | 40 |
| Protect the U.S. from terrorist strikes | 60 | 81 |
| Maintain U.S. military advantage | 30 | 68 |
| Sharing cost of maintaining world order | 30 | 70 |
| Limit power and influence of China | 36 | 63 |
| Defend human rights in other countries | 23 | 42 |
| Prevent spread of weapons of mass destruction | 62 | 66 |

*Source:* Mara Mordecai and Moira Fagan, "Americans' Views on Key Foreign Policy Goals Depend on Their Attitudes toward International Cooperation," PEW Research Center, April 23, 2021.

## Impact of Public Opinion

How much influence does public opinion have on American foreign policy? This question can be answered in two ways: (1) the type of impact and (2) the conditions necessary for it to exert an influence. Public opinion can have three types of impact on American foreign policy. It can serve as a constraint on innovation, a source of innovation, and a resource to be drawn on by policy makers in implementing policy. To the extent that the public is subject to unstable moods about foreign policy issues—as was frequently believed in the early Cold War period and by some today in the War on Terrorism—public opinion may act as a powerful constraint on U.S. foreign policy by defining the limits of what is politically feasible.

A case can also be made that the existence of too firm an outlook or too rigid a division of opinion is just as much a constraint. The deeply entrenched isolationist outlook of the American public during the 1930s made it extremely difficult for President Franklin Roosevelt to prepare the United States for World War II. A firm but divided opinion is cited by one major study as being responsible for the prolonged U.S. presence in Vietnam.[25] Faced by a "damned if they do and damned if they don't" dilemma, successive administrations are seen as having followed a strategy of perseverance until a public consensus developed for a strategy of either victory or withdrawal.[26]

Observers generally agree that public opinion rarely serves as a stimulus to policy innovation. One commentator argues that "no major foreign policy decision in the United States has been made in response to a spontaneous public demand."[27] However, public opinion today does appear to be capable of placing new items on the political agenda. What it tends to lack is the ability to overcome forces that push policy makers in the opposite direction. Such appears to be the case with regard to humanitarian interventions. In examining U.S. humanitarian interventions into Haiti, Somalia, Bosnia, and Kosovo, one study found that public support did increase congressional support, but political partisanship and ideology were strong enough to block congressional action.[28]

With regard to the conditions necessary for public opinion to exert an influence, work by public opinion pollsters suggests that it might be helpful to think about this influence in terms of **tipping points**.[29] Policies that have reached the tipping point share three characteristics:

(1) a majority of the public is in support of or opposed to a particular policy, (2) they feel intensely about it, and (3) they believe that the government is responsible for addressing the problem. Public opinion on most foreign policy issues does not meet these requirements. Recent current issues that are at the tipping point or have crossed it are the Iraq War, ISIS terrorism, illegal immigration, and outsourcing jobs.

# Elections

Almost invariably, the winning candidate in an election cites the results as a mandate for their policy program. Do elections really serve as a mechanism for translating the public voice into policy? The evidence suggests that claims of popular mandates are often overstated and based on a flawed reading of election returns.

A look back at the Lyndon Johnson–Barry Goldwater election of 1964 shows just how deceptive electoral outcomes can be. In 1964, Johnson won a landslide victory over Goldwater, who had campaigned on a platform of winning the war against communism in Vietnam "by any means necessary." The results were commonly interpreted as a mandate for continued restraint in the war effort. However, national surveys revealed that 63 percent of those who favored withdrawal and 52 percent of those who favored a stronger stand, such as invading North Vietnam, supported Johnson.[30]

## Voting and Foreign Policy

For elections to confer a mandate on the winner, three demands are made of the voters: (1) they must be knowledgeable, (2) they must cast their ballots on the basis of issue preferences, and (3) they must be able to distinguish between parties and candidates. Evidence on the first point is not encouraging. The lack of widespread public understanding about foreign affairs issues never ceases to amaze commentators. Consider the following:

1964: Only 38 percent knew that Russia was not a member of NATO.
1966: Over 80 percent failed to properly identify the Vietcong.
1979: Only 23 percent knew which countries were involved in the Strategic Arms Limitation Talks.
1993: 43 percent could not identify the continent on which Somalia is located.
2003: 68 percent believed that Iraq played an important role in the terrorist attacks of 9/11.
2022: 34 percent could identify Ukraine on a map.[31]

Do candidates win because of, or in spite of, their policy preferences? Historically, foreign policy has not been a good issue on which to conduct a campaign.[32] Party identification, candidate image, incumbency, or some other nonissue factors generally play important roles in deciding how the public votes. The "bump" a president gets from a foreign policy success may also be short-lived and is not easily transferred to other issues on the agenda. After Saddam Hussein was captured, George W. Bush's approval rating went up eight points. Three months later that bump was gone. Obama's rating immediately jumped nine points after Osama bin

Laden was killed. It also soon returned to its prior level, and the jump had virtually no impact on his low approval rating on economic issues. The increased polarization of American society may make obtaining lasting bumps ever more difficult. When asked about Trump's meeting with North Korean leader King Jong-un across the DMZ, 42 percent said it was a step toward peace, and 50 percent said it was a political act. The onset of the Ukraine War and the fact that it was going better than expected, with Russia encountering serious military problems, had little impact on Biden's standing in public opinion polls. Prior to the beginning of the conflict in February, his positive rating was about 40 percent. In May it had risen to only about 42 percent positive.

Charles Whalen, a former six-term congressman, sees the sporadic interest and low information level of constituents regarding foreign policy matters as a point of vulnerability for incumbents.[33] Challengers attempt to create policy differences with the incumbent and to cast the incumbent in a negative light. They find a powerful weapon in foreign affairs voting records. This dynamic also holds true at the presidential level, where foreign policy setbacks provide a strategic opening for the opposition party to put the president on the political defensive. Over the course of more than a century, the party out of power has sought to exploit setbacks in U.S.-China relations as evidence of incompetent or weak presidential leadership.[34] In the 1870s, Democrats called for a policy of curbing Chinese immigration into the United States; in the 1950s, Republicans blamed Truman for losing China; in the 1990s, Democrats attacked George H. W. Bush for his response to China's handling of the Tiananmen Square protests; and most recently Republicans have called on Biden to take a stronger stance against China.

The third prerequisite for elections to serve as a mandate is that voters must be able to distinguish between party and candidate positions. In U.S. elections this is rarely the case. When choice is present in a presidential campaign, it generally takes place in primaries, where candidates seek to separate themselves from their competitors by advancing boldly stated **positional issues** that lack detail but carve out valuable political turf.[35] During the general election, presidential candidates of both parties tend to stress **valence issues,** which find most people on the same side because of the need to form and hold together broad electoral coalitions.

In line with this reasoning, early in the 2015–2016 primary season Donald Trump called for building a wall along the U.S.-Mexico border and making Mexico pay for it, and advocated torture as a weapon to defeat terrorists; he also called upon South Korea and Japan to develop nuclear capabilities. As the Republican convention neared and his nomination appeared certain, Trump's tone changed. He now promised that "America is going to be strong again; America is going to be great again; it's going to be a friend again . . . we are going to finally have a coherent foreign policy, based on American interests and the shared interest of our allies . . . we want to bring peace to the world."

## Impact of Elections

What then is the impact of elections on U.S. foreign policy? For many observers, the greatest foreign policy impact of elections is not found in a single election but in the cycle of elections that defines a president's term in office.[36] The first year in office is generally characterized by policy experimentation, false starts, and overly zealous goals due to inexperience and the continued influence of overly simplistic foreign policy campaign rhetoric. During the second year, pragmatism becomes more evident because of the increased knowledge and skill of the administration and the realization that a foreign policy mishap may lead to the loss of House and Senate seats in the midterm elections. In the third year, foreign policy issues are evaluated largely in terms of their potential impact on the presidential reelection campaign. Potential successes are pursued vigorously, even if the price tag is high, while the administration tries to disengage from potential losses. The final year brings stalemate to the foreign policy process. "Foreign governments have long understood the difficulty of doing business with the U.S. in election years."[37]

The most propitious time for foreign policy undertakings is held to be the first year and a half of a second term. Here, there is an experienced president who has a foreign policy agenda and is operating under the halo effect of a reelection victory. By late in the second year of a president's second term, electoral considerations begin to overwhelm foreign policy again, as jockeying begins in both parties for their respective presidential nominations. At some point, the president comes to be regarded, both at home and abroad, as a "lame duck," limiting the ability to conduct foreign policy.

The influence of the election cycle competes with other factors, so its fit with any particular presidency is likely to be imperfect. However, indications of its influence may be seen in the experiences of recent presidents. Obama's first year in office was marked by frequent calls for resetting American foreign policy. His second year saw him adopt a pragmatic surge in troops to Afghanistan. Following the midterm elections, he moved to clear his foreign policy agenda by gaining high-stakes victories on the New Strategic Arms Reduction Treaty (New START) and ending the ban on gays in the military. In his third year, Obama announced the beginning of troop withdrawal from Afghanistan and moved on getting much-delayed trade legislation through Congress. In March 2012, Obama confided in Russian president Dmitry Medvedev that no agreement could come before the presidential election, indicating that after the election he would have "space." Obama's second term did not fully follow the script outlined by the election cycle argument. Partisan divisions between Republicans and Democrats and divisions within the Republican Party stalled efforts to pass immigration reform legislation.

Evidence for the election cycle argument can also be found in Trump's presidency in his first three years. He started off intent on dismantling existing polices. In his second year, with a change in key advisors, his foreign policy became more pragmatic. In his third year, with another change in advisors, he sought to get contentious foreign policy issues off the electoral agenda by completing multiple trade agreements, signing a nuclear agreement with North Korea, and backing away from a conflict with Iran. In the fourth year, Trump deviated somewhat by announcing the withdrawal date from Afghanistan and signing the Abraham Accords, a Middle East peace agreement between Israel and the United Arab Emirates. Biden, too, moved quickly to reverse inherited foreign policies and to fulfill campaign promises. The results were uneven. Exiting from Afghanistan was a political crisis, and changes in refugee immigration policy produced abrupt swings due to surging numbers and political backlash. His second year saw Biden make strides to establish himself as a global foreign policy leader, with his building of allied support for a unified response to the Russian invasion of Ukraine and his meetings with leaders abroad and at international conferences.

# Interest Groups

The third avenue open to the public for expressing its outlook on foreign policy issues is interest group activity. A wide variety of groups actively try to influence U.S. foreign policy. Consider U.S. policy toward China.[38] A representative list of interest groups active in this policy area includes such diverse groups as the AFL-CIO, Amnesty International, the Christian Coalition of America, the Committee of 100 for Tibet, and the U.S.-China Business Council.

Groups wishing to influence U.S. foreign policy make their views known to policy makers either directly or through interest brokers (lobbyists). Not surprisingly, former policy makers are among the most prominent interest brokers because of their access to policy makers and policy-making institutions. Key White House foreign policy officials from the George W. Bush administration who established lobbying or strategic consulting firms after leaving office include Condoleezza Rice (secretary of state and national security advisor), Stephen Hadley (national security advisor), and Robert Gates (secretary of defense).

## Types of Interest Groups

The most active foreign policy interest groups can be divided into four broad categories: business groups, ethnic groups, foreign lobbyists, and ideological/politically involved public interest groups. Before examining the efforts of today's interest groups to influence U.S. foreign policy, we turn back the clock in the "Historical Lesson" section to look at the 1940 America First Committee.

### Historical Lesson

### The America First Committee, 1940

The roots of the America First Committee can be traced back to informal discussions by students at Yale University in the spring of 1940. Officially established in September 1940, General Robert Wood, head of the board of Sears, Roebuck and Co., served as its national chairman. Also on the committee were a former commander of the American Legion; Chester Bowles, future diplomat; and American aviator Charles Lindbergh. Prominent advisors to the board included William Benton, vice president of the University of Chicago and future Republican senator from Connecticut; Phillip La Follette, a former governor of Wisconsin; Democratic senator Burton Wheeler of Montana; and Republican congressman Karl Mundt of South Dakota. Its total national membership was estimated to be between 800,000 and 850,000, with the great majority located in the Midwest and Northeast.

Five core principles guided the America First Committee's approach to foreign policy:

- Our first duty is to keep America out of foreign wars. Our entry would only destroy democracy, not save it.
- Not by acts of war abroad but by preserving and extending democracy at home can we aid democracy and freedom in other lands.
- In 1917 we sent our American ships into the war zone and this led us to war. In 1941 we must keep our naval convoys and merchant vessels on this side of the Atlantic.
- We must build a defense, for our own shores, so strong that no foreign power or combination of powers can invade our country by sea, air, or land.
- Humanitarian aid is the duty of a strong, free country at peace. We should feed and

clothe the suffering and needy people of England and the occupied countries and so keep alive their hope for the return of better days.

These principles led the America First Committee to oppose Franklin Roosevelt's lend-lease proposal and a proposed revision of the Neutrality Act so that American merchant ships could enter war zones. Convinced that Nazi Germany could not defeat Great Britain but that Great Britain could not win without full U.S. military support, the America First Committee recommended exploration of the possibility of a negotiated peace. In June 1941, the committee called for a national advisory referendum on war and peace as part of its campaign to influence Congress and the president. There was disagreement within the America First Committee on several points. Initially it banned pacifists from joining but soon abandoned this policy; the America First Committee would later cooperate informally with pacifist groups. Disagreement also existed about whether building U.S. defenses extended to a defense of the Western Hemisphere.

In addition to distributing material through the mail, the America First Committee actively used the media to promote its noninterventionist foreign policy views though newspaper advertising, pamphlets, radio addresses, motion pictures, press releases, and use of cartoon services. The committee also lobbied Congress and the president. It provided congressmen with policy bulletins and helped them write speeches. Most importantly, it urged sympathizers to demonstrate their support for its cause by writing to the president and Congress, indicating that "your pen is your last weapon against war." While

they failed to change the overall direction of U.S. foreign policy, these efforts were not without impact. Accounts describing Franklin Roosevelt's foreign policy note the impact of the America First Committee on his decision making.

Critics rallied opposition by highlighting the extent to which committee views were consistent with and supported the efforts of communist, pro-fascist, and anti-Semitic groups. Charges of anti-Semitism were especially damaging given the committee's association with such prominent anti-Semitic individuals as Henry Ford, who briefly served on the national committee; followers of member Father Charles Coughlin, who had begun attacking Jews in 1938; and Charles Lindbergh, who at a September 1941 rally stated that the three most important groups pushing the United States to war were the British, the Roosevelt administration, and Jews.

The America First Committee passed from the scene with the Japanese attack on Pearl Harbor. Four days later, it voted to dissolve, urging members to "give their full support to the war effort of this country until the conflict with Japan is brought to a successful conclusion."

## Applying the Lesson

1. How similar is the America First Committee's foreign policy to Donald Trump's America First foreign policy?
2. Would the America First Committee's foreign policy agenda have much popular support today?
3. Identify any current organizations or policy makers today that hold the same foreign policy beliefs as the America First Committee.

### Business Groups

The long-standing cliché at the heart of business lobbying is that "what is good for General Motors is good for the United States." This view is endorsed both by those who feel threatened by foreign competition and seek protection (such as the auto, steel, and textile industries and farmers) and by those who depend on open access to foreign markets or natural resources. An example of the latter is lobbying during Obama's presidency by Exxon (then headed by Trump's first secretary of state, Rex Tillerson) to obtain a Treasury Department waiver to sanctions that would prohibit Exxon from partnering with Russia on oil-drilling projects in the Black Sea. Earlier it had received a waiver to search for oil in the Arctic; under that plan, Exxon and the Russian firm agreed to invest $3.2 billion.

The extent to which U.S. businesses depend on foreign trade and access to markets is captured in table 5.3, which lists the top ten states in terms of international trade as a share of their GDP in 2017. The auto industry is most responsible for Michigan's high ranking; its top import partner is Mexico, and its top export partner is Canada. For Louisiana, crude oil is the most important foreign trade industry; its major partners are Russia, Saudi Arabia, Venezuela, and Iraq. Washington has a highly globalized economy due to its aerospace industries.

Nowhere is business foreign policy lobbying more controversial than when it is carried out by defense industries. Their activities bring forth images of what President Dwight Eisenhower referred to in his farewell address as the **military-industrial complex**.[39] At the core of this negative image is the assertion that a dominating political force consisting of professional soldiers, industrialists, and government officials exists within U.S. policy-making circles that acts in unison to determine policy on defense-related matters.[40] The resulting policies are based on an ideology of international conflict that requires high levels of military spending, a large defense establishment, and a belligerent, interventionist foreign policy. In the 1960s, the concept of a military-industrial complex became a major theme in the writings of those who opposed U.S. involvement in Vietnam.

Central to the effectiveness of the military-industrial complex are the linkages between its various elements. A 2012 study found that 70 percent of retired three- and four-star generals took jobs with defense contractors or served as consultants to them. Perhaps the most important dimension of its operation is the extensive lobbying efforts of defense contractors directed at Congress and the White House. Collectively, Lockheed Martin, Boeing, Northrop Grumman, and Raytheon spent more than $50 million on lobbying in 2017. In 2019, Lockheed Martin and the Pentagon reached agreement on a $34 billion deal for F-35 fighters, the largest contract ever signed. Especially important to these firms are their sales to Saudi Arabia, which came under attack in Congress following the assassination of Saudi dissident Jamal Khashoggi and the uncovering of links to the Saudi government. Raytheon's chief executive announced the firm's continuing support for Saudi Arabia, stating, "We have supported the Kingdom of

| Table 5.3 | International Trade as a Share of GDP, 2017 (Top 10) | | |
|---|---|---|---|
| **State** | **GDP (billions)** | **Exports + Imports (billions)** | **Trade Share of GDP (%)** |
| Michigan | $514.5 | $200.1 | 38.9 |
| Louisiana | $243.3 | $94.1 | 38.7 |
| Kentucky | $204.4 | $78.0 | 38.1 |
| Tennessee | $344.7 | $112.2 | 32.6 |
| South Carolina | $218.9 | $69.7 | 31.9 |
| Texas | $1,692.0 | $527.4 | 31.2 |
| Indiana | $359.5 | $92.4 | 25.7 |
| Washington | $503.1 | $127.0 | 25.3 |
| New Jersey | $589.3 | $124.2 | 25.0 |
| Illinois | $818.2 | $200.9 | 24.6 |

*Source*: Mark Perry, "How Important Is International Trade to Each U.S. State's Economy?," May 11, 2018, https://seekingalpha.com/article/4155383-important-international-trade. Data is from U.S. Census and Bureau of Economic Analysis.

Saudi Arabia in securing defense for more than 50 years . . . we are lock step behind them." The Aerospace Industries Association echoed Trump's call for standing with the Saudi government, asserting that it would continue "to support U.S. national security and foreign policy goals."

*Ethnic Groups*

The most successful ethnic lobbies have relied on three ingredients to give them political clout: (1) the threat of switching allegiances at election time, either from one party to another or from one candidate to another in the same party; (2) a strong and effective lobbying apparatus; and (3) the ability to build a case around traditional American symbols and ideals.[41]

The Jewish American lobby possesses the most formidable combination of these elements. The centerpiece of the Jewish lobbying effort for Israel is the highly organized, efficient, and well-financed American Israel Public Affairs Committee (AIPAC), which serves as an umbrella organization for pro-Israeli groups. It "promptly and unfailingly provides all members [of Congress] with data and documentation, supplemented, as circumstances dictate, with telephone calls and personal visits on those issues touching upon Israeli national interests."[42]

High levels of funding for pro-Israeli candidates are a key component of the lobbying strategy, as are pro-Israeli political action committees (PACs). A study by the Federal Election Commission found that, from 1998 to 2006, Jewish PACs made over $13 million in contributions to congressional candidates. The next highest level of contributions was by a Cuban American PAC ($1 million). Money alone does not explain the strength of Jewish American lobbying efforts. They have also been successful because their message resonates well with Americans: a country founded by settlers who were displaced from their homelands with a common sense of destiny and mission as a chosen people who are threatened by enemies.[43]

One of the challenges AIPAC faces is that the demographics of its support base are changing. Its primary supporters were once liberal Democrats; now they are conservative Republicans and, especially, evangelical Christians. African Americans were once staunch supporters of Israel but now increasingly align with Palestinian causes. AIPAC's core base has also aged. A 2008 poll showed that, while more than one-half of Jewish Americans older than age 65 felt that the Israel-Palestine relations were a major issue in the U.S. election, more than 66 percent of young non-Orthodox Jewish students did not feel this way. This change in support base has contributed to the emergence of competing groups.[44] The most significant of these is J Street; formed in 2008, it defines itself as "the political home for pro-Israel, pro-peace Americans" and advocates a two-state solution to the Israeli-Palestinian conflict. It lobbied against AIPAC's position on such issues as Obama's nuclear agreement with Iran and imposition of economic sanctions on Iran, and disagreed with Trump's decision to recognize Jerusalem as Israel's capital outside of formal peace negotiations.

AIPAC's many sources of strength do not guarantee success. Citizens for a Nuclear Free Iran, an AIPAC affiliate, worked with a $20 million advertising budget to stop Obama's nuclear deal with Iran, and ran ads in forty states. It was unable to mobilize sufficient votes in Congress to block the agreement. Decades earlier, in 1981, over AIPAC's objections Ronald Reagan had agreed to sell AWACS (Airborne Warning and Control Systems aircraft) to Saudi Arabia in what was then the largest arms sale in U.S. history.[45]

No Arab American lobbying force equal to AIPAC has yet emerged.[46] In 1972 a central organization called the National Association of Arab Americans (NAAA) was founded, and in the mid-1980s it had field coordinators in every congressional district and a membership of some one hundred thousand Arab American families. Also active in encouraging the participation of Arab Americans in the political process is the Arab American Institute, which was founded in 1985. From 1998 to 2006 Arab American PACs spent some $500,000 on congressional campaigns.

A major obstacle to creating an effective Arab American lobbying force is their ethnic diversity. Until 1948, most Arabs coming to the United States were Christians from Syria and Lebanon. Since 1978, most have been Muslims. As a result, no single political agenda exists for Arab Americans. Consensus exists only on the broad issues of pursuing a comprehensive peace plan in the Middle East and establishing better U.S. relations with the Arab world.

By the mid-1980s, African Americans had made great strides toward meeting two of the three prerequisites listed at the beginning of this section. First, as the Reverend Jesse Jackson's 1984 bid for the presidency made clear, blacks make up an important constituency within the Democratic Party, strengthening the threat of switching allegiances. Second, an organizational base, TransAfrica, now exists. The major focus of black lobbying in the mid-1980s was reorienting U.S. policy toward South Africa. Following the successful resolution of this issue, African Americans have had a more difficult time mobilizing on foreign policy issues.[47] TransAfrica's primary agenda today focuses on promoting global justice for the African World and bringing human rights to the center of U.S. foreign policy.

Ethnic diversity is also a problem for Hispanic American lobbying on foreign policy.[48] Mexican immigration, which has been motivated largely by economic considerations, is concentrated in the Southwest and is largely Democratic. In 1980, Jimmy Carter got 72 percent of this vote. Cuban immigration is concentrated on the East Coast; it has been motivated largely by foreign policy concerns, and is politically conservative and Republican. Ronald Reagan received 59 percent of Florida's Hispanic vote.

Two additional fissures within the Hispanic community make the establishment of an effective lobbying force difficult. One pits American-born Hispanics against immigrants.[49] The only real area of overlapping concern is immigration policy. American-born Hispanics give greatest weight to domestic issues such as education, crime, economic growth, and the environment. The second fissure is generational. This came through clearly in the differing reactions to President Obama's announcement that the United States and Cuba would move toward establishing normal diplomatic relations. By and large, longtime Cuban exiles in Florida denounced Obama as a traitor and liar, while younger Cuban Americans expressed the view that the time was right for a change in U.S.-Cuba relations. In reversing Obama's opening to Cuba, Trump was seen as appealing to this older generation of Cuban American voters for electoral support. Some also argued that this was a key element in his support for removing socialist Nicolás Maduro from power in Venezuela; Trump had shown little interest in Venezuela but was strongly pushed by Florida's Republican senator Mark Rubio. A similar dynamic played out early in Biden's presidency. Following up on a campaign promise, he announced his intent to reverse many of Trump's restrictions on trade with Cuba as well as to reinstate the family reunification program. Objections from Cubans in Florida (and members of Congress) who are adamantly opposed to the current authoritarian government caused Biden to put the decision on hold, only to move ahead with it again as pressure built with a different stated purpose, "to further support the Cuban people" and empower the private sector.

The most famous Hispanic lobby is the Cuban American National Foundation (CANF).[50] Established in 1981, CANF was vehemently opposed to Fidel Castro, was intent on ending communist rule in Cuba, and had a long history of opposition to any change in American policy toward Cuba. Among the major legislation that it supported was the 1992 Cuban Democracy Act. Passed by Congress in an election year and endorsed by both presidential candidates in an effort to gain the support of the Cuban American community, the act prohibited foreign affiliates of U.S. firms from doing business in Cuba.

CANF did a dramatic about-face in April 2009. Just days before President Obama announced that he was lifting long-standing restrictions on family reunification and remittances to Cuba, CANF issued a white paper calling for a new direction in U.S.-Cuba relations based on people-to-people exchanges and the promotion of Cuban civil society, and targeting bilateral and multilateral diplomacy.

### Foreign Lobbyists

Both foreign governments and groups within their societies engage in lobbying. While their most common concerns are foreign aid legislation and arms sales, foreign governments pursue a wide range of interests.[51] A point of controversy behind their lobbying efforts is the legal requirement that advocates of foreign organizations register as lobbyists and provide details of their fees and activities. Often individuals recruited by foreign organizations argue that they are not lobbyists but are legitimately acting as individuals to promote good foreign policy decisions. This was the position taken by Rudolph Giuliani, former New York City mayor and personal attorney to Donald Trump, who had not registered as a foreign agent even though Brazil, Colombia, and an Iranian dissident group, Mujahedeen-e-Khalq (MEK), were among his clients.

One of the most active foreign lobbyists is Saudi Arabia. In 2017, it had twenty-eight lobbying contracts. Only Japan had more, with forty-seven. In 2015, Saudi Arabia spent $7.7 billion on lobbying and consulting activities in the United States. This amount jumped to $27.6 billion in 2016, primarily because of a resolution in Congress to end U.S. support for Saudi bombing in Yemen. In the weeks leading up to a vote on this resolution, Saudi Arabian lobbyists had 759 contacts with members of Congress, staffers, academics, and reporters. Another reason was the election of Donald Trump, who had attacked Saudi Arabia during the campaign. Shortly after his election, Saudi Arabia hired six additional lobbying firms. Three days after Khashoggi's death and rising demands in Congress for action against the country, Saudi Arabia again invested in lobbying firms, adding the McKeon Group founded by former Republican chair of the House Armed Services Committee Robert McKeon for $450,000.

MEK provides an ongoing example of nonstate foreign lobbying. Founded by Iranian students who embraced Marxism, overthrow of the shah, and the establishment of an Islamic state, it was identified by the State Department as a terrorist organization. A series of MEK attacks in the early 1970s resulted in the deaths of several U.S. soldiers. The organization formally renounced terrorism in 2001. Among those speaking out on its behalf were two former CIA directors, a former House Speaker, and a former head of the Joint Chiefs of Staff. Secretary of State Hillary Clinton removed MEK from the terrorist list in 2012, but it continues to be at the center of controversy for its lobbying efforts. Shortly after Elaine Chao was confirmed as Trump's secretary of transportation, she acknowledged receiving $50,000 from MEK for a five-minute speech.

Another nonstate foreign lobby is the Kurds, an ethnic group found along the borders of Turkey, Iraq, Syria, Iran, and Armenia that hopes to create its own state out of this territory.

The United States has relied on the Kurds heavily to promote its interests in the Middle East. The Kurds have targeted many of their efforts toward bureaucracy. One of their goals has been to obtain $18.4 billion from U.S. construction funds dedicated to the Kurdish region of Iraq. When the State Department opposed their efforts, the Kurdish lobbying effort switched its focus to the Commerce Department, which identified this region as the "gateway" for U.S. firms going to Iraq.

### *Ideological/Politically Involved Public Interest Groups*

This category includes a wide variety of groups. At one extreme are highly institutionalized and well-funded organizations that are not normally thought of as interest groups. Part of the mission of these think tanks is the propagation and advancement of ideas about how to address public policy problems. The Brookings Institution is one of the most prominent foreign policy think tanks. It has long advanced a liberal-democratic foreign policy agenda but has become more moderate and centrist in orientation. Two of the most visible think tanks now occupy positions at the conservative end of the political spectrum: the Cato Institute, a libertarian organization that has advanced a restrictive—if not isolationist—foreign policy agenda, and the Heritage Foundation. In the view of many of its past supporters, the Heritage Foundation has moved away from its traditional orientation—as a source of conservative ideas about a foreign policy based on a strong military defense, limited involvement in humanitarian undertakings, and free market principles in international trade—to a more activist and combative orientation. Also playing prominent roles as producers of ideas are the American Enterprise Institute (AEI), New America, and the Center for Strategic and International Studies (CSIS).

Think tanks make their mark on Washington in many ways. Their members serve as a source of expertise, as either outside experts or employees, on which administrations and congressional committees can draw. Perhaps most significantly, they serve as a focal point for bringing together like-minded individuals to address common concerns. For example, think tanks were prominent members of the "blue team," a loose alliance of members of Congress, staffers, conservative journalists, and lobbyists for Taiwan who worked to present China as a threat to the United States. More recently, the Heritage Foundation, AEI, and the Foreign Policy Institute joined forces in a "defend defense" initiative to protect the Pentagon's budget from major cutbacks.

Recently, think tanks have come under close scrutiny for receiving large sums of money from foreign governments without acknowledgment.[52] Since 2011, at least sixty-four foreign governments and their officials have contributed money to twenty-eight major U.S. research organizations. CSIS has disclosed a list of thirteen foreign government donors, including Germany and China. The Atlantic Council has acknowledged accepting funds from twenty-five countries since 2008.

Also included in this category are more traditional societal groups, the most prominent of which today might be the "religious right."[53] Pat Robertson's Christian Broadcasting Network gave $3 to $7 billion to U.S.-backed anticommunist forces in Central America. In 2003, Robertson defended Liberian leader Charles Taylor against charges that he was a war criminal. Robertson later called for the assassination of Venezuelan president Hugo Chávez.

Evangelical groups also have become active in shaping U.S. foreign policy in Africa; U.S. policy on AIDS was heavily influenced by the beliefs of and lobbying by Focus on the Family.[54] As with other groups active in influencing foreign policy, divisions exist among evangelicals. For example, a 2017 poll showed that 76 percent of evangelicals aged sixty-five or above had a favorable view of Israel, compared to 58 percent in the 18–34 age group. Some 30 percent of those in this latter group were unsure, about twice as many as in the older age group.[55] The religious right does not hold a monopoly on interest group activity by religious organizations. During the prelude to the Iraq War, groups were active on both sides. Fundamentalist groups tended to support the war, but the Catholic Church, the Religious Society of Friends (Quakers), the World Council of Churches, the Muslim Peace Fellowship, and the Shalom Center all spoke out against it.

## Impact of Interest Groups

Establishing an interest group's influence on a specific policy is difficult. More is required than just revealing the presence of group activity. A concrete link must be established between the group's actions and the actions taken by those who were influenced. Efforts to establish the validity of assertions about the influence of the military-industrial complex on U.S. foreign policy have produced mixed results. The influence of the military-industrial complex is greatest in the industrial arena and far less in the military one, where it faces strong competition from ideological, economic, and other nonmilitary influences.

Two additional factors must be considered in assessing the influence of interest group lobbying. First, to a considerable degree, success or failure may be due to factors beyond the control of interest groups, such as the existence of an economic problem or a change in the political climate. For example, a surge in populism within the United States fueled the election of Donald Trump, whose America First campaign promised to protect American businesses from unfair foreign competition. Second, interest group successes may have negative political side effects. Trump's tariffs on steel and aluminum were designed to protect those industries, but the tariffs are likely to harm the auto industry and result in higher prices unless exceptions are granted, which would undermine the benefits of the tariffs. Moreover, China retaliated by placing tariffs on soybeans and other products produced in the United States, hurting the U.S. farmers that were one of Trump's strongest support groups.

# Political Protest

The public voice on foreign policy matters is not just expressed through officially sanctioned avenues. It can also be heard in a variety of forms that challenge policy makers to take notice of positions often at odds with official policies. Protests range from the acts of single individuals, such as Cindy Sheehan challenging President George W. Bush's position on the Iraq War by camping outside his ranch in Crawford, Texas, to antiwar marches involving thousands, such as the one that occurred in Washington, DC, in 2010 on the seventh anniversary of the Iraq War.

Modern technology has added a new dimension to protest movements: the *virtual protest march*. In October 2003, when tens of thousands of protesters marched in Washington calling for an end to the occupation of Iraq, other protesters flooded congressional offices with emails stating their opposition to the war. A similar tactic was used to pressure Congress into investigating prewar intelligence claims made by the George W. Bush administration; more than four hundred thousand people from every state contacted members of Congress.

Political protests are valued for their ability to alter the political landscape by bypassing existing power centers and introducing new or marginalized voices into the political debate. The antiglobalization protests that began in Seattle in 1999 ensured that environmental, labor, and democracy issues could not be totally ignored. Pro-immigration protests have brought many Hispanics into the political process for the very first time.

The ability of political protests to have this impact may be especially important today. In large part this is because an *apathetic internationalism* is reshaping American politics, encouraging policy makers to ignore foreign policy problems and empowering *squeaky wheels*, those who make the loudest noise about foreign policy problems. More often than not, this condition favors those organized interests that can mobilize their supporters most effectively to pressure policy makers. However, when thousands of protesters repeatedly take to the streets, a new element is added to the equation.[56]

There is nothing automatic about the success of protest movements. Major foreign policies are not easily reversed, and it is often difficult to sustain the political momentum needed to change policies. Such was the situation facing the antiglobalization protestors at a 1999 meeting of the World Trade Organization in Seattle and climate change protestors who marched in New York City in 2014. Protest movements can also give birth to counterprotests, which can be cited by policy makers as justification for their policies. Such was the case in September 2005 when Iraq War supporters marched in Washington, DC.

## The Media and American Foreign Policy

To this point, the chapter has looked at how the public conveys its views to policy makers, but it has not yet examined how the public obtains information about the world. In analyzing this issue, the sources of information on which the public relies are presented first, followed by an examination of how those sources can shape their thinking. Chapter 7 examines how presidents interact with the media to advance their agendas.

### Newspapers and Television

For generations of Americans, newspapers were the primary—if not the only—means of keeping up with news. One of the early, most often cited examples of the influence of the media on U.S. foreign policy is the Spanish-American War. At the turn of the twentieth century, the Hearst and Pulitzer newspaper chains engaged in sensationalistic **yellow journalism** to increase circulation. Their coverage of the sinking of the USS *Maine* in Havana Harbor is routinely cited as contributing to the onset of the war by stirring up American public opinion. More recent scholarship cites the greater importance of more fundamental foreign policy issues dividing the United States and Spain, but the imagery of the press being able to lead the United States to war remains strong.

Over time, television also transformed the coverage of foreign policy issues. Network evening news broadcasts were only fifteen minutes long in 1962 and relied heavily on video of international events that were at least a day old. About the October 1962 Cuban missile crisis, Robert McNamara, President Kennedy's secretary of defense, observed, "I don't think that I turned on a television set during the whole two weeks of that crisis."[57] During the Cuban missile crisis, the Kennedy administration knew about the missiles in Cuba six days before the information was broadcast to the American people. Consider how differently the crisis might have played out had it occurred in the 1990s[58] following the transformation of television coverage of foreign policy issues by the arrival of CNN's 24-7 news coverage in 1980. CNN dramatically changed the political time clock for presidents to inform the public about their responses to events. Today, the bottom line is that presidents must develop a television policy to accompany their foreign policy. They have not always succeeded. During the Persian Gulf War, the George H. W. Bush administration was able to frame the policy issue on its own terms and to control media coverage.[59] Uncertain about how to proceed in Haiti, Bosnia, and Somalia, his administration and that of Bill Clinton were unable to present a coherent story with which the media could frame its pictures.[60]

The ability of the press to shape public opinion declined with the arrival of competing news sources and increased costs. By 1993, slightly more Americans reported watching network news regularly than reading the newspaper (60 percent versus 58 percent). By 2008, more people were going online three or more times per week (37 percent) than listening to radio news (34 percent) or reading the newspaper (34 percent).[61] The percentage of front-page foreign news stories in U.S. newspapers has also declined steadily. In 2007 it was at 14 percent, down from 27 percent in 1987 and 1977. Table 5.4 presents an overview of the extent to which different media sources are relied upon to obtain news.

## The New Media and American Foreign Policy

Today the internet and the sharing of information, ideas, personal messages, videos, and other content via social media have become a major if not the dominant source of foreign policy news and information. By 2003, 77 percent of Americans who used the internet did so to get or share information on the Iraq War. One in five internet users stated that it helped shape their thinking about the war.[62] Today, most voters receive their foreign policy news from TV, but younger voters turn most heavily to social media sources.

**Table 5.4**  **Frequency of News Platforms Used, 2021**

| Frequency Used | Digital (%) | Television (%) | Radio (%) | Print Publication (%) |
|---|---|---|---|---|
| Never | 8 | 12 | 22 | 32 |
| Rarely | 8 | 20 | 27 | 23 |
| Sometimes | 33 | 32 | 36 | 34 |
| Often | 51 | 36 | 15 | 10 |

*Source:* Katerina Matse and Sarah Laseer, "News Platform Fact Sheet," PEW Research Center, November 8, 2021.

The new media helps shape public views on foreign policy in two ways. First, it serves as a source of raw information and images. One way it does this is through leaking secret documents. Nowhere was this more in evidence than in July 2010 when WikiLeaks released over ninety-one thousand secret documents about Afghanistan and other foreign policy matters on its website. Another way is by carefully managing the information it provides. For example, the Syrian civil war is described as the most socially mediated conflict in history. Social media images were carefully managed by "gatekeepers." Violent images were designed to delegitimize the Assad regime to the outside world, encourage further extremism and polarization in the conflict, and demobilize others from intervening militarily for fear of becoming the next victims.[63]

Second, the internet allows individuals to connect in a personal and direct manner with U.S. foreign policy. Foreign policy blogs abound. The White House arranged for President Obama's June 2009 speech in Cairo to be sent out in text-message format in four languages, translated into thirteen languages, and broadcast on Facebook. President Trump uses tweets rather than news conferences or press briefings as the primary way to present his views to the public and connect with his political base.

## Shaping the Public's View

It has become commonplace to speak of the media as driving foreign policy decisions through the **CNN effect**, the ability to place "breaking" news stories before the public all day, every day. Evidence suggests that a more complex relationship between the media and policy makers drives coverage of foreign events. In the traditional view, the media does not so much discover foreign policy problems as it takes cues about what to report from the political debate in Washington. This practice is referred to as *indexing*. If there is no debate in Washington, then there is no debate in the media, and coverage of a topic may all but disappear. Journalists look first to the White House for cues on how to define a problem, creating what one White House official characterized as an echo chamber. "All of these newspapers used to have foreign correspondents. Now they don't. They call us to explain to them what's happening in Moscow and Cairo. . . . They literally know nothing."[64]

Two very different consequences of the manner in which the traditional media frames its foreign policy stories have been identified. The first is the **rally-around-the-flag effect** in which the public moves to support the president in times of conflict and crisis. Initially, the American public was sharply divided on using military force against Iraq in 1991. Support for war hovered around the 50 percent mark until President George H. W. Bush's January 16, 1991, speech announcing the beginning of the bombing campaign. Support then shot up to 72 percent.

There is nothing automatic in media coverage of a major foreign policy issue that automatically produces a significant boost in support for the administration's foreign policy. Biden's public opinion rating in June 2022 (41 percent positive) was virtually identical to his rating in February, just prior to the Russian invasion of Ukraine. Among the factors contributing to this unchanged view are the growth in the number of media outlets from which news can be obtained, the growing and deepening polarization of public opinion, and the lack of direct U.S. military involvement in the war.

A second consequence of media framing of foreign policy stories is a **spiral of silence**. When individuals hold opinions that they do not hear reaffirmed in the voices of others, they exercise self-censorship as a way of protecting themselves from criticism. The opposite reaction takes place among those who receive positive reinforcement for their views; they become even more vocal and confident in their beliefs, leading the dissenters to exercise even more self-censorship. Many saw this spiral at work in public opinion on the Persian Gulf War. Networks all but ignored antiwar stories in the lead-up to the war. Of 2,855 minutes of network news coverage of the war during this period, only 29 minutes showed popular opposition to the ongoing American military buildup.

These traditional consequences of media coverage of foreign policy continue to exist. But they now coexist with new forms of impact. First, the media can serve as a supporter of foreign policy agendas and even a driving force behind them. This is possible because the vast number of news sources now available and the preference for individuals to follow only those news sources they agree with has created a type of silo effect in which individuals do not hear all sides of a policy debate but only one. Fox News during the Trump administration became the leading example of this phenomenon. Seventy-one percent of voters who watched Fox News supported strong national security border policies and limiting legal and illegal immigration. This contrasted with 46 percent of voters overall. So attentive was President Trump to what Fox News broadcasts were saying about his policies that it was often said that Fox News effectively had "an audience of one."

Second, as evidence of Russian efforts to influence the 2016 presidential election reveals, the new media can also serve as a powerful tool to manipulate information covertly for political purposes.[65] Russian operators published more than 131 messages on Twitter, uploaded more than a thousand videos to YouTube, and reached 126 million users on Facebook. Russian efforts to influence public attitudes in the United States pre-date the 2016 election. One of its most important propaganda instruments was the state-backed news channel RT (Russia Today), which the U.S. intelligence community defined as Russia's "principal international propaganda outlet."

The Russian influence campaign was based on producing misinformation and sheltered social media sites of its own making as well as promoting misinformation from existing platforms run by Americans. In spreading its messages, Russian operatives relied on standard Facebook technologies that allowed them to send specific news stories, messages, and ads tailored to people who had unknowingly just visited a Russian site.

## States and Cities: The New Foreign Policy Battleground

Because the foreign policy agenda has increasingly become one in which both domestic and foreign policy concerns are present simultaneously (*intermestic*; see chapter 2), the public voice on foreign policy is being directed away from a singular focus on Washington to include state capitals and major cities. The attention of many allies has also been directed away from Washington in what some diplomats refer to as the *donut strategy*: when you have a problem in the middle, you work around the edges to build networks and encircle it. States and cities have responded by increasing their profiles abroad.[66] For example, Los Angeles now has a deputy mayor for international affairs.

One foreign policy area in which states and cities have become increasingly active is immigration policy. During the Trump administration the most publicized entry into foreign policy making was the *sanctuary city movement*. It began in response to Trump's promise to carry through on his campaign promise to deport illegal immigrants. Mayors across the United States asserted that they would not cooperate with such a program. In March 2019, eight states including California, Massachusetts, New Jersey, and Illinois had declared themselves to be sanctuary states. There were 178 cities and counties in twenty-seven states that had also declared themselves to be sanctuaries. Included among them were Los Angeles, San Francisco, Denver, Chicago, New Orleans, and Philadelphia. In response to the sanctuary city movement, the Trump administration threatened to revoke or withhold federal law enforcement funding from these jurisdictions. In 2019, Trump raised the possibility of transporting immigrants detained at the border to sanctuary cities. The administration officials termed the policy proposal a viable option to deal with overcrowding at the border. Comments made by others, including Trump, suggested that the policy was retaliation against these cities, which largely vote Democratic.

In the Biden administration, state foreign policy activity on immigration moved in the opposite direction. Twenty states having Republican governors successfully brought forward court action designed to stop Biden from lifting Title 42 border controls. Texas went one step further. On April 6, Governor Greg Abbott issued a safety inspection order on trucks crossing from Mexico into Texas. The average stop time ran ten to twelve hours. Abbott justified the policy on the need to deal with illegal immigration and drug smuggling, but since Texas officials could not look inside trucks, that rationale did not hold. Instead, it was widely seen as a political statement. Abbott raised the order on April 15. Estimates placed the lost money for the Texas economy at $4 billion.

## Policy Makers' Responses

The prevailing view among policy makers holds that foreign policy is too important to be rooted in public perceptions of world affairs. Public attitudes should be formed and shaped rather than followed. Consider comments made by two past secretaries of defense. At a press conference, Leon Panetta (under Obama) stated, "We cannot fight wars by polls." Dick Cheney (under George H. W. Bush) said, "I do not look upon the press as an asset. Frankly, I look on it as a problem to be managed."[67]

The tendency of policy makers to discount the positive contribution of the public voice to foreign policy making shows up when they look to uncover that voice. A State Department official observed, "If a given viewpoint different from our own does not have congressional expression, forget it."[68] A congressional staffer could not remember the last time he was asked to do a foreign policy poll. The inevitable result of this perspective is to greatly narrow the range of public attitudes that are taken into account in making policy. Additionally, policy makers often appear not to understand how the public thinks about foreign policy issues. In a 2004 poll, 76 percent of the public said that the United States should participate in the International Criminal Court. When asked about the issue before poll results were released, only 32 percent of government officials and 15 percent of congressional staffers anticipated that a majority of the public would hold this view.[69]

Policy makers may not be totally off base in their lack of attention to public opinion. One study suggests that, depending on the type of foreign policy problem, presidents can safely ignore what the public thinks. For a noncrisis issue, what matters to the public is that the president takes action; judgments of success and failure do not enter into public thinking because of the long time needed for such issues to be resolved. In a crisis, what matters is not the decision of whether to use force or intervene, but whether the effort failed or succeeded.[70]

Kori Schake challenges thoughts of dismissing the public's input into foreign policy as self-destructive hubris.[71] She, along with many other commentators, argues that instead the foreign policy elite must become more responsive to the public by working with civil society groups and nongovernmental organizations to gain the sustained public support necessary for foreign policy to succeed.

## Over the Horizon: An Intelligence-Industrial Complex?

As we noted earlier, in his farewell address, President Eisenhower warned about the need to guard against the influence of the military-industrial complex. The 2013 revelations by Edward Snowden regarding the existence of a secret NSA domestic electronic data gathering program have many warning against a new threat to the public's ability to effectively express its voice on foreign policy matters: an *intelligence-industrial complex*. As with the military-industrial complex, critics see the intelligence-industrial complex as a potentially unaccountable political force rooted in the perception of significant national security threats to the United States. In contrast to the military-industrial complex, which gains influence through the production of military power, the intelligence-industrial complex gains influence through the collection and production of information. As former NSA director Lieutenant General Keith Alexander put it, the challenge is that "you need a haystack to find a needle." For the NSA and other intelligence agencies, building a haystack required the cooperation of commercial communication firms.[72] In the early postwar era of the twentieth century, Western Union and others provided government access to telegraph communications. Later the government turned to AT&T for help in tapping into underwater fiber cables. Then Microsoft provided the NSA with the capability of circumventing its own encryption program.

The issue of whether or not the intelligence-industrial complex represents a threat to civil liberties finds Americans and Congress divided. A March 2016 CBS poll found that 50 percent supported the FBI's insistence that Apple unlock the mobile phone linked to the 2015 San Bernardino terrorist attack, and 43 percent supported Apple's refusal to comply. In 2019, a bipartisan group of lawmakers petitioned Secretary of State Mike Pompeo and Director of National Intelligence Dan Coats to formulate a strategy to ensure that surveillance tools are not exported to foreign countries with records of human rights abuses, which might use them against political dissidents, the press, and U.S. citizens.

## Critical Thinking Questions

1. Which of the means of exercising the public voice discussed in this chapter (public opinion, elections, lobbying, and political protest) is most effective, and why?

2. Is the media best seen as a threat to the president's ability to conduct foreign policy or an important tool? Explain your answer.

3. Should policy makers listen to the public or use their professional judgment in making foreign policy decisions? Explain your answer.

## Key Terms

CNN effect, 106
military-industrial complex, 98
positional issues, 94
rally-around-the-flag effect, 106
spiral of silence, 106

think tanks, 86
tipping point, 92
valence issues, 94
Vietnam syndrome, 90
yellow journalism, 104

# Congress 6

## Learning Objectives

Students will be able to:

1. Identify the constitutional powers of Congress in making foreign policy.
2. Explain why the structure of Congress is important for understanding U.S. foreign policy.
3. Describe how the relationship between Congress and the president has changed over time.
4. Evaluate the overall impact of Congress on U.S. foreign policy. Does the Ukraine example fit this assessment?

## On the Agenda: Aid for Ukraine

No shortage of views exists regarding the role that Congress plays in making foreign policy. Frequently it is characterized as an obstacle course for presidential foreign policy initiatives to navigate. One dissenting view holds that Congress is not really an obstacle course for presidents.[1] They tend to get their way. A second dissent argues that, even if it is a hard obstacle course, congressional participation in foreign policy making is critical to raising public awareness about issues and providing additional information to policy makers.[2] In this "On the Agenda" section, the pathway followed by Congress in providing assistance to Ukraine in the lead-up to the 2022 midterm elections is reviewed.

In December 2021, shortly after Biden warned Russian president Vladimir Putin of "strong economic and other consequences" should Russia invade Ukraine and two months before it did so in February 2022, Congress passed the National Defense Authorization Act. It included $70 million in aid for Ukraine. The act was passed just prior to adjourning for the Christmas break. Its passing was marked by intense partisan and intraparty conflicts. Top congressional officials met behind closed doors to assemble a bill that could quickly pass both chambers without amendments being put forward.

As 2022 began, Biden publicly stated that he expected a Russian invasion of Ukraine. This pronouncement brought into public view a significant rift within the Republican Party separating traditional hawks who occupied most leadership positions and a group still loyal to Trump's America First instincts and pro-Russian sentiment. Traditional hawks demanded that Biden get tougher on Russia by putting in place immediate sanctions on Russian energy exports and providing Ukraine with more military aid. Those embracing Trump's view on Russia and global involvement questioned why the United States should get involved and why it should side with Ukraine. Representative Marjorie Taylor Greene compared sending billions of dollars to Ukraine to "a money laundering scheme."

The first point of conflict in the new year was a vote over a proposal by Republican senator Ted Cruz to impose sanctions on the controversial Nord Stream 2, a natural gas pipeline that was about to provide Russian natural gas to Western Europe. Allowing this vote was the price Democrats paid to get Cruz to drop his hold on Biden's ambassador nominations. Cruz argued that his bill would impose heavy economic costs on Russia prior to any invasion and blunt its influence on Western Europe. Democrats, with White House support, argued that doing so would take away important leverage from the United States in ongoing talks with Russia and alienate European allies. Ukrainian president Volodymyr Zelensky urged its passage. In order to avoid a potentially embarrassing defeat, Democrats unveiled their own Russia sanctions bill, which they claimed would trigger "severe costs to Russia's economy." Senior State Department officials met with nearly twelve swing-vote Democratic senators to build support for their competing bill. The Cruz bill was defeated by a 55–44 vote. Sixty votes were needed for it to pass.

Just days before the Russian invasion of Ukraine, on February 19, 2022, Congress was unable to agree on the Democratic sanctions bill. On paper, bipartisan support existed for providing Ukraine with support through sanctioning Russia, but agreeing on the "mother of all sanctions bills" proved to be beyond their reach. Only Senators Rand Paul and Bernie Sanders publicly opposed it. The bill would have placed immediate penalties on some Russian officials and business interests and would have authorized Biden to use the Lend-Lease Act of 1941 to lend additional military equipment to Ukraine. With no agreement coming on the proposal as it stood, Republicans introduced a new sanctions plan that would have given Ukraine another $500 million in military financing. Democratic senator Robert Menendez, chair of the Senate Foreign Relations Committee, denounced the plan as "partisan posturing." Congress settled instead for a strongly worded statement criticizing Putin for a "provocative and reckless" military buildup and then passed a nonbinding resolution before adjourning for a week.

Less than one month later on March 9, the House passed a bill to avoid a government shutdown that included $13.6 billion in military, economic, and humanitarian aid for Ukraine and authorized the Biden administration to enforce sanctions it had already announced against Russia. The Senate passed the bill the next day. An earlier version of the bill included language to end normal trade relations with Russia and ban imports of Russian oil. Democrats removed the trade section at Biden's request so that he would have more time to coordinate a response with allies. Biden had already issued an executive order banning the import of Russian oil. Early in the debate over the budgetary package, Republican senator Rick Scott unsuccessfully sought to separate funding for Ukraine from the package, a move that would have allowed Republicans to vote for aid and against the budget bill. Thirty-one Senate Republicans voted against the $1.5 trillion spending bill, including Scott, who termed the bill wasteful and filled with lawmakers' pet projects.

Just over one week later, more than two dozen Senate Republicans who voted against the bill called on Biden to take a more aggressive stance in providing aid to Ukraine. An important stimulus here was a virtual presentation President Zelensky made to Congress requesting help. Scott, who was considered to be a possible presidential candidate, called for providing planes and antiaircraft defense systems or enforcing a no-fly zone. Josh Hawley, another potential presidential candidate who earlier called for a greater focus on China and rejected admitting Ukraine to NATO, now called for Biden to "step up." Only a day before these statements, Biden had announced that over $800 million in weaponry would be sent to Ukraine that week. While significant, it still fell short of the sophisticated weapons that Zelensky sought.

In early April, Congress broke the ongoing stalemate by passing legislation that punished Russia for invading Ukraine and provided Ukraine with aid. In neither case did the legislation fundamentally change U.S. policy, as the content of both measures had already been implemented by Biden. A trade bill passed the Senate 100–0 and the House 420–3 that took away Russia's "permanent normal trade relations" status. A second bill that banned Russian energy imports to the United States passed the Senate 100–0 and the House 413–9. Controversy was not totally absent. Senator Rand Paul objected to language in the trade bill that allowed for sanctions against Putin allies for "serious" human rights violations rather than "gross" violations. The Senate also passed a bill unanimously that would allow the United States to activate World War II "lend-lease" weapons funding policy to aid Ukraine. The House did not act on this bill.

Congress passed another stand-alone Ukraine aid bill, the 2022 Additional Ukraine Supplemental Appropriations Act, in late May just prior to adjourning for a week's recess. The House voted 368–57 to support the bill, and the Senate passed it by an 88–11 margin. All the no votes came from Republicans, some of whom cited "America First" in doing so. The $40 billion aid package was larger than Biden had requested. As with other efforts to provide aid to Ukraine, this initiative was marked by political conflict. The administration had urged quick congressional action since money was running out from the last supplemental funding bill. As it began to stall in Congress, Biden announced his support for separating World War II–type "lend-lease" funding from the larger bill, which would allow the government to purchase equipment for U.S. stockpiles and lend it to Ukraine. He signed that bill on May 9. Quick action was blocked by Senator Rand Paul, who demanded that the bill include a provision for a special inspector general to oversee how the funds were spent. Paul argued that "we cannot save Ukraine by dooming the U.S. economy." Under Senate rules, one senator can hold up a vote if the vote is to take place under accelerated voting procedures. The vote ultimately was taken on the day that Biden had said funding would run out.

This chapter first looks at the constitutional basis of Congress's power to participate in foreign policy and the methods at its disposal to exercise its voice.[3] Next, the impact of Congress's operating structure and procedure on its participation in foreign policy making is examined. The chapter then analyzes how Congress's relationship with the president in making foreign policy changes over time.

## Constitutional Powers

The division of power found in the Constitution provides the foundation on which congressional participation in foreign policy rests. It comprises four powers: (1) the power of advice and consent in making treaties, (2) the power to confirm presidential appointments, (3) a set of war powers, and (4) the power to regulate commerce.

### Treaty-Making Power

The Constitution states that the president, by and with the advice and consent of the Senate, has the power to make treaties. The president's role in the treaty-making process generally has not been a source of serious controversy. The president nominates the negotiators, issues instructions to them, submits the treaty to the Senate for its advice and consent, and, if consent is given, decides whether to **ratify** the treaty and make it a law. Far more controversial have been the nature of senatorial advice and consent, the topics to be covered by treaties, and the role of the House of Representatives in the treaty-making process.

*Senatorial Advice and Consent*

The Senate has given its consent to well over 1,500 treaties and has rejected only 22. Fifteen of those rejections occurred between 1789 and 1920. Some, such as the Treaty of Versailles, were rejected twice. One of the most recently approved and controversial treaties was President Obama's New Strategic Arms Reduction Treaty (New START) in December 2010. It was passed by a vote of 71–26. In order to secure its passage and block crippling amendments, the administration agreed to spend an additional $84 billion over ten years to modernize the U.S. nuclear weapons program. The most recent treaty rejected by the Senate was the International Disability Treaty that was signed by President George W. Bush. It was defeated by a 61–38 vote in December 2012, five short of the sixty-six votes needed. Supporters argued that it was modeled on the Americans with Disabilities Act. Opponents argued that, by allowing international authorities to dictate the treatment of Americans with disabilities, it undermined U.S. sovereignty and the ability of American citizens to hold policy makers accountable for their actions.[4] A list of rejected treaties is presented in table 6.1.

Omitted from this count are treaties negotiated by presidents but never voted on by the Senate and those to which the Senate consented only after prolonged delays. Some eighty-five treaties have been withdrawn from consideration. President Jimmy Carter's withdrawal of the Strategic Arms Limitation Talks II (SALT II) Treaty from consideration after the Soviet invasion of Afghanistan is one example of a major Senate "nonrejection."

Thirty-seven treaties have been submitted to the Senate for its advice and consent on which it has not yet voted. A 1949 International Labor Organization Convention supporting labor's right to organize has still not come up for a vote. A 2013 arms trade treaty establishing international norms regulating the sale of weapons, including small handguns, was considered "dead on arrival" because over fifty senators had made their opposition known even before it was signed. It never came up for a vote, and Trump officially withdrew the United States from the treaty in 2019.

**Table 6.1**　**Rejected Treaties**

| Bilateral | Multilateral |
| --- | --- |
| Suspension of Slave Trade/Columbia, 1825 | Treaty of Versailles, 1920 |
| Property Rights/Switzerland, 1836 | World Court, 1935 |
| Annexation/Texas, 1844 | Law of Sea Convention, 1960 |
| Commercial Reciprocity/Germany, 1844 | Montreal Aviation Protocol, 1983 |
| Transit and Commercial Rights/Mexico, 1860 | Comprehensive Test Ban, 1999 |
| Cuban Claims Commission/Spain, 1860 | Convention on the Rights of Persons with |
| Arbitration of Claims/United Kingdom, 1869 | Disabilities, 2012 |
| Commercial Reciprocity/Hawaii, 1870 | |
| Annexation/Dominican Republic, 1870 | |
| Interoceanic Canal/Nicaragua, 1885 | |
| Fishing Rights/United Kingdom, 1888 | |
| Extradition/United Kingdom, 1889 | |
| Arbitration/United Kingdom, 1897 | |
| Commercial Rights/Turkey, 1927 | |
| St. Lawrence Seaway/Canada, 1934 | |

In addition to treaty ratifications and rejections, it is also important to look at senatorial attempts to change treaties. A treaty needs sixty-seven votes to pass, but Senate amendments to treaties only need a majority. Between 1947 and 2000, the Senate attached reservations to 162 of the 796 treaties that came before it.[5] In the heated debate over the Panama Canal Treaties, 145 amendments, 76 reservations, 18 understandings, and 3 declarations were proposed. The Senate's attachment of amendments and reservations to treaties is far from random.[6] *High-politics* treaties—those dealing with national security issues and questions of U.S. sovereignty—are far more likely to be saddled with reservations. Economic treaties are also likely to attract reservations.

The motivations behind the introduction of treaty amendments are many. Some senatorial changes are designed to improve a treaty; others are meant to kill it by introducing unacceptable provisions.[7] For example, the Senate approved the Intermediate Nuclear Forces Treaty by a vote of 93–5 in 1988; it rejected more than a dozen killer amendments, including one that required removal of U.S. troops from Europe after withdrawal of U.S. missiles. Still others seek to protect domestic economic interests, reassert senatorial powers, or make a policy statement. An example of the latter is the 1997 Chemical Warfare Convention, which directed the secretary of defense to increase U.S. military ability to operate in areas contaminated by chemical or biological weapons.

Finally, note that the president and the Senate may continue to clash over the provisions of a treaty long after senatorial advice and consent have been given. A key issue here is the power to interpret treaty language that could potentially change the meaning of the treaty. A significant presidential-congressional clash over the language of the Antiballistic Missile (ABM) Treaty spanned three presidencies. The centerpiece of the dispute was whether a president could reinterpret the language of a treaty without congressional approval. President Reagan did so when he asserted that his administration could legally test elements of the proposed Strategic Defense Initiative shield. The controversy continued when the Clinton administration approached Russia about modifying the language of the treaty to permit the deployment of mobile defensive systems against intermediate missiles. Senate leaders responded that the administration should not try to put any change into effect without the approval of the Senate. The Clinton administration ultimately conceded this point and recognized the Senate's right to review the revised treaty language. President George W. Bush formally withdrew the United States from the ABM Treaty in June 2002. Thirty-one members of Congress unsuccessfully brought legal action against his administration, asserting that the president lacked the constitutional power to do so. President Trump withdrew the United States from two international treaties that the Senate had given its consent to: the Open Skies Treaty and the Intermediate Nuclear Forces Treaty.

### *The Role of the House*

Under the Constitution, the House is a spectator in the treaty-making process. It has no formal role. This is changing, as the House has seized on its budgetary powers as the vehicle for making its voice heard. Treaties are not always self-executing. They typically require enabling legislation and the expenditure of funds before their provisions take effect. The Constitution gives the House control over the budget and, in the process, the ability to undo agreements between the Senate and the president.

A case in point is the Panama Canal Treaties. According to one observer, the House came quite close to destroying them by inserting language into the implementing legislation that disagreed with and contradicted parts of one of the treaties just approved by the Senate by identical 68–32 votes.[8] Primary jurisdiction over the implementing legislation was held by the Merchant Marine and Fisheries Committee; its chair opposed the treaty and proposed his own version of the implementing legislation. Eventually, the Carter administration found it necessary to abandon its own bill in favor of the committee bill. This angered Panamanian leaders, who cited almost thirty articles of the House bill that violated provisions of the negotiated treaty. Final congressional approval was given to the implementing legislation only four days before the treaty was scheduled to take effect.

## Appointment Powers

As originally envisioned, the power to approve or reject presidential appointments was closely related to the power to give advice and consent to treaties. By exercising a voice about the persons negotiating a treaty, the Senate could influence its content. In practice, this linkage was never fully put into place, and it has long since unraveled. The Senate has failed to exercise its confirmation powers actively or systematically. Frequently, it has not hesitated to approve ambassadors appointed solely for political purposes and without any other apparent qualifications for the post. This practice is heavily criticized by Foreign Service professionals due to appointees' lack of expertise. However, it is defended by others, who argue that political appointees bring more political clout to the position of ambassador than careerists and can therefore be of value to the president. Typically, 30 percent of ambassadorial positions now go to political appointees or noncareerists. During the Reagan administration, this number reached a high of 38 percent. Under Clinton and Carter, it fell to 27 percent, and in 2019 it rose to 49 percent in the Trump administration before falling to 40 percent. Typically, many ambassadors are major campaign contributors. Obama's political ambassadorial appointments had given $13.6 million to Democratic campaigns. Biden reduced this number to 33 percent, with most of these being "campaign bundlers" who raised over $100,000 in his election campaign.

The impact of polarization in Congress was very much in evidence in the difficulty Biden had in getting the Senate to approve his nominees to be ambassadors. In October 2021, only four ambassadors had been approved (all of them former senators or their widow). Republican senator Ted Cruz had blocked the remainder as part of his political battle with the Biden administration to force a vote on sanctioning Russia for the Nord Stream 2 gas pipeline from Russia to Germany. In December 2021, on the final day the Senate met for the year, a deal was struck. In January a vote would be taken on Cruz's sanctions bill, and in return nearly fifty ambassadors would be approved.

## War Powers

The war powers of the Constitution are split into three parts. Congress is given the power to declare war and the power to raise and maintain an army and a navy. Presidents are designated as commander in chief of the armed forces. In the abstract, these powers fit together very nicely. In practice, their exact meaning is unclear. Alexander Hamilton saw this grant of presidential power as a symbolic grant of power, with the actual power to decide military strategy and tactics held by professional soldiers. Many presidents have taken this grant of power quite literally. Franklin Roosevelt participated actively in formulating military strategy and tactics during World War II, and Lyndon Johnson took part in selecting bombing targets during Vietnam.

A further complicating factor is defining when a state of war exists. Is it any instance where U.S. troops are placed into combat, or must a war be declared into existence? In its Prize Cases decision of 1862, the Supreme Court ruled that the existence of a war was found in the prevailing conditions and not in a formal congressional declaration. U.S. practice has borne this out. Out of the over 125 "wars" that the United States has fought, Congress has declared only five: the War of 1812, the Spanish-American War, the Mexican War, World War I, and World War II.

The most visible means available to Congress in trying to limit the president's use of force is the 1973 **War Powers Resolution** (see the "Historical Lesson"), which was passed over President Nixon's veto. It requires the president to:

1. "In every possible instance," consult with Congress before committing U.S. troops in "hostilities or into situations where imminent involvement in hostilities" is likely.
2. Inform Congress within forty-eight hours after the introduction of troops if there has been no declaration of war.
3. Remove U.S. troops within sixty days (or ninety days in special circumstances) if Congress does not either declare war or adopt a concurrent resolution approving the action.

Congress also can terminate U.S. military involvement before the sixty-day limit by passing a concurrent resolution. Such a resolution does not require the president's signature and therefore cannot be vetoed.

## Historical Lesson

### War Powers Act

The 1973 War Powers Resolution is the starting point for most contemporary discussions about the proper relationship between Congress and the president. It was a highly controversial piece of legislation when passed and continues to be so today. The bill was passed over President Nixon's veto, and no president has yet recognized its constitutionality. Members of Congress and scholars have called for its repeal. Others have proposed amendments.

Crises in both foreign policy and domestic policy provided a highly charged backdrop for a multiyear political tug-of-war between Nixon, the House, and the Senate over the question of placing limits on the president's ability to deploy troops into combat without prior consultation with Congress. The principal foreign policy crisis was the Vietnam War. In the 1964 Gulf of Tonkin Resolution, Congress provided President Lyndon Johnson with the authority to take "all necessary measures" to repel any armed attack against the forces of the United States and to prevent further aggression. The facts of the Gulf of Tonkin incident, in which U.S. naval vessels were attacked by North Vietnamese forces, remain contested even today. Johnson maintained that he did not need this congressional endorsement to carry out the U.S. war effort.

Nixon took the same position in continuing and expanding the war to include the 1970 invasion of Cambodia. On the domestic scene, increased opposition to the Vietnam War and controversies surrounding the 1972 presidential election campaign created an electrifying political atmosphere that spurred congressional efforts to control presidential war powers. One incident was the 1972 Watergate break-in at the Democratic Party headquarters and subsequent efforts to cover it up. A second was the October 1973 Saturday Night Massacre in which Nixon's attorney general and his deputy both refused to fire Archibald Cox, the special prosecutor appointed to investigate the Watergate affair. Both of them, along with Cox, resigned in protest.

The Senate acted first. In 1969 it passed a resolution proclaiming that U.S. forces could not be committed to combat "only from affirmative action taken by the executive and legislative branches . . . by means of a treaty, statue, or concurrent resolution." In 1970, the House approved legislation requiring presidents, after placing troops into combat, to report to Congress on the circumstances leading to this action and its military scope. A House Foreign Affairs subcommittee considered seventeen war powers bills and resolutions in putting forward the bill. No prior approval from Congress was required. The House passed the legation by a 288–39 vote. Congress adjourned without the Senate taking any action.

In 1971, the House again passed this legislation. The Senate Foreign Relations Committee took up the proposed House bill, but its approach to limiting presidential war-making power was quite different. The legislation sent forward by the Senate specified conditions under which a president could commit troops to combat without congressional approval and set a time limit for how long such a deployment could last. The competing House and Senate bills eventually went to a conference committee, but only one meeting took place and Congress adjourned without reaching an agreement.

In 1972, both the House and Senate acted quickly to reintroduce their respective war powers legislation. Significant points of disagreement remained, including limitations on the president's right to send troops into combat without prior consent and the president's time line for reporting to Congress. The House had a 120-day reporting deadline, while the Senate's deadline was 30 days. In July, the competing versions of the bill again went to a conference committee. On October 4 it emerged from committee and was approved by both the House (238–123) and the Senate (75–20). As promised, President Nixon vetoed the bill on October 24. There was no doubt that the Senate would vote to override Nixon's veto. The House vote was less certain. Presented as pitting congressional power against presidential power, the House voted to override Nixon's veto by four votes; eighteen House members who had voted against the bill nevertheless voted to override Nixon's veto, while fifteen who supported the bill supported Nixon's veto.

From the outset, the War Powers Resolution has been controversial. Senator Jacob Javits saw in it the basis for a new foreign policy compact between the president and Congress. Senator Thomas Eagleton, originally a supporter of the legislation with Javits, voted against it because he claimed that it gave the president powers he never had—the power to commit U.S. troops abroad without prior congressional approval.

## Applying the Lesson

1. What does the War Powers Resolution case reveal about Congress's ability to influence the use of military force by the president?
2. Which is preferable: the War Powers Resolution or an Authorization of the Use of Military Force? Why?
3. What is the proper role of Congress in making decisions about the use of military force?

Presidents have submitted over 168 reports to Congress referencing the War Powers Resolution.[9] In 110 of these cases they were forty-eight-hour reports involving the new entry of U.S. forces rather than a report of an ongoing situation. Biden submitted two reports in 2020, both involving the use of force in Syria. Trump submitted five reports, and Obama submitted

| **Table 6.2** | **Stated Purpose or Mission of Use of Force by Presidents, Forty-Eight-Hour Reports (through December 31, 2019)** | |
|---|---|---|
| Respond to Threat | | 20 |
| Protect U.S. Citizens/Property | | 17 |
| Evacuation | | 16 |
| Rescue/Hostage Recovery | | 4 |
| Humanitarian | | 15 |
| Stabilization | | 19 |
| Advise/Assist | | 13 |
| Other | | 1 |

*Source:* Tess Bridgeman, *Presidential Practice and the Use of Armed Forces Abroad, 1973–2019*, War Powers Resolution Reporting Project, January 2020.

twenty-eight reports.[10] As seen in the rationales cited by presidents in table 6.2, not all uses of force are equal in their purposes and objectives.

In submitting their reports, presidents have not recognized the constitutionality of the War Powers Resolution. In reporting the Mayaguez rescue operation in 1975, President Gerald Ford stated that he was "taking note" of the War Powers Resolution but that he acted on the basis of his commander-in-chief powers. In 2011, President Obama used language frequently employed by past presidents when he did not seek congressional approval in establishing the no-fly zone in Libya. In his notification to Congress, he stated that "this is a limited . . . operation which does fall in the president's authority" and that he was informing Congress "consistent" with the War Powers Resolution.

One source of presidential hostility to the War Powers Resolution is the provision granting Congress the right to terminate hostilities after they have begun through the use of a **legislative veto**. It allows Congress to approve or disapprove executive branch actions after the fact, in a form short of legislation. In addition to the War Powers Resolution, Congress has inserted legislative vetoes into a wide range of foreign policy legislation, including arms sales and the export of nuclear fuel and facilities.[11] Presidents have maintained that only congressional action approved by the president or passed by Congress over a presidential veto is legally binding. On January 23, 1983, in a landmark case, the Supreme Court agreed with the presidential interpretation in making its ruling in *U.S. v. Chadha*. The closest that the legislative veto came to being used was with the transfer of nuclear material to India in 1980 and the sale of an AWACS and F-15 enhancement package to Saudi Arabia in 1981.

Another sore point with presidents is the sixty-day time limit imposed by the War Powers Resolution. Presidents have challenged the time limit on constitutional grounds and ignored it in practice. In 1999, for example, U.S. military operations in Kosovo passed the sixtieth day. Bill Clinton did not seek a thirty-day extension. Thirty-two members of Congress and others brought the case to court to try to block continued military action. The court ruled that they did not have legal standing and dismissed the case. A more recent controversy over the sixty-day limit came during the Obama administration; it argued that no report back to Congress was necessary since the operations being conducted in Libya did not qualify as "engaging in hostilities."

The War Powers Resolution is not the only legislative document that presidents have at their disposal related to the use of military force. Another is the Authorization for Use of Military Force (AUMF). The most frequently invoked AUMF was issued after the 9/11 attacks. It gave presidents the authority to "use all necessary and appropriate force against anyone who committed or aided the attacks of September 11, 2001, or harbored such an organization or person in order to prevent a future attack." As passed, it is of unlimited geographic scope and duration.

By February 2018, AUMFs had been cited by presidents as the justification for forty-one military operations in nineteen countries, beginning with Operation Desert Storm against Iraq in 1991. An excerpt of the most recent AUMF authorization, made in 2002 during the Iraq War, appears in box 6.1. An AUMF permitting Obama to use military force in Syria was introduced in 2015 but never came up for a vote. In 2022, Representative Adam Kinzinger introduced a joint AUMF resolution that would permit the use of force to defend Ukraine.

Presidents do not see a universal need for AUMFs. When questioned about military deaths in Niger in 2017, the Trump administration's position was that an AUMF was not necessary since the presence of U.S. forces was permitted by separate legislation related to training and assistance missions. Obama rejected the need for an AUMF in participating in the 2013 responsibility to protect (R2P) UN intervention in Libya that removed Gaddafi from power, arguing that it did not constitute a military hostilities situation. Biden supported an unsuccessful repeal of the 2002 AUMF.

## Commerce Powers

The Constitution gives Congress the power to regulate commerce with foreign nations. In theory, this power belongs exclusively to Congress. In practice, power sharing between the two branches has been necessary. Congress may have the power to regulate foreign commerce, but only the president has the power to negotiate treaties.

Power sharing in the area of commerce has produced cooperation and conflict. The first innovative power-sharing arrangement was the 1934 Trade Agreements Act, by which Congress delegated to the president the authority to "implement into domestic law the results of trade agreements as they relate to tariffs." This authority greatly enhanced the president's power position in multilateral trade negotiations; it removed the threat of congressional obstructionism in the formal approval and implementation of the negotiated agreement. Congress periodically renewed this grant of authority for a succession of presidents, changing only the time frame and permitted value of the reduction and inserting legislative veto provisions.

The Trade Reform Act of 1974 introduced the second major innovative power-sharing arrangement when it created a *fast-track* reporting procedure; Congress was required to vote yes or no on trade legislation that came before it within ninety days and was prohibited from adding any amendments. Presidents often have found it difficult to obtain this negotiating authority, now renamed **trade promotional authority**. Proponents of fast-track authority argue that, without it, countries are unwilling to enter into agreements with the United States, since Congress may reject or amend the agreements. Fast-track authority is also seen as valuable because it protects Congress from domestic trade protectionist pressures. Critics are concerned that presidents will sacrifice environmental

> **Box 6.1**
>
> ### Excerpt: House Resolution Authorizing the Use of Military Force against Iraq, October 2, 2002
>
> #### Section 1
>
> This joint resolution may be cited as the "Authorization for the Use of Military Force against Iraq."
>
> #### Section 2: Support for United States Diplomatic Efforts
>
> The Congress of the United States supports the efforts by the president to:
>
> a. strictly enforce through the United Nations Security Council all relevant Security Council resolutions applicable to Iraq and encourages him in those efforts; and
> b. obtain prompt and decisive action by the Security Council to ensure that Iraq abandons its strategy of delay, evasion and noncompliance and promptly and strictly complies with all relevant Security Council resolutions.
>
> #### Section 3: Authorization for Use of United States Armed Forces
>
> a. Authorization. The president is authorized to use the Armed Forces of the United States as he determines to be necessary and appropriate in order to
>
>    1. defend the national security of the United States against the continuing threat posed by Iraq; and
>    2. enforce all relevant United Nations Security Council Resolutions regarding Iraq.
>
> b. Presidential determination. In connection with the exercise of the authority granted in subsection (a) to use force the president shall, prior to such exercise or as soon thereafter as may be feasible, but no later than 48 hours after exercising such authority, make available to the Speaker of the House of Representatives and the president pro tempore of the Senate his determination that
>
>    1. reliance by the United States on further diplomatic or other peaceful means alone either (A) will not adequately protect the national security of the United States against the continuing threat posed by Iraq or (B) is not likely to lead to enforcement of all relevant United Nations Security Council resolutions regarding Iraq, and
>    2. acting pursuant to this resolution is consistent with the United States and other countries continuing to take the necessary actions against international terrorists and terrorist organizations, including those nations, organizations or persons who planned, authorized, committed or aided the terrorist attacks that occurred on Sept. 11, 2001.
>
> c. War powers resolution requirements:
>
>    1. Specific statutory authorization. Consistent with section 8(a)(1) of the War Powers Resolution, the Congress declares that this section is intended to constitute specific statutory authorization within the meaning of section 5(b) of the War Powers Resolution.
>    2. Applicability of other requirements. Nothing in this resolution supersedes any requirement of the War Powers Resolution.
>
> #### Section 4: Reports to Congress
>
> a. The president shall, at least once every 60 days, submit to the Congress a report on matters relevant to this joint resolution, including actions taken pursuant to the exercise of authority granted in section 2 and the status of planning for efforts that

are expected to be required after such actions are completed, including those actions described in section 7 of Public Law 105338 (the Iraq Liberation Act of 1998).

b. To the extent that the submission of any report described in subsection (a) coincides with the submission of any other report on matters relevant to this joint resolution otherwise required to be submitted to Congress pursuant to the reporting requirements of

Public Law 93-148 (the War Powers Resolution), all such reports may be submitted as a single consolidated report to the Congress.

c. To the extent that the information required by section 3 of Public Law 102-1 is included in the report required by this section, such report shall be considered as meeting the requirements of section 3 of Public Law 102-1.

protection, food safety, intellectual property rights, and labor standards in the name of furthering free trade.

Bill Clinton was forced to allow his fast-track authority to lapse as part of the political price for Senate ratification of the treaty establishing the World Trade Organization. In December 2001, the House of Representatives passed a bill restoring fast-track authority to George W. Bush by a vote of 215–214. In 2015, Obama succeeded in obtaining fast-track authority for a three-year period, which was seen as necessary to gain approval of the Trans-Pacific Partnership (TPP) then being negotiated. Soon after becoming president, Donald Trump announced his intention to withdraw from the TPP and initially showed little interest in gaining fast-track authority. This changed when a successor agreement to NAFTA, the United States–Mexico–Canada Trade Agreement (USMCA), was under negotiation. In July 2018, Congress approved a three-year extension of fast-track authority with little controversy. The House approved the USMCA by a vote of 385–41. The Senate followed suit and approved it 89–10. The USMCA went into effect on July 1, 2020.

# Congressional Structure and Foreign Policy

The four constitutionally based powers are brought to bear on foreign policy problems through Congress's internal structure and its standard operating procedures. This section highlights four important by-products of these features: reliance on blunt foreign policy tools, the absence of a single voice that can speak for Congress, the presence of policy entrepreneurs, and significant power possessed by staff aides.

## Blunt Foreign Policy Tools

Foremost among the tools for influencing policy on which Congress relies are its general legislative, budgetary, and oversight powers. Although these powers are formidable, Congress often finds itself frustrated in its efforts to fine-tune U.S. foreign policy or to give it a new sense of direction because of their bluntness and essentially negative character.

*General Legislative Powers*

Four basic forms of congressional action exist:

- *simple resolution*, a statement made by one house
- *concurrent resolution*, a statement passed by both houses
- *joint resolution*, a statement made by both houses that if signed by the president becomes law
- *legislative bill*, passed by both houses and signed by the president

Congress can override the president's veto of joint resolutions and legislative bills. This occurred just prior to the 2016 presidential election, when the Senate voted 97–1 and the House voted 348–77 to override Obama's veto of a bill that would allow families of those killed in the 9/11 attacks to sue Saudi Arabia if it were found to have aided al-Qaeda. Obama had opposed the bill for setting a possibly dangerous precedent that other countries might use against the United States in response to military or intelligence activities. Congress failed to override Trump's presidential veto of joint resolutions to block $8.1 billion in arms sales to Saudi Arabia and the United Arab Emirates that he authorized by using emergency powers in the Arms Export Control Act.

An early post–World War II study of Congress found that, while presidential policy proposals were primarily presented as bills, congressionally initiated actions tended to be expressed as simple resolutions.[12] The challenges facing legislation originating in Congress is illustrated by the fate of comprehensive immigration reform. The foundational law governing U.S. immigration and citizenship policy is the 1952 McCarran-Walter Act. It was vetoed by President Truman for being un-American and discriminatory and was then passed over his veto. The last comprehensive immigration reform legislation passed by Congress occurred in 1986 during the Reagan administration. Both George W. Bush and Barack Obama identified comprehensive immigration reform as high-priority items and failed.

**Barnacles** is the term often used to describe the amendments that Congress attaches to foreign policy legislation sought by the president.[13] One type of barnacle is *earmarking*, or designating funds contained within a piece of legislation for a specific country. Foreign aid earmarks for Israel are among the most prominent and recurring examples of funds designated for specific purposes. For example, the December 2010 budget resolution directed that $205 million be given to Israel to help construct a missile defense system. A different type of barnacle can be found in the House 2014 budget bill. It forbade the Obama administration from spending funds to transfer detainees at Guantanamo Bay to the United States, and from U.S. military involvement in Syria unless approved by Congress.

*Budgetary Powers*

In fall 2017, press reports observed that "rank and file senators are eyeing the annual defense bill . . . as a chance to challenge President Trump's recent controversial moves on national security." When the budget was passed in March 2018, it was described as a "broad rebuke" to Trump's policy agenda. While providing him with a sizable increase in funding for the military, Trump was prohibited from building a concrete wall along the Mexican border. Instead, money was provided for thirty-three miles of fencing, which had already been authorized under previous legislation. The budget bill also rejected Trump's proposed 30 percent cut in State Department funding and the administration's request to start a new round of base closures, as well as more money for specific pieces of military hardware.

In December 2021, Biden signed the $768 billion National Defense Authorization Act. It was $25 billion more than Biden had requested in an earlier proposed budget act, which was rejected by Congress out of concern that it did not sufficiently counter Russian and Chinese military buildups. The bill includes $7.1 billion for a Pacific Deterrence Initiative designed to help defend Taiwan, $300 million for assistance to Ukraine, and $4 billion of the European Defense Initiative. In signing the bill, Biden also stated his opposition to several provisions that he defined as "constitutional concerns or questions of construction." They included restricting the use of funds to transfer or release individuals detained at the Guantanamo Bay Detention Center. His administration had plans to close the detention center.

Undercutting the perception that Congress can use its budgetary powers to influence policy is the reality that these powers are difficult to use because of how the budget is constructed. Authorization decisions are made separately by the committees with legislative jurisdiction over the relevant policy areas. Appropriations decisions are made by the House and Senate appropriations committees and their subcommittees. The omnibus spending bill passed by the House in January 2014 comprised funds found in twelve different spending bills.

Three problems for foreign and defense policy stand out:

1. *Coherence.* In 2015, the Senate passed a $600 billion defense policy bill authorizing the sale of lethal offensive weapons to Ukraine. It then voted down a bill authorizing the government to spend money to pay for it.
2. *Inconsistency in application.* Foreign aid allocated by the State Department comes under far more scrutiny than aid distributed by the Pentagon. In Afghanistan, the State Department had to verify, among other things, that the programs were sustainable and transparent and that the Afghan government was taking steps to reduce corruption, empower women, and protect human rights before releasing its funds. The Pentagon faced no such constraints.
3. *End runs.* The primary vehicle for end runs, the Overseas Contingency Operations (OCO) account, was created to fund temporary war-related costs in frontline states, most notably Afghanistan, Pakistan, and Iraq. However, it has been used to fund war-related operations in places such as Yemen, the Horn of Africa, and the Philippines to circumvent serious objections that might be encountered if the expenditures surfaced in other spending bills.

A second problem with using the budget as an instrument to shape the direction of U.S. foreign policy is that programs cost money, but "policies" may not. Policies are able to raise expectations, place U.S. prestige on the line, or commit the United States to a course of action in the eyes of other states. Congress tends to find that it has little choice but to support (i.e., fund) policy initiatives, at least on the surface. Senator John Kerry spoke to this point in expressing his opposition to the congressional resolution supporting the Persian Gulf War: "I hear it from one person after another—I do not want the President to look bad. . . . The President got us in this position. I am uncomfortable—but I cannot go against him."[14]

A third problem with Congress's ability to influence foreign policy lies with the implementation of congressional budgetary decisions. In 1971 Congress appropriated $700 million for a new manned bomber. The funds went unspent because the Nixon administration opposed the project. The reconstruction of Iraq provides another example of the limited ability of Congress's budgetary powers to influence the implementation of American foreign policy. In 2003, the Bush administration called for a quick infusion of money into Iraq to speed its recovery and transformation in the aftermath of the war. Yet in June 2004, just days before power was transferred to a new Iraqi government, none of the $500 million for health care, $400 million for roads and bridges, or $4.2 billion for water and sanitation improvements had been spent.

### Oversight

The term **oversight** refers to the actions of Congress regarding the bureaucratic implementation of policies. It is no easy matter. For political and bureaucratic reasons, getting presidents to reverse policies is difficult. Two general approaches exist: firefighting and police patrolling. *Firefighting oversight* occurs after the fact.[15] Firefighting investigations often take on a highly charged political atmosphere, as is evidenced by congressional hearings into the rapid and disorganized exit from Afghanistan. Earlier examples include investigations into the 2012 attack on the U.S. government buildings in Benghazi and into Russian interference in the 2016 presidential election. The latter case is discussed in box 6.2.

*Police patrolling* is oversight carried out on a regular basis to keep informed about an ongoing situation and to anticipate problems. It can be carried out in public sessions, such as one by the Senate Armed Services Committee in 2017 on foreign cyber threats, or closed-door briefings, such as those on Syria's civil war and North Korea's nuclear program. It can also be carried out by congressional visits to foreign policy hot spots. The purpose here is often twofold. On the one hand it seeks to obtain information. It also may seek to strengthen its political hand in decision making, either for Congress as a whole or for one party. Numerous congressional trips were made to Ukraine for these purposes. Congressional trips can also raise political concerns, such as when House Speaker Nancy Pelosi expressed interest in going to Taiwan in 2022, the Biden administration objected for fear of antagonizing China. Pelosi was not the first member of Congress to visit Taiwan, and her arrival produced an angry response from China announcing that military exercises near Taiwan would take place and claiming that her visit violated the United States' one-China policy. Biden stated that there was no change in U.S. policy.

In addition to holding briefings, Congress often establishes **reporting requirements** that must be met. Three major types are used. One standard tool is to require government agencies to provide periodic reports on their activities and events abroad. The State Department must submit a number of annual reports. Numbered among them are ones on human rights, terrorism, religious freedom, and narcotics control. Typically, countries identified as not meeting U.S. performance standards in a policy area must be recertified in order to qualify for foreign aid and trade preferences. As will be discussed in chapter 10 on diplomacy, in the Trump administration many of these reports became extremely controversial because of changes made that later were reversed under Biden.

Box 6.2

## Investigating Russia's Involvement in the 2016 Presidential Election

Oversight is one of Congress's most fundamental powers in exercising its voice in foreign policy. One of the most difficult challenges in using that power is getting members of Congress to agree about what to investigate and what conclusions to draw. This was quite evident in the House Intelligence Committee hearings into Russian involvement in the 2016 presidential election. For Democrats, the main issue was Russian meddling through social media and interactions with the Trump campaign. For Republicans, the primary concern was the behavior of the FBI and intelligence agencies in carrying out its investigation of Russian links to the Trump campaign. Particularly controversial during this investigation were the actions of committee chair Devin Nunes (R-CA); he collaborated with White House officials to secretly examine classified intelligence files, which revealed that Trump and his campaign had been caught up in the FBI surveillance operations. Nunes then briefed Trump on this information and went public with it.

The House report, issued by the Republican majority without Democratic input, found no evidence of collusion or coordination between the Trump campaign and Russian operatives. It also found "significant intelligence tradecraft failings." The Democratic rebuttal stated that the Department of Justice had provided the Foreign Intelligence Surveillance Court, which approves domestic covert intelligence gathering, with "contemporaneous evidence" of Russia's interference in the 2016 election and information related to Russian links and outreach to Trump campaign officials.

The controversy did not end there. It continued after Justice Department special counsel Robert Mueller III finished his two-year investigation into Russian interference in the 2016 presidential election. His report charged thirty-four people, including seven Russian nationals. He obtained guilty pleas from seven individuals, including several from the Trump administration. The Mueller Report did not find sufficient evidence to charge the Trump presidential campaign with conspiring

with Russia to influence the election, but did present evidence that Russia spread disinformation in a systematic fashion over social media and stole and disseminated personal emails from Clinton campaign officials. While arguing that sitting presidents cannot be charged with wrongdoing through the criminal justice system, it also presented evidence of the Trump administration's efforts to block the investigation. In his testimony before the House Judiciary and Intelligence Committees on July 24, 2019, Mueller reaffirmed that his report did not totally exonerate President Trump or say that there was no obstruction. Mueller also warned that Russia was preparing to interfere in the 2020 presidential election.

Mueller's testimony was reinforced by the release of the first of four volumes of a highly redacted investigative report by the Senate Intelligence Committee. A later volume will examine Russia's use of social media. The report concluded that all fifty states had been targeted by Russia in the 2016 presidential election in what it termed "an unprecedented level of activity against state election infrastructure." This included the ability to change or delete voter data in Illinois. The Intelligence Committee report went on to conclude that Russia and other adversaries would seek to interfere in the 2020 elections, and that other countries were working to replicate what Russia had done.

These hearings and reports did not lay an immediate foundation for congressional action. At the time they were released, the Democrat-controlled House had just passed legislation that would provide states with hundreds of millions of dollars in grants to improve election security. Senate majority leader Mitch McConnell has blocked Senate consideration of the bill, arguing that it is highly partisan, built around the conspiracy theory of Trump's collaboration with Russia, and that it ignores the progress made in correcting the Obama administration's failure to prevent Russian interference.

A second type of reporting requirement is a onetime report. For example, in the 1986 Anti-Apartheid Act, Congress identified ten issues on which it wanted the president to furnish information. The third type is notification that a particular type of foreign policy action has been or will be taken. Most of these reports do not concern politically charged issues, but on occasion they do. Recently, reporting issues have arisen around military operations. The National Defense Authorization Act for Fiscal Year 2018 (Defense Bill for short) required the secretary of defense to promptly submit written notices to congressional defense committees of any sensitive military cyber operations no later than forty-eight hours after they are carried out.

One long-standing sensitive reporting policy area involves covert action. Initially, there was little if any meaningful congressional control over the CIA. When asked if the committee he chaired had approved funding for a thirty-six-thousand-man "secret" army in Laos, Senator Allen Ellender, chairperson of the Senate Appropriations CIA subcommittee, replied, "I did not know anything about it. . . . I never asked. . . . It never dawned on me to ask about it. I did see it published in the newspaper some time ago."[16]

Beginning in 1974, Congress's attitude toward the intelligence community began to change.[17] One factor prompting the new outlook was a series of revelations about CIA wrong-doing and excess. The two most publicized events were one implicating the CIA in a desta-bilization campaign directed at bringing down the socialist government of Salvador Allende in Chile, and another including allegations that the CIA had violated its charter by under-taking surveillance of U.S. citizens inside the United States. In their aftermath, Congress passed the Hughes-Ryan Amendment to the 1974 Foreign Assistance Act. The amendment required that, except under exceptional circumstances, the CIA must inform members of six congressional committees "in a timely fashion of the nature and scope of any CIA operation conducted for purposes other than obtaining information."

According to the terms of the Hughes-Ryan Amendment, the president was also required to make a "finding" that each covert operation is important to national security. **Presidential findings** have included such information as the time and duration of the activity, the risks involved, funding restrictions, their relationship to prior National Security Council (NSC) decisions, policy considerations, and proposal origin.[18] This has not always meant that Congress has been well informed. The presidential finding for the Iran arms transfers carried out by the NSC was signed after the operation began, and Director of Central Intelligence William Casey was instructed not to inform Congress. The 1975 presidential finding supporting U.S. activities in Angola was so vague that the entire continent of Africa was identified as the location of the operation.[19]

## The Absence of a Single Voice

Traditionally, the work of Congress has been done in committees. It is here that political deals are made and the technical details of legislation are worked out. Congress, as a whole, was expected to quietly and expeditiously give its consent to committee decisions; more often than not, it did. Beginning in the early 1970s, the focus of decision making shifted from the full committee to the subcommittee. The result has been an even greater decentralization of Congress in a number of different ways.

First, the executive branch must give increased attention to the foreign policy views of all members of Congress, because foreign-policy-relevant legislation now springs from a greater variety of sources. As one State Department official put it, "It used to be that all one had to do was contact the chairman and a few ranking members of a committee, now all 435 members plus 100 senators have to be contacted."[20] In 2000, legislation allowing the sale of food to Cuba was part of an agricultural spending bill. A prohibition on spending funds for planning related to the Kyoto Protocol was inserted as an amendment to an appropriations bill for the Environmental Protection Agency.

Second, there is the growing tendency for prospective pieces of legislation to be referred to more than one committee. Multiple referrals are necessary because of the lack of fit between the jurisdictions of congressional committees and policy areas. At least three Senate committees and seven subcommittees claim jurisdiction over cybersecurity. A dozen Senate committees are involved in foreign economic policy, and nearly fifty subcommittees are involved in foreign policy regarding the Third World.[21]

## Policy Entrepreneurship

A change in attitude has accompanied the trend toward increasing decentralization. Policy individualism has replaced party loyalty as the motivation behind much congressional action. As a result, the long-standing congressional norms of deference and apprenticeship have been replaced by expectations of power sharing and policy input. *Entrepreneurship* is the label frequently attached to this new outlook. A **policy entrepreneur** is someone who is looking for opportunities to make political capital out of policy gaps.[22] Many saw policy entrepreneurship at play in the establishment of a select committee to investigate the Benghazi attacks six months before the midterm elections. This perception was reinforced by comments made by Republican House majority leader Kevin McCarthy; he stated that the hearings had achieved the desired result because Hillary Clinton's positive image in polls had declined.

The entrepreneur is different from the traditional foreign policy **gadfly**, someone who raises issues to influence the terms of the policy debate and is concerned with long-term policy gains.[23] Gadflies are found across the political spectrum. Among the most outspoken gadflies of late have been John McCain and Ron Paul. Before his death, McCain was identified as the "critic in chief" of the Trump administration's foreign policy. Paul has been a leading congressional critic of the NSA electronic surveillance program and the presidential use of military power without explicit congressional approval.

## Staff Aides

A shortage of information has always been a problem for Congress when it comes to making foreign policy. Few members can hope to acquire the background and expertise to understand the full range of topics that may come before them. They rely heavily on staff aides for information. The number of staff aides has grown dramatically. In 1947, there were roughly five hundred committee staffers and two thousand personal staffers. By the 1990s, the House was employing some eleven thousand staffers and the Senate another six thousand. The major House and Senate foreign policy committees (Armed Services and Foreign Affairs/Foreign Relations) each have over fifty staffers.

The emergence of numerous and well-informed staff aides has given the problem a new focus.[24] Concerns have been expressed about (1) whether the staffers are serving Congress or just leading willing members from issue to issue, and (2) whether an activist staff might be overloading Congress with new issues, robbing it of the time needed for debate and deliberation. Congress as a whole has also increased its information-gathering and information-processing capabilities by establishing or increasing the size of the Congressional Research Service (established in 1914), the Government Accountability Office (which dates back to 1921 under a different name), and the Congressional Budget Office (established in 1974). Representatives and senators can also draw on the products of private nonprofit research institutes and think tanks (see chapter 5) such as the Brookings Institution, the Cato Institute, and the Heritage Foundation.[25] Until the 1970s, think tanks were relatively few in number. Today, they are prominent fixtures on the Washington, DC, political landscape.

## Influence of Party and Region

It is clear that Congress's difficulty in speaking with one voice on foreign policy greatly complicates its efforts at efficiency. This difficulty is brought into even greater focus by examining the influence of party and region on foreign policy decisions. The overwhelming majority of votes occur along party lines, a tendency that has become more pronounced since the 1980s. One area in which partisanship appears to surpass all other factors in influencing congressional involvement in foreign policy involves control of presidential war powers. The single best predictor of whether Congress will remain quiet or vocally oppose presidential calls for the use of force is its partisan composition. When the opposition party is in control, Congress raises its voice.

Strong as it may be, party affiliation cannot withstand all of the competing pressures facing representatives and senators when they vote. Splits within the Republican and Democratic parties are a recurring problem. In the late 1990s, senior Republican leaders embraced an internationalist outlook rooted in Cold War foreign policy triumphs, while more junior Republicans tended to have a different worldview.[26] They opposed supporting loan guarantees to Mexico and expensive new weapons systems, favored privatization of foreign aid, and showed little interest in bipartisan resolutions supporting the president in Bosnia or elsewhere.

The arrival of Tea Party members into Congress after the fall 2010 election accentuated this split. A revolt against Republican leadership by Tea Party members defeated legislation that would have extended the provisions of the Patriot Act for one year. The bill had to be introduced a second time to get it passed. Tea Party members also tend to be *budget hawks*, who are less willing than the party leadership as a whole to spare the defense budget from cuts. This divide was quite visible as Congress grappled with how to respond to Obama's call for a vote on military action in Syria.

The Democratic Party is beset with its own internal struggles on foreign policy, which have split conservatives and liberals. This came through quite clearly in the conflict over revelations that the National Security Agency had engaged in a covert electronic communications collection program that gathered data on Americans. Democratic senator Dianne Feinstein, chair of the Senate Intelligence Committee, strongly supported the NSA. Democratic committee members Mark Udall and Ron Wyden were vocal opponents of the program, arguing that it violated the Fourth Amendment.

Polarization is evident along two dimensions when looking at political parties in Congress today. First, each has within it competing factions, although they are not evenly split. Within the Republican Party are traditional conservative internationalists and adherents of an "America First" foreign policy. Democrats continue to be split within the party between more middle-of-the-road adherents and those on the political left. The second dimension of polarization is the combative spirit it has produced and that separates the two parties. As some put it, the political middle has hollowed out, leaving little space on which to build compromise or to establish the joint ownership of a policy, something very evident in the efforts to craft legislation.

Geographic interests are also a significant influence on congressional votes. Today, as in the past, U.S. involvement in the global economy has an uneven impact on different areas of the country, producing regional conflict over how to define the American national interest.[27] U.S. foreign policy can be seen as driven by a coalition of the South and the West, regions that benefit from a foreign policy designed to promote free trade and ensure international stability. Opposed to this view is the Northeast; although it once benefited from such policies, it now sees itself as economically disadvantaged by them and favors protectionism and cuts in defense spending. Geography and economics come together to influence foreign policy votes in other ways as well. Those representing districts negatively affected by foreign imports from oppressive regimes raise human rights issues more often than those whose districts rely more heavily on foreign markets.[28] The potential for tension between party and region was very much in evidence in the congressional Republican reaction to Trump's efforts to use tariffs as leverage in trade talks with China. Those from states with aging industries supported it; those in farming states, against whom China was retaliating with tariffs of its own, urged caution or were opposed.

Members of Congress are also especially protective of how their constituents fare in receiving government funds. In 2019, House minority leader Kevin McCarthy stopped a bipartisan effort to prevent Chinese companies from contracting with U.S. transit systems because one of those firms had a plant in his district. During the Cold War, Henry "Scoop" Jackson, who sat on the Armed Services Committee, was known as the "Senator from Boeing" for his ability to steer aircraft contracts to the Boeing Company, which was headquartered in his home state of Washington. This concern for "pork" extends beyond the committee system. At one time, the contract for the B-1 bomber had subcontracts in more than 400 of the 435 districts of the House.

## Outsourcing Foreign Policy

Congress has turned with increasing frequency to another mechanism for overcoming the many forces that impede efficiency in making policy and exercising oversight: the special commission. These may be composed of outside experts, retired government officials, or hand-picked members of Congress. Commissions deal with the inefficiency problem in a number of ways. First, the appointment of a commission represents a positive symbolic response to a perceived foreign policy problem. Second, commissions remove political pressure from policy makers by providing them with political cover for making difficult decisions. Third, commissions provide opportunities for educating the public and for information gathering that extends beyond the closed network of congressional staffers, committee and subcommittee chairs, and executive branch officials.

Commissions have been created to deal with several different types of problems. One type is formed to investigate and make recommendations on a particular policy issue or problem. The National Commission on Terrorist Attacks upon the United States (the 9/11

Commission) was this type of committee. Calls have also been heard for a similar commission to investigate the fall of Afghanistan to the Taliban and the subsequent U.S. exit. A second type is set up to investigate and report back on an ongoing problem. The Commission on Wartime Contracting is an example; of particular concern to this commission have been questions of waste, fraud, and financial abuse stemming from the increased use of private contractors in combat theaters. The third type of committee is created to provide Congress with policy options to deal with a problem. The Defense Department Base Realignment and Closure (BRAC) Commission was created for this purpose. Closing military bases is a politically unpopular decision given the economic impact on local communities. Instead of having Congress identify which bases to cut, the BRAC Commission was established. Five BRAC rounds have taken place, in 1988, 1991, 1993, 1995, and 2005. More than 350 military installations have been closed by this process.

There is nothing automatic about action on commission proposals. Many of the recommendations of the 9/11 Commission were ignored. The December 2005 "report card" issued by members of the 9/11 Commission gave the administration five Fs and twelve Ds for its follow-through in implementing its recommendations. It received only one A, for its antiterrorism finance efforts.[29] Commissions can also produce political backlash because of their recommendations. Since 2005, presidents, including Trump, have been unsuccessful in establishing a new BRAC round. Congress has forbidden the Pentagon from spending any funds "to propose, plan, or execute" the base-closing process.

Not everyone is pleased with the increasingly frequent use of commissions. In addressing the Senate in 2002 on the subject of special commissions, specifically the creation of the 9/11 Commission, Trent Lott observed that, in his opinion, congressional commissions were "an abdication of responsibility." Why, he wondered, "do we have an Armed Services Committee, an Intelligence Committee, a Government Affairs Committee, or a Foreign Affairs Committee?"[30]

## Congress and the President: The Changing Relationship

The relationship between Congress and the president is not static. One way to capture the changing relationship is by analyzing the degree to which Congress has been assertive and active in its dealings with the president on foreign policy matters.[31] Combining these two dimensions produces four patterns. A *competitive* Congress is both active and assertive in foreign policy and thus is quite willing to challenge a president's lead. A *disengaged* Congress is neither active nor assertive and tends to readily follow a president's foreign policy preferences. A *supportive* Congress is active but not aggressive. It cooperates with the president on a broad range of foreign policy initiatives without challenging him. Finally, a *strategic* Congress is not particularly active but is willing and able to challenge a president on specific issues that conflict with its foreign policy agenda.

From the end of World War II until about 1958, a *supportive Congress* existed. Relations between the two branches were largely harmonious. Bipartisanship was the order of the day. The president was the acknowledged architect of American foreign policy, and Congress's role was to reaffirm his policy initiatives and provide him with the means to act. Often its participation took on a plebiscitary character, with the passage of area resolutions such as those on the Middle East, Taiwan, and Latin America. Periods of dissent did occur, such as after the "loss of China" and during the McCarthy hearings, but overall the Cold War consensus held.

The next decade, 1958–1968, saw the emergence of a *strategic Congress*. The Cold War principles around which the earlier bipartisan consensus was built began to fray. Congress was not in open revolt against the president; proclamations of support were still present, most notably for the Gulf of Tonkin Resolution, and failures such as the Bay of Pigs invasion did not evoke partisan attacks. However, pockets of resistance formed, and Congress moved to challenge the president selectively. Two key points of confrontation were the Vietnam War and the existence of a missile gap.

From 1968 into the mid-1980s, Congress was both active and assertive. This *competitive Congress* not only sought to limit the president's ability to conduct foreign policy by passing such measures as the War Powers Resolution and the Case-Zablocki Act, but it also resisted many of the president's most important foreign policy initiatives. The Jackson-Vanik Amendment undermined Nixon's détente policy, and Carter was challenged on the Panama Canal Treaties.

The period from the mid-1980s until September 11, 2001, marked a return to a *strategic Congress*. Once again, Congress selectively engaged the president on foreign policy issues. In some cases, such as the annual vote on most favored nation status for China, the interactions became almost ritualistic. On other occasions, such as the Comprehensive Nuclear Test Ban Treaty, ratification of NAFTA, and granting of fast-track trade authority, the conflicts were highly partisan and spirited.

The terrorist attacks of 9/11 led to the emergence of a *disengaged Congress* willing to cede the authority to the president in making crucial foreign policy decisions. Nowhere is this more evident than in George W. Bush's ability to obtain an AUMF resolution from Congress against Iraq by votes of 77–23 in the Senate and 296–133 in the House. Congress was not totally compliant, but it did not challenge the president directly. Objections to the Bush administration's proposed language authorizing the president "to use all means that he determined to be appropriate" were addressed in behind-the-scenes meetings and led to mutually acceptable language being found. This disengaged Congress did not last long. It soon showed signs of moving back toward a *strategic Congress*, which by 2005 was firmly in place as Bush and Congress sparred regularly over the Iraq War.

By the end of Obama's presidency, a *competitive Congress* had reemerged, with Congress often acting in a preemptive manner, as highlighted by two examples from 2015. In March, Israeli prime minister Benjamin Netanyahu addressed a joint session of Congress at the invitation of House Speaker John Boehner. Obama was not consulted on the invitation. In his speech, Netanyahu spoke out strongly against a nuclear arms agreement with Iran. In December, after Obama promised world leaders at the Paris climate conference that the United States would be in the lead in responding to global climate change, the House joined the Senate in passing a resolution preventing the Environmental Protection Agency from enforcing tighter standards.

Trump also faced a *competitive Congress*. One area of deep competition was the Yemen War. In March 2015, Saudi Arabia and its allies began military operations in Yemen designed to restore the government that had been forced out of power by an Iranian-supported alliance. Initially the Obama administration supported the Saudi alliance's military effort. Congress had limited interest in the Yemen War. Its focus was on the Iranian nuclear agreement and ISIS in Syria. In 2017, Trump's increased support for the Saudi forces, plus a major new offensive, led to renewed congressional action. A concurrent resolution was introduced calling for an end to support for Saudi Arabia's military intervention into Yemen, but House leaders effectively blocked a vote. Instead, a vote was taken on a non-binding version expressing concern about the conflict without calling for an end to U.S. involvement. It passed by a vote of 366–30. Tension between Congress and the Trump administration continued to grow in 2018 with the introduction of a joint resolution to remove U.S. forces from conflicts that have not been authorized by Congress. The motion was tabled on a procedural vote. Matters came to a head in 2019. In February, with the Democrats now in control of the House, legislation was passed by a vote of 248–177 ending military support for Saudi Arabia. This was the first time in history that the War Powers Resolution was invoked. On April 4, the House passed that bill by a vote of 247–175. On April 16, Trump exercised the second veto of his presidency, refusing to sign the resolution. This did not end congressional attempts to end U.S. support for the Saudi bombing campaign; in September 2019, Congress inserted an amendment into the defense authorization bill for that purpose.

The competitive relationship between President Trump and Congress reached new heights in October 2019, when the House began to move forward with impeachment hearings over his conduct of foreign policy. The immediate spark was a whistleblower report related to a July 25 phone call between Trump and the president of Ukraine in which Trump sought to use his presidential powers to advance his reelection.

As seen in the "On the Agenda" section at the beginning of this chapter—with Biden's difficulty in getting Congress to authorize aid for Ukraine, the holdup in confirming his ambassadorial nominations, and congressional hearings into the exit from Afghanistan—a competitive relationship continues to exist. An added dimension to the competitive relationship was the quick call by members of both parties for sanctions against Saudi Arabia for its unexpected October 2022 decision to make deep cuts in its oil production in cooperation with OPEC and Russia.

The existence of a competitive Congress does not by definition preclude cooperation between the two branches of government. One example is the innovative way in which congressional participation was handled in approving the Iranian nuclear accord. Obama had initially claimed the authority to enter into a nuclear agreement with Iran without congressional approval. When this proved to be politically untenable, Obama agreed to a compromise. The legislation was structured in a way that would allow Congress to exercise its voice by voting its disapproval but at the same time give Obama the upper political hand since his veto would be difficult to overcome.

## Over the Horizon: A New War Powers Act?

The fundamental problem facing Congress in exercising its foreign policy voice in the future will continue to be the challenge of managing the contradictory pressures of efficiency and participation. Nowhere does this challenge appear more difficult to resolve than in the exercise of congressional and presidential war powers. The focal points of the debate over how to proceed are the requirements of the War Powers Act and the use of AUMFs to justify a wide range of military activities. Efforts to modify or end the use of these grants of presidential authority have become increasingly common in recent years.

In January 2014, Senators Tim Kaine and John McCain put forward the War Powers Consultation Act. They characterized the act as bipartisan legislation to strengthen the current ineffective consultative process between Congress and the president regarding whether and when to engage in military action. The act was based upon a 2008 bipartisan National War Powers Commission report,[32] with a number of key provisions: consultation between the president and Congress before deploying U.S. troops into significant armed conflict, the creation of a permanent Joint Congressional Consultation Committee, and a congressional yes/no vote on significant armed conflicts within thirty days. For some, this did not go far enough. In November, Senator Rand Paul called for Congress to vote on a declaration to proclaim war against ISIS. His declaration would have limited military action to one year and placed significant restrictions on the use of ground forces.

The following year, Representative Chris Gibson, along with thirty-four cosponsors, introduced a bill to reform the War Powers Resolution. Among its provisions was the requirement that in every possible instance the president must submit a written report to Congress before introducing U.S. armed forces into hostilities or situations in which involvement in hostilities is imminent. It also prohibited the use of available military forces unless specific legal or operational conditions were met.

In 2017, Senator Paul, through an amendment to the 2018 National Defense Authorization Act, sought to repeal the 2002 AUMFs used to send military forces to Afghanistan and Iraq. During congressional testimony, the Trump administration asserted that it was not interested in Congress passing a new AUMF and that, if it did, the agreement should be of unlimited duration. The amendment was tabled by a 61–36 vote.

The question of the president's right to place troops into combat situations came up again in 2019 with the Iranian crisis that was triggered by Iran's downing of a U.S. drone, which led to plans for U.S. military action that could take place without congressional approval. As the threat of war faded, Senate majority leader Mitch McConnell announced that he would permit a vote on a bipartisan amendment to the defense authorization bill currently before Congress to require congressional approval for any military action against Iran. The amendment required sixty votes to be included in that bill. It failed with a 50–40 vote. Four Republicans voted with the Democratic majority in support of the bill.

Following U.S. airstrikes authorized by Biden in 2021, Senators Kaine and Todd Young reintroduced bipartisan legislation to repeal the 1991 and 2002 AUMFs. Kaine argued that the need existed "to review and revise the way in which our leaders collectively choose whether or not to wage war. In July the House voted 268–161 to repeal the 2002 AUMF that provided justification for the Iraq War and later military campaigns. Democrats and Republicans, as well as the Biden White House, supported the repeal. The Senate, however, failed to act on the legislation. A vote had been scheduled for December, but it got pushed off the agenda under pressure to pass the defense authorization bill before Congress adjourned.

Public support for repealing the AUMF authorizations is strong. A 2022 poll found that 59 percent of all respondents favored repeal of the 2001 AUMF. Bipartisan support existed for doing so, as 65 percent of Democrats, 52 percent of Republicans, and 63 percent of independents favored repeal.[33]

## Critical Thinking Questions

1. Is there a need for a new War Powers Act? Why or why not?
2. Is party identification or geography (state or district represented) a more important influence on how members of Congress vote on foreign policy issues? Support your answer.
3. What changes would you make to Congress's internal structure and operating procedures to make its voice more effective in foreign policy?

## Key Terms

barnacles, 124
gadfly, 129
legislative veto, 120
oversight, 126
policy entrepreneur, 129

presidential finding, 128
ratify, 114
reporting requirement, 126
trade promotional authority, 121
War Powers Resolution, 118

# Presidency 7

## Learning Objectives

Students will be able to:

1. Identify the constitutional powers of the president in making foreign policy.
2. Describe the four types of presidential personality.
3. Compare the strengths and weaknesses of the different types of presidential managerial styles.
4. Assess the relative and overall importance of the "other White House voices" in making U.S. foreign policy.

## On the Agenda: Biden's First One Hundred Days

Presidential performance can be judged by any of a number of different standards. One that continues to be embraced is what they accomplished during their first one hundred days. This builds on a sense of high expectations (and sometimes fear) that a newly elected president will move quickly to implement campaign promises. The mystique surrounding a president's first one hundred days in office began with the election of Franklin Roosevelt in 1932 at the height of the Depression. In his first one hundred days, Congress passed fifteen major pieces of legislation as part of the New Deal economic recovery program. First one hundred days' performance since then has been spotty, especially in foreign policy. In this "On the Agenda," an overview of Joe Biden's first one hundred days is presented. For details on John F. Kennedy's first one hundred days in office, see the "Historical Lesson."

In his campaign for the presidency, Joe Biden promised to "bring America back to the table," reversing the U.S. exit from international organizations and agreements that took place in Donald Trump's administration and reestablishing relations with U.S. allies. On day one in office, the United States rejoined the Paris Climate Agreement. Biden also rescinded the announced withdrawal from the World Health Organization and indicated that the United States would resume its funding obligations. On day two, Biden proposed extending the New START arms control agreement with Russia that was set to expire on February 5, 2021. That agreement was extended on February 3, 2021, to stay in force through February 4, 2026. In other early actions, Biden announced that the United States would reengage with the United Nations Human Rights Council; he attended a G7 Summit virtual meeting; he hosted the first virtual meeting of the Quad, the Quadrilateral Security Dialogue (Australia, India, Japan, and the United States); and in late April he hosted an in-person meeting of the leaders of forty countries in the Leaders' Summit on Climate.

One major policy area in which Biden had promised to reverse Trump policies involved Mexican border controls and restrictions on immigration into the United States. His success in doing so was mixed. On day one Biden issued an executive order halting funding for the wall and repealed Trump's travel ban from Muslim-majority countries. A few days later his administration overturned the Trump administration's zero-tolerance policy, which had resulted in the separation of over three thousand migrant families at the Mexico-U.S. border. In early February he ordered a legal review of several immigration policies, most notably the Remain in Mexico policy. On February 14, his administration ended that policy. In August the Supreme Court ruled that it had to be reinstated while the case to prevent that from happening was under review. In June 2022 it ruled that Biden could end the program.

Also in early February, the administration announced that it would admit up to 62,500 refugees for that fiscal year with a goal of admitting 125,000 the following fiscal year. For several weeks no actions were forthcoming. No executive order was issued. Then in April the administration announced that it would keep Trump's refugee limit at 15,000. The pause and the change of direction were due to the political and economic impact of a surge in the number of individuals seeking to cross the border. Within hours Biden's decision produced another backlash from Democrats. The White House quickly reversed direction again, indicating it would support increased border crossings, but it did not specify how many would be allowed.

Biden's first one hundred days also saw him address a variety of ongoing national security issues. In late February, Biden authorized military strikes against ISIS in Syria in retaliation for rocket attacks on U.S. troops. In April, after weeks of back-channel talks, the United States and Iran agreed to begin informal talks through representatives from other countries to the nuclear arms control agreement exploring how the 2015 Joint Comprehensive Plan of Action (JCPOA) nuclear agreement that Trump withdrew from in 2018 might be rejuvenated. These new talks were suspended in December. Also in April, Biden announced that the withdrawal of U.S. forces from Afghanistan would begin on May 1 as Trump had agreed to, with September 11, 2021, the twentieth anniversary of the 9/11 terrorist attack on the United States, set as the target date for withdrawing all U.S. forces.

Relations with Russia and China were also on Biden's first-one-hundred-days agenda. On March 17, Biden referred to Russian president Vladimir Putin as "a killer" and said that he would pay a price for interfering in U.S. elections. Earlier Biden had suggested that he had little interest in improving relations with Russia. The next month Biden signed an executive order imposing widespread sanctions on Russia for the SolarWinds interference in the 2020 elections. Biden also imposed two sets of sanctions on China that month. One was directed at Chinese officials for "serious human rights abuses" against Uighur Muslims. The second was directed against Chinese and Hong Kong officials as a result of new national security laws seen as suppressing pro-democracy individuals and groups.

The historical record suggests that focusing too heavily on a president's first one hundred days is not necessarily a good indicator of what foreign policy is to come in the 1,361 days that follow. However, the standard will continue to be used and comparisons made. This chapter looks at the president and foreign policy from various perspectives to provide a better foundation for evaluation. It examines the president's constitutional powers, then turns to the president as a person and the presidency as an institution. It begins by noting the ongoing debate over whether presidents are strong or weak leaders.

### Historical Lesson

#### John F. Kennedy's First One Hundred Days

John Kennedy's first one hundred days in office were among the most active insofar as foreign policy was concerned. The results were both good and bad. Kennedy was inaugurated on January 21, 1961. Three days later he announced that, via an executive order, he was establishing the Peace Corps as a pilot program,

naming George McGovern as its director. Congress would be asked to establish it on a permanent basis.

On February 22, Kennedy sent a letter to Nikita Khrushchev, head of the Soviet Communist Party, in which he extended an invitation to hold personal talks on foreign policy matters of interest to both countries. Earlier, Khrushchev had sent Kennedy a congratulatory letter following the election. Kennedy's advisors urged him not to hold such a meeting. They feared that he would misread Khrushchev's personality and intentions. (The meeting was held in Vienna in June, after the one-hundred-day period, with Berlin and Laos as the major points of discussion. Initially the summit was seen as a diplomatic success, but that assessment soon changed. Kennedy did not fare well in the private discussions, and Khrushchev appears to have come away from the summit with the view that Kennedy was an inexperienced leader who could be outmaneuvered.)

In March, Kennedy announced an ambitious ten-year plan for economic growth and development in the Western Hemisphere. A central feature of the plan was an economic partnership between the United States and Latin American countries. This partnership became the Alliance for Progress, which officially came into existence in August 1961. The short-term impact of the Alliance for Progress was significant, as the amount of U.S. foreign aid to the region virtually tripled. Long-term assessments were not as positive, as much of the money flowing into the region benefited U.S. corporations that returned profits to the United States rather than local economies.

The most significant foreign policy decision made by Kennedy in his first one hundred days came in April 1961, when he approved the Bay of Pigs operation. It called for covert training of Cuban exiles into a paramilitary force. The force would secretly be sent back to Cuba, where it would help spawn a popular uprising designed to overthrow Castro. The plan was developed by the CIA during the Eisenhower administration's final year in office. During the 1960 presidential campaign, both Kennedy and Richard Nixon called for taking a hard-line stance against

Castro, with Kennedy asserting that Eisenhower had not done enough to end his rule. Kennedy was elected president on November 8, 1960, and on November 18 he was briefed on the invasion plan. On January 3, 1961, the Eisenhower administration broke diplomatic relations with Cuba. Kennedy was briefed again on January 28, 1961. At these briefings he called for changes in the invasion plan, one of which was to move the landing to the Bay of Pigs in order to further hide its link to the United States. At an April 12 press conference, when asked what the United States would do to help support anti-Castro Cubans, Kennedy said that the United States had no intention of intervening in Cuban affairs.

The Bay of Pigs invasion took place on April 17, 1961. Little went right. Overwhelmed by Cuban military forces, the U.S.-backed Cubans quickly surrendered. When confronted with news of the invasion's imminent collapse, Kennedy rejected calls to openly provide additional U.S. assistance. The failure was not a surprise to many. Both the chairman of the Joint Chiefs of Staff and the secretary of defense had voiced their doubts about the CIA plan, as had former secretary of state Dean Acheson and current members of Kennedy's State Department.

### Applying the Lesson

1. What standard should be used in assessing presidential performance in the first one hundred days, and why?
2. How deeply should presidents be involved in the decision-making process? Explain your answer.
3. What is more important in the first one hundred days of a presidency: continuity with the past or changing the direction of foreign policy? Explain your answer.

## Weak President or Strong President

Some see the president as a weak leader, little more than a clerk lacking the power to command others to act who must rely on the ability to persuade.[1] Far from running the government, the president struggles simply to make sense of events.[2] Information does not come to presidents automatically, nor can they count on speed and secrecy in making and carrying out decisions. In 2003, George W. Bush had a conversation with Secretary of Defense Donald Rumsfeld and Paul Bremer, who headed the Coalition Provisional Authority in Iraq. Bush asked who was in charge of finding weapons of mass destruction in Iraq. Rumsfeld said it was Bremer; Bremer said it was Rumsfeld.[3]

Others see the president as, at least potentially, a strong and powerful leader capable of taking unilateral action.[4] Being a **unilateral president** is not a matter of usurping congressional powers as much as it is taking advantage of ambiguities in the constitutional distribution of powers; the existence of vaguely worded legislative language; and the inherent difficulties that Congress, the courts, and other political competitors face in acting in a unified fashion.

## Presidential Power and Supreme Court Decisions

The Constitution is not self-interpreting; that task falls to the Supreme Court. Their decisions can both free presidents to conduct foreign policy as they wish or place limits on what they can do. In the first years of the Biden administration, the Supreme Court has made rulings that have both blocked actions it has taken to alter the Mexican border policy and supported them. As such, before looking at how presidents use their constitutional powers, we want to look at four key Supreme Court decisions that have been especially important to U.S. foreign policy. The first two increased presidential powers. The second two cases placed limits on it. A very early case was *Ware v. Hilton* (1796). In this case a treaty signed with Great Britain conflicted with a Virginia state law. The Treaty of Paris by which the United States obtained its independence required that British debts be paid. The Virginia law allowed the debt not to be paid. The Supreme Court ruled that treaties took precedence over state law. In a second case, *U.S. v. Belmont* (1937), the Supreme Court ruled that executive agreements were just as binding on states as were treaties. The case involved an agreement between the United States and Russia reestablishing diplomatic relations. At issue was a process by which the United States would take control of the bank accounts of firms nationalized by Russia and use those funds to settle claims against Russia. New York refused to do so, saying it conflicted with state laws and that no treaty had been signed. The Supreme Court ruled that executive agreements were equivalent to treaties and thus took precedence over state law.

A third case, *Youngstown Sheet and Tube Company v. Sawyer*, better known as the "Steel Seizure Case" (1952), involved a presidential effort to nationalize the steel industry after a labor strike had closed them down. President Truman issued an executive order nationalizing steel companies (and thus ending the ability of unions to strike), citing his presidential commander-in-chief powers and the need for steel because of the Korean War. The Supreme Court ruled against Truman, asserting that it found nothing in the commander-in-chief powers that permitted seizing private property. The final case is the 1971 "Pentagon Papers Case." President Nixon sought to stop the *New York Times*, the *Washington Post*, and others from continuing to publish portions of a forty-seven-volume classified Department of Defense history of the Vietnam War that Daniel Ellsberg had secretly obtained and released to the press. The Supreme Court ruled in *New York Times Co. v. United States* against the U.S. government, asserting it could find no justification for prior restraint on free speech and blocking publication.

## The President and the Foreign Affairs Constitution

The Constitution binds both the president and Congress, but over time presidents have developed a number of strategies for circumventing its restrictions. This section examines four of the most important strategies at the president's disposal: using executive agreements, issuing signing statements, employing unofficial ambassadors, and engaging in undeclared wars. This does not mean that presidents will always get their way or that their actions will go unchallenged. When Congress did not act on immigration reform, Obama issued an executive order providing deportation relief to illegal immigrants in the United States. A federal court judge ruled the order unconstitutional, and the administration was forced to appeal the case to the Supreme Court. On a tied vote, the Supreme Court held that Obama's immigration reform policy was illegal.

## Executive Agreements

From the outset, presidents have claimed the constitutional authority to engage in international agreements by means other than treaties. Over time, this alternative, known as an **executive agreement**, became the favored presidential method for entering into understandings with other states. Unlike a treaty, an executive agreement does not require the consent of the Senate before coming into force. The U.S. Supreme Court has ruled that it carries the same legal force as a treaty. The principal limit on its use is political, not legal: the fear that an angry Congress would retaliate by blocking other presidential foreign policy initiatives.

The proportion of executive agreements to treaties has increased steadily over time. Between 1789 and 1839, the United States entered into sixty treaties and twenty-seven executive agreements. A century later, between 1889 and 1939, those numbers had grown to 524 treaties and 917 executive agreements. Because Obama preferred to act through executive orders and memorandums, he did not make as much use of executive agreements as his predecessors. Midway through his last year in office, Obama had entered into 183 executive agreements, compared to 291 for George W. Bush. However, many were for high-profile foreign policy issues, such as a 2012 strategic partnership agreement with Afghanistan (establishing the outlines for U.S.-Afghanistan relations after U.S. combat forces left in 2014), the 2015 climate agreement, and the nuclear agreement with Iran.

Consistent with its America First perspective, the Trump administration has not embraced executive agreements to the extent of its predecessors, preferring instead to leave previously established agreements, such as the Asia-Pacific Trade Agreement and the Paris Climate Agreement. The major exception is Trump's pursuit of the U.S.-Mexico-Canada Agreement. A numerical comparison shows that the United States entered into seventy-six executive agreements or treaties in 2018 and only twenty-three as of June 2019. This compares to an average of just over one hundred in previous years.[5]

The Senate has attempted to curb the president's use of executive agreements on a number of occasions. Two efforts have been particularly noteworthy. The first, the **Bricker Amendment**, would have required that executive agreements receive the same two-thirds vote of approval from the Senate as treaties. In 1954, the Bricker Amendment failed by one vote to get the two-thirds Senate majority needed to set into motion the amendment ratification process at the state level.

The second was the 1972 Case-Zablocki Act, which required that Congress be informed of all executive agreements so that it could take action to block them if it saw fit.[6] This act was seen as necessary because executive agreements have not always been made public. Particularly revealing in this regard is the history of secret presidential agreements with Saudi Arabia.[7]

Both Harry Truman and John Kennedy entered into agreements to use military force to protect the Arab nation under certain conditions. However, the Case-Zablocki Act has not ended the practice of secret executive agreements. In part, the problem is definitional. In 1975, Representative Les Aspin estimated that four hundred to six hundred agreements had not yet been reported to Congress because the White House claimed that they were understandings, oral promises, or statements of political intent, not executive agreements.[8] Included among these were a 1973 secret message that President Nixon had sent to North Vietnam promising reconstruction aid in return for a peace agreement, Henry Kissinger's 1975 understanding with Israel and Egypt that U.S. personnel would be stationed in the Sinai as part of the disengagement process, and the 1975 Helsinki Accords.

## Signing Statements

Presidents may also act unilaterally by issuing **signing statements**. Some amount to little more than claiming credit for a piece of legislation or thanking key supporters. Others are statements of constitutional rights and prerogatives. Such was the case in 2005 following the passage of anti-torture legislation. Two weeks after its public signing, Bush quietly attached a signing statement dealing with the rights of detainees. It stated that he would interpret the legislation "in a manner consistent with the constitutional authority of the President to supervise the unitary executive branch and as Commander in Chief and . . . in achieving the shared objective of the Congress and the President in . . . protecting the American people from further terrorist attacks."[9] In effect, this statement claimed presidential authority to conduct the War on Terrorism as the executive saw fit.

Trump and Biden have embraced signing statements. In signing the $716 billion defense bill in August 2018, Trump raised objections to fifty provisions of the bill, including one that called for formal consultations with South Korea and Japan before reducing the size of the U.S. military footprint in South Korea. Trump did not say he would refuse to abide by these provisions but indicated that he would implement them "consistent with his authority as commander in chief." Biden issued a signing statement with regard to the 2022 National Defense Authorization Act. One of the act's provisions bars the use of funds to transfer Guantanamo Bay detainees to the effective control of other countries. His statement said in part that these limitations "constrain the flexibility of the executive branch with respect to its engagement in delicate negotiations with foreign countries. . . . I urge the Congress to eliminate these restrictions as soon as possible."

## Executive Orders, Spending, and Administrative Powers

Presidents also have a number of more subtle options to pursue their foreign policy agendas.[10] One is to issue *executive orders*, directives issued to U.S. government agencies. These differ from executive agreements, which the president enters into with other countries. Obama issued executive orders in a variety of foreign policy areas. In 2016, he signed an executive order ending a twenty-year-old economic sanctions program against Iran for its pursuit of nuclear weapons. The order revoked four previous executive orders and modified a fifth one. Eight executive orders imposing sanctions on Iran remained in place. During his second term, Obama issued controversial executive orders involving cybersecurity. One provided for expanded information sharing and collaboration between the government and the private sector and the development of a voluntary framework for cybersecurity standards and best practices. Another allowed his administration to impose sanctions on groups or individuals engaged in cyberattacks or commercial espionage in cyberspace.

Trump has used foreign policy executive orders for a variety of issues, including drone strikes, trade violations and abuses, and the imposition of economic sanctions on Venezuela and Iran. Trump's most controversial executive order was his travel ban. Drafted largely within the White House and during the transition, it did not follow the vetting system traditionally used in formulating executive orders. Typically, the White House staff sends a proposed executive order to Congress for comment. It is then sent for review to the Office of Management and Budget, which in turn sends it to relevant departments for comment. The president is also required to obtain guidance from the Justice Department's Office of Legal Counsel. In the case of the travel ban, input was restricted to Trump's appointees and did not involve professional staffers. NSC officials raised concerns and presented lengthy comments. Secretary of Defense Jim Mattis was not given an opportunity to comment on the proposal.

Executive orders played an important part in Biden's response to Russia's invasion of Ukraine. Four of the thirteen he signed from January to May 2022 dealt with it. All totaled, Biden issued some ninety executive orders in his first eighteen months in office. Among those passed in 2021 were establishing a National Space Council and a Termination of the Emergency with the International Criminal Court. Biden also signed an "instrument" to rejoin the Paris Climate Agreement and a "proclamation" to stop construction of the border wall.

Presidents may also use their spending and administrative powers to advance foreign policy initiatives blocked by Congress:

- In 1999, the Senate rejected the Comprehensive Nuclear Test Ban Treaty. Yet Bill Clinton helped fund a global network of monitoring stations that were vital to detecting illegal tests.
- The United States has not yet signed the 1997 treaty banning land mines, yet it has avoided producing, transferring, or deploying new ones. It is also the world's leading funder of de-mining projects and helps fund follow-up meetings on the treaty's progress.
- The United States has not signed the treaty establishing an International Criminal Court (ICC), yet Bush supported a UN resolution referring Darfur to the ICC. Obama sent U.S. forces to Africa to help capture ICC fugitive Joseph Kony and turned over a Congolese warlord to the ICC after he surrendered to a U.S. embassy.

## Informal Ambassadors

Presidents have also reduced the Senate's confirmation powers from what was originally intended by using personal representatives as negotiators. President Franklin Roosevelt relied heavily on Harry Hopkins in making international agreements, leaving Secretary of State Cordell Hull to administer "diplomatic trivia." President Jimmy Carter had Hamilton Jordan conduct secret negotiations during the Iranian hostage crisis. The Reagan administration relied on National Security Council (NSC) staffers and private citizens to carry out the Iran-Contra initiative. Obama turned to informal ambassadors for dealing with a number of high-profile foreign policy problems, most notably reopening relations with Cuba; negotiations were conducted by two White House officials and begun without the knowledge of

Secretary of State John Kerry. Biden picked Kerry to be his climate envoy. In this position he has a seat on the National Security Council and was the first senior Biden administration official to visit China.

A similar problem confronts the Senate if it wishes to influence the type of advice the president receives. Presidents are free to listen to whomever they please. Under Woodrow Wilson, Wilson's friend and confidant Colonel House was more influential than Secretaries of State William Jennings Bryan and William Lansing. Today it is widely recognized that the national security advisor often has more influence on presidential thinking than the secretary of state. Yet the former's appointment is not subject to Senate approval.

Two informal ambassadors rose to prominence in the Trump administration. One was Rudolf Giuliani, Trump's personal lawyer who also headed a lucrative international consulting firm. Giuliani emerged as a central figure in foreign policy to Ukraine, for which Trump was impeached. Giuliani made contact with key Ukrainian individuals and pushed for the removal of key State Department officials. The second was Jared Kushner, Trump's son-in-law, who held the title of senior advisor. Kushner was put in charge of formulating the administration's Middle East peace plan, which led to the Abraham Accords.

It also must be remembered that presidents can serve as their own ambassador. Such is the case when engaging in direct talks with foreign leaders. Often this occurs at international meetings and summit conferences, which we will look at in chapter 10, but it may also occur on a variety of trips they make abroad. Table 7.1 presents a listing of ten presidents who made the most visits. By mid-2022, Biden had made seventeen visits.

## Undeclared Wars

By one count, the United States has used force over three hundred times.[11] However, it has declared war only five times. The passage of the 1973 War Powers Resolution (see the "Historical Lesson" in chapter 6) did little to redress this imbalance. Rather than willingly abide by it, many presidents have submitted reports to Congress declaring that they were doing so voluntarily and characterized their decisions to use force as lying beyond the jurisdiction of the War Powers Resolution. Carter did not engage in advance consultations with Congress in carrying out the Iranian hostage rescue effort, claiming that it was a humanitarian action.

**Table 7.1** **Number of Foreign Visits Made by Presidents (Top Ten)**

| President | Foreign Visits Made |
| --- | --- |
| George W. Bush | 140 |
| Bill Clinton | 133 |
| Barack Obama | 120 |
| George H. W. Bush | 60 |
| Franklin D. Roosevelt | 52 |
| Ronald Reagan | 49 |
| Richard Nixon | 42 |
| Dwight Eisenhower | 37 |
| Donald Trump | 34 |
| Jimmy Carter | 31 |

*Source*: Travels Abroad by the President, Office of the Historian, Department of State.

Reagan used the same logic in bypassing Congress on the invasion of Grenada. He would later argue that, because U.S. Marines were invited in by the Lebanese government, they were not being sent into a combat situation, so the War Powers Resolution did not apply. This assertion lost much of its support when 241 U.S. soldiers were killed in a terrorist attack. Even though George H. W. Bush did obtain a congressional resolution supporting the 1991 Persian Gulf War, he continued to stress that "I don't think I need it . . . I feel that I have the authority to fully implement the United Nations resolution." In a twist on this situation that occurred well before the War Powers Resolution, President Grover Cleveland went so far as to tell Congress that even if it declared war against Spain over Cuba, he would not honor that vote and begin a war.

Obama's thinking on presidential war powers evolved during his presidency. As a presidential candidate, Obama stated, "The president does not have the power under the Constitution to unilaterally authorize a military attack in a situation that does not involve stopping an actual or imminent threat to the nation." As president, his position was consistent with that of his predecessors. Obama sought congressional approval neither for military action against Gaddafi nor for the continuance of military operations there after the mandated sixty-day reporting period established by the War Powers Resolution. Approval, he held, was not necessary because it was a humanitarian operation. Later, he asserted that the sixty-day reporting requirement did not apply because U.S. military activities in Libya fell short of "hostilities."[12]

Trump similarly rejected congressional efforts to control his use of military power. In contemplating the use of military force against Iran in response to its downing of a U.S. drone, Trump talked with congressional leaders but did not seek official congressional support or inform them that he had authorized an attack, or that one was underway, only to be recalled as he changed his mind.

As senator, Biden voted against the Persian Gulf War Authorization for Using Military Force (AUMF) Resolution, and he asserted that Clinton needed congressional approval to send ground forces to Kosovo. Yet he also embraced the idea of broad presidential war powers. These two opposing views have surfaced in his administration. He argued that his commander-in-chief powers were sufficient to launch air strikes against ISIS in Syria but invoked the 2002 AUMF in approving air strikes in Somalia. He also supported repealing the 2002 AUMF.

## When Does the President Matter?

In a study of twentieth-century U.S. foreign policy, John Stoessinger was struck by how few individuals made crucial decisions shaping its direction.[13] He found that *movers* (exceptional individuals who, for better or worse, not only find turning points in history but help create them) have been far outnumbered by *players* (individuals caught up in the flow of events, who respond in a standard and predictable fashion). One explanation for this imbalance is that relatively few situations may exist in which the personal characteristics of the president or other policy makers are important for explaining policy.

A useful distinction can be made between action indispensability and actor indispensability.[14] **Action indispensability** refers to situations in which a specific action is critical to the success or failure of a policy. The identity of the actor is not necessarily a critical factor in explaining the action. It is possible that any individual (player) in that situation would have acted in a similar manner. **Actor indispensability** refers to those situations in which the personal characteristics of the involved individual are critical to explaining the action taken. In Stoessinger's terms, the individual involved is a mover, increasing the odds of success or failure by bringing unique qualities to bear on a problem.

A crucial element of action indispensability is the degree to which the situation permits restructuring. Some situations are so intractable or unstable that it is unreasonable to expect the actions of an individual policy maker to have much of an impact. In concrete terms, the identity of the president will have the greatest impact on policy under four conditions, all of which were met by the events of 9/11:

1. *The issue is new on the agenda.* Although the administration of Bill Clinton had given terrorism more attention than the incoming George W. Bush administration, no firm plan of action was in place.
2. *The issue is addressed early in the administration.* The terrorist attacks occurred early in the Bush administration.
3. *The president is deeply involved in ongoing issues.* Bush was deeply involved in decision making following the attacks.
4. *The issue is in a state of precarious equilibrium, and events are primed to move in any number of directions.* Certainly, from the viewpoint of key individuals in the administration, the terrorist attacks presented the United States with a unique opportunity to remake the political map of the Persian Gulf.

Students of the presidency have focused most heavily on two aspects of the president as an individual in attempting to understand U.S. foreign policy. The first is presidential personality. The second is the president's managerial or leadership style.

## Presidential Personality

Textbooks and newspaper accounts of U.S. foreign policy are dominated by references to policies that bear a president's name, such as the Monroe Doctrine and the Truman Doctrine. Personalizing the presidency in this way suggests that the identity of the president matters greatly and that if a different person had been president, U.S. foreign policy would have been different. Is this really the case?[15] A persuasive case can be made that situational factors, role variables, and the common socioeconomic backgrounds of policy makers place severe constraints on the impact of personality on policy. This section first looks at a leading effort to capture presidential personality and then examines the conditions under which presidential personality should be expected to make a difference.

The most famous effort to classify presidential personality and explore its implications for policy is that of James David Barber, who defines personality in terms of three elements.[16] The first element is *worldview*, which Barber defines as an individual's politically relevant beliefs. The second is *style*, an individual's habitual ways of responding to political opportunities and challenges through "rhetoric, personal relations, and homework." Both are heavily influenced by the third and most important component of personality: *character*, which develops in childhood. *Character*, the way individuals orient themselves toward life, involves two dimensions: energy and personal satisfaction. Presidents are classified as either passive or active by the amount of energy they put into the presidency. A president who derives personal satisfaction from the job is classified as positive, and one who gets no personal satisfaction from it is classified as negative. Together, these two dimensions produce four presidential personalities. Each type of **presidential personality** has different implications for U.S. foreign policy.

*Active-positive* presidents, such as Truman, Kennedy, Carter, Clinton, George H. W. Bush, and Obama, put a great deal of energy into being president and derive great satisfaction from doing so.[17] They are achievement oriented, value productivity, and enjoy meeting new challenges. The primary danger facing active-positives is the possibility that pragmatism will be seen as "flip-flopping." Carter's handling of the Panama Canal Treaties illustrates the ability of active-positives to engage productively in coalition-building efforts and accept the compromises necessary to get a policy measure passed. Carter's presidency also illustrates the problem with active-positive presidents: they may overextend themselves by pursuing too many goals at once and may be insensitive to the fact that the irrationalities of politics can frustrate even the best-laid plans. Carter was roundly criticized for being too flexible in the search for results and for trying to do too many things at the outset of his administration: negotiate a SALT II treaty, negotiate a Panama Canal treaty, and reorder U.S. foreign policy priorities by emphasizing human rights and economic problems over the Soviet threat.

*Active-negative* presidents, such as Johnson and Nixon, are compulsive individuals who are driven to acquire power as a means of compensating for low self-esteem. Active-negatives adopt a domineering posture toward those around them and have difficulty managing their aggressive feelings. The great danger of active-negatives is that they will adhere rigidly to a disastrous foreign policy. Woodrow Wilson did so during the League of Nations controversy; Johnson with Vietnam; and Nixon with his actions in the Watergate scandal and the impeachment proceedings.

Donald Trump exhibited many of the characteristics of the active-negative president in his decision making. Trump actively used his presidential powers of communication to advance his policy positions and attack those who challenged him. At the same time, Trump's frustration by his limited ability to fully exercise what he saw as his presidential powers and the lack of credit for what he accomplished—including winning the presidency—have been noted repeatedly. There were numerous accounts of him lashing out at aides for a failure to implement his policies. Most significantly, Trump often found himself locked in losing or overly costly policy disputes, such as building a wall along the Mexican border, his embrace of Vladimir Putin, rejecting findings about Russian influence in the 2016 presidential election, his trade war with China, and revelations that he took highly classified documents, including ones dealing with nuclear weapons and strategy, with him upon leaving the presidency.

*Passive-negative* presidents, such as Eisenhower, get little satisfaction from the job and use few of the powers available to them. They are in politics only because others have encouraged them to be, and they feel a responsibility to meet those expectations. Their actions are plagued by low self-esteem and feelings of uselessness. They do not enjoy the game of politics. Rather than bargain and compromise, they seek to avoid confrontation by emphasizing vague principles and procedural arrangements.

*Passive-positive* presidents, such as Reagan, are directed individuals who seek affection as a reward for being agreeable. They do not make full use of the powers of the presidency but feel satisfied with the job as they define it. Most frequently, Biden is identified as a passive-positive president. He is characterized as optimistic, flexible, and one who places a great deal of emphasis on teamwork. He is a uniter rather than a divider. After Saudi Arabia announced a cut oil production, Biden spoke out in anger but then worked quietly to restore relations. Using jet fighters, the United States secretly launched a show of force against Iran when warnings were received of planned missile and drone attacks on Saudi Arabia. Placing Biden and Reagan in the same category highlights the point that ideology is not a defining characteristic of presidential personality. What matters is how the individual approaches the task of being president.

Passive-positive and passive-negative presidents are especially prone to two problems. The first is policy drift. Problems may go unaddressed, and opportunities for action may be missed. The second potential danger is the absence of accountability. Without the energetic involvement of the president in making policy, an inevitable question arises: "Who is in charge?"

Placing a president in one of Barber's categories involves a great deal of subjective judgment. Consider the case of Eisenhower, whom he defined as a passive-negative president. Recent evidence suggests that this may not have been the case.[18] Eisenhower may have deliberately cultivated the image of not being involved in policy making in order to deflect political pressures. His "hidden-hand leadership" combined a behind-the-scenes activism with a low public profile.

An even more significant complicating factor is that Barber's personality traits may not be permanent. Change may occur over time, because multiple traits are present. George W. Bush is a case in point.[19] Bush can be seen as passive in his delegation of authority to others, his preference for focusing on a few select themes, and his engagement in binary black-and-white thinking, which allowed him to make decisions without getting into the deeper questions involved in an issue. At the same time, he had a very active side. Bob Woodward, who chronicled the Bush administration's decisions to go to war in Afghanistan and Iraq, said that Bush's decision-making style "bordered on the hurried. He wanted actions, solutions. Once on course, he directed his energy at forging on, rarely looking back, scoffing at—even ridiculing—doubt and anything less than 100 percent commitment."[20]

## Presidential Managerial Style

Presidents do not lead by personality alone. Just as important to the outcome of their presidency is the managerial style they embrace to get others to follow. In addition, while the influence of presidential personality might be greatest under a limited set of conditions, a president's managerial and leadership style can be expected to have a more uniform effect on U.S. foreign policy. Getting others to follow is not easy.

Presidential managerial styles can be described in any number of ways. Zbigniew Brzezinski gave the following thumbnail sketches of how the first three post–Cold War presidents managed foreign policy.[21] George H. W. Bush had a "top-down" managerial style that placed him firmly in command of decisions. This did not mean that he was always happy with the way the system worked, however. Commenting on discussions about dealing with Soviet pressure on Lithuania, Bush later said, "I was dissatisfied with this discussion since it did not point to action and I wanted to take action."[22] Bill Clinton had a kaffeeklatsch (informal get-together over coffee) approach to decision making. His meetings lacked an agenda, rarely began or ended on schedule, were frequently marked by the spontaneous participation of individuals who had little reason to be there, and often ended without any clear sense that a decision had been reached. George W. Bush is described as having "strong gut instincts" along with a "propensity for catastrophic decisiveness" and a temperament prone to "dogmatic formulations."

Viewed from a more analytical perspective, four basic managerial options have been employed by presidents to bring order and coherence to their foreign policy.[23] None is, by definition, superior to another. All have contributed to foreign policy successes and failures. The first is a **competitive system**, which places a great deal of emphasis on the free and open expression of ideas. Jurisdictions and grants of authority overlap, as individuals and departments compete for the president's attention in putting forward ideas and programs. Franklin Roosevelt is the only president who successfully employed such a model. Johnson is seen as having tried and failed.

A second leadership style involves setting up a **formalistic system**, in which the president establishes orderly routines and procedures for organizing the administration's policy deliberations. The system is hierarchically structured, with the president deeply involved as the final arbitrator in defining strategy and policy choices. Truman, Eisenhower, Nixon, Ford, Reagan, and Obama each set up variations of formalistic systems.

The third management style centers on the creation of a **collegial system**, in which the president tries to bring together a group of advisors to operate as a problem-solving team. Kennedy, Carter, George H. W. Bush, and Clinton set up this type of system. Biden's managerial style is very much in the mode of a congenial system. It has been described as "a team of buddies," made up of officials who have a long experience of working collaboratively with one another. This does not mean that Biden accepts the consensus among his advisors. He has been known to reject their position in favor of his own. The most notable case is his rejecting the military's position that U.S. troops not be withdrawn from Afghanistan.

The fourth management style, employing a **chief executive officer (CEO) system**, was introduced by George W. Bush. In spirit, it harkens back to a Nixon-style attempt to govern by stressing loyalty, tightly controlling the flow of information, and surrounding the president with an "iron triangle" of aides to the exclusion of others in the White House. There have been noticeable differences in implementation of the CEO system. In contrast to the Nixon NSC system, which stressed hierarchy and centralized control, Bush put into place a flattened power structure in which the president set the overall direction of policy but delegated responsibility for carrying through on policy to key individuals.

Trump's managerial system left no doubt that foreign policy decisions resided with him. As one observer noted, "It's a presidency of one person," or as Trump put it, "I alone can fix it." His foreign policy decisions, often expressed as tweets, routinely contradicted comments made by key advisors and department heads. Trump's CEO system differed from that of his predecessors in that rather than operating in a system with tight controls over information and decision making, Trumps' managerial system had multiple centers of power vying for his attention, creating what some have called a "team of rivals." Additionally, compared to other presidents, Trump came to the White House without a large and skilled set of foreign policy advisors and staff to consult for advice. A significant number of Republican foreign policy experts declared that they would not join his administration, and many of those whose names were put forward for key foreign policy positions were rejected by the Trump transition team for their lack of loyalty. The end result was referred to by administration officials as a "lean administration" that had "shed excess baggage"; others saw it as lacking the skills or resources to comment on and implement Trump's foreign policy effectively.

# The National Security Council

Leadership requires more than getting individuals to work together toward a common set of goals. It also has an organizational foundation. Bureaucracies are needed to provide advice, develop policy alternatives, and implement policies. Experience has taught presidents that bureaucracies are not easily moved. As a result, presidents have been forced to look elsewhere for organizations that will allow them to lead. The central foreign policy structure on which presidents rely is the National Security Council (NSC) system, which is composed of three parts: an advisory body of cabinet-rank officials, a national security advisor, and a professional staff.

According to the 1947 National Security Act that founded it, the purpose of the NSC was to advise the president "with respect to the integration of domestic, foreign, and military policies relating to national security."[24] The NSC has gone through several different phases in its history. Each altered the manner in which foreign policy problems come to the president.

The first phase of the NSC's history ran from 1947 to 1960. During this period, the NSC gradually became overly institutionalized. Truman was the first president to have the NSC, and he was cautious in using it. He particularly wanted to avoid setting any precedents that would give the NSC the power to supervise executive branch agencies, or establishing a norm of group responsibility for foreign policy decisions. For Truman, foreign policy was the responsibility of the president alone. The NSC was to be an advisory body and nothing more. To emphasize this point, Truman did not attend early meetings of the NSC. The outbreak of the Korean War changed Truman's approach. He started using the NSC more systematically and began attending its regularly scheduled meetings. All national security issues were now to be brought to his attention through the NSC system; the NSC staff was reorganized, and the emphasis on outside consultants was replaced by a senior staff served by staff assistants.

The institutionalization and involvement of the NSC in policy making continued under Eisenhower, who created a Planning Board to develop policy recommendations for the president and an Operations Coordinating Board to oversee the implementation of national security decisions. Eisenhower also established the post of assistant for national security affairs (commonly known as the president's national security advisor) to coordinate the national security decision-making process more forcefully. This NSC system never really functioned as envisioned. Instead of producing high-quality policy recommendations, decisions were made on the basis of the lowest common denominator of agreement. Rather than increasing presidential options, it limited them. Policy implementation continued to be governed by departmental objectives and definitions of the problem rather than by presidential goals and perspectives.[25]

During the second phase of the NSC's history, which began with the Kennedy administration and lasted until 1980, it became overly personalized. Kennedy adopted an activist approach to national security management grounded in informal operating procedures. The emphasis was on multiple lines of communication, direct presidential contacts with second- and third-level officials, and securing outside expert advice. Ad hoc interagency task forces replaced the formal NSC system as the primary decision-making unit. Within the NSC system, emphasis switched from the council itself to the NSC staff.

In Kennedy's revamped management system, the national security advisor played a key role. This person was responsible for ensuring that the staff operated from a presidential perspective. McGeorge Bundy held this post under Kennedy and in the first part of the Johnson administration. He was replaced by Walt Rostow in 1966. The change in advisors brought with it a change in operating style. Bundy saw his role as a facilitator or honest broker whose job was to encourage the airing of ideas and policy alternatives. Rostow was more of an ideologue, concerned with policy advocacy over process management.

Like Kennedy, Lyndon Johnson took an activist stance and favored small, informal policy-making settings over the formal NSC system. Major decisions about Vietnam were made at the Tuesday lunch group that brought together Johnson and his key foreign policy advisors. According to William Bundy, the Tuesday lunch group was a "procedural abomination," lacking a formal agenda and clearly stated conclusions, wearing on participants, and confusing to those at the working levels.[26] The end result was that the NSC was often bypassed as key decisions were made in the White House.

Nixon began his presidency with a pledge to put the NSC system back at the center of the foreign policy decision-making process, but instead foreign policy decision making remained in the White House.[27] He selected Henry Kissinger as his national security advisor and William Rogers as his secretary of state. The combination of a strong, opinionated, and activist national security advisor and a secretary of state with little foreign policy experience guaranteed that foreign policy would be made in the White House. Nixon also created an elaborate NSC committee and staff system with Kissinger at its center; Kissinger was allowed to direct the flow of paper in the direction he wanted, bringing the NSC system into play on certain issues and cutting it out of others. By the end of the Nixon administration, the NSC was largely "on the outside looking in." It met only three times in 1973, compared with thirty-seven times in 1969. Such important decisions as the invasion of Cambodia, Kissinger's trip to China, the Paris peace negotiations, and bombing in Vietnam were made outside the NSC system.

Carter dismantled the elaborate Nixon-Ford-Kissinger committee system in favor of two committees. The Policy Review Committee handled long-term projects. A Special Coordinating Committee dealt with short-term problems, crisis situations, and covert action. Collegiality also returned, as evident in the prominent policy-making roles played by the Friday foreign policy breakfasts (attended by Carter and his key foreign policy advisors), but at a price. The Friday foreign policy breakfasts became substitutes for full NSC meetings; decisions made during the breakfasts were not always fully integrated into the NSC system, nor did they necessarily result in clearly articulated positions.[28]

During the Reagan administration, the NSC entered a third phase. Pledging to depersonalize the system, Reagan pushed too far in the opposite direction, causing it to go into decline. The national security advisor became a "nonperson," with little foreign policy influence or stature. The NSC staff moved in two different directions. On the one hand, it became preoccupied with bureaucratic trivia. There were twenty-five committees, fifty-five mid-level committees, and some one hundred task forces and working groups. On the other hand, it became involved in the actual conduct of foreign policy in the Iran-Contra initiative. Only with the arrival of Colin Powell as national security advisor and the passing from the cabinet of such powerful and highly opinionated figures as Secretary of Defense Caspar Weinberger and Director of Central Intelligence William Casey did a coherent foreign policy agenda appear.[29]

In the George H. W. Bush and Clinton administrations, decision making in the NSC was transformed again, becoming more collegial in nature. Both presidents selected low-key national security advisors who were expected to stay out of the public limelight. The final result was less than anticipated. The primary problem encountered in George H. W. Bush's administration was too much homogeneity in outlook. Bill Clinton failed to make his collegial system work because he was unable to provide a constant vision to guide his team or to construct an effective division of labor among its members.

George W. Bush and Obama continued to try to construct a collegial system. Central to George W. Bush's advisory system was the "War Cabinet," consisting of some twelve key Bush advisors on the War on Terrorism. Instead of operating in a collegial fashion, however, this system became highly competitive and split over how to conduct foreign policy.[30] Commenting on the decision to invade Iraq, one CIA official recalled that "there was no meeting; no policy options papers, no showdown in the Situation Room where the wisdom of going to war was debated or the decision to do so made."[31]

In setting up his NSC system, President Obama created an advisory system that emphasized his role as the key foreign policy decision maker. Rather than serving as a stimulus for effective decision making, Obama's deep involvement was characterized as one of micromanagement that often resulted in paralysis and an endless decision loop. Director of National Intelligence Dennis Blair was moved to note that, at any one time, there was not one national security advisor in the Obama administration but at least three and as many as five.[32] Obama's national security system also continued a controversial trend. Under Carter, the NSC had twenty-five staffers; under George W. Bush, it had reached two hundred. Under Obama it doubled in size to four hundred staffers. Critics of this growth saw it as reducing the input of the State Department, Defense Department, and other foreign policy bureaucracies. Defenders saw it as reflecting the changed nature of foreign policy making; the more important role of domestic political considerations require the White House to play a more active and controlling role.

A new phase in the evolution of the NSC system occurred in the Trump administration. Both the national security advisor and the NSC staff were routinely sidelined in a decision-making process described as disconnected and disused. Instead, voices outside the NSC system held great influence over Trump's foreign policy decision making. Trump's first national security advisor, retired general Michael Flynn, resigned after twenty-four days. Flynn was replaced by General H. R. McMaster, who quickly moved to reorganize the operation of the NSC by removing White House chief strategist Steve Bannon from the NSC's cabinet-level Principals Committee. McMaster was a forceful, independent thinker who often disagreed with Trump, most notably on Russia, a situation that led to his removal after slightly more than one year in the position. In April 2018, John Bolton became Trump's third national security advisor in fourteen months. Where McMaster held regular NSC meetings, Bolton isolated the council. Bolton also reached out regularly to members of Congress to advance his views and engaged in social media postings. Bolton served 520 days as national security advisor before being fired by Trump (or, as he claimed, resigning). While both hold hawkish foreign policy views, Bolton and Trump differed on using military force and entering into diplomatic talks with adversaries. Trump also came to view Bolton's loyalty with suspicion. By summer 2019, Bolton was isolated from decision making on an Afghanistan/Taliban peace agreement, the details of which were advanced by Trump and pursued by a small circle of Trump advisors without input from the National Security Council. Robert O'Brien replaced Bolton as national security advisor. O'Brien was a strong Trump supporter. Where Trump was routinely described as inattentive to details and uninterested in briefings, O'Brien characterized him as "laser focused on issues." The political nature of O'Brien's appointment became an issue when he was accused by the acting head of Homeland Security of suppressing evidence of Russian interference in the United States.

In addition to moving back to a more congenial management style, Biden has brought about a number of structural changes in the NSC system. He has expanded its focus by adding new directorates on such topics as Russia, China, and technological competiveness, as well as reinstating directors terminated by Trump on pandemics, democracy and development, and climate. With this expansion has come an expansion in the size of the NSC staff. Under Trump it had shrunk in size. Biden increased it roughly back to the size it was under Obama: 350–370.

## Other White House Voices

The NSC system is not the only body close to the president that exercises influence over the making of U.S. foreign policy. Four other voices have grown in prominence: the vice president, the U.S. trade representative (USTR), the president's chief of staff, and the First Lady.

### The Vice President

Political folklore assigns the vice president little more than a ceremonial position in the policy-making process, barring the death of the president. There is often great truth in these images. Harry Truman spoke with Franklin Roosevelt only eight times and knew nothing of the development of the atomic bomb or Roosevelt's discussions with Winston Churchill and Joseph Stalin about the shape of the post–World War II international system.

Of late, much has changed. More and more, vice presidents are playing selective but important foreign policy roles.[33] Dan Quayle, George H. W. Bush's vice president, became the administration's most active voice on Latin American affairs, and his decidedly pro-Israel position was important in maintaining the Persian Gulf War alliance against Iraq. Al Gore, Bill Clinton's vice president, established himself as a key administration expert on Russia. Joe Biden continued in the role of activist vice president as part of the Obama administration. In 2013 Biden traveled to China, where he played the administration's "bad cop," publicly criticizing Chinese leaders for their attempts to silence American media criticism by blocking their websites in China. Most significantly, Biden played a leading role in organizing and overseeing Obama's policy toward Ukraine and the 2014 Russian takeover of Crimea, an experience that heavily influenced his views on the 2021 Ukraine crisis.

In some respects, Mike Pence followed in Biden's footsteps, being sent abroad to advance and defend the Trump administration's foreign policy. However, Pence has also advanced his own foreign policy agenda based on his conservative Christian worldview. He has spoken out for religious freedom, criticizing countries such as Myanmar more forcefully than Trump for its persecution of Muslims. Undercutting Pence's influence in foreign policy was Trump's administrative style. Commentators have noted that Trump had no real understanding of how presidents interacted with vice presidents. One result was that Pence would attend meetings without knowing the agenda or being briefed in advance. Kamala Harris has spent considerable time abroad meeting with government leaders individually and in conferences as part of Biden's efforts to reestablish American global involvement and leadership. These undertakings have produced mixed results. In March 2021, Biden tasked Harris with leading the effort to address the root causes of Central American migration to the United States across the Mexican border. Her public "do not come" comment in Guatemala was not well received. Subsequent trips to Singapore and South Vietnam, Poland, and Japan took place against a backdrop of rising global concern over U.S. policies to Afghanistan, Ukraine, and China complicating her efforts to build support for the United States.

By far the most active and influential vice president in making foreign policy decisions was Dick Cheney, George W. Bush's vice president. He assembled a national security staff larger than that of any previous vice president and brought a clear-cut perspective on foreign policy matters, along with considerable foreign policy experience, having served as secretary of defense under George H. W. Bush.[34] After the 9/11 attacks, Cheney became a powerful voice for taking the war to Iraq, often engaging in spirited exchanges with Secretary of State Colin Powell, who opposed such a move. Both before and after the invasion of Iraq, Cheney vehemently and publicly asserted that Iraq possessed weapons of mass destruction and that a link existed between Iraq and al-Qaeda. Bush and Cheney were not always in agreement in foreign policy matters, and by the end of his presidency the distance between their views had grown.[35]

## The U.S. Trade Representative

Up until the early 1960s, the State Department had the primary responsibility for conducting international economic negotiations. That changed with the passage of the 1962 Trade Expansion Act, which created the Office of the Special Trade Representative to head an interagency trade organization located in the White House. The move, which was led by Congress, was seen as necessary because the State Department was not viewed as a strong enough advocate of American economic interests.

The USTR is charged with the responsibilities of overseeing U.S. activity in multilateral trade negotiations and of negotiating trade issues with other states and within the UN system of organizations. It was Trade Representative Robert Zoellick, rather than Secretary of State Colin Powell, who accompanied George W. Bush to meet with Latin American leaders in hopes of laying the foundation for the Free Trade Area of the Americas. Zoellick also supervised U.S. negotiations at the Doha Round of World Trade Organization talks.

Robert Lighthizer, Trump's USTR, was a longtime Trump supporter who worked on trade issues in the Reagan administration, had a reputation as a tough negotiator, and was an advocate of high tariffs as an instrument of foreign policy. A critic of China's trade policies, Lighthizer opposed its entry into the World Trade Organization and charged it with intellectual property theft. In response to COVID-19, Tai played a leading role in formulating policy in international trade meetings and was an advocate of waiving intellectual property right protections for pharmaceuticals. In early May 2022 Tai announced that the administration supported waiving those rights. In October, on the day Biden announced new trade sanctions against China, she openly criticized its "state-directed industrial dominance policies," and called for a U.S. industrial policy aimed at protecting national security.

## The White House Chief of Staff

By convention, a division of labor has evolved in White House decision-making circles between the chief of staff (COS) and the national security advisor. Each acts as a principal source of advice for the president—the COS for domestic policy and the national security advisor for foreign policy. This division of labor is disappearing; more and more, the COS has come to have an important voice in foreign policy matters.[36] Several reasons for this change stand out. Foremost is the blurring of the boundary between foreign and domestic policy. As discussed in chapter 2, many of today's traditional foreign policy problems can be characterized as *intermestic* issues, with elements of both foreign and domestic policy. As a consequence, the COS's domestic political expertise has become relevant to decisions on many foreign policy issues. As Carter's COS, Hamilton Jordan, recalled, he sought to play the role of an early-warning system to alert officials to potential domestic political problems embedded in foreign policy decisions.

In addition to providing advice, the COS acts as a **gatekeeper**, regulating those who have access to the president. Leon Panetta, Bill Clinton's second COS, insisted that all decision papers, including those from the NSC, go to the president only after his review. The influence of domestic considerations filtered through the COS's office affects not only what decisions are made, but also how foreign policy decisions are communicated. Brent Scowcroft, George H. W. Bush's national security advisor, noted that he had expected the NSC to write the first draft of the president's national security speeches because the language was so very important. Instead, White House speechwriters took the lead, with the result that foreign policy speeches often sounded like campaign speeches laced with dramatic rhetoric.

Examples of the prominent foreign policy role played by the COS in recent administrations are easy to find. Andrew Card, George W. Bush's first COS, was one of those placed in charge of the Homeland Security Council after the 9/11 attacks. As the Bush administration moved toward war with Iraq, Card established the White House Iraq Group to make sure that the various parts of the White House were working in harmony on Iraq. Secretary of Defense Gates was highly critical of Obama's COS Thomas Donilon, complaining that decisions about military intervention in Libya were made without significant military input. At one point, Gates told the Pentagon not to give the White House staff too much military information because they did not understand it.

The foreign policy influence of the COS in the Trump administration was heavily muted by the frequency with which he changed COS and their inability to tell Trump something he did not want to hear. Trump expected them to take a "hands-off approach." The more they sought to control his foreign policy impulses, the more Trump sidelined them. His best-known COS was General John Kelly. He was charged with bringing order to the White House. To a large extent he succeeded in managing the flow of paper and the number of people who had access to Trump. What Kelly was unable to do was impose discipline on Trump; after initially welcoming Kelly's presence, Trump grew to resent it, along with Kelly's efforts to modify his foreign policy thinking on such issues as the border wall. When asked how to evaluate his tenure as COS, Kelly responded that it was best measured by what the president did *not* do. Biden selected Ron Klain to be his chief of staff. Klain served as chief of staff for Biden when he was vice president and for Vice President Al Gore. He also served as Obama's Ebola czar. Klain has stayed well behind the headlines in Biden's foreign policy making in comparison to his involvement in domestic policy, which has on occasion been controversial, especially as it relates to working with Congress.

## The First Lady

According to traditional thinking, First Ladies play largely ceremonial foreign policy roles. It is important to recognize that, while the most common one, this is not the only role that first ladies have played. First ladies have long been involved informally in making U.S. foreign policy. Abigail Adams lobbied President John Adams on a treaty with the Netherlands in 1799. Edith Wilson served as Woodrow Wilson's communication link with both foreign governments and others in the U.S. government while he was incapacitated by a stroke. While generally neutral on policy matters, she tried but failed to get Wilson to accept Senator Henry Cabot Lodge's reservations about the League of Nations. Eleanor Roosevelt engaged in a wide series of debates with President Franklin Roosevelt during his presidency.

Two recent first ladies who adopted a much more visible and active role in foreign policy were Rosalynn Carter and Hillary Clinton. The signature foreign policy undertaking of Rosalynn Carter's stay in the White House was a June 1977 trip to Latin America. With Jimmy Carter heavily involved in completing the Panama Canal Treaties, the Middle East peace process, and arms control talks with the Soviet Union, the decision was made to send her to Latin America as a sign of U.S. interest in the region and of its commitment to human rights. In preparation for the trip, Rosalynn Carter met with scholars and representatives from the State Department, Treasury Department, National Security Department, and Organization of American States. As First Lady, Hillary Clinton's signature foreign policy initiative involved advocacy for women's rights and her attendance at the Fourth United Nations Conference on Women, held in Beijing in September 1995. In addressing that body, she strongly criticized China's treatment of women.

Melania Trump embraced the traditional passive foreign policy role of first ladies, advancing in a low-key manner her signature foreign policy agenda: highlighting the role of U.S. foreign aid in helping children. Similarly, Laura Bush was seen much more than heard, but she did have a focal point for her foreign policy activities, including freedom in Burma. Michelle Obama's primary area of international involvement was youth engagement. First Lady Jill Biden also has embraced a largely passive role in foreign policy matters. Her first major foreign policy undertaking occurred in early May 2022 when she visited Romania and Slovakia to talk with Ukrainian women and children refugees, highlight their plight, and promise U.S. support. This visit included an unannounced trip into Ukraine. Later that month, Jill Biden traveled to Central America where she stressed the positive role that the United States was playing in addressing regional issues and the value of partnering with the United States.

# Over the Horizon: Improving Presidential Transitions

As noted at the outset of this chapter, for many, the first one hundred days of a president's term in office are seen as sending important signals as to what the future holds for their presidency. For others, just as important—and perhaps even more important—are the seventy-two days between their election as president in November and their inauguration the following January, when the transition from one president to another takes place. Trump only conceded defeat on November 23, 2020, almost three weeks after the election. During that time period, he instructed agencies not to talk to Biden's transition team. Even after that date, certain agencies were barred from meeting with Biden's team. This included the National Security

Agency and the Defense Intelligence Agency. From the November election until Inauguration Day on January 20, 2021, Trump actively pursued his foreign policy agenda by making a series of decisions, such as leaving the Open Skies Treaty and pulling U.S. forces out of Somalia, as well as engaging in what was described as a postelection purge of personnel, such as firing Secretary of Defense Mark Esper in a tweet.

The stressful and complicated nature of the Biden transition to president promises to bring additional pressures to bear on reforming the time between Election Day and Inauguration Day. It also brings into sharp focus the potential problems that newly elected presidents face whose predecessor was from a different party and the number of common challenges that exist in constructing an effective and efficient transition process. According to Kurt Campbell and James Steinberg, six stand out: (1) government by amateurs, (2) solving the jigsaw puzzle, (3) promises to keep, (4) the clean slate syndrome, (5) fumbled information handoffs, and (6) only one president at a time.[37]

Prior to 2008, very little formal transition planning took place to help overcome these problems. Transitions were largely ad hoc affairs consisting of occasional national security briefings after the election. 9/11 changed that. As one senior George W. Bush administration official involved in both the 2000 and 2008 transitions noted, "Thank goodness it was September 11 and not February 11 because we would have been completely incapable of dealing with them." Still, another official noted that in 2008 "we were kind of making it up as we went along."

The desire to better prepare a presidential candidate to become president led to the creation of the nonpartisan Partnership for Public Service. In studying the 2008 transition, it found that both McCain and Obama began transition planning in spring 2008; McCain's campaign was less aggressive, believing that he would face fewer problems succeeding a Republican president. Fears of appearing overly presumptuous or overly confident about victory were major psychological and political impediments to transition planning. The report recommended that future presidential candidates appoint transition directors within two weeks of gaining the nomination, and that by January 1 the president-elect should give Congress the names of the nominees for the top fifty State Department, Defense Department, national security, and economic positions. The Senate should vote on them on or shortly after Inauguration Day.

In March 2016, Congress passed legislation establishing a set of deadlines that both presidential candidates and the administration had to meet, which Obama signed into law. That very month, transition coordinators from some forty different agencies met to discuss transition planning. The legislation had established a May deadline, six months before the election, for a president to create a transition coordinating council at the White House and in federal agencies. Another reform was announced in March 2019; two former CIA officials created an unclassified briefing book on major challenges facing the United States, which is being given to announced presidential candidates in an effort to help them address issues arising from fake news and foreign election interference.

## Critical Thinking Questions

1. Where does presidential responsibility begin and end in foreign policy making, and why?
2. Is there a "best" type of presidential personality for foreign affairs? Explain your answer.
3. Is the way the NSC is organized or presidential management style more important in determining presidential success in foreign policy? Explain your answer.

## Key Terms

action indispensability, 146
actor indispensability, 147
Bricker Amendment, 142
chief executive officer (CEO) system, 150
collegial system, 150
competitive system, 150

executive agreement, 142
formalistic system, 150
gatekeeper, 156
presidential personality, 148
signing statement, 143
unilateral president, 141

# Bureaucracy 8

## Learning Objectives

Students will be able to:

1. Identify the strengths and weaknesses of the State Department as an instrument of U.S. foreign policy.
2. Describe the bureaucratic culture within the State Department, Defense Department, and intelligence community.
3. Compare the foreign policy approaches of domestic bureaucracies to those of the State Department, Defense Department, and intelligence community.
4. Evaluate the manner in which policy makers respond to the bureaucracy in making foreign policy.

# On the Agenda: Fixing the State Department

Viewed in terms of lines on an organizational chart, the foreign affairs bureaucracy provides presidents with a powerful set of tools to use in promoting their foreign policy agendas. Examined more closely, these organizations cannot be used freely. They have their own histories, operating styles, and concerns. The inherent tension within these conflicting perceptions often leads to policy disputes, feelings of frustration, and laying blame. It can also lead to calls for organizational reform and the creation of new organizations.

From the very beginning of the Trump presidency, reorganizing the State Department was a primary focus of his efforts to reshape the foreign affairs bureaucracy. This was not surprising. Two prominent themes of Trump's campaign were "Make American Great Again" and put "America First." Trump asserted that too many existing international agreements were bad deals, in which other countries took advantage of the United States.

The Trump administration's agenda included wide-ranging reforms of its structure, personnel system, and policies. Not all were implemented, but taken as a whole they had a major impact on the conduct and content of U.S. foreign policy. One proposal that Trump was unable to implement was the merger of the State Department and the U.S. Agency for International Development (USAID), which operates as an independent agency under the guidance and supervision of the secretary of state. The purpose of this reorganization was to concentrate under a single umbrella foreign aid programs that are spread across many military and civilian agencies. The fear in the State Department was that this would result in a smaller and more politicized foreign aid budget.

Another structural challenge involved internal day-to-day operations. Here, public attention centered on the Trump administration's proposal to cut the State Department budget by as much as 33 percent. This proposal was widely considered to be "dead on arrival" by members of Congress. Secretary of Defense Jim Mattis went so far as to state, "If you don't fund the State Department fully, then I need to buy more ammunition." Trump never achieved the deep cuts he sought, but he constantly returned to it. His FY 2021 proposed budget called for a 22 percent cut.

Less visible were changes in the internal structure of the State Department. Secretary of State Rex Tillerson quickly expanded the size of the policy planning staff attached to his office. One consequence of this expansion was to isolate Tillerson from input by State Department professionals, creating blockages in State Department decision making. Some within the State Department characterized his new advisors as a praetorian guard. There also came steps to reduce the size of the State Department, with one proposal calling for eliminating as many as 2,300 positions in the department. A hiring freeze ordered by Tillerson reduced the number of new Foreign Service officers from 366 in 2016 to 100 in 2018. By November 2017, the number of minister counselors (the equivalent of two-star officers) had declined by 15 percent, career ministers (three-star officers) by 42 percent, and career ambassadors (four-star officers) by 60 percent as a wave of resignations swept through the State Department.

The Trump administration's reform agenda included changes in the State Department's mission. Some took the form of decisions made by Tillerson, such as removing Afghanistan, Burma, and Iraq from the list of countries ineligible for some forms of military aid because they were identified as using child soldiers. Others included removal of references to reproductive rights for women and of the term "occupied territories" (i.e., Israel's presence in Gaza and the West Bank) from the State Department's annual human rights report. Under Mike Pompeo, who succeeded Tillerson as secretary of state, a new advisory commission on human rights was established to reevaluate how human rights are thought about in U.S. diplomacy. Most fundamentally, there occurred a change in the State Department's official mission statement. On May 1, 2019, it read:

> The U.S. Department of State leads America's foreign policy through diplomacy, advocacy, and assistance by advancing the interests of the American people, their safety and economic prosperity.

In the State Department's Fiscal Year 2015 Report and on its website, the following statement appeared:

> The [State] Department's mission is to shape and sustain a peaceful, prosperous, just and democratic world, and foster conditions for stability and progress for the benefit of the American people and people everywhere.

The Trump administration saw reorganization as long overdue. The controversy over whether and how to reform the State Department did not begin with Trump nor has it ended. Among those also calling for reforms today are former Foreign Service officers who look back and reflect on their careers. They too see problems that need to be solved but make very different recommendations.[1] A sampling of their reform agenda includes:

- The decision-making process needs to be delayered and decentralized; it is too lumbering and conservative.
- The personnel system needs added diversity and a new outlook for examining foreign policy problems; it has become too rigid and is out of date.
- Foreign Service officers need to become public affairs and public diplomacy diplomats; they must reach out to the public and be open.

This chapter examines the organizational structure and internal value systems of the State Department, the Department of Defense, and the intelligence community and takes a brief look at key domestic bureaucracies and other agencies that have a foreign policy role. The chapter concludes with an examination of how policy makers respond to the challenges of dealing with the foreign affairs bureaucracy.

# Presidents and the Bureaucracy

According to Henry Kissinger, "the purpose of bureaucracy is to devise a standard operating procedure that can cope effectively with most problems."[2] Doing so frees high-level policy makers to concentrate on the unexpected and the exceptional and to pursue policy innovations. While true in theory, this view is misplaced. In practice, two problems arise:

1. Policy makers expect far more from bureaucracy than help in dealing with the normal— probably too much more. Consider President Gerald Ford's statement about the U.S. involvement in Vietnam: "We could have avoided the whole darn Vietnam War if somebody in the Department of Defense or State had said, 'Look here. Do we want to inherit the French mess?'"[3] As discussed in chapter 4, the reality of U.S. involvement in Vietnam was far more complex.
2. Policy makers often feel trapped by the bureaucracy. Obama put it this way: "There's a playbook in Washington that presidents are supposed to follow. It's a playbook that comes out of the foreign policy establishment. . . . But the play book can also be a trap that can lead to bad decisions."[4]

One important player in the bureaucratic foreign policy playbook is the U.S. State Department.

# The State Department

Then called the Department of Foreign Affairs, the State Department was created in 1789 as the first department under the new Constitution. According to historical tradition and government documents, the president looks first to the State Department in making foreign policy.

## Structure and Growth of the State Department

The State Department serves as a transmission belt for information between the United States and foreign governments, and as a source of expertise and skills on which senior policy makers can draw. These are daunting tasks. Dean Rusk, secretary of state under Presidents John Kennedy and Lyndon Johnson, estimated that he saw only six of every one thousand cables sent to the State Department each day and that the president saw only one or two.[5] By the end of the twentieth century, the State Department was electronically processing over fourteen thousand official records and ninety thousand data messages each day, and over twenty million email messages per year.

Annually, the State Department represents the United States in over fifty major international organizations and at over eight hundred international conferences. In 2019, the United States had diplomatic relations with 191 countries and had 170 embassies, along with consulates and liaison and branch offices. Together, these overseas posts represented thirty different government agencies. Present in a typical embassy are representatives from the U.S. Agency for International Development; the Departments of Defense, Agriculture, Commerce, and the Treasury; the CIA; the Centers for Disease Control and Prevention; and the Export-Import Bank.

The concept of a **country team** was developed to bring coherence to the welter of agencies and programs now represented at an embassy. The ambassador heads the country team. In practice, ambassadors have found it quite difficult to exercise enough authority to transform a set of independent and often competing policies into a coordinated and coherent program. For example, in 2005, the Pentagon requested that it be allowed to put special operations forces into a country without the explicit approval of the ambassador. Also complicating the problem is the ambassador's background. Frequently, the ambassador is not a career diplomat. A study of ambassadorial appointments from 1960 to 2014 found that in twenty-nine countries and diplomatic missions such as the United Nations, 81–100 percent of ambassadors were political appointees.

The State Department's basic structure remained largely unchanged for the duration of the Cold War. Beneath the secretary of state were two deputy secretaries of state and six undersecretaries with responsibility for such matters as political, economic, and management affairs and international security. The remainder of the State Department was organized around geographical areas and functional tasks. While the number and identity of the regional areas held steady, the functional bureaus showed considerable change over time. Certain units, such as the Education and Culture Bureau, disappeared, and others, such as the Refugee Bureau and a bureau responsible for human rights and humanitarian affairs, were created. Today a very different picture exists. There are over fifty bureaus and offices covering geographic regions, policies (e.g., population, refugees, and migration; arms control, verification, and compliance), and administrative issues. There are also special coordinators (Tibetan issues, Israel and the Palestinian Authority) and special representatives (Iran, Venezuela), along with special envoys and ambassadors at large.

Running parallel to this significant organizational growth is a "shrinking presence" overseas. In June 2008, there were 6,636 **Foreign Service officers** (FSOs). A part of Biden's FY 2022 budget request was funding for an additional 500 FSOs and civil service positions in the State Department. In April 2022, the administration announced that it had hired 170 new FSOs.

## The State Department's Value System

Capturing the essence of the State Department's value system is best done by looking at how secretaries of state have defined their roles and how the FSO corps approach their jobs.

### The Secretary of State

The job of secretary of state is not an easy one. All too frequently, post–World War II secretaries of state have left under a cloud of criticism. Among the charges leveled are lack of leadership (Dean Rusk), aloofness and arrogance (Dean Acheson), and overly zealous attempts to dominate foreign policy making (Henry Kissinger). Secretaries of state have also found themselves excluded from key decisions. Cyrus Vance resigned from the Carter administration partly in protest over his exclusion from decision making on the Iranian hostage rescue effort.

In order to participate effectively in foreign policy making, secretaries of state, like their counterparts at the Department of Defense and the CIA, need a power base from which to work. In practice, this has required them to either become advocates of the State Department perspective or serve as loyal allies of the president.[6] Neither guarantees success, and each power base has its dangers and limitations. Adopting the first perspective makes them suspect in the White House, while the second makes them suspect within the State Department and runs the risk of letting the department drift for lack of effective oversight. Under President George W. Bush, Colin Powell's primary role orientation was as a spokesperson for the State Department perspective. Condoleezza Rice built her power base around the close personal ties she had developed with Bush during the campaign and as national security advisor.

The greatest danger comes with the failure to establish any power base, a situation most recently experienced by Trump's first secretary of state, Rex Tillerson. Tillerson failed to establish support within the State Department. Referred to as "the phantom of Foggy Bottom," his decisions were not seen as efforts to improve the State Department but as an act of obedience to Trump. He also never gained the trust of Trump, who only met Tillerson after winning the presidency and was attracted to him by his reputation as a global deal maker. Once in office, Trump came to see Tillerson as weak, and the two were seldom on the same page. When Tillerson talked of negotiating with North Korea, Trump tweeted that "he is wasting his time trying to negotiate with Little Rocket Man." After fourteen months, Trump used Twitter to fire Tillerson.

Mike Pompeo, who was an enthusiastic defender of Trump's foreign policy as head of the CIA, replaced Tillerson. Pompeo took office announcing his intention to get the State Department's "swagger" back. However, by the end of the administration, especially during the transition to Biden, Pompeo was seen as working with Trump to carry out a campaign of "fire-sale diplomacy" by implementing controversial policies intended to hamper Biden in his efforts to change the direction of U.S. foreign policy. In short order, Cuba was declared to be a state supporter of terrorism, Yemen's Houthi rebels were declared to be a foreign terrorist organization, and Iran was declared to be the home of al-Qaeda and new sanctions were imposed.

Antony Blinken assumed the position of secretary of state already having a strong power base with Biden, having worked with him in the Senate and when Biden was vice president, and during the presidential campaign. Blinken also previously served in the State Department and the National Security Council, which led to his appointment being well received there.

### Foreign Service Officers

At the heart of the State Department system is its FSO corps. The Foreign Service was created in 1924 by the Rogers Act. Foreign Service officers were intended to be generalists, "trained to perform almost any task at any post in the world."[7] The principal organizational device for producing such individuals is to rotate them frequently among functional tasks and geographic areas. The State Department relied on civil service, which existed apart from the FSO corps, to perform its "lesser" technical and administrative tasks. Increasingly, FSOs feel themselves under siege by the blurring of the line between civil service and Foreign Service personnel and by the increasing politicization within the State Department. Senior positions are routinely filled with short-term political appointees, a process referred to as **political creep**.

The distinction between FSOs and civil servants in the Foreign Service has long been the subject of controversy. In 1954, a reorganization proposal developed by Henry Wriston led to the merger of these two personnel systems. "Wristonization" was not a complete success. The hope had been that this merger would "Americanize" the Foreign Service by bringing in individuals with backgrounds different from those of the typical eastern, Ivy League, and upper-class officers. This broadening of outlook was seen as necessary; many viewed FSOs with suspicion for becoming aloof and separate from American society. They were a prime target of the McCarthy investigations into un-American activities. In 1953 alone, some 70–80 percent of the highest-ranking FSOs were dismissed, resigned, or were reassigned to politically safe positions.[8]

The representativeness of the FSO corps continues to be a major problem. In 1976, a class-action discrimination lawsuit was brought against the State Department. That year, only 9 percent of FSOs were women. In late 1993, the FSO corps was 56 percent white male, 24 percent white female, 7 percent minority male, and 4 percent minority female. In 2019, 6.3 percent of FSOs were Hispanic, 5.4 percent were African American, and 4.8 percent were Asian; 41.2 percent were female. In 2020, 90 percent of the Foreign Service was white and 69 percent were male. Less than 3 percent were African Americans. In the first five months of the Trump administration, three senior African American officials and a senior Hispanic official resigned or were removed abruptly. Among those who left was Linda Thomas Greenfield, who later became Biden's UN ambassador.

Additional problems surround the nature of key overseas appointments. For example, under George W. Bush, there were only three Hispanic FSOs serving as ambassadors, all in Latin America. Only one of the thirty-two diplomats heading embassies or U.S. missions in Europe in 2009 was black.[9] In 2018, only 26 percent of ambassadors were women and none were African American.

## Impact of the State Department on Foreign Policy

Once the centerpiece of the foreign affairs bureaucracy, the State Department has seen its power and influence steadily erode. It has gone from being the leading force behind such policies as the Marshall Plan, NATO, and containment to largely playing the role of the critic who finds fault with the proposals of others. It has become defensive and protective in interdepartmental dealings, unable to centralize and coordinate the activities of the foreign affairs bureaucracy.[10] One indicator of the problems it faces is its budget. Currently foreign affairs spending consists of 1.3 percent of the federal budget. Defense spending takes up 13.9 percent. Its problems are also evident when its budgetary allocations are looked at over time. Table 8.1 presents such an overview. The surge in money allocated to the State Department and foreign operations in FY 2021–2022 is due to the Ukraine War.

| Table 8.1 | Department of State, Foreign Operations, and Related Programs: Budget Requests and Appropriations, FY 2014–2022 (in billions of dollars) | | | | | | | | |
|---|---|---|---|---|---|---|---|---|---|
| **Year** | *2014* | *2015* | *2016* | *2017* | *2018* | *2019* | *2020* | *2021* | *2022* |
| Request | 51.96 | 55.01 | 54.83 | 60.21 | 40.21 | 41.66 | 43.10 | 44.21 | 71.37 |
| Funded | 50.89 | 54.39 | 54.52 | 59.78 | 54.18 | 54.38 | 57.37 | 71.38 | 66.51 |

*Source:* Department of State, "Foreign Operations, and Related Programs: Budget Requests and Appropriations, FY 2023," Congressional Research Service, April 18, 2022.

Two complaints are frequently voiced about the State Department's performance. The first centers on the FSO corps value system, which consists of a clearly identifiable world outlook and a set of guidelines for survival within the State Department bureaucracy.[11] The FSO is empirical, intuitive, and cautious.[12] Risk taking in the preparation of analysis or processing of information is avoided. The FSO mission is to keep intact the policy inherited from predecessors.[13]

Second, State Department recommendations are insensitive to the presidential perspective on foreign policy matters. Because it fails to frame proposals in ways that will produce political support for, or at least minimize political costs to, the president, State Department recommendations are easily dismissed. In the eyes of many, it has become more of a spokesperson for foreign viewpoints within the U.S. government than an advocate of U.S. national interests. This situation is not universally condemned. Some feel that it is an appropriate role for the State Department to play and that it should stop trying to perform functions for which it is no longer suited.[14]

Efforts are underway to change the FSO system and the culture of the State Department. One change is in how FSOs are selected. Beginning in June 2022, a candidate's score on the Foreign Service Officer Test will not be the primary factor in determining if they pass. It will be combined with their education, work history, and written responses to questions. The State Department has termed this as the most significant change since 1930.

# The Department of Defense

For most of its history, the military security of the United States was provided by forces under the command of the War Department and the Department of the Navy. No political or military authority, other than the president, existed to coordinate and direct the affairs of these two departments. During World War II, the ineffectiveness of this system became apparent, leading U.S. policy makers to take a series of ad hoc steps to bring greater coherence to the U.S. war effort. In 1947, the National Security Act formalized many of these arrangements by establishing a Department of the Air Force, giving legal standing to the Joint Chiefs of Staff (JCS), and creating a National Military Establishment and the position of secretary of defense. Further changes were made in 1949 when the National Military Establishment was redesignated the Department of Defense.[15]

## Structure and Growth of the Department of Defense

A number of different organizational reform issues have arisen since the Department of Defense was created. In the early 1980s, the pressing issue was improving the operational efficiency of the armed forces. The failed 1979 hostage rescue effort, the 1983 terrorist attack on the marines in Beirut, and problems encountered during the 1983 invasion of Grenada were cited by military reformers as proof that reforms were needed, beginning at the very top.[16] Over the objections of the executive branch and many in the military, Congress passed two pieces of legislation in 1986 designed to remedy the perceived shortcomings. The Goldwater-Nichols Act strengthened the position of the JCS relative to that of the individual services. It also gave added weight to those areas of the Pentagon with an interservice perspective. The second piece of legislation, the Cohen-Nunn Act, established a unified command for special operations and created an assistant secretary of defense for special operations and low-intensity conflict.

A recurring organizational challenge is budget size. Advocates of increased defense spending routinely identify four great waves of post–World War II defense budget neglect.[17] Each followed the end of a major U.S. military commitment but also reflected the onset of additional economic and social problems facing the military. The first (1945–1950) followed the end of World War II, the second (1970–1980) followed the end of the Vietnam War, the third (1991–2000) followed the end of the Cold War, and the most recent period began in 2009 with the decisions to withdraw from Iraq and Afghanistan. President Trump aggressively moved to end this fourth period in seeking a $54 billion increase over Obama's proposed 2017 defense budget. He requested a $716 billion defense budget for 2019 and a $750 billion budget for 2020. Russia's invasion of Ukraine has spurred a further increase in defense spending. The Pentagon's budget in FY 2022 was $722 billion. Biden proposed an increase to $737 billion for FY 2023.

A second, complex set of recurring challenges involves personnel issues. The military is facing a numbers crunch. In 2018, the army missed its recruiting goal for the first time since 2005. With a goal of seventy-six thousand (reduced from the initial target of eighty thousand), the army signed up fewer than seventy thousand recruits, despite offering waivers for previous marijuana use, bad conduct records, and health problems. Compounding matters, the army is much smaller than it was at the end of the Cold War. At that time it had 732,403 active-duty soldiers. In 2022 the army announced that it would fail to meet its FY 2022 recruiting goal by 23 percent and that as a result the size of the army would be reduced in FY 2023 from 485,000 to 476,000.

One part of the solution has been to **outsource** many tasks to private contractors. These tasks range from cleaning military facilities to supervising supply lines, operating combat systems, and training troops. At one point there were more than sixty private firms with twenty thousand employees in Iraq. While typically seen as a means of saving money and dealing with personnel shortfalls, outsourcing can also be used for political purposes, such as when the use of U.S. forces would arouse negative public opinion or run against congressional limits on the size of U.S. military operations. Another part of the solution to the personnel shortage problem has been to rely more heavily on National Guard and reserve forces. By 2005, almost 400,000 of the nearly 870,000 members of the reserves had been activated since 9/11. This represents the greatest proportional use of the National Guard and reserves since World War II.

Related to the numbers crunch problem is how representative the military is of American society and how individuals are treated by the military. More and more, the military has come to rely on young men and women from economically depressed rural areas. There has also been a decline in the number of African American recruits. The "Historical Lesson" reviews the path toward integrating African Americans into the military. Today, much of the focus is on its treatment of women, LGBTQ+, and immigrants. At issue here are both the roles they are allowed to play and the respect they are shown.

A third challenge involves the value of the United States' military presence abroad. Presidents George H. W. Bush, George W. Bush, and Bill Clinton closed hundreds of overseas military bases. Still, even after the withdrawals from Afghanistan and Iraq, it is estimated that the United States has some 750 military bases overseas that the U.S. owns or leases in seventy countries. Additional bases, often referred to as lily pads, are owned by the national governments and "host" U.S. forces. Iraq fits into this category today. Bases range in size from small cities to isolated radar installations. Beyond their cost, $55 billion annually, at issue is their value. For some they are necessary to maintain global order and U.S. security. For others they serve as launching pads for U.S. foreign military involvement and help stabilize authoritarian regimes. Table 8.2 provides a listing of the twelve countries with the most U.S. bases in 2021.

| Table 8.2 | Countries with Overseas U.S. Military Bases, 2021: Top Twelve |
|---|---|
| **Country** | **Number of Bases** |
| Germany | 119 |
| Japan | 119 |
| South Korea | 76 |
| Italy | 44 |
| United Kingdom | 25 |
| Portugal | 21 |
| Turkey | 13 |
| Bahrain | 12 |
| Belgium | 11 |
| Panama | 11 |
| Saudi Arabia | 11 |
| Kuwait | 10 |

*Source:* David Vine et al., "Drawdown: Improving US and Global Security through Military Base Closings Abroad," Quincy Brief #6, Quincy Institute for Responsible Statecraft, September 20, 2021.
*Note:* Refers to bases owned by United States or leased to United States; it does not include bases on U.S. territories.

## Historical Lesson

### Integrating the Military

On July 26, 1948, President Harry Truman signed Executive Order 9981:

> WHEREAS it is essential that there be maintained in the armed services of the United States the highest standards of democracy, with equality of treatment and opportunity for all those who serve in our country's defense:
>
> NOW THEREFORE, by virtue of the authority vested in me as President of the United States, by the Constitution and the statutes of the United States, and as Commander in Chief of the armed services, it is hereby ordered as follows:
>
> 1. It is hereby declared to be the policy of the President that there shall be equality of treatment and opportunity for all persons in the armed services without regard to race, color, religion or national origin. This policy shall be put into effect as rapidly as possible, having due regard to the time required to effectuate any necessary changes without impairing efficiency or morale. . . .

Executive Order 9981 went on to create a President's Committee on Equality of Treatment and Opportunity in the Armed Services, one of whose tasks was to examine how rules, procedures, and practices might be altered or improved upon to carry out this policy.

The history of black American participation in the military shows a continued pattern of white reluctance to allow it, along with the military necessity that it occur. From the very outset, free and slave blacks fought on both sides in the American Revolution. New England states offered freedom to slaves who fought, as a means of meeting their quota of troops in the Continental Army. Some southern states did likewise, but to a lesser degree. For its part, the British also offered freedom to blacks who joined with them.

During the Civil War, manpower shortages led Congress to pass legislation to allow blacks to fight but required them to serve in racially segregated military units; 180,000 blacks fought for the North. It is estimated that one-fifth of the Northern army was black. After the war, many of those promised freedom remained in slavery. After the war, four black regiments were established, which fought in the Indian wars and the Spanish-American War.

This policy of segregated military units was still in effect when World War II began. An additional policy was a quota system, which limited the number of blacks in the military to their percentage of the total American population. Once again, the pressures of wartime led to de facto changes in policy. With an insufficient number of Allied forces available to counter the German offensive at the Battle of the Bulge, black soldiers were allowed to volunteer to fight alongside white soldiers rather than serve in support roles but were placed in separate platoons.

After the end of World War II, political pressures mounted for ending segregation. A 1945 army report called ending discrimination a desirable goal but concluded that it was impractical. In 1947, the army permitted states to determine the level of integration of their National Guard above the company level. New Jersey ended military segregation at that point. As a result, some states had partially integrated reserve units, but the active military was still segregated.

Also in 1947, A. Philip Randolph helped establish the Committee against Jim Crow in Military Service and Training as part of a broader civil rights movement effort to end discrimination in the military. The focal point of their concern was Truman's plan for universal military service; while it did not endorse discrimination, it was perceived by committee founders to endorse segregation. It was against this backdrop that Truman issued his executive order. It came shortly after he was nominated to run for president, an election many expected him to lose, especially since southern democrats, unhappy with the party's endorsement of civil rights, decided to run their own

candidate for president under the banner of the Dixiecrats.

Truman's executive order encountered resistance and was not uniformly accepted. In 1949, the secretary of the army was forced into retirement for refusing to desegregate the army. That same year, 32 percent of white army personnel opposed integration in any form. During the Korean War, a shortage of white enlisted men and increasing black enrollment created yet another crisis. Ninety-eight percent of blacks still served in segregated units, and black soldiers were trained at a segregated military base. In 1951, while General Douglas MacArthur was still the commanding officer in Korea, evidence surfaced that far more black soldiers than white soldiers were being court-martialed. The National Association for the Advancement of Colored People (NAACP) sent Thurgood Marshall to investigate. He defined the military situation there as one of "rigid segregation." As a result of his investigations, charges against most black soldiers were dropped. In September 1954, under the Eisenhower administration, the last all-black military unit was abolished. Many consider the endpoint of segregation in the military to be July 26, 1963, when Secretary of Defense Robert McNamara ordered an end to discrimination against blacks outside of military bases.

## Applying the Lessons

1. Did Executive Order 9981 go far enough to address discrimination and segregation in the military? Explain your answer.
2. To what extent should the military be representative of all groups in society?
3. How do you measure the extent to which real change takes place in the military, the Foreign Service, intelligence agencies, or other national security bureaucracies?

On December 3, 2015, Secretary of Defense Ashton Carter announced that the Defense Department would open all combat jobs to women. "There will be no exceptions." When the announcement was made, the navy and air force had already opened most of their combat positions to women, and the army was moving in that direction. In September of that year, the marine corps, which was 93 percent male, had asked for an exemption for its infantry and armor positions. With this announcement, their request was denied. An estimated 220,000 military jobs were now available to women.

While the history of women serving in combat positions in the military goes back to the American Revolution, it was not until the passage of the Army Reorganization Act in 1901 that women could formally join the military (through the Army Nurse Corps). The 1948 Women's Armed Forces Integration Act gave women a permanent place in the U.S. military but limited the number of women to 2 percent of the enlisted force and 10 percent of the officer corps. Since the 1970s, the military has repeatedly turned to the question of the role of women in combat. An early 1990s Presidential Committee on the Assignment of Women in the Armed Forces called for determining military assignments on the basis of qualifications, not gender. The War on Terrorism and the military conflicts in Afghanistan and Iraq, both of which lacked clearly defined combat zones, brought this issue into sharp focus. Women soldiers searched homes and people for weapons, engaged in door-to-door neighborhood patrols, and were embedded in special operations forces. By the end of 2015, at least 161 women had died and 1,016 had been injured in these conflicts.

The role of women goes beyond their ability to engage in combat. It extends to the problem of harassment, which potentially affects all active-duty service members. In 2015, the Pentagon reported 6,131 cases of sexual assault, more than double the number in 2007. In 2018, that number jumped to 7,623. According to estimates, about 20,500 service members (13,000 women and 7,500 men) were sexually assaulted in FY 2018, up from 14,000 in 2016.

In 2013, Senator Kirsten Gillibrand introduced legislation to reform the military justice system with respect to how it handles sex crimes, moving control out of the hands of commanders to independent prosecutors. The military consistently and vehemently argued against such a move. Opposition began to lessen in 2021 when General Mark Milley, chairman of the Joint Chiefs of Staff, dropped his opposition to changing the system and an independent panel created by Secretary of Defense Lloyd Austin also recommended that changes be made. Austin endorsed its recommendations while Gillibrand indicated that the panel's proposal did not go far enough. As the congressional calendar raced to a conclusion, support for Gillibrand's bill, which had become part of the defense appropriations bill, encountered stiff opposition. In the end, that bill largely contained the wording of the Pentagon report. The decision as to whether or not to bring forward charges will be in the hands of a special prosecutor, but commanders will continue to conduct trials, pick jury members, approve witnesses, and grant immunity.

Controversy over the ability of gays to serve in the military long centered on the "don't ask, don't tell" policy put in place in 1994, which allowed gays to serve but did not stop them from being discharged. In December 2010, after months of political maneuvering by opponents in Congress, along with a Pentagon study supporting the policy, President Obama signed legislation repealing "don't ask, don't tell."

A major point of controversy in the Trump administration was the ability of transgender individuals to serve in the military. A June 2016 directive banned the military from involuntarily separating transgender individuals in the military, and allowed them to begin receiving medical treatment. In June 2017, just before the new policy was to take effect, Mattis delayed its implementation. One month later, Trump announced on Twitter that transgender individuals would not be allowed to serve in the military, calling their presence disruptive and overly expensive. In March 2018, Trump issued a revised order, which took a step back from the previous total ban on transgender troops and deferred implementation to the Pentagon. To many observers, it echoed the "don't ask, don't tell" policy. Five days into his presidency, Biden issued an executive order reversing Trump's ban. A follow-up executive order in March returned the transgender guidelines to where they were during the Obama administration.

## The Value System of the Department of Defense

Understanding the internal value system of the Department of Defense requires examination of how secretaries of defense and the professional military have defined their jobs.

### The Secretary of Defense

Secretaries of defense generally have adopted one of two roles.[18] The first is that of the generalist. *Generalists* recognize and defer to military expertise. They are concerned with coordinating and integrating the judgments they receive from military professionals, and they see themselves as representatives of the Department of Defense in the policy process. In contrast, the *functionalist* is concerned with consolidating management and policy control in the office. Functionalists reject the notion that a unique area of military expertise exists, and they see themselves as first among equals in defense policy decision making. Above all, the functionalist seeks to manage the system efficiently in accordance with presidential policy objectives.

James Forrestal, the first secretary of defense, adopted the generalist perspective. As secretary of the navy, he had opposed creating a unified military establishment, and his tenure as secretary of defense was marked by repeated efforts by the services to protect their standing as independent organizations. Since Forrestal, the most prominent secretaries of defense have adopted a functionalist perspective. Robert McNamara, who served as secretary of defense during the Vietnam War, was a functionalist who sought to move decision-making power out of the hands of the military services and into those of civilians in the Office of the Secretary of Defense. To do so, he brought Planning, Programming, and Budgetary System (PPBS) analysis to the Department of Defense. Instead of organizing the budget by department (army, navy, air force), the PPBS examined spending by its principal missions, such as conventional defense of Europe or nuclear deterrence.[19]

Donald Rumsfeld, George W. Bush's first secretary of defense, sought to alter the fundamental direction of American military policy and organization. Military professionals saw his presence as a "hostile takeover."[20] Victory against the Taliban in Afghanistan and early military success in Iraq appeared to vindicate his positions. However, subsequent problems with the occupation and reconstruction of Iraq led to open questioning of his ideas and management style.

Trump had two secretaries of defense, neither of whom was able to establish strong working relationships with him. In mid-2020, Trump declared that he never had a secretary of defense who was fully aligned with his foreign policy views and accused the Pentagon of trying to undermine him. Retired marine corps general Jim Mattis, Trump's first secretary of defense, was also a functionalist. He took office with a clearly defined set of views regarding the structure and operation of the military. He resigned over Trump's decision to remove U.S. forces from Syria and Afghanistan, the downgrading of NATO, and the threat that Russia posed to U.S. security. Mark Esper was very much the generalist, having little military experience. He served as secretary of defense for less than one year and found himself in frequent conflicts with Trump over the use of military power.

Lloyd Austin, a retired general, is Biden's secretary of defense and has adopted a generalist perspective. He is the first African American to hold this position. One of the primary tasks given to Austin was to develop a plan to address the COVID-19 pandemic in the military. He moved quickly to remove Trump political appointees from posts within the Pentagon. Austin also participated in numerous foreign travels to meet with leaders as part of Biden's efforts to rebuild America's presence abroad.

*Professional Military*

To understand the system of values inside the Defense Department, it is necessary to examine the outlook of the professional military toward policy making at two different levels. At the highest level is the general pattern of **civil-military relations.** Two different sets of perspectives have long shaped thinking about this relationship.[21] The *traditional* view sees professional soldiers as above partisan politics. They are expected to restrict themselves to speaking out only on those subjects that fall within their sphere of expertise. In turn, policy makers stay out of military matters. In the *fusionist* perspective, the professional soldier must acquire and use political skills in order to exercise an effective voice on military matters.

Neither approach is without its problems. The line separating military decisions from political ones is anything but clear, making it difficult—if not impossible—for the professional to stand above politics. The challenges to a president created by an embrace of the fusionist perspective were on full view in recent administrations. Obama, Trump, and Biden all received guidance from the military not to engage in a rapid withdrawal from Afghanistan, a line of policy that, while it had military logic to it, was not consistent with the political context within which these decisions were being made. Concerns exist, however, that while it may have been hard for the professional military to stand above politics over the past three decades, there has occurred a "hollowing out" and lessening of civilian control of the military. Military professionals may not directly challenge civilian control, but in retirement they have become active voices in political battles, and while on active duty they have often delayed and selectively implemented executive orders and other forms of presidential guidance as well as preempted civilian analysis and input in decision making.[22]

One level down from civil-military relations, there are differences in outlook among the military services, each of which has a different "personality."[23] It is said that the navy worships at the altar of tradition, the air force at the altar of technology, and the army at the altar of country and duty. The services also have different views of their own identities. The navy sees itself, above all, as an institution with a stature and independence that must be protected. The air force sees itself as the embodiment of the idea that air power is the key guarantor of national security in the modern age. The army views itself as artisans of warfare. A challenge facing the U.S. Army today is how to conceptualize modern warfare. The success of the Persian Gulf War in 1991 gave impetus to the idea of a **Revolution in Military Affairs,** in which technological advances are central to success on the battlefield. At the same time, the development of counterinsurgency (COIN) warfare thinking (see chapter 4) emphasizes the soldiers and their interaction with the local population.[24]

## Impact of the Defense Department on Foreign Policy

The professional military's impact on foreign policy is a subject that is often discussed with great emotion, as evidenced by concerns expressed about Trump's appointment of Mattis,

Mike Flynn, and H. R. McMaster as national security advisors and John Kelly as chief of staff. All were retired generals whom Trump often referred to collectively as "my generals." The fear was that the generals would set a confrontational tone to Trump's foreign policy and use military force rather than diplomacy as the foreign policy instrument of choice. Reality proved to be more complex. Trump's initial foreign policy did take a hawkish turn, but it was only after the exit of the generals and their replacement by civilians that U.S. foreign policy took on a more aggressive and high-risk profile. In fact, Trump was often quite dismissive of the military. In a July 2017 meeting arranged by his advisors, who were concerned about Trump's lack of experience in dealing with foreign policy matters, Afghanistan was discussed, at which point Trump lashed out at the generals, calling them "a bunch of dopes and babies" and saying that "you're all losers . . . you don't know how to win anymore."[25]

Overall, historical evidence suggests that military professionals are not necessarily more aggressive than their civilian counterparts.[26] Where the military professional and the civilian policy maker part company is over how and when to use force, not whether to use it. The military prefers to use force quickly, massively, and decisively and is skeptical of making bluffs that involve the threatened use of force. Diplomats, on the other hand, prefer to avoid using force as long as possible because they see its use as an indication of a failure in policy; they are positively predisposed to making military threats.

The military's real policy influence comes through its ability to set the context of a decision through the presentation of information, capabilities, and tactics. Bob Woodward, author of *The Commanders*, similarly reflects on the variability of military influence on decisions regarding the use of force.[27] The Pentagon, he notes, "is not always the center of military decision making. . . . When the President and his advisors are engaged, they run the show."

## The CIA and the Intelligence Community

The intelligence community comprises sixteen agencies plus the Office of the Director of National Intelligence (ODNI). The director of national intelligence (DNI) is the head of the intelligence community. Until this position was created in 2004, the director of central intelligence (DCI) served as head of both the Central Intelligence Agency (CIA) and the intelligence community. Members of the intelligence community are charged with working independently and collaboratively to gather the information necessary to conduct foreign relations and national security activities.

### Structure and Growth of the CIA and the Intelligence Community

Two points must be stressed before turning attention to three of the most prominent members of the intelligence community: the CIA, the National Security Agency (NSA), and the ODNI. First, the intelligence community is not a static entity. Its composition, and the relative importance of its members, has changed over time as new technologies have been developed, the international setting has changed, and bureaucratic wars have been won and lost. The status of charter membership is best conferred on the CIA; the State Department's intelligence unit, the Bureau of Intelligence and Research (INR); and the intelligence units of the armed forces. All of these were given institutional representation on the National Security

Council at the time of its creation in 1947. Three institutions that have a long-standing but lesser presence in the intelligence community are the Federal Bureau of Investigation (FBI), the Treasury Department, and the Atomic Energy Commission (AEC), which is now part of the Energy Department. The newest addition to the intelligence community is the Department of Homeland Security.

Second, the concept of a community suggests the existence of a group of actors who share common goals and possess a common outlook on events. In these terms, U.S. intelligence is a community in only the loosest sense. More accurately, it is a federation of units with varying degrees of institutional autonomy that both work together and challenge one another.

This point can be illustrated through several examples. The CIA and the Defense Intelligence Agency (DIA) have often been in conflict over matters of intelligence analysis. The DIA was created in 1961 for the purpose of unifying the overall intelligence efforts of the Department of Defense. During the Vietnam War, the CIA and DIA were often at odds over estimates of North Vietnamese and Vietcong troop strength; CIA estimates were far more pessimistic than those of the DIA. During the Iraq War, the challenge to the CIA came from a newly created Office of Special Plans (OSP) within the DIA; its mission was to provide independent review of raw intelligence and dispute the mainstream interpretations by the intelligence community.

Our selective examination of members of the intelligence community begins by looking at the CIA. For most Americans, the CIA is the public face of the intelligence community. In addition, since its director was also the head of the intelligence community until the DNI came into existence, it long enjoyed the status of first among equals within the intelligence community.

The organizational predecessor of the CIA was the Office of Strategic Services (OSS), which was created by a 1942 military order and tasked with collecting and analyzing strategic information and conducting special operations. At the end of World War II, Truman disbanded the OSS and assigned its intelligence duties to units within the State Department, the army, and the navy. The 1947 National Security Act reestablished the CIA as a stand-alone intelligence unit.[28]

The CIA began a major reorganization in 2015. According to CIA director John Brennan, the goal was to break down organizational "stovepipes" that artificially separate CIA personnel into different operating units, making communication between them difficult. Central to the new organizational structure are mission centers that bring together analysts and covert action operators on a day-to-day basis. The mission centers are modeled on the CIA's Counterterrorism Center, which brought together analysts and covert operations officials. They focus on such issues as terrorism, weapons proliferation, global issues, and the Middle East. In October 2021, CIA director William Burns created two new mission centers: China and Transnational and Technology. Sitting above the mission centers on the CIA's organizational chart are five directors. The two best known are the Directorate of Intelligence and the Directorate of Operations. The Directorate of Intelligence has been the primary producer of government intelligence documents, which range in frequency from daily briefs to weekly, quarterly, and yearly summaries and occasional special reports. The best known of these reports are the National Intelligence Estimates (NIEs). The Directorate of Operations, more recently identified as the National Clandestine Service, has had three basic missions: the secret collection of information, counterintelligence, and covert action. Those missions will continue to exist, but the National Clandestine Service will now focus on recruiting and training personnel to be assigned to the centers. The three other directorates are the Directorate of Science and Technology, the Directorate of Personnel, and the Directorate of Digital Innovation. This last directorate is the newest one and is tasked with such responsibilities as cyber espionage, protecting the CIA's internal email system, and monitoring global social media and other open-source information outlets.

The second prominent member of the intelligence community, the NSA, was the first major addition to the intelligence community. It came into existence in 1952 and operates as a semiautonomous agency of the Department of Defense.[29] In 2013, the NSA became the center of unwanted public attention when the media began reporting on the existence of a secret domestic surveillance program. Controversy over the NSA's intelligence collection practices resurfaced more recently. In 2017, there was a major leak of its highly classified hacking tools by a group calling itself the Shadow Brokers. In 2019, it was revealed that Chinese intelligence agents already possessed these NSA hacking tools and had redirected them for cyberattacks on U.S. allies and private companies operating abroad.

The NSA has also undergone major internal organizational changes. In 2009, the U.S. Cyber Command (USCYBERCOM) was created and placed inside the NSA under a "dual-hat arrangement," in which the head of Cyber Command was also the head of NSA. Its focus was to be on developing policy and legal frameworks for the defense of the military's computer systems, along with protecting private-sector computers that provide a potential entryway into government computer systems. In 2013, following a Department of Defense study concluding that the military was unprepared for a full-scale cyberattack, the Pentagon began a major expansion of its cybersecurity force capabilities. Three different missions now have been identified for the expanded Cyber Command: (1) national mission forces to protect computer systems and other infrastructures from foreign attack, (2) combat mission forces to plan and execute offensive operations, and (3) cyber protection forces to strengthen the computer networks of the Department of Defense. In 2017, USCYBERCOM was elevated to the status of a full and independent unified combatant command operating under a dual-hat arrangement: the head of NSA is in charge of both organizations. Calls have come for ending this dual-hat command structure, and in his last year in office, Trump tried to do this but ran into strong objections in Congress, which accepted the argument that the dual-hat system was required to ensure the speed, agility, and collaboration needed to operate effectively in a digital world.

The third organization is the newest agency involved in intelligence; the ODNI came into existence as part of the post-9/11 reforms of the intelligence community. Its head, the DNI, is identified as the principal intelligence advisor to the president and is charged with overseeing and directing the implementation of the National Intelligence Program. The two principal organizational subunits within the ODNI focus on collection and analysis.

Two broad areas of concern have been raised about the operation of the ODNI. The first is its size. As originally envisioned, the ODNI was to be a lean management organization sitting atop the intelligence community. It quickly grew into an organization with a staff of over 1,500 people. In 2010, the President's Intelligence Advisory Board concluded that the ODNI had become "bureaucratic and resource heavy" to the point that its ability to coordinate the intelligence community was impeded. A second concern is the powers of the office, particularly its budgetary powers and ability to shape intelligence programs. Only the CIA exists as a separate organizational entity within the intelligence community. All other organizations are parts of larger departments, most often the Department of Defense. Consequently, the other members of the intelligence community look with only one eye to what the DNI demands while keeping the other eye firmly fixed on departmental positions and priorities. Shortly after its creation, the FBI moved 96 percent of its intelligence budget into units that were not under the jurisdiction of the DNI. More recently, the DNI reached an agreement in principle with the Department of Defense that the civilian portion of the Pentagon's intelligence budget will come under its control. The Pentagon's covert action/spy budget will remain under Pentagon jurisdiction.

## The Intelligence Community's Value System

Periodically throughout its history, the CIA has found itself an institution under siege, both because of covert action and intelligence failures. Senator Daniel Patrick Moynihan was so outraged over the CIA's failure to anticipate the fall of communism in the Soviet Union that he called for its abolition.[30] One area that has received a great deal of attention is the manner in which both its top leadership and its professionals approach their jobs. The Senate Intelligence Committee's report placed a major portion of the blame for the intelligence failures on Iraq and preceding 9/11 on "a broken corporate culture and poor management." Let's turn our attention to the informal organizational side of the CIA.

### The Director of Central Intelligence

Because the DCI was simultaneously head of the intelligence community and head of the CIA, the office has had many role orientations available from which to choose. Three outlooks have been dominant: managerial, covert action, and intelligence estimating. Only John McCone (1961–1965) gave primacy to the intelligence-estimating role, and he was largely an outsider to the intelligence process before his appointment. Allen Dulles (1953–1965) and Richard Helms (1966–1973) both stressed the covert action aspect of the agency's mission. Since the replacement of Helms by James Schlesinger, DCIs have tended to adopt a managerial orientation. Although their particular operating styles have varied, a common theme has been to increase White House control over the CIA. Mike Pompeo, Trump's first head of the CIA, very much fit this mold. He has been characterized as the most openly political head of the CIA in a generation. Not only was he a strong public supporter of Trump's foreign policy agenda, but he actively participated in White House policy discussions. Pompeo received a mixed reception at the CIA, where he was valued for his support of intelligence-gathering operations but faced misgivings over his contradictory public statements; on occasion they supported the intelligence community's analyses, but other times they echoed Trump's criticism of intelligence. Pompeo's successor, Gina Haspel, a career professional described by some in the intelligence community as "the consummate insider," also adopted a managerial orientation on taking the position. During her confirmation hearings, she called for returning the CIA to its traditional mission of focusing on foreign states and less on counterterrorism. Haspel's nomination was politically controversial because of her involvement in the CIA's post-9/11 torture programs, but her appointment was welcomed by those within the agency, who saw it as placing intelligence professionals back in charge of the CIA. William J. Burns was Biden's choice to head the CIA, and he has adopted a managerial perspective. A professional diplomat who served as an ambassador and deputy secretary of state, Biden nominated him saying that "intelligence must be apolitical."

According to critics of the managerial role orientation, one frequent result of this outlook is politicization of the intelligence process. In other words, the heads of the CIA have used their managerial control over intelligence products to ensure that its findings are consistent with the policy preferences of the administration rather than reflecting the judgment of intelligence professionals. **Politicizing intelligence,** a charge directed at William Casey, Robert Gates, and George Tenet, was a major concern raised from the outset of the Trump presidency. While some concern was directed at Pompeo's deep engagement in policy making and his open support of Trump's agenda, most (from retired DCIs Michael Hayden, John Brennan, and James Clapper) pointed to Trump's repeated public attacks on the intelligence community's findings concerning Russian interference in the 2016 election. Especially troubling to the intelligence community was his statement at the Helsinki summit with Vladimir Putin: "They said they think it's Russia; I have President Putin, he just said it's not Russia. . . . I will say this: I don't see any reason why it would be. I have great confidence in my intelligence people, but I will tell you that President Putin was extremely strong and powerful in his denial today."

A reverse case of politicization of the intelligence process marked Haspel's tenure as head of the CIA. Trump wanted intelligence gathered on Russian interference in the 2016 election to be made public, believing it would prove him right. Haspel refused to release the information citing the need to protect information and sources that could not be easily fixed. She was also criticized by members of the administration for briefings given to Congress on issues that had not fully been decided, leading to charges of insubordination.

### The Director of National Intelligence

The DNI is torn by the same types of role conflicts that have afflicted DCIs: the need to establish a power base and the need to define an orientation to intelligence. There has been considerable turnover in the position since its establishment in 2005. John Negroponte, the first DNI, moved quickly to solidify his position as the president's primary intelligence advisor by personally presenting the president's daily intelligence briefing. Later DNIs have struggled to establish an effective working relationship with both the president and the intelligence community. Dan Coats, Trump's first DNI, joined with DCI Pompeo in resisting an attempt by Steve Bannon and Jared Kushner to bring in a political ally to head a White House review of the intelligence community. In another step in the direction of politicizing intelligence in the new administration, at Trump's request Pompeo rather than Coats began briefing the president on intelligence. Coats resigned in 2019 following a series of conflicts with Trump over intelligence assessments on North Korea and Russia and Trump's critiques of the intelligence community. Following Coats were three acting DNIs. Avril Haines became the first woman to hold the position when she was nominated by Biden and approved by the Senate.

### Intelligence Professionals

Views on intelligence within the intelligence community are far from uniform. Differences exist both between and within organizations.[31] For example, some suggest that, within the Cyber Command, four different outlooks can be identified, all of which should be present: cyber priests (who think in terms of deterrence), cyber prophets (adaptation), cyber designers (resilience), and cyber detectives (resistance).[32]

With these outlooks in mind, it is possible to identify four tendencies in the approach to intelligence by members of the intelligence community.[33] One tendency is to be a current-events-oriented "butcher," cutting up the latest information and presenting the choicest pieces to the consumer. A second tendency is for analysts to adopt a "jigsaw theory" of intelligence. Here the analyst acts like a "baker"; everything and anything is sought after, classified, and stored, on the assumption that at some point in time, it may be the missing ingredient to solving a riddle. Similar to the butcher's role, the baker's orientation is consistent with the policy maker's notion of intelligence as a free good and the assumption that the ambiguity of data can be overcome by collecting more of it.

A third tendency is the production of "intelligence to please" or "backstopping." This occurs when consumers desire only the intelligence that supports their policy preferences, ignoring efforts at providing anything but supportive evidence. The final role orientation is the "intelligence maker," who acts as an organizational broker, forging a consensus on the issue at hand. The danger here is that the consensus reached may not be based on an accurate reading of events. Facts bargained into existence provide an equally suitable basis for consensus but can lead to policy failures.

### Impact of the CIA and the Intelligence Community on Foreign Policy

Intelligence is not easily integrated into the policy process.[34] For example, Trump was most interested in information about his personal relationships with world leaders and the size and power of U.S. military resources. He showed little interest in national security policy or secret weapons programs. The relationship between intelligence and policy makers is marked by a series of tensions that often serve to make the impact of intelligence on policy less than what it could be under optimum circumstances. As Paul Pillar, who once served as deputy director of the CIA's counterterrorism center, observed about the Iraq War, "had Bush read the intelligence community's report, he would have seen his administration's case for the invasion stood on its head."[35]

A starting point to understanding the challenges that intelligence faces in influencing policy is the view held by many policy makers that facts are self-interpreting. Intelligence is about connecting the dots, not providing meaning to the data.[36] The limitations on the influence of intelligence produced by this perspective are reinforced by the tension between the logic of intelligence and the logic of policy making.[37] The logic of intelligence is to reduce policy options by clarifying issues, assumptions, and consequences. The logic of policy making is to keep options open for as long as possible and build policy support. As such, policy makers are most eager to get information that will help them convince Congress or the public about the merits of a policy.[38] Finally, intelligence produced by the intelligence community is not the only source of information available to policy makers. Interest groups, lobbyists, the media, and personal acquaintances all compete with intelligence, and presidents are free to listen to whichever intelligence they choose.

## The Domestic Bureaucracies

The most recent additions to the foreign affairs bureaucracy are organizations that traditionally have been classified as domestic in their concerns and areas of operation. Their foreign policy involvement parallels a development after World War II when the Defense Department, rather than the State Department, was instrumental in shaping global arms development programs and international security arrangements.[39]

Integrating these newcomers into the foreign affairs bureaucracy has not been an easy task. At the core of the problem is finding an agreed-on balance between foreign policy and domestic concerns. In the early post–World War II period, the foreign policy goal of containing communism dominated over private economic goals; more recently, domestic goals have become dominant and are often pursued at the cost of achieving broad foreign policy objectives.

## Treasury, Commerce, and Agriculture

Of all the domestic bureaucracies, the Department of the Treasury (also called the Treasury Department) plays the most prominent role in foreign policy. By the mid-1970s, its influence had made the State Department become more of a participant than a leader in the field of international economic policy. It now takes a strong secretary of state to neutralize the influence of the Treasury Department and its domestic allies.[40]

The two departments approach international economic policy from quite different perspectives. Like the other domestic bureaucracies, the Treasury Department takes an **"America first" perspective** (a term used long before being embraced by Trump), placing the needs of its clients at the center of its concerns. One author describes it as having an "undifferentiating adversary attitude" toward world affairs.[41] In contrast, the State Department's tendency is to adopt a long-range perspective on international economic problems that is sensitive to the positions of other states. A type of standoff for influence in the policy process currently exists between the State Department and Treasury Department; however, Treasury has been ascending in importance due to the rise in the use of economic sanctions, the recent global economic downturn, and the central role played by China in holding U.S. debt and maintaining an undervalued currency. Treasury gained additional importance as a foreign policy actor when, along with trade restrictions, economic sanctions began to include financial sanctions directed at individuals.

The Department of Commerce (also called the Commerce Department) has also emerged as a major foreign affairs bureaucracy. However, it is more involved in administrative or operating issues than policy ones. Until 1969, the Commerce Department's primary foreign policy involvement stemmed from its responsibility for overseeing U.S. export control policy. These controls were aimed largely at restricting the direct or indirect sale of strategic goods to communist states. Since 1980, the Commerce Department has become the primary implementer of nonagricultural trade policy and the chief administrator of U.S. export and import programs. The Commerce Department is not without its own challengers for influence on trade policy. The Office of the U.S. Trade Representative has also benefited at the expense of the State Department, and its activities enjoy a great deal of congressional support.

The Department of Agriculture (also called the Agriculture Department) remains a junior partner in the foreign affairs bureaucracy. Along with administering U.S. food export programs, its best-known foreign policy role is as administrator of PL 480, the Food for Peace program, which provides free export of government-owned agricultural commodities for humanitarian and developmental purposes. In 2003, the Agriculture Department became embroiled in controversy for providing export help to American tobacco companies. Its Foreign Agricultural Service provided market information to firms about where the demand for American cigarettes was high and where control laws were weak.

Numerous others play occasional roles as well. The Drug Enforcement Agency (DEA) has eighty-six foreign offices in sixty-seven countries where it carries out bilateral investigations, sponsors and conducts counternarcotics training, participates in intelligence-gathering activities, and provides assistance in developing drug control laws and regulations. The DEA gained notoriety recently when its agents accompanied Honduran counternarcotics police in two firefights with cocaine smugglers. One of these incidents left four people dead, leading to demands that the agency leave the country.

The Food and Drug Administration (FDA) has become more active in foreign policy issues through its inspection program of drug and food imports into the United States. Some 150 countries export FDA-regulated products to the United States. As of 2008, the FDA operated foreign offices in China and India, as well as in Europe and Latin America. Movement in the opposite direction (decreases in influence) have also taken place. In 2017, the Trump administration closed the Department of Energy's Office of International Climate and Technology, which was established in 2010 to provide technical advice to countries trying to reduce greenhouse gas emissions.

## Homeland Security

The Department of Homeland Security (DHS) is an uneasy fit in the foreign affairs bureaucracy. It has elements of both foreign and domestic policy, given the wide range of activities that fall under its jurisdiction. The DHS was established on November 25, 2002, as a response to the terrorist attacks of 9/11. Its creation combined twenty-two different agencies from eight different departments, with a total of 170,000 employees and had a projected budget of $37.45 million. It absorbed all of the Federal Emergency Management Agency (FEMA), the Coast Guard, the Secret Service, the Immigration and Naturalization Service, and the Customs Service and was charged with overseeing the new Transportation Security Administration. The FBI and the CIA were not directly affected by the creation of the DHS, but the new department was given an "intelligence and threat analysis" unit that would serve as a customer of FBI and CIA intelligence for assessing threats, taking preventive action, and issuing public warnings. In 2017, the DHS had an estimated two thousand individuals stationed in over seventy countries who engaged in activities ranging from flying surveillance aircraft to questioning travelers at airports.

The DHS has encountered problems in virtually all aspects of its work, beginning with the ineffective color-coded terrorist warning system put into place after 9/11 and the tracking of activities of peaceful war protestors. As recently as 2015, it faced the possibility that Congress would deny it operating funds. In December 2017, the DHS announced the creation of a new office to deal with weapons of mass destruction. Between 2015 and 2017, it was at the center of the political controversy over Trump's travel ban on people from seven Muslim countries. John Kelly, then head of the DHS, took responsibility for failing to hold up the policy announcement until Congress had been briefed. A DHS study contradicted Trump's assertion of the existence of a terrorist threat requiring the ban. Later, Kelly's successor, Kirstjen

Nielsen, was roundly blamed in cabinet meetings for DHS's failure to effectively secure the southern border from illegal immigration. More recently DHS was accused by the agency's inspector general of delaying and altering an intelligence report on Russian interference in the 2020 election. In the Biden administration DHS has been beset with internal conflicts over the proper approach for reducing border crossings and managing the border.

## Policy Makers' Response to Bureaucracy

Policy makers have adopted three different strategies for dealing with bureaucracies that are perceived to be failing them.[42] The first is to replace senior leaders. Perhaps nowhere was this strategy more evident than with the recent history of Voice of America (VOA). Created in 1942, it is an international radio broadcaster producing material in forty-seven languages and is overseen by the U.S. Agency for Global Media, which is an independent agency of the U.S. government. Early in the Trump administration, a strong supporter of his polices took over as head of VOA. By midyear, the heads of Middle East Broadcasting, Radio Free Asia, and Radio Free Europe/Radio Liberty were fired and their governing boards dissolved. The purge continued through the remainder of the administration. Hours after his inauguration, Biden moved to remove key Trump appointees, including the head of VOA. Other dismissals soon followed, and a new head of VOA was appointed.

The second is to reorganize bureaucracies. Rare is the bureaucracy that is simply eliminated. Instead, the solution is to combine the offender with another or rearrange its internal structure. In the extreme, this solution takes the form of creating a new bureaucracy to address an ongoing problem. Recall that the Department of Defense and the Office of the Director of National Intelligence came into existence this way. Finally, policy makers may simply choose to ignore the bureaucracy, either by becoming their own experts or by establishing an informal in-house body of experts to produce policy guidance. This last strategy is not without its shortcomings that can affect the content and quality of foreign policy. In 2019 the British ambassador to the United States characterized the Trump administration as "clumsy and inept." Two years earlier, revelations in the Mueller Report showed that Russian officials were frustrated in dealing with the incoming Trump administration because it could not find out who was in charge of matters.

It also needs to be noted that bureaucrats have their own view of the problem of integrating the bureaucracy with policy makers. When asked by President Kennedy what was wrong with the State Department, career diplomat Charles Bohlen replied, "You are."[43] Indications are that this sentiment still exists. In January 2017, some nine hundred State Department employees signed a dissent cable criticizing Trump's travel ban on citizens from seven Muslim-majority countries. The year before, fifty-one State Department employees signed a letter to President Obama in which they asserted that his policy toward Syria would not end the civil war and called for the ousting of Syrian president Assad.

## Over the Horizon: U.S. Space Command

This chapter began by recounting efforts by the Trump administration to restructure the State Department, an existing foreign affairs bureaucracy. It ends by looking over the horizon to the challenge of thinking how best to organize the **military after next**,[44] one geared to addressing future defense needs: Trump's plan to create a U.S. Space Command.

Trump first advocated the establishment of a separate military space force in March 2018. In June of that year he signed an executive order directing the Pentagon to construct a space force as the sixth branch of the military (the other five are the army, navy, air force, marine corps, and coast guard). This was followed in December by a memorandum authorizing the Department of Defense to create a new space command.

A U.S. Space Command had existed from 1985 to 2002 and had been given the task of coordinating the army, naval, and air force space forces. The command was disbanded after the 9/11 terrorist attack so that homeland security efforts could be better funded. Its operations were taken over by the U.S. Strategic Command and the air force. The first political steps in the direction of creating a true space command came in 1999 when Congress established a Commission to Assess United States National Security Space Management and Organization. Advocates argued that this was necessary because treaties had negotiated away the U.S. space advantage. The commission's report warned against the dangers of a "Space Pearl Harbor" and called for creating a military department for space operations. In 2017, a bipartisan proposal was introduced in Congress to create a separate space service within the air force along the lines of the marine corps' status in the Department of the Navy. The proposal was defeated.

Trump's endorsement and authorization of a space command provided few details on what was to be created and left many obstacles in place. The most significant obstacle is that only Congress can create a new military service. While Congress contains supporters of the concept of an independent space command, it also has powerful opponents who serve on the House Armed Services Committee. Many senior military officials, especially those in the air force, argue that creating a separate space force would only complicate national security decision making, weaken the military capabilities of existing services, and create internal conflict within existing branches of the military.

Another complicating factor is the nature of space warfare. James Moltz argues that Cold War–era thinking about the nature of space warfare and space power is obsolete[45] and needs to be reshaped, with greater attention to the idea of networked power and the collaboration of military and commercial/entrepreneurial space power resources. Doing so may require creating a space command quite different from the one being proposed.

In February 2019, Trump issued Space Policy Directive (SPD) 4, centralizing all military space functions under a new Space Force Command led by a civilian undersecretary of the air force and a four-star general. This announcement marked a step back from creating a sixth military service but found added support in Congress. In December 2019, Congress approved limited funding for the Space Command.

A potentially significant bureaucratic player in space policy is NATO. In 2019 it declared space to be a fifth domain of military action. At present NATO neither owns nor operates space-based military systems. It is estimated that more than half of the three thousand active satellites orbiting the earth belong either to NATO countries or to firms based in them. In early 2022, NATO identified four key roles it would carry out in its space policy: space support, space domain awareness, deterrence, and defense and resilience. The international politics of space became more complicated later in 2022 when Russia announced that it would withdraw from the International Space Station project, a multinational collaborative scientific undertaking, after 2024, ending one of the last areas of cooperation between Russia and the United States.

## Critical Thinking Questions

1. Is the formal structure of a bureaucracy or the value system of its members more important to the quality of bureaucratic performance? Explain your answer.
2. Is there a place for the domestic bureaucracies identified as making American foreign policy, or should their tasks be taken over by more traditional foreign policy agencies? Explain your answer.
3. Can the State Department lead in the making of U.S. foreign policy? Should it lead? If not, who should lead?

## Key Terms

"America first" perspective, 180
civil-military relations, 173
country team, 164
Foreign Service officer, 164
military after next, 183

outsource, 168
political creep, 165
politicizing intelligence, 178
Revolution in Military Affairs, 173

# Policy-Making Models 9

## Learning Objectives

Students will be able to:

1. Describe the four decision-making models introduced in the chapter (rational actor, bureaucratic politics, small-group decision making, and elite theory/pluralism).
2. Evaluate the ability of the four models to provide insight into decision making in the Cuban missile crisis.
3. Explain why models are important for understanding decision making.
4. Develop an argument for and against giving more attention to individuals in decision-making models.

# On the Agenda: Ukraine War Decision Making

Russia's 2022 invasion of Ukraine was not unexpected. Months of growing evidence pointed in this direction. The Biden administration responded by moving down two different tracks. The first was diplomatic. Two video conferences between Biden and Putin took place in December 2021. In his meetings with Putin, Biden urged him to de-escalate tensions with Ukraine and indicated that the United States did not plan to place offensive weapons in Ukraine. Biden also warned that Russia faced "serious costs and consequences" such as sending additional U.S. forces to NATO members. Russia would respond to Biden's comments stating that if a solution to Russia's security concerns was not soon forthcoming, it would "take every necessary action . . . to eliminate unacceptable threats to our security." On January 10, 2022, bilateral talks between Russia and the United States on the situation in Ukraine were held in Geneva. Two days later a meeting of the NATO-Russia Council was held to discuss the growing crisis. Secretary of State Antony Blinken described his meeting as "not a negotiation but a candid exchange of concerns and ideas." Discussions were also held with Ukrainian leaders to convince them of the serious nature of the Russian threat and the need for them to take action.

The second track involved putting together a team of national security officials in November to identity scenarios of how the United States and its allies should respond to the outbreak of war. Known as the Tiger Team, it examined how the United States might respond to a variety of paths that the war might take, ranging from a limited military incursion to a mass-casualty invasion. With Biden's endorsement, it also developed a novel strategy for seeking to counter Russia's moves toward war by declassifying and publicly broadcasting U.S. intelligence about Russian moves and intentions in an effort to undercut Putin's plans and broaden public opposition. An important factor in the decision to go public with U.S. intelligence was the unwillingness of Obama to do so in 2014 when Putin successfully invaded Crimea.

These two tracks worked in tandem. Just days before Biden and Putin held a video conference, a U.S. intelligence report based on satellite images was made public showing the positions of Russian troops and military equipment, indicating that a multifront offensive was being planned. The United States would later release information about a plan to install a puppet government in Ukraine and a plan to create a false-flag social media video that would show Ukrainian forces attacking civilians in Russia or Russian-speaking people in Ukraine. Intelligence information was also shared with allies in an effort to create a united front against Russia.

On February 10, new evidence arrived pointing to an accelerated Russian time line for an invasion. That night two hastily arranged meetings of Biden's national security team were held in the White House. The next morning Blinken and National Security Advisor Jake Sullivan gave warnings that an attack could occur "at any time." That invasion occurred on February 24.

Shortly after the Russian invasion, on February 28, Sullivan created a second Tiger Team. It explored such matters as the Russian use of chemical, biological, or nuclear weapons; attacks into NATO territory against weapons and aid conveys headed for Ukraine; and the expansion of fighting into neighboring countries. It also examined the question of how to prepare Europe for a massive influx of refugees. As with the work of the first Tiger Team, its analyses were shared with U.S. allies when Biden met with NATO leaders for the first time after the invasion. Sullivan also created a second team of officials to go beyond the immediate questions of how Russia will fight the war and examine the long-term opportunities for the United States to improve its geopolitical position as a result of the Russian invasion, based on the assumption that Putin acted in error in launching the invasion.

After the Ukraine War began, Biden's decision making again moved in two directions simultaneously. This time, however, they did not interact to fully support each other but often were in competition. The first dimension was a highly personalist impulsive response to the onset of war. On March 16, Biden stated that Putin was "a war criminal." The next day he called Putin a "murderous dictator, a pure thug who is waging an immoral war against the people of Ukraine." In a March 26 speech in Poland, Biden went off script at the very end of his speech in speaking about Putin to say, "For God's sake, this man cannot remain in power." This comment set off a scramble by his advisors to clarify that Biden was not calling for regime change in Russia but only that Putin should not be allowed to "exercise power over his neighbors or the region." On his return to Washington, when he was asked about the comment and whether it represented a change in policy, Biden said, "I was expressing moral outrage . . . and I make no apologies for it."

The second dimension finds Biden working with allies to reach a consensus. Realizing that the European Council was set to meet in late March, his administration moved quickly to organize a meeting with NATO leaders that he would attend. The agenda focused on the EU role in placing sanctions on Russia and export controls, and NATO's role in providing assistance to Ukraine and trying to deter Russia. Biden also moved to arrange a meeting of the G7 to coincide with these meetings. Biden sought to create a consensus even if it meant abandoning his own policy preference. In early March, House Speaker Nancy Pelosi spoke out publicly for ending Russian energy imports: "I'm all for it—ban it." Biden and his advisors were not as supportive. They wanted Congress to hold off on passing legislation banning Russian oil and gas imports until they had built up more support with allies. Days later that bill was moving forward in Congress with bipartisan support. That night Biden spoke with Pelosi by phone and asked that the House delay acting on it. Pelosi said they could move forward with it. The next day Biden announced his support for the energy ban.

Russia's invasion of Ukraine is widely seen as a defining moment in twenty-first-century international politics, bringing back echoes of past military conflicts in Europe and the Cold War standoff between Russia and the United States. White House decision making both in the prewar period and after fighting began was very much aware of the dangers they faced in making decisions under conditions where the action of one side may produce a quick response by the other. While each move may be calculated, the sum effect of the moves in what is referred to as an *action-reaction cycle* is the loss of control and escalating violence. In the case of the Russia-Ukraine War, a consensus existed that war was probably unavoidable because Putin was committed to attacking Ukraine. The greater fear was that the action-reaction cycle would produce a dangerous escalation in the fighting, perhaps involving nuclear weapons as Putin would threaten. Action-reaction cycles do not automatically occur or result in war. A 2019 action-reaction cycle involving the United States and Iran over the downing of a U.S. drone did not lead to war. One that did led to World War I, the so-called war to end all wars (see the "Historical Lesson").

It is one thing to recount key aspects of an important foreign policy decision, but how do you decide which influences were important in shaping the key decisions? One way to answer this question is to employ foreign policy decision-making models. This chapter surveys four of the most frequently used models, highlighting both their strengths and weaknesses.[1] It illustrates how they can be used to understand U.S. foreign policy making by applying three of them to the Cuban missile crisis.

## Foreign Policy Decisions and Models

One former foreign policy maker has observed that "the business of Washington is making decisions."[2] What is a foreign policy decision? What is it we are trying to understand? Answering these questions is complicated by a number of factors. First, the notion of a decision is itself somewhat misleading. It suggests the existence of a specific point in time at which a conscious judgment is made about a problem. Reality is often far less organized. Decisions are seldom final or decisive, they tend to lack concrete beginnings and endpoints, and they often amount to only temporary breathing spells or truces before the same issue arises again. In addition, decisions are often made with far less attention to their full meaning and consequences than is commonly recognized: "A government does not decide to inaugurate the nuclear age, but only to try and build the bomb before its enemy does."[3]

A second complicating factor is the relationship of the policy process to policy outcomes. Our intuitive sense is that if the policy process can be made to work properly, the policy outcome should also work. So, bad policy can be attributed to bad decision making. Unfortunately, the link between the two is imperfect. Good decision making does not ensure good policy. According to a provocative account of the U.S. experience in Vietnam, the fundamental irony of Vietnam is that, while U.S. policy has been roundly criticized, the policy-making system worked;[4] it achieved its basic purpose of preventing a communist victory until domestic political opinion coalesced around a strategy of either victory or withdrawal. The political system produced policies responsive to the wishes of the majority and near the political center, while at the same time allowing virtually all views to be aired. The bureaucracy selected and implemented measures designed to accomplish these ends, and these policies were undertaken without illusions about their ultimate chances of success.

In an effort to make sense out of the complicated business of making decisions, models have been developed to help explain, describe, predict, and evaluate how U.S. foreign policy is made. **Models** are analytical tools that are designed to serve as simplified representations of reality. As simplifications, they leave out much of the detail and texture of what goes on in the policy-making process. Models can be distinguished from one another in terms of how they seek to capture and depict reality.

Before turning to descriptions of the models, two caveats need to be raised. First, these models can help us understand what happens during the policy-making process, but they are not necessarily chosen consciously by policy makers. Second, they should not be judged in terms of right or wrong; a more useful standard is how helpful they are for explaining, describing, or evaluating the workings of the foreign policy process for the particular policy being studied.

## The Rational Actor Model

The most frequently employed policy-making model is the **rational actor** model. At its core is an action-reaction process; foreign policy is viewed as a calculated response to the actions of another actor. In carrying out these calculations, the state is seen as being unitary and rational. Unitary means viewing the state as calculating and responding to external events as if it were a single entity; there is no need for the analyst to delve into the intricacies of governmental organization, domestic politics, or personalities in trying to understand why a policy was selected. The state can be treated as a **black box**, responding with one voice to the challenges and opportunities confronting it. For example, this model is employed implicitly when speaking of Chinese goals or Soviet adventurism.

The basic elements of a rational decision process are the following: (1) goals are clearly stated and ranked in order of preference, (2) all options are considered, (3) the consequences of each option are assessed, and (4) a value-maximizing choice is made. Broadly speaking, there are two ways of carrying out a rational actor analysis of policy making. The first is *inductive*, which is frequently employed in diplomatic histories. Analysts try to understand the foreign policy decision by placing themselves in the position of the government taking the action. The objective is to appreciate the situation as the government sees it and to understand the logic of the situation. The second approach, *deductive*, is best exemplified by game theory; it is frequently employed by military strategists and deterrence theorists. Here it is assumed that "a certain kind of conduct is inherent in a particular situation or relationship."[5] Rather than relying on actual events to support its analysis, the deductive approach relies on logical and mathematical formulations of how states should (rationally) behave under given conditions.

The rational actor model is attractive because it places relatively few informational demands on the observer. However, it is frequently criticized for essentially the same reason. Foreign policy is not just made in response to external events; it is heavily influenced by domestic political calculations, personalities, and organizational factors. In addition, the rational actor model assumes that "important events have important causes." Doing so downgrades the importance of chance, accidents, and coincidence in foreign affairs. Critics also contend that the model's information-processing demands exceed human capabilities. Goals are seldom stated clearly or rank ordered. The full range of policy options and their consequences are rarely evaluated. In making decisions, the need for value trade-offs is denied more often than it is faced.

Critics of the assumption of rationality often advance two other models. One is based on the concept of *incremental decision making*, in which goals are only loosely stated, a limited range of options is examined, and the policy selected is one that "satisfices" (is satisfactory and sufficient) rather than optimizes.[6] Another decision-making model, known as **prospect theory**, asserts that individuals tend to value what they have more than what they do not have, they prefer the status quo more often than one would predict, and they tend to be risk averse with respect to gains and risk accepting when it comes to losses. Prospect theory implies that leaders will take more risks to defend their state's international position than to enhance it, and that, after a loss, leaders tend to take excessive risks to recover their previous position.[7]

A final challenge to the rational actor model centers on its methodology. Carried out either inductively or deductively, the rational actor model relies heavily on personal judgment in interpreting actions or in weighting policy payoffs. Graham Allison has captured this criticism in his rationality theorem: there is no pattern of activity for which an imaginative analyst cannot find objectives that are maximized by a given course of action.[8]

## The Bureaucratic Politics Model

Bureaucratic politics is the "process by which people inside government bargain with one another on complex public policy questions."[9] As this definition suggests, the **bureaucratic politics** model approaches policy making in a completely different way from the rational actor model. Policy making is seen as a political process dominated by conflict resolution, not problem solving. Politics dominates the decision-making process because power is shared, and the individuals who share power disagree on what should be done because they are located at different places within the government and see different faces of the problem.

Using military force to punish terrorists looks different to a secretary of state, who must balance the diplomatic pluses and minuses of such a move, than it does to the military chiefs of staff, whose forces would be used, or to a presidential aide, who is most sensitive to the domestic implications of the success or failure of such a mission. Not everyone in the government is a participant in a particular policy-making "game." Fixed organizational routines define the issue, produce the information on which policy decisions are made, link institutions and individuals together, and place limits on the types of policy options that can be implemented.

Furthermore, the players in the game are not equal in their ability to influence the outcome of the bargaining process. Deadlines, the rules of the game, and **action channels** confer power on some and deny it to others. Rules determine what kind of behavior is permitted and by whom. Can unilateral statements be made? Can information be leaked? Action channels link policy makers and determine who is in the best position to make a unilateral statement or to be included in a committee that approves action. Deadlines, which force issues by accelerating the tempo of the decision-making process and creating pressure for an agreement, take many forms and may include a meeting with a foreign head of state, a presidential speech, or congressionally established reporting deadlines.

Rarely do policy problems enter or leave the policy process in a clearly definable manner. More frequently, they flow through it in a fragmented state and become entangled in other ongoing policy issues. The result is that policy is not formulated with respect to any underlying conception of the U.S. national interest. Instead, its content is heavily influenced by the way in which the problem first surfaces and how it interacts with the other issues on the policy agenda.

In putting all of this together, advocates of the bureaucratic politics model argue that policy is not, and cannot be, a product of deliberate choice. Instead, policy is either a result of a political bargaining process or the product of organizational **standard operating procedures**.[10] In either case, a new policy is not likely to differ greatly from the existing policy because bargaining is an expensive, time-consuming process. In addition, policy makers are often committed quite deeply to their positions. The need for agreement pushes policy makers toward acceptance of a minimal decision that will allow all sides to claim a partial victory. The inflexible and blunt nature of organizational routines and procedures reinforces the tendency for policy to change only at the margins. Administrative feasibility is a constant check on the ability of policy makers to tailor policy options to meet specific problems. In sum, from the bureaucratic politics perspective, the best predictor of future policy is not the policy that maximizes U.S. national interests, but the one that is only incrementally different from current policy.

The bureaucratic politics model makes important contributions to understanding U.S. foreign policy by highlighting the political and organizational nature of policy making. However, it has also been subjected to extensive criticism. First, by emphasizing compromise, bargaining, and standard operating procedures, this model makes it very difficult to assign decision-making responsibility.[11] Second, it misrepresents the mechanism of bargaining by overstating the extent to which policy simply emerges from the policy process.[12] Third, the bureaucratic politics model is chastised for artificially separating the executive branch bargaining process from the broader social and political context. Attention must also be given to the domestic political forces and the values of policy makers, not just to how policy-making games are played. Finally, the model is criticized for being too complex, a virtual "analytic kitchen sink" into which almost anything can be thrown that might be related to how an issue is resolved.[13] The result is a story that may make for interesting reading, but it violates a fundamental rule: all things being equal, simple explanations are better than complex ones.

## The Small-Group Decision-Making Model

A third policy-making model focuses on the dynamics of **small-group decision making**. Advocates of this perspective hold that many critical foreign policy decisions are made neither by an individual policy maker nor by large bureaucratic forces. From a policy maker's perspective, small-group decision making offers a number of advantages over its bureaucratic counterpart:

- The absence of significant conflict; there are few viewpoints to reconcile.
- A free and open interchange of opinion among members; there are no organizational interests to protect.
- Swift and decisive action.
- Possible innovation and experimentation.
- The possibility of maintaining secrecy.[14]

Three different types of small groups can be identified:[15]

1. *Informal small group that meets regularly but lacks an institutional base.* The Tuesday lunch group in the Johnson administration and the Friday breakfast and Thursday lunch groups of the Carter administration are prominent recent examples.

2. *Ad hoc group created to deal with a specific problem, then ceases to function once its task is completed.* In the first week of the 1950 Korean crisis, six small-group meetings were held. During the Cuban missile crisis, the key decisions were made by the Executive Committee (ExCom), an ad hoc group of about fifteen individuals brought together by President John Kennedy specifically to deal with this problem.

3. *Permanent small group that possesses an institutional base and is created to perform a series of specified functions.* The subcommittees of the National Security Council (NSC) fall into this category. During the Carter administration, a Special Coordinating Committee (SCC) was set up to deal with crisis situations; during the Iranian hostage crisis it met at 9:00 a.m., at first daily and later less frequently, to go over an agenda put together by the NSC staff.[16] Following the terrorist attacks of September 11, 2001, the George W. Bush administration established a "War Cabinet" consisting of some dozen people, including Vice President Dick Cheney, Secretary of State Colin Powell, Secretary of Defense Donald Rumsfeld, and National Security Advisor Condoleezza Rice.

Despite its advantages, small-group decision making often results in policy decisions that are anything but rational or effective. Pearl Harbor, the Bay of Pigs invasion, and key decisions in Korea and Vietnam have all been analyzed from a small-group decision-making perspective.[17]

Policy failures are seen as the result of strong in-group pressures on members to concur in the group's decision. This pressure produces a "deterioration of mental efficiency, reality testing, and moral judgment" that increases the likelihood of the group's making a potentially defective decision.[18] Irving Janis coined the term **groupthink** to capture this phenomenon. He also identified eight symptoms that indicate its presence and divided them into three categories: overestimation of the group's power and morality, closed-mindedness, and pressures toward conformity. Janis argued that the more symptoms are present, the more likely it is that concurrence-seeking behavior will result and that defective decisions will be made. Table 9.1 aligns Tower Commission Report observations about the decision making on the Iran-Contra Affair with Janis's elements of groupthink. Although the match is not perfect (e.g., illusion of unanimity is better seen as an illusion of presidential support), the parallels are striking.

Groupthink is a phenomenon that occurs regardless of the personality traits of group members. It is not an inevitable product of a tight-knit decision group, nor is it necessarily the cause of a policy fiasco. Poor implementation, changed circumstances, or accidental factors also produce policy failures. Groupthink exists as a tendency that is made more or less likely by three sets of antecedent conditions: the coherence of the decision-making group, structural faults of the organization, and the nature of the decision context. At its core is the assumption that concurrence-seeking behavior is an attempt on the part of group members to cope with stress by developing a mutual support base.[19]

Because groupthink is a tendency and not a condition, in theory it can be avoided. Recognizing that each proposed solution has its own drawbacks, Janis puts forward several measures to improve the quality of small-group decision making.[20] They include establishing multiple groups for the same task (multiple advocacy), establishing a devil's advocate, and having a "second chance" meeting at which decisions can be reconsidered one final time.

Three general lines of criticism have been directed at the groupthink approach to small-group decision making. First, Janis's proposed solutions probably will not work. Consider

| Table 9.1 | Groupthink and the Iran-Contra Affair |
|---|---|

| Element of Groupthink | Findings of the Tower Commission Report |
|---|---|
| Illusion of invulnerability | The president "was all for letting the Israelis do anything they wanted at the very first briefing" (McFarlane, p. 131). |
| Unquestioned belief in group's morality | The president distinguished between selling someone believed able to exert influence with respect to the hostages and dealing directly with the kidnappers (p. 39). |
| | The administration continued to pressure U.S. allies not to sell arms to Iran and not to make concessions to terrorists (p. 65). |
| Collective efforts to discount warnings | "There is a high degree of risk in pursuing the course we have started, we are now so far down the road that stopping . . . could have even more serious repercussions. We all view the next step as confidence building" (North, p. 167). |
| Stereotyping the enemy | Release of the hostages would require influence with Hezbollah, which could involve the most radical elements of the Iranian regime. The kind of strategy sought by the United States, however, involved what were regarded as more moderate elements (p. 64). |
| Self-censorship | Evidence suggests that he [Casey] received information about the possible divergence of funds to the Contras almost a month before the story broke. He, too, did not move promptly to raise the matter with the president (p. 81). |
| | Secretary Shultz and Secretary Weinberger, in particular, distanced themselves from the march of events (p. 82). |
| Illusion of unanimity | "I felt in the meeting that there were views opposed, some (presidential support) in favor, and the President didn't really take a position, but he seemed to, he was in favor of this project somehow or other" (Shultz, p. 183). |
| | "As the meeting broke up, I had the idea the President had not entirely given up on encouraging the Israelis" (Casey, p. 198). |
| Direct pressure against | "Casey's view is that Cap [Weinberger] will continue to create roadblocks until he is told by you that the President wants this move NOW" (North to Poindexter, p. 232). |
| Emergence of mindguards | "I don't want a meeting with RR, Shultz, and Weinberger" (Poindexter, p. 45). |
| | North directed that dissemination be limited to Secretary Weinberger, DCI Casey, McFarlane, and himself. North said McFarlane had directed that no copy be sent to the secretary of state and that he, McFarlane, would keep Secretary Shultz advised orally on the NSC project (p. 149). |

*Source:* President's Special Review Panel, *The Tower Commission Report* (New York: Bantam, 1987). Citations from Robert McFarlane, national security advisor, 1983–1985; Colonel Oliver North, national security council staffer; George Shultz, secretary of state; William Casey, director of central intelligence; Adm. John Poindexter, national security advisor, 1985–1986; Caspar Weinberger, secretary of defense.

the idea of multiple advocacy, which attempts to ensure that all views, "however unpopular," will receive serious attention.[21] Two dangers exist here. In each case, they are brought on by overloading the intellectual capabilities of policy makers and by highlighting the ambiguity of the evidence before them. One outcome is that policy makers will simply choose whatever policy option is in accord with their preexisting biases. If a wide range of options are all made to appear respectable and doubts exist about the effectiveness of each, why not "let Reagan be Reagan" and select the one that best fits his image of the world? The other, equally undesirable, outcome is paralysis. Confronted with too many policy options, all of which appear to have problems, policy makers may end up doing nothing.

Second, criticism is directed at the criteria used to establish a good decision.[22] The standard used (vigilant appraisal) virtually duplicates the logic of the rational actor model. The point remains: if the rational actor model is an unrealistic benchmark for judging decision making, isn't the same true for vigilant appraisal?

A third criticism is more theoretical in nature. The groupthink approach is grounded in a conflict model of individual decision making. According to this model, individuals often confront decision-making situations in which they feel "simultaneous opposing tendencies to accept and reject a given course of action."[23] According to the cybernetic approach to decision making, individuals do not necessarily attempt to resolve value conflicts and tensions in making decisions. From this vantage point, attention should be directed toward how uncommitted thinkers make decisions.[24]

Even with these problems, recent decision-making studies continue to point to the importance of groupthink.[25] The approach has also been extended from just explaining a defective decision to explaining shifts in a stream of policy decisions. These include the War on Terrorism and the invasion of Iraq.[26]

## Elite Theory and Pluralism

During the 1960s and early 1970s, elite theory and pluralism served as the focal point for an intense debate raging among political scientists over how best to understand the process of public policy making. Although no longer the center of attention, they remain important approaches for understanding how U.S. foreign policy is made.

**Elite theory** represents a quite different perspective on foreign policy making than the three approaches examined so far. It is concerned with the identities of those individuals who make foreign policy and the underlying dynamics of national power, social myth, and class interests. Elite theory stresses the ties that bind policy makers rather than the forces that divide them.

From this perspective, foreign policy is formulated as a response to demands generated by the economic and political system. Not all demands receive equal attention, and those that receive the most attention serve the interests of only a small sector of society. These special interests are transformed into national interests through the pattern of office holding and the structure of influence that exists within the United States. Those who hold office are seen as a stable and relatively cohesive group of people who share common goals, interests, and values.

Disagreements among elites exist only at the margins; they surface most frequently as disputes over policy implementation, not policy goals. Those outside the elite group are held to be relatively powerless. Furthermore, public reactions are often "orchestrated" by the elite rather than being expressions of independent thinking on policy matters. This explains why certain policy proposals routinely fail to attract serious attention: ideas that do not build on the relatively narrow range of value assumptions shared by the elite and rooted in the underlying dynamics of the socioeconomic structure are rejected as unworkable, fundamentally flawed, or fatally naive. Elite theory also suggests that the basic directions of U.S. foreign policy will change slowly, if at all.

Although consensus is broad, elite theorists do disagree on a number of points:

1. *Constraints on elite behavior.* Some elite theorists see few, if any, constraints on the type of policies that elites can pursue. Others see a more open policy process subject to periodic "short-circuiting" by the public.
2. *Conspiring elites.* Some elite theorists pay great attention to the social backgrounds and linkages among members of the elite class, but others deemphasize these features in favor of attention to the broader and more enduring forces of a capitalistic economic system that drives U.S. foreign policy to be expansionist, aggressive, and exploitive.[27]

Several recent administrations have been the subject of conspiratorial-style elite analysis. In the case of the Carter administration, the object of attention was the presence of large numbers of members of the Trilateral Commission in policy-making positions. The Trilateral Commission was formed in 1973 to foster cooperation among the United States, Western Europe, and Japan. During the Reagan administration, analysis focused on links between his appointees and the Committee on the Present Danger, a group established in the 1970s to warn against the continuing threat posed by the Soviet Union. In the George W. Bush administration, the focus was the influence of neoconservatives on foreign policy decisions. Unlike the other two groups, the neoconservatives were not part of an institution; rather, *neoconservative* refers to a broad philosophical outlook on America's role in world politics.

**Pluralism** is regarded as the orthodox interpretation of how the U.S. policy-making system works. Like elite theory, no single comprehensive statement of the argument exists. Still, six common themes can be identified:

1. Power in society is fragmented and diffused.
2. Many groups in society have power to participate in policy making.
3. No one group is powerful enough to dictate policy.
4. An equilibrium among groups is the natural state of affairs.
5. Policy is the product of bargaining among groups and reflects the interests of the dominant group(s).
6. The government acts as an umpire, supervising the competition and sometimes compelling a settlement.

Pluralists acknowledge that power resources are not distributed evenly throughout society. However, they hold that merely possessing the attributes of power (wealth, status, etc.) is not equal to possessing power itself[28] because the economic and political sectors of society are considered separate. In addition, power resources may be substituted for one another. Large numbers may offset wealth; leadership may offset large numbers; and commitment may overcome poor leadership. One example of pluralism was the grassroots movement in the United States to force South Africa to end apartheid. What began as a movement on college campuses in the late 1970s and early 1980s to force companies to disinvest from South Africa gradually succeeded in sensitizing policy makers and the American public to the problem; as a result, by 1985, U.S. policy toward South Africa began to show signs of change.

A number of flaws have been suggested in the pluralists' argument.[29] Pluralists assume that competition between groups produces policy makers who compete over the content of policy. What happens when policy makers do not compete over policy but instead are so fragmented that they rule over separate and self-contained policy areas? Theodore Lowi suggests that such conditions better describe the operation of the U.S. government than the pluralist model; when this happens, the government is not an umpire but a holding company. Pluralism, then, exists without competition, as interest groups capture different pieces of the government and shape its policies to suit their needs. New groups or the poorly organized are effectively shut out of the decision-making process. Just as important, interest group liberalism reduces the capacity of the government to plan because it is unable to speak with one voice or to examine problems from a national perspective.

## Historical Lesson

### The War to End All Wars

Known to many simply as "the Great War," World War I was an international system–changing event. The action-reaction cycle setting World War I in motion began with the assassination of Archduke Ferdinand, the heir to the Austrian-Hungarian throne, by a Serbian nationalist on June 28, 1914.

Existing alliance systems that divided the European great powers into two groups contributed to the speed with which events unfolded. Britain, France, and Russia formed the Triple Entente. Germany, Austria-Hungary, and Italy made up the Triple Alliance.

On July 23, Austria-Hungary issued to Serbia a set of ten demands that were deliberately constructed to be unacceptable. When they were rejected, Austria-Hungary broke off diplomatic relations, mobilized its troops, and declared war on Serbia on July 28, 1914. The next day, Russia mobilized its forces in support of Serbia. Germany asked Russia to cease mobilization and drop its support. Germany also sent a communication to France requesting that it not support Russia. When Russia refused, Germany declared war on Russia. Germany then demanded that France remain neutral but began mobilizing in accord with the Schlieffen Plan, Germany's pre-war military plan, which saw invasion of France as necessary to protect its western borders before sending troops to fight Russia. On August 3, Germany declared war on France. On August 4, Britain declared war on Germany. The United Sates declared war on Germany on April 6, 1917.

By the time World War I ended on November 11, 1918, with a death toll exceeding nine million, a number of significant events had occurred. Four empires had been destroyed: Germany, Russia, Austria-Hungary, and the Ottoman Empire. Russia had experienced one of the world's most important revolutions; in 1917, Russia's czar was overthrown and a communist government came to power, committed in principle to the overthrow of capitalism around the world. The United States had established itself as a major power and brought to that role a very different interpretation of international politics than the European great powers. The League of Nations was created. The map of Europe was redrawn as Poland, Finland, Czechoslovakia, Yugoslavia, Hungary, Austria, Estonia, Lithuania, Latvia, Estonia, and Turkey came into existence as independent states.

Given these far-reaching consequences, you would think that avoiding the onset of the Great War would have been a major concern to policy makers and the public alike. Yet this was not the case. For almost a hundred years, the great powers had worked together through a series of alliances that had provided them with a mechanism for managing political and military affairs in Europe in a way that minimized the potential occurrence of systemic disruptions. Public fears of a system-changing war were calmed by Norman Angell's argument in *The Great Illusion*, first published 1909; he argued that, while war was not impossible, it would be economically harmful to both the winners and losers due to the dynamics of economic interdependence. The conclusion was clear: war should be rejected, and reason and respect for international law should be embraced as the logical path to follow in managing world affairs.

You might also expect national memories of World War I to be consistent, yet they differ greatly. France looks back upon it as a tragic but noble cause. Great Britain views it with mixed feelings. Germany came out of the war humiliated and required to pay heavy reparations to the victors, a combination many see as laying the domestic political foundations on which Hitler rose to power.

Japan also emerged from World War I with a sense of having been dishonored; as a victorious Allied power, Japan entered the Paris Peace Talks expecting to gain control of German colonies in Asia just as France and Great Britain had acquired control over territories ruled by Germany and the Ottoman Empire in Africa and the Middle East. Japan also expected to be treated as an equal; to that end, it put forward a racial equality clause for inclusion in the League of Nations charter. Neither goal was realized. For its part, the United States championed the concept of a League of Nations and then declined to join it, instead adopting a policy of disengagement from the power politics of Europe and Asia.

While debates continue over whether World War I made World War II possible, caused it, or was irrelevant to it, it is clear that World War I did not end global wars. What is unclear is the possibility of a reappearance of the factors that contributed to its outbreak. Niall Ferguson suggests that many of those factors are already in place in today's international system: (1) imperial overstretch (Great Britain was showing signs of tiring in its role as the keeper of global peace and prosperity); (2) growing imperial rivalry (between Germany and Russia); (3) instability of existing alliance systems; (4) support by rogue regimes (e.g., Serbia) of international terrorism (the assassination of Archduke Ferdinand); and (5) the rise of a revolutionary terrorist group hostile to capitalism (the emergence of the Bolsheviks).[30] Today, Ferguson argues that the United States is overstretched militarily, a rivalry is growing between the United States and China, NATO is struggling to define its role, states are sponsoring international terrorism or are reluctant to challenge it, and al-Qaeda is much more of an Islamo-Bolshevist terrorist group than an Islamofascist group.

### Applying the Lesson

1. Are today's crises different from the one that set off World War I? Explain your answer.
2. What is the most dangerous step to be avoided in an action-reaction cycle, and why?
3. What decision-making models are best suited for studying crises, and why?

# Integrating Models

Given the complexity of the situations faced and the variety of factors that might go into selecting a course of action, it stands to reason that no single foreign policy model will be able to help us understand a foreign policy decision or outcome completely. Such an understanding often requires integrating several different models. Typically, integration can be attempted in four ways. The first is to shift from model to model as the focus of the analysis changes. For example, from the rational actor perspective, the decision to send U.S. troops to Korea in 1950 is a single decision. From the bureaucratic or small-group perspective, a series of separate decisions might be identified. A distinction can also be made between the sociopolitical aspects of policy making and the intellectual task of choosing a response.[31] The pluralist and bureaucratic politics models help us understand why policy makers act as they do once they are "in place," but they tell us little about how they got there or the values they bring to bear in addressing a problem. To answer these questions, we might turn to elite theory or the rational actor model for insight.

A second way to integrate policy-making models is to recognize that some are more appropriate for analyzing some problems or issue areas than for others. Generally, the more open the policy process and the longer the issue is on the policy agenda (as is typically the case for structural and strategic issues), the more useful the bureaucratic and pluralist models will be. For more closed processes and quicker responses, the rational actor, elite theory, or small-group model are more applicable.

A third way to integrate these models is to shift from one to another as the policy problem develops over time. The elite or rational actor model might be especially helpful for understanding how the United States got involved in Vietnam, but the small-group or bureaucratic politics model might be most helpful for understanding key decisions during the course of the war. The **poliheuristic decision-making** model suggests another way to combine approaches, arguing that individuals only engage in a rational calculation of the costs and benefits of a limited number of alternatives in a second stage of decision making, after most alternatives have been eliminated.[32] Similarly, individuals are likely to approach policy implementation differently than policy selection.

A final way of integrating these models is based on the values that guide analysis. As has already been suggested, although the rational actor model may be deficient as a description of the policy-making process, it is still valuable for the purpose of evaluating the process. However, one should be careful in using models in this way, for embedded in each are assumptions about how policy should be made that are not always readily apparent. For example, implicit in the rational actor model is a belief in the desirability of a strong president and the ability to act quickly. The model does not place great value on widespread participation in decision making or on a system of checks and balances.

# The Cuban Missile Crisis

This section examines the Cuban missile crisis, one of the most important events in U.S. foreign policy. Many consider it the defining foreign policy crisis of the Cold War. The section begins with an overview of how the crisis unfolded and then employs three models—rational actor, bureaucratic politics, and small-group decision making—to show how models can help in understanding foreign policy.

## The Crisis: An Overview

The Cuban missile crisis, which took place over thirteen days (October 16–28, 1962), is widely regarded as a major turning point in the Cold War.[33] Never before and never after did the United States and the Soviet Union appear to be on the brink of nuclear war. At the time of the crisis, President John Kennedy estimated that the odds of averting such an outcome were between one in three and 50/50.[34]

Soviet weapons shipments to Cuba had been taking place since the summer of 1960. A slowdown occurred in early 1962, but the pace quickened again in late July. By September 1, the inventory of Soviet equipment in Cuba included surface-to-air missiles (SAMs), cruise missiles, patrol boats, and large quantities of transportation, electrical, and construction equipment, as well as over five thousand technicians and other military personnel.[35] The first strategic missiles, medium-range ballistic missiles (MRBMs) with a range of 1,100 nautical miles, arrived secretly in Cuba on September 8. Forty-two of these missiles reached Cuba before the crisis was resolved. Equipment for the construction of intermediate-range ballistic missiles (IRBMs) and IRBM sites also began arriving, although no IRBMs actually reached Cuba. Finally, Soviet shipments in September included IL-28 jet bombers and MiG-21 jet fighters, plus additional SAMs, cruise missiles, and patrol boats.

Intelligence on the exact dimensions of the Soviet buildup in Cuba came from a number of different sources: refugee reports, CIA agents operating in Cuba, analyses of Soviet shipping patterns, and U-2 spy plane overflights. Not all of the information was reliable, nor did it all come together at the same time and place for analysis. For example, refugees were reporting the presence of Soviet missiles in Cuba before Cuba began receiving weapons of any kind from the Soviet Union, and great care had to be taken in processing reports from agents operating inside Cuba. The United States Intelligence Board met on September 19 and approved an intelligence estimate indicating that the Soviet Union would not introduce offensive missiles into Cuba.

This conclusion was not shared uniformly in the administration. In late August, Director of Central Intelligence (DCI) John McCone told President Kennedy, Secretary of Defense Robert McNamara, and Secretary of State Dean Rusk that the Soviet Union was preparing to place offensive missiles in Cuba. In late September others began to agree with McCone, and a U-2 overflight over western Cuba was considered. No U-2 overflights over this area had been authorized since September 5 because of recent mishaps with U-2 overflights in Asia. Fearful that all U-2 flights might be canceled if another incident occurred, the Committee on Overhead Reconnaissance (COMOR) had decided not to send any U-2s over western Cuba, where SAM sites were known to be under construction. On October 4, COMOR did approve a U-2 overflight over western Cuba. A jurisdictional dispute between the Defense Department and the CIA over who would conduct the mission led to an unsuccessful flight on October 9, and it was not until October 14 that a successful U-2 flight took place. Its photographs firmly established the presence of Soviet offensive missiles in Cuba. On October 22, President Kennedy went on national television to announce the discovery.

Kennedy called together a special ad hoc advisory group known as the ExCom of the National Security Council (NSC) to deal with the crisis. During ExCom's first meeting on October 16, it began to identify the options open to the United States. Six major options surfaced: (1) no action, (2) diplomatic pressures either at the United Nations or on the Soviet Union, (3) a secret approach to Castro with the option of "split or fall," (4) invasion, (5) a surgical air strike, and (6) a naval blockade.[36] The first option seized on was the surgical air strike.[37] The blockade was not lobbied for strongly until the end of the day, and Kennedy's initial response to this option was skeptical, as he was not sure how a blockade would get Soviet missiles out of Cuba.

By the end of the first day, Kennedy identified three options. Participant accounts suggest that attention focused primarily on two of these, the surgical air strike and the blockade. (The third option appears to have been invasion.) In his October 22 statement, Kennedy also announced that a naval quarantine would be imposed on Cuba on October 24; he threatened future action if the missiles were not removed. The blockade was chosen both for what it did and for what it did not do. It was a visible, forceful, military response, but it did not put the Soviet Union into a position where it had no choice but to fight. In fact, it placed responsibility for the next move back on Soviet chairman Nikita Khrushchev. A number of additional measures were taken publicly to impress on the Soviets the depth of U.S. resolve and to make credible Kennedy's threat of additional action: Squadrons of U.S. tactical fighters were moved to points from which they could attack Cuba, an invasion force of two hundred thousand troops was readied in Florida, some fourteen thousand air force reserves were called up, and U.S. forces around the world were put on alert.[38]

The air strike remained a live option. One had tentatively been scheduled for October 20 but was postponed in favor of the blockade. At an ExCom meeting on October 27, one day before Khrushchev offered to remove the missiles, Kennedy approved plans for an October 29 air strike on Soviet missile silos, air bases, and Cuban and Soviet antiaircraft installations. At that same meeting, ExCom concluded that an invasion would follow. McNamara held that an "invasion had become almost inevitable," and he felt that at least one missile would be launched successfully at the United States.[39]

The blockade did bring an end to Soviet military shipments to Cuba, but it did not bring a stop to the construction of Soviet missiles and missile sites in Cuba. SAMs became operational during the crisis and shot down a U-2 on October 23. According to President Kennedy's original orders, if this happened the United States would destroy the site that had launched the missile. However, when the incident occurred, Kennedy delayed retaliating to allow additional time for quiet diplomacy to bring about the withdrawal of the Soviet missiles.

Recent accounts of the Cuban missile crisis suggest that Kennedy would not have ordered an air strike had Khrushchev not responded favorably to U.S. demands, and that the president was prepared to pursue additional negotiations—perhaps through the United Nations—to resolve the crisis.[40] These accounts also argue that U.S. policy makers felt a sense of urgency in their deliberations, not out of a fear that Soviet missiles might soon become operational, but because the longer the missiles remained in Cuba, the more legitimate they would come to be seen by other states.

On October 28, Khrushchev agreed publicly to remove Soviet missiles in Cuba in return for a U.S. pledge of nonintervention into Cuba, allowing both sides to achieve their publicly stated goals. The United States got the missiles out of Cuba, and the Soviet Union could claim that it had succeeded in protecting Cuba from U.S. aggression (which was the justification given for having placed the missiles in Cuba when confronted by Kennedy). Recently released documents reveal the existence of a secret agreement between Kennedy and Khrushchev with terms different from those that officially ended the crisis. In order to entice Khrushchev into removing the missiles from Cuba, Kennedy promised to remove U.S. missiles from Turkey. The secret offer was made by Robert Kennedy to Soviet ambassador Anatoly Dobrynin on October 27. Dobrynin was also told that a commitment was needed from the Soviets the next day if the crisis was to end on these terms. For reasons of domestic politics and international prestige, Kennedy refused to publicly accept this trade-off, which had been repeatedly called for by the Soviets and suggested to him by some members of ExCom. Implementation of the U.S. part of the agreement was made conditional on the Soviets' maintenance of secrecy about the agreement.

October 28 marks the conventional ending point for the Cuban missile crisis, but it in fact continued for several more weeks as both sides struggled with implementation of the agreement. Particularly troublesome issues involved defining what was meant by "offensive" weapons (the United States insisted that the IL-28s be removed) and establishing a date for ending the blockade (the Soviets wanted the blockade ended and a no-invasion pledge issued before removing the bombers). Within the U.S. government, the earlier debate on how to proceed was repeated: take unilateral military action to resolve the issue, tighten the blockade, or concede the point and go on to other matters? Diplomacy again came to the rescue when, on November 20, Kennedy announced that the Soviet Union had agreed to remove the IL-28s and that the blockade was coming to an end.

## Applying the Rational Actor Model to the Crisis

The preceding account of the Cuban missile crisis is largely consistent with a rational actor interpretation of U.S. foreign policy making. It emphasizes the thorough canvassing of alternatives once a problem has been identified and the selection of a value-maximizing choice. For U.S. policy makers, the goal directing the search for policy options was clear: get the Soviet missiles out of Cuba without appearing to appease the Soviets and without starting a war. A hard-line stance was dictated in part by domestic political considerations. Cuba had become an important and recurring emotional issue in American electoral politics since Fidel Castro had come to power there in 1959, and Kennedy was vulnerable. The Bay of Pigs fiasco had made Cuba his political Achilles' heel, raising questions about his judgment and leadership. The Republican Senate and congressional campaign committees had already identified Cuba as the major issue in the upcoming 1962 election. Therefore, inaction (a possibility suggested at one point by McNamara) and quiet diplomacy were not policy options capable of achieving both the removal of the missiles and a demonstration of political resolve. The air strike was rejected because the Air Force could not give Kennedy a 100 percent guarantee that the missiles would be knocked out. Similar problems confronted the option of invasion. The blockade, coupled with highly visible signals of further military action, was selected as the option that offered the greatest likelihood of getting the missiles out and demonstrating U.S. resolve without running a high risk of setting off a war between the United States and the Soviet Union.

As the rational actor model suggests, the blockade itself was structured to fit the needs of U.S. policy makers. It was not implemented until U.S. officials were sure that Soviet leaders had been able to communicate with Soviet ship captains, and the blockade was placed closer to Cuba than was militarily prudent in order to give the Soviet leadership the maximum amount of time to formulate a peaceful response. The first ship stopped—a U.S.-built World War II Liberty ship registered in Lebanon, owned by a Panamanian firm, and under lease to the Soviet Union—was carefully selected to minimize the possibility of a hostile Soviet response; it did not carry missiles. Two ships that clearly did not carry missiles were allowed to pass through the blockade.

A similar analysis of policy options and consequences late in the crisis would identify Kennedy's secret offer to remove U.S. missiles from Turkey as the logical follow-up move. The blockade did buy time and show U.S. resolve; however, it could not, in and of itself, remove the missiles. Domestic political considerations again limited Kennedy's options, as did the continued inability of the military to guarantee that an air strike or invasion would prevent Soviet missiles from reaching the United States. Kennedy's publicly announced deadline ensured that the military option, with all of its drawbacks, would be used unless Khrushchev could be convinced to take the missiles out of Cuba. The key was to find a face-saving way out for the Soviets that was also true to Kennedy's stated objectives. This was accomplished by the combined secret agreement and public pledge of the removal of Soviet missiles from Cuba in return for a nonintervention pledge by the United States.

## Applying the Bureaucratic Politics Model to the Crisis

The bureaucratic politics perspective on decision making during the Cuban missile crisis paints a very different picture. Rather than emphasizing the logic of policy making, it stresses its political and organizational context. Politics is first evident in the discovery of missiles in Cuba. Consider the following:

- As early as August, DCI McCone had voiced concern about Soviet offensive missiles being placed in Cuba, but he was overruled by McNamara and Rusk.
- No U-2 flights were directed over the area most likely to have Soviet missiles from September 5 until October 14.
- The October 14 flight had been authorized on October 4, but a jurisdictional dispute over who would fly the aircraft and which aircraft would be used delayed it. (The agreed-upon solution was that an air force officer in uniform would fly a CIA plane.)

Moreover, evidence now points to the fact that the United States underestimated by one-half the number of troops (forty-two thousand) the Soviet Union had sent to Cuba. Had this figure been known or had the United States discovered the missiles earlier, the nature of policy options considered, the reading of Soviet goals, and U.S. objectives might have been quite different.

The "logic" of the blockade also suffers when the air strike option is examined more closely. First, the air force did not specifically design an option to meet ExCom's goal of removing the Soviet missiles. Instead, it merely dusted off an existing contingency plan that also called for air strikes against arms depots, airports, and artillery batteries opposite the U.S. naval base at Guantanamo Bay. Second, air force calculations of its ability to destroy the Soviet missiles were based on an incorrect labeling of the missiles as mobile field-type missiles; they were actually movable missiles that required six days to be switched from one location to another. Because the air force believed that the Soviet missiles might be moved between the time the last reconnaissance mission was flown and the time of the air strike, it was only able to offer Kennedy a 90 percent guarantee that it could knock out all of them. The limits of rational choice are also revealed in the implementation of the blockade. The navy, like the air force, did not tailor its plans to meet ExCom's needs. After-the-fact reconstructions of the timing of ship stoppings show that, contrary to Kennedy's orders, the navy placed the blockade in the location originally proposed rather than moving it closer to Cuba.

The bureaucratic politics model also raises a number of troubling questions about the logic of the agreement that ended the Cuban missile crisis. One point centers on the nature of Soviet goals. No one in ExCom gave serious consideration to the possibility that the Soviet Union was genuinely concerned with deterring a U.S. invasion of Cuba. Evidence now suggests that this, along with balance-of-power considerations, was one of Khrushchev's goals. Moreover, it appears that it was the possibility that the United States might use the crisis as a pretext for invading Cuba, not the threat of nuclear retaliation, that led to the decision to remove the missiles. The formal ending of the crisis on the Soviet side also raises troubling questions. Early accounts suggested that Khrushchev was not in full control of the Politburo, so contradictory messages were being received in Washington concerning the terms for ending the crisis. Evidence now suggests that faulty intelligence, not lack of political control, may have been responsible for the mixed messaging. The first, more conciliatory note was sent when Soviet intelligence was indicating an imminent U.S. attack on Cuba. The second, more stringent communiqué was sent once it became clear that there would not be an invasion.

## Applying the Small-Group Decision-Making Model to the Crisis

Early accounts of the Cuban missile crisis from the small-group decision-making perspective praised ExCom for not falling victim to groupthink. Janis credits ExCom with actively trying to understand what led the Soviets to try to place missiles in Cuba secretly, rather than stereotyping them.[41] Janis cites Robert Kennedy's concern about a Pearl Harbor in reverse as evidence of sensitivity to the moral dilemmas involved in the air strike option. He also notes that members of ExCom frequently changed their minds and eventually came to the conclusion that there were no good policy options at their disposal. President Kennedy is credited with having learned from the Bay of Pigs fiasco and practicing a leadership style that maximized the possibility of ExCom producing quality decisions. To encourage free debate, Kennedy did not attend all of its meetings, and he split ExCom into smaller groups to debate the issues and reexamine the conclusions reached by other participants.

More recent accounts of ExCom's deliberations suggest that its escape from groupthink was far less complete than was originally believed.[42] At least three decision-making defects surfaced that are fully consistent with the groupthink syndrome:

1. ExCom operated with a very narrow mandate. It was to consider the pros and cons of a variety of coercive measures. Kennedy had declared off-limits any consideration of either acquiescence to the Soviet move or diplomacy. True to that mandate, 90 percent of ExCom's time was spent studying alternative uses of troops, bombers, and warships. So it did not engage in a full search for policy options or operate as an open decision-making forum.
2. Those who sought to expand the list of options under consideration and break out of the group consensus were ostracized. U.S. ambassador to the United Nations Adlai Stevenson initially opposed the use of force and wrote Kennedy a note cautioning him on the dangers of this option. Kennedy was annoyed by the note and blocked efforts by McNamara and Stevenson to include diplomacy on the options list. Stevenson also suggested a trade of Soviet missiles for U.S. missiles in Turkey or for the Guantanamo Bay Naval Base. He came under sharp personal attack by Kennedy and was frozen out of the core decision-making group for these suggestions.
3. Theodore Sorensen, special counsel and advisor to President Kennedy, and Attorney General Robert Kennedy acted as surrogate leaders, reporting back to the president on the discussion and pushing group members to reach a consensus. Here, too, the impact was to limit the number of policy alternatives and stifle discussion. Stevenson observed that "we knew little brother [Robert Kennedy] was watching and keeping a little list where everyone stood." On Friday night, October 25, President Kennedy informed ExCom

that he had chosen the blockade. The very next day, the consensus within ExCom for the blockade began to unravel. At that point, Kennedy told his brother to "pull the group together quickly." Sorensen would tell the group that they were "not serving the president well," and Robert Kennedy would tell them that the president could not possibly order an air strike.

## Models: A Policy Maker Critique

As you have seen, decision-making models involve dissecting a complex set of political activities. Inevitably, the result is that certain features of the decision-making process receive greater attention and are accorded greater importance than others. For these reasons, policy makers often are uncomfortable with decision-making models. They see the models as oversimplifying policy decisions by putting forward a mechanistic, highly segmented interpretation of a process that is better seen as a seamless web of activity involving efforts at consensus building, problem definition, and problem solving. They contend that generalizations about decision making are dangerous because each situation is unique in terms of both the problem at hand and the domestic political context in which decisions are made. A rebuttal would point out that while each situation is to some extent unique, overemphasizing uniqueness can make us blind to learning lessons of the past.

## Over the Horizon: Individual-Centered Models

One factor frequently downplayed in decision-making models is the importance of individuals. The manner in which Donald Trump engaged in foreign policy decision making added weight to the importance of doing so. Two possible starting points for directing more attention to the importance of individuals in decision making are also suggested by Trump's presidency: intuitive decision making and impulsive decision making. On the surface, both are consistent with Trump's statement about how he makes decisions: "I don't think about them . . . I don't think about, you know, how I make them. I make what I consider the right decision."[43]

*Intuitive decision making* operates on the basis of knowledge stored in long-term memory and moves to a decision automatically at a subconscious level. Intuitive decision making examines multiple pieces of information simultaneously and immediately arrives at a judgment without any conscious awareness of how the decision was reached. The dangers of intuitive decision making include overconfidence, inappropriate application of past experiences, a lack of openness regarding the reasons that decisions are made, limited consideration of alternatives, and prejudice, which causes flawed experiences to overrule accepted facts and evidence.

*Impulsive decision making* can be broken down into four dimensions:

1. *Urgency.* Feeling the need to act quickly with a strong sense of purpose and force.
2. *Lack of premeditation.* Insensitivity to potential long-term consequences.
3. *Lack of perseverance.* An inability to remain focused.
4. *Sensation seeking.* Taking pleasure in making the decision.

Based on these traits, impulsive decision making leads to risky decisions that focus on short-term gains and jeopardize long-term goals.

The challenge is how to incorporate individual decision making into the array of policy-making models currently used to study foreign policy.[44] Possible approaches include examining whether intuitive and impulsive decision making are more likely under certain circumstances than others or in certain issue areas. Another approach is to look at how these decision-making styles link up with different stages in the decision-making process and the models with which they are best paired. For example, former secretary of defense Mattis is known to have ignored or resisted directives from Trump or limited the options presented to him regarding military action against North Korea, Iraq, and Iran. Trump is known to allow dissent but not disloyalty or self-promotion in the media to advance a position.[45]

## Critical Thinking Questions

1. What are the strengths and limitations of using models to understand U.S. foreign policy making?

2. How might the pluralist and elitist models explain the Cuban missile crisis?

3. Which model might be most helpful in trying to understand the foreign policy of China, Iran, or Russia, and why?

## Key Terms

action channels, 190
black box, 189
bureaucratic politics, 190
elite theory, 194
groupthink, 192
model, 188

pluralism, 195
poliheuristic decision making, 198
prospect theory, 189
rational actor, 189
small-group decision making, 191
standard operating procedures, 191

# Diplomacy 10

## Learning Objectives

Students will be able to:

1. Distinguish between the various forms of diplomacy.
2. Evaluate the effectiveness of arms transfers as an instrument of foreign policy.
3. Explain what is meant by the political use of force and how it has been done.
4. Define conference diplomacy and assess the extent to which the climate agreements reflect its strengths and weaknesses.

# On the Agenda: The Paris Agreement

Diplomacy is a process of communication between governments that is the primary means by which states seek to protect and promote their interests. The negotiation of the 2015 Paris Agreement on climate change, Donald Trump's decision to leave it, and Joe Biden's decision to reenter it are examples of this process in action.

Marking the culmination of six years of negotiations, the 2015 Paris Agreement was a treaty formulated at the twenty-first annual United Nations Climate Change Conference, attended by 195 states and the European Union. Officially coming into effect in November 2016, the agreement, which needed a unanimous vote and required all sides to compromise on their demands, broke new ground in dealing with the problem of climate change.

The Paris Agreement set the goal of reducing the global temperature increase to 1.5 degrees Celsius above preindustrial levels. This target is to be met by submission of nationally developed contribution plans by each country. These targets are not legally binding, and no enforcement mechanism was put in place. This marks a change from previous treaties, which sought to set legally binding commitments, producing opposition from the United States and others. Instead, a "name and shame" mechanism was put in place where peer pressure and publicity would serve as the primary enforcement mechanisms. Virtually all states are required to submit reports on a regular basis using agreed-upon measures to judge the progress of their efforts. The first public reports are due in 2023. In addition, every state is tasked with resubmitting its national plan targets every five years.

A recurring area of controversy in climate negotiations has been the issue of responsibility for global climate damage. Another aspect of this debate centers on who should bear the financial burden of actions needed to address "loss and damage" problems associated with the adverse effects of climate change. This was the first time that the phrase "loss and damage" was included in a climate treaty, at the insistence of smaller island countries. According to the Paris Agreement, developed countries should take the lead in mobilizing climate finance, but it does not establish a specific dollar amount they are obligated to provide.

A key element of U.S. support for the Paris Agreement was Obama's commitment. He personally attended the conference and lobbied the heads of key developing countries such as India and Brazil. A weakness in the U.S. commitment was the continuing conflict between Obama and Republicans in Congress. Prior to the conference, more than one hundred members of Congress sent a letter to foreign leaders indicating that Obama did not have their support.

On June 1, 2017, President Donald Trump announced that the United States was withdrawing from the Paris Agreement. He promised to cancel the agreement during his presidential campaign. His announcement came some months later than expected, largely due to conflict within his administration. Chief strategist Steve Bannon was a strong advocate of leaving the Paris Agreement while Secretary of State Rex Tillerson argued against it. In making his announcement, Trump asserted that the Paris Agreement was a "draconian deal." Proclaiming that "I was elected to represent the citizens of Pittsburgh, not Paris," he termed the agreement to be an attack on U.S. sovereignty that imposed unfair environmental standards on U.S. businesses and workers. There is no penalty for withdrawing from the Paris Agreement, but states who signed cannot leave until November 4, 2020, making that the effective date of U.S. withdrawal.

On his first day in office, President Joe Biden announced that the United States would rejoin the Paris Agreement. According to the agreement, there is a thirty-day reentry process. On February 19, 2021, the United States officially rejoined.

The Paris Agreement serves as an example of what diplomacy can accomplish and how fragile those accomplishments can be. It marked the third time since the initial United Nations Framework Convention on Climate Change (UNFCCC) was signed in Rio de Janeiro in 1992 that a climate agreement was reached. The first two agreements were the Kyoto Protocol and the Copenhagen Accord (see the "Historical Lesson"). This chapter first examines the fundamental choices and dilemmas facing policy makers in using diplomacy. It then turns to the major forms of diplomacy in which the United States has engaged, beginning with a broad overview of bilateral and multilateral diplomacy and then looking at more specific types including summit diplomacy, UN diplomacy, public diplomacy, and variations on the political use of force.

# Diplomacy: Choices and Dilemmas

For many, diplomacy remains the classic policy instrument best suited to producing lasting and workable solutions to foreign policy problems. Others point out that the use of diplomacy is not without its dangers. Negotiations also hold the potential for exacerbating hostilities, strengthening an aggressor, preparing the way for an attack, and eroding the moral and legal foundations of peace because they can be used to stall for time, obtain information, or make a propaganda play.[1]

## The Diplomatic Tool Kit

Diplomacy is closely identified with government-to-government **bargaining** and **negotiation**, but the diplomatic tool kit extends well beyond these processes. Most significantly, diplomatic efforts have often involved the use of military and economic power. States now also rely on individuals and private-sector groups to reach out and communicate with foreign governments as part of the negotiation process, a strategy known as *Track II diplomacy*. In addition, as captured by the concept of public diplomacy (described later in the chapter), diplomacy today also reaches out directly to the people of another state in hopes of laying a foundation favorable to U.S. foreign policy initiatives.

One of the challenges faced today in conducting diplomacy is that while the diplomatic tool kit is large, it is not without problems. Not all tools are equally effective in dealing with every problem, and often the temptation is to keep using those that work and avoid tools

| Table 10.1 | Budgets for Selected International Affairs Programs, FY 2022 | |
| --- | --- | --- |
| **Program** | **FY 2021** | **FY 2022** |
| HIV/AIDS | $330 million | $330 million |
| Tuberculosis | $770 million | $775 million |
| Global Health Security | $190 million | $700 million |
| Disaster Assistance | $4.4 billion | $3.91 billion |
| Migrants and Refugees | $3.43 billion | $2.91 billion |
| Development Assistance | $3.5 billion | $4.14 billion |
| Democracy Fund | $2.91 million | $3.41 million |
| Food for Peace | $1.74 billion | $1.74 billion |
| UN Operations | $1.46 billion | $1.5 billion |
| Economic Support Fund | $3.15 billion | $4.1 billion |

Source: "Congress Finalizes FY22 Spending," US. Global Leadership Coalition, March 17, 2022.

that have recently failed. Using multiple diplomatic tools can create confusion if different messages are received; under certain circumstances, they can also be self-defeating, if one undermines the effectiveness of another. Today three diplomatic silos are said to exist.[2] The first is the power silo, which is directed at managing issues that are seen as affecting U.S. national security. In dealing with adversaries, this involves deterrence and containment. In the case of allies, it involves creating and maintaining alliances. A second diplomatic silo involves stabilization issues. Here, the focus is on de-escalating conflicts and stopping their spread through such activities as peacekeeping and military assistance. The final silo is the governance silo. Its focus is on reordering internal government systems. Human rights, democratization, and economic aid are key tools. Commentators note that while these silos often interact in U.S. diplomacy, such as in Afghanistan, they are seldom integrated into a coherent strategic whole. Another way of thinking in terms of diplomatic silos is to look at the variety of programs the State Department funds. A sampling of these programs is presented in table 10.1.

The diplomatic tool kit lends itself to a variety of approaches to conducting foreign policy. This comes through clearly in looking at how Trump and Biden have approached using it. Trump viewed diplomacy in very personal terms. This was evident both in his preference for bilateral diplomacy over multilateral diplomacy for negotiating deals and in his view of deal making as a personal undertaking. His diplomacy had a short-term focus. In seeking to unravel existing foreign policy or establish a new policy, he gave far less attention to the long-term implications of his foreign policy decision. For example, for three years in a row, neither Trump nor a high-ranking cabinet member attended a summit meeting with Asian allies. Third, Trump tended to center his diplomacy in self-contained silos, focusing on narrow objectives. Another case in point is South Korea, a longtime critical ally of the United States in Asia. In February 2017, Trump announced that he was considering terminating a trade agreement with South Korea because of its high trade surplus with the United States. This statement left unrecognized South Korea's strong support of economic sanctions against North Korea and that South Korea had only recently agreed to allow the United States to place a missile defense system there. A significant break with this pattern was the September 2020 signing of the Abraham Accords, a statement brokered by the United States and signed by it along with Israel and the United Arab Emirates (UAE) in which the

UAE officially recognized Israel and began the process of normalizing relations between Israel and Arab states.

Biden came into office promising to reset U.S. diplomacy with a greater focus on collaboration and away from unilateral actions. He presented diplomacy as a "force multiplier" that increased U.S. influence abroad. A major theme in his travels and those by key administrative officials was that the goal was not to make other countries take a side in U.S. power diplomacy but to be partners with the United States in mutual beneficial undertakings. Implementing this reset occasionally ran into problems. A surprise agreement with Australia on purchasing U.S. submarines that undercut an agreement it had with France produced a backlash. So too did a Summit of the Americas conference with Latin American states on democracy promotion and climate change that was designed to promote U.S. leadership but excluded Cuba, Nicaragua, and Venezuela.

The remainder of the chapter examines major forms of diplomatic activity, starting with a closer look at bilateral diplomacy.

## Bilateralism versus Multilateralism

While countries may prefer to act unilaterally because of the high degree of freedom it affords, unilateralism is rarely a viable option. Instead they must choose between some combination of *bilateral diplomacy*, in which two states interact directly with each other, and *multilateral diplomacy*, in which many states participate. Bilateral relations are assuming a new prominence today because, without the Cold War to frame negotiations, diplomacy has become heavily influenced by country- and situation-specific considerations.

Multilateral diplomacy has not vanished completely, however. Many issues of concern to policy makers require the cooperation of multiple countries if they are to be addressed effectively. Multilateralism is not without its own drawbacks as a diplomatic problem-solving strategy.[3] One set of obstacles is domestic. U.S. public opinion tends to support acting through the United Nations and other multilateral bodies, but only up to a point, because unilateralism runs deep in the American national style[4] (see chapter 3). A second set of obstacles is international. What form of a multilateral partnership should be entered into? The choice at its most fundamental level is between **alliances**—such as membership in the North Atlantic Treaty Organization (NATO) and international organizations such as the World Trade Organization (WTO)—and creating ad hoc **coalitions** of states that share a common interest with regard to a specific problem, be it genocide, Iraq, or the environment.

## Process versus Product

Another point of tension is whether diplomacy should be viewed as a process or a product (an outcome). According to some observers, this long-standing tension is growing; while interest in diplomacy-as-process is on the rise, the preconditions needed for diplomacy-as-product are on the decline.[5] Three of the most important factors standing in the way of the success of diplomatic efforts today are (1) the absence of shared principles on which to base international agreements, (2) the increased presence of nonnegotiable goals, and (3) the growing role of public opinion in foreign policy making. The first two make compromise difficult and greatly reduce the common ground on which solutions can be built. The third complicates the ability of governments to implement agreements.

## Incentives versus Sanctions

One of the most difficult decisions that must be made in conducting diplomacy is the choice between employing sanctions and offering incentives. **Sanctions** are penalties generally directed at adversaries. The most frequently employed sanctions are economic in nature and will be discussed in more detail in the next chapter. *Diplomatic sanctions* include threatening to withhold or actually withholding recognition of a government and recalling an ambassador. One such episode during the Trump administration involved the European Union (EU). In 2018, without any formal announcement, the administration downgraded the diplomatic status of the EU's representative in Washington. Trump had been referring to the EU as a "foe" in economic competition with the United States. It also opposed his Iran policy. In 2019, that decision was reversed, and the EU representative was again given ambassador rank.

The historical record shows that sanctions have often been used against both allies and friends. Many argue that sanctions potentially are most effective against friends; when relations are minimal or already strained, sanctions may do little additional damage, so there is little reason for states to comply. U.S. trading partners were the frequent targets of economic sanctions by Trump as he sought to redress "bad deals." One such bad deal was the North American Free Trade Agreement (NAFTA), which he had renegotiated (see "On the Agenda" section in chapter 11).

Diplomatic sanctions strike many as being more symbolic than economic sanctions and thus less costly to employ. However, there are costs associated with the use of diplomatic sanctions.[6] First, there is a loss of intelligence. When the United States closed its embassy in Kabul, Afghanistan, it lost the ability to engage in human intelligence collection and was forced to rely heavily on Pakistan's intelligence service for information about the Taliban government. Second, diplomatic sanctions may also lead to misperceptions because of the inability to communicate directly. Because China's warnings to the United States that it would intervene in the 1950 Korean War went through India (there was no U.S. embassy in China), they were not believed. Third, a country loses the ability to promote a positive image, which can be a valuable resource for building negotiations with other states and influencing global public opinion.

Engagement of other states through offers of incentives is less well studied than sanctions.[7] Incentives can include the removal of sanctions or offers of additional trade or foreign aid. Offering incentives to a friend or ally is easy, but it is much more controversial when the target state is a foe. Yet it is precisely with these states that the strategy of engagement may offer its greatest benefits because it provides an avenue for dialogue that did not previously exist. Trump's nuclear negotiations with North Korea, his administration's support for peace talks with the Taliban, and Obama's talks with Cuba illustrate this point.

# Bilateral Diplomacy: Allies, Friends, and Adversaries

Countries enter into three different types of bilateral relationships: allies, friends, and adversaries. Each has its own unique set of characteristics. Dealings with allies are marked by high levels of commitment to the negotiation process, recognition of the existence of a wide area of common interests, and willingness to address the specific issues involved in a dispute. Leaks of the existence of covert National Security Agency (NSA) programs to intercept communications among foreign leaders brought home the reality that being an ally does not preclude being the target of intelligence-gathering efforts. The NSA captured communications among allies, including the European Union, Germany, Mexico, Spain, France, and Brazil. The reputed goal was to obtain information regarding their policy positions on global issues. The diplomatic fallout from the leaks escalated into a high-profile conflict between the United States and its allies.

Relations with adversaries are also marked by a high degree of commitment and attention; the difference is a lack of any sense of shared interests. Instead, there is an underlying sense of conflict and distrust. As a result, much of the bilateral dialogue centers on finding formula-based solutions for problems, such as those reached in U.S.-Soviet arms control agreements.

Today, China is seen as the primary U.S. adversary both in a trade war and a military buildup in the South Asian Sea centering on Taiwan. This adversarial relationship produced diplomatic interactions that became characterized by hard-hitting Chinese rhetoric, such stating the United States would not get away with "blackmail," which is often referred to as *wolf warrior diplomacy*, referencing a highly patriotic and popular 2015 Chinese film. Steps toward placing boundaries on these conflicts came about in November 2022 during the G-20 Summit. Biden and Xi met for the first time. Their discussion did not resolve these issues but opened new lines of communication. Biden stated the U.S.-China relationship "should not veer into conflict" and that competition must be managed "responsibly."

Finally, bilateral relations among friends are relations between states that are on good terms but lack extensive dealings with one another. As a result, it is often difficult to strike a deal, as each side advances its own particular interests in the absence of widely perceived common interests. U.S. relations with Saudi Arabia are one example. Saudi Arabia is an important friend in the Middle East, one which has received much military aid from the United States and who has worked with it to ensure a stable global supply of oil. The Biden administration was caught off guard in 2022 when Saudi Arabia announced that, along with OPEC and Russia, it would reduce the amount of oil produced. This followed a meeting between Biden and Crown Prince Mohammed bin Salman in which the United States thought it had an agreement not to cut oil supplies.

A fourth category of (non)relations can also be said to exist. During the George W. Bush administration, the most prominent countries with which the United States lacked formal diplomatic relations were the three members of the so-called axis of evil: Iran, North Korea, and Iraq. Consistent with Obama's pledge to reach out to all states, the United States began reestablishing relations with several countries, the most prominent of which was Cuba.

## Shuttle Diplomacy

In many respects, the choice between bilateral and multilateral diplomacy is a false one. Bilateral diplomacy can be an important component of any multilateral diplomatic undertaking. This is notably the case in **shuttle diplomacy**. Here, because the political distance between two states is so great that they are unable to engage in face-to-face negotiations, a trusted third party travels between them in an effort to end the diplomatic stalemate.

Shuttle diplomacy is most famously associated with Henry Kissinger, who served as national security advisor and later secretary of state under President Richard Nixon. His shuttle diplomacy occurred following the 1973 Yom Kippur War. A coordinated surprise attack by Egyptian and Syrian forces seriously weakened Israeli forces and raised the possibility of defeat. Eventually, Israeli forces launched a successful counterattack. A UN-arranged truce failed, and fighting continued until October 25, when efforts by the United States and the Soviet Union ended the fighting. A UN peace conference began in December 1973 and ended in failure in early January 1974. On January 14, 1974, Kissinger flew to Egypt to discuss the terms of a possible peace agreement. For the next week, Kissinger would repeatedly fly between Egypt and Israel in an effort to narrow the differences between the two states. On January 18, a peace agreement placing UN peacekeeping forces in the Sinai as a buffer between the two states was announced. Kissinger then turned his attention to the Syria-Israel standoff. Beginning in mid-March and running through most of April, he met separately and regularly with Syrian and Israeli embassy officials in Washington. Feeling that the foundations of an agreement had been identified, Kissinger left on May 1 for another round of shuttle diplomacy that ultimately produced a peace agreement on May 31.

Obama's secretary of state, John Kerry, also engaged in shuttle diplomacy. Over the course of five months in 2013, Kerry made six trips to the Middle East and engaged in what were termed "marathon sessions" with leaders on both sides for the purpose of restarting negotiations. His efforts failed. Rex Tillerson undertook a shuttle diplomacy mission in the Middle East in 2017 to resolve a crisis that pitted Qatar against Saudi Arabia, Egypt, the United Arab Emirates, and Bahrain. The dispute threatened to undermine counterterrorism efforts in the region and endangered two U.S. military bases. Tillerson spent a week shuttling among these countries but failed to end the conflict.

## Summit Diplomacy

The most visible of all forms of diplomacy is summit diplomacy, in which heads of state meet personally with one another at conferences. **Summit conferences** dominated headlines in the Cold War. Today summits have been overshadowed by the increased use of virtual meetings and phone calls as a pathway for leaders to interact. One such virtual summit was hosted by Biden in December 2021. The Summits of Democracy brought together government, civil society, and private-sector leaders with an agenda that focused on defending against authoritarianism, fighting corruption, and promoting human rights.

Summit conferences continue to perform a number of valuable services that these other forms of communication do not.[8] Foremost is establishment of a strong personal relationship between leaders that sensitizes each to the domestic constraints operating in the other's political system. A second potentially valuable service is energizing the bureaucracy and setting a deadline for decision making. The benefit here is not so much the summit itself but the preparations for it.

Aligned against these virtues of summit diplomacy are a number of potentially negative consequences.[9] First, the personal contacts established through face-to-face negotiations may result in an inaccurate reading of the adversary's character and the constraints under which they operate. This appears to have happened at the 1961 Kennedy-Khrushchev summit in Vienna. Khrushchev reportedly came away with the impression that Kennedy could be intimidated; many link the Soviet attempt to place missiles in Cuba to this meeting. Similarly, summit deadlines offer the recalcitrant state a golden opportunity to exploit the other's eagerness for resolution.[10] Misreading of intentions also appears to have played a role in the failure to achieve a U.S.–North Korea nuclear agreement. Trump came away from the 2018 meeting in Singapore claiming that he and Kim Jong-un had established a close personal bond and that Kim had written him "beautiful letters." Kim appears to have come away from that meeting with the view that Trump's flowery comments were evidence of his desperation to make a deal. Their second summit, in 2019, adjourned unexpectedly without an agreement.

Energizing the bureaucracy does not necessarily guarantee the emergence of a coherent policy, which is only realized when the planning process is given time and political attention. Moreover, it may only intensify the ongoing bureaucratic struggle, resulting in only a lowest-common-denominator position being brought to the summit. Summit deadlines may also politicize or impede decision making. This point is raised most forcefully with reference to annual economic summitry, but as the many accounts of U.S.-Soviet arms control talks reveal, it is equally applicable to other forms of international diplomacy.[11] Other commentators suggest that periodic meetings are a questionable device for addressing a continuously evolving problem. Agreements reached in April become obsolete in November, when the next summit is still months away.

More generally, summit conferences have been criticized for unfairly raising public expectations. They are part of a cycle characterized by "a burst of publicity about new initiatives or special envoys, followed by policy drift and an unwillingness to push either side," until "eventually the effort goes dormant, sometimes for months, until yet another approach is crafted."[12]

## Economic Summits

Beginning in 1975, the heads of state of the six major Western economies (the United States, Great Britain, France, Germany, Japan, and Italy) have been meeting at an annual summit. Originally known as the Group of Six (G6), today (with the addition of Canada) it is the Group of Seven (it was the G8 until Russia was expelled after the 2014 Ukraine crisis). These meetings began as a means for informal discussion among the leaders of the major economic powers as they dealt with the effects of the post–Arab-Israeli War oil crisis, global inflation, and the removal of the dollar from the gold standard.

In mid-2007, a financial crisis began to work its way through the international economic system. As the need for a global response to the financial crisis (rather than separate national responses) became evident, the search for a proper forum for conducting negotiations began. The G8 was seen as having too narrow a membership to construct a global solution, so attention shifted to the Group of Twenty (G20). The G20 was created as a response to the 1997–1998 Asian financial crisis and included developed and developing economies such as Saudi Arabia, Brazil, India, China, Mexico, and South Africa. The G20 held its first formal summit in 2008 to address the financial crisis. At the September 2009 G8 summit, it was agreed that the G20 would replace the G8 as the main forum for international economic discussions. Over time, however, regardless of the setting, political and military questions have also become prominent agenda items.[13] As early as 1996, the G8 agenda was broadened to include terrorism and international crime. At the 2013 G20 summit, Obama sought to build global support for a military strike against Syria for its use of chemical weapons. At the 2019 G7 summit, Trump sought to have Russia invited back as a member but failed.

In October 2021, the G20 broke new ground by endorsing a proposal developed by the OECD (Organization for Economic Cooperation and Development) to establish a 15 percent minimum global corporate tax rate. The plan had previously been endorsed by the G7 and G20. The objective was to provide poor countries with additional operating funds and to stop the "race to the bottom" in which corporations would play off states against one another as they sought to attract multinational firms with the lowest tax rate. The United States was a major advocate of the plan, and it was endorsed by over 140 countries representing over 90 percent of the world's economic output. The plan requires that each country implement the standards, which could take time and arouse domestic opposition. Not all in the United States supported the tax plan. Republicans argued that the Biden administration was sacrificing the U.S. tax base for a symbolic victory.

## East-West Superpower Summits

East-West summit conferences were a frequent, if irregularly spaced, feature of the Cold War. The early summits, from 1955 to 1967, dealt with European security issues. Later they became an important mechanism for institutionalizing détente (see chapter 1). They produced more than twenty-four agreements, including SALT I and SALT II. Reagan and Gorbachev conducted a series of post-détente summit conferences, the most famous of which was the 1986 Reykjavik summit. There, Reagan proposed abolishing all ballistic missiles, and Gorbachev countered with a proposal to eliminate all strategic arms. Nothing came of these initiatives because they would have prohibited Reagan from engaging in Strategic Defensive Initiative testing beyond the laboratory, something he was determined to do. With the disintegration of the Soviet Union and the end of the Cold War, East-West summits declined in overall strategic importance.[14]

The post-Cold War summit that drew the most attention was between Trump and Russian president Vladimir Putin and took place on July 18, 2018, in Helsinki. Controversy quickly arose on two points. One centered on Trump's approach to diplomacy. No National Security Council meetings were held in preparation for the summit, nor was a post-summit meeting held. Prior to the meeting, advisors had covered such matters as the Crimea conflict and the 2016 election and urged Trump to take a firm position with Putin. Instead, they noted that Trump made a "game-time decision" to handle it differently, referring to Putin as a competitor rather than an adversary. Where Putin struck observers as in control and with a strategy for moving forward, Trump appeared to improvise with vague promises.

The second issue involved what was said and agreed upon at the meeting. Trump and Putin met for two hours without advisors or note takers. Trump confiscated the notes of his interpreter. No agenda was published for their discussion, and no communiqué was issued afterward. Director of National Intelligence Dan Coats acknowledged that he did not have any details about what was discussed. Russian leaders asserted that "important verbal agreements" had been reached, including keeping the New START and INF arms control agreements. Complicating matters further, Trump appeared to accept Putin's assertion that Russia had not interfered in the 2016 presidential election, even though the intelligence community concluded this was the case.

Biden's June 2021 summit meeting with Putin had a very different tone. Biden's approach to their discussions was described as one of pessimism. He had little expectation of achieving watershed or breakthrough agreements. "I'm going to make clear to President Putin that there are areas where we can cooperate if he chooses, and if he chooses not to cooperate … then we will respond." The structure of the summit was also different. Biden met Putin accompanied either by Secretary of State Blinken or by aides, and no joint news conference was held to avoid surprise statements.

# Conference Diplomacy

**Conference diplomacy** starts from the logic that some problems in international politics affect the interests of too many states to be solved unilaterally, bilaterally, or at summit conferences. Instead, what is needed is to bring all of the concerned states together at a regional or global level. Conference diplomacy is a central but not necessarily effective vehicle for international environmental policy making. The complexity of issues coupled with the imperatives of American domestic politics has often made it difficult for the United States to exert leadership and placed it at odds with the rest of the world.

Three different forms of conference diplomacy can be identified. The first centers on the operation of formal international organizations such as the World Trade Organization. The second involves regularly scheduled meetings of states that share a common concern. Conferences on human rights and environmental protection fall into this category. The third is impromptu or irregularly scheduled meetings designed to address a common problem, the end product of which can be described as a *coalition of the willing*. Prominent recent examples include George W. Bush's creation of a coalition of the willing to support the Iraq War and the coalition of states that came together to take military action against Gaddafi, which led to his downfall and death during the Obama administration.

## The General Agreement on Tariffs and Trade and the World Trade Organization

In the area of trade, the United States has relied heavily on international conferences to accomplish its foreign policy objectives. Historically, the most important of these centered on meetings of the General Agreement on Tariffs and Trade (GATT). The last GATT conference, which ran from 1986 to 1994, was known as the Uruguay Round. It culminated with the signing of an agreement that established the World Trade Organization (WTO) to supervise international trade law and formally bring the GATT process to an end.

From its first meeting in Geneva in 1947, GATT had been seen as a transitional body that would deal with international trade matters only until an International Trade Organization (ITO) was set up. Because of political opposition in the United States to the broad powers that were to be given to the ITO, President Harry Truman never submitted the treaty to Congress for approval. Similar concerns about the loss of U.S. sovereignty were expressed when the WTO was proposed. Only a last-minute compromise reserving the right of the United States to leave should the WTO consistently rule against the United States cleared the way for the treaty's approval by the Senate.

Four conflict areas dominated the agenda at the Uruguay Round, and these continue to be the principal areas in which meaningful agreements have eluded WTO negotiators. The first is trade in agriculture. At the heart of the problem is the need for more markets for agricultural goods, the widespread presence of subsidies and quotas that protect farmers from foreign competition, and the unwillingness of governments to antagonize the politically powerful agricultural interests in their states. A second area of disagreement involves strengthening international protection for intellectual property. U.S. firms charge that Third World states routinely disregard copyrights and patents in the production of such items as books, pharmaceuticals, and computer software. A third area of controversy centers on the demands of the United States and Europe for international labor standards with regard to child labor, convict labor, minimum wages, and unions. Fourth, over Third World objections, the United States and Europe have pressed for the establishment of a body to examine the environmental impact of global trade agreements.

WTO meetings have struggled to achieve success. The 2001 WTO meeting in Doha took place two months after the 9/11 attacks and was viewed by many in the United States and abroad as an opportunity to promote global cohesion. The talks were set to produce an agreement in 2005, but it was not until December 2013 that an agreement was reached. Trump's election as president created a new and deeper set of problems. Trump characterized the WTO as "a disaster" and "very unfair." He also roundly criticized the WTO for its failure to put an end to China's unfair trade practices, asserting that the WTO had come under China's control. Instead of working through the WTO to achieve his foreign policy goals, Trump relied on economic policies based on national security needs. While doing so ran counter to the spirit and intent of WTO regulations, tariffs were permitted if defined as a matter of national security. Trump also blocked new members to the WTO appeals board, which undermined its ability to resolve trade disputes.

For the most part, Biden has shared Trump's reservations and policies, such as blocking new appointments to the WTO appeals board while publicly stating support for it. One result has been that the WTO is finding itself bypassed as a global economic rule maker and enforcer, with member countries increasingly moving to bilateral agreements or agreements outside of the WTO.[15]

## Historical Lesson

### The Kyoto Protocol and Copenhagen Accord

Under the terms of the initial UNFCCC, signatory states were required to develop programs to reduce the emission of greenhouse gases. No targets or requirements were included in the treaty. President George H. W. Bush signed the agreement, and the Senate ratified it following Bush's promise that targets and timetables from future agreements would be sent to the Senate for ratification.

The agreement reached at the 1992 UNFCCC mandated annual meetings to continue work on the problem of global warming. The first follow-on agreement came in 1997 with the signing of the Kyoto Protocol, formally an amendment to the Rio Treaty. The legal requirement of the Kyoto Protocol was a 5 percent reduction in greenhouse emissions from 1990 levels by 2012 by all developed states that signed and ratified the agreement. Six greenhouse gases were identified as requiring action. Three strategies were specified, including removal of greenhouse gases from the atmosphere by such measures as planting trees, investing in clean technologies, and trading emissions. Regarding the latter measure, states that had reduced greenhouse emissions to a point lower than the required target could sell emissions credits to countries that were not meeting them. Countries that failed to meet their targets would be assessed a 30 percent penalty in future reduction rounds. Developing countries, of which China claimed—and continues to claim—to be one, were exempt from any requirement to reduce greenhouse emissions.

For the Kyoto Protocol to come into force, fifty-five countries responsible for at least 55 percent of the total carbon dioxide emissions in 1990 had to ratify the agreement. The fifty-fifth country signed in 2002, but the percentage requirement was not met until 2004, when Russia ratified it. The United States signed the Kyoto Protocol under President Bill Clinton, who called it "environmentally strong and economically sound." While it was being negotiated, Congress passed a resolution stating that the United States should not sign any climate agreement without targets and timetables for all countries, or any agreement that seriously hurt the American economy. President George W. Bush withdrew the United States from the agreement in 2002 without sending it to the Senate for ratification, calling it "fatally flawed."

The second attempt at negotiating a climate treaty came in December 2009 when the fifteenth annual meeting following the signing of the Rio Treaty took place in Copenhagen. The basic outline of the agenda and the agreement to be negotiated had been set two years earlier at the 2007 meeting in Bali. The two weeks of negotiations to flesh out the "Bali Road Map" that took place in Copenhagen were described as raucous, disorganized, and frantic. Documents leaked by Edward Snowden in 2014 revealed that the United States had spied on other delegations and possessed details about their negotiating positions. One account characterized the negotiations as a textbook case of how *not* to do a deal.

No agreement was in hand as the conference was about to adjourn on December 18. Press reports suggested that only a weak political statement might be announced. At that point, state leaders, including President Obama, had only recently arrived for a ceremonial signing of the final document. What followed in the remaining thirteen hours was intense, round-the-clock negotiations among the United States, China, India, Brazil, and South Africa. Obama was particularly active, rejecting calls from some states that the United States should simply sign the Kyoto Protocol, making an agreement in Copenhagen unnecessary. It has been reported that he entered, without invitation, a meeting between Chinese leaders with other heads of state. In the end, an agreement was reached.

Advocates called it a historic step forward. Others complained that they had not yet seen the agreement and had been excluded from these last-minute negotiations. This proved to be its downfall. Under United Nations procedures, unanimous consent is needed for any agreement to become official. This rule held at Kyoto and Paris. At Copenhagen, angered at their exclusion and objecting to some of its terms, some countries, notably Bolivia, Venezuela, Sudan, and Tuvalu, objected. As a result, when the meeting conference ended on December 19, rather than being adopted, the agreement, officially known as the Copenhagen Accord, was merely "taken note of." It was not a legally binding document.

The initial response in the United States was mixed. Obama called it a "meaningful and unprecedented" agreement. Among the breakthroughs it contained were recognition of the need to keep temperatures from rising more than 2 degrees Celsius, pledges of aid to developing countries, and recognition that all countries must reduce emissions. An aide to Senator Richard Lugar called it a "home run." Senator McCain called it a "nothing burger." The longer-term political reaction in the United States and elsewhere was to pull back from seeking a new global climate agreement. The next climate meeting was held in Cancún in December 2010. The Center for Climate and Energy Solutions noted that the Cancún meetings basically stayed close to the script of the Copenhagen Accord, leaving all options open and setting no clear path forward to a binding climate agreement.

### Applying the Lesson

1. Should all states have an equal say in negotiating a climate treaty? Should there be a unanimity rule? Explain your answers.
2. How would you rank the Paris Agreement, the Copenhagen Accord, and the Kyoto Protocol in terms of their significance, and why?
3. What criteria should be used to measure the success and failure of international conferences, and why?

## Environmental Conferences

Environmental conference diplomacy did not begin with Kyoto or Copenhagen. The first effort was the 1987 Montreal Protocol on Substances that Deplete the Ozone Layer.[16] Following in the wake of the Chernobyl nuclear reactor accident, the Montreal Protocol was hailed for the cuts it was able to make in the production and consumption of ozone-depleting materials and for establishing a framework for addressing environmental problems. The second conference was the 1992 UN Conference on Environment and Development held in Rio de Janeiro, Brazil. Better known as the Earth Summit, it resulted in the signing of seven major pacts and initiatives. The United States was the only major state not to sign a biodiversity treaty. It was later signed by Bill Clinton. The United States was also virtually alone in its objections to a treaty on protection against global warming, agreeing to support it only after references to binding targets and timetables were dropped.

Efforts to protect the environment have continued after Paris. In April 2021, Biden organized a virtual meeting of forty countries to address the problem of climate change: the Leaders' Summit on Climate. A UN climate change conference, officially known as the Twenty-Sixth UN Climate Conference of the Parties (COPA 26), took place in November. A main goal of COPA 26 was getting countries to lock into the voluntary emission standards established at Paris and keep the Paris target reduction of 1.5 degrees Celsius alive. The overall outcome of the conference was seen as limited and as reflecting lingering concerns about U.S. diplomacy and fears that it might change direction again with little warning as it did with Trump's election. Under pressure from its allies and poor countries, at COP 27 (2022) the United States dropped its long-standing opposition to the principle of creating a "loss and damage fund" to help poor counties cope with damages growing out of climate change.

## Human Rights Conferences

The subject matter of international human rights conferences varies greatly. Topics range from commonly defined rights, such as those associated with the 1948 Universal Declaration of Human Rights, to concerns of more specific groups of individuals, such as women and children, the disabled, or refugees and displaced persons. The United States has often been an active participant in these conferences. It played an active role in the September 2015 Global Leaders' Meeting on Gender Equality and Women's Empowerment held in Beijing. At the same time, the United States has tended to participate in human rights conferences only when the proposed treaty or agenda involves advancing and protecting traditionally defined political and civil liberties. One prominent decision to abstain took place in 1996; the United States was absent from the Ottawa Conference on land mines, which resulted in a treaty banning the production and development of antipersonnel mines that has now been signed by over 150 countries. One reason given by the United States for not signing the treaty is the continued need for such mines along the demilitarized zone along the border between North and South Korea. In 2014 the United States announced that it would limit land mine use to the Korean Peninsula. Under Trump this policy was reversed, but in 2022 Biden announced a return to the 2014 policy.

The U.S. record in promoting human rights is also marked by a reluctance to ratify international human rights treaties. As of 2019, the United States had approved only five of eighteen such treaties on topics such as civil and political rights, racial discrimination, the rights of children, and torture. In some cases the refusal to ratify an agreement reflects the lack of consensus within the United States and the challenge that domestic politics can present to treaty ratification. In other cases it reflects the conflict between advancing human rights and other items on a president's agenda. The United States has also refused to participate in international conferences on racism because of concerns over the language in proposed treaties. A recurring example is a UN conference to end racism and discrimination. Obama did not send a delegation to the 2009 Durban Review Conference because it equated racism with Zionism. The George W. Bush administration balked at participating in the 2001 conference because of this language and the inclusion of a proposal calling for reparations for slavery.

The promotion of human rights did not play a major role in the Trump administration's foreign policy. In 2017, for the first time, the United States did not participate in a review meeting of the Inter-American Commission on Human Rights (IACHR). Created in 1959 as an autonomous unit within the Organization of American States, the IACHR reviews petitions filed about violations of human rights. The 2017 meeting was called to review a petition concerning Trump's Muslim travel ban. In meetings with Chinese president Xi Jinping, Trump resisted economic sanctions while a trade agreement with China was under negotiation. Trump only acted in support of the Uighurs in 2020 when he signed the Uighur Human Rights Policy Act one day after it was revealed in a book by John Bolton, Trump's second national security advisor, that he gave his approval to plans for building Uighur concentration camps. On the last day of his administration, Trump officially referred to China's Uighur policy as genocide.

Biden's human rights record reflects a similar tension between promoting human rights and other goals. Examples of positive steps to promoting human rights include making one-half of a security aid package to Egypt contingent on its ending persecution of civil society organizations. Past administrations had cited national security concerns as a justification for waiving human rights conditions in awarding aid. Biden also raised the issue of the Uighurs in a virtual meeting with Xi in November 2021. The following month he signed the bipartisan Uighur Forced Labor Prevention Act.

## Global Health Conferences

G. John Ikenberry notes that at its height the liberal international system consisted of a series of organizations, or clubs, that countries joined in order to achieve their objectives. Once in the club, countries acted consistent with its set of norms and rules.[17] Today, the international system is less a series of clubs than it is a shopping mall made up of countless stores that countries can enter and leave as they wish and which lack any unifying set of values or purpose.

Global health diplomacy, especially as it relates to COVID-19, is operating in a shopping mall. No one international organization or set of organizations has taken the lead in responding to the pandemic, nor has a coherent response framework been established. In March 2021, the Quad (the United States, India, Japan, and Australia) agreed to a plan where U.S. vaccines made in India would be purchased by Japan and distributed in South and Southeast Asia by Australia. It was a plan designed to counter China as much as it was to help people. The plan was derailed by the surge of COVID in India. In April 2021 a plan came before the WTO to waive the patent rights of pharmaceutical companies so that vaccines would be more readily available to poor countries. The plan sparked controversy both among countries and within countries. The Biden administration was divided over how to proceed. Those opposing the idea treated vaccines as a commodity, while those supporting it viewed vaccines as a public good. This controversy is at the heart of many health diplomacy disputes. In October 2021, the G20 announced the creation of a Joint Finance-Health Task Force to improve planning among wealthy countries to respond to pandemics with added financial and health resources. The plan was put forward with no commitment to new financing.

At their meeting, the G20 also agreed to a plan to vaccinate 70 percent of the world population by mid-2022. Commentators noted that at this time only 14 percent of a promised 1.8 billion vaccines had been delivered. The United States had delivered some two hundred million doses. The month before at a virtual Global Summit of World Leaders organized by Biden, he announced that the United States would double the amount of Pfizer vaccines it would give to poor countries at no cost, unlike Russia and China, which were selling their vaccines. Making reference to the United States as the "arsenal of democracy" in World War II, Biden promised that the United States would be the "arsenal of vaccines."

Embedded in these promises of action is a second point of tension in global heath diplomacy. Targeting a specific disease, providing vaccines, and then leaving the infected area the vaccines are given to is referred to as *vertical health diplomacy*. What many commentators argue is needed is *horizontal health diplomacy* in which health resources and facilities are provided to address daily ongoing health issues across entire countries.

## UN Diplomacy

Viewed from one perspective, the U.S. diplomatic relationship with the United Nations (UN) has shown great variation over time. In its early years, the United Nations existed as a virtual extension of the State Department, so support from the UN General Assembly could be taken as a given. This began to change in the 1960s as colonial areas gained independence and sought to use the United Nations as a tool for advancing their own agendas. The United States used its veto power for the first time in 1970 and today often finds itself on the defensive.

At the same time, there is great consistency in how the United States has approached the United Nations. U.S. policy toward the UN represents an amalgam of four different roles:[18]

1. *International reformer.* Viewed from this perspective, the UN is an important instrument deserving of U.S. support because it holds the potential to transform world politics.

2. *Custodian.* The United States sometimes usurps or resists the powers of the UN because its agenda conflicts with the greater purposes of the UN as identified and defined by the United States.
3. *Spokesperson for the American public.* A problem here is that policy makers do not necessarily have a clear sense of what the public thinks.
4. *Protector of American national interests.* This is exemplified by such actions as applying international sanctions against Iraq, vetoing resolutions condemning Israel, and opposing an international criminal court.

The Obama administration's UN diplomacy reflected a relative balance among these four role orientations. In the Trump administration, this balance was replaced by a strong emphasis on the UN as an instrument for advancing and protecting the U.S. national interest. It turned to the Security Council to impose sanctions on North Korea, and it withdrew from the UN Human Rights Council for its frequent criticism of Israel's treatment of Palestinians. In addition, Trump announced that the United States would not pay more than 25 percent of the cost of UN peacekeeping operations. Biden's approach to the UN was consistent with the international reformer perspective as evidenced by his UN speech calling for a unified front to tackle global issues. Biden's 2022 budget met regular U.S. financial obligations to the UN and provided a "sizable" down payment for money owed to the UN for peacekeeping.

## Public Diplomacy and Digital Diplomacy

**Public diplomacy** consists of the statements and actions of leaders that are intended to influence public opinion in other countries. It contrasts with classic diplomacy that emphasizes secrecy and confidential bargaining among government officials. As a result it has been largely neglected and often disparaged as propaganda. Public diplomacy is more than just words, however. It is a set of institutions, programs, and practices designed to accomplish three strategic objectives:

1. Inform the world accurately, clearly, and swiftly about U.S. policy.
2. Represent the values and beliefs of the American people.
3. Explain how democracy produces prosperity, stability, and opportunity.

An inherent tension exists in public diplomacy undertakings: is it an alternate source of information for citizens in these countries or an instrument of U.S. foreign policy? The Voice of America (VOA) is the best example of an information source, and Radio Marti is the most prominent example of how it serves as a foreign policy tool. VOA, which began broadcasting during World War II, eventually came under the control of the U.S. Information Agency (USIA). During the Cold War, USIA radio broadcasts reached into the Soviet Union and Eastern Europe through Radio Liberty and Radio Free Europe. Both were heavily funded (covertly) by the Central Intelligence Agency. Radio Marti was set up by the Reagan administration in 1983 to broadcast into Cuba. From the outset, its broadcasts contained a strong anti-Castro flavor.

The War on Terrorism breathed new life into America's public diplomacy through the increased interest in using social media technologies. Some refer to this development as the beginnings of **digital diplomacy**; others call it Public Diplomacy II. In 2003, a U.S. Office of eDiplomacy was established. By 2012, it was operating an estimated six hundred social media platforms, including blogs (*DipNote*), Twitter accounts (@StateDept), and Facebook pages (*eJournal USA*). A rapid response unit was created to monitor social media responses to ongoing situations that impact U.S. national interests.

Recent presidents have engaged in public diplomacy with varying degrees of success. Clinton is widely recognized as one of its most skilled practitioners, bringing an American-style political campaign atmosphere to his trips abroad that won foreign publics over to his cause. Reagan's forays into public diplomacy tended to have a hit-and-run quality to them. Reagan's references to the Soviet Union as the "evil empire" played well at home but scared the public abroad.[19]

Trump largely abandoned public diplomacy as a soft-power tool. Instead he used public statements as hard-power tools to force others to agree to his policy initiatives. This was especially true for U.S. allies and their leaders, about whom Trump often tweeted caustic and critical comments. He called Canadian prime minister Justin Trudeau Canada's "easily worst president yet." More often than not, such comments have been followed up by assertions of positive close working relations. Biden broke new ground in public diplomacy during the lead-up to Russia's invasion of Ukraine when on several occasions he made intelligence reports on Russian military activity public in an effort to build a global coalition against it and undercut its rationale for an invasion. The Biden administration also met with TikTok officials in an effort to ensure that the U.S. case against Russia would be effectively communicated through social media.

The newfound emphasis on public and digital diplomacy is not without its critics. There are two broad areas of criticism. At the strategic level, those who see soft power as being difficult to use perceive public diplomacy as only helping at the margins and as incapable of addressing the underlying images of distrust or dislike that may exist abroad.[20] At the tactical level, many are critical of continued attempts to use public diplomacy channels for partisan political purposes, such as presenting U.S. foreign policy in overly favorable terms or keeping critical stories about the president off the air.[21]

# The Political Use of Force

By its very existence, American military power serves as an instrument of diplomacy. Without ever having to be used or even referenced, it heightens U.S. prestige and gives importance to U.S. proposals and expressions of concern. The knowledge that both conventional and nuclear military power exist in the shadows of international crises influences both the manner in which U.S. policy makers approach problems and the positions adopted by other states.

## Coercive Diplomacy

The use of conventional military force for political purposes by the United States is not new. Researchers identified 218 incidents between 1946 and 1975 in which the United States did so.[22]

To qualify as a political use of force, the military action had to involve a physical change in the disposition of U.S. forces and had to be done consciously to achieve a political objective without going to war or trying to physically impose the U.S. position on the target state. On average, the political use of force lasted ninety days. Actions taken ranged from a port visit by a single warship to the deployment of major land, sea, and air units in conjunction with a strategic alert and reserve mobilizations. In any given year, as many as twenty incidents or as few as three took place.

The end of the Cold War did not end America's interest in using military power for political ends. In fact, a number of factors made the political use of force very attractive. Using a slightly different definition of the political use of force than was used at the beginning of this section, a recent study examined instances of post–Cold War **coercive diplomacy**. It found that of sixteen cases in which military power was used to persuade rather than defeat the opponent, success was realized only five times. Coercive diplomacy clearly failed in eight cases. The limited success rate is not surprising. Studies of attempts at coercive diplomacy during the Cold War documented an even lower success rate.

Although none of them guarantees success, three factors seem to have contributed to the limited success enjoyed by coercive diplomacy:

1. *Positive inducements.* Offering positive inducements to the other state to adjust its policy was important.
2. *Timing of inducements.* Inducements were most effective when offered *after* the demonstrative use of force or after threatening force. Inducements had little positive effect if they were offered *before* such shows of resolve.
3. *Consequences.* It was important to be able to demonstrate clearly to the opponent what would happen to their military forces should war occur, and that failure of their military strategy was inevitable.

Interestingly, the type of demand made by the United States had little relation to success or failure.

The increased prominence of international crises caused by domestic security threats (as opposed to cross-border conflicts) has created an additional problem for the conduct of coercive diplomacy today: the challenge of legitimizing the use of force for political purposes. In 2011, in the case of Libya, this was accomplished through a UN resolution invoking the responsibility to protect doctrine (R2P), which holds that sovereignty is not just the right of a government to rule but includes a responsibility for protecting and advancing the lives of its citizens. When a government is unable to do so, the international community has a responsibility to intervene, with force if necessary and as a last resort. Critics of R2P argue that, as in Libya, R2P is little more than a cover for countries to intervene to protect their own interests.

The Trump administration has engaged in a number of very different coercive diplomacy undertakings. One was an extension of the Obama administration's show of force in the South China Sea, where the United States and China have been engaged in a prolonged series of military provocations and countermoves over the political, military, and economic status of the region (see the "On the Agenda" section in chapter 14). Biden has engaged in the coercive use of force in a number of settings. His efforts to induce Russia not to invade Ukraine or to limit its military actions included joint military exercises between Ukraine and NATO, sending additional troops to Europe, and establishing a permanent military headquarters in Poland.

## Nuclear Diplomacy

In contemplating the use of military power for political purposes, American policy makers have not limited themselves to thinking in terms of conventional weapons. On at least two occasions, they have threatened to use nuclear weapons in an effort to compel others into action.[23] Evidence suggests that Dwight Eisenhower made a **compellence** threat in 1953 as part of his plan to bring an end to the Korean War. Richard Nixon also made such a threat in 1969 in an attempt to end the Vietnam War.[24] Unlike the Eisenhower case, when the threat of using nuclear weapons was presented as part of a deliberate U.S. strategy, Nixon cast his in quite different terms, telling his chief of staff H. R. Haldeman:

> I call it the Madman Theory, Bob. I want the North Vietnamese to believe I've reached the point that I might do anything to stop the war. We'll just slip the word to them that "for God's sake, you know Nixon is obsessed about Communism. We can't restrain him when he is angry and he has his hand on the nuclear button." Ho Chi Minh himself will be in Paris in two days begging for peace.[25]

On October 10, 1969, U.S. nuclear forces were put on alert "to respond to possible confrontation by the Soviet Union." The actions taken were designed to be picked up by Soviet intelligence but still not be visible to the American press or public. It was Nixon's hope that this would be part of a lead-up to a massive conventional offensive in Vietnam and would stampede the Soviets into working toward a diplomatic solution to the war. In fact, Nixon had already decided against such a military operation for two reasons: the domestic opposition it would unleash in the United States and military doubts about its effectiveness. Although Soviet leaders did not respond to this political use of nuclear power in any meaningful way, it does appear that Soviet intelligence recognized the change in nuclear readiness.

Two significant points emerge from a detailed look at the history of this episode. First, the military did not automatically and uniformly implement Nixon's alert order. The Strategic Air Command balked, as did Secretary of Defense Melvin Laird, suggesting that Nixon was in far less control of the U.S. nuclear forces than he believed or than most commentators thought. Second, to the Nixon administration, it was obvious that this was nuclear signaling over Vietnam. However, at that same time, the Soviet Union and China were involved in an intense border dispute. Chinese leaders had been evacuated from Beijing, and its nuclear forces were on alert. From both the Chinese and Soviet perspectives, the U.S. nuclear alert could have just as easily been seen in light of this separate conflict.

# Arms Transfers

**Arms transfers** have established themselves as a favorite instrument of policy makers.[26] The Arms Export Control Act of 1976 requires that all arms transfers valued at $25 million or more, or those involving the transfer of significant combat equipment, be reported to Congress. Soon thereafter, one study found that over a hundred arms transfers were being reported yearly.

No single measure exists on how to calculate the size of arms sales. Some studies use purchase price. Others calculate the unit production costs of the weapons being sold. Regardless

| Table 10.2 | Arms-Sales Notifications to Congress, January 1, 2022–June 23, 2022 | |
|---|---|---|
| **Country** | **Amount ($ million)** | **Details** |
| France | 388 | MQ-9 support ($300m) and sensor pods ($88m) |
| Greece | 233 | F-16 engine maintenance |
| Egypt | 5,846 | Chinook helicopters ($2.6b); C-130J Hercules aircraft ($2.2b); TOW 2A missiles ($691m); air defense radar ($355m) |
| Jordan | 4,280 | F-16s ($4.21b); rockets ($70m) |
| United Arab Emirates | 65 | missile defense spares/repairs |
| Saudi Arabia | 23.7 | missile defense terminals |
| Taiwan | 315.0 | ship spare parts ($120m); support services for Patriot program ($100m); contractor assistance ($95m) |
| Indonesia | 13,900 | F-15s |
| Poland | 6,000 | Abrams battle tanks |
| Kuwait | 1,000 | headquarters construction |
| Australia | 643 | HIMARS launchers ($385m); countermeasures for large aircraft ($122m); guided missiles ($94m); tactical radio systems ($42m) |
| Spain | 950 | MH-60R multimission helicopters |
| United Kingdom | 1,068.53 | ballistic missile defense radar ($700m); Tomahawk support ($368.53m) |
| Bahrain | 175.98 | multiple rocket launch systems upgrades |
| Bulgaria | 1,673 | F-16 C/D fighter aircraft |
| Argentina | 73 | T-6 aircraft sustainment |
| Nigeria | 997 | AH-1Z attack helicopters |
| Ukraine | 165 (via emergency declaration) | nonstandard ammunition |
| Netherlands | 117 | AIM-9X missiles |
| NATO | 22.7 | precision-guided munitions |
| **TOTAL** | **37,935.9** | |

*Source:* Major Arms Sales (via FMS) Notification Tracker, Forum on the Arms Trade.

of how it is calculated, the overall picture remains the same. In the calendar years 2017–2021, the United States was the leading exporter of major weapons systems, controlling 38.6 percent of the world's market. From 2015 to 2019, the United States sold weapons to at least ninety-six countries. A listing of major arms sales reported to Congress between January 1, 2022, and June 23, 2022, is presented in table 10.2.

States sell and buy weapons for a number of different reasons. The relationship between buyer and seller has been compared to a reciprocal bargaining process in which each tries to use the other to accomplish goals that are often incompatible.[27] For arms sellers, three strategic rationales are most often advanced:

1. Arms transfers can provide influence and leverage abroad by serving as a symbolic statement of support for a regime and providing access to elites.
2. They can be used to protect specific security interests abroad and further regional stability.
3. They can be used as barter in acquiring access to overseas bases.

None of these rationales is without problems. One problem is that arms sales can provoke retaliation. For example, in 2019 China threatened the United States with sanctions after it announced the sale of jet fighters to Taiwan, the first such arms sale since 1992. Second, leverage tends to be a transitory phenomenon in world politics, and an arms transfer relationship can just as easily promote friction and set off regional arms races as it can cement ties. In 2019, Turkey—a member of NATO—defied Trump's threats to cancel an F-35 fighter sale and purchased a Russian antimissile system after being unable to purchase the U.S. Patriot system.

There have been six major turning points in the development of U.S. arms transfer policy prior to the Biden administration. The first came in the early 1960s, when the Kennedy administration made a distinction between **arms sales** and arms transferred abroad as foreign aid. Kennedy turned to arms sales in an effort to counter the growing U.S. balance-of-payments problem, which had been brought about in part by the high cost of stationing U.S. troops in Europe. The second turning point came during the Nixon administration. Arms transfers became a cornerstone of the Nixon Doctrine, which stressed the need for Third World allies of the United States to assume the primary responsibility for their own defense. Sales also replaced aid as the primary vehicle for transferring arms, and the quality of the transferred weapons increased dramatically. No longer were arms transfers dominated by obsolete weapons in the U.S. inventory. Measured in constant dollars, U.S. arms transfers increased 150 percent between 1968 and 1977. Just as important, the Middle East now became the primary region for U.S. arms transfers.

The third turning point in the evolution of U.S. arms transfer policy came with the Carter administration. Carter sought to make arms transfers an "exceptional tool of foreign policy rather than a standard one."[28] Gradually, the Carter administration found it difficult to work within its own guidelines. Carter eventually abandoned all signs of restraint by approving weapons sales to Israel and Egypt as part of the Camp David Accords, and to Saudi Arabia after the shah fell and the Soviet Union invaded Afghanistan. The fourth turning point in U.S. arms transfer policy came with the arrival of the Reagan administration, which moved quickly to use arms transfers as a tool in its global struggle against communism. In its first three months, the Reagan administration offered approximately $15 billion in weapons and other forms of military assistance to other states.

The fifth period in arms sales policy began after the 9/11 terrorist attacks. One of the most notable features of this period is the embrace of arms transfers to developing countries that were once on restricted lists. Armenia, Azerbaijan, India, and Pakistan, all of which are key allies in the War on Terrorism, now received U.S. arms. In the case of India, 2002 marked the end of a nearly forty-year period during which no export licenses were granted. As the Obama administration came to an end, some brakes were put on the sale of weapons abroad. His Conventional Arms Transfer Policy (CAT) stressed considering the second- and third-order long-term consequences of arms sales, both for the United States and the recipient, in such areas as human rights and regional stability.

Trump shifted direction again and energetically embraced arms sales. In April 2018, he rescinded Obama's CAT policy, calling it overly restrictive and unfair to American defense industries. He changed the logic of approval to allow the United States to act proactively rather than responsively in arms sales in order to expand export opportunities for American industry and create American jobs. In May 2019, Trump also broke from accepted arms sales policies when he announced that he was using his emergency powers to sell $8 billion worth of precision-guided weapons and combat aircraft arms to Saudi Arabia and the United Arab

Emirates. Acting in this manner took Congress out of the standard approval process and ignored a bipartisan congressional resolution to ban arms sales to Saudi Arabia that resulted from its involvement in the Yemen Civil War.

During his presidential campaign, Biden gave indications that he would change Trump's arms sales policy. This proved not to be the case. While he quickly launched reviews of arms sales to Persian Gulf states and suspended arms sales to Saudi Arabia, arms sales have continued, with agreements being signed early in his administration with Saudi Arabia, Egypt, and the Philippines, among others. After the Russian invasion of Ukraine, three arms sales agreements were entered into with Taiwan in a six-month period.

## Over the Horizon: Coalitions of the Willing

According to one unnamed State Department official, the War on Terrorism expanded the role of the military and intelligence agencies to the point where, "in a lot of ways, diplomacy is a historical anachronism."[29] The discussion in this chapter provides evidence that this is not yet the case, but it has also identified how difficult and complex diplomacy is today and explained that many of its challenges have long histories.[30] Over the horizon, there may be increased emphasis on a middle course of diplomacy emerging as *coalitions of the willing.*

Protecting the global environment is one policy arena in which there have already been calls for forming coalitions of the willing due to frustration with both the pace and content of global environmental negotiations. Under this form of diplomacy, the United States would partner with interested countries to the exclusion of others.[31] A key area in which climate coalitions of the willing may be able to expand climate protection beyond current levels is enforcement. The argument is that, given the strong norm requiring universal consensus in international conference decision making, any form of meaningful enforcement may be impossible. It becomes politically more feasible when a smaller group of like-minded countries can agree on credible enforcement obligations and establish sufficient incentives to pursue them.[32]

A second potential area where coalitions of the willing might become important international actors is health diplomacy, especially dealing with pandemics. With international organizations such as the WHO and G20 struggling to find the financial resources and political clout to act on pandemics in an effective fashion, many commentators are now suggesting that coalitions of the willing are the best way to move forward. One such coalition proposed is a COVID charter that would bring together rich and poor states as well as private-sector and philanthropic organizations committed to promoting health security.[33]

## Critical Thinking Questions

1. Under what conditions should the United States *not* enter into diplomatic negotiations with another country or group of countries? Explain your answer.
2. Is it wise for the United States to use weapons as an instrument of diplomacy? Why or why not?
3. Confronted with an international crisis, would you turn first to bilateral, multilateral, or public diplomacy? Which is most needed to solve the problem in the long run? Explain your answers.

## Key Terms

alliance, 210
arms sales, 227
arms transfers, 225
bargaining, 208
coalitions, 210
coercive diplomacy, 224
compellence, 225

conference diplomacy, 216
digital diplomacy, 223
negotiation, 208
public diplomacy, 222
sanctions, 211
shuttle diplomacy, 212
summit conference, 213

# Economic Instruments 11

## Learning Objectives

Students will be able to:

1. Distinguish free trade from strategic trade and assess in which category NAFTA and USMCA fit best.
2. Identify the reasons why sanctions can fail.
3. Compare the six different types of foreign aid.
4. Describe how trade wars end.

# On the Agenda: United States–Mexico–Canada Agreement (USMCA)

During his 2016 presidential campaign, Donald Trump repeatedly referred to the 1994 North American Free Trade Agreement (NAFTA) as "the worst trade deal maybe ever signed anywhere." (See the "Historical Lesson" at the end of this section for details about this agreement.) He promised that on his first day in office he would announce plans to renegotiate it.

Day one came and went with no NAFTA announcement. Instead, Trump's rhetoric suggested otherwise; he threatened to abandon NAFTA much as he had already done with the Trans-Pacific Partnership (TPP). However, in late March 2017, the administration circulated an eight-page draft document that did not contain a threat of withdrawal. Instead, it put forward negotiating points consistent with the views of many free trade pro-NAFTA Republicans in Congress.

Just under thirty days later, the pendulum swung in the opposite direction and then back toward negotiation. Stories emerged that Trump was going to announce a new executive order putting the withdrawal process in motion. This set off a wave of activity, including phone calls from the president of Mexico, the prime minister of Canada, and congressional Republicans warning against doing so. By that evening, Trump announced that he would not withdraw. The White House asserted that the confusion following word of his upcoming announcement had energized Mexico and Canada into coming to the negotiating table. Critics noted that Canada and Mexico were already at the table, as they had already made trade concessions and were waiting for the United States. Some two weeks later, on May 18, Trump sent a short notice to Congress indicating that he planned to renegotiate NAFTA, a legal necessity (Congress had to be given ninety days' notice of such a decision). Unlike the earlier draft sent to Congress, this announcement was vague regarding the changes that would be sought.

Negotiations began in August, with the Trump administration defining NAFTA as having "fundamentally failed." Each country brought its own set of concerns to the table. The United States was concerned with reducing the trade deficit, forcing carmakers to use more parts made in the United States, and increasing U.S. influence in NAFTA's dispute resolution process. Canada's main concerns were with low wages in Mexico and right-to-work laws that weakened labor unions. Among Mexico's primary concerns was revitalization of its energy industry. All three countries agreed that NAFTA had to be modernized to take telecommunications and digital trade into account. This was not seen as difficult, since such provisions had already been incorporated into the TPP and could now be placed into the new NAFTA agreement. More contentious were calls by the United States for a sunset clause that would allow the treaty to end after five years unless all three countries agreed to renew it.

Negotiations dragged on into the spring of 2018. President Trump became increasingly impatient. In March he announced that he was considering new tariffs on steel and aluminum but told Mexico and Canada that they might be exempted if they completed renegotiations. On May 31, Trump announced that he was imposing these tariffs on Mexico, Canada, and the European Union. Administration officials also indicated that Trump now wished to proceed with bilateral negotiations rather than multilateral ones.

On August 27, 2018, Trump announced that a breakthrough in bilateral negotiations with Mexico had produced an agreement in principle to replace NAFTA. Talks between the United States and Canada moved forward quickly. On September 30, with time running out on a self-imposed deadline set by negotiators for the two countries, Canada agreed to join the United States–Mexico–Canada Agreement (USMCA).

The United States was the last to act on approving USMCA. The House only signaled its willingness to ratify the USMCA in December 2019. In doing so, a new problem arose. Mexico objected to new language that would send U.S. diplomats to Mexico to verify that it was upholding labor standards. This issue was resolved by reassuring Mexico that no violation of sovereignty was involved. The Senate approved the USMCA in January 16, 2020. Trump signed the agreement on January 29, 2020. The USMCA officially entered into force on July 1, 2020.

This chapter begins with an overview of the concept of economic statecraft and then presents an inventory of economic options and strategic outlooks available to policy makers. This is followed by a discussion of different forms of trade agreements, economic sanctions, foreign aid, and trade with China. It concludes by raising the question of how trade wars end.

## Economic Statecraft

Defined as a deliberate manipulation of economic policy to promote the goals of the state, **economic statecraft** is an age-old instrument of foreign policy. Past examples include the Louisiana Purchase, dollar diplomacy in the late 1800s, the Lend-Lease Act during World War II, and the Marshall Plan for rebuilding Europe after World War II. More recently, it has been described as a "lost art" of U.S. foreign policy.[1] This may no longer be the case as economic statecraft was rediscovered in the Trump administration.

Supporters see the use of economic statecraft as part of the legitimate pursuit of American national interest, but critics often see the exercise of American economic power as part of a foreign policy of **imperialism** and domination. No matter its purpose or context, American economic power exerts its influence by its ability to lure other countries to the U.S. economic system and then trap them in it. For that reason, many refer to it as America's "*sticky power.*"[2] Less recognized is that this American sticky power can also entrap the United States, limiting its ability to pursue foreign policy initiatives. China, for example, has jumped to the forefront as a trading partner and holder of U.S. debt, complicating efforts to deal with it in strictly adversarial terms.

A major complicating factor in the use of economic statecraft is uncertainty over judging its successes and failures.[3] Its supporters argue that economic statecraft is dismissed as ineffective all too frequently. Four arguments are made in its defense:[4]

1. Day-to-day economic exchanges under the heading of **free trade** are generally—and incorrectly—defined to be outside the scope of economic power.
2. Economic power is often said to fail when it does not produce a change in policy in the target state. Underappreciated is the added cost that economic sanctions place on the target state, even without a policy change.
3. Economic power has often been judged a failure because it is examined out of context. Policy makers often turn to it when no other instruments are available or to accomplish the almost impossible, such as removing Fidel Castro from power.
4. Economic statecraft suffers because writers on world politics underestimate the importance of symbolic actions to policy makers and domestic pressure groups.

Critics of an overreliance on economic statecraft raise two cautionary points in rebuttal. First, the successful use of economic power increasingly requires global cooperation and coordination to succeed. Unilateral use of economic power or by coalitions of the willing is not enough. Second, the use of economic power can often have damaging effects that reverberate through the economies of other countries and the global economy.[5]

## Inventory of Options

Should American policy makers decide to employ U.S. economic power, they have several options at their disposal, including tariffs, nontariff barriers, embargoes, boycotts, and quotas.

A **tariff** is a tax on foreign-made goods entering the country. Typically tariffs are applied either to protect domestic industry against foreign competition or to raise revenue, but they can also be manipulated to serve foreign policy goals. More than once in the post–World War II era, the United States manipulated tariffs to accomplish foreign policy goals. It used its tariff system as a lever in dealing with communist states, excluding them from equal access to the U.S. market. During détente, the United States sought to use access to the U.S. market and most favored nation status as an inducement for Soviet cooperation in noneconomic areas, such as the Strategic Arms Limitation Talks (SALT) negotiations.

The primary danger inherent in the excessive use of tariffs is retaliation. The most serious instance took place in the early 1930s after the United States passed the Smoot-Hawley Tariff intended to help solve the Great Depression. The highest tariff in U.S. history, it taxed imports at an average rate of 41.5 percent of their value. Retaliation by foreign governments led to a sudden and dramatic drop in U.S. exports, which only worsened the ongoing depression. The Trade Agreements Act of 1934 broke the spiral of raising tariffs by authorizing the president to lower existing tariffs by as much as 50 percent to those countries making reciprocal concessions.

Manipulating **nontariff barriers (NTBs)** to trade is a second policy option. NTBs are a modern variation on traditional tariffs and can range from labeling requirements, health and safety standards, and license controls to taxation policy; they have become powerful tools to protect firms from foreign competition or to remedy a balance-of-payments problem. U.S. use of NTBs dates from the 1930s when the Buy American Act required the government to purchase goods and services from U.S. suppliers if their prices were not unreasonably higher than those of foreign competitors.

The third economic instrument of foreign policy is an **embargo,** a refusal to sell a commodity to another state. Embargoes (and the more subtle concept of export controls) played an important role in U.S. Cold War foreign policy. Building on the Trading with the Enemy Act of 1917, the United States embargoed financial and commercial transactions with North Korea, the People's Republic of China, Cuba, and North Vietnam. Trade with communist states was also controlled by the Export Control Act of 1949. During the Korean War, the list of restricted items reached one thousand. Many of these controls are still in place. In 2016, Obama lifted an arms embargo against Vietnam that had been in place since 1975.

A **boycott,** a refusal to buy a product or products from another state, represents the fourth economic instrument available to policy makers. One celebrated case involved U.S. participation in UN-sponsored sanctions against Rhodesia (Zimbabwe).[6] Off and on, these sanctions lasted for over a decade. They were first imposed by President Lyndon Johnson in a 1968 executive order to force the white-minority Rhodesian government into accepting the principle of majority rule. The U.S. commitment to the boycott was never firm, however. Congress amended the boycott in 1971 to allow the export of raw chromium and other critical materials to Rhodesia.

The fifth policy tool is the **quota**, a quantitative restriction on goods coming from another state. Because of GATT, quotas have not played a large role in foreign economic policy making for most of the post–World War II era. This changed as concerns grew over the international competitiveness of U.S.-made products. Canada has often been the target of U.S. quotas. In 1994, Clinton threatened to limit the amount of Canadian grain entering the United States. In 2004, attempting to end a trade dispute, the United States offered to replace tariffs with a quota system for imports of Canadian lumber.

## Strategic Outlooks

There is no single strategic outlook that forms the basis for economic statecraft. This section provides overviews of two outlooks: free trade and strategic trade.

### Free Trade

Free trade is both an instrument of foreign policy and a strategic orientation for organizing economic power.[7] There is nothing inevitable or natural about free trade. International free trade systems exist because they serve the interests of the dominant power. This was true of Great Britain in the nineteenth century and of the United States in the post–World War II era. From about 1944 to 1962, access to U.S. markets was used as an inducement to get other states to adopt policies favored by the United States. Included among those Cold War goals were strengthening military alliances, promoting the economic recovery of Western Europe, ensuring access to strategic raw materials, and stimulating economic growth and political stability in the Third World. American policy makers were also sensitive to the limits of free trade. On a selective basis, they permitted or encouraged discrimination against U.S. goods if it would further these broader U.S. foreign policy goals. At the strategic level, the United States used free trade to create an international system that allowed the U.S. economy to prosper and placed it at the center of international economic trade and monetary transactions.

## Strategic Trade

Strategic trade competes with free trade as the foundation for American international economic policy.[8] Its advocates maintain that the comparative advantages enjoyed by states in international trade is due not to a country's resource base or historical factors but to imperfections in markets that have been deliberately created by government policy. Only by actively intervening in the international marketplace to create comparative advantages for selected industries can the United States hope to remain a world leader. Critics argue that strategic trade policy often crosses the line into protectionism and away from world leadership.[9]

The driving force behind post–World War II strategic trade was the inability to put a dent in the U.S.-Japan trade imbalance. In 1988, concern with the trade imbalance gave rise to the Omnibus Trade and Competitiveness Act. Section 301, commonly referred to as "Super 301," provides for retaliatory sanctions against states that engage in unfair trading practices against the United States. Presidents identify "priority countries" and set a timetable for resolving the dispute, after which time the sanctions will take effect. While its use has declined, concern remains. The 2022 annual report of the Office of the U.S. Trade Representative placed seven countries on its priority watch list, including China, Russia, Venezuela, and India. Twenty countries are on its watch list, including Canada, Mexico, Pakistan, Egypt, and Turkey.

Strategic trade policy requires two things of the U.S. government. First, it must identify which high-growth industries are crucial to the overall global competitiveness of the American economy. Second, it must ensure that these firms are not shut out of foreign markets. Neither task is easy. Identifying industries for special treatment is a politically charged decision. Just as members of Congress fight to prevent military base closures in their districts, they also fight to ensure that their districts get a fair share of research and development money. A related problem is how to address the problems faced by industries, such as steel, that are no longer competitive internationally but retain enormous political clout. An overly aggressive strategic trade policy runs the risk of spawning a trade war in which U.S. goods are singled out for retaliation.

## Monetary Strategies

Financial transactions can also be used to further foreign policy goals. This may occur at the strategic level, such as when the United States allowed the value of the dollar to float or provided debt relief funding after the 2008 global financial crisis. It may also occur at the tactical level, such as in blocking the ability of an individual, corporation, or government to access its funds held in the United States or in other countries.

The United States helped create two important international financial institutions as part of the **Bretton Woods system**: the International Monetary Fund (IMF) and the International Bank for Reconstruction and Development (IBRD or, more commonly, the World Bank). The IMF was intended to regulate international currencies to ensure that they did not suddenly and violently change in value. The World Bank was to provide additional funds that were believed necessary for European economic recovery. Virtually from the outset, the financial aspects of the Bretton Woods system did not function as anticipated. American dollars became the international currency of choice, and American foreign economic and military aid provided the necessary funds for economic recovery.

By 1960 the situation began to change, and the outflow of dollars reached the point where U.S. officials began to worry about the trade deficit. The Bretton Woods system ended in 1971 when President Nixon announced that the U.S. dollar would no longer be convertible to gold. Since then, international monetary management has taken the form of periodic exercises in crisis management rather than systemic reform.

The most recent exercise of crisis management came in 2008, with the largest financial and economic crash in over seventy-five years. It set in motion concerns within the United States about two aspects of China's international monetary policy for U.S. economic and national security. The first was China's manipulation of the renminbi, its official currency. As China grew in economic power through exports, it devalued the renminbi, making its goods cheaper to buy than those made elsewhere. U.S. officials argued that this cost American workers jobs and slowed the American economic recovery. The second was China's massive holding of U.S. debt.

In 2019, China held $1.12 trillion of U.S. debt, making it the United States' largest debt holder. It was feared that large debt holdings would give China foreign policy leverage over the United States through a massive sell-off of its U.S. debt that would drive down the value of the dollar in retaliation for a U.S. foreign policy decision it opposed.

Donald Trump's strategic international economic outlook fit into the strategic trade category. Trump's preferred economic instrument was the tariff, going so far as to identify himself as "Mr. Tariff." Trump's embrace of a strategic trade policy is not a radical break from the past.[10] Trump's highest strategic trade priorities were state autonomy and maximizing state power. He viewed economic transactions from a conflictual and zero-sum, win-lose perspective. Trump embraced bilateral trade agreements over regional and global ones, asserting that "what we will no longer do is enter into large-scale agreements that tie our hands, surrender our sovereignty, and make meaningful enforcement impossible."

## Varieties of Trade Agreements

There are a number of varieties of trade agreements. The United States engages in three different types: bilateral, regional, and global.

### Bilateral Trade Agreements

*Bilateral trade agreements* govern the terms of trade between two countries. For much of the post–World War II era, bilateral trade agreements were viewed as a second-best method for strengthening the U.S. economy and promoting U.S. interests abroad. Regional and global multilateral agreements were preferred, since they promised to open more markets to American goods more quickly. This began to change in the post-9/11 era as dissatisfaction with regional and global trade agreements grew.

Virtually all of the bilateral agreements negotiated by President George W. Bush ran into domestic political problems. One problem Bush faced was that his **fast-track** presidential authority to sign trade agreements, which would limit Congress to a yes/no vote, expired. Many of these agreements were opposed by domestic interest groups that felt they would harm their constituents' interests. With fast-track authority expired, they were now in a position to demand modifications. Key bilateral free trade agreements with Singapore, Chile, and Australia were approved by Congress, but when Bush left office, agreements with South Korea, Colombia, Panama, and Vietnam had not yet been approved.

During his presidential campaign, Barack Obama voiced concern about these treaties, but his administration was largely silent on trade issues during his first year in office. This changed in 2010 when Obama announced a major initiative to double U.S. exports as a way of spurring job growth in the United States. Bilateral export agreements were central to the success of this initiative. Difficult negotiations were entered into with South Korea (over trade in autos and beef imports), Colombia (over treatment of union officials), and Panama (over taxation policy). Congress approved the agreements in successive separate votes in 2011, and they took force in 2012.

In response to what he argued was foreign exploitation of the United States, Donald Trump typically initiated his bilateral trade negotiations with announcements of significant and punitive tariff rate increases on high-profile items such as steel and aluminum, which would be implemented unless a new trade agreement is reached by his deadline. That strategy produced agreements with smaller states such as Brazil and Argentina but was not as successful in creating agreements with larger trading partners, but it often did compel them to begin negotiations and offer up concessions. Trump had to delay or suspend the implementation of tariffs on cars and auto parts in 2019 with Japan and Europe when negotiations stalled. One problem noted in Trump's high-profile imposition of tariffs followed by low-profile reversals was the challenges allies often faced in responding to his demands. In short order, South Korea found itself attacked by Trump for an unfair bilateral trade agreement that he threatened to cancel, and congratulated on the signing of a new agreement, only to have Trump threaten not to sign it depending on progress in nuclear negotiations with North Korea.

## Regional Trade Agreements

*Regional trade agreements* have held an uneven place in U.S. thinking about their merits in conducting international economic policy. The "Historical Lesson" and the "On the Agenda" sections in this chapter examine the original NAFTA agreement and the new USMCA agreement, respectively. This section looks at two recent failed attempts at creating regional trade agreements: the Trans-Pacific Partnership (TPP) and the Transatlantic Trade and Investment Partnership (TTIP) and the newest agreement negotiated by the Biden administration.

On February 4, 2016, the United States and eleven other states signed the Trans-Pacific Partnership, creating what would be the world's largest free trade agreement. In 2008, George W. Bush announced that the United States would join talks that had begun in 2003 to negotiate free trade issues relating to investment and financial services. Obama announced that his administration would continue these free trade talks, and a negotiating framework was announced in November 2011.

TPP negotiations proceeded at an uneven pace. Agreements in some areas were reached with relatively little controversy, while talks in other areas stalemated and threatened to block consensus on a treaty. Among the issues that raised serious domestic political and economic consequences for some states were the length of patents for drugs held by pharmaceutical companies; protection of the environment, wildlife, and worker rights; and reducing tariff protections for dairy, beef, and poultry producers.[11]

The Obama administration hailed the TPP as a model twenty-first-century trade agreement. Critics argued that its economic benefits were being oversold and that at best they would be distributed unevenly, with low-income workers and industries benefiting the least. An often-voiced counterpoint was that critics underestimated the political and strategic importance of the TPP in overall U.S. foreign policy. Noting that China was not a member of the TPP, supporters argued that the TPP was an important vehicle for ensuring a highly visible and effective U.S. presence in the Pacific. On his third day as president, Trump announced that the United States withdrawal from the TPP, which never entered into force.

The Transatlantic Trade and Investment Partnership is another agreement that did not come into existence. The concept of a transatlantic free trade area, which had been raised off and on since the 1990s, is often described as an "economic NATO." Obama advocated such a plan in his 2013 State of the Union address. Talks for creating a TTIP between the United States and the European Union began in July 2013, with November 2014 set as the target date for an agreement. Trump suspended these talks upon taking office to pursue bilateral agreements with European states that were characterized as trade wars. Trade talks would later resume but end again in 2019 when European negotiators declared them to be "obsolete and no longer relevant."

In May 2022, Biden announced an agreement with twelve Asian-Pacific states to create an Indo-Pacific Economic Framework. Among those who joined are India, South Korea, Vietnam, and the Philippines. The announcement came five months after a China-sponsored organization, the Regional Comprehensive Economic Partnership, began operating. Most of the countries participating in the U.S.-led group also belong to that led by China. Many of those joining with the United States had called for it to simply rejoin the TPP. The Biden administration saw that as all but politically impossible. It also negotiated an agreement that was built around cooperation in areas such as fighting corruption and promoting clean energy rather than commitments to reduce tariffs or provide market access so that the agreement could be implemented via executive agreements and not require congressional approval. The soft nature of the agreement raised questions about its economic impact but also pointed to what all agreed was its primary purpose, which was to counter Chinese influence and provide the United States with a platform for reentering the region.

## Global Trade Agreements

At the global level, free trade in the form of *global trade agreements* became a major U.S. foreign policy priority for the post–World War II international system. It played a central role in establishing the Bretton Woods system. Through a series of negotiations, one of its core institutions was the General Agreement on Tariffs and Trade (GATT), which succeeded in lowering national tariffs and other barriers to free trade. Out of the last series of GATT talks, the Uruguay Round (held from 1986 to 1994), came an agreement to set up the World Trade Organization (WTO).

WTO talks encountered problems from the outset. A 1999 meeting in Seattle to launch a new Millennium Round of trade talks ended in failure. Not only were the countries attending the meeting divided, but the event drew large numbers of antiglobalization protestors. U.S. interest in WTO talks only returned after the 9/11 attacks when the Bush administration saw advancing global economic growth as a key part of its strategy to defeat terrorism.

Launched in Doha, Qatar, in November 2001, the first round of WTO talks stalled. In December 2013, what many saw as a last-ditch effort to save the Doha Round was held in Bali, Indonesia. An agreement was reached when negotiators gave up on achieving a comprehensive agreement in favor of a more limited one.

One of the WTO's few major successes was the creation of a dispute settlement procedure. Under the GATT, a dispute settlement panel was set up only if requested, and its report was adopted only if there was a consensus in favor of it. Under the WTO, the report of a standing dispute settlement panel is adopted unless there is a consensus against it. This change transformed the WTO dispute settlement process into a compulsory and automatic instrument for resolving trade disputes. The United States has been the most actively involved of all countries in the dispute resolution system, having brought some 125 cases and been the defendant in some 150 cases. In cases involving the United States and China, the United States won twenty of twenty-three cases it brought to the WTO against China between 2002 and 1019. China won five cases it brought during this time period. Regardless of the outcome of WTO decisions, the very existence of the dispute resolution system has produced fears about the potential loss of sovereignty and the nondemocratic nature of the decision-making procedures; it was one of Trump's primary objections to the WTO.

## The China Trade War

When trade agreements fail, one possible result is trade wars. While Donald Trump often claimed that tariff wars were easy to win, most see them as often holding serious negative consequences. Here we review the evolution of the U.S.-China trade war.

Early in his candidacy for president, Trump identified China as stealing American technology, taking American jobs, and "ripping off" the U.S. economy. Following his election, Trump moved away from this rhetoric. He did not label China as a currency manipulator and held out the promise of improved trade relations in return for help in dealing with North Korea. Movement toward a trade war began to build midway through Trump's first year in office with the announcement that his administration was opening an investigation into China's trade practices. In January 2018, he imposed a new 30 percent tax on solar panels. In March, new import taxes on steel and aluminum were announced. China responded that it would take "proper measures to safeguard its legitimate rights and interests." One month later, it announced $2.4 billion in tariffs on U.S. exports. Trump retaliated by identifying 1,300 Chinese goods that could face 25 percent tariff hikes totaling $50 billion. China countered by producing a list of 106 American goods that could face the same tariff increase.

Tensions eased in late June when Trump and Xi met at the 2019 G20 summit in Tokyo and agreed to restart trade talks. Those talks took place in late July and did not go well, with Trump later arguing that China kept changing its position and reneged on its commitment to buy agricultural goods. The United States claimed that China had agreed to buy $200 billion worth of U.S. products by 2020. Chinese officials claimed that no such firm agreement had been reached. China responded by announcing $75 billion in retaliatory tariffs, stating that they were forced to do so by the "unilateralism and trade protectionism of the United States." A few days earlier, Trump had defended the trade war by indicating that "this is not my trade war . . . this is a trade war that should have taken place a long time ago by other presidents."

As a candidate for president, Biden indicated a lack of support for Trump's China trade policy, saying it hurt American consumers, farmers, and companies. Once in office Biden has moved in several directions in trade relations with China. In late 2021, Biden said that he would consider lifting some sanctions. Soon after that, his administration blacklisted more than twelve Chinese firms, citing national security concerns. In December he banned U.S. investment in a Chinese artificial intelligence firm specializing in facial recognition software for violating human rights. Following Russia's invasion of Ukraine, his administration reinstated tariff exemptions for over 350 types of Chinese exports to the United States. This was followed by a May 2022 announcement that the United States was considering lifting tariffs on some Chinese goods in order to combat inflation. In June the Uighur Forced Labor Protection Act took effect, banning the import of products made in Xinjiang unless it could be certified that forced labor was not used. In late October far-reaching restrictions were placed on selling semiconductors and chip-making technology to China. The Biden administration argued this action was needed to slow China's access to critical technologies it needed to advance its military programs and develop domestic surveillance systems on dissidents.

# Economic Sanctions

Economic sanctions have long been a popular way of exercising American economic power. As noted in discussing trade with China and responding to Russia's invasion of Ukraine, it is an option Biden has embraced. Obama put in place five hundred sanctions in his first term. Trump nearly doubled this amount and put some seven hundred sanctions in place in one day. It is estimated that in 2020 the United States had over eight thousand sanctions in place. In some cases they are directed at specific countries, such as Cuba, China, Iran, and Russia. In others, they are problem oriented, such as those in place against terrorism, diamond trading, narcotics trafficking, and weapons proliferation.[12] This section examines how sanctions are used in general, and then how they have been applied in three specific cases.

## Using Sanctions

What exactly constitutes an economic sanction is highly contested. This text adopts a middle-of-the-road definition of economic sanctions: "the deliberate withdrawal of normal trade or financial relations for foreign policy purposes."[13] Once announced, sanctions must be enforced. Policy makers have two broad choices: whaling and fishing.[14] A *whaling strategy* involves pursuing relatively few and major cases where sanctions are violated and imposing heavy fines when violations are found. Here, violations are expected to be deterred because of the penalties assessed. A *fishing strategy* pursues a broad-ranging enforcement focus in identifying violators and imposes relatively small fines. In this case, deterrence rests on the likelihood of being caught. George W. Bush adopted a fishing strategy in enforcing his sanctions on Cuba, Iran, Sudan, and others. Obama adopted a whaling strategy in focusing on Iranian sanctions and violations by financial institutions. Table 11.1 provides a list of major banks fined for breaking U.S. sanctions policy against Iran.

It is also important to recognize that sanctions are "not forever." They are intended to bring about change in targeted countries, and when that is accomplished, they are to be removed. Determining when sufficient changes have been made is no easy matter and is not

| Table 11.1 | Major Sanctions/Fines Paid by Banks for Violations of Iran Sanctions | | |
|---|---|---|---|
| **Bank** | **Date** | **Amount Paid** | **Violation** |
| UBS (Switzerland) | 2004 | $100 million | Unauthorized movement of U.S. dollars to Iran and others |
| ABN Amro (Netherlands) | December 2005 | $80 million | Failing to fully report financial transactions involving Bank Melli |
| Credit Suisse (Switzerland) | December 2009 | $536 million | Illicitly processing Iranian transactions with U.S. banks |
| ING (Netherlands | June 2012 | $619 million | Concealing movement of billions of dollars through the U.S. financial system for Iranian and Cuban clients |
| Standard Chartered (United Kingdom) | April 2019 | $639 million | Dubai branch of Standard Chartered processed Iran-related transactions to or through Standard Chartered–New York. |
| Standard Chartered (United Kingdom) | August 2012 | $340 million | Settlement paid to New York State for processing transactions on behalf of Iran |
| Clearstream (Luxembourg) | January 2014 | $152 million | Helping Iran evade U.S. banking restrictions |
| Bank of Moscow (Russia) | January 2014 | $9.5 million | Illicitly allowing Bank Melli to access the U.S. financial system |
| BNP Paribas | June 2014 | $9 billion | Amount forfeited for helping Iran (and Sudan and Cuba) violate U.S. sanction. |

*Source:* "Iran Sanctions," Congressional Research Service, February 2, 2020.

without controversy.[15] Economic sanctions against Cambodia were in place for seventeen years (1975–1992), while those against Japan ran for just twenty-four days in 1985. Evidence suggests that a major factor in determining how long sanctions will stay in place is whether they were imposed by Congress or by the president. Presidential sanctions are twice as likely to be lifted after one year. After five years, about 70 percent of congressional sanctions remain in place, compared to 30 percent of presidential sanctions.[16]

The effectiveness of sanctions can be undermined by a variety of factors. A 2014 study concluded that at best the success rate of sanctions is between 33 and 50 percent, leading some to argue that the most effective sanctions may be those threatened that do not have to be enforced. One problem standing in the way of success is the pursuit of incompatible goals. For example, George W. Bush imposed broad sanctions against Syria for its support of terrorism in 2004. All exports to Syria were barred except for food and medicine. Yet Bush delayed implementing the measure and indicated that he would continue to permit the sale of telecommunications equipment and aircraft spare parts. The telecommunications exemption was justified because of the need to promote the free flow of information. Critics argued that Bush really did this to protect the economic interests of the telecommunications industry.

A second problem is that economic sanctions are often imposed because policy makers find themselves needing to demonstrate resolve when they are unwilling or unable to use military force. In such cases, critics argue that sanctions amount to nothing more than "chicken soup diplomacy." They give the appearance of taking action and make people feel good without having to pay a cost.[17] One example was the Iran-Libya Sanctions Extension Act of 2001. It kept sanctions approved by Congress in 1996 in effect that were about to expire, even though no firms had been sanctioned under their terms.

A third problem is the response by other countries. Often described as *black knights*, some states provide economic support to the sanctioned country for political reasons, which lessens sanction effectiveness. During the Cold War, the Soviet Union was a black knight for Cuba in the face of U.S. sanctions. In the post–Cold War period, Venezuela has been Cuba's black knight, while Russia has played that role for Syria and Iran. What holds true for getting around sanctions against governments also holds true for sanctions against rebel groups. In Syria, Sudan sold Chinese-made weapons to Qatar, which arranged for their delivery to Syrian rebels through Turkey. Recent studies suggest that help from black knights is of limited value unless it is accompanied by sanction-busting actions of corporations interested in profit.[18] Cuba, for example, has benefited from investments by Canadian and European firms.

A very different criticism of sanctions is that, in reality, the primary targets of sanctions are ordinary people. The rich escape the pain. This gave rise to the concept of **smart sanctions**, so called because they target the ability of government, businesses, and terrorist leaders to access personal funds and are intended to protect vulnerable social groups from economic harm. The initial round of sanctions against Russia for invading Ukraine was heavily focused on elite supporters of Putin. Initial evaluations of smart sanctions are not encouraging.[19] They do not appear to be significantly more successful than conventional ones. The fundamental problem is the same—a lack of political will to enforce them.

## Sanctions in Action: Iran, Cuba, Russia

This discussion of economic sanctions concludes by examining three different types of situations and the policies employed by the United States to address them.

### Iranian Sanctions

The United States has a long history of imposing economic sanctions against Iran. Carter ordered a freeze on all Iranian assets under the jurisdiction of the United States after the American embassy was seized and hostages were taken in 1979. Reagan imposed sanctions against Iran for its ties to the bombing of the marine barracks in Beirut in 1984. Clinton instituted a boycott against Iran in response to evidence that it was seeking to acquire nuclear technology, and issued an executive order banning U.S. oil companies and their subsidiaries from trading with Iran. In 1996, Congress passed the Iran-Libya Sanctions Act (now the Iran Sanctions Act), which permitted the United States to issue penalties against foreign firms dealing with Iran. Originally set to terminate in 2001, the Iran Sanctions Act has been extended several times. After 9/11, George W. Bush issued an executive order freezing the assets of individuals, organizations, and financial institutions supporting terrorism. Many of those now on the list are Iranian, including corporations, banks, and the Revolutionary Guard.

Obama continued sanctions against Iran but coupled them with a willingness to engage in talks. With little progress being made in July 2010, he signed the Comprehensive Iran Sanctions, Accountability, and Divestment Act. It extended the Iran Sanctions Act to include trade in refined petroleum products and expand the types of sanctions that presidents could apply. Under pressure from Congress in 2011, Obama accepted new sanctions against Iran, preventing foreign banks from opening an account in the United States or limiting the funds in an existing account if that bank processed payments through Iran's central bank.

This reduced Iran's ability to sell oil abroad. When Congress passes sanction legislation, presidents generally are permitted to waive the sanctions under specified circumstances. By mid-2012, twenty countries, including China and all of Iran's major purchasers, had received exemptions.

The Joint Comprehensive Plan of Action (JCPOA), signed in July 2015, placed limits on Iran's stockpiles of enriched uranium and called for a reduction in UN nuclear-related sanctions and U.S. sanctions against other countries for doing business with Iran. The United States also agreed to ease sanctions against Iran. Unaffected were U.S. sanctions against firms conducting business with Iran and sanctions against support for terrorism, human rights abuses, and missile production. Under the terms of the 2015 Iran Nuclear Agreement Review Act, presidents must certify that Iran is acting in accord with the JCPOA every ninety days. Trump repeatedly denounced the JCPOA during his presidential campaign but certified Iran's compliance in April and July 2017. In September 2017, Trump extended waivers on Iran's sanctions, but in October he declined to do so. In May 2018, the United States officially withdrew from the JCPOA. In August of that year the administration began reinstating U.S. economic sanctions. More than seven hundred individuals, organizations, aircraft, and vessels were sanctioned.

Trump further tightened sanctions in 2019. In April, he announced the end of exemptions that had been given to countries the previous November, allowing them to import oil from Iran without sanctions. Those now subject to U.S. sanctions included China, India, Japan, South Korea, and Turkey. This was followed by an announcement in early May of sanctions on Iran's steel and mining industries that would effectively end Iran's ability to export those goods. The cumulative effect of these sanctions on Iran's economy were significant and contributed greatly to the rising tensions that led to the ongoing crisis in the Persian Gulf and domestic riots in Iran.

In February 2022, Biden restored a sanctions waiver that would allow other countries to work with Iran on select nonproliferation activities needed to return to JCPOA. In May the administration announced its intention to resume those sanctions if the talks failed.

### Cuban Sanctions

When Fidel Castro came to power in 1959, Cuba was heavily dependent on the United States; 67 percent of its exports went to the United States and 70 percent of its imports came from the United States. Under the terms of legislation passed in 1934, the United States purchased the bulk of Cuban sugar at prices substantially above world market rates. Relations between the United States and Castro deteriorated quickly. In February 1960, Castro concluded a barter deal with the Soviet Union in which Cuban sugar was exchanged for Soviet crude oil. After U.S.-owned oil refineries refused to process the Soviet oil, Castro took them over. The United States responded by terminating all remaining foreign aid programs and canceling all purchases of Cuban sugar for the remainder of the year. Castro retaliated with additional nationalizations of U.S. property. Next, the United States imposed an embargo on all exports to Castro except for food and medicine. Cuba then entered into more economic agreements with the Soviet Union; in response, the United States broke off diplomatic relations.

Throughout the Cold War, economic sanctions were tightened periodically, often as a result of electoral considerations. In 1992, Congress passed the Cuban Democracy Act, which placed heavy penalties on U.S. firms that engaged in trade with Cuba through foreign subsidiaries. In 1996, the Helms-Burton Act threatened sanctions against countries that provided Cuba with foreign aid, and it allowed U.S. nationals to sue foreign firms that now controlled properties seized during the Cuban Revolution. Opposition from American allies to this last provision has been intense, and presidents have routinely waived it.

President Obama moved to restore normal diplomatic and economic relations with Cuba. While he was unable to convince Congress to end economic sanctions, Obama did issue a series of executive orders easing regulations covering travel, trade, financial transactions, and commerce. President Trump entered office determined to reverse Obama's policy change; among the economic sanctions his administration put in place were limitations on the amount of money that could be remitted back to Cuba and on tourist access to Cuba.

In 2022, Biden began easing the "maximum pressure" sanctions Trump had placed on Cuba but fell short of returning to an Obama-era normalization-of-relations policy. One important change Biden made was to allow for the remittance of funds to Cuba. Prior to the close of airports in 2019 due to the COVID pandemic, some $3.7 million in remittances were sent to Cuba. Other changes involved easing travel restrictions and providing greater access to U.S. internet sources. Biden did apply new sanctions at one point in response to Cuban human rights violations in dealing with protests.

### Russian Sanctions

Cold War sanctions against the Soviet Union were commonplace. The first significant post–Cold War sanctions were placed in response to Russia's annexation of Crimea and its role in the Ukrainian crisis. In 1954, the Soviet Union had transferred control over Crimea to Ukraine. The action was described as largely symbolic, because Ukraine was then part of the Soviet Union. This transfer of control took on a great deal of significance in 1991 with the fall of the Soviet Union. As an independent country on its borders, the foreign policy of Ukraine was of great importance to Russian leaders. Matters came to a head in February 2014 when public protests forced Ukraine's pro-Russian president out of office. Russian ground forces and pro-Russian Ukrainian militia soon seized control of Crimea. On March 21, Crimea became part of Russia.

With no credible military options at his disposal, President Obama turned to economic instruments of foreign policy. First, Russia lost its membership in the G8, and Obama announced economic sanctions targeting the financial holdings of Putin's key political and economic allies along with Russian banks. In late April, additional business leaders and companies linked to Putin's supporters were targeted by financial and travel sanctions. In July, sanctions were placed on Russia's largest financial, energy, and defense industries, restricting their access to foreign capital. Later in 2014, U.S. companies were prohibited from doing business in Crimea. Judgments about the effectiveness of these sanctions are mixed. Defenders argue that they imposed significant financial, societal, and political costs on Russia.[20] Critics argue that any success was due to a general downturn in the global economy.[21]

Sanctions against Russia became highly controversial under Trump, who repeatedly praised Russian president Vladimir Putin. Trump offered to end the Crimea sanctions if Russia agreed to nuclear arms control talks. Trump's reluctance to place sanctions on Russia over interference in the 2016 presidential election and cyberattacks on U.S. energy grids put him at odds with both Republicans and Democrats in Congress. Disagreement over sanctions against Russia also existed within his administration, as he and UN ambassador Nikki Haley publicly disagreed in 2018 about the imposition of new sanctions on Russia over its support for Syria's use of chemical weapons.

Ultimately, after Congress passed the Countering America's Adversaries through Sanctions Act in July 2017 with a veto-proof majority, Trump found that he had little political choice but to impose sanctions. That bill required him to produce a list of individuals and government organizations by January 2019 that could be subjected to sanctions, and a list of businesses that dealt with Russian defense and intelligence programs by October 2018. The administration missed both deadlines. When the lists were finally announced, many viewed them as largely symbolic since many had already been sanctioned by Obama, and Trump lifted sanctions against a firm whose owner was linked to Russian meddling in the 2016 presidential campaign.

Where Trump sought to avoid placing sanctions on Russia, it became a primary target of sanctions in the Biden administration. A first set of sanctions were put in place in response to evidence of Russian interference in U.S. elections and cyberattacks. These were described as the first significant sanctions against Russia in years. In April 2021, the United States announced the expulsion of ten Russian diplomats, as well as targeting thirty-two individuals and six cybersecurity companies with sanctions. It also barred U.S. financial institutions from buying bonds from Russia's central bank and other financial institutions.

In response first to the buildup of Russian forces for its invasion of Ukraine and then its invasion in February 2022, there occurred wave after wave of sanctions. Days prior to the invasion, Biden issued an executive order stopping new investments into Russia as well as exports or imports. He also put in place sanctions against two major Russian financial institutions that support critical Russian defense industries. Immediately after the invasion, the Treasury Department sanctioned the Sberbank stock company of Russia, requiring all U.S. financial institutions to close its current accounts and not engage in future transactions. It also froze the assets of several Russian banks in the United States and sanctioned thirteen major Russian state-owned companies as well as private companies owned by Russian oligarchs. Biden would also suspend all normal trade relations with Russia. In late June, the U.S. Treasury Department implemented a G7 ban on importing Russian gold and placed new financial sanctions on seventy Russian organizations and twenty-nine individuals. By late November 2022 these and additional sanctions were clearly having an effect as Putin created a new council to coordinate military supplies.

## Foreign Aid

A perennial debate exists regarding the purpose of U.S. foreign aid. Are its primary goals found in the areas of humanitarian assistance, development, and democratization, or is the purpose of foreign aid to advance core American national security interests? The existence of multiple goals means that foreign aid policy often runs the risk of working at cross-purposes: foreign aid given to support governments fighting terrorism or promoting regional stability may negate efforts to promote democracy.

Several underlying conditions need to be kept in mind in thinking about foreign aid as an instrument of foreign policy: First, the size of the U.S. foreign aid program has varied greatly. Calculated in 2015 dollars, the high point for foreign aid came in 1949 ($65.9 billion), and the low point came in 1997 ($19.5 billion). In 2015, it was estimated at $48.6 billion. Compared to other areas of government spending, the foreign aid budget is small, amounting to some 1.3 percent of the total federal budget. Second, U.S. foreign aid is not distributed evenly around the world but is concentrated in a few states. Table 11.2 provides a comparative listing of the top ten recipients of U.S. foreign aid in 1999, 2009, and 2019.

Third, U.S. foreign aid is often given with restrictions; however, these restrictions may be overridden by national security concerns. In October 2009, Obama approved a $7.5 billion, five-year aid program to Pakistan, which officials there quickly characterized as "insulting and unacceptable." Among the conditions attached by the United States were the establishment of monitoring mechanisms to see how the money was spent and the enactment of procedures for promoting military officers. In 2012, Obama announced that the United States would resume military aid to the new government in Egypt and waive restrictions that made such aid conditional on progress toward democracy. Fourth, a very high percentage of U.S. foreign aid funds are spent on U.S. products. The Congressional Research Service estimates that 90 percent of food aid is spent on U.S. goods and services.

## Types of Foreign Aid

There is no standard method for categorizing the different types of U.S. foreign aid programs. The Congressional Research Service identifies six basic categories, which will be followed here. However, before examining the breakdown of official U.S. foreign aid, it is important to note three major trends in the organization and disbursement of foreign aid.

First, *remittances*, private foreign aid from individuals living abroad, are now among the most important sources of funds for Third World states. In 2018, $4.8 billion in remittances was sent to Honduras, and $9.5 billion was sent to Guatemala. For countries such as these, the value of the remittances far exceeds the value of U.S. foreign aid (which totaled $2.6 billion for the region) and has a more direct impact on their lives; for example, Guatemala spent

**Table 11.2 — Top Recipients of U.S. Foreign Aid, FY 1999, 2009, 2019 (millions of dollars)**

| Country | FY 1999 | Country | FY 2009 | Country | FY 2019 |
|---------|---------|---------|---------|---------|---------|
| Israel | $3,030.4 | Afghanistan | $8,964.4 | Afghanistan | $4,983 |
| Egypt | $2,214.0 | Iraq | $5,694.4 | Israel | $3,308 |
| Russia | $1,601.8 | Israel | $2,423.3 | Jordan | $1,723 |
| Jordan | $381.9 | Egypt | $1,989.9 | Egypt | $1,467 |
| Colombia | $325.5 | Pakistan | $1,174.2 | Iraq | $959 |
| Ukraine | $297.8 | Sudan | $1,156.8 | Ethiopia | $923 |
| Indonesia | $256.7 | West Bank and Gaza | $1,040.3 | Yemen | $810 |
| Peru | $231.5 | Ethiopia | $865.1 | Colombia | $801 |
| Bangladesh | $229.7 | Colombia | $863.6 | Nigeria | $794 |
| Bosnia and Herzegovina | $220.6 | Jordan | $528.3 | Lebanon | $791 |

*Source:* Foreign Assistance: An Introduction to U.S. Programs and Policy, Congressional Research Service, January 10, 2022.

$241 per person on health care in 2016. One consequence is that threats to cut off foreign aid (such as Trump's threats against Guatemala in 2019 in an attempt to reduce the flow of migrants to the United States) may have a limited effect in ending the exit of individuals seeking jobs and income.

Second, it is becoming increasingly common to speak of a distinction between traditional and nontraditional official foreign aid. *Traditional foreign aid* is distributed by the State Department and affiliated agencies such as the U.S. Agency for International Development (USAID). *Nontraditional foreign aid* flows from other agencies, such as the Environmental Protection Agency, the National Institutes of Health, the Department of Energy, and, most importantly, the Department of Defense.

The third trend is the increased importance of public-private collaboration and philanthropic foreign aid. The bottom line is that USAID, the primary source of foreign aid in the U.S. government, is now a minority shareholder in foreign aid.[22] One example of public-private collaboration is USAID's Global Development Alliance, which includes corporations such as Coca-Cola and Wal-Mart. The overall goal is to share expertise and information and carry out projects more efficiently.

The first of the six categories of official U.S. foreign aid is *economic aid* given for the purpose of advancing U.S. political and security objectives. This is the biggest category. Monies given in this category have supported such diverse programs as the Camp David Accords, the building of democracy, antinarcotics efforts, antiterrorism plans, and attempts to counter weapons proliferation.

A particularly challenging problem confronting economic aid in the 1980s and 1990s was debt relief. The sums were staggering. In 1988, Mexico's debt stood at $107.4 billion. At first the United States approached the problem as solvable through a combination of government austerity measures and prudent lending policies by banks and international organizations. When this proved inadequate, the United States sought to increase the level of funding available (the Baker Plan). This was followed by a program of limited and voluntary debt forgiveness with international guarantees of the remaining loan amounts (the Brady Plan). It, too, failed to solve the debt problem completely.

The second-largest category of foreign aid is *military assistance*. These monies go to help allies maintain and train their armed forces, as well as to fund purchases of U.S. military equipment. Included in this category are economic support funds, loans to countries that are not eligible for development assistance but are considered strategically important. Of growing concern here is the inability to account for the weapons that were provided. In 2014, the Pentagon discovered that 156,000 pieces of military equipment valued at almost $500 million could not be found in Afghanistan. Some of it was likely broken and discarded, while other pieces were probably stolen and sold to hostile forces.

The third category is *bilateral development assistance*. These aid programs are generally administered by USAID and have a long-term development focus on strengthening the economy, environment, health care delivery systems, and political institutions of recipient states. Funding for the Peace Corps and debt relief falls into this category. One of the major complaints about development assistance aid is that, rather than being transitional, it has become permanent, creating dependent societies and stifling rather than promoting development.[23]

The fourth category of foreign aid is *humanitarian economic assistance*. This aid tends to be short term and emergency focused. Refugee assistance, emergency food aid, and disaster relief account for the bulk of this spending. The amount of money involved has fluctuated greatly from year to year, largely because of the unpredictability of the natural disasters that set such aid in motion. Providing humanitarian aid is often complicated by other policy goals. In 2011, the Obama administration had to relax restrictions on prohibiting aid to terrorist groups or their supporters in order to get relief to famine victims in Somalia.

The fifth category is *multilateral development assistance*. The smallest segment of the foreign aid budget, it consists of funds contributed to such international development organizations as UNICEF, the World Bank, and the African Development Bank. U.S. aid to multilateral organizations is affected by a number of concerns, such as organizations' international planning policies and conflicting goals.

The final category of foreign aid is *nonemergency food aid*. The Food for Peace program, also known as PL 480, is the primary instrument for distributing nonemergency food aid. It makes surplus U.S. agricultural goods available to Third World states in local currency and at concessionary prices. Critics of the Food for Peace program have noted that tension has always existed between the humanitarian and political purposes of this aid and that politics tends to triumph. Often those countries receiving PL 480 funds are not the neediest by objective measures but are valuable U.S. allies. Egypt, for example, has always ranked among the leading recipients of PL 480 funds.

## Cold War Foreign Aid

The relative importance of military and economic aid varied considerably during the Cold War. The Truman administration's foreign aid program was dominated by economic development initiatives such as the Marshall Plan and the Point Four Program. Ninety-six percent of Truman's foreign aid budgets consisted of development funds. With the outbreak of the Korean War, policy makers increasingly viewed foreign aid as an instrument for furthering American national security; more than 60 percent of foreign aid was being given for military purposes. The geographic focus of American foreign aid also changed. At one time, Europe received 86 percent of U.S. foreign aid, but it received only 6 percent between 1958 and 1961. The share of American aid to the Third World increased to 68 percent during this same period.

During the presidency of John Kennedy, the proportion of economic aid to military aid changed again so that by the mid-1970s, economic aid accounted for 75 percent of all U.S. foreign aid. However, within the economic aid category, greater emphasis was given to loans (which had to be repaid) than to grants (which did not). With the deepening American involvement in Vietnam, the pendulum swung back in favor of military aid, which constituted 70 percent of U.S. foreign aid by the mid-1970s. After the American withdrawal from Vietnam, economic aid grew to 80 percent of the total, then faded again under the Reagan administration.

## Post–Cold War Foreign Aid

During the first decade of the post–Cold War era, three issues dominated the foreign aid agenda. The first centered on foreign aid to Russia, with the major goal of helping Russia denuclearize by providing it with funds to destroy chemical and nuclear weapons, establish safeguards against proliferation, and assess the environmental damage done by nuclear waste. The 1991 Nunn-Lugar Threat Reduction Program was designed with this goal in mind. Formally terminated in 2013, the Nunn-Lugar program remains operational in a modified form that includes a worldwide focus on chemical and biological weapons. At the time of its termination in 2013, it had helped deactivate 7,616 strategic warheads (82 percent of its goal) and destroy 914 intercontinental ballistic missiles (88 percent of its goal).

### Historical Lesson

### NAFTA

The North American Free Trade Agreement (NAFTA) among Mexico, Canada, and the United States came into effect in 1994. NAFTA talks began in 1991. On October 7, 1992, a two-thousand-page agreement was signed. Congress gave its approval in November 1993 by votes of 234–200 in the House and 61–38 in the Senate. President Bill Clinton signed the agreement into law on December 8, 1993. At the core of the NAFTA agreement were provisions to eliminate most tariffs on goods traded between the three countries. Some were to be eliminated immediately, while others were to be phased out over fifteen years. Particularly affected by the NAFTA agreement were agriculture, automobiles, and textiles. Other portions of NAFTA established intellectual property rights protections, labor and environmental safeguards, and a dispute resolution system. George H. W. Bush, whose administration negotiated NAFTA, promised to negotiate labor and environmental protections in order to secure getting fast-track authority from Congress. These safeguards were included in the agreement, but many considered them to be insufficient.

The negotiating path that led to NAFTA's signing began with President Ronald Reagan's advocacy of a North American Common Market during his 1980 presidential campaign. Armed with fast-track authority that Congress gave him in 1984, the United States and Canada entered into trade negotiations that led to the 1989 Canada-U.S. Free Trade Agreement. The agreement was widely regarded as the most extensive bilateral trade agreement ever negotiated, and it contained several groundbreaking elements that would appear in later free trade agreements.

By this time, Mexico had also become interested in a continent-wide free trade agreement. In the 1960s, Mexico pegged its development hopes on an import-substitution strategy that would protect domestic industries from foreign competition. It was now clear that this strategy had failed. From an economic perspective, the most attractive alternative was integration into the U.S. market. Politically, however, this was an unattractive option due to fears that doing so would lead to Mexican dependence on the American economy. Instead, Mexico proposed a North American free trade zone.

George H. W. Bush embraced the concept in his 1988 campaign, but once in office his administration was divided over the wisdom of entering into talks with Mexico. The National Security Council, the Commerce Department, and the State Department supported the idea. The Department of Agriculture and the Office of the U.S. Trade Representative were less enthusiastic.

Bush looked on the NAFTA agreement as a vehicle for generating Republican votes in Texas and California in the upcoming 1992 presidential election. Instead, NAFTA became a controversial campaign issue. Leading the early charge against it was onetime supporter Ross Perot, who said NAFTA was the product of a conspiracy among

Washington insiders, foreign lobbyists, and huge corporations that would cost the United States some five million jobs. He warned, "You're going to hear a giant sucking sound of jobs being pulled out of this country."[24] Bill Clinton straddled the fence on NAFTA during the presidential campaign. When he finally announced his support for NAFTA, it was conditioned on adding supplemental agreements to cover "serious" omissions dealing with the potential for a sudden inflow of large amounts of foreign goods into the U.S. market, as well as with the environment and labor.

Bill Clinton did not immediately push for congressional approval of the NAFTA agreement. Many of those who supported his candidacy for president opposed NAFTA, as did a large number of Democrats in Congress. When it did act, it first negotiated a series of executive agreements with Mexico that were not officially part of the treaty and side deals with members of Congress. In one he promised that textile quotas would be phased out over fifteen years instead of ten. In another he pledged to protect peanut, wheat, tomato, and citrus growers by restricting imports to prevent lowering prices. Other

side deals had nothing to do with NAFTA, such as Bill Clinton's promise to a New York congressman to support a Small Business Administration pilot urban project in his district.

NAFTA continued to be at the center of political controversy after it came into effect in 1994, largely out of concern for its real or perceived impact on American workers, crime, illegal immigration, and drug trafficking. During the 2008 presidential campaign, John McCain supported the agreement, but the other major candidates attacked it. Barack Obama blamed it for the loss of American jobs. Both he and Hillary Clinton promised to amend the treaty or withdraw from it. Ron Paul called for abolishing NAFTA.

### Applying the Lessons

1. Is fast trade authority (trade promotion authority) a good idea? Is it necessary?
2. Are regional trade agreements in the U.S. national interest?
3. Should trade agreements come with expiration dates?

A second area of controversy surrounded funding for health and social programs. In particular, conflicts arose over combating human immunodeficiency virus/acquired immunodeficiency syndrome (HIV/AIDS) and aid for family planning programs. In 1984, in what is known as the "Mexico City policy," Reagan prohibited USAID from providing funds to foreign governments, international organizations, and nonprofit organizations that engaged in family planning programs. This ban was suspended by Clinton, put back into place by George W. Bush, suspended again by Obama, and put back in place (and expanded) by Trump. Biden rescinded the ban through a presidential memorandum upon taking office.

The third area of controversy involved efforts to stop international drug trafficking. The most ambitious undertaking was Plan Colombia, a $7.5 billion aid package intended to advance the peace process in Colombia, strengthen its national economy, stop the production of drugs, promote justice and human rights, and foster democracy and social development. Both defenders and critics of Plan Colombia acknowledge that drug production has not so much been curtailed as moved elsewhere, most notably to Mexico.

## Post-9/11 Foreign Aid

After 9/11, foreign aid came to be viewed in a more positive light by those who had long criticized it, under the assumption that it can make a major contribution to fighting terrorism. Almost immediately after 9/11, the George W. Bush administration sought authority from Congress to waive all existing restrictions on U.S. military assistance and weapons exports for five years to any country determined to be helping in the War on Terrorism. A similar pattern existed in the area

| Table 11.3 | Millennial Challenge Corporation Categories and Indicators for Granting Funds |
|---|---|

**Ruling Justly**

Civil Liberties
Political Rights
Voice and Accountability
Government Effectiveness
Rule of Law
Control of Corruption

**Investing in People**

Immunization Rate
Public Expenditures on Health
Girls' Primary Education Completion Rate
Public Expenditure on Primary Education
Natural Resource Management

**Economic Freedom**

Inflation Rate
Trade Policy
Land Rights and Access
Regulatory Quality
Fiscal Policy
Business Start-Up

*Source:* https://www.mcc.gov.

of trade; the administration proposed dropping trade restrictions on eight Central Asian countries that emerged out of the Soviet Union after its fall, even though all had questionable records in the areas of human rights and democratization. In addition to being used as a carrot, trade restrictions were also used as a stick. In 2003, the Bush administration announced that it was suspending military aid to some thirty-five countries because they failed to meet a congressionally imposed deadline exempting Americans from prosecution in the new International Criminal Court. Congress exempted twenty-seven states, including NATO members Israel and Egypt, from the loss of aid.

One new foreign aid plan put forward was the Millennium Challenge Corporation (MCC). The MCC targets low-income countries to support economic growth and reduce poverty.[25] Money is given only to countries that meet a demanding set of criteria, and programs are implemented by the recipient country's government. The seventeen indicators used to judge eligibility are presented in table 11.3. They fall into three categories: (1) good government ("ruling justly"), (2) economic freedom, and (3) investing in people. In 2021, twenty-nine compacts (five-year projects) had been completed since its founding. There were eleven active compacts and eight threshold programs where details were being finalized on a compact. As an independent government aid agency, a concern raised with the MCC's efforts is its potential impact on the coherence of U.S. foreign aid initiatives. Colin Powell described the relationship as one of the MCC "pulling" countries forward and USAID "pushing" them.[26]

## Contemporary Foreign Aid

Donald Trump left little doubt about how he viewed foreign aid upon becoming president. In a speech to the United Nations (UN), he declared, "We are only going to give foreign aid to those who respect us, and, frankly, are our friends." UN ambassador Nikki Haley followed up this statement by saying that the United States was taking note of those states that voted against the U.S. recognition of Jerusalem as Israel's capital. While this comment stunned many, it was not without precedent. The United States has collected statistics on UN votes since the Reagan administration.

Overall, Trump sought to reduce the level of foreign aid spending drastically. His proposed 2020 budget called for reducing funding for humanitarian aid, refugee assistance, and global health by more than $9 billion. Trump frequently asked what the United States was getting in return for its aid. He called past foreign aid expenditures, such as those in the Middle East, "a mistake." His preference was to provide loans rather than grants. Following this logic, he was reluctant to provide foreign aid for rebuilding war-torn states in the region. In 2018, Iraq requested $88 billion for this purpose. The United States offered only $4 billion and asked its allies to cover the rest. A funding conference in Kuwait resulted in the failure to secure any funding.

In his initial budget request, Biden sought to dramatically increase U.S. foreign aid spending. He requested almost $64 billion for his International Affairs Budget, an increase of just over $6 billion. Congress approved a $58 billion budget, an amount only slightly larger than the existing budget. Ukraine has become a major recipient of U.S. aid. Multiple agencies provide this funding. The approved International Affairs Budget for FY 2022 included $6.9 billion in emergency aid. In FY 2021, the Defense Department provided it with $275 million in security assistance. By mid-FY 2022, it had provided an additional $950 million in security assistance. USAID has provided some $55 million in humanitarian aid.

## Over the Horizon: How Trade Wars End

The U.S.-China trade war has taken its toll on both economies. Imports of American-made goods fell by 22 percent in August 2019, and as of September 2019, the growth rate in China had slowed to its lowest level in thirty years. As noted earlier in this chapter, the U.S.-China trade war has not ended. No single ending exists for trade wars. A number of possibilities must be considered. Five deserve particular attention:

- *One side wins.* One side is able to exert sufficient pressure and costs on the other to obtain an agreement largely consistent with its goals.
- *A draw.* Neither side is able to achieve its goals. Exhaustion plus high domestic costs dictate ending the war and moving on; this outcome may require a change in leadership to one that is not committed to winning the war.
- *A cease-fire.* Neither side can achieve victory, but rather than walk away, each prepares for a future trade war that they see as inevitable and as needed to restore national honor.
- *Return to a global free trade system.* Both sides lose. Neither is in a position to impose its will; rather than a cease-fire, the remaining global economic powers reassert the logic of a global free trade system through a modified WTO.
- *The emergence of trading blocs.* The trade war ends in the establishment of competing trading blocs, each with its own economic and political rules. Nationalist economic competition rather than cooperation now guides global economic interactions.

It remains to be seen which of these will be the ultimate outcome of the U.S.-China trade war and the extent to which others factors such as the COVID pandemic and the impact of the Ukraine War have on the strength of their economies and the preference for continuing the trade war or ending it.

## Critical Thinking Questions

1. Which type of free trade agreement—bilateral, regional, or global—is of most value to the United States today, and why?

2. Should economic sanctions be used against friends or just foes? Explain your answer.

3. How do you think the U.S.-China trade war will end?

## Key Terms

boycott, 234
Bretton Woods system, 235
economic statecraft, 232
embargo, 234
fast track, 236
free trade, 233

imperialism, 232
nontariff barrier, 233
quota, 234
smart sanctions, 242
tariff, 233

# Military Instruments
## Big Wars

## Learning Objectives

Students will be able to:

1. Identify the key elements in U.S. nuclear strategy.
2. Describe the difference between deterrence and preemption.
3. Distinguish between arms control and disarmament and assess in which category North Korean denuclearization fits best.
4. Explain why defense has been the missing element in nuclear policy and what policies have been tried.

# On the Agenda: North Korean Denuclearization

In his first one hundred days in office, Biden put out feelers to North Korea about restarting **denuclearization** talks but was met with silence. In March 2022, North Korea conducted its first intercontinental ballistic missile (ICBM) test since 2017. It was said to have the ability to strike the East Coast of the United States and could carry multiple warheads. By the end of 2022, it had launched more than eighty-eight ballistic and other missiles and had completed preparations for a nuclear test.

The first North Korean nuclear weapons agreement was negotiated by the Clinton administration. Talks began in June 1993 and culminated in an Agreed Framework in October 1994. North Korea agreed to freeze its nuclear program in return for fuel oil, economic cooperation, the international construction of two proliferation-resistant nuclear reactors, and the promise of improved diplomatic relations with the United States. This agreement collapsed early in the Bush administration as evidence showed consistent violations by North Korea. In April 2003, the Bush administration entered into the Three-Party Talks attended by the United States, China, and North Korea. Eventually, two agreements were reached. Under the terms of a 2005 agreement, North Korea agreed to abandon all nuclear weapons and return as soon as possible to the Non-Proliferation Treaty (NPT), which it had left in 1994. For its part, the United States confirmed that it had no intention to attack or invade North Korea. All participants agreed to promote economic cooperation with North Korea. The 2007 agreement (which became a Six-Party Agreement including Japan, South Korea, and Russia) required North Korea to shut down and seal the Yongbyon nuclear facility under international supervision. In return, North Korea would receive emergency energy assistance and would be removed from the U.S. list of state sponsors of terrorism.[1]

Early on in his presidency, advisors urged Trump to enter into negotiations with North Korea because of fears that it could build a nuclear weapon in six to seven weeks. In late February 2017, Trump agreed to informal talks, only to change his position hours later. Instead, the administration chose to step up the deployment of an anti–ballistic missile system in South Korea and increase pressure by financial institutions if North Korea's nuclear missile program was not restrained. In July, North Korea countered with its first successful test of an intercontinental ballistic missile. In early September, it detonated its sixth nuclear bomb; Trump responded with the pledge that even the threat of North Korea using nuclear weapons "will be met with massive military response." In late September, Trump issued an executive order placing strong financial sanctions on individuals, aircraft, ships, and firms trading in goods, services, or technology with North Korea. He also chided Secretary of State Rex Tillerson for proposing talks with North Korea.

In 2018, Trump's rejection of diplomacy in favor of military and economic pressure took a sudden about-face. In March, he accepted on the spot a meeting invitation from North Korean leader Kim Jong-un, which was passed to him by South Korean president Moon Jae-in during a visit to Washington. That meeting was held in Singapore on June 12, 2018. Although short, the road to the meeting was not easy. On May 24, Trump canceled the summit in response to the strongly worded negative response by North Korea to Pence's suggestion that the Libyan model (denuclearization and removal of leadership/change in government) would be in order if no agreement were reached. The next day Trump changed his mind about canceling the summit, citing "a very nice statement" from North Korea.

Trump's negotiation style and approach to these talks differ greatly from those of his predecessors. Clinton and George W. Bush pursued *bottom-up negotiations,* in which the details of the agreement were reached by lower-level officials. Trump's approach emphasized *top-down negotiations,* in which leaders meet and seek an agreement with little preparatory work by staffers. No National Security Council preparatory meeting was held. Trump asserted that "within the first minute" he would know if Kim was serious. At the summit's conclusion a brief joint statement was signed, pledging both sides to establish more positive relations, build a lasting and stable peace on the Korean Peninsula, and work together to recover MIA/POW remains. North Korea also pledged to honor an existing commitment to denuclearize the Korean Peninsula, but denuclearization was not defined. Trump also announced the end of "provocative" joint military exercises between the United States and South Korea and his hope to remove the thirty-two thousand U.S. troops in South Korea, and he proclaimed that "there is no longer a nuclear threat from North Korea."

The sense of goodwill generated by the summit soon disappeared. In July, Secretary of State Mike Pompeo flew to North Korea to create a nuclear inventory for denuclearization. Kim refused to see him, and North Korea issued a statement complaining of the U.S. "unilateral and gangster-like demand" for denuclearization. In August, Trump canceled a follow-up trip by Pompeo. North Korea countered by announcing its intent to strengthen its nuclear forces.

With negotiations stalemated, Trump announced his desire for a new summit. It was held in Hanoi in February 2019. The conference ended abruptly, without a signed statement, after Trump walked out.[2] He had proposed that North Korea denuclearize, trading all of its nuclear weapons, materials, and facilities for an end to economic sanctions. This offer was virtually the same as those offered by Clinton and Bush. North Korea rejected it, proposing to dismantle its Yongbyon nuclear facility in exchange for an end to sanctions put in place by the United Nations in 2016. Kim's position was also virtually the same as North Korea had put forward in the past: denuclearization (with a still-contested meaning) would proceed in stages, but sanction relief would come immediately. Each side blamed the other for the failure of the Hanoi Summit, then returned to past policies. The United States imposed new sanctions. North Korea tested a series of new weapons. The United States seized a North Korean ship for running the blockade.

To the surprise of most observers, a third Trump-Kim meeting took place in June 2019. Following the G20 meeting in Japan, Trump flew to the DMZ and entered North Korea to talk with Kim. The meeting was judged to be largely symbolic, but it was agreed that working-level nuclear talks between the United States and North Korea would resume in July. Once again, optimism about a resolution soon faded. When the United States and South Korea announced their determination to go ahead with their annual joint force exercise in August, North Korea indicated that it would resume nuclear testing. Within one month, it carried out seven weapons tests, including launches of two short-range ballistic missiles. Trump downplayed the tests, saying, "He likes testing missiles. Many nations test those missiles." More tests followed in December, and North Korea set the end of 2019 as the hard deadline for beginning negotiations. No agreement was reached.

This chapter begins by looking at the use of nuclear weapons and large-scale conventional forces for preemption, deterrence, and war fighting. It then looks at arms control efforts.

# Cold War Nuclear Thinking

The United States' nuclear strategy during the Cold War was not static; it changed several times. It also lacked internal consistency.[3] There often was a distinction between how policy makers described their strategy and what it actually meant in terms of action. Recall from chapter 1 that the former is known as *declaratory policy* and the latter as *action policy*. To fully appreciate this difference, the discussion begins by looking at the development of U.S. and Soviet nuclear arsenals and then examines the strategies built upon them.

## The U.S. Cold War Strategic Arsenal

On July 16, 1945, the first atomic bomb was detonated at 5:30 a.m. in the New Mexican desert. On August 6, Hiroshima was destroyed by an atomic bomb. On August 9, Nagasaki was similarly destroyed by a plutonium bomb. These two attacks effectively depleted the U.S. (and the global) inventory of atomic weapons. As World War II came to a close, a divided Truman administration looked out to the post–World War II era. Many decisions would have to be made, not the least of which was determining what to do with the nuclear bomb; for one proposed action, see the "Historical Lesson."

The U.S. nuclear arsenal grew slowly. Two weapons were stockpiled at the end of 1945, nine in July 1946, thirteen in July 1947, and fifty in July 1948.[4] None of these weapons was preassembled; it took thirty-nine people over two days to put them together. The U.S. nuclear monopoly ended in 1949 when the Soviet Union detonated its first atomic bomb. The United States responded by developing a more powerful weapon, the hydrogen bomb (H-bomb). The United States successfully tested an H-bomb in November 1952. The Soviet Union duplicated the feat in August 1953.[5] By 1957, it is estimated that the United States probably had three thousand nuclear bombs, and the Soviet Union had a few hundred.[6]

Reinforcing this U.S. numerical advantage in bombs was a marked superiority in delivery systems. The Soviet bomber fleet was small and had to travel a great distance to strike the United States. The United States could use bases in Western Europe to attack the Soviet Union. This advantage disappeared in 1957 when the Soviet Union successfully tested an ICBM and launched Sputnik into orbit. With these two actions, the Soviet Union demonstrated the theoretical capability to deliver a nuclear attack on U.S. cities and its overseas military bases.

Fearing the development of a "missile gap" in which the Soviet Union would have a significant advantage in nuclear weapons, the United States stepped up production of its own ballistic missile force. As it turned out, no missile gap developed because the Soviet Union did not engage in a crash buildup of its nuclear forces. The result was overwhelming U.S. nuclear superiority.

The U.S. nuclear arsenal reached its peak size in 1966 with an estimated thirty-two thousand nuclear warheads. At that time, the Soviet Union possessed about seven thousand nuclear warheads. The long-predicted Soviet buildup got underway in the mid-1960s; by 1978, it held a slight numerical advantage over the United States: 25,393 Soviet warheads to the United States' 24,826. Beginning at this time, the term *parity* was used to characterize the U.S.-Soviet nuclear relationship.

## U.S. Cold War Nuclear Strategy

For the first eight years of the nuclear age, virtually no such thing as nuclear strategy existed at either the declaratory or action level. The uniqueness of nuclear weapons was not yet appreciated. They were simply treated as the largest explosive devices yet created. It was expected that the next war would be fought along the lines of World War II. Long-range bombers would deliver nuclear weapons against Soviet cities, industries, and military support facilities. When the small stockpile of atomic bombs was exhausted, plans called for using conventional bombs and a general mobilization of U.S. forces.[7] The first war plan to identify atomic bomb target lists was *Broiler* in the fall of 1947, which called for thirty-four bombs to be dropped on twenty-four cities.[8]

There was a certain degree of unreality to early war plans. Documents leaked to the press indicate that nuclear weapons remained in U.S. war plans in 1958 and involved defending Taiwan from a Chinese attack. That year China engaged in heavy shelling of islands controlled by Taiwan.[9] The U.S. military urged the first use of nuclear weapons against China to defend Taiwan. The likely risk of Russian nuclear retaliation against the United States was acknowledged by the military. One factor pushing support for the idea was the need to avoid another prolonged war in Asia so soon after the Korean War. Eisenhower rejected the plan in favor of continuing to rely on conventional weapons to defend Taiwan. The crisis ended when China broke off its attacks.

Writing in 1946, Bernard Brodie questioned whether nuclear weapons could be used in the same way as other weapons, or if deterrence (the use of force to prevent something unwanted from happening) rather than war fighting was their sole credible use.[10] Moreover, if deterrence was the principal purpose of nuclear weapons, then thought was necessary about how to accomplish it. Deterrence could not simply be assumed to exist.

The first formal statement of nuclear strategy was put forward by the Eisenhower administration as part of its New Look defense posture. The nuclear component of this strategy was **massive retaliation**. It was intended to deter a wide spectrum of Soviet attacks, guaranteeing not only the security of the United States but also that of its allies by threatening the Soviet Union with massive destruction in retaliation for aggressive behavior. No details were given; all that was promised was "retaliation instantly, by means and places of our own choosing." The lack of specificity was intentional. The Eisenhower administration felt that the Truman administration's pledge of help to any country threatened by communism had given the initiative to the Soviet Union. Massive retaliation was designed to give it back to the United States.

Two recurrent lines of criticism of massive retaliation were leveled. The first concerned its credibility. Critics asserted that deterrence required more than just the capability to inflict damage. The threat also had to be believable. Threatening the Soviet Union with massive destruction for an attack on the United States was one thing; to make the same threat for attacks on allies was quite another. Soviet leaders would find the former credible, but not the latter; therefore, they would not be deterred, leaving the United States with the distasteful choice between implementing its threat and doing nothing. The second line of criticism was that massive retaliation was ill suited to the changing U.S.-Soviet nuclear relationship. Massive retaliation assumed the existence of an invulnerable retaliatory force, which was no longer the case. The growing vulnerability of nuclear forces to attack transformed deterrence from a certainty into one based on a "delicate balance of terror."[11]

Massive retaliation was U.S. declaratory policy. Action policy was reflected in U.S. war plans. Evidence suggests that these plans were tailored to meet the two primary contingencies spoken of by policy makers: retaliation and **preemption** (striking first in self-defense when a threat is imminent). Instead, U.S. war plans had become capability plans. They were constructed in such a way as to employ all of the nuclear weapons in the U.S. inventory and provide a rationale for acquiring additional weapons.[12]

The first coordinated effort to establish a nuclear action policy came in 1960 when President Dwight Eisenhower approved the establishment of a National Strategy Target List (NSTL) and a Single Integrated Operational Plan (SIOP) for using nuclear weapons. Planners selected 2,600 separate installations for attack out of an overall list of 4,100 targets.[13] Plans called for launching all 3,500 nuclear warheads if sufficient warning time existed. According to one calculation, the SIOP assigned three hundred to five hundred kilotons of weapons to accomplish the level of destruction caused by a single bomb on Hiroshima.

The Kennedy administration differed in how to structure deterrence and gave attention to a problem not yet fully addressed: how to fight a nuclear war. Kennedy replaced massive retaliation with the concept of **flexible response**, under which the United States would have a range of conventional and nuclear options from which to choose in deterring and responding to Soviet aggression. To make this happen, the Kennedy administration incorporated three new features into U.S. nuclear thinking:

1. More attention was given to the use of tactical nuclear weapons in the hope that, because of their less destructive nature, they might be more manageable.
2. A new targeting policy was adopted that emphasized attacks on military forces and avoidance of population centers.
3. The administration looked into two measures that might limit the damage done to the United States in case of a nuclear war: civil defense and damage limitation.[14]

The value of these changes in nuclear strategy was called into question by the 1962 Cuban missile crisis (see chapter 9).[15] Attention now shifted back to formulating a nuclear posture built on the ability to inflict widespread devastation on the enemy. To be credible, Robert McNamara initially estimated that U.S. forces must possess **assured destruction,** the capability to destroy 25–30 percent of the Soviet population and 66 percent of its industrial capacity.

Movement from massive retaliation to flexible response and then to assured destruction implied a parallel set of changes in U.S. targeting policy. Although changes in the SIOP did occur, SIOP remained a capabilities (action) plan rather than an objectives (declaratory) plan.[16] The most significant targeting change took place when the Nixon administration introduced the principle of **sufficiency**, which required strategic equality between the United States and the Soviet Union rather than the possession of a minimum level of retaliatory threat.[17] This was seen as providing crisis stability so that neither side had an incentive to go first with its nuclear weapons in a crisis. A new Nuclear Weapons Employment Policy (NUWEP) emphasized the destruction of Soviet economic recovery assets as the primary objective of U.S. nuclear forces. It stipulated that, under all circumstances, the United States must be able to destroy 70 percent of the Soviet industrial capacity needed for postwar economic recovery. The major notable and controversial addition to U.S. nuclear strategy made by the Reagan administration was to add the requirement that the United States must be able to "prevail" and "force the Soviet Union to seek the earliest termination of hostilities on terms favorable to the U.S."

## Historical Lesson

### The Baruch Plan

After World War II ended, on one side of the debate about what to do with the nuclear bomb was Secretary of War Henry Stimson, who argued that the United States could not keep a nuclear monopoly for long. It would only be a matter of time before the Soviet Union and other countries acquired the scientific knowledge and technological capacity to build nuclear weapons. To prevent such nuclear **proliferation**, he favored placing nuclear power under international control. Aligned against Stimson was a group led by Secretary of State James Byrnes. Distrustful of Soviet motives and fearful of its power, Byrnes argued against any sharing of nuclear secrets. From this perspective, a monopoly over nuclear weapons would be crucial to maintaining the postwar balance of power. Truman was divided on the matter but ultimately supported Stimson's perspective.

In September 1945, the first international discussions about the future of nuclear power took place in Washington among representatives from the United States, Great Britain, and Canada, all of whom had worked on various aspects of the Manhattan Project responsible for development of the nuclear bombs that leveled Hiroshima and Nagasaki. This was followed by a foreign ministers meeting in Moscow in December, during which the United States, Great Britain, and the Soviet Union agreed in principle to create a United Nations (UN) commission to work for the peaceful use of nuclear power and to advise on the destruction of existing nuclear weapons (which only the United States possessed). In January 1946, to help formulate a U.S. position, Stimson appointed Undersecretary of State Dean Acheson to chair a committee that would draft a U.S. nuclear energy policy. Acheson formed a technical advisory group to support his committee's deliberations chaired by David Lilienthal, who also chaired the Tennessee Valley Authority.

The Acheson-Lilienthal Committee issued its report in March 1946. Its fundamental conclusion supported Stimson's position. International inspections of atomic energy facilities were unlikely to stop their spread and the diversion of atomic energy for military purposes. Accordingly, the best solution was to place atomic energy under the control of a new international agency, the Atomic Development Authority, and make it available in small quantities to all countries for peaceful use. In return for the United States taking this step, all other countries would agree not to develop nuclear weapons. The committee's approach was consistent with the prevailing view of the early post–World War II era that the primary obstacles to developing a bomb were not technological and scientific problems but access to raw materials.

After receiving the report, Truman arranged for it to be given to Bernard Baruch, whom he had appointed as the U.S. representative to the UN Atomic Energy Commission. Baruch proceeded to make important changes in the Acheson-Lilienthal Plan, the most significant of which dealt with modifying the enforcement procedures that could be wielded by the new Atomic Development Authority. Baruch eliminated the possibility that decisions by the Atomic Development Authority might be vetoed by participating countries. Only then did he believe that the phrase "immediate and direct enforcement" would carry any weight. Baruch also inserted additional language that Truman accepted. With Baruch's change in wording, the Baruch Plan was presented to the UN Atomic Energy Commission on June 14, 1946. Truman's about-face appears to be tied to steadily deteriorating relations with the Soviet Union that made conflict appear far more likely than cooperation.

Baruch opened his presentation by telling the assembled delegates that they faced a choice between the "quick and the dead." His plan gave the Atomic Energy Authority the power to inspect nuclear facilities, made it illegal to possess an atomic bomb, and allowed for the seizure of facilities. The United States would end its nuclear monopoly in stages and destroy its nuclear weapons only when the Baruch Plan was fully implemented. The Soviet Union quickly rejected the plan, objecting to its loss of a veto and calling for the United States to end its nuclear monopoly as a precondition for participation. In December 1946, the Baruch Plan was approved by a 10–0 vote, with the Soviet Union and Poland abstaining. Since a unanimous vote of all twelve members of the UN Atomic Energy Commission was needed, the plan was defeated. The Soviet Union detonated its first nuclear device on September 23, 1949.

### Applying the Lesson

1. Could the Baruch Plan have slowed down or stopped nuclear proliferation? Why or why not?
2. Some argue that Truman knew the plan would be rejected and was not serious about it. What do you think?
3. What would a new Baruch Plan have to look like to stop nuclear proliferation by North Korea or Iran?

# Post–Cold War Nuclear Thinking

The end of the Cold War did not bring with it an end to nuclear weapons. Questions continued over the proper size of the U.S. nuclear arsenal and strategies for its use. Additionally, questions were raised about whether nuclear weapons were still a stabilizing force in world politics or a source of instability.[18] Two different dynamics were at work here. The first involved the expanded number of states with nuclear capabilities and the variety of strategies that emergent nuclear powers might employ, which greatly complicated the challenges of deterrence for the United States.[19] The second was the pursuit by both Russia and the United States of low-yield nuclear weapons; some saw this as a dangerous development because it threatened to lower the threshold for their use.

## The U.S. Post–Cold War Strategic Nuclear Arsenal

At the beginning of 2022, the U.S. nuclear inventory totaled 5,428 nuclear weapons, of which 1,744 were deployed. The remainder were held in reserve or were classified as retired and awaiting disarmament. Of the deployed warheads, 1,344 are on ballistic missiles, 300 are on strategic bombers, and 100 tactical bombs are deployed in Europe.[20] Table 12.1 presents an overview of the global nuclear inventory in 2022.

| Table 12.1 | World Nuclear Forces, January 2022 | | |
|---|---|---|---|
| Country | Deployed Warheads | Reserve/Stored Warheads | Total Inventory |
| Russia | 1,588 | 2,889 | 5,977 |
| United States | 1,744 | 1,664 | 5,428 |
| France | 280 | 10 | 290 |
| China | — | 350 | 350 |
| United Kingdom | 120 | 60 | 225 |
| Israel | — | 90 | 90 |
| Pakistan | — | 165 | 165 |
| India | — | 160 | 160 |
| North Korea | — | 20 | 20 |

*Source:* SIPRI Yearbook 2022, https://www.sipri.org/media/press-release/2022/global-nuclear-arsenals -are-expected-grow-states-continue-modernize-new-sipri-yearbook-out-now.
*Notes:* Deployed warheads are found on intercontinental missiles, at heavy bomber bases, and on bases with operational short-range delivery systems. Reserve warheads are in storage and not deployed on launchers. Total inventory includes retired warheads that are still intact but in line for dismantlement.

Since nuclear inventories are classified and kept secret, there is always some debate over the exact number of nuclear warheads countries possess, including the United States. Two other debates exist today over the size of the U.S. nuclear force. One deals with the readiness and reliability of U.S. nuclear warheads, especially those designed in the 1950s and early 1960s. In 2005, Congress began funding the Reliable Replacement Warhead program to address this concern. In 2014, Pentagon studies documented serious deficiencies in the nuclear weapons infrastructure, such as aging blast doors in nuclear silos and an aging submarine fleet. The second debate centers on the cost of modernizing and expanding the U.S. nuclear arsenal. Trump's 2018 Nuclear Posture Review (NPR), discussed shortly, had a price tag of $1.2 trillion to be spent over the next twenty years.

## U.S. Post–Cold War Nuclear Strategy

U.S. nuclear thinking continues to bear the imprint of Cold War thinking. The first presidential statement of U.S. post–Cold War policy was Bill Clinton's 1997 Presidential Decision Directive 60 (PDD-60). According to PDD-60, the U.S. military should no longer prepare to win a protracted nuclear war but instead to deter the use of nuclear weapons against the United States and its allies. It continued to call for the existence of a wide range of nuclear strike options against Russian nuclear forces and its civilian and military leadership. It also contained a requirement to plan for nuclear strikes against states that have "prospective access" to nuclear weapons or that may become hostile to the United States.

The major change in George W. Bush's nuclear weapons policy was to add flexibility to U.S. nuclear strategy by constructing a wider range of scenarios in which nuclear weapons might be employed. Operations Plan (OPLAN) 8010 contained nuclear strike options against combat forces and options for use of support equipment against six potential enemies: Russia, China, North Korea, Iran, Iraq, and Syria. Obama reaffirmed the fundamental role of nuclear weapons in U.S. security policy but moved to reduce the size of the U.S. nuclear arsenal and to minimize the role of nuclear weapons in defense planning.[21] These efforts met with mixed results. On the one hand, he announced the retirement of nuclear-armed, submarine-launched cruise missiles. On the other hand, he committed to modernizing the U.S. nuclear arsenal in return for obtaining Senate approval of the New Strategic Arms Reduction Treaty (New START).

President Trump's 2018 Nuclear Posture Review endorsed Obama's support for nuclear modernization but parted company with Obama in a number of important respects. It held that new arms control agreements were "difficult to envision" given changes in the dynamics of world politics and the growing threats from China and Russia. Trump's NPR called for maintaining the U.S. nuclear triad of land-based, sea-based, and air-launched missiles and for developing low-yield submarine-launched ballistic missiles and a new generation of cruise missiles that hug the ground after launch. One of the most controversial aspects of his NPR was advancing the integration of nuclear and conventional forces in military planning and training exercises, especially in identifying situations in which nuclear weapons might be used.

In October 2022 an unclassified version of Biden's NPR was released. It identified China and Russia as the major nuclear threats and defined the purpose of nuclear weapons as: (1) deterring strategic attacks, (2) assuring allies and partners, and (3) achieving U.S. objectives if deterrence fails. "Our nuclear posture is intended to complicate an adversary's entire decision calculus, including whether to instigate a crisis, initiate armed conflict, conduct strategic attacks using non-nuclear capabilities, or escalate to the use of nuclear weapons on any scale."

In terms of the structure of the U.S. nuclear force, emphasis was placed on modernization and integrating conventional and nuclear weapons planning rather than expanding its size. Work on the nuclear sea-launched cruise missile endorsed by Trump, but opposed by Presidents George H. W. Bush through Obama, was terminated. It also retreated from a no-first-use policy that Biden advanced during his presidential campaign and Trump's embrace of low-yield nuclear weapons.

The NPR put forward an overall positive position on arms control, asserting that "mutual, verifiable nuclear arms control offers the most effective, durable and responsible path to achieving a key goal: reducing the role of nuclear weapons in U.S. strategy."[22]

## Bridging the Nuclear-Conventional Divide

Where do we draw the line between using conventional and nuclear weapons?[23] The long-standing fear exists that, without a clearly defined **firewall** separating the two, a conventional war might escalate into a nuclear one.

Careful thinking about the interaction of nuclear and conventional weapons is especially important in two of the most controversial areas of contemporary U.S. military strategy: deterrence and preemption. Deterrence is controversial because some now argue that some U.S. enemies cannot be deterred. Preemption is controversial because of its offensive character and the possibility of its being carried out on the basis of incorrect information. Both of these concerns have been raised in the Ukraine War where on occasion Putin has threatened the use of nuclear weapons.

## Deterrence

The United States is concerned with deterring attacks both on its own homeland (*direct deterrence*) and against its allies (*extended deterrence*). Up until the terrorist attacks of 9/11, it was taken for granted that direct deterrence was more easily achieved than extended deterrence. Now both are suspect.

Two different strategies have been used to implement a deterrence strategy. The first is to set *trip wires*. This typically took the form of American troops stationed abroad—most notably in Germany and South Korea—that would stand in the way of any enemy attack. During the Cold War, the presence of American troops abroad was seen as a sign of strength and resolve. Today, troops have become targets of opportunity for terrorists and insurgents.

A second strategy is to leave the door open to a nuclear response should deterrence fail. By threatening to take a crisis to the brink of nuclear war, it was assumed that the enemy would abandon its unwanted line of action. Reportedly, President Eisenhower threatened the use of nuclear weapons against China if it did not help bring about an end to the Korean War.

You can begin to understand the problems faced in constructing a successful deterrence strategy if you look at its past failures.[24] Two primary failure patterns exist:

1. *A fait accompli.* Hostile policy makers detect no U.S. commitment and feel that they can control their risks in challenging the United States. The 1950 North Korean attack on South Korea is an example of this type of deterrence failure. The attack was not irrational because no clear U.S. commitment existed, and the risks appeared to be controllable. Public statements by leading U.S. diplomats and military figures had placed South Korea outside of the U.S. "defense perimeter" and referred to it as a "liability" in the event of war in the Far East. The most likely response to an attack was expected to be diplomatic protest or a minimal military action.

2. *A limited probe.* The challenging action is easily reversed or expanded depending on the nature of the U.S. response. In these cases, the U.S. commitment is unclear, and the risks still seem to be controllable. The Berlin Wall crisis of 1961 is one example. The Soviet Union and East Germany moved at midnight on May 12 to close the Berlin border crossing by constructing a barbed-wire wall on East Berlin territory. Only when the minimal nature of the U.S. response was clear (the Western powers did not make a protest for four days) did they move to construct a more substantial and permanent wall with only a few well-guarded openings.

Failure patterns such as these led the George W. Bush administration to move away from deterrence to preemption.

Deterrence is not doomed to fail. According to advocates of deterrence, it is important to recognize that deterrence has two dimensions. It contains both a threat, "Cross this line and we will attack," and a promise, "If you do not cross this line, we will not harm you." Viewed from this perspective, recent U.S. deterrence failures such as those against Saddam Hussein in Iraq and Bashar al-Assad in Syria result from implementing only the first part of the deterrence equation. Instead of a promise not to do harm, the United States has treated its adversaries as villains who could not be trusted and had to be replaced. Similarly, efforts described in the opening to this chapter about reaching an agreement that would deter North Korea from building a larger nuclear force suffered from references to employing the Libyan model, which saw Gaddafi give up his nuclear weapons only to be captured and killed following Western military intervention into Libya in 2011.

A reemerging deterrence challenge facing the United States involves NATO. It is both external and internal. The internal deterrence challenges to NATO come from two directions.[25] A general challenge is found in the internal politics of member states with the rise of authoritarian leaders. A more specific challenge comes from Trump's questioning of NATO's value. During his presidential campaign, Trump spoke of NATO as an obsolete organization that was a financial drain on the United States because member states were not paying their fair share. Several times early in his presidency, Trump went so far as to raise the matter of withdrawing from NATO with his national security staff. Members may withdraw from NATO after a one-year notification period. Dissension within NATO reached the point that, in 2019, a seventieth-anniversary meeting in Washington scheduled to be attended by heads of government was downgraded to a foreign ministers' meeting. The 2022 Russian invasion of Ukraine breathed new life into NATO by serving as a unifying force among existing members and leading to the expansion of NATO to include Finland and Sweden shoring up its eastern flank and creating a situation Russia has long feared.

The external challenge comes from Russia's growing military presence in Europe and came into focus with its 2014 annexation of Crimea and 2022 invasion of Ukraine. Both times the United States responded with an increased presence of NATO ground forces in the region and sending training and equipment supplies to strengthen Ukraine's army. Russia is also modernizing its navy and has altered its naval doctrine to include developing a Russian presence in strategic areas such as the Mediterranean Sea and the blue-water Atlantic (the deep waters of its open oceans). Especially troubling to the United States and its European allies is Russia's increasing military presence and military exercises in the Baltics. One such exercise, Zapad-2017, involved almost a hundred thousand military personnel and employed nuclear-capable missiles. This last point is significant because Russia's nuclear doctrine includes an escalate-to-deescalate strategy, in which low-yield nuclear weapons could be employed to prevent military action by the United States and NATO.

## Preemption

As indicated earlier in the chapter, *preemption* is striking first in self-defense when a threat is imminent. When a threat is not imminent but is still held to be real, striking first in self-defense is referred to as a *preventive strike*. Technically speaking, the George W. Bush administration ignored this long-standing distinction in putting forward its policy and combined both scenarios under the single heading of preemption. Preemption is not a new U.S. strategy. Ronald Reagan justified the invasion of Grenada in 1983 as a preemptive move. Lyndon Johnson did so when he sent troops to the Dominican Republic in 1965. In the more distant past, Woodrow Wilson's decision to send troops to Mexico in 1914 could be considered consistent with the logic of preemption.

The Iraq War represented the Bush administration's attempt to implement a policy of preemption. Particular attention has been directed at the *shock-and-awe* strategy used in its opening stage. The expectation was that, by rapidly overcoming the enemy's ability and will to fight, the United States would immobilize the enemy, and reconstruction would be less expensive. The subsequent occupation problems in Iraq led to debate over the wisdom of using a small military force in this manner. Defenders of the strategy maintain that Operation Iraqi Freedom was not a good test case for a shock-and-awe strategy. They argue that operational difficulties and the less-than-perfect knowledge of the enemy reduced it to a mere slogan instead of a strategy. They cite a military conflict with China as a potential case in which it might be better applied.[26]

Even if the logic of striking first in self-defense is accepted, questions remain to be answered.[27] Perhaps the most pressing issues include the following: How long should a country have to wait before acting? And how should it respond? Here again the influence of Cold War thinking can be seen. In a bipolar nuclear world, preemption was focused on responding to national security superpower nuclear threats. Today, many crises are domestic rather than cross-border in nature. In addition, they are not necessarily nuclear in nature. Even when the threat is nuclear, the argument is increasingly being made that the increased lethality of conventional weapons makes them better suited for responding to certain types of nuclear threats than the use of nuclear weapons.

## Using Large-Scale Conventional Military Force

Conventional military power can be used for many purposes.[28] This section examines the large-scale use of conventional military power for fighting wars. It looks at past uses of force and future challenges. The next chapter returns to its use in the context of peacekeeping operations and as a stability force. While few countries possess nuclear forces, conventional armed forces are universally possessed. Table 12.2 provides a ranking of the conventional power capabilities of the twenty most powerful countries in 2022. The index weighs fifty different factors. Included among them are manpower, naval power, oil reserves, airports, external debt, defense budget, tank strength, rocket projectors, land area, and coastline coverage. The lower the power index score, the greater is a country's theoretical conventional war-fighting power.

During the Cold War, the U.S. military fought two big wars: Korea and Vietnam. Three times since the fall of the Berlin Wall in 1989, the United States has sent large numbers of armed forces abroad to engage the enemy in conflict. The first occurred in 1991, when the United States led a United Nations–sanctioned war against Iraq after its invasion of Kuwait. A massive bombing campaign was initiated on January 17. The offensive military actions that followed met ineffective Iraqi resistance, and after a hundred hours of fighting, President George H. W. Bush declared a cease-fire. The 2003 Iraq War got off to a similarly effective start. A massive shock-and-awe bombing campaign was followed by twenty-one days of combat, which began on March 20 and encountered little resistance. Baghdad fell on April 9. There followed, however, a long and protracted unconventional war in which U.S. forces did not fare as well. In October 2011, Obama announced that the last U.S. troops would leave Iraq by the end of the year, bringing the war to a close. In 2019 there

| Table 12.2 | Global Conventional Power Index: Top Twenty Countries | | |

| Rank/Country | Power Index Score | Rank/Country | Power Index Score |
|---|---|---|---|
| 1. United States | .0453 | 11. Italy | .1801 |
| 2. Russia | .0501 | 12. Egypt | .1809 |
| 3. China | .0511 | 13. Turkey | .1961 |
| 4. India | .0979 | 14. Iran | .2104 |
| 5. Japan | .1195 | 15. Indonesia | .2251 |
| 6. South Korea | .1261 | 16. Germany | .2322 |
| 7. France | .1283 | 17. Australia | .2372 |
| 8. United Kingdom | .1382 | 18. Israel | .2621 |
| 9. Pakistan | .1572 | 19. Spain | .2801 |
| 10. Brazil | .1695 | 20. Saudi Arabia | .2966 |

*Source:* Global Fire Power, 2022 Military Strength Ranking, https://www.globalfirepower.com/countries-listing.php.
*Note:* The lower the power index score, the greater the country's theoretical conventional war-fighting power.

were still an estimated 5,200 troops in Iraq as part of a security agreement to provide military support and advice to defeat Islamic terrorist groups. The Trump administration also sought to shift U.S. forces from Syria to Iraq and keep U.S. forces in Iraq in order to monitor Iran.

The third major involvement of U.S. forces has been in Afghanistan. This was covered in depth in the opening chapter. Here it is important to note that U.S. involvement in Afghanistan can be divided into two phases. The first phase, which came immediately after 9/11, had the goals of removing the Taliban from power and capturing or killing Osama bin Laden. It relied heavily on air power and special forces that operated in alliances with local resistance leaders. The second phase began in 2008 when U.S. forces began entering Afghanistan in large numbers. The Taliban insurgency had regrouped, forming an alliance with al-Qaeda and threatening the control of the U.S.-backed Afghan government. By 2010, the number of U.S. troops in Afghanistan had reached ninety-four thousand.

War fighting has always been the ultimate measure of a state's power. For much of the post–World War II period, American military policy was cast in terms of a *two-war capability*, meaning that the United States needed the ability to fight two wars at the same time. This has not always been the case, however. Under Nixon the standard was 1.5 wars, and under Reagan it was 3.5 wars. After 9/11, the United States began moving away from this baseline. The 2015 National Military Strategy stated that "if deterrence fails . . . our military will be capable of defeating a regional adversary in a large-scale, multi-phased campaign while denying the objectives of—or imposing unacceptable costs on—another aggressor in a different region."[29] This was characterized as a *one-plus strategy*. Today, the primary attention of defense planners has again been directed toward the possibility of major military conflict with China rather than toward terrorism or a regional adversary.

Concern over possible conflict with China centers on the South China Sea and led to the development of the *Air-Sea Battle strategy* in 2010. At the low end of the conflict continuum, the Air-Sea Battle strategy was intended to provide policy makers with enough flexibility to be able to move military forces outside a specific theater of conflict, conduct a show of force, or engage in limited military strikes. At the higher end of the conflict continuum, the Air-Sea Battle strategy was designed to provide the ability to defeat aggression and maintain escalation advantages in the face of advanced weapons systems. One version of the Air-Sea Battle strategy called for U.S. bombers and submarines to incapacitate China's long-range intelligence capabilities and precision missile systems, followed by larger air and naval assaults on Chinese targets. In 2015, the Air-Sea Battle strategy was replaced by the *Joint Concept for Access and Maneuver in the Global Commons.* The change was intended to direct attention to two elements missing from the Air-Sea Battle strategy, which included no role for the army and no detailed attention to the question of U.S. strategy after gaining access to denied territory.

The Joint Concept for Access and Maneuver in the Global Commons directs attention to problems of anti-access/area denial (A2/AD) in the South China Sea. These problems have long been a focus of military planners dealing with small-war contingencies. *Anti-access (A2) challenges* refer to efforts by the adversary to prevent the United States from entering a theater of operation and block it from prepositioning forces near or moving forces to that area. Tactics range from denial of basing rights and overflight rights, expulsion from existing bases, terrorism, cyberattacks, opening alternative fronts requiring U.S. military engagement, and the use of weapons of mass destruction and ballistic missiles. *Area denial (AD) challenges* refer to possible steps taken by an adversary to resist and limit the freedom of action open to the U.S. military once it has entered an area. Area denial tactics include the use of ballistic missiles, mines, electronic warfare, and social media.

## Reducing the Danger of War: Arms Control and Disarmament

In the earliest years of the Cold War, two general strategies were pursued to lessen the likelihood of nuclear war: disarmament and arms control. **Disarmament** has as its ultimate goal the systematic elimination of weapons, whereas **arms control** seeks to place restraints on the use of weapons. For the most part, disarmament tended to be pursued at the level of declaratory policy through formal treaties. Arms control did not always involve formal agreements or treaties. Instead, it took the form of more flexible and informal *traffic rule* agreements, such as arrangements to give advance notification of tests or military exercises to reduce the possibility that these actions might be incorrectly interpreted and spiral into military conflict. The rationale for pursuing such traffic rule agreements was that a treaty in and of itself did not produce arms control.

These multiple paths to arms control continue today, as does the tendency for disarmament to remain at the declaratory level. More recently, a third strategy, defense, has also been pursued. Before examining each of these as ways of controlling or preventing big wars, note that an often underappreciated dimension to the problem of controlling nuclear weapons involves accidents. In 1979, a training video of a Soviet attack was accidently played and set off warnings of a nuclear attack. Even more serious were a series of Soviet missile, bomber, and submarine accidents between 1983 and 1987 that grew out of fears of a NATO first strike.[30] Most recently, a nuclear explosion at a Russian military testing site in August 2019 killed five scientists and released radiation off its northern coast. Russia provided little information about the accident. Speculation centered on the testing of a new type of nuclear-propelled cruise missile. Evidence later emerged that the explosion occurred underwater or near the surface when Russia was trying to salvage a sunken missile.

## The Cold War Record

From 1946 to 1957, disarmament proposals dominated the international negotiating agenda. Little of significance was achieved, as proposals were put forward with an eye more to their propaganda value than to their substantive merits. The first nuclear disarmament proposal to command global attention was the Baruch Plan, which was highlighted in the "Historical Lesson." Presented by the United States at the United Nations in 1946, it sought to place all aspects of nuclear energy production and use under international control, but it was rejected by the Soviet Union.

Proposals for lessening the danger of nuclear war were not forthcoming again until the Eisenhower administration. Its first proposal was the 1953 Atoms for Peace plan. This was followed in 1957 by the Open Skies proposal. Atoms for Peace was a disarmament plan only in an indirect sense. It sought state cooperation on the peaceful development and use of atomic power. Eisenhower's proposal led to the creation of the International Atomic Energy Agency, but it did not produce movement in the direction of disarmament. The proposed Open Skies Treaty focused on reducing the fear of surprise attack by exchanging blueprints of military installations and allowing each side to carry out aerial surveillance of the other's territory. It, too, failed to serve as a first step toward disarmament. Rather than accepting the plan as a way of sidestepping the question of on-site inspection, the Soviet Union interpreted it as a device for legitimizing U.S. spying.

The first major breakthrough in arms control came in 1963 following the Cuban missile crisis, with the signing of the Limited Test Ban Treaty. This treaty outlawed nuclear explosions (testing) in the atmosphere, underwater, and in outer space. A second milestone was reached in 1968 with the signing of the Treaty on the Non-Proliferation of Nuclear Weapons, commonly referred to as the Non-Proliferation Treaty (NPT). Up until that time, the primary proliferation concern shared by the United States and the Soviet Union was stopping the spread of nuclear weapons in Europe, especially to West Germany. With the signing of the NPT, attention shifted to the Third World. The NPT represented an agreement between nuclear and nonnuclear states. Those states that had nuclear weapons promised not to provide them to nonnuclear states and to negotiate in good faith to reduce their nuclear stockpiles. They also pledged to help nonnuclear states develop nuclear energy for peaceful purposes. In return, the nonnuclear states agreed not to try to obtain nuclear weapons.

In addition to spurring interest in multilateral arms control treaties, the Cuban missile crisis also nudged the United States and the Soviet Union toward bilateral arms control efforts. The first major product was the hotline (actually a telegraph link) between the White House and the Kremlin. During the crisis, it had taken nearly twelve hours for a key communication from Soviet leader Nikita Khrushchev to reach President John Kennedy and be decoded. The hotline was first used in 1967 during the Arab-Israeli War, when the Americans and Soviets informed each other of the movements of their navies.

The negotiation of a formal arms control treaty between the United States and the Soviet Union had to wait until their nuclear inventories had grown to the point at which each side felt that a balance of power existed. The breakthrough agreements came with the 1972 Anti-Ballistic Missile (ABM) Treaty and an agreement called the Strategic Arms Limitation Talks (SALT; it became SALT I upon introduction of the second, SALT II agreement). The ABM Treaty was of unlimited duration and was modified in 1975. Its key provisions limited each side to one ABM deployment area and prohibited the development, testing, or deployment of ABM components. Among the key provisions of SALT I were limits on the number of fixed launchers for ICBMs and numerical limits for submarine-launched ballistic missiles.

The SALT I agreement on offensive forces was set to expire in 1977. The expectation was that it would lead to a second agreement (SALT II). A first step in this direction was the November 1974 signing by President Ford of the Vladivostok Accords, which set ceilings on the total numbers of strategic launchers that each side could possess and the number of vehicles that could carry multiple independently targeted warheads. Movement from the Vladivostok Accords to SALT II did not proceed smoothly, in part because Jimmy Carter sought to achieve deeper cuts upon becoming president. As it finally emerged, SALT II was a complicated, multilayered document to which the U.S. Senate has never given its consent; it has now technically expired.

In his campaign for the presidency, Ronald Reagan attacked the SALT II treaty as fatally flawed because it placed the Soviet Union in a position of military advantage. Reagan's first concrete arms control proposal was directed at the problem of intermediate-range nuclear weapons in Europe. These weapons had become NATO's main defense against the conventional military advantage held by Warsaw Pact troops. By the late 1970s, their military value was seriously challenged by the Soviet Union's introduction of mobile SS-20 missiles. In November 1981, Reagan presented his solution to this problem. His *zero option* called on the Soviet Union to eliminate its existing intermediate-range ballistic missiles (IRBMs) targeted at Europe in return for a U.S. pledge not to deploy a new generation of missiles there. The idea of a zero option was quickly rejected by the Soviet Union. The resulting deadlock was not broken until September 1987 with the signing of the Intermediate Nuclear Forces (INF) Treaty.

During the same speech in which he unveiled his zero option, Reagan indicated that his administration was preparing proposals for a new round of strategic arms talks, to be known as the Strategic Arms Reduction Talks (START). Little visible movement was forthcoming, and public concern began to mount over the administration's commitment to arms control and its loose language about nuclear war.[31] Ultimately, the Reagan administration presented a series of arms control proposals that the Soviet Union rejected as "old poison in new bottles." Still, negotiations continued, and a START framework was agreed upon by the time Reagan left office. The agreement was signed by President George H. W. Bush and Mikhail Gorbachev in July 1991.

## The Post–Cold War Record

The dynamics of arms control changed with the end of the Cold War. Rather than engaging in many rounds of protracted treaty negotiations, the United States and the Soviet Union entered into a series of unilateral cuts. For example, in September 1991, Bush ordered all tactical nuclear weapons, except those dropped from planes, to be removed from the U.S.

arsenal; all nuclear cruise missiles and bombs to be taken off naval ships, attack submarines, and land-based naval aircraft; and all strategic bombers to be taken off high-alert status. He also halted the development and deployment of mobile ICBMs. Gorbachev responded by calling for the elimination of all land-based tactical nuclear weapons and the removal of all nuclear arms from ships, submarines, and land-based naval aircraft.

The failed August 1991 coup against Gorbachev raised concerns in the United States that, should the Soviet Union disintegrate, the government and military's ability to exert command and control over the immense Soviet nuclear arsenal would also disappear, with potentially catastrophic proliferation consequences. In November 1991, to try and minimize the dangers inherent in thousands of "loose nukes," Congress passed the Cooperative Threat Reduction Program (better known as the Nunn-Lugar Program) to help the Soviet leadership secure and dismantle its nuclear stockpile.

The United States and Russia returned to formal arms control agreements in January 1993 with the signing of START II. It never came into force, however. Domestic and foreign policy issues in both countries led to the treaty languishing in limbo. Russia delayed final approval as a sign of its disapproval of U.S. military action in the Balkans. In the United States, attention shifted to the politically charged question of whether it should withdraw from the ABM Treaty so that a national missile defense system could be created. This issue was settled when, in December 2001, President George W. Bush gave the required six-month notice that the United States was withdrawing from the ABM Treaty.

Russian president Vladimir Putin called the decision to withdraw from the ABM agreement a "mistake," but it did not stop him from signing a new arms control agreement with the United States in May 2002; the Strategic Offensive Reductions Treaty (SORT) broke new ground in treaty language. It starts from the premise that Russia is a friend of the United States and not an enemy. The agreement was negotiated in six months and contains only ten sentences. In essence, the treaty permitted each side to do as it pleased as long as its nuclear arsenal was reduced to 2,200 deployed warheads by December 31, 2012. SORT expired on December 21, 2012.

With START I set to expire in December 2009, at a July 2009 summit meeting, President Obama and Russian president Dmitry Medvedev announced that they had agreed upon the outlines of a new arms control agreement: New START. Obama encountered significant problems in getting Senate approval. Many in Congress argued that its inspection provisions were inadequate and that the U.S. nuclear inventory needed upgrading. Obama succeeded in gaining Senate approval of New START in December 2010 by committing to a ten-year, $85 billion nuclear weapons modernization program. According to the terms of the treaty, both sides can deploy no more than 1,550 strategic warheads and 700 launchers seven years after the treaty is ratified. On-site inspection agreements established in START I also would resume. New START was activated in February 2011 and would remain in force until 2021, with an option to extend its life to 2026.

Trump showed little interest in extending New START, something he called a one-sided agreement. Instead he called for creating a new agreement, which would include Chinese nuclear forces and cover Russian nuclear forces not currently controlled by a treaty. In April 2019, Trump gave instructions to his staff to prepare for trilateral nuclear arms control talks. Such a trilateral treaty would be an unprecedented arms control accomplishment. From the outset observers were skeptical that this line of arms control negotiations could produce a meaningful agreement due to the short time within which to create an agreement before New START would expire. Moreover, China was seen as having little interest in placing limits on nuclear weapons. These concerns led many arms control experts to conclude that Trump was more interested in ending New START than he was in reaching a new agreement.

Early in his presidency Biden and Putin agreed to extend New START. The arms control value of that agreement was cast into doubt by Russia's invasion of Ukraine and deteriorating U.S.-Soviet relations. At one point early in the fighting, Putin placed Russian nuclear forces on high alert in an attempt to counter U.S. efforts to send arms to Ukraine and build a global coalition to stop the invasion. The United States publicly dismissed his declaration as being typical of his pattern of manufacturing threats to justify his actions.

Another area of controversy involved the INF treaty. U.S.-Russian nuclear relations took an antagonistic turn here in 2014, when the United States accused Russia of violating the 1987 INF Treaty by testing a prohibited ground-launched cruise missile. That agreement banned producing or testing low-flying, ground-launched cruise missiles with a range of 310 to 3,420 miles. Although it had begun testing this missile in 2008, Russia denied the allegation. In 2015, the Obama administration determined that, despite Russia's violations, it was not in the interest of the United States to withdraw from the INF treaty.[32]

President Trump reached the opposite conclusion, announcing in October 2018 that the United States was planning to withdraw from the INF Treaty. In February 2019, following unsuccessful talks between the United States and Russia over preserving the treaty, the United States formally suspended its participation. Ending the INF Treaty allows the United States (and Russia) to legally begin testing and developing a new generation of land-based, intermediate-range cruise missiles. It also allowed the United States to address the Chinese buildup of cruise missiles. Since China was not a party to the INF Treaty, its ability to build these weapons was not limited; it now had an inventory of more than two thousand ballistic and cruise missiles, presenting U.S. forces in the region with a growing military challenge. On August 18, 2019, sixteen days after the official U.S. withdrawal, the United States tested a Tomahawk cruise missile that would have been illegal had the INF Treaty still been in place. Trump followed this up by withdrawing from the Open Sky agreement.

The post–Cold War era has also seen the reemergence of nuclear proliferation as a central national security problem for the United States. In spite of the NPT, nuclear proliferation has become a political and strategic reality. India and Pakistan acquired nuclear weapons (in 1974 and 1998, respectively), and Israel is recognized to have possessed them since 1979. South Africa, Iraq, and Libya are known to have had or to have been in pursuit of nuclear weapons at one time. Attention today is focused on the nuclear ambitions of two states identified by Bush as part of the "axis of evil": Iran and North Korea.

As noted in the "On the Agenda" section opening this chapter, repeated efforts to negotiate North Korean denuclearization have accomplished little. Negotiations with Iran did produce an agreement, but success was short-lived. On July 14, 2015, after eighteen months of talks, the United States and its negotiating partners (Great Britain, France, Russia, and China, plus Germany, collectively known as the P5+1) and Iran reached an agreement on limiting Iran's nuclear program. Known as the Joint Comprehensive Plan of Action (JCPOA), it was controversial from the outset. President Obama stated that it would extend Iran's nuclear breakout time, the time it would take to produce enough weapons-grade uranium for a single nuclear bomb, to one year in its first decade, up from two to three months. It would do so by actions such as freezing the size of Iran's uranium stockpile, reducing the number of uranium-enriching centrifuges, and reducing the allowed level of enrichment. The agreement also contained provisions for unannounced, on-site inspections of all phases of its nuclear development program. Should Iran not comply, the United Nations could begin a *snapback* of sanctions (a reimposition of previously imposed sanctions). From Iran's perspective, the goal was removal of U.S. and international economic sanctions. The agreement contains a timetable for sanctions removal through a four-step process, defined as adoption day, implementation day, transition day, and termination day. Trump had campaigned against the treaty. In April and June 2017, he certified Iran's compliance, but in October 2017 he did not. In May 2018, fifteen months into his presidency, Trump officially withdrew from the JCPOA. In August 2020, Trump demanded the reinstitution of the snapback sanctions. The UN Security Council rejected the move. The Biden administration has engaged in indirect and direct talks with Iran to restart JCPOA, but with little success.

# Defense

According to one observer, "The great missing innovation in the nuclear age is the development of means to defend against nuclear attack."[33] Without this ability, it is impossible to protect a nation's population and territory without the cooperation of the enemy. Strategists have established that such tacit cooperation between enemies is possible and often takes place during war.[34] Still, many are troubled that the defense of the United States in the nuclear age is possible only with the cooperation of an adversary. Reagan gave voice to these concerns in a March 1983 speech:

> What if free people could live secure in the knowledge that their security did not rest upon the threat of instant U.S. retaliation to deter a Soviet attack; that we could intercept and destroy their strategic missiles before they reached our soil or that of our allies? Is it not worth every investment necessary to free the world from the threat of nuclear war?[35]

The terrorist attacks of 9/11 added a new dimension to the defense problem. Nuclear weapons did not have to be delivered by long-range missiles or aircraft. Weapons could be assembled in the target state or cross national borders in a variety of ways, and there would be no clearly defined set of targets for retaliation.

## The Strategic Defense Initiative

Reagan's solution to this dilemma was the Strategic Defense Initiative (SDI). He defined it as a long-term research and development program designed to identify viable policy options for creating a nuclear defense system. The decision as to which system—if any—to pursue was scheduled to be made in the 1990s. However, in early 1987, the Reagan administration began examining the possibility of an early deployment of SDI. As envisioned by most observers, Reagan's SDI system involved a series of defensive systems layered in such a way as to create a leak-proof umbrella or protective shield. Each layer in this system was to perform the same tasks: it would search out and detect targets, track them, discriminate between real targets and dummy targets, and intercept and destroy the real targets.

Although the goal was never formally abandoned, the scope of and funding for a "Star Wars" system were progressively cut back. The George H. W. Bush administration continued to seek funding for it under the guise of "brilliant pebbles," under which missiles possessing the ability to detect the launch of enemy missiles would be sent into space in layered orbits. SDI's short-lived existence formally came to an end during the Clinton administration. It was replaced by interest in developing follow-on missiles to the Patriot system used against Scud missiles in the Persian Gulf War. Instead of constructing a nuclear shield over the United States, the new goal would be to prevent attacks by short-range, ground-launched missiles.

## National Missile Defense Systems

The death of SDI did not mark the end of efforts to establish a national ballistic missile defense system. Surprise missile tests by Iran and North Korea in 1998 provided political support for creating such a system. In 2002, after George W. Bush withdrew the United States from the ABM Treaty, he put forward a national missile defense system plan calling for ground-based, long-range missile interceptors supported by a network of ground-based radars and space-based infrared sensors. Implementation of such a system in Alaska and California began in 2004. During his presidential campaign, Obama expressed skepticism about the merits of this missile defense shield. One of his first foreign policy initiatives was to terminate it. He also announced a comprehensive review of U.S. ballistic missile defense (BMD) policies, strategies, plans, and programs. The U.S. Congress also mandated such a review.

As a result of these reviews, in 2010 the Defense Department produced a Ballistic Missile Review Report. It concluded that the United States had the capability of defending the homeland against a ballistic missile attack from states such as North Korea or Iran for the foreseeable future. The report also called for greater international cooperation among allies on missile defense and the pursuit of regionally focused missile defense arrangements. Overall, the report recommended proceeding in a fiscally sustainable manner, making reasonable judgments about threats, and developing reliable capabilities.

It was not until January 2019 that the next Missile Review Report was released, again under a mandate from Congress and led by presidential directives on U.S. security goals. In announcing it, Trump invoked the rhetoric of Reagan and the imagery of SDI, claiming, "When it comes to defending America we will not take any chances. We will only take action. There is no substitute for American military power." The report moved in two directions. In terms of long-term goals and aspirations, it described attacking enemy missiles prior to launch or soon thereafter (the boost phase) and placing an array of sensors in outer space that could track missiles. In terms of concrete objectives, it largely continued down the path of the previous report, neither canceling existing initiatives nor announcing the beginning of a new weapons program. One major addition was reference to Russian and Chinese missile defenses, but it continues to focus on destroying missiles launched by smaller powers. A second change was dropping "Ballistic" from the report's title, indicating concern about countering cruise missiles and hypersonic vehicles (those that can travel at Mach 5 or higher—five times the speed of sound).[36] Biden issued a still classified Missile Defense Report to Congress in 2022.

The potential benefits of missile defense systems are a subject of intense debate.[37] Four issues dominate the discussion. The first is the wisdom of constructing an overly robust system that could potentially negate an opponent's nuclear capability. Many fear that such a system would force the targeted state to undertake large-scale expansions of their nuclear programs to deter the United States from acting unilaterally against them. The second issue is the military value of such systems, designed to protect the United States from rogue nuclear states. Where some see them as prudent, others see them as a largely symbolic response to domestic political pressures. The third issue is effectiveness. From 2004 to 2011, ten tests against incoming warheads were held on the West Coast, five of which failed. The fourth issue is cost. Over $70 billion has already been invested in building a ground-based interceptor system. The price tag for a space-based system has been estimated at over $1 trillion.

## Over the Horizon: A New Age of Nuclear Proliferation

The main nuclear proliferation concern for the United States during the Cold War was the growing size and sophistication of Russia's nuclear arsenal. With the end of the Cold War, attention shifted to the pursuit of nuclear weapons by **rogue states**, states that are considered to be threats to the peace and stability of the international system due to their refusal to act in accordance with global rules and norms. The most dangerous rogue states over the past several decades because of their pursuit of nuclear weapons have been Libya, North Korea, Syria, and Iran.

The possibility is now raised that we may be entering into a new era of nuclear proliferation, one no longer dominated by the actions of rogue states. Instead, the main proliferation threat will come from a group of states who are neither rogue states nor adversaries of the United States. They also are not among states considered to be strong allies. Leading possibilities cited include Saudi Arabia, Turkey, and Egypt. Their pursuit of nuclear weapons is not driven by fear of an attack or of an attempt to overthrow the government by the United States, but by a fear that the United States cannot or will not defend their security in a time of crisis.[38] Theirs is a hedging and leveraging strategy: (1) develop a nuclear capability but stop short of building bombs, and (2) use this capability as a bargaining chip with the United States to ensure that it meets its defense commitments. One major proliferation change this strategy may bring about is that the pursuit of nuclear weapons may not be covert. To be an effective bargaining chip requires that the pursuit of nuclear weapons be known.

This nuclear proliferation challenge is not without precedent. In some respects it repeats the challenge presented by South Korea's interest in nuclear weapons in the 1970s when it had doubts about U.S. security commitments. The global context, however, is different. The increase in the size of China's nuclear arsenal plus concerns over the unsettled nature of U.S. domestic politics have accentuated these fears today, perhaps making past ways of addressing the proliferation challenge less likely to succeed. Simply applying force or threatening action may result in political and security backlashes from them. Creating international coalitions against these states also may not be as easy as doing so against rogue states.

## Critical Thinking Questions

1. Are nuclear weapons a usable military tool? Why or why not? Under what conditions should their use be considered instead of conventional weapons?

2. Should we be optimistic or pessimistic about the future of arms control efforts? Explain your answer.

3. Can arms control efforts become counterproductive? Explain your answer.

## Key Terms

arms control, 268
assured destruction, 259
denuclearization, 255
disarmament, 268
firewall, 263

flexible response, 259
massive retaliation, 258
proliferation, 260
rogue state, 275
sufficiency, 260

# Military Instruments
## Small Wars

# 13

## Learning Objectives

Students will be able to:

1. Distinguish between humanitarian operations and stability operations.
2. Identify the different stages of counterinsurgency warfare.
3. Explain the underlying dynamics and characteristics of cyber warfare.
4. Recognize the variety of conventional weapons proliferation challenges that exist today.

# On the Agenda: Cyber Warfare

**Cyber warfare** refers to attacks on computers or information networks. Two statements capture the current state of thinking about cyber warfare. The first is from Admiral Mike Rogers, former National Security Agency (NSA) director and head of the U.S. Cyber Command: "Every conflict around the world now has a cyber-dimension." The second is from Michael Hayden, former director of the CIA and the NSA: "Rarely has something been so important and so talked about with less clarity and understanding [as cybersecurity]." While both observations may be overstated, evidence suggests that they are right on target.

On the first point, you need look no further than President Trump's decision to authorize cyberattacks on Iran's missile system after deciding not to employ military force in the June 2019 crisis following Iran's downing of a U.S. drone. For years, Iran had been linked to a series of cyberattacks against Saudi Arabia. Following the tightening of economic sanctions in 2012, Iran began targeting U.S. banks and businesses. Iran reduced its attacks on U.S. targets with the onset of the 2015 nuclear agreement, but a noticeable increase in its cyber activity followed U.S. withdrawal from the agreement.

The U.S. attacks on Iran soon were followed by revelations that the United States had shifted from a defensive posture to an offensive one in using cyber weapons against Russia. Russia had successfully broken into the Pentagon's classified communications system in 2008 and had shut off power to hundreds of thousands of people in Ukraine in 2014 as part of the conflict over Crimea. It was also determined that Russia had made significant inroads into the U.S. energy grid. Since 2012, the United States had been putting reconnaissance probes into the control systems of Russia's electrical grid in order to determine weaknesses and to signal that the United States was in a position to cripple the system in a retaliatory strike.

The cyberattacks were not the first time the United States went on the cyber offensive against Iran. In 2010, in cooperation with Israel, the United States launched the Stuxnet virus attack on Iran's nuclear weapons program. Information made public as part of the 2013 NSA leaks revealed that the United States carried out 231 offensive cyber operations in 2011 alone, all of which were on a far smaller scale than the Stuxnet attack. In 2014, cyberattacks on North Korea's nuclear forces were ordered to sabotage its missiles prior to or just after launch. In 2015, Obama approved cyberattacks on North Korea in retaliation for its attack on Sony Pictures over a movie release that included a satirical assassination plot against North Korea's leader. ISIS has also been the target of cyberattacks; in 2016 it was revealed that attacks were being carried out in order to disrupt communications and interrupt electronic transfers of money.

Four separate issues are raised by Hayden's observation in the first paragraph of this section. The first involves launch authority. Obama's Presidential Policy Directive 20 had required high-level discussions among agencies before the Department of Defense could launch aggressive cyberattacks. Reportedly, the State Department often blocked proposed attacks. Under Trump's National Security Presidential Memorandum 13, the Department of Defense can act unilaterally on many types of cyberattacks. Accounts suggest that the military did not brief Trump in any detail about these operations for fear that he would overrule them or would discuss the information with foreign officials in an offhand manner.

The second issue involves evaluating cyberattack effectiveness. Evaluations of Obama's cyberattacks on North Korean missiles were mixed. The success rate of North Korea's missile launches went down, but it was not clear if this was the result of the cyberattacks or multiple problems existing in the North Korean military establishment. Varying evaluations also have been put forward of the 2010 Stuxnet virus attack on Iran's Natanz nuclear enrichment facility. Before the attack, Israeli officials had stated that an Iranian nuclear capability was imminent. Afterward, they said that it would not happen before 2015. Press accounts only two years later spoke of how quickly Iran was recovering from the attack. A similar debate has taken place over Russia's use of cyberattacks against Ukraine in 2022. Dire predictions of the impact of cyberattacks (cyber Pearl Harbors) did not occur.

Some commentators argue that effectiveness should not focus solely on military consequences. They assert that cyberattacks can also produce significant political consequences for the targeted country in terms of monetary costs, the political standing of leaders, and uncertainty about the security of its secrets.[1] These concerns have arisen in the controversy over Russian interference in the 2016 U.S. presidential election; they also ensued following the Stuxnet attack, prompting Iran's supreme leader to restart nuclear negotiations with the West. In 2020 it was revealed that Russian hackers known as Cozy Bear penetrated the computer system of SolarWinds, a U.S. network and software management company, allowing them to gain access to files of the Treasury, Commerce, and Homeland Security Departments, among others.

The third issue is the nature of cyber power and how it should be used.[2] Is it a powerful new weapon for which there are no strategic precedents, or is it best seen as the most sophisticated version of past weapons, including sabotage, espionage, and subversion?[3] Is it a preemptive weapon that produces cyber-9/11s, or a weapon of deterrence and retaliation?[4]

The fourth issue is how to think about countering cyberattacks. Should one use a strategy of deterrence or preemption, or is another approach necessary? One alternative strategy emphasizes *resilience*. It is based on the reality that completely stopping cyberattacks is probably impossible. What is needed is a strategy to detect them quickly, respond, and adjust and adapt so that the impact of a cyberattack is short-lived and contained.

Cyber warfare is only one of many varieties of small wars. This chapter examines the range of forms that small wars take (conventional military force, hybrid wars, covert action, counterinsurgency operations, counterterrorism, and cyber warfare) as well as the role of arms control in such conflicts.

## Separating Big Wars from Small Wars

No clear dividing line or formula exists for distinguishing between big wars and small wars. The number of casualties, length of combat, and impact on domestic society are the most frequently cited distinctions. In spite of the implications of the label, small wars have the ability of presenting large challenges to powerful states.

Big wars and small wars tend to have their own language. Large wars have combatants and are fought according to rules of law that are generally accepted (in the West). Small wars have insurgents and often appear to be fought without rules. Different language is also used to discuss the origins and dynamics of big and small wars. The starting points most frequently used to describe big wars are the logic of geopolitics, the influence of geography, and the power considerations of national security policy. **Windows of opportunity**, calculations by leaders that they can win, are contrasted with **windows of fear**, consequences of inaction so dire that leaders feel forced to try to go to war. This language also underlies efforts to stop big wars. Deterrence is intended to convince an opponent that no window of opportunity exists. Arms control seeks to close windows of fear and reduce the potential for and consequences of accidents. In all cases, it is assumed that a major threat to the national interest is at work.

Small wars often appear to be wars of choice rather than wars of necessity, language implying that other means existed for solving the dispute that gave rise to the conflict. Major sources of small wars involve access to energy supplies, water, and food supplies. Ethnicity is also a cause. In some cases, this takes the form of *separatism*, where one ethnic group seeks to leave a state and form a new one in order to better protect itself. In other cases, it takes the form of *irredentism*, where a state reaches out and tries to bring its kin group into the state by expanding its boundaries. In still other cases, it takes the form of *genocide*, as one group seeks to eliminate another ethnic group from its territory.

Deterrence and arms control become more complex in small wars. For example, some argue that deterrence against terrorism can only be partially successful; for deterrence to work, terrorist networks must be broken down into their component parts and different deterrence strategies employed against each segment.[5] Arms control efforts can easily flounder when the target of concern is viewed by key states as a matter of domestic politics. This has been the case with conventional arms control efforts in the United States amid concerns that they would violate the right to bear arms outlined in the Second Amendment to the U.S. Constitution.

## Exiting Small Wars

While small wars may be more a matter of choice than big wars, this does not mean they are easy to end. Just as with big wars, ending a small war requires both achieving an agreement with the enemy and having sufficient domestic political support to act. A major diplomatic initiative by Obama in 2014 designed to help broker a peace in Afghanistan ended when Republicans in Congress voiced strong opposition to an agreement whereby five Taliban prisoners in Guantanamo Bay would be released in return for the release of one captured U.S. soldier. The strong negative political backlash to this agreement ended further efforts at negotiating a peace agreement.[6] Donald Trump called for leaving Afghanistan as early as 2012, but early in his presidency he said little about it. Movement in that direction gained speed in 2018 as the United States and the Taliban entered into peace talks. After ten months of negotiations, an agreement in principle was reached. Some 5,000 U.S. troops would leave within 135 days after the agreement was signed. Most of the remaining 9,500 U.S. troops and the 8,600 NATO troops would be withdrawn in phases. In return, the Taliban agreed not to allow ISIS, al-Qaeda, or other terrorist groups to operate in Afghanistan. The Taliban also agreed to begin talks with the Afghan government, which was not part of the peace talks. With an agreement in hand, President Trump sought to bring the Taliban and the Afghan government leaders to Camp David to iron out the final details. Neither the Taliban nor Afghan government leaders desired to go to Camp David, and congressional leaders reacted with disbelief that Trump would invite terrorists to Camp David. At that point, Trump canceled the meeting and declared peace talks with the Taliban "dead."[7]

# Types of Small Wars

From January to March 2015, the Cato Institute think tank estimated that U.S. Special Forces were deployed in over eighty countries. None of these situations is exactly alike, but one thing they tend to share is that they are asymmetric wars, military conflicts between forces that have significantly different power resources and strategies. In contrast to conventional warfare, in which victory is achieved by defeating enemy military forces and taking control of land leading to surrender, in asymmetric warfare the path to victory lies in inducing exhaustion that erodes the enemy's will to fight and leads to the collapse of its military and political base.[8] The United States faces three major asymmetric conflict challenges today: **hybrid warfare**, insurgencies, and terrorism. The distinctions between them are fluid, and elements of each may be present to some degree in any given conflict situation.

## Hybrid Warfare

**Hybrid warfare** is a term with many different meanings. Perhaps the most frequently used definition is that by Frank Hoffman, who defines a hybrid war as one that "incorporate(s) a range of different modes of warfare, including conventional capabilities, irregular tactics, and formations, terrorist acts including indiscriminate violence and coercion, and criminal disorder."[9] By 2010, the U.S. Army had already begun to alter its training programs to put greater emphasis on hybrid conflicts. Its Hybrid Threat Training Circular presented three hybrid conflict scenarios: offensive operations, defensive operations, and stability operations.[10]

Most observers agree that hybrid warfare is not a new form; instead, it combines different forms of warfare into a coordinated and controlled strategy of war that emphasizes avoiding predictability and engaging in combat in *contested zones* (areas that are highly populated and/or of economic importance). Most accounts of hybrid warfare also recognize the importance of using information resources such as social media and the press to defeat the adversary.[11]

The Iran crisis during the Trump administration had many of the characteristics of a hybrid war. Found in it are a combination of traditional military operations in the downing of a U.S. drone, naval operations involving the seizure of British and Iranian commercial ships, cyber retaliatory attacks by the United States against Iranian targets, proxy attacks by Houthi rebels who are supported by Iran against Saudi Arabian oil targets, and the dispatch of additional U.S. forces to the region.

It is important to note that hybrid warfare may be carried out by both nonstate actors and states. Hezbollah's campaign against Israel is an example of the former, and Russia's military operations in Crimea and Ukraine are examples of the latter. In 2014 Russia sent in armed forces without uniforms, professional soldiers in uniforms without marking, and agents acting with indigenous separatist groups to seize public buildings in Ukraine. It also relied upon local agitators (a variety of militia groups). In 2022 Russia relied upon mercenary soldiers (the Wagner Group) to mount the invasion. Sophisticated military technology such as antiaircraft weapons and surface-to-air missiles were provided to local fighters, who also employed terrorist techniques and engaged in sabotage. Russia sought to control the information about the conflict and to engage in deception through such means as Russia Today, a Russian-controlled news network.

## Counterinsurgency

The *U.S. Army/U.S. Marine Counterinsurgency Field Manual defines an insurgency as* "an organized movement aimed at the overthrow of a constituted government through the use of subversion and armed conflict." **Counterinsurgency (COIN),** the strategy the United States employs to defeat insurgencies, is defined by the 2006 field manual (FM3-34) as a protracted conflict that involves a mix of offensive, defensive, and stability operations. It requires that soldiers be both "nation builders as well as warriors."[12] COIN is a strategy designed to get the support of the people, which requires the coordinated use of military, paramilitary, political, economic, psychological, and civic actions.

Using a medical analogy, COIN operations are seen as moving through three stages:

*Stage 1: Stopping the bleeding by providing the patient with emergency first aid.* The goal at this stage is to protect the population and break the insurgency's momentum.

*Stage 2: Inpatient care.* The goal is to restore the patient's health and move him on the way to a successful long-term recovery.

*Stage 3: Outpatient care.* The goal of this third stage is to move the patient to self-sufficiency, with more and more of the governing functions being carried out by the patient.

At each stage, attention needs to be given to a wide range of activities, including providing security and essential services and promoting good governance and economic development.

COIN is primarily associated with U.S. military involvement in Iraq and Afghanistan. Two major criticisms have emerged. The first has to do with the prerequisites for COIN success, most notably the character of the host government. COIN seeks to partner with the government-in-power to restore or enhance its legitimacy, diminishing the insurgents' military capability and isolating them from the public, who will turn their loyalty to the government. As Iraq and Afghanistan demonstrated, not all local partners are in a position to capitalize on the successes of COIN. Rather than seeing their legitimacy increase, the result is a growing political void that invites a renewed insurgency.

A second question focuses on COIN's internal logic. It has three main strategic goals: force protection, distinction between combatants and noncombatants, and the physical destruction of insurgents. However, according to some analysts, at any one time COIN is only capable of achieving two of its goals.[13] In the case of the U.S. surge in Iraq, COIN's focus on protecting U.S. forces and civilians by distinguishing between them and enemy combatants came at the expense of destroying the insurgents. In Afghanistan, COIN focused on discriminating between civilians and enemy combatants and physically destroying the insurgents at the cost of increasing the risks faced by U.S. troops.

COIN is not without its defenders. Instead of being inherent in the concept of counterinsurgency, they see many of the problems identified by critics as a product of a military culture that was slow to embrace the idea (and then did so with little enthusiasm) and of policy makers who made military decisions on going to war without plans following its conclusion. In the final analysis, some argue that "counterinsurgency is sometimes the least bad option available."[14]

## Counterterrorism

As discussed in chapter 2, *terrorism* is violence employed for the purpose of political intimidation. Where counterinsurgency strategies focus on winning the collective "hearts and minds" of the public, military-oriented antiterrorism policies focus on taking out individual leaders and crippling terrorist organizations. The weapon of choice in combating terrorism is air power. Since mid-2015, air strikes against ISIS economic targets such as oil wells, tanker trucks, oil pipelines, and buildings containing stores of cash have been major targets of U.S. air power. In 2016, it was estimated that its production of oil had fallen by 30 percent, and revenues from its oil sales were down some 50 percent. Moreover, ISIS had lost 47 percent of its territory in Iraq and 20 percent in Syria. Its fighting force fell from thirty-three thousand in 2015 to between eighteen and twenty-two thousand in mid-2016. In December 2017, ISIS controlled less that 5 percent of Syria, and in March 2019 it was defeated. Yet, in early 2022, ISIS showed renewed strength even though it did not control any territory when it carried out a ten-day attack on a prison to release ISIS members held there.

The air power of greatest importance in fighting terrorism are drones (shorthand for unmanned aerial vehicles or remotely piloted vehicles). The use of drones for military purposes does not represent a revolutionary strategic or tactical military breakthrough. They date back to World War I, when pilotless vehicles were launched by catapults. By the Vietnam War, their role had expanded from serving as reconnaissance aircraft to being employed as combat decoys and missile launchers. Drones next played a major role in U.S. military operations in Bosnia in 1995. After the 9/11 attacks, the mission assigned to drones expanded yet again to include killing suspected terrorists. Under the George W. Bush administration, the use of drones to kill terrorists was limited. Trump embraced the use of drones even more. Shortly after taking office, parts of Yemen and Somalia were declared to be war zones; doing so removed the need for White House approval and provided the military and the CIA with increased freedom to launch drone strikes. Trump also relaxed the standards used to justify drone strikes outside of war zones. There no longer needed to be an "imminent threat" or a "near certainty" that civilians would not be killed. He also terminated the annual report on drone strikes outside war zones, which detailed strike numbers and numbers of civilian casualties. Over the course of his presidency, it is estimated that Obama approved 542 drone strikes, an average of one every 5.4 days. Through March 2017, Trump approved thirty-six drone strikes in forty-five days, an average of one every 1.25 days.[15] In the first two years in office, accounts place Trump's use of drones at about 240. Table 13.1 presents an overview of drone strikes during the Obama and Trump administrations.

The most notable drone strike by Biden occurred in late July 2022 when Ayman al-Zawahiri, the leader of al-Qaeda and a mastermind behind the 9/11 attacks, was killed at his apartment in Kabul. The strike was carried out in such a manner that no one else was killed. The drone attack was considered by most observers not to be militarily significant given the reduced level of operations of al-Qaeda, most of which were being carried out by affiliated

| Table 13.1 | Number of U.S. Drone Strikes, 2011–2019: Somalia, Yemen, and Pakistan | | |
| --- | --- | --- | --- |
| *Year* | *Somalia* | *Yemen* | *Pakistan** |
| 2011 | 1–4 | 11 | 75 |
| 2012 | 2 | 37 | 50 |
| 2013 | 1 | 22 | 27 |
| 2014 | 3 | 17 | 25 |
| 2015 | 11 | 21 | 13 |
| 2016 | 14 | 37 | 3 |
| 2017 | 35 | 127 | 5 |
| 2018 | 45 | 36 | 1 |
| 2019 (May) | 38 | 7 | 0 |

*Source*: Statista.com/statistics.
* Strikes carried out under CIA command.

groups in Africa. The attack was politically significant in many ways. In the United States, it represented a continuing commitment to take action against the 9/11 terrorists. In Afghanistan it was seen as possibly creating pressure on the Taliban government, which was aware of al-Zawahiri's location, to take retaliatory action against the United States.

The attractiveness to policy makers of targeted drone strikes is readily apparent. They greatly reduce the human cost to the U.S. military. Prior to their use, the primary means of targeting terrorist or insurgent leaders was to send U.S. troops into contested territory, a tactic that held high risks for those troops with no guarantee of success. Drone critics raise two questions. First, is the military effectiveness of drone strikes largely restricted to short-term successes rather than long-term goals? Second, does the military success of drone strikes come at the cost of losing popular support? Critics contend that drone strikes may undermine efforts to promote human rights and build democracy.

## The Return of Small Wars?

With the passing of the Cold War, small wars came to be seen by most observers as the dominant form of future military conflict. The Trump administration's foreign policy strategy sought to reverse this thinking and reposition threats from powerful states, most notably Russia and China, at the center of U.S. national security policy. This has not proven to be easy, as evidenced by the prominent role played by crises in Syria, Niger, the Persian Gulf, and Yemen in the Trump administration's foreign policy. Many explanations for the difficulty of making this pivot have been given. For organizational and professional reasons, many in the Department of Defense favor continuing to engage in small wars—albeit at a lower level— while simultaneously focusing more on great-power competition; this has resulted in defense budget proposals calling for significant expenditures on both forms of warfare.[16] Reinforcing this unwillingness to break away from small wars, many policy makers hold the perception that, while these conflicts cannot be easily won—if at all—stalemates are politically preferable to losing. Andrew Bacevich argues that this outlook reflects the acceptance of war as a normal condition that can be managed and used for political purposes.[17]

While the Biden administration has continued Trump's focus on Russia and China as the primary national security threats to the United States, he broke with Trump in a May 2022 announcement authorizing the Pentagon to deploy hundreds of special operations forces in Somalia. Trump had ordered the withdrawal of almost all of the seven hundred U.S. ground troops stationed there. Biden also gave permission for standby authority for the Pentagon to order attacks on some twelve suspected leaders of the al-Qaeda-affiliated Somali terrorist group al-Shabaab. Up until that time, air strikes against al-Shabaab leaders were largely limited to cases where local allies were facing an immediate threat. Adding to the Biden administration's interest in sending troops to Africa is the perceived need to counter Russia's and China's growing presence there.

Rarely has Africa been a high-priority foreign policy issue for the United States. The Africa Command (AFRICOM), only established in 2007, is headquartered in Germany. During the Cold War, American involvement was spurred by concern for Russian support of procommunist governments and guerilla movements in Africa. With the end of the Cold War, the U.S. presence in Africa briefly centered on providing humanitarian aid, a foreign policy orientation that abruptly ended with the 1993 Battle of Mogadishu, highlighted in the "Historical Lesson." Since 9/11, local Islamic terrorist groups affiliated with ISIS and al-Qaeda have been the key motivating factors for U.S. involvement in Africa. Concern has centered on their impact in Africa as well as their ability to use the continent as a launching pad for attacks in the Middle East. Most recently, this antiterrorism orientation has been joined by concern about growing Russian and Chinese involvement in Africa. Russian involvement is perhaps most visible in the Central African Republic. It began with an arms deal and has expanded to include military training and exploration of the potential for mineral resource mining. China has built its first overseas military base in Djibouti. It is located only a few miles from one of

**Table 13.2** **U.S. Military Bases in Africa, 2019**

| Country | Enduring Bases | Non-Enduring Outposts |
|---|---|---|
| Djibouti | 2 | — |
| Uganda | 1 | — |
| Kenya | 1 | — |
| Gabon | 1 | — |
| Burkina Faso | 1 | — |
| Senegal | 1 | — |
| Ascension Island | 1 | — |
| Niger | 2 | 4 |
| Chad | 1 | — |
| Mali | — | 1 |
| Tunisia | — | 1 |
| Cameroon | — | 2 |
| Libya | — | 2 |
| Somalia | — | 5 |
| Kenya | — | 1 |

*Source:* Nick Turse, "Pentagon's Own Map of U.S. Bases in Africa Contradicts Its Claim of 'Light' Footprint," *Intercept*, February 27, 2020, https://theintercept.com/2020/02/27/africa-us-military-bases -africom.

*Note:* "Enduring" bases provide "strategic access and use to support United States security interests for the foreseeable future." "Non-enduring" outposts—also known as "contingency locations"—are defined as supporting and sustaining "operations during contingencies or other operations." Contingency locations can be categorized as initial, temporary, or semipermanent.

the United States' largest military bases. China also has 2,400 peacekeepers in Africa and has become an important source of financial and development aid.[18] Table 13.2 presents a listing of African countries where AFRICOM had bases or outposts in 2019.

## Small Wars by Other Means

We routinely think about wars as being fought by armies. There are, however, other instances—often referred to as gray zones—in which adversaries engage in hostile actions that fall just below the level of overt military conflict. One example of this is *coercive diplomacy*, which was discussed in chapter 10. Two types of gray-zone conflicts not involving the use of military power are covert action and cyber warfare. Because the "On the Agenda" section has already discussed cyber warfare, only a few additional observations will be added here. Most of the discussion is devoted to Cold War and post–Cold War covert action.

### Cold War Covert Action

As its name implies, **covert action** is conducted in secret. It seeks results by altering the internal balance of power in a foreign state. As is the case with cyber operations, a great deal of confusion exists over its fundamental characteristics. In popular usage, covert action is all but synonymous with secret paramilitary operations. A review of U.S. Cold War covert action shows that at least five different forms have been employed by the United States.[19] No instrument of foreign policy is more controversial or difficult to control. In its report, the Tower Commission, which investigated the Iran-Contra Affair during the Reagan administration, stated, "Covert action places a great strain on the process of decision making in a free society."[20]

The most common form of covert action has been and remains providing clandestine support for individuals and organizations. This support takes many forms (financial, technical, or training) and can be directed at many targets (politicians, labor leaders, journalists, unions, political parties, church groups, or professional associations). Clandestine support for pro-U.S. political leaders and parties was the major focus of CIA efforts in France, Italy, and West Germany in the immediate post–World War II era.[21] A widely publicized case of clandestine CIA support outside Europe involved efforts to block the election of Salvador Allende in Chile by training Chilean peasants and slum dwellers as anticommunist organizers.[22]

A second category of covert action is propaganda. The CIA has used a number of techniques for dispensing propaganda, including radio broadcasts and placing stories in newspapers. One of the most primitive involved using loaded balloons with an assortment of leaflets, pamphlets, and newspapers in an effort to exploit dissatisfaction and increase internal unrest in China in the early Cold War era.[23]

A third category of covert action involves economic operations. According to one account, comparatively few economic operations have been undertaken by the CIA, and they have not been very successful.[24] Economic operations were an integral part of the CIA's efforts to stop Salvador Allende, with the goal "to make the economy scream." The most persistent target of CIA covert economic operations was Fidel Castro's Cuba. One of the most notorious programs was Operation Mongoose.[25] It succeeded in getting European shippers to turn down Cuban delivery orders and sabotaging British buses destined for Cuba. Other economic anti-Castro covert action programs included an effort at weather modification against Cuba's sugar crop and infecting Cuban pig herds with an African swine flu virus.

The fourth category of covert action involves **paramilitary** undertakings, defined as furnishing covert military assistance and guidance to unconventional and conventional foreign forces and organizations. It is argued to be a highly valuable "third option" that falls between dispatching military troops and doing nothing.[26] Initially, paramilitary operations were targeted against the Soviet Union and its Eastern European satellite states.[27] Almost uniformly, they failed. In one effort, to establish an underground apparatus for espionage and revolution in Poland, Polish secret service co-opted the network and used it to acquire gold and capture anticommunist Poles.

More significant CIA paramilitary operations took place in the Third World. In 1953, the United States and Great Britain undertook a joint venture, Operation Ajax, to bring down the government of Iranian prime minister Mohammad Mosaddegh and return the shah to power.[28] In 1954, the CIA helped bring down the government of Jacobo Arbenz in Guatemala.[29] As was the case with Iran, the paramilitary operation itself was relatively small in scale, and it was preceded by a propaganda campaign designed to frighten Arbenz into fleeing the country.

As the 1950s ended, so too did the string of CIA successes. Its greatest embarrassment came in 1961 with the Bay of Pigs invasion of Cuba. A brigade of some 1,500 Cuban exiles was put ashore in Cuba, where they were to link up with Cuban opposition forces and topple the Castro regime. Everything went wrong. On the first day of the invasion, two of the four supply and ammunition ships were sunk, and the other two fled. On the second day, the brigade was surrounded by twenty thousand loyal, well-armed Cuban soldiers. On the third day, the 1,200 surviving members of the invasion force surrendered. Almost two years later, most were released in exchange for $53 million in food and drugs.

The Bay of Pigs put a temporary dent in Washington's fascination with paramilitary covert action programs, but it did not put an end to it. By the mid-1970s, a controversial covert paramilitary operation was underway in Angola.[30] In January 1975, a transitional coalition government in Angola was formed, intending to unite rival pro-independence groups, one communist and one anticommunist. After this agreement was reached, the CIA secretly paid the pro-U.S., anticommunist group to attack the Soviet-supported, communist group. The CIA claimed that no U.S. personnel were directly involved in the fighting and that it was not directly supplying funds to one side. Discovering that this was not true, Congress passed the Tunney Amendment in 1975 and the Clark Amendment in 1976, which attempted to cut off all government spending in Angola.

The most controversial of the CIA's paramilitary programs in the 1980s was its Nicaraguan operation. The impetus for CIA involvement in Nicaragua was evidence collected in the late 1970s that the Nicaraguan Sandinista government was increasing its shipments of arms to El Salvadoran rebels and becoming the site of a substantial Cuban-backed military buildup. In 1981, the Reagan administration authorized a $19.5 million covert action program to stop the flow of arms to El Salvador. By November 1981, the program's goals had expanded to include creating an anti-Sandinista force (the Contras).[31] The CIA's paramilitary program in Nicaragua is credited with having slowed down the shipment of arms to El Salvador and with hampering Sandinista offenses, but it also became the object of intense criticism for going too far and trying to overthrow the Nicaraguan government. Congress responded by passing Boland Amendments forbidding the CIA from funding the Contras for the purpose of overthrowing the Nicaraguan government.

The largest Third World covert operation run by the CIA was a Cold War paramilitary program in Afghanistan. In FY 1985, the CIA spent about $250 million (more than 80 percent of its covert action budget) helping Afghan guerrillas evict Soviet forces. The operation was not without long-term costs. After defeating the Russian forces, U.S. weapons remained in Afghanistan and came under the control of the Taliban.

A final form of covert action involves the assassination of foreign leaders. The most thorough investigation into U.S. involvement in an assassination plot was carried out by the Church Committee, which investigated five cases of alleged U.S. involvement.[32] The committee concluded that only the cases of Fidel Castro and Patrice Lumumba (Belgian Congo) involved plots conceived by the United States to kill foreign leaders. It found concrete evidence of at least eight CIA plots to assassinate Fidel Castro between 1960 and 1965. One former CIA official characterized these efforts as ranging from "the vague to the weird."[33] Proposed assassination devices included arranging an "accident," poison cigars, poison pills, poison pens, placing deadly bacterial powder in Castro's scuba-diving suit, and rigging a seashell to explode while Castro was scuba diving.

In 1972, following the kidnapping and assassination of Chilean general René Schneider, Director of Central Intelligence Richard Helms issued a directive banning assassinations.[34] This ban was later included in presidential executive orders. Following the terrorist attacks on the World Trade Center and the Pentagon, President George W. Bush asserted that the ban on assassinations did not prohibit the United States from assassinating terrorists or acting in self-defense.

## Post–Cold War Covert Action

Covert action programs did not disappear with the end of the Cold War. President-elect Barack Obama received a briefing on nine different types of ongoing covert action operations in over sixty countries targeting terrorism, weapons of mass destruction (WMD) proliferation, genocide, and drug trafficking. In 2013, Obama authorized a covert program to fund and assist Syrian rebels who sought to remove Bashar al-Assad from power. Training Syrian rebels did not go well. Very few recruits who joined the battle against Assad or ISIS distinguished themselves in combat, and some CIA weapons intended for the rebels were stolen by Jordanian intelligence officers and sold on the black market.

Earlier, the CIA ran a Cold War–style operation against Saddam Hussein between 1992 and 1996. The goal was to remove him from power by encouraging a military coup and reducing his control over Iraq's outlying regions, such as Iraqi Kurdistan. The cost of the program is estimated to have approached $100 million. Little was achieved. In June 1996, Saddam Hussein arrested and executed more than a hundred Iraqi dissidents and military officers associated with the CIA plan.

The most controversial post–Cold War covert action program became public on September 6, 2006, when George W. Bush acknowledged the existence of a *rendition program*; suspected terrorists were kidnapped and taken to prisons located outside the United States, where they were subjected to what he referred to as "tough" but "safe and lawful and necessary" interrogation methods. Others condemned the methods as torture. Interrogation techniques included feigned drowning (*waterboarding*), extreme isolation, slapping, sleep deprivation, semi-starvation, and light and sound bombardment.[35] Public reports identified Thailand, Egypt, Indonesia, Poland, Romania, and Libya among the countries to which suspects were taken. In August 2009, Obama announced that his administration would continue the rendition program but would monitor the interrogation methods more closely by assigning oversight responsibility to the National Security Council.

## The Covert War against Osama bin Laden

Osama bin Laden was killed on May 2, 2011, in an attack carried out by U.S. Special Forces on his safe house in Abbottabad, Pakistan. Efforts to capture him predated the terrorist attacks of 9/11.[36] Perhaps the earliest involved kidnapping bin Laden so that he could be taken out of Afghanistan by U.S. Special Forces. The CIA contacted and recruited at least three proxy forces in the region to try and capture or kill bin Laden.

Formal authorization for the CIA to pursue bin Laden had been obtained in 1998; it followed the bombings of the American embassies in Kenya and Tanzania, when Bill Clinton signed the first of a series of findings consistent with the Hughes-Ryan Amendment. The original finding emphasized the goal of capturing bin Laden but permitted the use of lethal force. This was later expanded to include using lethal force against bin Laden even when there was little chance of capturing him, including shooting down private or civilian aircraft.[37] Another expansion permitted the intelligence community to target his top aides.

## Cyber Warfare

This section includes two observations about cyber warfare in addition to those included in the "On the Agenda" section. First, on several occasions the United States has considered engaging in a cyberattack, only to decide against doing so. One was an offensive cyber warfare campaign against Libya in the early period of the uprising against Gaddafi. The plan was rejected for fear that it would set a precedent that might be used by Russia or China to justify a future offensive cyberattack. The use of cyber weapons against the Syrian military and President Bashar al-Assad's communication networks was also proposed. Obama rejected it, in part because Syria was not of sufficient strategic value to the United States to justify the accompanying risks. The Obama administration constructed—but did not implement—a cyberattack plan, Nitro-Zeus, with the mission of disabling Iran's air defenses, communications systems, and crucial parts of its power grid if an arms control agreement was not reached.

Second, cyber threats are not static. Because they evolve and change over time, strategies and tactics to use (and defeat) cyber power must be geared to specific situations and threats. Four common stages in the life cycle of cyber threats have been identified:[38]

1. The discovery of a vulnerability and the development of a cyber tool to exploit it.
2. At the introduction stage, the existence of the cyber tool is not well known. No defense is likely to exist, giving an attacker a major advantage.
3. Knowledge of the cyber tool is still limited in the growth stage, but it is known to exist. At this point the attacker has an incentive to use the cyber tool aggressively, since defenses will soon be developed.

4. In the maturation stage, defenses are in place, and the offensive value of the cyber tool steadily diminishes. At the same time, the cyber tool is no longer under tight control. It is now possessed by a large number of states and other actors, which use it for their own purposes on a wide range of targets; many of them are still vulnerable.

### Cyber Lessons from the Ukraine War

The Ukraine War was the first major international conflict involving the large-scale use of cyber operations.[39] Estimates are that eight different sets of destructive cyber software were used by Russia shortly before the invasion and in the opening phases of the conflict. More than fifty cyberattacks were conducted from December 2021 to March 2022. Most of the attacks were conducted by Russian intelligence agencies, but some also involved foreign hackers. Early targets included government websites, energy and telecom operations, financial institutions, and media outlets. The goal of these operations appears to have been to create uncertainty and disorder in Ukraine and to weaken its defensive abilities.

The end result was far from what Russia had expected. Initial evaluations pointed to several problems. Most significantly, Russian cyber planning was inadequate, and the cyberattacks were poorly coordinated with each other and with the Russian military. Studies suggest that the lack of coordination is not a problem unique to the Ukraine War. Another problem was the aid and assistance Ukraine received from private-sector companies and supporting countries in countering Russian cyberattacks. Also important were lessons Ukraine learned from Russia's use of cyberattacks in the 2014 war. It issued a National Cybersecurity Strategy in 2016 that helped create redundancy and resilience for data along with expanded use of encryption.

## Small Wars for Peace

Two other forms of military action, often involving the use of conventional forces short of engaging in traditional interstate wars, have had a recurring presence on the international scene. Even though they are small wars, humanitarian/peacekeeping operations and stability forces hold the potential for the involvement of large numbers of military forces.

### Humanitarian/Peacekeeping Operations

Operation Restore Hope (Somalia), Operation Provide Comfort (northern Iraq), Operation Restore Democracy (Haiti), and Operation Odyssey Dawn (Libya) are prominent examples of post–Cold War U.S. military interventions that, at least in part, can be classified as humanitarian in nature. The United States is the largest source of money for United Nations (UN) peacekeeping operations; the United States provides about one-quarter of UN funds for peacekeeping, but it is among the least active in providing personnel, with only eighty-two military personnel and police officers assigned.

Humanitarian military operations grew out of an earlier generation of efforts referred to as **peacekeeping operations**. Carried out by neutral UN forces, their original purpose was to provide a way to stabilize an international or domestic conflict without involving U.S. or Soviet forces or creating a situation in which one side had "lost," providing a second-best solution for each side. Peacekeeping forces did not arrive until all parties to the conflict were ready to end the fighting. Over time, the scope of these efforts has been expanded to include interventions undertaken outside of the UN system in which fighting continues. In these situations, the word *peacemaking* is often used to describe the challenge facing the intervening military forces.

Opposition to humanitarian and peacekeeping undertakings has been expressed across the political spectrum. Neo-isolationist commentators have questioned whether humanitarian interventions are really in the American national interest. They compare it to bungee jumping: "a risky undertaking for which there is no compelling need."[40] Advocates of humanitarian military interventions reject this argument, contending that definitions of the American national interest that focus only on the physical security of the United States or the health of its economy are much too narrow. One of the most controversial peacekeeping and stability operations undertaken by the United States was in Somalia in 1993. An overview of that mission and its tragic outcome is presented in the "Historical Lesson."

## Historical Lesson

### The Path to Mogadishu

On October 3, 1993, a 160-person special assault team consisting of Army Ranger and Delta Force troops, nineteen aircraft, and twelve vehicles targeted the Olympic Hotel in Mogadishu, Somalia, to apprehend warlord Mohamed Farrah Aidid and two of his top leaders. The raid was expected to be completed in one hour. Instead, it became a seventeen-hour overnight battle in which eighteen U.S. soldiers died and eighty-four were wounded before being rescued by an international military force.

Little went right in the October 3 military raid, although it did reach its intended target. Minutes after beginning their withdrawal from the area of the hotel, U.S. forces were attacked by Somali militia and armed civilians who blocked their path. They pushed back repeated attempts by Somali groups to overrun their positions. Two U.S. Black Hawk helicopters were shot down and its crew members killed, captured, or pinned down by enemy fire. Highly emotional TV images of the Battle of Mogadishu showed the bodies of U.S. servicemen being dragged through the streets. Estimates of Somali deaths ranged from 315 (by Aidid) to 1,000–2,000 (by U.S. diplomatic officials).

The path to Mogadishu began in January 1991 when Somalia's dictator was overthrown by an alliance of tribal warlords. With his removal from power, the alliance collapsed and the warlords began competing for control of the government. By September, fighting had become so widespread and intense that an estimated 4.5 million Somalis were on the verge of starving to death. By the end of the year, an estimated two hundred thousand people had been killed or injured. In response, a cease-fire was organized by the United Nations, and relief efforts began. In July 1992, a small UN mission was sent to Somalia to oversee the distribution of food. In August, the UN initiated Operation Provide Comfort to further the relief effort. The United States provided transportation to move aid workers and relief supplies to Somalia. Its efforts were frustrated and undermined by continuing fighting among the warlords and their seizure of an overwhelming majority of the relief supplies. General Mohamed Farrah Aidid, one of the key players in bringing down the Somali government and its self-proclaimed new head, was now demanding that UN peacekeepers leave and that no new peacekeepers be sent.

The inability of Operation Provide Comfort to alleviate the suffering and stabilize the situation in Somalia led to a proposal to the UN by President George H. W. Bush that U.S. combat troops be sent in to protect the humanitarian operation, on the condition that they not be placed under a UN command. That offer was accepted, and in December it was announced that some twenty-five thousand troops would be sent to Somalia under the heading Operation Restore Hope. Bush stressed that Operation Restore Hope was not an open-ended military mission but would be concluded by the time Bill Clinton was inaugurated as president in January 1993.

In March 1993, the mission of UN forces in Somalia was officially changed from providing humanitarian aid to nation building and promoting stability throughout the country. Upon taking office, Clinton had expressed a desire to reduce the U.S. military presence in Somalia; with the change in mission, he arranged for reducing the number of U.S. forces and having them replaced by troops from other UN member nations. By June 1993, only 1,200 U.S. troops remained in Somalia.

A principal challenge facing the UN mission was disarming the warlords. On June 5, 1993, the full extent of the challenge became clear when twenty-four Pakistani troops were ambushed and killed and another fifty-seven wounded while they were inspecting a weapons storage facility. Three American soldiers were also wounded. A UN emergency resolution called for international efforts to capture those responsible. Evidence pointed to Aidid.

U.S. and UN troops repeatedly attacked locations in Mogadishu the following week searching for Aidid. He was not found, but several buildings were destroyed and a number of Somalis were killed. In August, four U.S. military police were killed by a remotely detonated land mine. A four-hundred-person U.S. military task force was sent to Somalia in September. That month it carried out six missions in an attempt to apprehend Aidid. Also in September, the Clinton administration rejected requests for armed reinforcements and began secret planning to negotiate with Aidid.

The path out of Mogadishu was not smooth. Shortly after the attack, President Clinton ordered the remaining U.S. Ranger troops to leave Somalia on the grounds that the mission had changed from a military one to a diplomatic one (seeking a political settlement to the ongoing civil war). Additional U.S. troops were sent to Somalia in order to prevent greater violence, but they were restricted to defensive operations. March 1994 was set as the withdrawal date for all U.S. forces. All remaining UN forces left in 1995. However, in 2016, fifty U.S. troops returned to Somalia to help fight terrorism.

### Applying the Lesson

1. What should be the lesson of Mogadishu for U.S. foreign policy?
2. Can future Mogadishu's be prevented? How?
3. Who holds primary responsibility for dealing with domestic unrest and civil wars in Africa, and why?

## Stability Operations

Peacekeeping and humanitarian interventions focus on developments in a state and generally occur after a crisis has already begun. **Stability operations**, in contrast, may focus on internal situations but may also have a broader focus, such as seeking to prevent interstate violence from breaking out or stopping an international conflict from spilling over into neighboring states.

A recent example of international stability operations is Libya. The Libyan case is instructive for understanding the challenges that can be faced using conventional military power to address threats to domestic and regional stability. When asked to identify the biggest mistake of his presidency, Barack Obama pointed to the lack of planning for the post-Gaddafi era that followed the 2011 bombing of Libya.

Protests against the government of Muammar Gaddafi, which grew out of the Arab Spring movement, began in mid-February 2011. Obama's advisors disagreed over whether to use military force to protect Libyan civilians and remove Gaddafi from power. Secretary of Defense Robert Gates warned against becoming involved in another big land war, asking, "Can I finish two wars before you guys go looking for a third one?" Director of National Intelligence James Clapper suggested that the end result of the crisis would be the emergence of two or three ministates. Secretary of State Hillary Clinton joined with National Security Council staffer Samantha Powers and United Nations ambassador Susan Rice in supporting military action. Obama approved military action with the caveat that no U.S. troops would be involved and that it would be a limited and finite operation.

Operation Odyssey Dawn began on March 19, 2011, with air attacks on armored Libyan government units near Benghazi and on Libya's air defense system. The U.S. effort was part of a broader UN undertaking to impose a no-fly zone and use "all necessary means" to protect civilians. The operation ended on October 31 when Gaddafi died at the hands of rebel forces. Odyssey Dawn was hailed by many as a model of humanitarian intervention. It was not long before pessimism set in. Libya could not form a national unity government and became a jihadist magnet, attracting as many as 6,500 fighters to ISIS training camps.

President Trump raised the possibility of a domestic stability operation in November 2019 when, following the murder of nine members of an American family in Mexico by a drug gang, he announced plans to designate Mexican drug cartels as foreign terrorist organizations. Mexican officials strongly objected, arguing that this designation would be a violation of Mexican sovereignty. It also voiced fears over the possible use of drones by the United States in Mexico.

# Conventional, Cyberspace, and WMD Arms Control

Nuclear weapons receive most of the attention when arms control is discussed, but they are not the only proliferation problem facing policy makers today. The proliferation of chemical and biological weapons (along with their missile delivery systems) and of conventional weapons has also been the subject of arms control efforts. Collectively, chemical, biological, and nuclear weapons are referred to as **weapons of mass destruction (WMDs).**

## Chemical and Biological Weapons

Chemical and biological weapons may be constructed to deliver a number of different agents. Among the most significant chemical agents are mustard gas, which causes blistering over the entire body, blindness, and death by respiratory failure, and sarin, which interrupts the flow of oxygen to cells. Significant biological agents and toxins include anthrax, which causes pneumonia and organ failure; ricin, which attacks the circulatory system; and smallpox, which many consider the most deadly biological agent.

The modern historical record documenting the use of chemical and biological weapons dates to World War I when Germany used chemical weapons. Saddam Hussein employed chemical weapons, principally sarin and mustard gas, against Iran during the Iran-Iraq War, as early as 1983. Hussein then used poison gas and possibly anthrax against Kurds in northern Iraq to solidify his hold on power following that war. In late 2013, evidence began to mount that Syria had used chemical weapons against rebel groups seeking to overthrow the government. At the time, Syria had one of the world's largest stockpiles of chemical weapons. It had begun to acquire them in large numbers in the 1970s and 1980s to offset Israel's superior strength in conventional weapons. Commonly discussed means for the delivery of WMDs include dispersal from an aircraft or drone, artillery shells, rockets, ballistic missiles, and cruise missiles. Of most concern are ballistic and cruise missiles because of their long-range ability to strike targets.

The military value of chemical and biological weapons is disputed. For example, sarin is most effective against large concentrations of troops but is not very useful for fighting insurgent forces in close-contact situations. There is also the danger that, if winds change direction, government forces and their supporters might be affected. At the same time, it is recognized that the use of chemical weapons could have a devastating psychological impact on rebel forces and might succeed in denying opposition forces access to large areas due to the poison's long-lasting effects. The use of biological weapons faces similar problems. Microbes used for biological weapons often lose their effectiveness when exposed to sunlight, water, and other natural elements. They are also difficult to use militarily because of the challenges involved in spreading them out over large areas.

International treaties are in place regulating both chemical and biological weapons. The United States has signed and ratified the Chemical Weapons Convention, which outlaws the production, stockpiling, and use of chemical weapons; the treaty entered into force in 1997. With over thirty-five thousand tons of declared chemical weapons stockpiled, the United States had the second-largest quantity of chemical weapons to destroy. April 2012 was set as the destruction target, but this date was not met. As of January 2012, the United States had destroyed 90 percent of its chemical weapons. A Biological Weapons Convention also exists, but the United States has not signed it. The Obama administration followed the path pursued by the Bush administration to support a more limited global biological weapons monitoring system.

## Recovering Loose WMD Material

An additional serious arms control problem in the area of WMDs involves preventing vulnerable WMD material from falling into the hands of terrorists, rogue governments, or criminals. The challenge is immense. From 2004 to early 2011, the United States recovered 4,996 discarded chemical weapons in Iraq alone. Not all were lethal in their present condition. Some were found abandoned. Others had been purchased secretly by the CIA in 2005–2006 as part of Operation Avarice. All were manufactured in the 1980s and early 1990s. They were destroyed by open-air detonation.

Following a 2009 address in Prague in which he highlighted the dangers posed by unsecured nuclear material, President Obama organized a series of Nuclear Security Summits to address this problem. The first took place in 2010. The fourth—and last—took place in 2016. Their focus was on increasing security around vulnerable military and civilian nuclear material and identifying how to better deal with the potential problem of nuclear terrorism. At that time, it was estimated that twenty-four countries held nearly two thousand tons of nuclear weapons–grade material. Twenty countries had atomic stockpile facilities or nuclear power plants judged to be vulnerable to cyberattacks.[41] The largest amount of nuclear-grade material is held in Russia, which declined to attend the meeting due to worsening relations with the United States. In October 2016, as U.S.-Russian relations worsened over Syria, Russia announced that it was suspending its participation in a 2000 agreement to dispose of surplus weapons-grade plutonium. Among the conditions Russia identified for resuming its participation were removal of economic sanctions put in place after its annexation of Crimea, ending the deployment of NATO troops in the Baltics, and repeal of the Magnitsky Act, which targeted Russian officials for violations of human rights.

## Cyberspace

While much of the discussion to date has been over questions related to cyber warfare, the political contest to establish rules for the use of cyberspace is also underway.[42] For some, cyberspace is best seen as a region divided among states around which borders will be built and national legal and political rules will apply. For others, cyberspace is—and should remain—a global commons to which all should have equal access and to which internationally agreed-upon rules and norms should apply.

At present, the policy debate between these two perspectives centers on calls for a cyber-security treaty. In 2011, Russia and China jointly proposed a code of conduct among cyber powers. The stated goal was to keep cyberspace from becoming a battleground and heading off a cyber arms race. The United States objected, citing a provision asserting that states had the right to protect their information space from attacks and sabotage; the reason for the objection was that such a statement provided grounds for legitimizing censorship and curbing free speech. In 2014, the State Department's Office for Cyber Issues joined the discussion by calling for development of a set of confidence-building measures that would promote security in cyberspace and reduce the incentives for using it as a platform for attacks.[43]

The complexity and newness of cyberspace as an arms control issue have led many to call for shifting the focus of negotiations from cyberspace security to curbing cybercrime. Others argue that the Chemical Weapons Convention might serve as a model for a cybersecurity treaty.[44] Each country is responsible for enforcing the treaty's terms within its borders. The agreement also established an international office to provide help during crises.

## Conventional Weapons

Several different types of conventional weapons exist. A commonly used classification distinguishes between heavy weapons systems (such as missiles, tanks, attack helicopters, and advanced artillery systems); small weapons (pistols and rifles that can be carried by one person); light weapons (heavy machine guns and antitank and antiaircraft munitions that are carried by two or more people or transported in light vehicles); cluster bombs (air- or ground-launched weapons that release smaller munitions); and land mines (explosive devices that are hidden underground and activated on contact). Each has been subject to arms control efforts, with limited success.[45]

Traditionally, efforts to curb conventional weapons proliferation have focused on restricting the sale or transfer of major weapons systems from one state to another. For a brief period of time, it appeared that conventional arms transfers were becoming less pronounced in world politics. Between 1989 and 1991, worldwide sales fell 53 percent, and U.S. sales fell nearly 34 percent. This downward trend has since reversed. The volume of major weapons sold between 2011 and 2015 was 14 percent higher than during the 2006–2010 period. The United States was the largest exporter of weapons, accounting for 33 percent of the total.

The major international initiative in place to curb conventional proliferation is the UN Arms Transfer Register.[46] It identifies seven different categories of heavy conventional weapons; countries are requested to submit an annual statement of the number of these items it has exported or imported during the previous year. The goal is to bring a heightened degree of transparency to the arms transfer process and thereby reduce the military advantages that arms transfers bring to states. However, some fear that it may have the unintended effect of legitimizing registered arms transfers.

In 2001, a voluntary international agreement was reached that was designed to stop the international trade in small arms. The United States blocked efforts to include regulations on civilian ownership of military weapons and to restrict small arms trade to rebel movements. It continued to oppose such an agreement, even when, after seven years of negotiations, it finally produced a 2013 treaty covering trade in heavy, small, and light conventional weapons. Among the treaty's key features was a prohibition on selling weapons to countries that were engaged in genocide, war crimes, or crimes against humanity. While the United States voted for the treaty at the UN, it raised objections that almost scuttled the talks, insisting that any agreement "not impose any new requirements on the U.S. domestic trade in firearms or on U.S. exporters." In 2019, Trump officially withdrew the United States from the agreement without a vote ever having been taken in the Senate.

In 2008, ninety-four countries signed the Convention on Cluster Munitions, which banned the production, stockpiling, transfer, and use of explosive weapons that scatter submunitions over an area. That agreement came into effect in 2010. The United States opposed the agreement, maintaining that a separate treaty on cluster munitions was not needed and that it should be included in the broader conventional arms trade treaty then under discussion. Moreover, the United States argued that the development of "smart" munitions with automatic self-destruct capabilities had drastically reduced the scope of the problem and that a treaty banning their use was dangerous to civilians.

Although it did send an observer to the 2009 Review Conference, the Obama administration continued the existing policy of not signing the 1997 Ottawa Treaty banning the use, stockpiling, or transfer of antipersonnel land mines and allowing prosecution of offenders. The U.S. military has long opposed the ban, arguing that land mines are necessary to ensure the protection of U.S. forces abroad. Some one million land mines remain in place along the border between North and South Korea. Along with the United States, China, Russia, India, and Israel are the most prominent countries that have not signed the Ottawa Treaty.

## Counterproliferation

One final arms control and disarmament strategy is **counterproliferation**. Unlike the other approaches outlined here, which rely heavily on diplomacy, counterproliferation has historically involved the use of military force to deter countries from acquiring and using WMDs against the United States. Today, the use of force can be extended to include cyberattacks.

Proponents of counterproliferation start from the premise that nonproliferation efforts have failed. Not a new strategy, it continues to evolve and is controversial.[47] Its principal targets are smaller states such as Iran and North Korea. Few historical examples of counterproliferation exist.[48] The most frequently cited are Israel's 1981 raid on Iraq's Osiraq nuclear reactor, the bombing of Iraq's unconventional weapons during the first phase of Operation

Desert Storm in 1991, and U.S. cruise missile attacks on the Al-Shifa pharmaceutical plant in Sudan in 1998. Because the historical evidence is so limited, strategists have turned to war games and simulations to help them judge the potential value of a specific counterproliferation strike. A 2012 Pentagon assessment, based on a two-week war game that assumed Israel would attack four major Iranian nuclear sites, concluded that it would lead to a wide-ranging regional war.

## Over the Horizon: Drone Wars

Commentators uniformly agree that the drone genie is out of the bottle and that the United States no longer sits atop the playing field. In 2018, twelve states and several nonstate actors such as Hamas, Hezbollah, and Houthi were using armed drones. At least five other states had drone development programs underway. Accounting for over 60 percent of all sales, Israel is the leading exporter of military drones, followed by the United States and China. Iran and Turkey also export armed drones. Nigeria, Iraq, and Turkey rank among the most active users of armed drones within their own borders. Iran, Saudi Arabia, and the United Arab Emirates use armed drones in cross-border conflicts. Along with Egypt and Pakistan, the countries listed above are often characterized as the second generation of drone users. Standing ready to join them are Russia, India, South Korea, and several European states.[49]

Armed drones are not seen as having the potential to alter the fundamental nature of international politics in the way that nuclear weapons did, but their impact is potentially significant in several ways. First, a drone arms race is generally expected to develop as countries seek to acquire drones to offset their adversaries' advantages. China has already emerged as a leading provider of cheap reconnaissance drones. Within the United States, manufacturers of drones actively lobby Congress to approve sales of unarmed drones. In 2011, the drone industry's political action committees gave $2.3 million to the House Unmanned Systems Caucus in order to get Congress to lift restrictions on drone sales.

Second, although reconnaissance drones may increase deterrence by providing policy makers with additional information about a conflict situation, they bring an added element of uncertainty. As one observer asked, "Does sending a drone into a contested area signal commitment, or does it send a [message of a] lack of commitment because a nation wasn't willing to risk sending a person?"

Finally, there are no clear-cut international norms on the use of drones. The agreement currently governing their use is the 1987 Missile Technology Control Regime (MTCR). Use of the MTCR to establish guidelines on acceptable drone use is hindered by two problems. One is that, under the MTCR, drones are treated as missiles. Today, most observers argue that they are better thought of as a type of aircraft. Second, the MTCR is defined as an "informal political understanding among states." The problem here is that the view of drones appears to be changing, creating problems for the application of international norms. At one time, the use of drones was seen as relatively safe and occupied a low rung on the ladder of international conflict. Shooting down a drone created international tensions, but it fell far short of setting a military crisis in motion.

Fourth, while drones are attractive to policy makers because they are pilotless aircraft, innocent civilians can be killed. This happened in August 2021 when a U.S. drone strike in Afghanistan killed ten innocent civilians, producing a major domestic political problem for Biden as these deaths overshadowed the decline in drone strikes that had occurred in his administration. The majority of that decline took place outside of war zones (defined as Afghanistan, Iraq, and Syria). Trump had loosened restrictions on drone strikes outside of war zones, allowing commanders to order them. Biden tightened those out-of-war-zone restrictions, increasing the need for White House approval. Biden later authorized drone strikes in 2022 against al-Qaeda-linked terrorist leaders in Syria and Somalia. He also provided Ukraine with drones following the Russian invasion.

## Critical Thinking Questions

1. How can insurgents best be stopped from acquiring weapons?
2. What types of actions are best taken covertly and what actions should never be taken covertly, and why?
3. What is the most likely cause of a U.S. small war in the next five years? In the next ten years? Explain your answers.

## Key Terms

counterinsurgency (COIN), 282
counterproliferation, 296
covert action, 286
cyber warfare, 278
hybrid warfare, 281
paramilitary, 287

peacekeeping operations, 290
stability operations, 292
weapons of mass destruction (WMDs), 293
window of fear, 280
window of opportunity, 280

# Alternative Futures

## Learning Objectives

Students will be able to:

1. Identify the six competing visions of the future direction of U.S. foreign policy.
2. Distinguish between the key assumptions they make with regard to the threats facing the United States.
3. Compare how each of the competing visions defines U.S. responsibility to other states.
4. Assess the extent to which each of the competing visions feels the United States has an obligation to the global community.

## On the Agenda: The South China Sea

By definition, foreign policy is outward looking and seeks to promote the national interest. Disagreement exists over how best to anticipate threats and recognize opportunities found beyond state borders. Do we look at the structure of the international system, changing relations between countries, or specific events? Each of these focal points presents itself as the United States formulates a foreign policy to respond to Chinese actions in the South China Sea.[1]

Some 648,000 square nautical miles, the South China Sea is one of the world's largest semi-enclosed seas. Five countries (six if Taiwan is counted) with a combined population of about 270 million are found along its borders: China, Vietnam, the Philippines, Brunei, and Malaysia. All claim sovereignty over some or all of it. China argues that these islands have been Chinese territory "since antiquity." At issue is control not only over the waters and the airspace above it, but also over some four hundred to six hundred rocks, reefs, atolls, and islands. The two largest groupings of land in the South China Sea are the Spratly and Paracel Islands. Both have been the focal point of military-political conflicts involving competing claims made by China, Vietnam, and the Philippines. The United States has taken no official position on these conflicting territorial claims other than rejecting China's claim to sovereignty over virtually all of it.

Three geostrategic factors come together to frame the South China Sea foreign policy problem facing the United States. First, the South China Sea is a critical passageway for global commercial shipping and naval operations linking the Middle East and Africa to Asia. The amount of oil passing through its waters is six times larger than that going through the Suez Canal. Second, evidence points to the presence of potentially significant natural energy reserves beneath the South China Sea that the Chinese media refers to as "the second Persian Gulf." Third, the South China Sea is of great strategic importance to China. It is often spoken of in terms comparable to the United States' traditional view of the Caribbean Sea. To a considerable degree it was in recognition of China's growing economic and military power, along with the key role that the South China Sea played in China's foreign policy thinking, that President Obama called for a "pivot" to Asia when he became president.

Tensions between the United States and China have grown noticeably over the past decade. As China's military and economic power have increased, the United States has placed greater emphasis on Asia in its foreign policy. In November 2013, after China unilaterally claimed the right to police a contested portion of the airspace over the South China Sea, the United States sent two B-52 bombers into that zone without asking permission. In May 2014, without notice, China unilaterally placed a $1 billion deepwater oil-drilling rig on the shore of an island claimed by both China and Vietnam. The move was described in the press as a possible "game changer" because expansion of the Chinese navy would be required to protect its investment. Three months later, China rejected a U.S. call for a freeze on "provocative acts" in the South China Sea, stating that "as a responsible great power, China is ready to maintain restraint but for unreasonable provocative activities, China is bound to make a clear and firm reaction."[2]

Matters escalated considerably in 2015 when China began to build a "Great Wall of Sand" in the South China Sea; this effort was defined by China as a "lawful and justified" land reclamation project within its own borders. The project involves the construction of coral reefs and rocks within the Spratly Islands, along with harbors, piers, helipads, and possibly an airstrip. State Department officials characterized it as an unprecedented attempt to "militarize outposts on disputed land features." By early 2016, China had moved forward, placing surface-to-air missiles with a range of 125 miles on a disputed island. In a countermove, the United States announced that it was on track to reposition 60 percent of the navy to the Pacific by 2020. Later that year, the U.S. Navy sent a destroyer near a contested island. The government claimed that it was the first of what they defined as freedom of navigation patrols, intended to challenge China's "excessive maritime claims" and demonstrate the U.S. commitment to free maritime passage through the South China Sea. China countered by carrying on military exercises in disputed waters. The International Court of Justice in 2016 rejected China's claims of historical rights to most of the South China Sea, a ruling that China has not accepted.

During the 2016 presidential campaign, Donald Trump openly criticized Obama for not responding forcefully enough to China's expansionist South China Sea policies. However, early in his administration his interest was less on the South China Sea than on trade agreements with China. It was only after nuclear talks with North Korea faltered, due to what he saw as China's reluctance to bring pressure on North Korea, that Trump began to increase the U.S. presence in the South China Sea through B-52 bomber and surveillance flyovers and increased use of freedom of navigation patrols. The military effectiveness of these actions is unclear. In 2018, Admiral Philip Davidson, head of the U.S. Indo-Pacific Command, told Congress that "China is now capable of controlling the South China Sea in all scenarios short of war with the United States."

Tensions in the South China Sea escalated in 2020 when the Trump administration accused China of trying to take advantage of the COVID pandemic to increase its military and economic leverage in the region. The United States announced that it would conduct military operations with naval vessels and B-1 bombers "in support of a free and open Indo-Pacific region amidst the pandemic caused by coronavirus." China responded by urging the United States to "focus on its own business with pandemic prevention and control . . . and immediately stop military operations that are detrimental to regional security, peace, and stability." In his last week in office, Trump imposed one last set of sanctions on Chinese leaders and companies for the country's "violations of international standards of free navigation" in the South China Sea.

In his first year in office, Biden embraced the Trump administration's official position on the South China Sea that rejected virtually all of China's significant claims. Even though U.S. attention would soon shift to Russia with the invasion of Ukraine, the South China Sea remained a reoccurring issue high on the foreign policy agenda. In part this was due to public comments made by Biden on multiple occasions that the United States would provide military support to Taiwan should a conflict with China erupt. This statement was taken by some to be a rejection of the long-standing U.S. policy of strategic ambiguity with regard to Taiwan's defense that it adopted after recognizing China. Biden asserted that this was not the case. China responded that it had "no room for compromise" on Taiwan.

In 2022, Chinese foreign policy actions kept it on the agenda. First, China signed a security agreement with the Solomon Islands, which had only officially recognized China in 2019. The Solomon Islands stated that this was not a military agreement but one designed to strengthen the ability of the police to deal with riots. Next, it was revealed that China was secretly building a naval base in Cambodia. This would be China's second overseas naval base, the first being in Djibouti, Africa. The United States countered when Biden met with leaders of Japan and South Korea at the 2022 NATO Summit, a clear indication to China that NATO was expanding its focus to include the Asia-Pacific. Earlier in 2022 it was revealed that the United States had been sending troops to Taiwan to train its soldiers.

The conflict between the United States and China involving the South China Sea highlights the high stakes that can accompany foreign policy choices. This concluding chapter introduces six competing visions of the future direction that American foreign policy might take. In the "Historical Lesson" section, it looks at the first U.S. pivot to Asia: Commodore Perry's opening of Japan. It ends by raising the question of whether U.S.-China relations should be viewed as a new cold war.

# Foreign Policy Visions

Each of the six competing visions about to be introduced provides a different starting point for making policy choices. Three questions are asked of each alternative future: (1) What is the primary threat to U.S. national security? (2) What responsibility does the United States have to other states? and (3) What responsibility does the United States have to the global community? The answers reflect different views regarding the degree to which the United States should be involved in world politics, how much power it possesses, and the extent to which the future may differ from the past.

## The United States as an Ordinary State

For some, the key to the future is realizing that foreign policy can no longer be conducted on the assumption of American uniqueness or the idea that U.S. actions stand between anarchy and order. The American century is over, and the challenge facing policy makers is no longer managing alliances, deterring aggression, or ruling over the international system. It now requires adjustment to a new role orientation in which the United States is an **Ordinary State.**[3] This change in outlook is necessary because international and domestic trends point to the declining utility of a formula-based response to foreign policy problems—be it rooted in ideology, concepts of power politics, or some vision of regional order. Such a response forces the United States to pursue narrowly defined national interests at the expense of international collaborative and cooperative efforts. In this altered environment, flexibility, autonomy, and impartiality are valued more than one-sided commitments, name-calling, and efforts at the diplomatic, military, or economic isolation of states.

As an Ordinary State, the United States would not define its interests so rigidly that their defense would require unilateral American action. If the use of force is necessary, it should be a truly multilateral effort; if others are unwilling to act, there is no need for the United States to assume the full burden of the commitment. Stated as a rule, "The United States should not be prepared, on its own, and supported solely by its own means, to perform tasks that most other states would not undertake."[4] Ordinariness does not, however, mean passivity, withdrawal, or a purely defensive approach to foreign policy problems. The quality of U.S. participation in truly multilateral efforts to solve international problems will be vital, because the core ingredients of the international influence of the future will be found in fields in which the United States is already a leader: economics, diplomacy, and technology. The goal of these collaborative efforts should be to "create and maintain a world in which adversaries will remain in contact with one another and where compromises are still possible."[5] The following summarizes the Ordinary State perspective:

1. The greatest threat to U.S. national security lies in trying to do too much and in having too expansive a definition of its national interest.
2. Responsibility to other states must be proportionate and reciprocal to that of other states to the United States.
3. The United States' responsibility to the global community is to be a good global citizen—nothing more and nothing less.

The imagery advanced by the Ordinary State perspective—with its denial of American uniqueness, its lack of optimism, its focus on restraints rather than opportunities, and its admonition to not try to do too much—runs against the traditional American approach to world politics.[6] A variant of the Ordinary States perspective voiced today is that the United States must act like a Normal State. The Normal State perspective also taps into a feeling shared by many Americans that, although it should not retreat into isolationism, the United States should not be the first to take risks that others are not willing to run.

## Reformed America

According to proponents of the **Reformed America** perspective, U.S. foreign policy has traditionally been torn between pursuing democratic ideals and **empire** (one power center ruling a hierarchically structured grouping of states).[7] The United States wants peace, but only on its own terms; the United States supports human rights, but only if its definitions are used; the United States wants to promote Third World economic growth, but only if it follows the U.S. model and does not undermine U.S. business interests abroad. Historically, the thrust toward empire (whether called containment or détente) has won out, and democratic ideals have been sacrificed or only given lip service. U.S. policy makers have given highest priority to maintaining the United States' position of dominance in the international system and promoting the economic well-being of U.S. corporations.[8]

The Reformed America outlook argues that the need now exists to reverse this pattern. Democratic ideals must be given primary consideration in the formulation and execution of U.S. foreign policy. Not doing so invites future Vietnams and runs the risk of undermining the very democratic principles for which the United States stands. From this outlook, foreign policy and domestic policy are not seen as two separate categories. They are held to be inextricably linked; actions taken in one sphere have effects on behavior and policies in the other. Bribery of foreign officials leads to bribery of U.S. officials; an unwillingness to challenge human rights violations abroad reinforces the acceptance of discrimination and violations of civil rights at home; and a lack of concern for the growing disparity in economic wealth on a global basis leads to an insensitivity to the problems of poverty in the United States.

The Reformed America perspective demands global activism from the United States. The much-heralded decline in American power is not seen as being so great that it prevents the United States from exercising a predominant global influence. Moreover, the United States is held to have a moral and political responsibility to lead by virtue of its comparative wealth and power. The danger to be avoided is inaction brought on by the fear of failure. The United States cannot be permitted to crawl into a shell of isolationism or to let itself be "Europeanized" into believing that there are limits to its power and accepting the world "as it is." The power needed for success in creating what amounts to a new world order faithful to traditional American democratic values is not the ability to dominate others but to renew the American commitment to justice, opportunity, and liberty. The following summarizes the Reformed America perspective:

1. The primary threat to U.S. national security is a continued fixation on military problems and an attachment to power-politics thinking.
2. The United States' responsibility to other states is great, provided that they are truly democratic, and the United States must seek to move those that are not democratic in that direction.
3. The United States' responsibility to the global community is also great and centers on the creation of an international system conducive to the realization of traditional American values.

The values underlying this perspective were widely embraced in the early post–Cold War period, as many commentators urged presidents to move more aggressively toward a neo-Wilsonian foreign policy. After 9/11, a split occurred within the Reformed America movement. Some, labeled liberal hawks, advance a foreign policy that embraced the use of military power in places such as Iraq and Afghanistan to advance democracy and reconstruct societies. Others continue to express concern over how much the military has become the foreign policy instrument of choice to advance American foreign policy goals. Along these lines, some commentators argue that the United States is far more secure today than is commonly believed, thus providing an opportunity for rejecting power-politics thinking.[9]

## Pragmatic America

The **Pragmatic America** perspective holds that the United States can no longer afford foreign policies on the extreme ends of the political spectrum. Neither crusades nor isolationism serve America well. Some world problems require U.S. attention, but not all do. What is needed in U.S. foreign policy is *selectivity*, a strong dose of moderation in means and ends.[10] To supporters of this view, the end of the Cold War vindicated a policy of moderation.[11]

The United States must recognize that the American national interest is not identical to the global interest and that not all problems lend themselves to permanent resolution. The most pressing issue on the U.S. agenda is the development of a set of criteria for identifying these problems and then acting in moderation to protect American interests.

Pragmatic America emphasizes a utilitarian outlook on world politics and recognizes the lessened ability of military force to solve many foreign policy problems; it also recognizes that the nature of the problems facing the United States has changed. The Cold War dragon represented by the Soviet Union has been slain. The world confronting the United States is now populated by large numbers of poisonous snakes.

One national security practitioner suggests that the ideal practical method for moving forward and dealing with these poisonous snakes is through the creation of international posses.[12] Just as in the old American West, when security threats present themselves, the United States (the sheriff) should organize and deputize a posse of like-minded states that will end the threat and then disband. The following summarizes the Pragmatic America perspective:

1. The primary threats to U.S. national security continue to be military in nature.
2. The United States has a responsibility to other states on a selective basis, and only to the extent that threats to the political order of those states would lessen American security.
3. The United States' responsibility to the global community is limited. More pressing is a sense of responsibility to key partners, whose cooperation is necessary to manage a threatening international environment.

President George H. W. Bush, in his farewell foreign policy address, argued for a position that is consistent with this view.[13] Warning against becoming isolationist, Bush asserted that the United States can influence the future but that "it need not respond to every outrage of violence." Bush went on to note that no formula exists telling with precision when and where to intervene. "Each and every case is unique . . . we cannot always decide in advance which interests will require our using military force." When force is used, Bush urged that the mission be clear and achievable, that a realistic plan be in place, and that equally realistic criteria be established for withdrawing U.S. forces.

The Pragmatic America perspective is seen by some as well suited for an international system in a state of flux. Henry Kissinger argues that goals should be consistent over time, but the means to achieve them must be based on specific conditions.[14] This measured approach to solving foreign policy problems is also a fundamental weakness. Because pragmatism can be interpreted differently by different people, the policy it produces tends to move forward in a series of disjointed steps. The result is that defenders see it as producing flexibility and adaptability, but detractors see in it a foreign policy by lottery, in which the past provides little guidance for friends or enemies as they seek to anticipate America's position.

## American Crusader

The **American Crusader** sees the United States as having won the Cold War and now being intent on enjoying the fruits of its victory as the dominant global power.[15] Victory brings with it an opportunity to act on America's historical sense of mission. It builds on an important strain in the American national style that defines security in absolute terms. The objective is "unconditional surrender." "For more than two centuries, the United States has aspired to a condition of perfect safety from foreign threats," both real and imagined.[16] Unlike the Reformed America perspective, the American Crusader perspective identifies military power as the instrument of choice. It is rooted firmly in that part of the American national style that rejects compromise and seeks permanent, engineered solutions to political problems.

Faint echoes of the American Crusader perspective can be found in post–World War II foreign policy. During the Eisenhower administration, some commentators called for rolling back the Iron Curtain, feeling that containment was too passive and accommodating a strategy. During the Persian Gulf War, there was a moment when defeating Saddam Hussein had the characteristics of a crusade, at least at a rhetorical level. The American Crusader perspective is most associated with neoconservative thinking on foreign policy and burst onto the scene with full force following the 9/11 terrorist attacks on the World Trade Center and the Pentagon. The following summarizes the American Crusader perspective:

1. The international system holds real and immediate threats to American national security that must be unconditionally defeated.
2. The United States has a responsibility to help other states that are allies in its cause, because their security increases American security.
3. The United States' responsibility to the international community is great, but how that responsibility is defined is a matter for the United States to determine based on its historical traditions.

There are some who share the American Crusader view that the international system contains immediate and serious threats to American national security, but others question its wisdom as the basis for U.S. foreign policy. One concern is that this view overlooks the fact that superpower status does not convey total power to the United States. The challenge of bringing means and ends into balance is an ongoing one, and "superpower fatigue" becomes a real danger.[17] A second concern is that, by acting in this manner, the United States may hasten its own decline. Rather than staying on the American "bandwagon" as an ally, second-order states may decide that—because they too may become the object of an American crusade—it is necessary to build up their own power to balance that held by the United States.

## America the Balancer

Out of a conviction that unipolarity is bound to give way to a multipolar distribution of power in the international system, some commentators argue that the prudent course of action today is to adopt the role of balancer. The United States needs to stand apart from others yet be prepared to act in concert with them. It cannot and should not become a rogue superpower, acting on its own impulses and imposing its vision on the world.[18]

The starting point of wisdom from this **America the Balancer** perspective is that not all problems are threatening to the United States or require its involvement. The United States has a considerable amount of freedom to define its interests. In addition, the United States must recognize that one consequence of putting a global security umbrella in place is that it has discouraged other states and regional organizations from taking responsibility for preserving international stability. This situation must be reversed. Others must be encouraged to act in defense of their own interests. Otherwise, the United States runs the risk of becoming entrapped by commitments to unstable regimes.[19] Finally, the United States must learn to live with uncertainty. Absolute security is an unattainable objective and one that only produces imperial overstretch. The following is a summary of the America the Balancer perspective:

1. The primary national security threats to the United States are self-inflicted. They take the form of a proliferation of security commitments designed to protect America's economic interests.
2. The United States has a limited responsibility to other states, because the burden for protecting a state's national interests falls on that state.
3. The United States' responsibility to the global community is limited. American national interests and the maintenance of global order are not identical.

Many advocates of balancing see a return to multipolarity as all but inevitable and believe that trying to reassert or preserve American preeminence and suppress the emergence of new powers is futile.[20] Thus, there is little reason for the United States to become deeply involved in the affairs of other states on a routine basis. What is needed is a **hedging strategy**, one that will allow the United States to realize its security goals without provoking others into uniting against it or accelerating their separate pursuits of power. Blessed by its geopolitical location, the answer for some lies in adopting the position of an offshore balancer.[21] The United States is positioned to allow global and regional power balances to ensure its strategic independence. Only when others prove incapable of acting to block the ascent of a challenging hegemony should the United States step in to affect the balance of power. Given its continued power resources, such an intervention is likely to be decisive.

One issue that must be confronted by advocates of the America the Balancer perspective is how to exercise American military power most effectively. Traditionally, war has been the mechanism for preserving a stable balance of power in the international system. Commentators across the political spectrum have raised the question of whether wars can continue to play this role on a large scale. If they cannot, how is the balancer to enforce its will? One possibility is that, rather than using American power to deter or defeat an adversary, America the Balancer will play a central role in compelling adversaries to change their behavior. The distinction is potentially important. One commentator who has looked at *compellence* (see chapter 10) suggests that it is more of a police task than *deterrence* (see chapter 12), which is a military task.

## Disengaged America

The final alternative future calls for the United States to selectively, yet thoroughly, withdraw from the world.[22] It is a perspective most often associated with the libertarian perspective on U.S. foreign policy.[23] The **Disengaged America** perspective sees retrenchment as necessary because the international system is becoming increasingly inhospitable to U.S. values and unresponsive to efforts at management or domination. Increasingly, the choices facing U.S. foreign policy will be selecting what types of losses to avoid. Optimal solutions to foreign policy problems will no longer present themselves to policy makers; even if they do, domestic constraints will prevent policy makers from pursuing such a path. In the Disengaged America perspective, foreign policy must become less of a lance—a tool for spreading values—and more of a shield, a minimum set of conditions behind which the United States can protect its values and political processes.[24] In the words of one commentator writing after 9/11, the purpose of American foreign policy should be security first. Promoting democracy is fine so long as it is pursued by peaceful means and is seen as homegrown.[25]

### Historical Lesson

### The First Asian Pivot: Commodore Perry's Opening of Japan

For some two centuries, Japan had managed to severely limit the access of foreigners to its territory. In 1639, Japanese leaders had expelled missionaries, whom they had come to consider as overly zealous, and foreign traders, whom they saw as taking advantage of their people. By the mid-1800s this policy was becoming harder to maintain. In the 1830s, U.S. naval vessels stationed in China had already made several voyages to Japan in an effort to establish relations.

By the time Commodore Perry set sail to Japan, a combination of factors had made the opening of Japan a high-priority foreign policy issue. The annexation of California now provided the United States with Pacific Ocean ports, raising the possibility of expanding U.S. trade with China. Japan's geographic location and rumors of its large coal reserves made access to Japanese ports an important part of any move to increase the U.S. economic presence in Asia. American missionaries also lobbied for access

to Japan, convinced that Protestantism would be accepted by the Japanese, who had earlier rejected Catholicism. Stories of Japanese mistreatment of shipwrecked American sailors gave rise to even more calls for opening Japan.

Perry presented Japanese leaders with a letter from President Millard Fillmore outlining U.S. objectives. Before leaving, he informed them that he would return the following year. After his return, the Treaty of Kanagawa was signed on March 5, 1854; it was subsequently ratified unanimously by the Senate. The treaty provided the United States with two coaling stations and protection for shipwrecked sailors, but it did not include commercial concessions or the guarantee of trading rights. In 1858, a follow-on treaty gave the United States two additional coaling stations and trading rights and established the principle of *extraterritoriality* (American citizens arrested in Japan would be tried by U.S. courts). Because this provision was common to treaties between Western powers and Asian states at the time, such agreements came to be known as unequal treaties.

Within a decade, Japan turned these agreements to their fullest advantage, using them to spur reforms to its feudal political and economic systems. The resulting Meiji Restoration transformed Japan into an industrial and military power, as testified to by its victories in the Sino-Japanese War of 1894 and the Russo-Japanese War of 1904. The latter gave Japan control over Taiwan and much of Manchuria, as well as a dominant position in Korea. Theodore Roosevelt won the Nobel Peace Prize for helping bring about an end to the Russo-Japanese War.

Over the next several decades, Japan's growing power also set the stage for a series of military and diplomatic interactions with the United States that would steadily deepen America's involvement in Asian regional politics. One of the first points of dispute was the U.S. annexation of Hawaii in 1898. The Taft-Katsura Agreement of 1905 was designed to prevent future disputes over areas of influence. In return for recognizing American control over the Philippines, the United States recognized Japan's dominant role in Korea. This agreement was followed in short order by an American show of military strength and another agreement. In 1907, President

Theodore Roosevelt sent the entire American battle fleet of sixteen ships on an around-the-world tour, and Japan was one of its most important ports of call. At the time, the United States had the world's second-largest navy, and Japan's was the fifth largest. The next year both countries signed the Root-Takahira Agreement, promising to respect the political-military status quo in the Pacific, support the Open Door policy in China, and honor China's political independence and integrity. This agreement failed to hold; during World War I, Japan sought to extend its dominance over China by issuing the Twenty-One Points and seizing control of Germany's Asian colonial holdings.

### Applying the Lesson

1. How do the foreign policy goals regarding Asia held by recent administrations compare with those that motivated Admiral Perry's opening of Asia?
2. What lessons does Admiral Perry's opening of Asia have for current U.S. foreign policy toward China and Japan?
3. How would realists, neoliberals, and constructivists evaluate U.S. foreign policy toward Japan as described here? How would this assessment compare to their views on President Trump's Asia policy?

Becoming disengaged means that the United States will have to learn to live in a "second-best world," one that is not totally to its liking but one in which it can "get by." Allies will be fewer in number, and those that remain will have to do more to protect their own security and economic well-being. Nonintervention will be the rule for the United States, and self-reliance will be the watchword for others. The United States must be prepared to "let" some states be dominated and to direct its efforts at placing space between the **falling dominoes** rather than trying to define a line of containment. In the realm of economics, while supporting free trade, the objective should be to move toward autarchy and self-sufficiency so that other states cannot manipulate or threaten the United States. If the United States cannot dominate the sources of supply, it must be prepared to "substitute, tide over, [and] ride out" efforts at resource manipulation.[26] World order concerns must also take a backseat in U.S. foreign policy. As George Kennan has said about the food-population problem, "We did not create it and it is beyond our power to solve it."[27] Kennan argues that the United States needs to divest itself of its guilt complex and accept the fact that there is really very little that it can do for the Third World and very little that the Third World can do for the United States. The following summarizes the Disengaged America perspective:

1. The major threat to U.S. national security comes from an overactive foreign policy. Events beyond U.S. borders are not as crucial to U.S. security as is commonly perceived; moreover, the United States has little power to influence their outcome.
2. The United States' responsibility to other states is minimal. The primary responsibility of the United States is to its own economic and military security.
3. The United States' responsibility to the global community is also minimal. The issues on the global agenda, especially as they relate to the Third World, are not the fault of the United States, and the United States can do little to solve them.

From the Disengaged America perspective, traditional principles of defense planning are largely irrelevant.[28] Military power should no longer be employed to further human rights or economic principles beyond American borders. Rather than pursuing military goals, American foreign policy must concentrate on protecting American lives and property, the territorial integrity of the United States, and the autonomy of its political system. Consistent with these priorities, American military power should only be used for three purposes: (1) to defend the approaches to U.S. territory, (2) to serve as second-chance forces if deterrence fails or unexpected threats arise, and (3) to provide finite essential deterrence against attacks on the United States and its forces overseas.

The Disengaged America perspective has few qualms about the need to defend American interests or to take action unilaterally and forcefully in doing so. Preemption as a means for dealing with terrorists is not a repugnant strategy. The primary concern is that the War on Terrorism has as its objective not simply the defeat of the enemy, but its transformation. In the words of Pat Buchanan, an assistant and special consultant to Presidents Nixon, Ford, and Reagan, the purpose of American foreign policy is "America First—and Second, and Third." Some twenty-five years later, Buchanan reiterated this theme, writing, "This is not isolationism. It is putting our country first. . . . It used to be called patriotism."[29]

## Over the Horizon: A New Cold War?

China has become the central reference point for discussing the present and future direction of U.S. foreign policy. In 2019, General Mark Milley (who would soon become chairman of the Joint Chiefs of Staff) told Congress that China may be the primary threat to the U.S. military for a century.[30] In the Council on Foreign Relations' annual Preventive Priorities Survey in 2022, a poll of some four hundred scholars and practitioners ranked thirty challenges to U.S. interests.[31] A conflict between China and Taiwan that would draw in the United States was identified as a Tier 1 prevention priority with a moderate likelihood and high impact. An armed U.S.-China conflict was placed in Tier 2 with a low likelihood and high impact. President Trump's National Security Strategy stated that China was "a revisionist power that seeks to shape a world antithetical to U.S. values and interests." William Burns, President Biden's CIA director, defined China as "the most important geopolitical threat we face in the 21st Century."

Not surprisingly, comments such as these have led to characterizing U.S.-China relations as being in the early stages of a new cold war. Few doubt that future U.S.-China relations will be heavily competitive in nature and contain a potentially high degree of conflict that, given the military power of each, could hold serious consequences for global peace and security. What many doubt is whether the rhetoric and imagery of a new cold war is the proper foundation on which to build a grand strategy to protect and promote U.S. interests as well as preserving and advancing global interests. From this perspective, referring to U.S.-China relations as a new cold war obscures and distorts reality as much as it clarifies and explains the conditions under which the United States may need to make foreign policy choices and select among them.

In particular it is argued that the U.S.-Russia Cold War and a potential cold war between the United States and China differ in a number of important ways.[32] One is geography. At its core, the U.S.-Russia conflict was heavily land based, while the U.S.-China conflict is sea based. Second, ideology played a central role in the U.S.-Russia Cold War. Ideology matters little today, as China's rulers, compared to Russia's, rely far less on communism to bolster their domestic legitimacy and build foreign influence than they do on nationalism and China's record of economic success. Third, the U.S.-Russia Cold War was centered on military power. Conflict and competition between the United States and China involve military, economic, and technological power. Fourth, the dominant U.S. strategy during the U.S.-Russia Cold War was containment. What tends to be forgotten is that containment was not a single consistent set of policies but involved elements of cooperation, conflict, negotiation, rivalry, and deterrence. Overall, it fluctuated between policies of détente, massive retaliation, and "rolling back the Iron Curtain." Finally, where the economies of the United States and Russia during the Cold War had virtually no meaningful interaction, this is not the case with U.S.-China economic relations. The two economies are highly interactive and dependent on one another. While this does not make a cold war impossible, it makes using similar strategies difficult.

Three bottom-line conclusions of note have been put forward in the debate over whether or not a new cold war is in the offing. First, given the differences noted above, the need is to create a new strategy for interacting with China rather than dusting off an old strategy. Second, it is important that the United States not let its overall foreign policy be "hijacked" by a single country.[33] The focus of U.S. foreign policy may need to be on China, but it should not be so obsessed with China that it loses sight of other foreign policy problems. Third, the United States needs to avoid the *sleepwalker syndrome*.[34] It cannot ignore the challenges and possible threats that China may present or assume that they will pass, as European leaders did with rising tensions that led to World War I.

## Critical Thinking Questions

1. In selecting a foreign policy for the future, which of the three questions we ask is most important, and why?

2. Identify one foreign policy option that is missing and needs to be added to the list. Why is it needed?

3. What power resources are most needed by the United States in facing the future, and why?

## Key Terms

America the Balancer, 307
American Crusader, 306
Disengaged America, 308
empire, 303
falling dominoes, 309

hedging strategy, 307
Ordinary State, 302
Pragmatic America, 305
Reformed America, 303

# Glossary

**action channels** Decision-making linkages between organizations and individuals that determine who participates in bureaucratic decision-making games. Important because not everyone "plays" in these games. Players and their power are determined by where they fit in the action channels.

**action indispensability** Decision-making situations in which action by policy makers is critical to success or failure. The identity of the actor is not essential because the response was standard and expected.

**action policy** U.S. foreign policy as it is actually carried out with respect to a problem. Refers to what is done rather than what is said. Often contrasts with declaratory policy. Originally used in the context of U.S. nuclear policy.

**actor indispensability** Decision-making situations in which not only is action by policy makers critical to success or failure, but the identity of the actor is seen as being key to the outcome.

**alliance** A formal agreement among states to provide military assistance to each other. Alliances vary in the types of aid offered and the nature of the commitment.

**"America first" perspective** A perspective on foreign policy in which priority is given to the interests of American firms over those of other states. Identified with bureaucracies such as the Commerce and Agriculture Departments.

**America the Balancer** A possible future strategic orientation of U.S. foreign policy that is based on a limited and selective involvement in world affairs.

**American Crusader** A possible future strategic orientation of U.S. foreign policy that is based on the idea that the United States faces real and immediate security threats and has the power and moral responsibility to lead.

**analogy** Central method of reasoning in which comparisons are made between events and objects as the basis for making judgments about similarities and differences. Foreign policy often involves comparison of present with past events.

**arms control** Policy designed to bring about restraint in the use of weapons. Generally involves reduction in numbers of weapons but does not have to do this. Often contrasted with disarmament.

**arms sale** Purchase of weapons by one state from another. The distinguishing feature of arms sales is the quality of the weapons obtained. Unlike in the case of arms transfers, these weapons tend to be among the most preferred in the seller's inventory.

**arms transfer** Process of providing weapons to another state for free or at greatly reduced prices. Typically these weapons are characterized as being excess defense articles or emergency allocations.

**assured destruction** Nuclear strategy under Johnson predicated on U.S. ability to destroy a significant portion of the Soviet population and economic capability in retaliation for a Soviet attack on the United States.

**bargaining** Process by which two or more states reach agreement on a policy through a process of give and take. It can take place in formal settings or informally. A subtype of negotiations.

**barnacles** Riders or amendments that are attached to foreign policy legislation. Often needed to secure its passage, they can result in features being added that complicate the conduct of U.S. diplomacy. Reporting requirements are an example.

**bipartisanship** Situation in the domestic politics of American foreign policy where a policy is supported by both political parties. Seen as a sign of national unity and communicates resolve to opponents. It came into use following World War II when the foundations of containment policy were put into place.

**bipolar** Characterizes an international system that is conflict prone and divided into two competing and mutually exclusive blocs each led by a superpower. Often subdivided into loose and tight variants depending on the unity of the blocs and the distance separating them. The Cold War was a bipolar system.

**black box** Part of the rational actor decision-making perspective. Assumes that foreign policy is a response to actions and events in the international system. Therefore, one does not need to examine domestic politics, and events inside the state can be ignored or black-boxed.

**blowback** The negative consequences that result from foreign policy actions. Originally used with reference to CIA covert actions but now applied more generally to foreign policy initiatives.

**boycott** A refusal to buy or sell goods from a company or country. Alternatively, a refusal to attend a meeting or negotiations.

**Bretton Woods system** International economic order created after World War II consisting of the International Monetary Fund, the World Bank, and the General Agreement on Trade and Tariffs. Formally ended in 1974 when Nixon took the United States off the gold standard.

**Bricker Amendment** Failed attempt by Congress in the 1950s to limit the president's ability to use executive agreements in place of treaties as instruments of U.S. foreign policy. It would have required Senate advice and consent to executive agreements before they took effect.

**bureaucratic politics** Decision-making model that emphasizes the influence of bureaucratic factors, most notably self-interest. Policy is not decided upon so much as bargained into existence.

**chief executive officer (CEO) system** Presidential management system introduced by George W. Bush that emphasizes the importance of providing overall direction to policy and selecting qualified individuals and then removing oneself from the day-to-day affairs of governing.

**civil-military relations** The overarching relationship between professional military officers and civilian policy makers. Involves issues such as who has ultimate authority, the values to be pursued, and political neutrality.

**closed belief system** A belief system is a set of interrelated mental images about some aspect of reality. A closed belief system is one that does not change in spite of contradictory evidence. Contrasts with an open belief system.

**CNN effect** Phrase designed to convey increased importance of the media for determining the foreign policy agenda of the United States by its ability to arouse and shape public opinion and force policy makers to respond quickly to unfolding events.

**coalitions** Informal alignments of states that come together out of self-interest to deal with a specific problem. Common forms include voting blocs at an international organization and combinations of military forces such as those in the Persian Gulf War and the Iraq War.

**coercive diplomacy** Use or threatened use of force against another state for political purposes. Typically refers to military force but can include economic force. Purposes can include deterrence and compellence.

**cognitive consistency** The tendency of individuals to seek out information and stimuli that are supportive of their beliefs and attitudes.

**collegial system** Presidential management system that emphasizes cooperation, teamwork, and problem solving as primary values for top presidential aides and department heads.

**compellence** Use or threat of using military force to prompt another state to undertake a desired action. Contrasts with deterrence in which force is used or threatened to prevent an action from taking place.

**competitive system** Presidential management system that emphasizes playing off aides against one another and assigning the same task to multiple units in order to maximize information flow and freedom of maneuver.

**conference diplomacy** Category of diplomacy that focuses on large international gatherings that are generally open to all states. Typically they focus on a single problem or issue and attempt to lay down rules for addressing the problem. Differs from summit diplomacy where only a few states attend.

**constructivism** A theoretical perspective for studying international relations that emphasizes the subjectivity of actions. Emphasis is placed on understanding how the developments are viewed by the participants by examining ideas, culture, history, and the dynamics of interaction.

**containment** U.S. policy toward the Soviet Union for much of the Cold War. Predicated on the assumption that the potential for Soviet aggression was constant but could be checked by applying constant counterpressure to thwart it. Over time, this policy was expected to produce a mellowing of Soviet foreign policy.

**counterinsurgency (COIN)** The military strategy for fighting an insurgency, which is defined as an armed rebellion against a recognized government. The military strategy counterinsurgency also contains political, economic, and psychological dimensions.

**counterproliferation** Military strategy designed to prevent the spread of weapons. Most frequently talked about in the context of weapons of mass destruction, it can be seen as a preemptive use of force.

**country team** Comprises the representatives from all U.S. agencies represented in an embassy, headed by the ambassador. It is meant to signify that a united purpose exists to U.S. foreign policy in the country.

**covert action** Activities to influence military, economic, and political conditions abroad, where it is intended that the role of the U.S. government not be apparent.

**cyber warfare** A variety of attacks on computer and information systems for the purpose of causing damage or destruction through such means as computer viruses or denial-of-service attacks.

**declaratory policy** Public statements of U.S. foreign policy with regard to a problem. Refers to what is said rather than what is done. Often contrasted with action policy. Originally used in the context of U.S. nuclear policy.

**denuclearization** Process by which a state that has acquired or is pursuing a nuclear weapon reverses course and agrees to forgo it.

**détente** Foreign policy associated with Nixon. Rather than containing the Soviet Union, it sought to establish a working relationship by treating it as a legitimate power and engaging it in a series of mutually beneficial arms control and economic relationships that would reduce its threat to the United States, thus making global conflicts more manageable.

**deterrence** The use of power to prevent an unwanted action from taking place. Most frequently it refers to the use of military power, and in the context of the Cold War, the nuclear standoff between the United States and the Soviet Union.

**digital diplomacy** The use of the internet and information and communication technologies such as social media and Twitter to achieve diplomatic objectives.

**disarmament** Policy designed to reduce the number of weapons in existence. May be applied to specific weapons or to inventories in general. Logical endpoint is zero weapons but need not necessarily reach this point. Often contrasted with arms control.

**Disengaged America** A possible future strategic orientation of U.S. foreign policy that is based on minimal global engagement and learning to live in a second-best world.

**economic statecraft** The use of economic resources and tools to achieve foreign policy goals.

**elite theory** Decision-making model that stresses the overwhelming influence of economic class and ideology on policy. Contrasts with pluralism, arguing that there does not exist a system of checks and balances among competing interests.

**embargo** A prohibition of selling goods or services to another country.

**empire** A hierarchically structured grouping of states ruled from one power center. It is debated whether or not the U.S. position of dominance in the world qualifies it to be an empire. Similarly, it is debated how long the U.S. empire, if it exists, can survive.

**executive agreement** Arrangements entered into with other countries by the president that are not subject to a congressional vote. The Supreme Court has ruled that executive agreements hold force of law as do treaties.

**falling dominoes** Term associated with the Cold War, it denotes the possibility that a U.S. foreign policy failure in a given country or military engagement may set off a chain reaction leading to the fall of many states, resulting in a major national security crisis.

**fast track** Today known as trade promotional authority. Voted on by Congress for set periods of time, it gives the president the authority to enter into international trade negotiations, guarantees a prompt vote by Congress, and limits Congress's ability to modify treaties that come before it.

**firewall** A blockage or separation that is intended to stop the spread of a dangerous condition. In warfare, it is often used to signify attempts to create a dividing line between conventional and nuclear weapons.

**flexible response** Nuclear strategy under Kennedy that called for a wide range of military responses, including a variety of nuclear options to deal with Soviet challenges.

**Foreign Service officer** Professional diplomatic corps of the United States. Has been controversial at times for its values and degree of separation from American society as a whole.

**formalistic system** Presidential management system that employs strict hierarchical decision-making structure on decision-making processes.

**free trade** International economic policy based on the principle of the open and nondiscriminatory flow of goods across borders. Achieved through the removal of government-imposed barriers to trade.

**gadfly** A congressional orientation to foreign policy in which an individual raises concerns about the direction of U.S. foreign policy not out of an interest in short-term electoral gains but with an eye toward affecting the long-term direction of policy.

**gatekeeper** An individual who determines the types of information and which individuals have access to a policy maker. Gatekeepers are crucial to establishing effective decision-making routines and yet also a liability because they can distort the information on which policy is made.

**generational events** Those highly visible and psychologically significant events that influence the worldview of a generation of individuals, whether they were experienced directly or not. The Great Depression, Pearl Harbor, and Vietnam are often given as examples.

**globalization** Refers to the process of the growing pace and density of economic, political, and cultural interactions in international affairs. Viewed by some in a positive light as a force that unites peoples; others see it as a threatening condition that fosters conflict among people and countries.

**grand strategy** Overarching conceptual framework for integrating and applying all elements of power. Establishes the general direction, purposes, and logic of U.S. foreign policy. Often associated with presidential doctrines.

**groupthink** Common consequence of small-group decision-making dynamics. Concurrence-seeking behavior on the part of group members causes them to reach fundamentally flawed decisions.

**guerrilla war** Unconventional war strategy that emphasizes hit-and-run tactics and prolonged warfare rather than direct engagement of enemy forces in decisive battles. Ultimate objective is to get government to overreact and lose support of the people.

**hard power** The power to coerce. Generally associated with military power. It seeks to impose an outcome on an opponent.

**hedging strategy** A foreign policy strategy in which the United States acts cautiously to ensure that the failure of no single initiative can inflict great harm on U.S. national interests. It requires keeping open lines of communication with all states and not locking the United States into an all-or-nothing situation.

**hegemony** Domineering and uncontested leadership that is rooted in the political, economic, and military ability to impose one's will on others. Often used to characterize the position of the dominant state in a unipolar system and the U.S. position in the world after the end of the Cold War.

**hybrid warfare** A form of warfare that employs a combination of conventional and unconventional military strategies along with informational and other nonmilitary resources and societal resources to achieve victory.

**imperialism** A foreign policy of domination in which one state controls the people, resources, and political activity in other states generally by military force. Critics of U.S. foreign policy have often argued that it has been imperialist in dealings with developing countries.

**intermestic** Foreign policy problems that contain both domestic and foreign policy dimensions, thus complicating efforts to solve them and defy the traditional dichotomy of foreign versus domestic policy.

**internationalism** An orientation to world affairs that stresses the importance of taking an active role in global decision making in order to protect and promote national security and economic prosperity. Can be undertaken both in the pursuit of liberal or conservative goals.

**Iraq syndrome** Much speculated on possible negative public reaction to U.S. involvement in Iraq that will prevent policy makers from using force in the future, just as Vietnam syndrome did in the 1970s.

**isolationism** An orientation to world affairs that stresses the dangers of global involvement rather than its benefits. Strong defenses and unilateral action are seen as necessary to protect the national interest. A sharp distinction is drawn between the national interest and the global interest.

**legalism** Part of the American national style. The belief that foreign policy problems can be solved through the application of legal formulas and principles.

**legislative veto** A situation where Congress repeals presidential action or the decision of a federal agency by writing legislation so that it can be overridden by a majority of one or both Houses. Contained in the War Powers Resolution.

**Lippmann gap** The difference between a country's power resources and the goals it wishes to achieve. Named after political columnist Walter Lippmann, who argued that the larger this gap, the greater the likelihood that U.S. foreign policy would fail.

**massive retaliation** Nuclear strategy under Eisenhower that sought to deter Soviet aggression throughout the world by threatening a large-scale retaliatory strike on the Soviet Union.

**military after next** Phrase used to describe the need to think beyond immediate problems and focus on long-term bureaucratic requirements of U.S. foreign policy. Can also be "State Department after next" or "CIA after next."

**military-industrial complex** A phrase used in Eisenhower's farewell presidential address. Most narrowly used, it speaks to the unchecked influence of industry lobbyists and allies in the military to obtain funds for weapons systems and militarize American foreign policy.

**model** A simplified depiction of a complex process or structure used to generate insights into their nature. May be mathematical or descriptive.

**moral pragmatism** Part of the American national style. Brings together the belief that foreign policy ought to be driven by the pursuit of principles and that they can be solved by applying an engineering problem-solving logic.

**multipolar** Characterizes an international system in which there are at least five major powers. No permanent dividing line separates them into competing blocs; rather, the major states enter into a series of shifting alliances to preserve national interests. Nineteenth-century Europe is seen as a multipolar period.

**national interest** The fundamental goals and objectives of a state's foreign policy. Used as if it were self-explanatory, it is a contested concept that holds great emotional power in political debates.

**national style** Refers to deeply engrained patterns of thought and action on how to approach foreign policy problems and their solutions. More generally, it establishes the basis for how a country looks out at the international system and defines its role in world politics.

**negotiation** Broadly defined as a dialogue to resolve disputes. This result may be achieved through mediation, fact finding, or bargaining. On occasion, negotiations are entered into by states not to solve problems but to gain an advantage through obtaining information or the publicity it generates.

**neoliberalism** A theoretical perspective for studying international relations that stresses the ability of states to cooperate, solve problems, and defend their interests peacefully. Emphasis is placed on the importance of mutually beneficial economic interactions, the peaceful effects of democracy, and the importance of international laws and organizations.

**noise** Background clutter of irrelevant or misleading data that complicates the task of policy makers trying to identify important pieces of information or signals that will help them formulate policy.

**nontariff barrier** A nontax barrier to free trade. Generally takes the form of requirements to ship national vessels, purchase goods in a specific country of origin, or meet safety and health or environmental standards imposed on goods and their production.

**opportunity costs** In conducting foreign policy, states are faced with the reality of limited time and limited resources. The pursuit of any objective necessarily comes at the expense of pursuing other goals that now must be neglected.

**Ordinary State** A possible future strategic orientation of U.S. foreign policy that is based on the presumption that the United States has no greater responsibility for maintaining global order than does any other state.

**outsource** To rely on nongovernmental or private-sector agencies to carry out assigned tasks. Found throughout foreign policy area. Became controversial with large-scale use of private contractors during the Iraq War.

**oversight** Congressional regulatory supervision of the federal bureaucracy. The stated objective is not day-to-day managerial control but ensuring accountability of decisions made and improving performance.

**paramilitary** Operations carried out by forces or groups distinct from the professional military for which no broad conventional military capability exists. They are often carried out in hostile, politically sensitive, or denied areas.

**peacekeeping operations** Operations conducted in postconflict areas to observe the peace process and implement peace agreements. Although not exclusively military in nature, peacekeeping operations generally build upon a significant military presence in the country affected.

**pledge system** Form of international cooperation in which countries promise voluntarily to support an agreement. No enforcement mechanism is created.

**pluralism** Decision-making model that sees policy as the result of competing interest groups. The government is often pictured as a neutral umpire making policy to reflect the position of the strongest groups.

**policy entrepreneur** A congressional orientation to foreign policy whereby the individual takes positions on foreign policy legislation primarily with an eye toward the electoral advantage it might bestow rather than a long-range concern for the issue itself.

**poliheuristic decision making** A model of decision making that emphasizes the presence of a two-stage decision-making process, only the second of which involves engaging in an analysis of options.

**political creep** The tendency for political criteria and considerations to replace professional ones in the assignment of personnel to positions within the foreign policy bureaucracy. Once identified with the appointment of political fund-raisers to ambassadorships, it is now also an issue at lower levels of bureaucracies.

**politicizing intelligence**  Situation where professional expertise and objectivity of intelligence reports is replaced by partisan political considerations. Associated with phrases such as *intelligence-to-please* and *cherry-picking.*

**positional issues**  Refers to foreign policy issues in elections that find candidates taking opposite sides. The dominant logic of primary campaigns. A frequent result is to oversimplify issues.

**Pragmatic America**  A possible future strategic orientation of U.S. foreign policy that is based on the view that rapid changes in world politics make it inadvisable for U.S. foreign policy to be guided by a broad set of principles. Instead, it should focus on the particulars of each situation as they arise.

**preemption**  Striking first in self-defense. In classical usage, a distinction is drawn between preemption, which occurs when the threat is immediate, and prevention, when it is more long term or generic.

**presidential finding**  Mandated by the Hughes-Ryan Amendment, it requires that, except under exceptional circumstances, presidents inform key members of Congress in advance of the scope of CIA operations.

**presidential personality**  Refers to those traits of the president that are important for understanding how he defines problems and solutions as well as his outlook on the use of presidential power.

**proliferation**  Spread of weapons. Two different versions exist. Horizontal, in which weapons spread to additional countries, and vertical, in which case, the inventories of states already possessing the weapon grow larger.

**prospect theory**  Decision-making model that sees policy makers as far more willing to take risks to defend what they have than to pursue new goals and objectives.

**proxy war**  War fought on behalf of another state that does not actively participate in the war itself. Typically associated with a smaller or regional ally fighting on behalf of a major power.

**public diplomacy**  Diplomatic activity that is directed at the public at large in a target state. Contrasts with classical diplomacy, which is conducted in secret and involves government-to-government relations. Based on the belief that the public can influence the foreign policy decisions of adversaries.

**public goods**  Policy benefits that are not the object of competition among states and cannot be possessed by a state or group of states and denied to all others. Often characterized as goals that are in the global interest, such as a clean environment, absence of disease, or a stable international economic order.

**Quadrennial Defense Review**  Congressionally mandated four years of U.S. defense strategy. Used to identify scenarios that might confront the United States and forces that might be needed to meet that threat. In practice, it has often been largely a symbolic exercise.

**quota**  Quantitative restriction placed on the amount of goods allowed to enter a country from another country.

**rally-around-the-flag effect**  Tendency for public opinion to coalesce and support the president's foreign policy position in times of crisis. Reflects both the power of the presidency and media to shape public opinion as well as the lack of in-depth knowledge that many Americans have on foreign policy matters.

**ratify**  To give approval. Treaties in the United States are ratified by the president after the Senate has given its advice and consent by a two-thirds majority.

**rational actor**  Decision-making model that stresses foreign policy; it should be viewed as a deliberate and calculated response to external events and actions. Values are identified, options are listed, and a choice is made that best ensures that the most important values will be realized.

**realism**  A theoretical perspective for studying international relations that emphasizes the struggle for power carried out under conditions of anarchy. Conflict and competition are seen as permanent features of world politics. Security, not peace, is the central objective of foreign policy.

**Reformed America** A possible future strategic orientation of U.S. foreign policy that is based on the belief that the time is appropriate to give preference to traditional American values over narrowly defined security interests in dealing with global problems.

**reporting requirement** A statement added onto legislation requiring periodic reports by implementing agencies or the president on the status of a situation. They have been used by Congress as a means of keeping up the pressure on presidents to carry out foreign policy according to its wishes. Generally, escape hatches are included to give presidents freedom to act.

**Revolution in Military Affairs** Term used to capture the transformational power that modern information and communication technology were expected to have in the conduct of military campaigns. Widely used in U.S. defense planning and weapons procurement decisions after the Persian Gulf War. Now challenged by new emphasis on counterinsurgency warfare.

**rogue states** States that are considered to be threats to the peace and stability of the international system due to their refusal to act in accordance with global rules and norms.

**sanctions** Penalties or other means of enforcement used to create incentives for countries to act in accordance with policy edicts of the sanctioning state. Typically involves the use of economic instruments of foreign policy.

**shock and awe** Massive bombing campaign used by the United States in the opening of the Iraq War. Designed as much to psychologically intimidate an enemy as to defeat it on the battlefield. Associated with military logic of Revolution in Military Affairs.

**shuttle diplomacy** Negotiations or talks mediated by a third party who travels frequently between the counties that are involved in the dispute.

**signal** Piece of information that will help policy makers formulate policy. Often difficult to identify because of the presence of noise that masks their presence and significance.

**signing statement** Comments made by the president when signing legislation into law and used to identify which parts of the legislation he objects to and will not enforce. Effectively allows the president to veto certain parts of a bill without having to veto the entire bill.

**small-group decision making** A decision-making model that emphasizes the importance of interactions among individuals in formal or informal group settings.

**smart sanctions** Penalties or other measures that are targeted on specific groups or individuals in a target state. Adopted out of a concern that sanctions, particularly economic sanctions, unfairly punish all individuals in a society rather than just those engaging in the disputed behaviors.

**soft power** The power to influence and persuade. It attracts others to one side rather than forcing them to support a cause, as is the case with hard power. Often associated with diplomacy, positive economic incentives, and, more generally, the attraction of American culture, ideas, and values.

**sovereignty** The principle that no power exists above the state. The state alone decides what goals to pursue and how to pursue them. Its relevance as an absolute standard is questioned by many in today's world of globalization, terrorism, and large-scale power inequalities among states.

**spiral of silence** Tendency for those holding minority views to remain silent when they fail to see the media report stories that support their position. Results in an exaggerated sense of national unity.

**stability operations** Military operations undertaken to restore and maintain order and stability in regions or states where a competent civil authority no longer functions.

**standard operating procedures** Central part of bureaucratic politics model. States that policy is implemented not with an eye to the particulars of a situation or problem but in a routine and predictable fashion, with the result that policies often fail to achieve their intended purpose.

**sufficiency** Nuclear strategy under Nixon that emphasized strategic equality with the Soviet Union and the possession of a minimum retaliatory threat.

**summit conference** Category of diplomacy that involves meetings of the heads of government of a small number of states. Popularized during World War II and the Cold War. They are now less negotiating sessions and more occasions to sign agreements reached in other settings.

**tariff** Tax on foreign products coming into a country. May be put in place to raise revenue, protect domestic industries from foreign competition, or punish another state.

**terrorism** Violence employed for purposes of political intimidation. It may be employed in the support of any set of goals and carried out by nonstate actors or state agencies. It may exist as a strategy in its own right or as the first stage in a larger guerrilla war conflict.

**think tanks** Generic phrase used to describe organizations that engage in policy analysis and advocacy. They may be nonprofits, represent corporate interests, or be funded by governments.

**tipping point** Term used to describe foreign policy issues in which elite and public opinion are so divided that a shift in public opinion holds the potential for changing the direction of policy.

**trade promotional authority** Once known as fast-track authority. Voted on by Congress for set periods of time, it gives the president the authority to enter into international trade negotiations, guarantees a prompt vote by Congress, and limits Congress's ability to modify treaties that come before it.

**unilateral president** View of presidential power that emphasizes strength rather than weakness. By acting unilaterally to make policy statements, create organizations, appoint individuals to key positions, and take action, the president is seen as able to dominate the political agenda and outmaneuver Congress and the courts, placing them in a reactive position.

**unilateralism** Part of the American national style. It is an orientation to action that emphasizes the value of going it alone. When cooperation with others is needed, it must be carried out on one's own terms and with a minimal level of commitment to joint action.

**unipolar** Characterizes an international system in which one power dominates over all others. No balancing or competing bloc exists. Rare at the international level, it has been more common at the regional level such as in Latin America and East Europe. Some see the contemporary international system as unipolar.

**valence issues** Refers to electoral foreign policy issues that find all candidates taking the same side. Common in general elections. For voters, the choice becomes not what position to endorse but who they think is best capable of achieving the agreed-upon outcome.

**Vietnam syndrome** Refers to what many interpreted as the primary lesson of Vietnam. The perception that the American public will not again support long-term military engagements that result in the substantial loss of American lives. Consequently, any military action must be quick and decisive.

**War Powers Resolution** The major Cold War attempt by Congress to limit a president's ability to use military force without its approval. Its constitutionality has never been tested. No president has officially recognized its binding nature on their decision-making power.

**weapons of mass destruction (WMDs)** Overarching term used to describe nuclear, biological, and chemical weapons. Radiological weapons and delivery systems are also often included in the definition. During the Cold War, the term related almost exclusively to nuclear weapons.

**Wilsonianism** A set of foreign policy ideas associated with Woodrow Wilson. The core essence of these ideas is contested. Generally seen as foundational is the notion that the United States has a moral and national security obligation to spread democracy and create a liberal international order.

**window of fear** The onset of a set of short-term conditions that lead policy makers rationally to conclude that military action needs to be taken, regardless of how small the prospects of victory are, because conditions will only get worse in the future.

**window of opportunity** The onset of short-term conditions that lead policy makers rationally to conclude that military action needs to be undertaken because they possess a clear and distinct military advantage over the enemy.

**yellow journalism** Phrase used to characterize media coverage of foreign policy that stresses a provocative, overly dramatic, and sensationalistic treatment of events over measured reporting and a concern for factual accuracy.

# Notes

## Chapter 1: Defining American Foreign Policy Problems

1. Steve Strasser, ed., *The 9/11 Investigations* (New York: Public Affairs Press, 2004), 233.

2. Jim Hoagland, "Why Clinton Improvises," *Washington Post*, September 25, 1994, C1.

3. Bob Woodward, *Obama's Wars* (New York: Simon & Schuster, 2010), 278–79.

4. Jeffrey Jones, "Terrorism, Nuclear Weapons, China Viewed as U.S. Top Threats," Gallup.com, March 7, 2022.

5. Bruce Drake, "Americans Put Low Priority on Promoting Democracy Abroad," Pew Research Center, March 2, 2021.

6. Dina Smeltz, *Foreign Policy in the New Millennium* (Chicago: Chicago Council on Global Affairs, 2012), 14.

7. For recent efforts, see Ted Galen Carpenter, "Dealing with Bad Allies: The Case for Moral Realism," *National Interest* 140 (2015): 51–58; Derek Reveron and Nikolas Gvosdev, "(Re)Discovering the National Interest," *Orbis* 59 (2015): 299–316; and Bruce Jentleson, "Strategic Recalibration," *Washington Quarterly* 37 (2014): 115–36.

8. Humphrey Taylor, "The Not-so-Black Art of Public Diplomacy," *World Policy Journal* 24 (2007/08): 51–59.

9. "The Price of Detachment," *Economist*, March 23, 2013, 37.

10. Walter Lippmann, *The Cold War: A Study in US Foreign Policy* (New York: Harper, 1947). Also see Michael Mazarr, "A Strategy of Discriminate Power," *Washington Quarterly* 37 (2014): 137–50.

11. Chalmers Johnson, *Blowback: The Costs and Consequences of American Empire* (New York: Owl Books, 2000).

12. Charles Kupchan and Peter Trubowitz, "Grand Strategy for a Divided America," *Foreign Affairs* 86 (2007): 82.

13. John P. Lovell, "The Idiom of National Security," *Journal of Political and Military Sociology* 11 (1983): 35–51.

14. Glenn Kessler and Robin Wright, "A Case for Progress amid Some Omissions," *Washington Post*, June 29, 2005, A1; Omar Fekeiki, "The Toll of Communism," *Washington Post*, June 13, 2007, C1.

15. Bob Woodward, *The War Within, 2006–2008* (New York: Simon & Schuster, 2009), 189.

16. Maria Repnikova, "The Balance of Soft Power," *Foreign Affairs* 101 (July 2022): 44–51.

17. Ann Scott Tyson, "Gates Warns of Militarized Policy," *Washington Post*, July 16, 2008, A6.

18. Greg Whitlock, *The Afghanistan Papers* (New York: Simon & Schuster, 2021), 5.

19. "National Security Strategy of the United States," 2002, http://georgewbush-whitehouse.archives.gov/nsc/nss/2002.

20. Patrick Porter, "Why America's Grand Strategy Has Not Changed," *International Security* 42 (2018): 9–46.

21. Richard Betts, "The Grandiosity of Grand Strategy," *Washington Quarterly* 42 (2019): 7–22.

22. Paul Macdonald, "America First? Explaining Continuity and Change in Trump's Foreign Policy," *Political Science Quarterly* 133 (September 2018): 401–34.

23. Ernest Haass, "The Age of America First," *Foreign Affairs* 100 (November 2021): 85–98.

24. Jessica Matthews, "Present at the Re-Creation," *Foreign Affairs* 100 (March 2021): 10–16; and Jonathan Kirshner, "Gone but Not Forgotten," *Foreign Affairs* 100 (March 2021): 18–26.

25. Haass, "The Age of America First."

26. George Joffe, "Libya: Who Blinked and Why," *Current History* 103 (May 2004): 221–25.

27. Henry Kissinger, *A World Restored: Metternich, Castlereagh and the Problems of Peace* (New York: Grosset & Dunlap, 1964).

28. Stanley Hoffmann, "Requiem," *Foreign Policy* 42 (1981): 3–26.

29. Robert Tucker, "Reagan's Foreign Policy," *Foreign Affairs* 68 (1989): 1–27.

30. For a sampling of views on Trump's grand strategy, see Randall Schweller, "Three Cheers for Trump's Foreign Policy," *Foreign Affairs* 97 (September 2018): 133–43; Elliott Abrams, "Trump the Traditionalist," *Foreign Affairs* 96 (July 2017): 10–16; Hal Brands, "The Unexceptional Superpower," *Survival* 59 (2017): 7–40; and Richard Wolf, "Donald Trump's Status-Drive Foreign Policy," *Survival* 59 (2017): 99–116.

31. Woodward, *The War Within*, 32.

32. Eliot Cohen, "The Return of Statecraft," *Foreign Affairs* 101 (May, 2022): 117–29.

33. Daniel Drezner, "This Time Is Different," *Foreign Affairs* 98 (May 2019): 10–17.

# Chapter 2: The Global Context

1. For an assessment of the problems with the Russian war effort, see Lawrence Freeman, "Why War Fails," *Foreign Affairs* 101 (July 2022): 10–23.

2. Kenneth Waltz, *Theory of International Politics* (New York: McGraw-Hill, 1979).

3. Andrew Moravcsik, "Taking Preferences Seriously: A Liberal Theory of International Politics," *International Organization* 51 (1997): 513–53.

4. Alexander Wendt, *Social Theory of International Politics* (New York: Cambridge University Press, 1999).

5. David Calleo, "The Tyranny of False Vision: America's Unipolar Fantasy," *Survival* 50 (2008): 61–78.

6. "Troubled Waters, Murky Commitments: How Asia Sees Obama's Pivot to the Pacific," *Washington Post*, November 20, 2012, http://article.wn.com/view/2012/11/20/troubled_waters_murky _commitments_How_Asia_sees_obama_s_pivo. Also see Andrew Nation and Andrew Scobell, "How China Sees America," *Foreign Affairs* 91 (2012): 32–47.

7. Robert Tucker, *The Inequality of Nations* (New York: Basic Books, 1977).

8. Robert Gilpin, *War and Change in World Politics* (New York: Cambridge University Press, 1981). For a dissenting view on the decline of U.S. power, see Bruce Russett, "The Mysterious Case of Vanishing Hegemony; or, Is Mark Twain Really Dead?," *International Organization* 39 (1985): 207–32.

9. Bayliss Manning, "The Congress, the Executive and Intermestic Affairs: Three Proposals," *Foreign Affairs* 56 (1977): 306–24.

10. For discussions of the growth of nonstate actors, see Werner Feld, *International Relations, a Transnational Approach* (Sherman Oaks, CA: Alfred, 1979); Harold K. Jacobson, *Networks of Interdependence: International Organizations and the Global Political System* (New York: Knopf, 1979). For statistics, see the *Yearbook of International Organizations*, http://www.uia.be/ybvol1.com.

11. The three subsystems as well as the management problems they present are taken from Joan Edelman Spero, *The Politics of International Economic Relations*, 3rd ed. (New York: St. Martin's, 1985), 13–19.

12. William Dobson, "The Day Nothing Much Changed," *Foreign Policy* 156 (2006): 22–25; Patrick Porter, *A World Imagined: Nostalgia and Liberal Order* (Washington, DC: Cato Institute, 2018).

13. Joseph Nye, "The Future of American Power," *Foreign Affairs* 89 (2010): 2–12.

14. For a discussion of the concept of terrorism, see Anthony Richards, "Conceptualizing Terrorism," *Studies in Conflict and Terrorism* 37 (2014): 213–36.

15. David C. Rapoport, "The Four Waves of Modern Terrorism," and Audrey Kurth Cronin, "The Sources of Contemporary Terrorism," in *Attacking Terrorism: Elements of a Grand Strategy*, ed. Audrey Kurth Cronin and James Ludes, 46–73, 19–45 (Washington, DC: Georgetown University Press, 2004).

16. Audrey Cronin, "ISIS Is Not a Terrorist Group," *Foreign Affairs* 94 (2015): 87–98.

17. Audrey Kurth Cronin, "How al-Qaida Ends: The Decline and Demise of Terrorist Groups," *International Security* 31 (2006): 7–48.

18. Thomas Friedman, *The World Is Flat* (New York: Farrar, Straus and Giroux, 2005).

19. Richard Haass and Robert Litan, "Globalization and Its Discontents: Navigating the Dangers of an Entangled World," *Foreign Affairs* 77 (1998): 2–6.

20. For example, see Adam Posen, "The Post American World Economy," *Foreign Affairs* 97 (March 2018): 28–38.

21. Jonathan Haidt, "How Nationalism Beats Globalism," *American Interest* 12 (2106): 7–15.

22. Dani Rodrik, "Globalization's Wrong Turn," *Foreign Affairs* 98 (July, 2019): 26–33.

23. Niall Ferguson, "Sinking Globalization," *Foreign Affairs* 84 (2005): 64–77.

24. Ian Bremmer, *The End of the Free Market* (New York: Penguin, 2010).

25. Shannon K. O'Neil, "The Myth of the Global," *Foreign Affairs* 101 (July, 2022): 158–69.

26. Alexander Motyl, "Empire Falls," *Foreign Affairs* 85 (2006): 190–94; David Hendrickson, "Is America an Empire?," *National Interest* 162 (November 2017): 39–46.

27. Michael Mandelbaum, *The Case for Goliath: How America Acts as the World's Government in the Twenty-First Century* (New York: Public Affairs Press, 2005).

28. Thomas Wright, "The Rise and Fall of the Unipolar Concert," *Washington Quarterly* 37 (2015): 7–24.

29. Niall Ferguson, "Empires with Expiration Dates," *Foreign Policy* 156 (2006): 46–52.

30. Robert Kaplan, "The Post-Imperial Moment," *National Interest* 143 (2016): 73–76.

31. Michael Boyle, "The Coming Illliberal Disorder," *Survival* 58 (2016): 35–66.

32. John Mearsheimer, "America Unhinged," *National Interest* 129 (January/February 2014): 9–30; Micah Zenko and Michael Cohen, "Clear and Present Safety," *Foreign Affairs* 91 (2012): 79–93.

33. Stephen Brooks and William Wohlforth, "The Rise and Fall of the Great Powers in the Twenty First Century," *International Security* 40 (2015/16): 7–53.

34. Niall Ferguson, "Complexity and Collapse," *Foreign Affairs* 89 (2010): 18–32.

35. https://www.whitehouse.gov/wp-content/uploads/2022/10/Biden-Harris-Administrations-National-Security-Strategy-10.2022.pdf.

36. Michael Mazarr, "What Makes a Power Great," *Foreign Affairs* 101 (July 2022): 52–63.

37. Pew Global Attitudes Project, http://www.pewglobal.org/2013/07/18/americas-global-image.

38. Pew Global Attitudes Project, https://www.pewresearch.org/global/2021/09/14/in-response-to-climate-change-citizens-in-advanced-economies-are-willing-to-alter-how-they-live-and-work.

39. https://www.pewresearch.org/global/wp-content/uploads/sites/2/2021/06/PG_2021.06.10_us-image_REPORT.pdf.

40. Peter Katzenstein and Robert Keohane, "Anti-Americanisms," *Policy Review* 139 (2006): 25–37.

41. Anne Applebaum, "In Search of Pro-Americanism," *Foreign Policy* 149 (2005): 32–40.

42. *Global Trends 2040: A More Contested World* (Washington, DC: National Intelligence Council, 2021).

# Chapter 3: The American National Style

1. Michael Desch, "America's Liberal Illiberalism: The Ideological Origins of Overreaction in U.S. Foreign Policy," *International Security* 32 (2007/08): 7–43.

2. Robert Kagan, "Neocon Nation: Neoconservatism, c. 1776," *World Affairs* 170 (2008): 13–35; and Robert Kaplan, "Clash of Exceptionalisms," *Foreign Affairs* 97 (March 2018): 139–48.

3. Derek Reveron and Nikolas Gvosdev, "(Re)Discovering the National Interest," *Orbis* 59 (2015): 299–316.

4. Judith Goldstein, *Ideas, Interests, and American Trade Policy* (Ithaca, NY: Cornell University Press, 1993), 1–18.

5. Goldstein, *Ideas, Interests, and American Trade Policy.*

6. For discussions of containment and détente, see John Spanier, *American Foreign Policy since World War II,* 10th ed. (New York: Holt, Rinehart & Winston, 1985), 23–29, 189–200, 304–6, 316–21; Charles W. Kegley Jr. and Eugene R. Wittkopf, *American Foreign Policy: Pattern and Process,* 2nd ed. (New York: St. Martin's, 1982), 48–69; Henry T. Nash, *American Foreign Policy: A Search for Security,* 3rd ed. (Homewood, IL: Dorsey, 1985), 44–48, 249–50.

7. Cited in Robert Tomes, "American Exceptionalism in the Twenty-First Century," *Survival* 56 (2014): 27.

8. Stanley Hoffmann, "Foreign Policy Transition: Requiem," *Foreign Policy* 42 (1980/81): 3–26.

9. For a discussion of alternative interpretations of U.S. foreign policy and national style, see Kegley and Wittkopf, *American Foreign Policy,* 69–81. See also Bear Braumoeller, "The Myth of American Isolationism," *Foreign Policy Analysis* 6 (2010): 349–72.

10. Howard Bliss and M. Glen Johnson, *Beyond the Water's Edge: American Foreign Policy* (Philadelphia: Lippincott, 1975), 52–53.

11. Frank Klingberg, *Positive Expectations of America's World Role* (Lanham, MD: University Press of America, 1996).

12. Dexter Perkins, *The American Approach to Foreign Policy* (Cambridge, MA: Harvard University Press, 1962), 154.

13. Robert Dallek, *The American Style of Foreign Policy, Cultural Politics and Foreign Affairs* (New York: New American Library, 1983).

14. Max Lerner, cited in Cecil Crabb Jr., *American Foreign Policy in the Nuclear Age,* 4th ed. (New York: Harper & Row, 1983), 47; Richard Ullman, "The 'Foreign World' and Ourselves: Washington, Wilson and the Democratic Dilemma," *Foreign Policy* 21 (1975/76): 97–125.

15. For a discussion of these points, see Stanley Hoffmann, *Gulliver's Troubles, or the Setting of American Foreign Policy* (New York: McGraw-Hill, 1968); Spanier, *American Foreign Policy since World War II*; Perkins, *The American Approach to Foreign Policy*; Amos Jordan and William J. Taylor Jr., *American National Security, Policy and Process* (Baltimore, MD: Johns Hopkins University Press, 1981).

16. Kenneth Keniston, quoted in Bliss and Johnson, *Beyond the Water's Edge,* 110.

17. John Judis, "The Author of Liberty," *Dissent* (Fall 2005): 54–61. See also the special issue, "Religion and the Presidents," *Review of Faith and International Affairs* 9, no. 4 (2011).

18. Peggy Shriver, "Evangelicals and World Affairs," *World Policy Journal* 23 (2006): 52–58.

19. Walter Russell Mead, "God's Country," *Foreign Affairs* 85 (2006): 24–43.

20. For a discussion of unilateralism, see Gene Rainey, *Patterns of American Foreign Policy* (Boston: Allyn & Bacon, 1975), 19–43.

21. Robert Tucker, *The Radical Left and American Foreign Policy* (Baltimore, MD: Johns Hopkins University Press, 1971), 34.

22. James Schlesinger, "Reykjavik and Revelations: A Turn of the Tide?," *Foreign Affairs* 65 (1987): 431.

23. For a discussion of American foreign policy highlighting these themes, see Arthur Schlesinger Jr., "Foreign Policy and the American Character," *Foreign Affairs* 62 (1983): 1–16.

24. Paul Pillar, "The Role of Villain," *Political Science Quarterly* 128 (2013): 211–31.

25. Hoffmann, *Gulliver's Troubles,* 150.

26. Freeman Dyson, "On Russians and Their Views of Nuclear Strategy," in *The Nuclear Reader: Strategy, Weapons, War*, ed. Charles W. Kegley Jr. and Eugene R. Wittkopf, 97–99 (New York: St. Martin's, 1985).

27. David Watt, "As a European Saw It," *Foreign Affairs* 62 (1983): 530–31.

28. For a critical discussion of the impact of legalism, see George Kennan, *American Diplomacy, 1900–1950* (New York: Mentor, 1951).

29. Rainey, *Patterns of American Foreign Policy,* 36.

30. Robert E. Osgood, *Limited War: The Challenge to American Strategy* (Chicago: University of Chicago Press, 1957), 29.

31. Spanier, *American Foreign Policy since World War II,* 11.

32. Jackson Diehl, "War against Time," *Washington Post,* January 8, 2007, A15.

33. George Kennan, "On American Principles," *Foreign Affairs* 74 (1995): 116–26.

34. The material and quotation in this section are found in Adam Wolfson, "How to Think about Humanitarian War," *Commentary* 110 (July/August 2000): 44–48.

35. Michael Mandelbaum, "Bad Statesman, Good Prophet: Woodrow Wilson and the Post–Cold War Order," *National Interest* 64 (2001): 31–41.

36. Charles W. Kegley Jr., "The Neoidealist Moment in International Studies: Realist Myths and the New International Realities," *International Studies Quarterly* 37 (1993): 131–46; Arthur S. Link, *The Higher Realism of Woodrow Wilson* (Nashville, TN: Vanderbilt University Press, 1971).

37. Robert W. Tucker, "The Triumph of Wilsonianism?," *World Policy Journal* 10 (1993): 83–100.

38. David Fromkin, "What Is Wilsonianism?," *World Policy Journal* 11 (1994): 100–12.

39. Walter Russell Mead, "The Tea Party and American Foreign Policy," *Foreign Affairs* 90 (2011): 28–44.

40. Walter Russell Mead, "The Jacksonian Revolt," *Foreign Affairs* 96 (March 2017): 2–7.

41. Another outsider from the recent past is George McGovern; see Roberta Haar, "Insurgency and American Foreign Policy," *World Affairs* 180 (Summer 2017): 32–61.

42. Brian Rathbun, "Steeped in International Affairs? The Foreign Policy Views of the Tea Party," *Foreign Policy Analysis* 9 (2013): 21–37.

43. Ernest J. Wilson III, ed., *Diversity and U.S. Foreign Policy: A Reader* (New York: Routledge, 2004).

44. A. Trevor Thrall and Erik Goepner, *Millennials and U.S. Foreign Policy* (Washington, DC: Cato Institute, 2015).

# Chapter 4: Learning from the Past

1. Jenny Lei Ravelo, "World Is Dangerously Unprepared for Future Pandemics GHS Index Finds," DEVEX.com, December 9, 2021.

2. Richard Ned Lebow, *Between Peace and War: The Nature of International Crisis Behavior* (Baltimore, MD: Johns Hopkins University Press, 1981), 199.

3. Roberta Wohlstetter, *Pearl Harbor: Warning and Decision* (Stanford, CA: Stanford University Press, 1962), 70.

4. Roland Paris, "Kosovo and the Metaphor War," *Political Science Quarterly* 117 (2002): 423–50.

5. Wohlstetter, *Pearl Harbor,* 388.

6. On cognitive consistency and its application to world politics, see Robert Jervis, *Perception and Misperception in International Politics* (Princeton, NJ: Princeton University Press, 1976); John D. Steinbruner, *The Cybernetic Theory of Decision: New Dimensions of Political Analysis* (Princeton, NJ: Princeton University Press, 1974); Lebow, *Between Peace and War.*

7. Ole Holsti, "The Belief System and National Images: A Case Study," *Journal of Conflict Resolution* 6 (1972): 244–52.

8. *Washington Post,* December 23, 1984, 11.

9. An example of this is the lack of U.S. learning from Russia's experience in Afghanistan. See Larry Goodson and Thomas Johnson, "Parallels with the Past—How the Soviets Lost in Afghanistan, How the Americans Are Losing," *Orbis* 55 (2011): 577–99.

10. These points are discussed in George Quester, *Nuclear Diplomacy, the First Twenty-Five Years* (New York: Dunellen, 1970); Michael Mandelbaum, *The Nuclear Question: The United States and Nuclear Weapons, 1946–1976* (New York: Cambridge University Press, 1979).

11. Jervis, *Perception and Misperception,* 249–50.

12. Henry Kissinger, *The White House Years* (Boston: Little, Brown, 1979), 54.

13. Richard K. Betts, *Surprise Attack: Lessons for Defense Planning* (Washington, DC: Brookings Institution, 1982), 8.

14. See also Dominic Tierney, "Intelligent Failure," *Foreign Affairs* 98 (January 2019): 41–48.

15. Scott Sagan, "Why Do States Build Nuclear Weapons?," *International Security* 21 (1996/97): 58.

16. Kenneth Pollack, "Spies, Lies, and Weapons," *Atlantic Monthly* 293 (January 2004): 78–92.

17. Joshua Rovner, "Delusion of Defeat: The United States and Iraq, 1990–1998," *Journal of Strategic Studies* 37 (2014): 482–507.

18. Results of the public opinion poll are found in the *New York Times,* March 31, 1985, sec. 6, 34. Reagan's comments can be found in the *Weekly Compilation of Presidential Documents* 18 (February 18, 1982): 185.

19. John Stoessinger, *Why Nations Go to War,* 3rd ed. (New York: St. Martin's, 1982), 101.

20. *The Pentagon Papers as Published by the New York Times* (New York: Quadrangle, 1971), 263.

21. On this point, see Richard Barnett, *The Roots of War* (New York: Penguin, 1973), chaps. 4 and 5.

22. Ernest May makes this point in his treatment of Vietnam in *"Lessons" of the Past: The Use and Misuse of History in American Foreign Policy* (New York: Oxford University Press, 1978).

23. Robert Gallucci, *Neither Peace nor Honor: The Politics of American Military Policy in Vietnam* (Baltimore, MD: Johns Hopkins University Press, 1975), 33.

24. May, *"Lessons" of the Past,* 94.

25. May, *"Lessons" of the Past,* 98–99.

26. David Halberstam, *The Best and the Brightest* (Greenwich, CT: Fawcett, 1969), 212.

27. Halberstam, *The Best and the Brightest,* 356.

28. Halberstam, *The Best and the Brightest,* 643.

29. Ole Holsti and James N. Rosenau, "Vietnam, Consensus, and the Belief Systems of American Leaders," *World Politics* 32 (1979): 1–56.

30. For a first wave of writings on the Iraq War, see Larry Diamond, "What Went Wrong in Iraq," *Foreign Affairs* 83 (2004): 34–56; Bob Woodward, *State of Denial: Bush at War, Part III* (New York: Simon & Schuster, 2006); Thomas Ricks, *Fiasco* (New York: Penguin, 2006); Rajiv Chandrasekaran, *Imperial Life in the Emerald City* (New York: Knopf, 2007).

31. *The Iraq Study Group Report* (New York: Vintage, 2006).

32. FM 3-24, *Counterinsurgency.* Available at Army Knowledge Online, www.us.army.mil.

33. The extent to which the surge and COIN versus the Anbar Awakening are responsible for this drop in violence is a point of debate. See Stephen Biddle, Jeffrey Friedman, and Jacob Shapiro, "Testing the Surge," *International Security* 37 (2012): 7–40.

34. Anatol Lieven and John C. Hulsman, "Neo-Conservatives, Liberal Hawks, and the War on Terror: Lesson from the Cold War," *World Policy Journal* 23 (Fall 2006): 64–74.

35. Andrew Bacevich, "The Real World War IV," *Wilson Quarterly* 29 (Winter 2005): 36–61.

36. For comparisons of Vietnam and Iraq, see Stephen Biddle, "Seeing Baghdad, Thinking Saigon," *Foreign Affairs* 85 (2006): 2–14; Frederick Kagan, "Iraq Is Not Vietnam," *Policy Review* 134 (2005–2006): 3–14; Andrew Krepinevich Jr., "How to Win in Iraq," *Foreign Affairs* 84 (2004): 87–104.

37. Michael Fletcher, "Bush Compares Iraq to Vietnam," *Washington Post*, August 23, 2007, A1.

38. John Kerry, John McCain, and Bob Kerry, "Lessons and Hopes in Vietnam," *New York Times*, May 24, 2016, A21.

39. Melvin Laird, "Iraq: Learning the Lessons of Vietnam," *Foreign Affairs* 84 (2005): 22–43.

40. Lawrence Freedman, "Iraq, Liberal Wars and Illiberal Containment," *Survival* 48 (2006): 51–65.

41. Quoted in Biddle, "Seeing Baghdad, Thinking Saigon," 4.

42. Krepinevich, "How to Win in Iraq."

43. Biddle, "Seeing Baghdad, Thinking Saigon."

44. David Kilcullen, "Counter-insurgency *Redux*," *Survival* 48 (2006): 111–30.

45. Bush's speech can be found at http://www.cbsnews.com/news/bush-speech-full-text.

46. Douglas Porch, "Occupational Hazards," *National Interest*, June 1, 2003, 35–46.

47. Minxin Pei, "From Victory to Success: Afterwar Policy in Iraq," *Foreign Policy* 137 (July 2003): 1–55.

48. See Jon Finer, "The Last War—and the Next?," *Foreign Affairs* 98 (July 2019): 183–91.

49. Hal Brands and William Imboden, "Wisdom without Tears: Statecraft and the Uses of History," *Journal of Strategic Studies* 41 (2018): 916–46.

50. Bacevich, "The Real World War IV," 60.

51. Bob Woodward, *Obama's Wars* (New York: Simon & Schuster, 2010), 97.

52. For a sampling of lesson-drawing efforts, see Craig Whitlock, *The Afghanistan Papers* (New York: Simon & Schuster, 2021); Elliot Ackerman, *The Fifth Act: America's End in Afghanistan* (New York: Penguin, 2022); Russell K. Brooks and Brandon K. Brooks, "The End of Illusion?," *Small Wars Journal*, January 28, 2022; and David Petraeus, "Afghanistan Did Not Have to End This Way," *Atlantic*, August 8, 2022.

# Chapter 5: Society

1. Quincy Institute for Responsible Statecraft, https://quincyinst.org. The policy proposals listed later in this section can be accessed under the heading of policy briefs from its home page.

2. Daniel Deudney and G. John Ikenberry, "Misplaced Restraint," *Survival* 27 (July, 2021): 7–32.

3. Deudney and Ikenberry, "Misplaced Restraint."

4. Daniel Drezner, "What Do Neoconservatives and the Quincy Coalition Have in Common?," *Washington Post*, August 2, 2021.

5. Matthew Baum, "Circling the Wagons: Soft News and Isolationism in American Public Opinion," *International Studies Quarterly* 48 (2004): 313–38.

6. Kathryn Tempas, "Words vs. Deeds," *Brookings Review*, Summer 2003, 33–35.

7. Craig Katura and Dina Smeltz, "Who Matters for US Foreign Policymaking?," Chicago Council on Global Affairs, June 19, 2015.

8. On trade, see Max Ehrenfreund, "What Americans Really Think about Free Trade," *Washington Post*, March 25, 2016, https://www.washingtonpost.com/news/wonk/wp/2016/03/25/what-americans-really-think-about-free-trade.

9. Robert Erikson, Norman Luttbeg, and Kent Tedin, *American Public Opinion* (New York: Wiley, 1980), 44.

10. Barry Hughes, *The Domestic Context of American Foreign Policy* (San Francisco: Freeman, 1978), 31.

11. Ole R. Holsti and James N. Rosenau, *American Leadership in World Affairs: Vietnam and the Breakdown of Consensus* (Boston: Allen & Unwin, 1984), 218–20.

12. Lloyd Free and William Watts, "Internationalism Comes of Age . . . Again," *Public Opinion* 3 (1980): 46–50.

13. "American Isolationism, with a Very, Very Big Stick," *Foreign Policy*, May 17, 2016, http://foreignpolicy.com/2016/05/17/american-isolationism-with-a-very-very-big-stick-trump-clinton-election.

14. Center for American Progress, "America Adrift," May, 2019, https://www.americanprogress.org/article/america-adrift.

15. Pew Research Center, "Americans' Views of Key Foreign Policy Goals," April 15, 2021, https://www.pewresearch.org/fact-tank/2021/04/23/americans-views-of-key-foreign-policy-goals-depend-on-their-attitudes-toward-international-cooperation.

16. Economist/YouTube Poll, May 15–17, 2022, table 10A, https://docs.cdn.yougov.com/8ew54v1ohy/econTabReport.pdf.

17. Pew Research Center, "Conflicting Partisan Priorities for U.S. Foreign Policy," November 29, 2018, https://www.people-press.org/2018/11/29/conflicting-partisan-priorities-for-u-s-foreign-policy.

18. See Scott Clement, "Poll: Americans Also See Chemical Weapon 'Red Line' in Syria," *Washington Post*, December 20, 2012; Scott Clement, "Majority of Americans Say Afghan War Has Not Been Worth Fighting, Post-ABC News Poll Finds," *Washington Post*, December 12, 2013; Pew Research Center for the People and the Press, "Public Backs Diplomatic Approach in Syria, but Distrusts Syria and Russia," September 16, 2013.

19. Chicago Council on Global Affairs, "Americans Support Ukraine—but not with US Troops or a No Fly Zone," April 15, 2022, https://www.thechicagocouncil.org/sites/default/files/2022-04/Final%20US%20Ukraine%20Brief.pdf.

20. Bruce W. Jentleson, "The Pretty Prudent Public: Post-Vietnam American Opinion on the Use of Military Force," *International Studies Quarterly* 36 (1990): 49–74.

21. Miroslav Nincic, "Domestic Costs, the U.S. Public, and the Isolationist Calculus," *International Studies Quarterly* 41 (1997): 593–610; Robert Hormats, *The Price of Liberty: Paying for America's Wars* (New York: Times Books, 2007).

22. Marisa Abrajano and R. Michael Alvarez, "Hispanic Public Opinion and Partisanship in America," *Political Science Quarterly* 126 (2011): 255–85.

23. Washington Post–ABC Poll, August 13–17, 2014, reported in the *Washington Post*, http://apps.washingtonpost.com/g/page/politics/obama-and-iraq-post-abc-poll-aug-13-17-2014/1268.

24. Richard Eichenberg, "Gender Differences in Public Attitudes toward the Use of Force by the United States, 1990–2003," *International Security* 28 (2003): 110–41.

25. Leslie Gelb and Richard K. Betts, *The Irony of Vietnam: The System Worked* (Washington, DC: Brookings Institution Press, 1979).

26. Richard Sobel, *The Impact of Public Opinion on U.S. Foreign Policy since Vietnam* (New York: Oxford University Press, 2001).

27. Richard J. Barnett, *The Roots of War* (New York: Penguin, 1977), 243.

28. Timothy Hildebrandt, Courtney Hillebrecht, Peter Holm, and Jon Pevehouse, "The Domestic Politics of Humanitarian Intervention," *Foreign Policy Analysis* 9 (2013): 243–66.

29. Daniel Yankelovich, "The Tipping Points," *Foreign Affairs* 85 (2006): 115–25; "Poll Positions," *Foreign Affairs* 84 (2005): 2–16.

30. Gerald M. Pomper, *Elections in America: Control and Influence in Democratic Politics* (New York: Dodd, Mead, 1968), 251.

31. The figures through 1979 are discussed in Pomper, *Elections in America*, 19, and Hughes, *Domestic Context of American Foreign Policy*, 91. The 1993 data are from *Time* (October 4, 1993). The 2003 data are from Steven Kull, Clay Ramsey, and Evan Lewis, "Misperception, the Media, and the Iraq War," *Political Science Quarterly* 118 (2003): 569–98. The Ukraine data is from Morning Consult, https://morningconsult.com/2022/02/09/can-americans-find-ukraine-on-a-map.

32. Michael Abramowitz, "Terrorism Fades as Issue in 2008 Campaign," *Washington Post*, September 11, 2008, A6.

33. Charles Whalen, *The House and Foreign Policy* (Chapel Hill: University of North Carolina Press, 1982).

34. Peter Turbowitz and Jungkun Seo, "The China Card," *Political Science Quarterly* 127 (2012): 189–211.

35. William Schneider, "Conservatism, Not Interventionism: Trends in Foreign Policy Opinion, 1974–1982," in *Eagle Defiant: United States Foreign Policy in the 1980s*, ed. Kenneth Oye, Robert Lieber, and Donald Rothchild (Boston: Little, Brown, 1983).

36. William B. Quandt, "The Electoral Cycle and the Conduct of American Foreign Policy," *Political Science Quarterly* 101 (1986): 825–37.

37. Laurence Radway, "The Curse of Free Elections," *Foreign Policy* 40 (1980): 61–73.

38. Kerry Dumbright, "Interest Groups," in *Making China Policy: Lessons from the Bush and Clinton Administrations*, ed. Ramon Hawley Myers, Michel Oksenberg, and David L. Shambaugh (Lanham, MD: Rowman & Littlefield, 2001), 149–72.

39. C. W. Mills, *The Power Elite* (New York: Oxford University Press, 1956).

40. See Steven Rosen, ed., *Testing the Theory of the Military Industrial Complex* (Lexington, MA: Heath, 1973).

41. Martin Weil, "Can the Blacks Do for Africa What the Jews Did for Israel?," *Foreign Policy* 15 (1974): 109–29.

42. Charles McMathias Jr., "Ethnic Groups and Foreign Affairs," *Foreign Affairs* 59 (1981): 975–99.

43. Walter Russell Mead, "The New Israel and the Old: Why Gentile Americans Back the Jewish State," *Foreign Affairs* 87 (2008): 28–46.

44. Michael Abramowitz, "Jewish Liberals to Launch a Counterpoint to AIPAC," *Washington Post*, April 15, 2008, A13.

45. Mark Lander, "Potent Pro-Israeli Group Finds Its Momentum Blunted," *New York Times*, February 3, 2014, 4.

46. David J. Sadd and G. Neal Lendenmann, "Arab American Grievances," *Foreign Policy* 60 (1985): 17–29.

47. Fran Scott and Abdulah Osman, "Identity, African-Americans and U.S. Foreign Policy," in *Ethnic Identity Groups and U.S. Foreign Policy*, ed. Thomas Ambrosio, 71–92 (Westport, CT: Praeger, 2002).

48. Bill Richardson, "Hispanic American Concerns," *Foreign Policy* 60 (1985): 30–39.

49. Michael Jones-Correa, "Latinos and Latin America," in Ambrosio, ed., *Ethnic Identity Groups and U.S. Foreign Policy*, 115–30.

50. See Shawn Miller, "Trade Winds Stir Miami Storm," *Insight*, June 7, 1993; Carla Anne Robins, "Dateline Washington: Cuban-American Clout," *Foreign Policy* 88 (1992): 165–82.

51. "Shadow Diplomacy," http://100r.org/2013/07/shadow-diplomacy-african-nations-bypass-embassies-tap-lobbyists.

52. Eric Lipton, Brooke Williams, and Nicholas Confessore, "Foreign Powers Buy Influence at Think Tanks," *New York Times*, September 7, 2014, A1.

53. William Martin, "The Christian Right and American Foreign Policy," *Foreign Policy* 114 (1999): 66–80.

54. Asteris Huliaras, "The Evangelical Roots of U.S. Africa Policy," *Survival* 50 (2008–2009): 161–82.

55. Loveday Morris et al., "Long, Uneasy Love Affair of Israel and U.S. Evangelicals May Have Peaked," *Washington Post,* January 28, 2018, https://www.washingtonpost.com/world/the-long -uneasy-love-affair-of-israel-and-us-evangelicals-may-have-peaked/2018/01/27/6d751bd0-0051 -11e8-86b9-8908743c79dd_story.html.

56. James Lindsay, "The Apathy: How an Uninterested Public Is Reshaping Foreign Policy," *Foreign Affairs* 79 (2000): 2–8.

57. See "News Release," John F. Kennedy Library, January 24, 2012, https://www.jfklibrary.org/ About-Us/News-and-Press/Press-Releases/JFK-Library-Releases-Remaining-Presidential-Recordings .aspx.

58. See prepared statement by Michael R. Beschloss, "Impact of Television on U.S. Foreign Policy," hearing before the Committee on Foreign Affairs, House of Representatives, 103rd Cong., 2nd Sess. (April 26, 1994).

59. Trevor Thrall, "The Gulf in Reporting the Gulf War," *Breakthroughs* 2 (1992): 9–13.

60. Jacqueline Sharkey, "When Pictures Drive Foreign Policy," *American Journalism Review* 15 (December 1993): 14–19.

61. John Hamilton, *Journalism's Roving Eye: A History of American Foreign Reporting* (Baton Rouge: Louisiana State University Press, 2009), 459.

62. Lee Raine, Susannah Fox, and Deborah Fallows, *The Internet and the Iraq War: How Online Americans Have Used the Internet to Learn War News, Understand Events, and Promote Their Views,* Internet and American Life Project (Washington, DC: Pew Foundation, 2004).

63. Marc Lynch, Deen Freelon, and Sean Aday, *Syria's Socially Mediated Civil War, Peaceworks No. 91* (Washington, DC: U.S. Institute of Peace, 2014).

64. Paul Farhi, "Obama Official Says He Pushed a 'Narrative' to Media to Sell the Iran Nuclear Deal," *Washington Post,* May 6, 2016, https://www.washingtonpost.com/lifestyle/style/obama-official-says-he-pushed-a-narrative-to-media-to-sell-the-iran-nuclear-deal/2016/05/06/5b90d984 -13a1-11e6-8967-7ac733c56f12_story.html.

65. Paul Baines and Nigel Jones, "Influence and Interference in Foreign Elections," *RUSI Journal* 163 (March 2018): 12–19.

66. Simon Curtis and Michele Acuto, "The Foreign Policy of Cities," *RUSI Journal* 16 (December 2018): 8–17.

67. Cheney, as quoted in Herbert Abrams, "Weapons of Miller's Descriptions," *Bulletin of the Atomic Scientists* 60 (July/August 2004): 63; for Panetta's quote, see Paula Newton, "Panetta: Polls Won't Change Afghan Strategy," CNN, March 27, 2012, http://www.cnn.com/2012/03/27/politics/ panetta-afghanistan.

68. Bernard Cohen, *The Public's Impact on Foreign Policy* (Boston: Little, Brown, 1973), 117.

69. David Skidmore, *The Unilateralist Temptation in American Foreign Policy* (New York: Routledge, 2011), 36–38.

70. Thomas Knecht, *Paying Attention to Foreign Affairs* (University Park: Penn State University Press, 2010).

71. Kori Schake, "Back to Basics," *Foreign Affairs* 98 (May, 2019): 36–43.

72. Michael Hirsh, "How America's Top Tech Companies Created the Surveillance State," *National Journal,* July 25, 2013.

# Chapter 6: Congress

1. Norman Ornstein and Thomas Mann, "When Congress Checks Out," *Foreign Affairs* 85 (2006): 67–82.

2. Douglas Bennett Jr., "Congress in Foreign Policy: Who Needs It?," *Foreign Affairs* 57 (1978): 40–50.

3. For a study of congressional nondecisions, those where its voice is not raised, see Michael Hayes, "Congress and War Powers: Symbolism and Nondecisions in the Struggle for Influence," *Congress and the Presidency* 45 (2018): 185–207.

4. For a statement of this position, see Jon Kyl, Douglas Feithr, and John Fonte, "The War of Law: How New International Law Undermines Democratic Sovereignty," *Foreign Affairs* 92 (2013): 115–25.

5. David Auerswald and Forrest Maltzman, "Policymaking through Advice and Consent: Treaty Consideration by the United States Senate," *Journal of Politics* 65 (2003): 1102.

6. Auerswald and Maltzman, "Policymaking through Advice and Consent," 1097–1110; C. James DeLaet and James M. Scott, "Treaty-Making and Partisan Politics: Arms Control and the U.S. Senate, 1960–2001," *Foreign Policy Analysis* 2 (2006): 177–200.

7. See David Auerswald, "Senate Reservations to Security Treaties," *Foreign Policy Analysis* 2 (2006): 83–100.

8. William L. Furlong, "Negotiations and Ratification of the Panama Canal Treaty," in *Congress, the Presidency, and American Foreign Policy*, ed. John Spanier and Joseph Nogee, 77–107 (Elmsford, NY: Pergamon, 1981).

9. Matthew Weed, *The War Powers Resolution* (Washington, DC: Congressional Research Service, March 8, 2019), https://fas.org/sgp/crs/natsec/R42699.pdf.

10. War Powers Resolution Reporting Project, https://warpowers.lawandsecurity.org/findingsandanalysis.

11. Congressional Research Service, *Foreign Policy Effects of the Supreme Court's Legislative Veto Decision* (Washington, DC: Congressional Research Service, February 23, 1984).

12. James A. Robinson, *Congress and Foreign Policy Making: A Study in Legislative Influence and Initiative* (Homewood, IL: Dorsey, 1962), 110.

13. I. M. Destler, "Dateline Washington: Congress as Boss," *Foreign Policy* 42 (1981): 161–80.

14. *Congressional Record*, January 11, 1991, S250–S251.

15. Douglas Kriner and Eric Schickler, "The Resilience of Separation of Powers? Congress and the Russia Investigation," *Presidential Studies Quarterly* 48 (September 2018): 436–55.

16. Quoted in Victor Marchetti and John Marks, *The CIA and the Cult of Intelligence* (New York: Dell, 1980), 324.

17. For an account of why little has really changed, see Amy Zegart, "The Domestic Politics of Irrational Intelligence Oversight," *Political Science Quarterly* 126 (2011): 1–25.

18. William Corson, *Armies of Ignorance: The Rise of the American Intelligence Empire* (New York: Dial, 1977), 472.

19. John Stockwell, *In Search of Enemies: A CIA Story* (New York: Norton, 1978), 47.

20. Roger H. Davidson, "Subcommittee Government: New Channels for Policy Making," in *The New Congress*, ed. Thomas E. Mann and Norman J. Ornstein (Washington, DC: American Enterprise Institute, 1981).

21. Thomas L. Brewer, *American Foreign Policy: A Contemporary Introduction*, 2nd ed. (Englewood Cliffs, NJ: Prentice Hall, 1986), 119.

22. David Price, *Who Makes the Laws?* (Cambridge, MA: Schenkman, 1972), 330.

23. Joshua Muravchik, *The Senate and National Security: A New Mood*, Washington Paper #80 (Beverly Hills, CA: Sage, 1980), 57–60.

24. For a discussion of congressional staffs, see Michael J. Malbin, "Delegation, Deliberation, and the New Role of Congressional Staff," in Mann and Ornstein, *The New Congress*, 134–77; Muravchik, *The Senate and National Security*.

25. James A. Smith, *The Idea Brokers: Think Tanks and the Rise of the New Policy Elite* (New York: Free Press, 1991); David Newsom, *The Public and Foreign Policy* (Bloomington: Indiana University Press, 1996).

26. James Kitfield, "The Folk Who Live on the Hill," *National Interest* 58 (1999/2000): 48–55.

27. Peter Trubowitz, *Defining the National Interest* (Chicago: University of Chicago Press, 1998).

28. Ellen Cutrone and Benjamin Fordham, "Commerce and Imagination," *International Studies Quarterly* 54 (2010): 633–56.

29. Dan Eggen, "U.S. Is Given Failing Grades by 9/11 Panel," *Washington Post*, December 6, 2006, A1.

30. Trent Lott, "Special Commissions," *Congressional Record*, September 23, 2002, S9050–S9053.

31. James Scott and Ralph Carter, "Acting on the Hill," *Congress and the Presidency* 29 (2002): 151–69; Ralph Carter and James Scott, "Striking a Balance: Congress and U.S. Foreign Policy," in *American Foreign Policy Today: American Renewal?*, ed. Steven Hook and James Scott, 36–53 (Washington, DC: CQ Press, 2012).

32. Miller Center of Public Affairs, University of Virginia, *National War Powers Commission Report* (2008).

33. Responsible Statecraft, "Bipartisan Majorities Want More Control for 'the People' on War and Arms Sales," March 29, 2022, https://responsiblestatecraft.org/2022/03/29/bipartisan-majorities -want-more-control-for-the-people-on-war-and-arms-sales.

# Chapter 7: Presidency

1. Richard Neustadt, *Presidential Power, the Politics of Leadership* (New York: Free Press, 1960).

2. Hugh Heclo, "Introduction: The Presidential Illusion," in *The Illusion of Presidential Government*, ed. Hugh Heclo and Lester M. Salamon (Boulder, CO: Westview, 1981), 1.

3. Bob Woodward, *State of Denial: Bush at War, Part III* (New York: Simon & Schuster, 2006), 212.

4. Terry Moe and William G. Howell, "Unilateral Action and Presidential Power: A Theory," *Presidential Studies Quarterly* 29 (1999): 850–72.

5. See U.S. State Department, Treaties and Other International Acts Series, for a yearly listing and summary.

6. James A. Nathan and Richard K. Oliver, *Foreign Policy Making and the American Political System* (Boston: Little, Brown, 1983), 115.

7. Walter Pincus, "Secret Presidential Pledges over Years Erected U.S. Shield for Saudis," *Washington Post*, February 9, 1992, A20.

8. Charles W. Kegley Jr. and Eugene R. Wittkopf, *American Foreign Policy: Pattern and Process*, 2nd ed. (New York: St. Martin's, 1982), 418.

9. George W. Bush, "Statement on Signing the Department of Defense, Energy Supplemental Appropriations to Address Hurricanes in the Gulf of Mexico and Pandemic Influenza Act, 2006," *Weekly Compilation of Presidential Documents* (December 30, 2005), 1918–19.

10. David Kaye, "Stealth Multilateralism," *Foreign Affairs* 92 (2013): 113–24.

11. Ryan Hendrickson, *The Clinton Wars: The Constitution, Congress, and War Powers* (Nashville, TN: Vanderbilt University Press, 2002), 1.

12. Charlie Savage, "2 Top Lawyers Lost to Obama in Libya War Policy Debate," *New York Times*, June 17, 2011, 1.

13. John Stoessinger, *Crusaders and Pragmatists: Movers of Modern American Foreign Policy* (New York: Norton, 1979).

14. Fred I. Greenstein, *Personality and Politics* (Chicago: Markham, 1969).

15. Robert Jervis, "Do Leaders Matter and How Would We Know?," *Security Studies* 22 (2013): 153–79.

16. James David Barber, *The Presidential Character: Predicting Performance in the White House*, 3rd ed. (Englewood Cliffs, NJ: Prentice Hall, 1985). Also see Alexander George, "Assessing Presidential Character," *World Politics* 26 (1974): 234–82. For other formulations of presidential personality, see Lloyd S. Etheridge, "Personality Effects on American Foreign Policy, 1898–1968: A Test of Interpersonal Generalization Theory," *American Political Science Review* 72 (1978): 434–51; Stoessinger, *Crusaders and Pragmatists.*

17. On Obama, see Stanley Renshon, "Psychological Reflections on Barack Obama and John McCain: Assessing the Contours of a New Presidential Administration," *Political Science Quarterly* 123 (2008): 391–433, and "Understanding the Obama Doctrine," *White House Studies* 12 (2012): 187–202.

18. Fred I. Greenstein, *The Hidden Hand Presidency: Eisenhower as Leader* (New York: Basic Books, 1982).

19. See Ilan Peleg, *The Legacy of George Bush's Foreign Policy* (Boulder, CO: Westview, 2009), 75–98. Peleg classifies Bush as an active-negative.

20. Bob Woodward, *Bush at War* (New York: Simon & Schuster, 2002), 256.

21. Zbigniew Brzezinski, *Second Chance: Three Presidents and the Crisis of American Superpower* (New York: Basic Books, 2007), 11, 86–87, 137.

22. George Bush and Brent Scowcroft, *A World Transformed* (New York: Vintage, 1998), 225, 381.

23. Donald M. Snow and Eugene Brown, *Puzzle Palaces and Foggy Bottom: U.S. Foreign and Defense Policy-Making in the 1990s* (New York: St. Martin's, 1994), 44–70.

24. Zbigniew Brzezinski, "The NSC's Midlife Crisis," *Foreign Policy* 69 (1987/88): 80–99.

25. For a reinterpretation of the Eisenhower NSC experience, see Fred Greenstein and Richard Immerman, "Effective National Security Advising: Recovering the Eisenhower Legacy," *Political Science Quarterly* 115 (2000): 335–45.

26. William Bundy, "The National Security Process: Plus Change . . . ," *International Security* 7 (1982/83): 94–109.

27. On the Nixon NSC system, see John Leacacos, "Kissinger's Apparat," *Foreign Policy* 5 (1971): 2–27.

28. Robert E. Hunter, *Presidential Control of Foreign Policy: Management or Mishap*, Washington Paper #91 (New York: Praeger, 1982), 35–36.

29. Terry Diehl, "Reagan's Mixed Legacy," *Foreign Policy* 75 (1989): 34–55.

30. Colin Campbell, "Unrestrained Ideological Entrepreneurship in the Bush II Advisory System," in *The George W. Bush Presidency*, ed. Colin Campbell and Bert Rockman, 73–104 (Washington, DC: Congressional Quarterly Press, 2004).

31. Paul Pillar, "The Right Stuff," *The National Interest* 91 (2007): 53.

32. Bob Woodward, *Obama's Wars* (New York: Simon & Schuster), 289.

33. Paul Kengor, "Cheney and Vice Presidential Power," in *Considering the Bush Presidency*, ed. Gary Gregg II and Mark Rozell, 160–76 (New York: Oxford University Press, 2004); "The Vice President, Secretary of State, and Foreign Policy," *Political Science Quarterly* 115 (2000): 175–99.

34. James Oliver, "Pragmatic Fathers and Ideological Suns: Foreign Policy in the Administrations of George H. W. Bush and George W. Bush," *White House Studies* 7 (2007): 203.

35. Peter Baker, *Days of Fire: Bush and Cheney in the White House* (New York: Doubleday, 2013).

36. For a history of chief of staff–presidential relations, see Chris Wipple, *Gatekeepers: How the White House Chiefs of Staff Define Every Presidency* (Murfreesboro, TN: Diversified Publishing, 2017).

37. Kurt Campbell and James Steinberg, *Difficult Transitions* (Washington, D.C.: Brookings, 2008).

# Chapter 8: Bureaucracy

1. See William Burns, "The Lost Art of American Diplomacy," *Foreign Affairs* 98 (May 2019): 98–107; Uzra Zeya and Jon Finer, *Revitalizing the State Department and American Diplomacy* (New

York: Council on Foreign Relations, 2020); and Ian Brzezinski and Frank Carlucci, *State Department Reform* (New York: Council on Foreign Relations, 2007).

2. Henry Kissinger, "Conditions of World Order," *Daedalus* 95 (1966): 503–29.

3. "No Point in Being Bitter," *Washington Post*, December 31, 2006, B1.

4. Jeffrey Goldberg, "The Obama Doctrine," *The Atlantic*, April 1, 2016.

5. On the volume of State Department message traffic, see Werner Feld, *American Foreign Policy: Aspirations and Reality* (New York: John Wiley, 1984), 61; Gene Rainey, *Patterns of American Foreign Policy* (Boston: Allyn & Bacon, 1975), 175.

6. J. Anthony Holmes, "Where Are the Civilians? How to Rebuild the U.S. Foreign Service," *Foreign Affairs* 88 (2009): 148–60.

7. Donald Warwick, *A Theory of Public Bureaucracy: Politics, Personality and Organization in the State Department* (Cambridge, MA: Harvard University Press, 1975), 29–30.

8. Henry T. Nash, *American Foreign Policy: A Search for Security*, 3rd ed. (Homewood, IL: Dorsey, 1985), 141.

9. Paul Richter and Tom Hamburger, "Few Blacks Serve in Top U.S. Diplomatic Posts," *Los Angeles Times*, March 16, 2010.

10. Burns, "Lost Art of American Diplomacy."

11. In addition to other studies cited in this chapter, see Andrew Scott, "The Department of State: Formal Organization and Informal Culture," *International Studies Quarterly* 13 (1969): 1–18; Andrew Scott, "Environmental Change and Organizational Adaptation: The Problem of the State Department," *International Studies Quarterly* 14 (1970): 85–94.

12. John Harr, *The Professional Diplomat* (Princeton, NJ: Princeton University Press, 1969), 197–98.

13. I. M. Destler, *Presidents, Bureaucrats, and Foreign Policy: The Politics of Organizational Reform* (Princeton, NJ: Princeton University Press, 1972), 158.

14. Robert Pringle, "Creeping Irrelevance at Foggy Bottom," *Foreign Policy* 29 (1977/78): 128–39; Warwick, *Theory of Public Bureaucracy*, 72.

15. Richard Betts, "The National Security Act, Seventy Years On," *American Interest* 12 (March 2017): 75–84.

16. For a discussion on the pros and cons of reorganizing the JCS system, see William J. Lynn and Barry R. Posen, "The Case for JCS Reform," *International Security* 10 (1985/86): 69–97; MacKubin Thomas Owen, "The Hollow Promise of JCS Reform," *International Security* 10 (1985/86): 98–111; Edward Luttwak, *The Pentagon and the Art of War* (New York: Touchstone, 1985).

17. Peter Hussy, "The Four Great Waves of Defense Neglect," Gatestone Institute, January 10, 2014, https://www.gatestoneinstitute.org/4125/defense-neglect-hollow-military.

18. James Roherty, "The Office of the Secretary of Defense," in *American Defense Policy*, ed. John E. Endicott and Roy W. Stafford, 4th ed., 286–96 (Baltimore, MD: Johns Hopkins University Press, 1977).

19. Amos A. Jordan and William J. Taylor Jr., *American National Security: Policy and Process* (Baltimore, MD: Johns Hopkins University Press, 1981), 185.

20. Bob Woodward, *State of Denial: Bush at War, Part III* (New York: Simon & Schuster, 2006), 39.

21. John H. Garrison, "The Political Dimension of Military Professionalism," in Endicott and Stafford, *American Defense Policy*, 578–87.

22. Risa Brooks, Jim Golby, and Heidi Urben, "Crisis of Command," *Foreign Affairs* 100 (May 2021): 63–75.

23. Carl Builder, *The Masks of War: American Military Styles in Strategy and Analysis* (Baltimore, MD: Johns Hopkins University Press, 1989).

24. Christian Brose, "The New Revolution in Military Affairs," *Foreign Affairs* 98 (May 2019): 122–34.

25. Philip Rucker and Carol Leoning, *A Very Stable Genius: Donald J. Trump's Testing of America* (New York: Penguin, 2020).

26. Richard K. Betts, *Soldiers, Statesmen, and Cold War Crises* (Cambridge, MA: Harvard University Press, 1977), 4–5.

27. Bob Woodward, *The Commanders* (New York: Simon & Schuster, 1991), 33.

28. Mark Lowenthal, *U.S. Intelligence: Evolution and Anatomy,* Washington Paper #105 (New York: Praeger, 1984), 89–92; Stafford Thomas, *The U.S. Intelligence Community* (Lanham, MD: University of America Press, 1983), 45–63; and Amy Zegart, *Flawed by Design: The Evolution of the CIA, JSC, and NSC* (Stanford, CA: Stanford University Press, 1999).

29. James Bamford, *The Puzzle Palace: Inside the National Security Agency* (Baltimore, MD: Penguin, 1982).

30. See, for example, Herbert Meyer, "Reinventing the CIA," *Global Affairs* 7 (1992): 1–13; Marvin Ott, "Shaking up the CIA," *Foreign Policy* 93 (1993): 132–51.

31. For a discussion of these points, see Patrick J. McGarvey, *The CIA: The Myth and the Madness* (Baltimore, MD: Penguin, 1973), 148–59; Victor Marchetti and John D. Marks, *The CIA and the Cult of Intelligence* (New York: Dell, 1974), 235–77.

32. Chris Demchak, "Conflicting Policy Presumptions about Cybersecurity," *Atlantic Council Issue Briefs,* http://www.acus.org/files/publication_pdfs/403/_Demchakbrief.pdf.

33. Roger Hilsman, *Strategic Intelligence and National Defense* (Glencoe, IL: Free Press, 1956), 199–222; Thomas L. Hughes, *The Fate of Facts in a World of Men,* Headline Series #233 (New York: Foreign Policy Association, 1976), 36–60.

34. Sherman Kent, *Strategic Intelligence for American World Policy* (Princeton, NJ: Princeton University Press, 1966); Willmoore Kendall, "The Functions of Intelligence," *World Politics* 2 (1949): 542–52.

35. Paul Pillar, "Think Again: Intelligence," *Foreign Policy* 191 (January/February 2012): 52.

36. Hilsman, *Strategic Intelligence and National Defense,* 37–56.

37. Hughes, *Fate of Facts in a World of Men,* 47.

38. Thomas Hughes, "The Power to Speak and the Power to Listen: Reflections on Bureaucratic Politics and a Recommendation on Information Flows," in *Secrecy and Foreign Policy,* Thomas M. Franck and Edward Weisband (New York: Oxford University Press, 1974), 18.

39. Raymond Hopkins, "The International Role of 'Domestic Bureaucracies,'" *International Organization* 30 (1976): 411.

40. Hopkins, "International Role of 'Domestic Bureaucracies,'" 41.

41. Stephen D. Cohen, *The Making of United States International Economic Policy: Principles, Problems, and Proposals for Reform,* 2nd ed. (New York: Praeger, 1981), 40.

42. Morton Abramowitz and Leslie Gelb, "In Defense of Striped Pants," *National Interest* 79 (2005): 73–77.

43. Quoted in Destler, *Presidents, Bureaucrats, and Foreign Policy,* 155.

44. Paul Bracken, "The Military after Next," *Washington Quarterly* 16 (1993): 157–74.

45. James Moltz, "The Changing Dynamics of Twenty-First-Century Space Power," *Strategic Studies Quarterly* 13 (2019): 66–94.

# Chapter 9: Policy-Making Models

1. A short summary of additional models can be found in Thomas L. Brewer, *American Foreign Policy: A Contemporary Introduction,* 2nd ed. (Englewood Cliffs, NJ: Prentice Hall, 1986), 26–54.

2. Roger Hilsman, "Policy Making Is Politics," in *Perspectives on American Foreign Policy: Selected Readings,* ed. Charles W. Kegley Jr. and Eugene R. Wittkopf (New York: St. Martin's, 1983), 250.

3. Hilsman, "Policy Making Is Politics," 251.

4. Leslie H. Gelb and Richard K. Betts, *The Irony of Vietnam: The System Worked* (Washington, DC: Brookings Institution Press, 1979).

5. Patrick Morgan, *Theories and Approaches to International Politics: What Are We to Think?*, 3rd ed. (New Brunswick: Transaction, 1981), 110.

6. Herbert A. Simon, *Administrative Behavior: A Study of Decision Making Processes in Administrative Organization*, 3rd ed. (New York: Free Press, 1976).

7. Jack Levy, "Prospect Theory, Rational Choice and International Relations," *International Studies Quarterly* 41 (1997): 87–112.

8. Graham T. Allison, *Essence of Decision: Explaining the Cuban Missile Crisis* (Boston: Little, Brown, 1971), 35.

9. I. M. Destler, *Presidents, Bureaucrats, and Foreign Policy: The Politics of Organizational Reform* (Princeton, NJ: Princeton University Press, 1974), 52.

10. As originally presented by Allison in his *Essence of Decision*, two separate models were used to explain foreign policy making through organizational routines and governmental politics. Subsequently, Allison combined them into one model, as is done here. See Graham T. Allison and Morton H. Halperin, "Bureaucratic Politics: A Paradigm and Some Policy Implications," *World Politics* 24 (1982): 40–79.

11. Robert L. Gallucci, *Neither Peace nor Honor: The Politics of American Military Policy in Vietnam* (Baltimore, MD: Johns Hopkins University Press, 1975), 153.

12. Robert J. Art, "Bureaucratic Politics and American Foreign Policy: A Critique," in *International Politics: Anarchy, Force, Political Economy, and Decision Making*, ed. Robert J. Art and Robert Jervis, 2nd ed. (Boston: Little, Brown, 1985), 471; Stephen D. Krasner, "Are Bureaucrats Important? (or Allison Wonderland)," *Foreign Policy* 7 (1972): 159–79; Jerel Rosati, "Developing a Systematic Decision Making Framework: Bureaucratic Politics in Perspective," *World Politics* 33 (1981): 234–51.

13. Jonathan Bendor and Thomas H. Hammand, "Rethinking Allison's Models," *American Political Science Review* 86 (1992): 301–22.

14. Robert L. Wendzel, *International Politics: Policymakers and Policymaking* (New York: John Wiley, 1981), 439.

15. Wendzel, *International Politics*, 438.

16. Robert E. Hunter, *Presidential Control of Foreign Policy: Management or Mishap?*, Washington Paper #191 (New York: Praeger, 1982), 35–46.

17. Irving L. Janis, *Groupthink: Psychological Studies of Policy Decisions and Fiascos*, 2nd ed. (Boston: Houghton Mifflin, 1982).

18. Janis, *Groupthink*, 9.

19. Janis, *Groupthink*, 256.

20. Janis, *Groupthink*, 172, 262–71.

21. Richard K. Betts, "Analysis, War, and Decision: Why Intelligence Failures Are Inevitable," *World Politics* 31 (1978): 61–89.

22. Carol Barner-Barry and Robert Rosenwein, *Psychological Perspectives on Politics* (Englewood Cliffs, NJ: Prentice Hall, 1985), 247.

23. Irving L. Janis and Leon Mann, *Decision Making: A Psychological Analysis of Conflict, Choice, and Commitment* (New York: Free Press, 1977).

24. John Steinbrenner, *The Cybernetic Theory of Decision* (Princeton, NJ: Princeton University Press, 1974).

25. Mark Schafer and Scott Crichlow, "The Process-Outcome Connection in Foreign Policy Decision Making," *International Studies Quarterly* 46 (2002): 45–68; Alexander George and Erick Stern, "Harnessing Conflicts in Foreign Policy Making," *Presidential Studies Quarterly* 32 (2002): 484–508.

26. Dina Badie, "Groupthink, Iraq and the War on Terror," *Foreign Policy Analysis* 6 (2010): 277–96.

27. Compare Gabriel Kolko, *The Roots of American Foreign Policy* (Boston: Beacon, 1969), with C. Wright Mills, *The Power Elite* (New York: Oxford University Press, 1956).

28. Robert A. Dahl, "A Critique of the Ruling Elite Model," in *C. Wright Mills and the Power Elite*, ed. G. William Domhoff and Hoyt B. Ballard (Boston: Beacon, 1968), 31.

29. Theodore J. Lowi, *The End of Liberalism: Ideology, Policy, and the Crisis of Public Authority* (New York: Norton, 1969).

30. Niall Ferguson, "Sinking Globalization," *Foreign Affairs* 84 (2005): 64–77.

31. Glenn H. Snyder and Paul Diesing, *Conflict among Nations: Bargaining, Decision-Making, and System Structure in International Crises* (Princeton, NJ: Princeton University Press, 1977), 355.

32. Alex Mintz, "How Do Leaders Make Decisions? A Poliheuristic Perspective," *Journal of Conflict Resolution* 48 (2004): 3–13.

33. For a discussion of Cuban missile crisis decision making, see Graham T. Allison, *The Essence of Decision: Explaining the Cuban Missile Crisis* (Boston: Little, Brown, 1971); Theodore Sorensen, *Kennedy* (New York: Harper & Row, 1965); Richard Ned Lebow, *Between Peace and War: The Nature of International Crisis* (Baltimore, MD: Johns Hopkins University Press, 1981).

34. James A. Nathan and James K. Oliver, *United States Foreign Policy and World Order*, 3rd ed. (Boston: Little, Brown, 1985), 275.

35. Allison, *The Essence of Decision*, 103.

36. Allison, *The Essence of Decision*, 58–61.

37. Walter Pincus, "Standing at the Brink of Nuclear War," *Washington Post*, July 25, 1985, A10.

38. Allison, *The Essence of Decision*, 64.

39. "The Decision Would Take Out Only the Known Missiles," *Washington Post*, July 25, 1985, A1.

40. The most important of these is Raymond Garthoff, *Reflections on the Cuban Missile Crisis*, rev. ed. (Washington, DC: Brookings Institution Press, 1989). The revised edition contains insights into the crisis that came out of a joint U.S.-Soviet conference on the Cuban missile crisis held in 1987.

41. Janis, *Groupthink*, 132–58.

42. Lebow, *Between Peace and War*, esp. chap. 8.

43. See his comments at https://www.newsweek.com/donald-trump-how-he-makes-decisions-i-dont-think-about-them-1221314.

44. One classic model that does try is the decision-making model presented by Richard Snyder, H. W. Bruck, and Burton Sapin in "Decision Making as an Approach to the Study of International Politics," in *Foreign Policy Decision Making*, ed. Richard Snyder, H. W. Bruck, and Burton Sapin (New York: Free Press, 1963).

45. Ashley Parker and Philip Rucker, "You're the Prop in the Back," *Washington Post*, September 12, 2019, A1.

# Chapter 10: Diplomacy

1. Fred Ikle, *How Nations Negotiate* (New York: Harper & Row, 1964), ix.

2. Pamela Aall et al., "A New Concert? Diplomacy for a Chaotic World," *Survival* 62 (December 2020): 77–94.

3. Jonathan Terperman, "Some Hard Truths about Multilateralism," *World Policy Journal* 21 (2004): 27–36.

4. Antonia Chayes, "How American Treaty Behavior Threatens National Security," *International Security* 33 (2008): 45–81.

5. Jakub Grygiel, "The Diplomacy Fallacy," *American Interest* 3 (2008): 26–35.

6. Tara Miller, "Diplomacy Derailed: The Consequences of Diplomatic Sanctions," *Washington Quarterly* 33 (2010): 61–79.

7. Richard N. Haass and Meghan L. O'Sullivan, eds., *Honey and Vinegar: Incentives, Sanctions, and Foreign Policy* (Washington, DC: Brookings Institution Press, 2000).

8. For references to the positive contributions of summitry, see Robert Putnam, "Summit Sense," *Foreign Policy* 55 (1984): 73–91.

9. For a discussion of the negative contributions of summitry, see J. Robert Schaetzel and H. B. Malmgren, "Talking Heads," *Foreign Policy* 39 (1980): 130–42.

10. Adam B. Ulam, *Dangerous Relations: The Soviet Union in World Politics, 1970–1982* (New York: Oxford University Press, 1983), 186.

11. For the case of economic summits, see Ulam, *Dangerous Relations*, 138; for examples from arms control talks, see the discussion in Strobe Talbot, *Deadly Gambits* (New York: Vintage, 1984).

12. Quoted in Glenn Kessler, "Road Map Setbacks Highlight U.S. Pattern," *Washington Post*, October 6, 2003, 1.

13. George de Menil, "The Process of Economic Summitry," in *Economic Summitry*, ed. George de Menil and Anthony M. Solomon, 55–63 (New York: Council on Foreign Relations, 1983).

14. Richard Nixon, "Superpower Summitry," *Foreign Affairs* 64 (1985): 1–11.

15. Shannon O'Neil, "The Myth of the Global," *Foreign Affairs* 101 (July 2022): 158–69.

16. Richard Elliot Benedick, *Ozone Diplomacy: New Directions in Safeguarding the Planet* (Cambridge, MA: Harvard University Press, 1991).

17. G. John Ikenberry, "The Next Liberal Order," *Foreign Affairs* 99 (July, 2020): 133–42.

18. This discussion is based on W. Michael Reisman, "The United States and International Institutions," *Survival* 41 (Winter 1999–2000): 62–80, although the definition of roles is slightly different.

19. Katherine Brown et al., *Public Diplomacy and National Security in* 2017 (Washington, DC: Center for Strategic and International Studies, 2017).

20. Giacomo Chicozza, *Anti-Americanism and the American World* (Baltimore, MD: Johns Hopkins University Press, 2009).

21. Sanford Unger, "Pitch Imperfect," *Foreign Affairs* 84 (2005): 7–13.

22. Barry M. Blechman and Stephen S. Kaplan, *Force without War: U.S. Armed Forces as a Political Instrument* (Washington, DC: Brookings Institution Press, 1978).

23. On the question of nuclear weapons and coercion, see Todd Sechser and Matthew Fuhrmann, *Nuclear Weapons and Coercive Diplomacy* (Cambridge: Cambridge University Press, 2017).

24. Scott Sagan and Jeremi Suri, "The Madman Nuclear Alert," *International Security* 27 (2003): 150–83; William Burr and Jeffrey Kimball, "Nixon's Nuclear Ploy," *Bulletin of the Atomic Scientists* 59 (2003): 28–37, 72–73.

25. Sagan and Suri, "The Madman Nuclear Alert," 156.

26. For background data on arms transfers, their history, the policies of specific states, and a discussion of their rationale, see Stephanie G. Neuman and Robert E. Harkavy, eds., *Arms Transfers in the Modern World* (New York: Praeger, 1980); Andrew J. Pierre, *The Global Politics of Arms Sales* (Princeton, NJ: Princeton University Press, 1982); Michael T. Klare, *American Arms Supermarket* (Austin: University of Texas Press, 1984).

27. Edward Kolodiej, "Arms Transfers and International Politics: The Interdependence of Independence," in Neuman and Harkavy, *Arms Transfers in the Modern World*, 3.

28. Klare, *American Arms Supermarket*, 43–44.

29. Quoted in Karen DeYoung and Karin Brulliard, "U.S. Breach with Pakistan Shows Imbalance between Diplomatic, Security Goals," *Washington Post*, December 4, 2011.

30. For suggestions of how the United States might proceed, see the symposium "America's Alliances," *American Interest* 6 (Summer 2011): 37–69.

31. Thomas Hale, "A Climate Coalition of the Willing," *Washington Quarterly* 34 (2011): 89–101.

32. Stine Aakre, "The Political Feasibility of Potent Enforcement in a Post-Kyoto Climate Agreement," *International Environmental Agreements* 16 (2016): 145–59.

33. Rajiv Shah, "A New Development Model for a World in Crisis," *Foreign Affairs* 100 (September, 2021): 179–92.

# Chapter 11: Economic Instruments

1. Robert Blackwell and Jennifer Harris, "The Lost Art of Economic Statecraft," *Foreign Affairs* 95, no. 2 (March 2016): 99–110.

2. Walter Russell Mead, "America's Sticky Power," *Foreign Policy* 141 (2004): 46–53.

3. For a discussion of evaluating economic statecraft that focuses on foreign aid, see Mariann Lawson, *Does Foreign Aid Work?* (Washington, DC: Congressional Research Service, February 13, 2013).

4. David Baldwin, *Economic Statecraft* (Princeton, NJ: Princeton University Press, 1985), makes this point throughout. The statement is found on page 115.

5. See Barry Eichengreen, "What Money Can't Buy," *Foreign Affairs* 101 (July 2022): 64–73.

6. Stephen R. Weissman and Johnnie Carson, "Economic Sanctions against Rhodesia," in *Congress, the Presidency, and American Foreign Policy*, ed. John Spanier and Joseph Nogee, 132–60 (New York: Pergamon, 1981).

7. Baldwin, *Economic Statecraft*, 44–47, 207–9.

8. Theodore Moran, "Empirical Studies of Strategic Trade Policy," *International Organization* 50 (1996): 175–205.

9. Robert Merry, "Protectionism in America," *National Interest* 146 (2016): 28–36.

10. Kristen Hopewell, "The Liberal International Economic Order on the Brink," *Current History* 116 (November 2017): 303–8.

11. http://useconomy.about.com/od/Trade-Agreements/fl/What-Is-the-Trans-Pacific-Partnership.htm.

12. U.S. Department of the Treasury, "*Sanctions Programs*," http://www.treasury.gov/resource-center/sanctions/programs.

13. Meghan O'Sullivan, *Shrewd Sanctions: Statecraft and State Sponsors of Terrorism* (Washington, DC: Brookings Institution Press, 2003): 12.

14. Bryan Early and Keith Preble, "Going Fishing Versus Hunting Whales," *Security Studies* 29 (2020): 251–67.

15. Richard Nephew, "The Hard Part: The Art of Sanctions Relief," *Washington Quarterly* 41 (2018): 63–77.

16. Emre Hatipoglu, "A Story of Institutional Misfit," *Foreign Policy Analysis* 10 (2014): 431–45.

17. Meghan O'Sullivan, "Iran and the Great Sanctions Debate," *Washington Quarterly* 33 (2010): 7–21.

18. Bryan Early, "Unmasking the Black Knights," *Foreign Policy Analysis* 7 (2011): 381–402.

19. Arne Tostensen and Beate Bull, "Are Smart Sanctions Feasible?," *World Politics* 54 (2002): 373–403; and Edward Fishman, "Even Smarter Sanctions," *Foreign Affairs* 96 (November 2017): 102–10.

20. Valdislav Inozemtsev, "Yes, Sanctions Work," *Foreign Affairs* 94 (March 2015): 33–38.

21. Emma Ashford, "Not-So-Smart Sanctions," *Foreign Affairs* 95 (January 2016): 114–23.

22. See Carol Adelman, "Global Philanthropy and Beyond," *Georgetown Journal of International Affairs* 13 (2012): 15–24; James Stavridis and Evelyn Farkas, "The 21st Century Force Multiplier," *Washington Quarterly* 35 (2012): 7–20.

23. *Development and the National Interest* (Washington, DC: Agency for International Development, 1988).

24. "The 1992 Campaign; Transcript of 2d TV Debate between Bush, Clinton and Perot," *New York Times*, October 16, 1992.

25. Gene Sperling and Tom Hart, "A Better Way to Fight Global Poverty," *Foreign Affairs* 82 (2003): 9–14; Lael Brainard, "Compassionate Conservatism Confronts Global Poverty," *Washington Quarterly* 26 (2003): 149–69.

26. Colin Powell, "No Country Left Behind," *Foreign Policy* 146 (January/February 2005): 30–35.

# Chapter 12: Military Instruments: Big Wars

1. Gary Samore, "North Korean Verification," *Bulletin of the Atomic Scientists* 74 (2018): 312–16.

2. For an overview discussion of the problems of perceptions here, see Robert Jervis and Mira Rapp-Hooper, "Perception and Misperception on the Korean Peninsula," *Foreign Affairs* 97 (May 2018): 103–17.

3. For a recent commentary, see Christopher Fettweis, "Pessimism and Nostalgia in the Second Nuclear Age," *Strategic Studies Quarterly* 13 (Spring 2019): 12–41.

4. David Alan Rosenberg, "The Origins of Overkill: Nuclear Weapons and American Strategy, 1945–1960," *International Security* 7 (1983): 124.

5. There is an inherent upper limit to how much power can be generated by fission, but there is no upper limit for fusion.

6. Harvard Nuclear Study Group, *Living with Nuclear Weapons* (New York: Bantam, 1983), 79.

7. There are a number of excellent volumes dealing with the development of U.S. nuclear strategy. The major ones relied on in constructing this history are Rosenberg, "The Origins of Overkill," 3–71; Jerome H. Kahan, *Security in the Nuclear Age: Developing U.S. Arms Policy* (Washington, DC: Brookings Institution Press, 1975); Michael Mandelbaum, *The Nuclear Question: The United States and Nuclear Weapons, 1946–1976* (Cambridge: Cambridge University Press, 1979); Richard Smoke, *National Security and the Nuclear Dilemma: An Introduction to the American Experience* (Reading, MA: Addison-Wesley, 1984).

8. Thomas Gibbons-Neff, "Declassified: How the Pentagon Planned to Nuke the Soviet Union and China during the Cold War," *Washington Post*, December 28, 2015.

9. Charles Savage, "Risk of Nuclear War over Taiwan in 1958 Said to Be Greater than Publicly Known," *New York Times*, May 22, 2021.

10. Bernard Brodie, ed., *The Absolute Weapon* (New York: Harcourt Brace, 1946).

11. Albert Wohlstetter, "The Delicate Balance of Terror," *Foreign Affairs* 37 (1959): 211–56.

12. Rosenberg, "The Origins of Overkill"; Peter Pringle and William Arkin, *S.I.O.P.: The Secret U.S. Plan for Nuclear War* (New York: Norton, 1983).

13. Rosenberg, "The Origins of Overkill," 116–17.

14. On the ABM decisions, see Morton Halperin, *Bureaucratic Politics and Foreign Policy* (Washington, DC: Brookings Institution Press, 1974).

15. Mandelbaum, *The Nuclear Question*, 134.

16. Desmond Ball, "U.S. Strategic Forces," *International Security* 7 (1982/83): 34.

17. Warner R. Schilling, "U.S. Strategic Nuclear Concepts in the 1970s: The Search for Sufficiently Equivalent Countervailing Parity," *International Security* 6 (1981): 59.

18. Kier A. Lieber and Daryl G. Press, "The End of MAD," *International Security* 30 (2006): 7–44.

19. Vipin Narang, "Nuclear Strategies of Emerging Nuclear Powers," *Washington Quarterly* 38 (2015): 73–91.

20. Hans Kristensen and Matt Korda, "Nuclear Notebook," *Bulletin of the Atomic Scientists*, May 10, 2022.

21. Hans Kristensen, "Falling Short of Prague," *Arms Control Today*, September 2013.

22. Hans Kristensen and Matt Korda, "2022 Nuclear Program Review," *Federation of American Scientists*, October 27, 2022.

23. Andrew Krepinevich Jr., "The Eroding Balance of Terror, the Decline of Deterrence," *Foreign Affairs* 98 (January 2019): 62–74; and Rebecca Friedman Lissner, "Legacies of the First Gulf War," *Survival* 59 (2017): 143–56.

24. Alexander George and Richard Smoke, *Deterrence in American Foreign Policy: Theory and Practice* (New York: Columbia University Press, 1974).

25. Celeste A. Wallander, "NATO's Enemies Within," *Foreign Affairs* 97 (July 2018): 70–81.

26. Harlan Ullman, "Slogan or Strategy," *National Interest* 84 (2006): 43–49.

27. For a variety of critiques, see the various articles in the symposium "Is Preemption Necessary?," *Washington Quarterly* 26 (2003): 75–145.

28. See Richard Betts, *American Force: Dangers, Delusions, and Dilemmas in National Security* (New York: Columbia University Press, 2012), for a discussion of the challenges of using military force today.

29. *"The National Military Strategy of the United States of America,"* 2015, 6.

30. Sean Maloney, "Remembering Soviet Nuclear Risks," *Survival* 57 (September 2015): 77–104.

31. For a statement of the nuclear freeze position, see Randall Forsberg, "Call a Halt to the Arms Race: Proposal for a Mutual U.S.-Soviet Nuclear Weapons Freeze," in *Toward Nuclear Disarmament and Global Security: A Search for Alternatives*, ed. Burns H. Weston, 384–89 (Boulder, CO: Westview, 1984).

32. For a critique of the Obama record, see Steven Pifer, "Obama's Faltering Nuclear Legacy: The 3 R's," *Washington Quarterly* 38 (Summer 2015): 101–18.

33. Michael Mandelbaum, *The Nuclear Future* (Ithaca, NY: Cornell University Press, 1983), 43.

34. Thomas C. Schelling, *The Strategy of Conflict* (New York: Oxford University Press, 1960).

35. Reagan's speech is reprinted in Edward Haley, David M. Kethly, and Jack Merritt, eds., *Nuclear Strategy, Arms Control, and the Future* (Boulder, CO: Westview, 1985), 311–12.

36. On hypersonic missiles, see R. Jeffrey Smith, "Hypersonic Missiles Are Unstoppable. And They're Starting a New Global Arms Race," *New York Times Magazine* (June 19, 2019).

37. George Lewis and Frank von Hippel, "Limitations on Ballistic Missile Defense—Past and Possibly Future," *Bulletin of Atomic Scientists* 74 (2018): 199–209.

38. Eric Brewer, "Nuclear Proliferation: Is Past Prologue?," *Washington Quarterly* 44 (2021): 181–97.

# Chapter 13: Military Instruments: Small Wars

1. Travis Sharp, "Hiding in Plain Sight," *Survival* 60 (2018): 45–53.

2. David C. Gompert and Martin Libicki, "Waging Cyber War the American Way," *Survival* 57, no. 4 (2015): 7–28.

3. Thomas Rid, "Cyber War Will Not Take Place," *Journal of Strategic Studies* 35 (2012): 5–32; Richard Clarke and Robert Knake, *Cyber War* (New York: Ecco, 2010).

4. On the question of deterrence, see William Lynn III, "Defending a New Domain," *Foreign Affairs* 89 (2010): 97–108; Mike McConnell, "To Win the Cyber-War Look to the Cold War," *Washington Post*, February 28, 2010, B1; and Matthew Croston, "World Gone Cyber MAD," *Strategic Studies Quarterly* 5 (2011): 100–116.

5. Matthew Kroenig and Barry Pavel, "How to Deter Terrorism," *Washington Quarterly* 35 (2012): 21–36.

6. Craig Whitlock, *The Afghanistan Papers* (New York: Simon & Schuster, 2021), 271.

7. Whitlock, *The Afghanistan Papers*, 272–73.

8. On the strategy of exhaustion, see Lawrence Freedman, "Ukraine and the Art of Exhaustion," *Survival* 57, no. 5 (2015): 77–106; and Dan Altman, "Advancing without Attacking," *Security Studies* 27 (2018): 58–88.

9. Frank Hoffman, *Conflict in the 21st Century: The Rise of Hybrid Wars* (Arlington, VA: Potomac Institute, 2007), 14, http://www.potomacinstitute.org/images/stories/publications/potomac_hybridwar_0108.pdf.

10. *Hybrid Threats*, U.S. Army Training Circular, November 2010, http://www.benning.army.mil/mssp/security%20topics/Potential%20Adversaries/content/pdf/tc7_100.pdf.

11. Robert Chesney and Danielle Citron, "Deepfakes and the New Disinformation War," *Foreign Affairs* 98 (January 2019): 147–55.

12. *Counterinsurgency,* Field Manual 3-24, Department of the Army, December 2006.

13. Lorenzo Zambernardi, "Counterinsurgency's Impossible Trilemma," *Washington Quarterly* 33 (2010): 21–34.

14. The quote is from John Nagl, "COIN Fights: A Response to Etzioni," *Small Wars and Insurgencies* 26 (2015): 379. For the debate over COIN, see Amatai Etzioni, "COIN: A Study of Strategic Illusion," *Small Wars & Insurgencies* 26, no. 3 (2015): 345–76; Karl Eikenberry, "The Limits of Counterinsurgency Doctrine in Afghanistan," *Foreign Affairs* 92, no. 5 (2013): 59–74; John Nagl, *Knife Fights: A Memoir of Modern War in Theory and Practice* (New York: Penguin, 2014); and Gian Gentile, *Wrong Turn: America's Deadly Embrace of Counterinsurgency* (New York: Free Press, 2013).

15. Micah Zenko, "The (Not-So) Peaceful Transition of Power: Trump's Drone Strikes Outpace Obama," Council on Foreign Relations blog, March 2, 2017.

16. Benjamin Denison, "Confusion in the Pivot," *War on the Rocks* (February 12, 2019).

17. Andrew Bacevich, "Perpetual War in Afghanistan," *New York Times,* March 13, 2017, A23.

18. Joseph Guido, "The American Way of War in Africa: The Case of Niger," *Small Wars & Insurgencies* 30 (2019): 176–99.

19. *Foreign Affairs* 93 (July 2014) presented a series of retrospective commentaries on Cold War covert actions in Bangladesh, Iran, Congo, and Chile.

20. President's Special Review Board, *The Tower Commission Report* (New York: Bantam, 1987), 15.

21. Jeffrey Richelson, *The U.S. Intelligence Community* (Cambridge, MA: Ballinger, 1985), 228–29.

22. Morton Halperin, Jerry Berman, Robert Borosage, and Christine Marwick, *The Lawless State: The Crimes of the U.S. Intelligence Agencies* (New York: Penguin, 1976), 15–29.

23. Victor Marchetti and John Marks, *The CIA and the Cult of Intelligence* (New York: Knopf, 1974), 167.

24. Marchetti and Marks, *The CIA and the Cult of Intelligence*, 72; Richelson, *The U.S. Intelligence Community*, 230–31; Steven Metz, "New Challenges and Old Concepts: Understanding 21st Century Insurgency," *Parameters* 37 (Winter 2007/2008): 20–32.

25. Warren Hinckle and William Turner, *The Fish Is Red: The Story of the Secret War against Castro* (New York: Harper & Row, 1982).

26. Theodore G. Shackley, *The Third Option: An American View of Counterinsurgency Operations* (New York: Reader's Digest Press, 1981).

27. Trevor Barnes, "The Secret Cold War: The CIA and American Foreign Policy in Europe, 1946–1956," *Historical Journal* 24–25 (1981, 1982): 399–415, 649–70.

28. Ray S. Cline, *Secrets, Spies and Scholars: The Essential CIA* (Washington, DC: Acropolis, 1970), 132–33; Barry Rubin, *Paved with Good Intentions: The American Experience and Iran* (New York: Penguin, 1981), chap. 3.

29. Richard H. Immerman, *The CIA in Guatemala: The Foreign Policy of Intervention* (Austin: University of Texas Press, 1982).

30. John Stockwell, *In Search of Enemies: A CIA Story* (New York: Norton, 1978).

31. Christopher Dickey, "Central America: From Quagmire to Cauldron," *Foreign Affairs* 62 (1984): 669.

32. The five cases were (1) Cuba: Fidel Castro, (2) Congo (Zaire): Patrice Lumumba, (3) Dominican Republic: Rafael Trujillo, (4) Chile: René Schneider, and (5) South Vietnam: Ngo Dinh Diem.

33. Harry Rositzke, *The CIA's Secret Operations* (New York: Reader's Digest Press, 1977), 97.

34. Bob Woodward, *Obama's Wars* (New York: Simon & Schuster, 2010), 50–55.

35. Dan Eggen and Dafna Linzer, "Secret World of Detainees Grows More Public," *Washington Post*, September 7, 2006, A18; Dana Priest, "Officials Relieved Secret Is Shared," *Washington Post*, September 7, 2006, A17.

36. Information in this section is drawn from various newspaper accounts. See Barton Gellman, "Broad Effort Launched after '98 Attacks," *Washington Post*, December 19, 2001, A1; "Struggles Inside the Government Define Campaign," *Washington Post*, December 20, 2001, A1; Bob Woodward and Thomas Ricks, "U.S. Was Foiled Multiple Times in Efforts to Capture bin Laden or Have Him Killed," *Washington Post*, October 3, 2001, A1; Bob Woodward, "CIA Paid Afghans to Track bin Laden," *Washington Post*, December 23, 2001, A1; Steve Coll, *Ghost Wars* (New York: Penguin, 2004).

37. For critical accounts of the attempt to capture bin Laden, see Richard Clarke, *Against All Enemies* (New York: Free Press, 2004); Anonymous, *Imperial Hubris* (Washington, DC: Brassey's, 2004).

38. Ben Nenjamin, "The Life Cycle of Cyber Threats," *Survival* 58 (2016): 39–58.

39. James Lewis, "Cyber War and Ukraine," CSIS Report, June 16, 2022. Also see Nadiya Kostyuk and Erik Gartzke, "Why Cyber Dogs Have Yet to Bark Loudly in Russia's Invasion of Ukraine," *Strategist*, Summer 2022.

40. Ted Galen Carpenter, "Foreign Policy Peril: Somalia Set a Dangerous Precedent," *USA Today*, May 1993, 13.

41. See NTI Nuclear Security Index, http://ntiindex.org/data-results/country-profiles/?index=theft.

42. Louise Arimatsu, "A Treaty for Governing Cyber-Weapons," 2012, http://www.ccdcoe.org/publications/2012proceedings/2_3_Arimatsu_ATreatyForGoverningCyber-Weapons.pdf.

43. For a discussion of cyber confidence control, see Paul Meyer, "Cyber-Security through Arms Control," *RUSI Journal* 156 (2011): 22–27.

44. Kenneth Geers, "Cyber Weapons Convention," *Computer Law and Security Review* 26 (2010): 547–51.

45. Ulrich Kuhn, "The End of Conventional Arms Control and the Role of the US Congress," *Journal for Peace and Nuclear Disarmament* 2 (2019): 253–73.

46. Edward J. Laurance, "Conventional Arms: Rationales and Prospects for Compliance and Effectiveness," *Washington Quarterly* 16 (1993): 163–72.

47. Henry Sokolski, "Mission Impossible," *Bulletin of the Atomic Scientists*, March/April 2001, 63–68.

48. Robert Luttwak, "Nonproliferation and the Use of Force," in *Ultimate Security: Combating Weapons of Mass Destruction*, ed. Jane Nolan, Bernard Finel, and Bryan Finlay, 75–106 (New York: Century Foundation Press, 2003).

49. Michael Boyle, "The Race for Drones," *Orbis* (Winter 2015): 76–94; Paul Scharre, "The Coming Drone Wars," *National Interest*, July 25, 2017, https://nationalinterest.org/feature/the-coming-drone-wars-headache-the-making-american-foreign-21662; Drone Wars UK, *Drone Wars: The Next Generation* (Oxford, UK: Drone Wars UK, May 2018); Center for a New American Security, *Drone Proliferation: Policy Choices for the Trump Administration* (Washington, DC: Center for a New American Security, June 2017).

# Chapter 14: Alternative Futures

1. Robert Kaplan, "The South China Sea Is the Future of Conflict," *Foreign Policy* 188 (2011): 78–85; Andrew Scobell, "The South China Sea and U.S.-China Rivalry," *Political Science Quarterly* 133 (Summer 2018): 199–224.

2. Anne Gearon, "U.S., China Tussle over Sea Claims," *Washington Post*, August 10, 2014, https://www.washingtonpost.com/world/us-china-tussle-over-sea-claims/2014/08/10/2f613504-2085-11e4-8b10-7db129976abb_story.html.

3. Richard Rosecrance, "New Directions?," in *America as an Ordinary Country: U.S. Foreign Policy and the Future*, ed. Richard Rosecrance (Ithaca, NY: Cornell University Press, 1976). Reprinted in James O'Leary and Richard Shultz, eds., *Power, Principles, and Interests* (Lexington, MA: Ginn, 1985), 433–44.

4. O'Leary and Shultz, *Power, Principles, and Interests*, 443.

5. O'Leary and Shultz, *Power, Principles, and Interests*, 442.

6. Robert Kagan, "The Allure of Normalcy," *New Republic*, June 9, 2014, 14–31.

7. On this theme, see Robert A. Isaak, *American Democracy and World Power* (New York: St. Martin's, 1977); Robert C. Johansen, *The National Interest and the Human Interest: An Analysis of U.S. Foreign Policy* (Princeton, NJ: Princeton University Press, 1980).

8. Johansen, *The National Interest and the Human Interest*.

9. Micah Zenko and Michael Cohen, "Clear and Present Safety," *Foreign Affairs* 91 (2012): 79–93.

10. James Schlesinger, "Quest for a Post–Cold War Foreign Policy," *Foreign Affairs* 72 (1992/93): 17–28; Stephen Walt, "The End of Hubris," *Foreign Affairs* 98 (May 2019): 26–35.

11. Robert W. Tucker, "1989 and All That," in *Sea-Changes: American Foreign Policy in a World Transformed*, ed. Nicholas X. Rizopoulos, 204–37 (New York: Council on Foreign Relations Press, 1990).

12. Richard Haass, "Military Force: A User's Guide," *Foreign Policy* 96 (1994): 21–38.

13. George Bush, "Remarks at the United States Military Academy," *Public Papers of the President* (Washington, DC: U.S. Government Printing Office, 1993), 2230–31.

14. Henry Kissinger, "Universal Values, Specific Policies," *National Interest* 84 (2006): 13.

15. For an argument why the United States will remain the dominant power, see Michael Beckley, *Why America Will Remain the World's Sole Superpower* (Ithaca, NY: Cornell University Press, 2018).

16. James Chace and Caleb Carr, *America Invulnerable: The Quest for Absolute Security from 1812 to Star Wars* (New York: Summit, 1988), E318.

17. Graham Fuller, "Strategic Fatigue," *National Interest* 84 (2006): 37–42.

18. The merits of balancing are most often debated with reference to an offshore balancing strategy. For opposing views, see Hal Brands, "Fools Rush Out?," *Washington Quarterly* 38 (Summer 2015): 7–28, and John Mearsheimer and Stephen Walt, "The Case for Offshore Balancing," *Foreign Affairs* 95 (July 2016): 70–83.

19. Hilton Root, "Walking with the Devil," *National Interest* 88 (2007): 42–45.

20. Christopher Layne, "The Unipolar Illusion: Why Great Powers Will Rise," *International Security* 17 (1993): 5–51.

21. Christopher Layne is a major proponent of the end of unipolarity and the need for an offshore balancing strategy. See his "This Time It's Real," *International Studies Quarterly* 56 (2012): 203–13.

22. Earl C. Ravenal, *Never Again: Learning from America's Foreign Policy Failures* (Philadelphia, PA: Temple University Press, 1978). Also see Joseph Parent and Paul MacDonald, "The Wisdom of Retrenchment," *Foreign Affairs* 90 (2011): 32–47. For an opposing view, see Stephen Brooks, G. John Ikenberry, and William Wohlforth, "Don't Come Home, America," *International Security* 37 (2012/13): 7–51.

23. See "Toward a Libertarian Foreign Policy," Cato Policy Report, July/August 2015, for a discussion of what a more libertarian foreign policy would mean for the United States.

24. Ravenal, *Never Again*, 15.

25. Amitai Etzioni, "Security First," *National Interest* 88 (2007): 11–15.

26. Ravenal, *Never Again*, xv.

27. George Kennan, *Cloud of Danger: Current Realities of American Foreign Policy* (Boston: Little, Brown, 1977), 32.

28. Earl Ravenal, "The Case for Adjustment," *Foreign Policy* 81 (1990/91): 3–19.

29. Patrick Buchanan, "America First, and Second, and Third," *National Interest* 19 (1990): 77–82; and Patrick Buchanan, "Putting America First," *Newsmax*, April 15, 2016, https://www.newsmax.com/patrickbuchanan/cold-war/2016/04/15/id/724140.

30. "Trump's Pick to Lead Armed Forces Says China Will Be Largest Military Threat for 100 Years," *Business Insider*, July 12, 2019, https://www.businessinsider.com/china-main-us-challenger-over-next-century-says-military-chief-2019-7.

31. Paul Stares, "Preventive Priorities Survey, 2022," Council on Foreign Relations.

32. Odd Arne Westad, "The Sources of Chinese Conduct," *Foreign Affairs* 98 (September 2019): 86–95; Kurt Campbell and Jake Sullivan, "Competition without Catastrophe," *Foreign Affairs* 98 (September 2019): 96–124; Michael McFaul, "Cold War Lessons and Fallacies for U.S.-China Relations Today," *Washington Quarterly* 43 (2021): 7–39.

33. Ben Rhodes, "Them and Us: How America Lets Its Enemies Hijack Its Foreign Policy," *Foreign Affairs* 100 (2021): 22–32.

34. Joseph Nye Jr., "The China Sleepwalker Syndrome," Project Syndicate, October 4, 2021.

# Photo Credits

1   U.S. Marine Corps photo by Sgt. Samuel Ruiz/Released 210824-M-GQ845-1045. JPG. https://www.marines.mil/Photos/igphoto/2002838168/igsearch/kabul
20   Kathy deWitt/Alamy Stock Photo
40   Jinitzail Hernández/CQ Roll Call via AP Images
60   Lightboxx/Alamy Stock Photo
85   Morgan Louie/Alamy Stock Photo
111   American Photo Archive/Alamy Stock Photo
137   Melina Mara/Pool, *Washington Post* via AP Images
160   Luis M. Alvarez via AP Images
185   American Photo Archive/Alamy Stock Photo
206   © iStock/E+/franckreporter
230   Martin Mejia, File via AP Images
254   KRT via AP Video
277   Wikimedia Commons, https://commons.wikimedia.org/wiki/File:US_Navy_090401-N-0506A-559_A_landing_craft_air_cushion_from_Assault_Craft_Unit_(ACU)_5_leaves_a_beach_during_an_exercise_near_Camp_Lemonier,_Djibouti.jpg
299   Ivan Marc Sanchez/Alamy Stock Photo

# Index

Abbott, Greg, 108
Abraham Accords, 95, 145, 209–10
Abu Ghraib prison, 54, 78
Acheson, Dean, 8, 18, 47, 140, 165, 260–61
Acheson-Lilienthal Committee, 260–61
action channels, 190
action indispensability, 146–47
action policy, 6–7, 9, 257, 259
actor indispensability, 146–47
actor proliferation, 27, 28–29, 30
Adams, John, 55, 157
Adams, John Quincy, 86
administrative powers, 143–44
adversaries, 8, 127, 211, 215, 245, 268, 273, 281, 297, 303, 308; China-US, adversarial relationship between, 212, 232; diplomatic efforts toward, 153, 209, 213, 286; regional adversaries, 267; Trump reaction to, 9, 180; villains, U.S. treating adversaries as, 50, 264
Aerospace Industries Association, 99
Afghanistan, 30, 45, 82, 86, 106, 289; Afghan War, 6–7, 83, 91; Bush administration and, 3, 10–11, 15, 149; drone use in, 297–98; foreign aid for, 125, 246; foreign policy on, 142, 153, 162, 172, 174, 209, 304; Kabul as capital, 2, 11, 211, 283; Soviet invasion of, 10, 13, 14, 33, 54, 66, 69, 80, 89, 115, 227, 288; Taliban in, 132, 172, 280, 284; terrorism and, 32, 34, 81; U.S. presence in, 2, 10–11, 135, 171, 211, 247, 267, 282, 288; withdrawal from, 2–3, 4, 6, 8, 44, 49, 95, 126, 134, 139, 150, 155, 168, 173
Africa, 32, 68, 69, 103, 125, 128, 284, 287; Central Africa, 33, 63, 285; Chinese presence in, 285–86, 302; U.S. forces in, 144, 285
Africa Command (AFRICOM), 285–86
Agriculture Department, 180–81
Aidid, Mohamed Farrah, 291, 292
Airborne Warning and Control Systems aircraft (AWACS), 99
Air-Sea Battle strategy, 267–68
Albright, Madeline, 44
Alexander, Keith, 109
A-list threats, 5–6

Allawi, Iyad, 77
Allende, Salvador, 48, 128, 286
alliances, 10, 30, 45, 49, 56, 209, 210, 291, 302; Alliance for Progress, 140; alliance systems, 26, 196, 197; Global Development Alliance, 247; in Middle East, 11, 154, 267; military alliances, 29, 44, 133, 234
Allison, Graham T., 190
al-Qaeda, 2, 3, 124, 165, 197, 285; drone strike against leaders, 283–84, 298; Iraq as linked to, 79, 88, 155; ISIS affiliation, 31, 33; Taliban and, 10–11, 267, 280
Al-Shabaab, 32, 33, 285
"America first" perspective, 310; America First Committee, 96–97; Republican support for, 114, 131; Trump embrace of, 10, 15–16, 36, 44, 49, 87, 97, 103, 112, 142, 161, 180
American Crusader perspective, 306
American hegemony, 23, 31, 35–36
American Israel Public Affairs Committee (AIPAC), 99
American national style, 16, 43, 57, 58, 210, 306; building blocks of, 48–52; consequences of, 52–55; historical sources of, 46–47
Americans with Disabilities Act, 115
America the Balancer perspective, 307–8
Amnesty International, 54, 96
analogies, 64, 75, 79–81
anarchy and anarchism, 24, 25, 33, 302
Anbar Awakening, 79
Angell, Norman, 196–97
Angola, 128, 287
anti-access/area denial (A2/AD), 268
anti-Americanism, 38
Anti-Ballistic Missile (ABM) Treaty, 116, 270, 271, 274
antiterrorism, 33, 132, 247, 283, 285
apartheid, 88, 128, 195
Apple Inc., 130
appointment powers, 117
Arab Americans, 99–100
Arab-Israeli War, 214, 269
Arab Spring, 292
Arbenz, Jacobo, 48, 287

Area Foundation, 87

Argentina, 226, 237, 245

Armenia, 101, 227

Armitage, Richard, 83

arms control, 164, 244, 263, 280; for conventional weapons, 295–96; counterproliferation strategy, 296–97; détente and, 13, 31; disarmament and, 268–73; Iran arms control agreement, 139, 289; New START arms control agreement, 138, 215; Soviets and, 14, 18, 50, 157, 212, 214; WMD arms control, 293–95

Arms Export Control Act, 124, 225

arms sales, 18, 99, 101, 120, 124, 225–28

arms transfers, 13, 128, 225–28, 295–96

Army Reorganization Act, 124, 225

Asian Development Bank, 36

Asian pivot, 25, 300, 308–9

Asia-Pacific Trade Agreement, 142

Aspin, Les, 143

aspirational youth, 38

Assad, Bashar al-, 106, 182, 264, 288, 289

assassination, 98, 102, 196, 197, 278, 288

assured destruction, 259

asymmetric warfare, 333

Atlantic Council, 102

Atomic Development Authority, 260–61

Atomic Energy Commission (AEC), 175, 261

Atoms for Peace plan, 269

Austin, Lloyd, 171, 172–73

Australia, 7–8, 49, 63, 138, 210, 221, 226, 237, 267

Authorization for Use of Military Force (AUMF), 10, 119, 120–21, 122, 133, 134–35, 146

axis of evil, 18, 78, 212, 272

Azar, Alex, 62–63

Ba'ath Party, 7, 77

Bacevich, Andrew, 80, 86, 284

Bahrain, 169, 213, 226

Baker Plan, 247

balance-of-power politics, 48, 51, 56, 202, 270, 307

Bali Road Map, 218

Balkans, 29, 271

Ball, George, 74

Ballistic Missile Review Report, 274

Bannon, Steven, 153, 178, 208

Barber, James David, 147, 149

bargaining, 53, 190, 191, 195, 208, 222, 226, 275

barnacles of foreign policy legislation, 124

Baruch, Bernard, 260–61

Baruch Plan, 260–61, 269

Base Realignment and Closure (BRAC), 132

Battle of Mogadishu, 285, 291

Bay of Pigs, 48, 133, 140, 192, 201, 203, 287

Begin, Menachem, 13

Benghazi attack, 126, 129, 293

Benton, William, 96

Berlin Wall, 264, 266

Betts, Richard, 15

Biden, Joe, 106, 117, 119, 135, 143, 145, 168, 215, 217, 222, 228, 240, 255, 272; Afghanistan, withdrawal from, 2–3, 4, 6, 8, 173; AUMF, seeking repeal of, 121, 146; Biden administration, 7–8, 156–57, 164, 165, 166, 177, 178, 212; border policy, 41, 108, 141, 144, 250; climate change, reacting to, 208, 219; COVID-19 pandemic, handling of, 221; diplomacy, use of, 209, 210, 213, 223; drone strikes, authorizing, 283, 298; executive orders, 41, 113, 138–39, 171–72, 245; first one hundred days, 138–39; foreign aid spending, 252; foreign policy, 3, 10, 16, 44, 66, 95, 156; Indo-Pacific Economic Framework, 238; Iran, relations with, 243, 273; Missile Defense Report, 274; Nuclear Posture Review, 263; presidential style, 148–49, 150, 154; regional trade agreements, negotiating, 237; sanctions, use of, 243, 244, 245; Somalia, sending special forces to, 33, 284–85; Taiwan policy, 125, 302; trade agreement stance, 155–56; Trump policies, reversing, 41, 42–43, 49, 100, 126, 144, 182, 207, 220, 250; Ukraine policy, 8, 21, 94, 112–14, 134, 186–87, 224

bilateralism: bilateral development assistance, 247–48; bilateral trade, 236–37, 249; bilateral trade agreements, 236–37, 249; multilateralism vs. bilateralism, 210

Bin Laden, Osama, 10, 15, 54, 93–94, 267, 289

Bin Salman, Mohammed, 212

biological weapons, 116, 249, 293–94

bipartisanship, 8, 132

bipolar system, 26, 266

black box, state treated as, 189

black knights, 242

Blair, Dennis, 153

Blair, Tony, 77

Blinken, Antony, 165, 186, 187, 216

blowback, 7

Boehner, John, 133

Boeing Company, 98, 131

Bohlen, Charles, 214

Boland Amendments, 288

Bolton, John, 62, 153, 220

Border Patrol, 42, 43

Bosnia, 30, 92, 105, 130, 246, 283

bottom-up negotiations, 256

Bowles, Chester, 10

boycotts, 233, 234, 242

Bracero Program, 52–53

Brady Plan, 247

Brazil, 101, 207, 212, 214, 218, 219, 237, 267

Bremer, Paul, 77, 140–41

Bremmer, Ian, 35

Brennan, John, 175, 178

Bretton Woods system, 34, 235–36, 238

Bricker Amendment, 142

Brodie, Bernard, 258

Brookings Institution, 102, 130

Brooks, Stephen, 36

Bryan, William Jennings, 145

Brzezinski, Zbigniew, 149

Buchanan, Pat, 310

budgetary powers, 116, 124–26, 176

budget hawks, 130

Bundy, McGeorge, 74, 152

Bundy, William, 152

bureaucracy, 102, 151, 167, 170, 188; domestic bureaucracies, 161, 162, 179–82, 184; foreign policy bureaucracy, 153, 161, 163, 166, 179–80, 181; summit diplomacy and, 213–14

bureaucratic politics model, 190–91, 197–98, 202–3

Bureau of Intelligence and Research (INR), 174

Burkina Faso, 32, 285

Burma (Myanmar), 154, 157, 162

Burns, William J., 175, 177, 310

Bush, George H. W., 43, 94, 145, 168, 217, 249, 263, 274, 291; Bush administration, 154, 155, 156; Iraq and, 52, 106, 266; NSC decision process, making changes in, 152–53; Persian Gulf War and, 67, 105, 146; in post-

Cold War period, 270–71; presidential style, 148, 149, 150

Bush, George W., 41, 82, 93, 123, 133, 142, 145, 168, 216, 240, 250, 274, 283, 288, 305; 9/11, response to, 14–15, 17, 56, 156, 158, 192, 238, 242; ABM treaty, withdrawing from, 116, 271; Afghanistan and, 3, 10–11, 15, 159; "axis of evil," deeming Iraq as, 18, 78, 212, 272; Bush administration, 96, 155, 156, 165, 166, 172, 195; Bush Doctrine, 14–15, 43; Durban Review Conference and, 220; foreign policy, 4, 43; immigration stance, 53, 124; Iran and, 78, 262; Iraq War and, 8, 54, 77–78, 103–4, 140–41; Kyoto Protocol, withdrawing from, 218; nuclear weapons and, 115, 262; preemption strategy, 264, 265; presidential style, 149–50, 153, 256; Secure Fence Act, signing, 41; terrorism, fight against, 49, 79, 147, 242; trade talks and, 236, 237; Vietnam War, comparing to Iraq War, 80; War Cabinet, establishing, 153, 192

business groups, 96, 97–99

Buy American Act, 233

Byrnes, James, 260

Cambodia, 13, 70, 71, 73, 82, 118, 152, 241, 302

Camp David Accords, 13, 227, 247, 281

Canada, 30, 37, 63, 260; foreign trade and, 98, 234, 235; international relations, 214, 223; NAFTA, as part of, 249–50; in USMCA, 123, 142, 231–32

Card, Andrew, 156

Carter, Ashton, 170

Carter, Jimmy, 100, 150, 195; Carter administration, 153, 156, 164; foreign policy, 13, 17, 152, 227; human rights, focus on, 13, 17, 18, 28, 148; Iran hostage situation, 80, 144, 145, 242; Panama Canal Treaties, handling of, 117, 133, 148, 157; SALT II talks, 115, 270; in small-group decision-making model, 191–92

Casey, George, 18

Casey, William, 128, 152, 178, 193

Case-Zablocki Act, 133, 142–43

Castro, Fidel, 27, 43, 100, 140, 199, 201, 222, 233, 243, 286–87, 288

Catholic Church, 29, 103

Cato Institute, 87, 102, 130, 281

Center for Climate and Energy Solutions, 218

Center for Strategic and International Studies (CSIS), 102

Centers for Disease Control (CDC), 43, 63, 68

Central Intelligence Agency (CIA), 11, 48, 77, 164, 165, 222, 289, 294; Bay of Pigs invasion and, 140; CIA and the intelligence community, 174–79; covert action, involvement in, 7, 10, 128, 286–88

Chad, 32, 285

Chao, Elaine, 101

Chávez, Hugo, 102

chemical weapons, 6, 215, 245, 293–94, 295

Cheney, Dick, 108, 155, 192

Chertoff, Michael, 42

Chiang Kai Shek, 74

Chicago Council on Global Affairs, 90

Chile, 48, 128, 236–37, 286

China, 9, 13, 25, 38, 45, 51, 90, 154, 155, 180, 181, 235, 266, 296; Africa, presence in, 285–86, 302; Air-Sea Battle strategy against, 267–68; China mission center, CIA creating, 175; China trade war, 148, 239–40; COVID-19 pandemic, handling, 61–63, 221; as a cyberpower, 289, 295; developing country, claiming status as, 218; drone manufacturing, 297; economic power of, 5, 36; embargoes on, 234; environmental issues, reacting to, 39, 87; as a global power, 214, 267; human rights in, 31, 139, 157, 240; Japan and, 308, 309; "loss of China," 49, 74, 94, 133; military power of, 5, 7, 36; in new cold war with U.S., 310–11; Nixon administration and, 17, 152, 225; as a nuclear power, 36, 262, 263, 272, 275; nuclear strategy against, 258, 262, 264; one-China policy, 126; power and influence of, 36, 92, 267; in Regional Comprehensive Economic Partnership, 238; renminbi as official currency, 236; sanctions and, 139, 227, 240, 243; South China Sea, 31, 212, 224, 267, 268, 300–302; state capitalist system in, 35; Taiwan and, 102, 126; tariffs placed on U.S. products, 103, 131; in Three-Party Talks, 255; Trump China policy, 8, 148, 217, 239–40, 263, 284, 301–2, 310; U.S.-China relations, 94, 96, 145, 197, 211, 212, 232; Vietnam and, 72, 73; Xi Jinping as leader of, 61–62, 220, 240

Christian Broadcasting Network, 102

Church Committee, 288

Churchill, Winston, 154

Citizens for a Nuclear Free Iran, 99

civil-military relations, 173

Clapper, James, 178, 293

Clark Amendment, 287

Clay, Lucius, 82

Cleveland, Grover, 146

climate change, 37, 92, 104; Chinese efforts to mitigate, 39, 87; climate change conferences, 207, 219; Paris climate conference, 133, 207–8; as a security threat, 5, 28; Summit of the Americas, climate discussed at, 210

Clinton, Bill, 52, 105, 116, 123, 145, 168, 234, 242, 250, 274; appointment powers, 117; Clinton administration, 154, 156; on environmental issues, 218, 219; Kosovo policy, 64, 120, 146; managerial style, 150, 223, 256; migration policy, 41, 43; Mogadishu, lesson of, 292; NAFTA, support for, 249–50; nuclear strategy of, 144, 255, 262; presidential style, 148, 149, 152–53; terrorism during administration, 147, 289

Clinton, Hillary, 101, 127, 129, 250, 293

closed belief systems, 65

cluster munitions, 296

CNN effect, 106

Coalition Provisional Authority (CPA), 77

Coats, Daniel, 109, 178, 215

cognitive consistency, 64–65

Cohen, Eliot, 18

Cohen-Nunn Act, 167

Cold War, 25, 30, 49, 71, 131, 183, 187, 234, 243, 248, 264, 285, 306; arms control efforts, 269–70; covert actions against adversaries, 286–88; Cuba, spotlight on, 198, 242; diplomatic activities, 210, 213, 224; East-West system, 31, 54, 215; foreign policy and, 38, 50, 92, 234; government changes during era, 133, 164, 168; internationalist outlook of period, 76, 130; lessons of the Cold War, 79–80; NATO and, 21, 29; nuclear thinking, 257–60, 268, 275; Truman Doctrine as foundational, 12; U.S. hegemony as characterizing, 35–36; Vietnam War during, 74, 266; VOA broadcasts in response to, 222. *See also* Post-Cold War era

collegial system, 150, 153

Colombia, 32, 101, 115, 237, 246, 250

Commerce Department, 102, 180, 249

commerce powers, 121, 123

Commission on Wartime Contracting, 132

Commission to Assess U.S. National Security Space Management and Organization, 183

Committee against Jim Crow in Military Service and Training, 170

Committee on Overhead Reconnaissance (COMOR), 199

Committee on the Present Danger, 195

compellence, 225, 308

Comprehensive Iran Sanctions, Accountability, and Divestment Act, 242

Comprehensive Nuclear Test Ban Treaty, 133, 144

concurrent resolutions, 118, 119, 124, 134

Congressional Budget Office, 130

Congressional Research Service, 130, 246

consensus building, 204

constructivism, 24–25, 26, 37

containment, 12, 17, 43, 44, 49, 89, 166, 209, 303, 306, 309, 311

contested zones, 281

Contras, 14, 50, 193, 287–88

Conventional Arms Transfer Policy (CAT), 227

conventional weapons, 225, 258, 263, 266, 293, 294, 295–96

Convention on Cluster Munitions, 296

Cooperative Threat Reduction Program, 271

Copenhagen Accord, 208, 217–19

Coughlin, Charles, 97

Council on Foreign Relations, 310

Countering America's Adversaries Through Sanctions Act, 245

counterinsurgency (COIN), 11, 78–79, 81, 173, 282–83

counterproliferation, 296–97

counterprotests, 104

counterterrorism, 11, 34, 175, 177, 179, 213, 279, 283–84

country teams, 164

covert action, 7, 9, 44, 128, 152, 175, 177, 279, 286–89

COVID-19 pandemic, 28, 32, 43, 61–64, 69, 83, 155–56, 173, 221, 228, 244, 253, 301

Cox, Archibald, 119

Cozy Bear hackers, 279

Cruz, Ted, 112–13, 117

Cuba, 74, 82, 99, 115, 129, 146, 210, 222, 234; Bay of Pigs invasion, 48, 133, 140, 192, 201, 203, 287; covert action in, 286–87, 288; migration from Cuba to U.S., 42, 43, 100; Obama, repairing U.S. relations with, 100–101, 144, 211, 212; sanctions on, 240, 242, 243; Soviet support for, 27, 198–200, 202, 214, 242

Cuban American National Foundation (CANF), 100–101

Cuban Democracy Act, 101, 243

Cuban Missile Crisis, 48, 51, 105, 186, 188, 192, 198–204, 259, 269

Customs and Border Patrol (CBP), 42

cyberspace, 21, 126, 128, 176, 194, 263; cyberattacks, 176, 245, 268, 278–79, 281, 289–90, 294; Cyber Command, outlook of, 178–79; cybersecurity, 129, 143–44, 295; cyberterrorism, perceived threat of, 4, 5

Czechoslovakia, 54, 66, 196

Davidson, Philip, 301

Dayton Accords, 30

debt relief, 235, 247

decentralization, 25, 128, 129

declaratory policy, 6, 257, 259, 268

deductive analysis, 189, 190

defense budget, 130, 168, 266, 284

defense contractors, 98

Defense Intelligence Agency (DIA), 175

defense weapons, 273–74

demilitarized zone (DMZ), 73, 220

denuclearization, 249, 255–57, 272

Department of Homeland Security (DHS), 181–82

détente, 13, 17, 31, 44, 73, 133, 215, 233, 303, 311

deterrence, 12, 43, 49, 179, 189, 209, 263, 279, 280, 297, 311; deterrence strategies, 264–65; fishing strategy and, 240; as a military task, 308, 310; moving away from, 81, 267; NATO as engaging in, 183; nuclear deterrence, 172, 258–59, 261; Pacific Deterrence Initiative, 125

diffusion of power, 27

diplomacy, types of: bilateral diplomacy, 101, 210, 211–12; coercive diplomacy, 223–24, 286, 337; conference diplomacy, 216, 219; digital diplomacy, 222–23; diplomatic tool kit, 208–10; dollar diplomacy, 232; "fire-sale" diplomacy, 165; health diplomacy, 62, 221, 228; nuclear diplomacy, 225; public diplomacy, 22, 162, 208, 222–23; shuttle diplomacy, 212–13; summit diplomacy, 213–16; UN diplomacy, 221–22

Director of Central Intelligence (DCI), 174, 177–78, 193, 199, 202

Director of National Intelligence (DNI), 174, 175, 176, 177, 178

disarmament, 51, 77, 261, 268–70, 296

Disengaged America perspective, 308, 310

disengagement policy, 143, 197

dispute settlements, 239

Djibouti, 285, 302

Dobrynin, Anatoly, 200

Doha Round, 155, 217, 239

domestic politics, 16, 17–18, 19, 69, 189, 200, 216, 220, 275, 280

domestic surveillance, 57, 176

Dominican Republic, 48, 54, 82, 115, 265

Donilon, Thomas, 156

donut strategy, 107

Drezner, Daniel, 19

drones, 33, 144, 149, 293, 294; in counterterrorism efforts, 33, 283–84; drone wars, 297–98; U.S. drone, Iranian downing of, 135, 146, 188, 278, 281

Drug Enforcement Agency (DEA), 181

Dulles, Allen, 177

Dulles, John Foster, 47, 65, 71

Durban Review Conference, 220

Eagleton, Thomas, 119

earmarking, 124

Earth Summit, 219

East-West superpower summits, 215–16

East-West system, 31

Ebola, 68–69, 156

economic aid, 23, 73, 209, 247, 248

economic statecraft, 232–33, 234

economic summits, 214–15

Egypt, 220, 246, 251, 267, 275, 289. 297; arms sales to, 29, 226, 227, 228, 235; diplomacy efforts toward, 143, 213; PL 480 funds, as a recipient of, 248

Eisenhower, Dwight, 81, 145, 151, 170, 225, 306; Cuba and, 74, 140; military-industrial complex, addressing, 98, 109; nuclear strategy, 258–59, 264, 269; presidential style, 148, 149, 150; Vietnam and, 71, 72

elite theory, 194–96, 197, 198

Ellender, Allen, 128

Ellsberg, Daniel, 56, 141

El Salvador, 62, 287

embargoes, 27, 49, 233, 234, 243

embassies, 3, 64, 144, 166, 211, 213; posts at typical embassies, 163–64; U.S. embassies, assaults on, 13, 33, 66, 73, 242, 289

empires, 27, 35, 36, 196, 197, 303

engagement, 73, 89, 143, 149, 157, 178, 211, 268

engineering approach, 50

environmental conferences, 219

Environmental Protection Agency, 129, 133, 216, 247

escalate-to-deescalate strategy, 265

Esper, Mark, 158, 172

Espionage Act, 56

ethnic group lobbying, 96, 99–101

evangelicalism, 47, 99, 103

evolutionary trends in international system, 25, 27–31

exceptionalism, 43, 44, 48

executive agreements, 52–53, 141, 142–43, 238, 250

Executive Committee (ExCom), 192, 199–200, 202–4

executive orders, 173, 242, 288; of Biden, 41, 113, 138–39, 171–72, 245; of Obama, 142, 143–44, 244; of Truman, 141, 169–70; of Trump, 144, 183, 231, 255–56

Export Control Act of 1949, 234

extraterritoriality, 308

Exxon, 97–98

Facebook, 106, 107, 223

Fall, Bernard, 82

falling dominoes, 309

fast-track authority, 121, 123, 236, 249

Federal Bureau of Investigation (FBI), 109, 127, 175, 177, 181

Federal Election Commission, 99

Feinstein, Dianne, 130

Ferdinand, Archduke, 196, 197

Ferguson, Niall, 35, 197

Fillmore, Millard, 308

firefighting oversight, 126
firewall, 263, 276
first ladies, 157
flexible response, 259
Flynn, Michael, 153, 174
Food and Drug Administration (FDA), 28, 181
Food for Peace program (PL 480), 180, 209, 248
Ford, Gerald, 73, 120, 150, 152, 163, 270, 310
Ford, Henry, 97
foreign aid, 44, 101, 125, 130, 140, 157, 161, 211, 227, 243, 290; contemporary foreign aid, 251–52; Israel, foreign aid earmarks for, 124; post-9/11 foreign aid, 250–51; purpose of U.S. foreign aid, 245–46; reporting requirements for, 126; types of foreign aid, 246–48
Foreign Assistance Act, 128
Foreign Intelligence Surveillance Court, 127
foreign lobbyists, 96, 101–2, 250
foreign policy: American national style, applying to, 46–47, 52–55; cost considerations, 6–8; foreign policy problems, thinking about, 3–4; foreign policy results, assessing, 16–18; grand strategy approach, future of, 18–19; internationalist system, 27–31, 45–46; legalist approach to, 51–52; Mexican border as a foreign policy challenge, 41–43; moral pragmatism approach, 49–50; new media and U.S. foreign policy, 105–6; policy instrument selection, 9–10; presidential foreign policy doctrines, 11–16; public opinion, role in, 4–5; State Department, impact on, 166–67; unilateralism, addressing foreign policy with, 48–49
Foreign Service Officers (FSOs), 164, 165–66, 167
formalistic system, 150
Forrestal, James, 172
Fourteen Points, 55–56
Fourth Amendment, 130
Fox News, 88, 107
France, 29, 74, 78, 212, 226, 272, 286; as a global power, 214, 267; as a nuclear power, 262; submarine agreement with Australia, 7–8, 49, 210; U.S.-France relations, 7–8; Vietnam War and, 70, 71; in World War I, 196–97

free rider problem, 10
free trade, 24, 30, 44, 56, 131, 233, 234, 235, 309; bilateral free trade agreements, 236–37; Free Trade Area of the Americas, 155; global free trade system, 238–39, 252; NAFTA, 123, 133, 211, 231–32, 237, 249–50; TPP as world's largest free trade agreement, 237–38
Friedman, Thomas, 34
friendship between countries, 211–12
Fromkin, David, 56
fundamentalists, 10, 47, 103

Gaddafi, Muammar, 30–31, 54, 90–91, 121, 146, 216, 265, 289, 292–93
gadflies, 129
gatekeepers, 106, 156
Gates, Robert, 9, 81, 96, 156, 178, 293
General Agreement on Tariffs and Trade (GATT), 34, 216, 234, 238–39
General Motors, 29, 97
generational events, 65
Geneva Peace Accords, 70, 71–72, 74
genocide, 62, 210, 220, 280, 288, 296
Germany, 11, 12, 37, 62, 63, 78, 102, 115, 117, 212, 269, 309; AFRICOM as headquartered in, 285; as a global power, 29, 214, 267, 272; in post-WW II era, 65, 82, 286; U.S. troops stationed in, 169, 264; in World Wars, 48, 97, 196–97, 293
Ghani, Ashraf, 2, 3
Gibson, Chris, 135
Gillibrand, Kirsten, 171
Gilpin, Robert, 27
Giuliani, Rudolph, 101, 145
global bully pulpit, 6
Global Development Alliance, 247
globalization, 23, 30, 31, 34–35, 104, 238
Global Leaders' Meeting on Gender Equality and Women's Empowerment, 219
Global War on Terrorism, 15, 33, 49, 50, 79
Goldwater, Barry, 93
Goldwater-Nichols Act, 167
Gorbachev, Mikhail, 14, 49, 215, 270, 271
Gore, Al, 154, 156
Government Accountability Office, 130
government shutdown, 41, 113
grand strategy, 11–12, 15, 18–19
Great Depression, 35, 53, 233

Greece, 12, 37, 226
Greene, Marjorie Taylor, 112
Greenfield, Linda Thomas, 166
Grenada, 48, 54, 82, 146, 167, 265
Group of 6 (G6), 214
Group of 7 (G7), 138, 187, 215, 245
Group of 8 (G8), 31, 214, 244
Group of 20 (G20), 214–15, 221, 228, 240, 256
groupthink, 192–94, 203
Guantanamo Bay, 54, 124, 125, 143, 202, 203, 280
Guatemala, 48, 62, 155, 246, 287
guerrilla wars, 72, 75
Gulf of Tonkin Resolution, 70, 72, 80, 118, 133

Haas, Richard, 16
Hadley, Stephen, 78, 96
Haines, Avril, 178
Haiti, 43, 52, 91, 92, 105, 290
Halderman, H. R., 225
Haley, Nikki, 245, 252
Hamilton, Alexander, 55, 56, 117–18
Hanoi Summit, 256
hard power, 9, 31, 35, 223
Harris, Kamala, 154–55
Haspel, Gina, 177, 178
Hawley, Josh, 113
Hayden, Michael, 178, 278–79
H-bomb (hydrogen bomb), 257
hedging strategy, 275, 307
hegemony, 9, 23, 27, 31, 35–36, 307
Helms, Richard, 177, 288
Helms-Burton Act, 244
Helsinki, 45, 143, 178, 215
Heritage Foundation, 102, 130
Hezbollah, 193, 281, 291
high *vs.* low politics, 27–28
Hiroshima, 257, 259, 260
Hitler, Adolf, 90
Ho Chi Minh, 70, 71, 74, 225
Hoffman, Frank, 281
Holsti, Ole, 76
Homeland Security, 42, 154, 156, 175, 181, 279
Honduras, 62, 246
Hopkins, Harry, 144
hotline, 269
House, Colonel, 145
House Speakers, 101, 122, 126, 133, 187
Houthi rebels, 165, 281, 297

Hughes-Ryan Amendment, 128, 289
Hull, Cordell, 144
humanitarian economic assistance, 248
humanitarian operations, 146, 291
human rights, 5, 6, 14, 109, 125, 126, 131, 164, 243, 250, 284; Area Foundation as supporting, 87; Carter focus on, 13, 17, 18, 28, 148; in China, 31, 139, 157, 240; Cuba, human rights violations in, 244; diplomacy regarding, 162, 209, 213; in Disengaged America perspective, 310; as a foreign policy concern, 92, 100, 227; human rights conferences, 45, 216, 219–20; Magnitsky Act as targeting violations of, 295; in Reformed American perspective, 303, 304; Russia, human rights in, 31, 114; Trump, low value placed on, 16; United Nations Human Rights Council, 138, 222
Humphrey, Hubert, 65
Hussein, Saddam, 15, 67, 77, 78, 80, 90, 93, 264, 288, 293, 306
hybrid warfare, 279, 281–82

identity politics, 34
Ikenberry, G. John, 220–21
imperialism, 31, 54, 232
impulsive decision-making, 204–5
India, 138, 181, 207, 211, 218, 235, 243, 296, 297; as a global power, 214, 267; in Indo-Pacific Economic Framework, 238; as a nuclear power, 120, 262, 272; the Quad, as part of, 138, 221; U.S.-India relations, 181, 227
individual-centered models, 204–5
Indochina, 71, 73, 74
Indonesia, 13, 226, 239, 246, 267, 289
inductive analysis, 189, 190
informal ambassadors, 144–15
intellectual coherence, 17
intelligence-industrial complex, 109
Inter-American Commission on Human Rights (IACHR), 220
interest groups, 44, 96–103, 179, 196, 236
intergovernmental organizations (IGOs), 28
Intermediate Nuclear Forces (INF) Treaty, 215, 270, 272
intermediate-range ballistic missiles (IRBMs), 199, 270
intermestic issues, 28, 107, 156
International Affairs Budget, 209, 252

International Atomic Energy Agency, 269
International Bank for Reconstruction and
   Development (IBRD), 235
International Criminal Court (ICC), 108, 144,
   222, 251
internationalism, 45–46, 49, 52, 55, 76, 89, 104
International Monetary Fund (IMF), 34, 51, 235
International Space Station project, 183
international trade, 51, 98, 102, 155, 216, 235,
   296
International Trade Organization (ITO), 216
internet, 105–6, 244
interventionism, 46, 48
intuitive decision-making, 204
Iran, 67, 80, 89, 101, 164, 167, 242, 274, 287,
   293, 296; arms transfers to, 13, 50, 128;
   cyber warfare with, 278–79, 289; drones
   and, 135, 146, 188, 278, 281, 297; the
   enemy, perceived as, 50, 78, 80, 193; G. W.
   Bush and, 78, 262; Iranian hostage crisis,
   13, 80, 144, 145, 165, 192; Iranian nuclear
   agreement, 6, 54, 99, 133, 134, 142, 272–73;
   as a nuclear power, 4, 5, 18, 50, 139, 143,
   275, 278, 279, 297; sanctions against, 99,
   143–44, 165, 240, 242, 273; shah of Iran,
   33, 65, 67, 227; Trump and, 4, 95, 135, 146,
   205, 211, 243, 267, 278, 281
Iran-Contra Affair, 14, 18, 50, 144, 152, 192,
   193, 286
Iran-Iraq War, 293
Iraq, 15, 18, 55, 98, 162, 205, 210, 272, 280,
   294, 297, 304; al-Qaeda, link with, 88, 155;
   in "axis of evil,," 18, 78, 212, 272; COIN
   involvement in, 282; de-Ba'athification of, 7,
   77, 82; endless war in, 86, 171, 298; foreign
   aid for, 246, 252; G. H. W. Bush and, 52,
   106, 154; groupthink on Iraq invasion, 194;
   G. W. Bush and, 133, 149, 153, 156, 172;
   ISIS in Iraq, 33, 283; Kurdish population
   of, 101–2, 293; military force against Iraq,
   authorization for, 122–23, 133, 135; OCO
   account funds and, 125; Operation Desert
   Storm in, 90, 121, 296–97; outsourced
   contractors and, 168; public opinion on, 88,
   90, 91, 93, 104, 106; rebuilding Iraq, 82–83,
   126; Saddam Hussein as leader of, 67, 264,
   288; sanctions against, 222
Iraq Study Group, 78
Iraq syndrome, 69

Iraq War, 7, 67, 69; AUMF authorization for,
   121, 135; Bush administration and, 8, 15, 18,
   54, 103, 133, 216, 266; chronology of, 77–
   79; CIA involvement, 175, 179; past conflicts,
   analogies with, 79–81; in phase model of
   military activity, 76–77; public opinion on,
   45, 91, 93, 104, 105
Iron Curtain, 12, 66, 306, 311
irredentism, 280
Islamic State of Iraq and Syria (ISIS), 7, 135,
   278, 293; military operations against, 33, 79,
   283; Syria, ISIS in, 133, 139, 146, 288; as a
   terrorist group, 31, 32, 93, 280, 285
Islamic State of Iraq and the Levant (ISIL), 79
isolationism, 11, 12, 45–46, 48, 49, 52, 56, 76,
   89, 303, 304, 305, 310
Israel, 14, 37, 81, 91, 103, 133, 154, 164, 193,
   227, 267, 296; Abraham Accords, signing,
   95, 209–10; Arab-Israeli War, 214, 269;
   conventional weapons, strength in, 293;
   diplomacy with, 13, 143, 213; foreign aid
   for, 124, 246; human rights in, 162, 222; in
   hybrid conflicts, 281; Jerusalem as capital,
   U.S. recognizing, 99, 252; military drones, as
   exporter of, 297; as a NATO member, 251;
   as a nuclear power, 262, 272; Stuxnet virus
   attack, assisting U.S. with, 278, 279
issue proliferation, 27–28
Italy, 169, 196, 214, 267, 286

Jackson, Andrew, 55, 57, 58
Jackson, Henry ("Scoop"), 131
Jackson, Jesse, 100
Jackson-Vanik Amendment, 133
Janis, Irving, 192–94, 203
Japan, 27, 37, 101; Commodore Perry's opening
   of, 302, 308–9; as a global power, 30, 127,
   138, 195, 214, 221, 256, 267; nuclear
   concerns and, 94, 255; Pearl Harbor attack,
   64, 65, 67, 97; post-war conditions in, 82,
   197; sanctions on, 241, 243; as a U.S. ally,
   37, 143, 169; U.S.-Japan trade, 51, 235, 237;
   Vietnam and, 70, 71
Javits, Jacob, 119
Jefferson, Thomas, 55, 56–57
Jentleson, Bruce, 90
JNIM terrorist group, 32
Johnson, Lyndon, 234, 265; Johnson
   administration, 152, 163, 191; presidential

style, 148, 150, 152; Vietnam War and, 70, 72–74, 75, 93, 118, 148
Joint Chiefs of Staff (JCS), 72, 75, 167
Joint Comprehensive Plan of Action (JCPOA), 139, 243, 272, 273
Joint Concept for Access and Maneuver in the Global Commons, 268
joint resolutions, 122–23, 124, 134
Jordan, 226, 246
Jordan, Hamilton, 144, 156
Justice Department, 127, 144

Kaine, Tim, 135
Kaplan, Robert, 36, 200, 203–4
Karzai, Hamid, 11
Kellogg-Briand Pact, 51
Kelly, John, 156, 174, 181
Kennan, George, 17, 49–50, 309–10
Kennedy, Edward, 80
Kennedy, John F., 143, 182, 227, 248; Cuban Missile Crisis and, 105, 192, 198–202, 203–4; first 100 days, 139–40; Khrushchev and, 213–14, 269; presidential style, 148, 150, 151–52, 259; Vietnam War and, 70, 72, 73–75, 80–81
Kennedy, Robert, 203–4
Kenya, 33, 285, 289
Kerrey, Bob, 80
Kerry, John, 80, 145, 213
Khashoggi, Jamal, 98, 101
Khrushchev, Nikita, 139–40, 199–200, 201–3, 213–14, 269
Kilcullen, David, 82
Kim Jong-un, 214, 256
Kinzinger, Adam, 121
Kissinger, Henry, 17, 66, 73, 143, 152, 163, 164, 213, 305
Klain, Ron, 156
Kony, Joseph, 144
Korean Peninsula, 220, 256. See also North Korea; South Korea
Korean War, 29, 45, 49, 51, 91, 170, 234; China, role in, 74, 211, 258, 264; economic stability in wake of, 81, 82; Eisenhower and, 225, 258, 264; Truman and, 17, 141, 151, 248
Kosovo, 64, 92, 112, 120, 146
Kurds, 101–2, 293
Kushner, Jared, 145, 178
Kuwait, 80, 88, 90, 169, 226, 266

Kyoto Protocol, 129, 208, 217–18

La Follette, Phillip, 96
Laird, Melvin, 80, 225
land mines, 144, 220, 292, 295, 296
Lansing, William, 145
Laos, 13, 71, 128, 140
Leaders' Summit on Climate, 219
League of Nations, 24, 45, 48, 51, 56, 148, 157, 196–97
Lebanon, 14, 18, 33, 50, 55, 81, 91, 100, 201, 246
legalism, 48, 51–52
legislative bills, 124
legislative vetoes, 120, 121
Lend-Lease Act, 113, 232
liberalism, 24, 25, 196
Libya, 69, 91, 242, 285, 289; Libyan model, 256, 265; nuclear weapons, pursuit of, 17, 265, 272, 275; Operation Odyssey Dawn, 290, 293; R2P doctrine, applying to, 121, 224; stability operations, 292–93; U.S. military intervention in, 30–31, 51–52, 54, 86, 90, 120, 146, 156
Lighthizer, Robert, 155
Lilienthal, David, 260
Limited Test Ban Treaty, 269
Lindbergh, Charles, 96, 97
Lippman, Walter, 7, 103
Lippmann Gap, 7
Locke, John, 47
Lockheed Martin, 98
Lodge, Henry Cabot, 157
Lott, Trent, 132
Louisiana Purchase, 232
Lowi, Theodore, 196
Lugar, Richard, 218
Lumumba, Patrice, 288

MacArthur, Douglas, 170
Maduro, Nicolás, 100
Magsaysay, Ramon, 75
Malaysia, 37, 75, 300
Mali, 32, 285
Maliki, Nouri al-, 77–78
Manhattan Project, 260
manifest destiny, 11, 46
Mariel boatlift, 43
Marshall, Thurgood, 170

Marshall Plan, 45, 82, 166, 232, 248
massive retaliation, 81, 258–59, 311
Mattis, James, 144, 161, 171, 172, 173–74, 205
Mazarr, Michael, 36
McCain, John, 80, 129, 135, 158, 218, 250
McCarran-Walter Act, 124
McCarthy, Kevin, 129, 131
McCarthyism, 49, 74, 133, 166
McCone, John, 177, 199, 202
McConnell, Mitch, 127, 135
McGovern, George, 139
McKeon, Robert, 101
McMaster, H. R., 153, 174
McNamara, Robert, 105, 170, 172, 199, 200, 201, 202, 203, 259
Mead, Walter, 55
Médecins Sans Frontières (MSF), 68
medium-range ballistic missiles (MRBMs), 198–99
Medvedev, Dmitri, 95, 271
Menendez, Robert, 113
Mexico, 98, 100, 115, 212, 214, 247; border wall, 41–43, 58, 94, 124, 144, 148, 156; Bracero Program, 52–53; Cancun, climate meeting held in, 218; drug cartels, 28, 293; foreign policy on, 75, 118, 130, 235, 250, 265; NAFTA, as part of, 231–32, 249–50; in USMCA, 123, 142, 231–32; U.S.-Mexico border, 62, 107, 108, 138–39, 141, 155, 181–82
military after next concept, 183
military assistance, 209, 227, 247, 250, 287
military engagement, 73, 268
military-industrial complex, 98, 103, 109, 129
millennial foreign policy, 57–58
Millennium Challenge Corporation (MCC), 251
Milley, Mark, 171, 310
Minsk Peace Agreement, 22
missile gap, 133, 257–58
Missile Technology Control Regime (MTCR), 297
Moltz, James, 183
monetary strategies, 235–36
Monroe, James, 86
Monroe Doctrine, 11, 45, 48, 51, 147
Montreal Protocol, 219
Moon Jae-in, 256
moral pragmatism, 48, 49–50, 52
Morgenthau, Hans, 24

Mosaddegh, Mohammed, 287
Moynihan, Daniel Patrick, 177
Mueller, Robert, 127, 182
Mujahedeen-e-Khalq (MEK), 101
multilateral action, 9–10
multilateral development assistance, 248
multilateralism, 210
multipolar stratification, 26, 307
Mulvaney, Mick, 63
Mundt, Karl, 96
Munich analogy, 65, 74
Muslims, 33, 79, 100, 103; Muslim persecution, 154; Muslim travel ban, 138, 181, 182; Uighur Muslims, 139, 220, 240

Nagasaki, 257, 260
National Association for the Advancement of Colored People (NAACP), 170
National Association of Arab Americans (NAAA), 99–100
National Clandestine Service, 175–76
National Commission on Terrorist Attacks upon the US (9/11 Commission), 131–32
National Court of Justice, 301
National Defense Authorization Act, 112, 125, 128, 135, 143
National Guard, 168, 170
National Intelligence Council (NIC), 38
National Intelligence Estimates (NIEs), 175
National Intelligence Program, 176
national missile defense systems, 271, 274–75
National Security Act, 151, 167, 175
National Security Agency (NSA), 56, 57, 109, 129, 130, 157–58, 174, 176, 211–12, 278
National Security Council (NSC), 3, 11, 17, 62, 128, 144, 145, 151–54, 165, 192, 199, 215, 249, 256, 289, 293
National Security Strategy, 14–15, 310
National Space Council, 144
National Strategy Target List (NSTL), 259
national style, 46
National War Powers Commission, 135
Negroponte, John, 178
neoconservatism, 195, 306
neo-isolationism, 76, 291
neoliberalism, 24, 25, 26
Netanyahu, Benjamin, 133
Netherlands, 157, 226, 241
neutrality principle, 50

New America think tank, 87, 102

New Deal, 138

new media, 105–7

newspapers, 97, 104–5, 106, 128, 286

New Strategic Arms Reduction Treat (New START), 51, 95, 115, 138, 215, 263, 271–72

Ngo Dinh Diem, 70, 72, 75

Nicaragua, 14, 50, 91, 115, 210, 287–88

Nielsen, Kirstjen, 181–82

Niger, 32, 121, 226, 284, 285

Nigeria, 32, 68, 226, 246, 297

Nixon, Richard, 13, 74, 88, 148, 150, 213, 225, 236, 260, 267, 310; détente and, 17, 44, 133; foreign policy, 126, 140, 152; Nixon Doctrine, 12–13, 43–44, 227; Vietnam War and, 73, 81, 141, 143; War Powers Act and, 118–19

no-fly zones, 30, 90, 113, 120, 293

nonemergency food aid, 248

nongovernmental organizations (NGOs), 28, 29, 109

Non-Proliferation Treaty (NPT), 255, 269, 272

nonstate actors, 24, 28, 30, 31, 32, 38, 281, 297

nontariff barriers (NTBs), 233

nontraditional foreign aid, 247

Nord Stream 2, 112, 117

North American Free Trade Agreement (NAFTA), 123, 133, 211, 231–32, 237, 249–50

North Atlantic Treaty Organization (NATO), 11, 21, 28, 45, 91, 113, 166, 197, 210, 226, 251, 280; Asia-Pacific, expanding focus to include, 302; Baltics, NATO troops deployed in, 295; historical lesson on, 29–30; nuclear weapons and, 49, 268, 270; Russia and, 23, 93, 186, 187, 224, 227; space policy, as part of, 183; Trump dislike for, 52, 172, 265

Northern Alliance, 11

North Korea, 63, 220, 234, 264; axis of evil, as placed in, 78, 212; cyberattacks against, 278–79; denuclearization efforts, 255–57; economic sanctions against, 209, 222; nuclear weapons in, 4, 5, 18, 126, 214, 262, 265, 272, 274, 275, 296; Trump, relations with, 4, 8, 94, 95, 165, 178, 205, 211, 213–14, 237, 255–57, 301

North-South system, 30–31

North Vietnam, 2, 70, 72, 73, 75, 76, 80, 93, 118, 143, 175, 225, 234

nuclear forces, 17, 54, 66, 81, 87, 90, 115, 225, 293; China as a nuclear power, 36, 262; danger of nuclear war, reducing, 268–73; Iran as a nuclear power, 4, 5, 18, 50, 139, 143, 275, 278, 279, 297; Iranian nuclear agreement, 6, 54, 99, 133, 134, 142, 272–73; in North Korea, 4, 5, 18, 126, 214, 255–57, 262, 265, 272, 274, 275, 296; nuclear-conventional divide, bridging, 263–66; nuclear submarine agreement, 7–8, 49, 210; post-Cold War nuclear thinking, 261–63; Russia as a nuclear power, 14, 21, 51, 187, 188, 249, 255, 258, 261, 262, 265, 268–69, 271, 272, 275, 294; U.S. Cold War nuclear strategy, 258–60

Nuclear Posture Review (NPR), 262, 263

nuclear test ban treaties, 115, 133, 144, 269

Nuclear Weapons Employment Policy (NUWEP), 260

Nunes, Devin, 127

Nunn-Lugar Threat Reduction Program, 249, 271

Nye Committee, 49

Obama, Barack, 106, 124, 145, 156, 158, 163, 168, 220, 222, 227, 238, 283, 296; Afghanistan and, 4, 11, 54, 83, 173, 280; ambassadors and, 117, 144; Asian pivot, 25, 300; bin Laden and, 93–94; border and migration issues, 142; China and, 224, 301; climate change and, 207, 218; competitive Congress during administration, 133, 134; Cuba, repairing relations with, 100–101, 144, 211, 212; cyberattacks, 278–79; "don't ask, don't tell" legislation, repealing, 171; Ebola epidemic and, 68–69, 157; epidemic preparedness, 62; executive orders, 142, 143–44, 244; foreign aid, 246, 248; foreign policy, 18, 43, 95, 274; Gaddafi and, 54, 121, 146, 216, 292–93; Iranian nuclear agreement, 99, 134, 272–73; Iraq War, ending, 78, 79, 266; Libya and, 51–52, 146, 292–93; North Korea and, 278–79; NSC system, working with, 153, 154; nuclear weapons and, 115, 262–63, 294; Obama administration, 66, 97, 155, 213; presidential style, 148, 150; Russia and, 127, 186, 271; sanctions, use of, 240, 242, 245; Syria and, 6, 91, 130, 182, 214–15, 288, 289; trade issues during administration,

237, 250; transgender guidelines under, 172;
  Vietnam, lifting arms embargo against, 234;
  war powers and, 119–20, 146
O'Brien, Robert, 153–54
Office of Special Plans (OSP), 175
Office of Strategic Services (OSS), 175
Office of the Director of National Intelligence
  (ODNI), 174, 176, 182
Office of the Secretary of Defense, 172
Office of the U.S. Trade Representative, 180,
  235, 249
Omnibus Trade and Competitiveness Act, 235
one plus strategy, 267
Open Door Notes, 51
Open Door strategy, 12
Open Skies Treaty, 116, 158, 269, 272
Open Society Foundation, 87
Operation Ajax, 287
Operation Avarice, 294
Operation Desert Storm, 90, 121, 296–97
Operation Gatekeeper, 41
Operation Iraqi Freedom, 78, 266
Operation Mongoose, 286–87
Operation Odyssey Dawn, 290, 293
Operation Provide Comfort, 290, 291
Operation Restore Hope, 290, 292
Operation Rolling Thunder, 70, 72
Operations Plan (OPLAN), 262
opportunity cost in action policy, 7
Ordinary State, 303
Organization for Economic Cooperation and
  Development (OECD), 215
Organization of American States, 28, 51, 157,
  220
Organization of the Petroleum Exporting
  Countries (OPEC), 212
Osgood, Robert, 52
Ottawa Treaty, 296
outsourcing, 93, 131–32, 168
Overseas Contingency Operations (OCO), 125
oversight, 123, 126, 127, 131, 165, 289

P5+1 group, 272
Pakistan, 2, 3, 7, 37, 125, 235, 246, 289, 292;
  arms transfers to, 13, 227; drone strikes in,
  284, 292; as a global power, 267; as a nuclear
  power, 262, 272; Taliban, link with, 10, 11,
  211
Palestine Liberation Organization, 29, 33

Panama, 13, 48, 54, 82, 117, 169, 237
Panama Canal Treaties, 13, 116, 117, 133, 148,
  157
Panetta, Leon, 108, 156
paramilitary action, 140, 282, 286, 287–88
Paris Climate Agreement, 28, 51, 133, 138, 142,
  144, 207–8, 219
Paris Peace Talks, 73, 197
Partnership for Peace program, 29
Partnership for Public Service, 158
Passman, Otto, 75
Patriot Act, 130
Patriot missile system, 226, 227, 274
patron's dilemma, 10
Paul, Rand, 113, 114, 129, 135
Paul, Ron, 57, 250
Peace Corps, 139, 247
peacekeeping, 29–30, 91, 209, 213, 222, 290–
  91, 292
Pearl Harbor, 64, 65, 67, 89, 97
Pelosi, Nancy, 126, 187
Pence, Mike, 62, 154, 256
Pentagon Papers, 56, 72, 141
Perot, Ross, 249
Perry, Matthew (Commodore Perry), 308–9
Persian Gulf War, 67, 88, 90, 105, 107, 125,
  146, 154, 173, 274, 306
Petraeus, David, 78
Philippines, 13, 37, 45, 64, 75, 125, 228, 238,
  300, 309
Pillar, Paul, 50, 179
Planning, Programming, and Budgetary System
  (PPBS), 172
pledge system, 51
Ploughshares Fund, 87
pluralism, 194, 195–96
Point Four Program, 248
Poland, 37, 66, 155, 187, 196, 224, 226, 261,
  287, 289
policy entrepreneurship, 123, 129
poliheuristic decision-making, 198
political action committees (PACs), 99, 297
political creep, 165
political protest, 79, 103–4
Pompeo, Mike, 109, 162, 165, 177–78, 256
Porch, Douglas, 82
positional issues, 94
post-Cold War era, 24, 51, 224, 242, 284, 290,
  305; American hegemony during, 35–36; arms

control, 270–71; covert action during, 288–89; foreign aid, 249–50; foreign policy during, 149, 304; nuclear thinking, 261–63, 272
Powell, Colin, 152, 155, 165, 192, 251
Powers, Samantha, 293
Pragmatic America perspective, 305–6
preemption, doctrine of, 17, 43, 81, 259, 263, 264, 265–66, 279, 310
Presidential Committee on the Assignment of Women in the Armed Forces, 171
Presidential Decision Directive 60 (PDD-60), 262
presidential findings, 128
presidential personality, 147–49
President's Commission on Migratory Labor, 53
President's Intelligence Advisory Board, 176
preventive strike, 265
prospect theory, 189–90
protectionism, 44, 121, 131, 235, 240
Protestantism, 47, 308
proxy wars, 71
public awareness, 87–88, 112
public goods, 6
Public Health Service Act, 43, 62
Putin, Vladimir, 271; Biden and, 139, 186–88, 216, 272; Crimea, use of force in, 69, 186, 244–45; Trump and, 54, 148, 178, 215, 244; Ukraine invasion and, 21, 22–23, 112–14, 186–88, 242, 263

Qatar, 213, 239, 242
Quadrennial Defense Review, 28
Quadrilateral Security Dialogue (the Quad), 138, 221
Quayle, Dan, 154
Quincy Institute for Responsible Statecraft, 86–87
quotas, 170, 217, 233, 234, 250

Radio Free Europe, 182, 222
Radio Liberty, 182, 222
Radio Marti, 222
rally-around-the-flag effect, 106
Randolph, A. Phillip, 170
rational actor model, 189–90, 194, 197–98, 201–2
Raytheon, 98
Reagan, Ronald, 10, 28, 55, 100, 116, 124, 145, 150, 194, 249, 250, 267; appointment

powers, 117; arms transfers and sales, 99, 227; covert actions, authorizing, 70, 286, 287; Cuba policy, 43, 222; foreign policy, 14, 17–18, 146; Gorbachev and, 14, 215; Grenada, justifying invasion of, 265; Iran and, 50, 80, 144, 152, 242; migrant worker program, 53; presidential style, 148–49, 150; Reagan administration, 155, 248, 252, 310; Reagan Doctrine, 13–14, 56; SDI system, implementing, 273–74; Soviets, relations with, 13–14, 18, 195, 223, 260, 270
realism, 24, 25, 56
reconstruction, 27, 82, 126, 143, 172, 202, 266
Reformed America perspective, 303–4
regimes, 12, 26, 131, 168, 197, 307
regional diversity, 27, 30–31
Reliable Replacement Warhead program, 262
religious right, 102–3
remittances, 101, 244, 246
rendition program, 288–89
reporting requirements, 123, 126, 128, 146
Responsibility to Protect (R2P), 121, 224
restrained engagement, 89
Revolution in Military Affairs, 173
Reykjavik summit, 14, 49, 215
Rhodesia, 234
Rice, Condoleezza, 3, 8, 18, 96, 165, 192
Rice, Susan, 293
Rio Treaty, 217, 218
Robertson, Pat, 102–3
Rockefeller Brothers Fund, 87
Rodrik, Dani, 34
Rogers, Mike, 278
Rogers, William, 152
Rogers Act, 165
rogue states, 81, 275
Romania, 157, 289
Roosevelt, Franklin, 29, 64, 71, 92, 97, 118, 138, 144, 145, 150, 154, 157
Roosevelt, Theodore, 18, 48, 55, 309
Roosevelt Corollary, 48
Root-Takahira Agreement, 309
Rosenau, James, 76
Rosenberg, Ethel and Julius, 56
Rostow, Walt, 72, 75, 152
Rovner, Joshua, 69
Rubio, Marco, 100
Rumsfeld, Donald, 11, 140–41, 172, 192
Rusk, Dean, 74, 163, 164, 199, 202

Russia, 33, 36, 76, 78, 95, 154, 155, 172, 221, 235, 242, 267, 274, 285, 297; Crimea annexation, 21–22, 154, 214, 244, 265, 278, 281; cyberwarfare, engaging in, 90, 94, 95, 106, 112–13, 278–79, 289, 290; Exxon partnership, 97–98; foreign aid for, 246, 249; human rights in, 31, 295; military power of, 5, 21, 90, 125; NATO and, 29, 93; New START treaty, signing, 51, 271; as a nuclear power, 21, 51, 187, 188, 249, 255, 258, 261, 262, 265, 268–69, 271, 272, 275, 294; oil production in, 212; Ottawa Treaty, declining to sign, 296; Putin as president, 54, 139, 187, 215, 245, 271; sanctions on, 21, 97, 112–14, 117, 139, 187, 240, 242, 244, 295; in treaties and agreements, 31, 116, 138, 183, 218; Trump and, 153, 178, 182, 215, 227, 263, 271, 284; Ukraine, invasion, 5, 21–23, 31, 90, 94, 95, 106, 112–13, 144, 168, 186–88, 224, 240, 242, 265, 272, 281–82, 290, 298, 302; U.S. election interference, 31, 107, 126, 127, 148, 178, 215; in World War I, 196, 197
Russia Today (RT), 107, 282
Russo-Japanese War, 64, 309

Sadat, Anwar, 13
sanctions, 17, 51, 180, 227, 233, 235, 241, 253; Chinese sanctions, 62, 139, 220, 240, 301; Cuban sanctions, 27, 240, 243–44; diplomatic sanctions, 211; Iranian sanctions, 99, 143–44, 165, 240, 242, 273, 278; Iraqi sanctions, 222, 266; North Korean sanctions, 209, 222, 255–56; Rhodesian/Zimbabwean sanctions, 234; Russian sanctions, 21, 97, 112–14, 117, 139, 187, 240, 242, 244, 295
sanctuary movement, 108
Sanders, Bernie, 113
Sandinistas, 14, 50, 287
Saturday Night Massacre, 119
Saudi Arabia, 67, 90, 101, 142, 172, 213, 214, 278, 281, 297; arm sales to, 13, 98–99, 120, 124, 226, 227–28; oil production in, 212; as a U.S. ally, 169, 275; as a world power, 214, 267; Yemen War and, 133–34
say-do problems, 6
Schake, Kori, 109
Schlesinger, James, 49, 177
Schlieffen Plan, 196
Schneider, René, 288

Scott, Rick, 113
Scowcroft, Brent, 156
Scud missiles, 274
Secretary of Defense, role of, 167, 172–73
Secretary of State, role of, 164–65
Secret Service, 181
Secure Fence Act, 41
self-help system, 25–26
September 11 terror attacks, 31, 58, 80, 83, 93, 124, 133, 147, 177, 285; 9/11 Commission, 3, 131–32; bin Laden and, 10, 289; Bush administration and, 14–15, 17, 56, 158, 238, 242; foreign policy response to, 304, 306, 308; homeland security and, 156, 181–82, 183; intelligence community adjustments due to, 57, 176; military strategy in wake of, 121, 155, 192, 264, 267, 273, 283–84; post-September 11 foreign aid, 250–51; twentieth anniversary of, 2, 139
Shadow Brokers group, 176
Sheehan, Cindy, 103
shock and awe strategy, 77, 266
Shultz, George, 3
shuttle diplomacy, 212–13
signing statements, 143
simple resolutions, 124
Singapore, 155, 214, 236–37, 256
Single Integrated Operational Plan (SIOP), 259–60
Sino-Japanese War, 309
small-group decision-making model, 191–94, 198, 203–4
smart sanctions, 242
Smoot-Hawley Tariff, 233
Snowden, Edward, 56, 109, 218
soft power, 9, 31, 223
SolarWinds network, 279
Solomon Islands, 302
Somalia, 34, 63, 91, 93, 105, 146; drone strikes in, 283, 284, 298; humanitarian intervention in, 92, 248, 290; Mogadishu, ambush of, 285, 291–92; terrorists in, 10, 32, 285; U.S. forces in, 33, 158, 285
Sony Pictures, 278
Sorensen, Theodore, 203, 204
Soros, George, 87
South Africa, 88, 100, 195, 214, 218, 272
South China Sea, 31, 212, 224, 267, 268, 300–302

Southeast Asia Treaty Organization (SEATO), 49, 70, 71
South Korea, 13, 37, 63, 81, 238, 267, 275, 297; land mines at demilitarized zone, 220, 296; Trump and, 94, 143, 209, 220, 237, 243, 255–56; U.S. military presence in, 81, 143, 169, 257, 264; U.S.-South Korea relations, 257, 264, 302
South Vietnam, 2, 13, 70, 72–73, 75, 80, 81, 82, 155
sovereignty, 12, 13, 26, 38, 44, 70, 77, 115, 116, 208, 216, 224, 232, 236, 239, 293, 300
Soviet Union, 51, 56, 65, 157, 177, 213, 225, 287; Afghanistan invasion, 10, 13, 14, 33, 54, 66, 69, 80, 89, 115, 227, 288; arms control and, 14, 18, 50, 157, 212, 214; Baruch Plan, lesson of, 260–61; in Cold War, 79, 222, 244, 257–58, 269–70, 305; Cuba, support for, 27, 214, 242, 243; Cuban Missile Crisis and, 198–203, 269; deterrence against, 258, 259, 264; fall of, 21, 29, 31, 215, 251; as a nuclear power, 14, 257–58, 261; in post-Cold War period, 270–71; Reagan-Soviet relations, 13–14, 18, 195, 223, 260, 270; Truman Doctrine and, 12, 17; Vietnam and, 73, 89, 225
Space Command, 182–83
Space Policy Directive (SPD), 183
Spain, 48, 77, 78, 104, 115, 146, 212, 226, 267
Spanier, John, 54
Spanish-American War, 55, 104, 118, 170
Special Coordinating Committee (SCC), 192
special operations missions, 11, 21, 164, 167, 171, 175, 285
spiral of silence, 106
Spratly Islands, 300, 301
Sputnik launch, 257
squeaky wheels, 104
stability operations, 281, 282, 291, 292–93
Stalin, Josef, 12, 154
standard operating procedures, 123, 163, 191, 205
Star Wars program, 14, 274
state capitalism, 35
statecraft, 18, 52, 86–87, 232–33, 234
State of the Union addresses, 13, 14, 49, 56, 78, 238
Stevenson, Adlai, 203
Stimson, Henry, 260

Stoessinger, John, 146–47
Strategic Arms Limitations Talks (SALT), 13, 51, 93, 115, 148, 215, 233, 270
Strategic Arms Reduction Talks (START), 270
Strategic Command, 183
Strategic Defense Initiative (SDI), 14, 116, 273–74
Strategic Offensive Reductions Treaty (SORT), 271
strategic trade policy, 235, 236
stratification, 25, 26
Stuxnet virus attack, 278, 279
submarines, 7–8, 49, 210, 262, 263, 268, 270, 271
subnational actors, 29
Sudan, 91, 218, 240, 242, 246, 297
Suez Canal, 29, 300
sufficiency, principle of, 260
Sullivan, Jake, 187
summit diplomacy, 213–14
Summit of the Americas, 210
Super 301 sanctions, 235
surface-to-air missiles (SAMs), 198, 282, 301
Sweden, 37, 63, 265
swing votes, 113
Switzerland, 115, 241
Syria, 32, 34, 63, 80, 100, 101, 124, 213, 264, 284, 289, 298; chemical weapons use, 6, 214–15, 245, 293–94; G. W. Bush and, 78, 241; ISIS presence in, 33, 133, 139, 146, 283; military interventions, 69, 86; nuclear weapons and, 262, 275; Obama and, 130, 182, 214–15, 288; sanctions on, 241, 242; Syrian civil war, 106, 126; Trump, removing U.S. troops from, 172, 267; use of force in, 90, 91, 119, 121

Taft, William Howard, 52–53
Taft-Katsura Agreement, 309
Tai, Katherine, 155
Taiwan, 74, 102, 309; arms sales to, 226, 227, 228; Congressional action on, 132–33; defense of, 125, 258, 302, 310; in South China Sea, 212, 300; U.S.-Taiwan relations, 28, 62, 126
Taliban: in Afghanistan, 2–3, 132, 172, 288; al-Qaeda, alliance with, 10–11, 267; global terrorism and, 15, 32; peace agreement with, 4, 153; Taliban government, 14, 211, 280–81, 284

Tanzania, 33, 289

tariffs, 34, 44, 121, 155, 238, 249; on Chinese goods, 103; GATT and the World Trade Organization, 216–17; in inventory of policy options, 233–34

Taylor, Charles, 102

Taylor, Maxwell, 72, 75

Taylor-Rostow Report, 70, 72, 74

Tea Party, 57, 130

television, 104–5, 199

Tenet, George, 178

terrorism, 4, 18, 93, 126, 165, 214, 245, 255, 267, 268, 280, 294; in Africa, 33, 285; in asymmetric conflicts, 281; Bush strategies to defeat, 49, 147, 238; counterterrorism, 11, 34, 175, 177, 179, 213, 279, 283–84; covert action against, 288; cyberterrorism, perceived threat of, 4, 5; four waves of, 32–33; global terrorism, 11, 22, 32, 49, 50, 79, 81, 197; MEK denunciation of terrorism, 101; post-9/11 offensive against, 56, 132; sanctions against, 240, 241, 242–43; in Somalia, 33, 292; War on Terrorism, 7, 15, 92, 143, 153, 171, 194, 223, 227, 228, 250, 310

Tet Offensive, 70, 72–73

Thailand, 63, 289

think tanks, 86, 87, 102, 130, 281

Tiger Team, 186, 187

TikTok, 223

Tillerson, Rex, 97, 161–62, 165, 208, 213, 256

tipping points, 79, 92–93

Title 42 policy, 43, 62, 108

top-down managerial style, 149, 256

Tower Commission, 192, 193, 286

trade agreements, 21, 31, 155; bilateral trade agreements, 236–37, 249; global trade agreements, 217, 238–39; NAFTA, 123, 211, 231–32, 249–50; regional trade agreements, 237–38; Trade Agreements Act, 121, 233; Trump and, 52, 62, 95, 209, 220; USMCA, 123, 142, 231–32, 301

Trade Expansion Act, 183

trade promotional authority, 121

Trade Reform Act, 121

trade wars, 235, 238; China-U.S. trade war, 61, 148; how trade wars end, 252–53

Trading with the Enemy Act, 234

traditional foreign aid, 247

traffic rules, 268

TransAfrica, 100

Transatlantic Trade and Investment Partnership (TTIP), 237, 238

Trans-Pacific Partnership (TPP), 123, 231, 232, 238

Transportation Security Administration, 181

Treasury Department, 97, 157, 175, 180, 245

treaty-making, 114, 116

Treaty of Kanagawa, 308

Treaty of Paris, 141

Treaty of Versailles, 115

Trilateral Commission, 195

Trudeau, Justin, 223

Truman, Harry S., 71, 124, 143, 154, 175, 216; as a Cold War president, 257, 258, 260–61; executive orders of, 141, 169–70; Korean War and, 17, 141, 151, 248; presidential style, 148, 150; Truman Doctrine, 17, 147, 242

Trump, Donald, 50, 99, 100, 117, 132, 158, 162, 166, 176, 232, 265, 271, 293; Afghanistan and, 3, 4, 6, 8, 95; America First policy, 10, 15–16, 36, 44, 49, 87, 97, 103, 112, 142, 161, 180; arms sales authorizations, 227–28; AUMF, low regard for, 121, 135; border wall and, 41–43, 94, 124–25, 138–39, 148; China policy, 8, 148, 217, 239–40, 263, 284, 301–2, 310; COVID-19 pandemic response, 61–63, 301; cyberattacks and, 278, 279; diplomacy style, 209, 215, 222, 223, 224; environmental stance, 181, 207–8, 219; executive orders, 144, 183, 231, 255–56; foreign aid, seeking to reduce, 247, 250, 251–52; foreign policy, 49, 52, 55, 66, 129, 156, 165, 172, 174, 204, 284–85; generals, bringing out of retirement, 173–74; Giuliani as personal attorney, 101, 145; human rights, low priority for, 28; immigration policy, 107–8, 138–39; intelligence community challenges, 177, 178; Iran and, 4, 95, 135, 146, 205, 211, 243, 267, 278, 281; Jacksonian political agenda, 57, 58; managerial style, 150, 205; military power, use of, 145, 153, 168, 172, 283, 298; Mueller Report on, 127; North Korea and, 4, 8, 94, 95, 165, 178, 205, 211, 213–14, 237, 255–57, 301; NSC system, changes in, 153–54; Nuclear Posture Review, 262, 263; Putin and, 54, 148, 178, 215, 244; reporting requirements, 119, 126; Russia and, 112, 127, 148, 244–45, 284; sanctions, use of, 211, 240, 243, 244–45, 273; Saudis, relations with, 99, 101, 124, 133–34; signing statement, embracing, 143; South Korea and, 94, 143, 209, 220, 237, 243, 255–56; Space Command program, 182–83; Taliban, attempts to negotiate with, 280–81; tariffs, use of, 9, 103, 131, 232, 236; TPP, as against, 123, 238; trade war with China, 148, 239–40; travel ban, 138, 144, 181–82, 220; Trump Doctrine, 15–16; Twitter use, 103, 165, 171, 223; Ukraine and, 8; USMCA, pursuit of, 142, 231–32; withdrawal from prior agreements, 33, 115, 116, 142, 272, 296

Turkey, 101, 115, 196, 203, 242, 267; global presence, 227, 267; United States and, 12, 169, 235, 243; weapons of war and, 200, 201, 275, 297

Tuvalu, 63, 218

Twitter, 61, 103, 107, 165, 171, 223

two-war capability, 267

Udall, Mark, 130

Uighurs, 139, 240

Ukraine, 93, 126, 263; arms sales to, 226; Biden and, 94, 95, 106, 144, 154, 155, 168, 240; Crimea, 21, 69, 154, 186, 215, 244, 265, 278, 281, 295; cyber attacks on, 278, 279, 290; foreign aid for Ukraine, 112–14, 125, 246, 252; foreign policy toward, 8, 145, 157, 166; Russian invasion, 5, 21–23, 31, 90, 94, 95, 106, 112–13, 144, 168, 186–88, 224, 233, 240, 242, 265, 272, 281–82, 290, 298, 302

undeclared wars, 142, 145–46

unilateral action, 9, 10, 58, 141, 210, 256, 303

unilateralism, 48–49, 51, 52, 210, 240

Unipolar Concert, 35–36

unipolarity, 26, 307

United Arab Emirates (UAE), 2, 95, 124, 209–10, 213, 226, 227–28, 281, 297

United Kingdom, 29, 36, 48, 50, 63, 75, 115, 169, 226, 234, 241; as a global power, 214, 267, 272; as a nuclear power, 7–8, 260, 262; as a U.S. ally, 37, 78, 141, 287; in World Wars, 97, 196, 197

United Nations, 28, 36, 45, 51, 92, 122, 138, 164, 218, 269, 291, 293; Cuban Missile Crisis and, 199, 200, 203; sanctions put in place by, 256, 273; Trump speech to

UN, 251–52; UN Arms Transfer Register, 296; UN Conference on Women, 157; UN diplomacy, 221–22; U.S. membership in, 49, 146, 210, 260, 290

United Nations Framework Convention on Climate Change (UNFCCC), 208, 217

United States-Mexico-Canada Agreement (USMCA), 123, 142, 231–32

Universal Declaration of Human Rights, 219

Uruguay Round, 216, 217, 238

U.S.-Africa Leaders Summit, 68

U.S. Agency for International Development (USAID), 68, 161, 247–48, 250, 251, 252

U.S. Cyber Command (USCYBERCOM), 176, 178, 278

use of force, 26, 29, 69, 71, 121, 174, 258, 296, 303; political use of force, 207, 208, 223–25; presidential calls for, 52, 57, 72, 118, 119, 120, 130, 203; public opinion and use of force, 90–91

U.S. Information Agency (USIA), 222

U.S. Office of eDiplomacy, 223

U.S. trade representative (USTR), 154, 155

valence issues, 94

Vance, Cyrus, 164

Venezuela, 63, 98, 100, 102, 144, 164, 210, 218, 235, 242

vice presidency, office of, 154–55

Vietcong, 72, 75, 93, 175

Vietnam, 234, 237, 238. *See also* North Vietnam; South Vietnam

Vietnam War, 29, 33, 44, 45, 118, 133, 141, 163, 198, 266, 283; chronology of, 70, 71–73; COIN strategy and, 81, 82; costs of war, 69–70, 91, 168, 175; domestic consensus loss, 27, 89; Iraq War, comparing to, 69, 80–81; lessons learned from, 76; Nixon administration and, 12, 155, 225; opposition to, 55, 98; policy decision-making and, 73–75, 148, 188, 192; U.S. withdrawal from Vietnam, 66, 92, 98, 248; Vietnamization and, 13, 73; Vietnam syndrome, 69, 83, 90

virtual protest marches, 103–4

Vladivostok Accords, 270

Voice of America (VOA), 182, 222

Wagner Group, 23, 281

Wallace, Henry, 29, 30

War Powers Resolution, 57, 114, 117–20, 122–23, 133, 134, 135, 145–46

Warsaw Pact, 21, 29, 270

Washington, George, 11, 45

Washington Naval Disarmament Conference, 51

waterboarding, 289

Watergate scandal, 119, 148

weapons of mass destruction (WMD), 34, 181, 268, 288, 293; foreign policy goals regarding, 4, 92; Iraq, assumption of WMD in, 8, 15, 67, 80, 88, 141, 155; recovering loose WMD material, 294–95

Weather Underground, 33

Weinberger, Caspar, 152, 193

Western system, 30

Westmoreland, William, 70, 75

Whalen, Charles, 94

Wheeler, Burton, 96

White House Chief of Staff, 156–57

wicked problems, 4

WikiLeaks, 106

Wilson, Woodrow, 48, 55–56, 145, 148, 157, 265, 304

Wilsonianism, 24, 56

windows of fear and opportunity, 280

Wohlforth, William, 36

Wolfowitz, Paul, 11

wolf warrior diplomacy, 212

Women's Armed Forces Integration Act, 171

Wood, Robert, 96

Woodward, Bob, 149, 174

World Bank, 34, 36, 51, 235, 248

World Health Organization (WHO), 61, 62, 68, 138, 228

World Trade Center bombing, 33, 288

World Trade Organization (WTO), 31, 123, 155, 210, 217, 221, 238–39, 252

World War I, 28, 35, 47, 49, 53, 64, 118, 283, 293, 309; League of Nations in wake of, 24, 48; rising tensions leading to, 89, 311; as the war to end all wars, 188, 196–97

World War II, 12, 29, 52, 54, 91, 114, 168, 175, 197, 221, 258; Battle of the Bulge, 170; bombing targets, 66, 75; Franklin Roosevelt during, 71, 118; isolationist outlook prior to, 88, 92; Lend-Lease Act during, 113, 232; nuclear bomb debate at end of war, 257, 260; Pearl Harbor attack, 64, 65, 67, 89, 97; presidential authority during war, 167; VOA broadcast, beginning during, 222

Wriston, Henry, 166

Wyden, Ron, 130

Xi Jinping, 61–62, 220, 240

Yanukovych, Viktor, 21

yellow journalism, 104

Yemen, 63, 86, 101, 125, 133–34, 165, 228, 246, 283, 284

Yom Kippur War, 213

Young, Todd, 135

Yugoslavia, 30, 196

Zapad-2017 exercise, 265

Zawahiri, Ayman al-, 283–84

Zelensky, Volodymyr, 112–13

zero option, 270

Zoellick, Robert, 155

ZTE Corporation, 288

# About the Author

**Glenn P. Hastedt** is professor emeritus at James Madison University where he was chair of the Justice Studies Department and prior to that chair of the Political Science Department. At JMU he received awards for research and teaching and the career achievement award. He is author of *American Foreign Policy: Past, Present, and Future* (12th edition) and coauthor of *Introduction to International Politics: Global Challenges and Policy Responses* (2020). Hastedt served as coeditor of *White House Studies* and has authored articles on intelligence studies that have appeared in *Intelligence and National Security, Journal of Intelligence History, Defense Intelligence Journal,* and *International Journal of Intelligence and Counterintelligence,* as well as chapters in edited volumes on American foreign policy and intelligence studies.

Milton Keynes UK
Ingram Content Group UK Ltd.
UKHW051908050324
438969UK00021B/436